JAHR'S

CLINICAL GUIDE;

OR,

POCKET-REPERTORY

FOR THE TREATMENT OF

ACUTE AND CHRONIC DISEASES.

TRANSLATED AND EDITED, WITH ANNOTATIONS,

BY

CHARLES J. HEMPEL, M.D.

NEW-YORK:
WILLIAM RADDE, 322 BROADWAY.

1850.

ENTERED

According to the Act of Congress, in the year 1849, by

WILLIAM RADDE,

In the Clerk's Office of the District Court for the Southern District of New-York.

H. Ludwig & Co., Printers, N. Y.

THE

EDITOR'S PREFACE.

This work is not to be confounded with the original Manual of Jahr. The present Repertory is a record of the observations which Jahr has been collecting for the last nine years, at the bed-side of patients. It is therefore an eminently practical work, and its utility is enhanced by the fact, that the various articles treated of in this Repertory are arranged in alphabetical order, and can, therefore, be consulted with the greatest ease. The reader will find, in reading Jahr's preface, that he gives the preference to particular attenuations in the treatment of disease. The subject of doses has been subjected to a full and impartial examination in the "Pharmacopœia and Posology," a work which is now in press, and will soon be given to the public. All those who take an interest in the doctrine of doses, are referred to this work for more complete information.

CHARLES J. HEMPEL, M. D.

New-York, December, 1849.

THE

AUTHOR'S PREFACE.

THE present work is intended to offer the practitioner every thing which it is necessary to know, in such a manner that, in whatever way the desired information may be sought to be obtained, the practitioner will be sure to find it. I have given both the symptoms and the names of the diseases, and have not only given the pathogenetic indications with great completeness, from my own and other physicians' experience, but have endeavoured to complete these indications by referring the reader to kindred articles, and in this way, giving him an opportunity of studying the internal connection of the remedies, and their relation to the case for which they are recommended. It is true that this method will frequently lead the reader from one article to another through a long series; but, since in nature all things are connected, I consider this circumstance an advantage rather than a disadvantage, so much more, as I know by experience, that the speediest, safest and easiest way of obtaining a full and correct insight into the nature of a particular case of disease, is to study every thing which has a bearing upon it.

As regards the names of diseases, I have adopted the nomenclature of Peter Frank, with which physicians are more familiarly acquainted. In treating of fevers, epilepsies, hysteric affections, &c., I have left Schœnlein's pathology out of consideration, for this reason, that his system is not much respected by the pathologists of the old school, and is combated with a good deal of spirit by the professors of Berlin, Vienna and Prague.

After all, pathological symptoms do not amount to much, provided we prescribe in accordance with the totality of the symptoms; for, by pursuing this course, we cannot fail to prescribe for *the thing*, even if *the name* be left out of consideration, and provided always that Schœnlein's classification of "*uterine, testicular, thoracic* and other kinds of epilepsy" be correct. There is one work, however, which I regret not having had an opportunity of consulting previous to the publication of this Repertory; it is Hebra's work on Cutaneous Diseases. Hebra's system combines practical advantages with great clearness and simplicity, whereas all other systems of cutaneous diseases are confused and without much practical value. Even as early as 1840, when I first published my "KLINISCHEN ANWEISUNGEN" in French, I applied myself to the study of the German, French and English systems of cutaneous diseases: but the more I advanced in my study, the more I became convinced that it would be impossible to offer an intelligible nomenclature of these diseases to German, French and English practitioners. My "REPERTORY OF THE CUTANEOUS DISEASES" will supply this deficiency as nearly as possible. This Repertory will contain a table exhibiting the chief names of all cutaneous diseases which have been adopted by our most distinguished pathologists, referring, moreover, to the synonymes of these names in other systems, and the symptoms in our Materia Medica which characterize the different diseases. This table will be as complete as possible, though it may not prove satisfactory to all.

As regards the remedies which have been recommended for single symptoms as well as whole groups of symptoms, I have only named such as have proved themselves curative, either in the particular case before us, or by removing, incidentally, the symptoms before us when belonging to a more extensive group. Remedies which have been proposed more or less speculatively, are marked with an interrogation-point (?). A great many new remedies have been added to those that are mentioned in my original Manual. These remedies have all been successfully tried in practice, and may, therefore, either be marked with a cipher (0), or, in case they should already be mentioned in the Manual, with an asterisk (*). Those who consult Boenninghausen's Repertory, will likewise find many useful hints and remarks in this Pocket-Repertory, and a number of remedies that were not yet much used heretofore. As regards the classification of remedies in Nos. 1, 2, 3, I ought to state that, though this classification is essentially based upon experience and the relative importance of the remedies in the particular diseases for which they are indicated, yet the practitioner should never dispense with the trouble of comparing the symptoms of all the remedies mentioned, since one of those arranged under Nos. 2 or 3, may be more specifically indicated than the remedies mentioned under No. 1. This classification is not absolutely true, and it would be wrong to infer that, because a remedy is found under No. 2 or 3, it cannot, therefore, be as useful as one of those mentioned under 1. This classification is merely intended to show that the remedies which are indicated in No. 1, are, generally speaking, those which are more frequently used in this particular case of disease, and that the practitioner, in order to save time, had better examine the remedies under No. 1 first, before he compares those mentioned under Nos. 2 or 3.

It is needless to give any further rules relative to the use of this work. The diseases being alphabetically arranged, both in the index and the body of the work, all the practitioner has to do, is to look for the disease and then to study the paragraphs devoted to it. Beginners, however, will do well to first study the systematic index following immediately after this preface, and more particularly in the article, "*General diseases*," those subjects which are printed in italics. By this means they will become familiar with the plan of the work, and will know how to use it in particular cases. This is the plan which I have always pursued in teaching. For those who have never studied our Materia Medica, I have added the characteristic symptoms of our principal medicines; I ought to say, however, that this work has especially been written for those who possess my Symptomen-Codex, or some other kind of Materia Medica, which they may consult in important cases. To those who study our Materia Medica with care and attention, the work will prove a valuable vade mecum, and an excellent introduction to the study of larger works. The *characteristic symptoms* of our principal medicines have been appended for the benefit of those who are not yet acquainted with our Materia Medica, and who are at a loss to know how to commence that study. These characteristic symptoms will serve as central points round which the other and less important symptoms of the medicines can easily be grouped.

For the benefit of beginners, I will subjoin the following remarks on the selection of remedies according to symptoms, and on the magnitude and repetition of doses.

I know, from experience, that Hahnemann's rule, *to select a remedy in accordance with the totality of the symptoms*, is, in many cases, incorrectly apprehended by beginners, or by physicians who come over to our side from the allœopathic ranks. They do not always distinguish primary and secondary symptoms. This incorrectness is, in the first place, owing to the fact that the old school considerably restricts the meaning of the term "symptom;" and, in the second place, to this other fact, that what is technically termed "taking a record," consists simply in taking down the prominent symptoms without including other constitutional ailments, the treatment of which is postponed until the principal difficulty is removed. It is not supposed, for instance, by beginners, that piles and pneumonia, when occurring in the same patient, have any connection with each other. It is on this account that I have always taught not only to consider the symptoms *of the case*, but also the symptoms *of the patient*. And even then I have not always been properly understood. Many symptoms, which our school considers as manifestations of the general disease, were considered as independent diseases by the beginner, simply because they had particular names in the old school works on pathology. I have, therefore, refrained from using the word symptom in my lectures to beginners, and have worded my fundamental rule of treatment as follows: The proper selection of a remedy, in *chronic* and generally also in *acute* diseases, depends upon the following three points: "1. *The remedy must correspond to the pathognomonic symptoms of the case; 2, to the accidental symptoms which do not seem to be a part of the essential features of the disease; and 3, to all other diseases and morbid phenomena which we might discover in the patient.*" If a patient be afflicted with *pneumonia*, for instance, we should not only record the essential symptoms of pneumonia, but also the symptoms of any other affection of the eyes that might happen to coexist with the inflammation, such as: ectropion, pterygion, blepharoptosis, diplopia, amblyopia, &c., and, moreover, the general morbid phenomena of the organism, no matter whether the books speak of them as mere symptoms or as independent diseases. In all chronic diseases this mode of recording the symptoms should he strictly pursued; and even in acute diseases the proper remedy will always be found to correspond to these three series of phenomena, though it need not be selected with particular reference to the third series, provided the disease does not rest upon a chronic foundation, and was occasioned by some exceptional cause. The accidental symptoms, however, that is, those symptoms which are not essentially pathognomonic, should be carefully noted in acute diseases, and the remedy should be selected with especial reference to these accidental symptoms. Some time ago I treated a man of 40 years for acute bronchitis. The remedies which were indicated by the pathognomonic symptoms, such as *Acon.*, *Bell.*, *Bry.*, *Dulc.*, *Merc.*, had no effect. I then learned that the patient had a pain in the calf, as if bruised, with tension on setting the foot on the ground. The patient did not remember having ever hurt himself at that place. The spot looked reddish, green-yellow on the sides, and was painful to the touch. This led me to *Conium* 30, three globules in water. After the second dose the spot was less painful, the fever diminished, the cough looser, and the appetite improved.*

* The apparently accidental symptoms are frequently the more essential symptoms of the patient. He who knows how to distinguish them from the pathognomonic symptoms, will frequently be able to cure noma, dropsy, inguinal hernia, &c., with remedies which have never produced such diseases; remedies which are individually essential to a cure, and such remedies do not always correspond to the pathognomonic symptoms.

As regards the magnitude of doses, my rule is to give as little medicine as possible. Nevertheless, in spite of the careful attention with which I have hitherto followed the discussions relative to that subject, I have not yet been able to decide whether the higher or the lower attenuations are the weaker or stronger doses. I have known one drop of the pure tincture to act for weeks precisely in the same manner as the 30th attenuation has been supposed to do; I have seen violent effects from the 30th as well as from the 2d or 3d; and on the other hand, I have effected speedy cures, without any previous aggravations, by means of the tincture, and the 1st, 2d or 3d attenuation, as well as with the 30th. I have observed similar effects from the 100th up to the 3 and 8,000th potency. In some cases I have effected a cure by a mere change of potencies, and sometimes an attenuation which seemed to do no good whatever, would effect a speedy cure when the same remedy was given after two or three other medicines.

As regards the repetition of doses, it is my conviction, confirmed by abundant experience, that an unnecessary repetition of the same remedy is productive of mischief, especially if the remedy was not indicated by the symptoms, or was continued after it had produced an incipient improvement. I have seen bad effects from spoonful doses of a solution of a few pellets, just as much as if the original dose had been repeated. We know that from the fourth attenuation upwards, the medicines act rather dynamically than chemically, but what the real difference is between the first and thousandth attenuation, is as yet impossible to say. It is my belief that the attenuations, if carried up to a certain degree, act more speedily and more positively than the lower preparations, and that a spoonful of a solution of a few pellets is a milder dose than a drop of an alcoholic attenuation; but I am unable to offer any proofs in favour of my belief; what I know positively, is, that we do not yet know the limit how far the attenuating process can be carried without destroying the power of the medicine, and *that, under proper circumstances, a pellet of the* 8,000*th potency acts as well as a pellet of the 30th or 3d.*

From this we may infer, that an unnecessary repetition of the dose might prove injurious to the patient; that a frequent repetition of the dose is necessary in very acute diseases, such as cholera, or even in recent chancre; that a single dose will frequently suffice in many slighter affections; and that, in chronic diseases, a dose should be allowed to act a long time. This is probably owing to the fact, that in such diseases as steatomata, polypi, chronic pulmonary and liver complaints, old wens, ulcers and herpes, the retro-formative process takes place very slowly, and that therefore a too frequent repetition of the dose produces an aggravation before the curative process has commenced. In all chronic diseases I never give more than one dose, of three or four pellets, and allow it to act a long time; and even in acute diseases I never repeat the dose until the preceding one has exhausted its action. I, therefore, use a solution of from three to six pellets of the 30th potency, in a tumblerful of water, administering it in teaspoonful doses every two, three or six hours. Sometimes I use a higher potency as being a weaker one, especially if I want to ascertain whether I have hit the right remedy, for which purpose a small dose is just as effectual as a large one: for even the smallest dose of the proper remedy, if it do not effect an immediate cure, will at least make a favourable impression upon the disease. If no such impression be manifest, I would rather resort to another remedy than to prescribe a lower attenuation of the same remedy. The beginner in homœopathy should especially guard himself against prescribing for mere *names* of diseases, as is too much the case in the old school. This is the reason why I have given as many symptoms as possible, and why I invite the beginning practitioner not to content himself with my own indications, but, moreover, to consult the Materia Medica Pura in every case. The study of the Materia Medica Pura is indispensable to learn to distinguish medicinal symptoms from the natural symptoms of the disease. This is especially important in chronic diseases where new symptoms frequently make their appearance, which may require a change of remedies, according as they are either a medicinal aggravation, or a new development of the disease. The present work is therefore, not intended to supply the place of the Materia Medica Pura; it is simply what the title indicates, a Pocket-Repertory to aid the memory of older practitioners, and to be a guide for beginners.

G. H. G. JAHR.

Paris, May, 1849.

SYSTEMATIC TABLE

OF THE

VARIOUS ARTICLES CONTAINED IN THIS WORK,

IN ALPHABETICAL ORDER.

N. B.—Those headings in the following paragraphs which are printed *in italics*, should be studied first; the general information which they furnish will be found more or less useful in all particular cases.

I. General Remarks.—See the articles:

A. *Constitution*, age, sex and temperament; *causes* of disease; *conditions* of aggravation; *conditions* of improvement; *emotions; colds; suppression* of secretions and eruptions; *injuries; ill effects of heat;* ill effects of various kinds of nourishment; *weakness of stomach; diseases of drunkards;* ill effects of growth; *poisoning*, especially by alum, arsenic, valerian, prussic acid, lead; *abuse of cinchona; noxious vapours*; iron; adipic poison; ichtyotoxicon; crab-apple vinegar; poisonous honey; abuse of iodine; *abuse of coffee;* abuse of camphor; *abuse of chamomile;* poisoning by copper; abuse of magnesia; *abuse of mercury;* opium; *narcotism;* phosphorus; noxious mushrooms; glanders; saffron; sal ammoniacum; nitrate of silver; abuse of salt; sarsaparilla; hepar sulphuris; abuse of sulphur; mezereum; cantharides; stramonium; poisonous sumach; *abuse of tobacco;* abuse of tea; alcohol; tin.

B. Deadness of single parts; swelling of veins; aneurisms; *sanguinous congestions;* plethora; anæmia; *hæmorrhage;* rushes of blood; *inflammations;* arthrocace; hydrarthrus; arthritis; *arthralgia;* diseases of bones; *spasms; paralysis;* contraction of muscles; polypi; rhachitis; *rheumatism; mucous derangement; paroxysms of pain;* scurvy; scrophulosis; tuberculosis; *typical affections; dropsy.*

C. Emaciation; *debility:* atrophy of scrofulous children; deficient exhalation; *dread of motion;* cyanosis; chlorosis; eclampsia; epilepsy; adiposis; jaundice; catalepsy; *diseases of children; dread of air;* marasmus senilis; *nervous debility;* fainting; *apparent death;* apoplexy; *asthenia:* consumption; indolence; awkwardness; chorea; hydrophobia; worm-affections; tremour.

II. Cutaneous and External Diseases:—See:

A. Formication; acne; lepra; *eruptions;* variola; blood-blisters; *petechiæ;* boils; eczema; *exanthemata; herpetic eruptions;* phagedenic blisters; rash; zona; itching of the skin; ichthyosis; itch; lichen; measles; nettle-rash; plague; pemphigus; purple-rash; ecthyma; rubeolæ; scarlatina; varicella; rupia; impetigo; *syphilis;* varioloid. Tinea capitis; *eruptions in the face;* mentagra; herpes praeputialis.

B. Excrescences; steatoma; chilblains; fungus articularis; moles; polypi; tuberculosis; *fungus excrescences* (fungus hæmatodes, &c.); sycoma; *sycosis; warts.*

C. *Abscesses, gangrene; glandular diseases; suppurations; tumours; ulcers;* rhagades; *indurations of the skin;* anasarca; stings of insects; *diseases of bones; diseases of nails* and panaritia; œdema; *erysipelas;* scurvy; *scrofulous affections; indurations; injuries; sore skin.*

D. Cyanosis; chlorosis; bloody sweat; jaundice; pitiriasis; erythrema; dropsy.

III. Morbid Sleep.—See: Night-mare; yawning; *morbid sleep; sleeplessness;* sopor; *dreams,* (see under morbid sleep.)

IV. Fever.—See: *Inflammatory fevers;* gastric (mucous and bilious fevers); yellow fever; catarrhal (and rheumatic fever); nervous fever (typhus); plague; morbid sweat; febris anglica; deficient warmth; fever and ague; dentition-fever (see under diseases of children); hectic fever.

V. Mental Diseases.—See: Paroxysms of anguish; idiocy;

delirium; *weak memory* and *mind; mental derangement;* emotions; *morbid emotions;* home-sickness; hypochondria; hysteria; unhappy love; anthropophobia; diseases of drunkards; *melancholy;* mania of suicide; awkwardness.

VI.–VII. Diseases of the Head and Brain.—See: *Delirium;* meningitis; concussion of the brain; hydrocephalus; debility of the brain; congestions of the brain; apoplexy; vertigo.

VIII. External Head.—See: Open fontanelle; large head; falling off of the hair; tinea capitis; bones of the skull; plica polonica.

IX. Diseases of the Eyes.—See: Hæmorrhage from the eyes; *ophthalmia; running of the eyes;* cancer of the eyes; blepharophthalmitis; blepharospasmus; blepharoplegia; *pains in the eyes; weakness of the eyes* (and alterations of vision); contraction of the lids; ulceration of the eyes; paleness of sight; stye; short-sightedness; photophobia; hemeralopia; strabismus; cataract; glaucoma; nyctalopia; fistula lachrymalis; bleareyedness; far-sightedness.

X. Diseases of the Ears:—See: *Deficient hearing; excessive irritation of hearing;* otorrhœa; parotitis; otitis; herpes of the ear; *otalgia;* polypus of the ears.

XI. Diseases of the Nose.—See: *Anosmia; excessive irritation of the sense of smell;* bleeding of the nose; suppuration of the nose; swelling of the nose; cancer of the nose; polypus of the nose; coryza.

XII. Face.—See: Swelling of the cheeks; *eruption in the face; complexion;* erysipelas of the face; *prosopalgia;* trismus; mentagra; swelling of the lips.

XIII. Teeth.—See: Diseases of the gums; toothache; dentition (see under: Diseases of children.)

XIV. Buccal Cavity.—See: Ranula; hæmorrhage of the

mouth; stomacace; fetor of the mouth; aphthæ; ptyalism; deficiency of speech; diseases of the tongue.

XV. Throat and Fauces.—See: Angina faucium; angina tonsillaris; dysphagia; pharyngitis; œsophagitis.

XVI. Taste and Appetite.—See: *Loss of appetite; malacia; alterations of taste;* loss of taste; canine hunger; *weakness of the stomach,* (and ill effects of certain kinds of nourishment.)

XVII. Gastric Derangement.—See: Hæmatemesis; cholera and cholerine; *gastric* (and bilious) derangement; *derangement of the stomach;* hiccough; heartburn and eructations.

XVIII. Diseases of the Stomach. — See: Gastroenteritis; gastritis; gastromalacia; cardialgia, and pains in the stomach.

XIX. Hypochondria.—See: Hepatitis; induration of the liver; splenitis; diaphragmitis.

XX. Abdomen and Groin.—See: Distention of the abdomen; abdominal congestions; enteritis; peritonitis; colic; abdominal tubercles; ascites; pot-bellied; ileus; tympanitis.—Hernia; bubo.

XXI. Stool and Anus.—See: Hæmorrhage of the anus; itching of the anus; diarrhœa; cholera and cholerine; hæmorrhoids; fistula recti; prolapsus of the rectum; dysentery; constipation; worm-affections.

XXII. Urine and Urinary difficulties.—See: Catarrh of the bladder; cystitis; hæmorrhoids of the bladder; cystospasmus; cystoplegia; polypus of the bladder; thickening of the bladder; urinary secretion; *urinary difficulties;* urinary fistula: hæmorrhage of the urethra; urethritis; gonorrhœa; stricture; diabetes; retention of urine; nephritis; calculi renales; lithiasis.

XXIII. Male sexual parts.—See: Balanorrhœa; *sexual instinct; sexual power;* gonorrhœa; hernia scrotalis; orchitis;

induration of the testes; phimosis; prostatitie; herpss præputialis; sycosis; syphilis.

XXIV. Female sexual parts, and Diseases of women.—See: Diseases of the ovaries; hæmorrhage of the uterus; metritis; cancer of the uterus; *diseases of the uterus;* prolapsus of the uterus; herpes præputialis; swelling of the pudendum.—*Menstrual difficulties;* ' amenia; chlorosis; leucorrhœa; *sexual instinct; sexual power; pregnancy; confinement; labour;* puerperal fever; *nursing; breasts and nipples.*

N. B. Diseases of children, infants at the breast and new-born infants, (see under: *Diseases of children.*)

XXV. Trachea and Cough.—See: Croup; influenza; hoarseness (and aphonia); *cough; catarrh;* catarrhal fever; laryngitis; laryngeal phthisis; whooping-cough; tracheitis; tracheal phthisis; *catarrh.*

XXVI. Chest, Respiration and heart.—See: Asthma Wigandi et Millari; *asthma spasmodicum;* asthma thymicum; angina pectoris; congestions of the chest; inflammation of the chest; pleuritis; *pains in the chest;* hydrothorax; orthopnœa paralytica; *diseases of the heart*) and palpitation of the heart); hæmorrhage of the lungs; pneumonia; paralysis of the lungs; pulmonary phthisis.

XXVII. Back, small of the back and neck.—See: Lumbago; nephritis; atrophia spinalis; spinitis; arthralgia; diseases of the bones; spasms; paralysis; rhachitis; rheumatism; paroxysms of pain; scrophulosis.

XXVIII. Upper extremities.—See: Deadness of single parts; arthrocace; hydrarthrus; tumours; *arthritis;* chiragra; *arthralgia;* diseases of the bones; paralysis; contraction of muscles; *rheumatism; paroxysms of pain; diseases of the nails* (and panaritia).

XXIX. Lower extremities.—See: Arthrocace; hydrarthrus;

arthralgia; tumours; *ulcers; arthritis;* coxagra; gonitis; diseases of the bones; paralysis; diseases of the nails; œdema; podagra; psoitis; contraction of muscles; erysipelas; *rheumatism; paroxysms of pain; diseases of the nails.*

N. B. The full names of the remedies recommended in this work, will be found at the end of the work, in the "*Characteristic Symptoms;*" in the body of the work the abbreviated names have been used.

CLINICAL GUIDE;

OR,

POCKET-REPERTORY;

FOR THE HOMŒOPATHIC TREATMENT

OF

ACUTE AND CHRONIC DISEASES.

N. B.—The classification of remedies which I have used in this Repertory, is the same as that which has been used in my Manual. The remedies under No. 1 are those that have acquired authority both from our provings and from experience at the sick-bed; the remedies under No. 2 are likewise authoritative, but not in the same absolute sense as those under No. 1. The remedies under No. 3 have only been confirmed by single cases, or are simply indicated theoretically; and the remedies marked with an interrogation-point (?), have never been used in practice, and are proposed upon a mere theoretical suggestion.

CLINICAL GUIDE

For the Homœopathic Treatment of

ACUTE AND CHRONIC DISEASES.

ABSCESSES, INTERNAL AND EXTERNAL.—§ 1. Internal abscesses generally require the same remedies as external.

A preference should be given:

a) for *acute* abscesses, to: *Ars. asa. bell. bryon. cham. hep. led. mezer. phosph. puls. sulph.*

b) for *chronic* abscesses, whether cold or occasioned by congestions, to: *Asa. aurum. calc. carb-veg. con. hep. iod. laur. lycop. mang. merc. merc-corr. nitr-ac. phos. sep. sil. sulph.*

§ 2. Particular indications:

ARSEN.: for intolerable, burning pains, during the fever; or when the abscess threatens to become gangrenous, or is accompanied with great debility.

ASA: for abscesses discharging a colorless, serous pus; violent pains on contact, and great sensitiveness of the adjoining parts.

BELLAD.: Pressure, burning and stinging in the abscess; cheesy and flocculent pus.—Is especially suitable for hepatic abscesses.

BRYON.: The tumor is either *very red* or *very pale*, with tensive pain.

MEZER.: for abscesses of *fibrous parts* and of *tendons*, or for abscesses arising from abuse of Mercury.

PULSAT.: When the abscess bleeds readily, with stinging or cutting pains; or when an *itching*, burning and stinging is experienced in the surrounding parts; especially varices.

RHUS.: especially for abscesses of the *axillary* or *parotid* glands, when the swelling is painful to the touch, or discharges a *bloody-serous pus.*

ACNE.—For acne in the face of young people: *Bell. carb-veg. hep.* or *sulph.*

For acne arising from *sexual abuse*, principally: *Calc. phos-ac.* and *sulph.*

For acne of *drunkards: N-vom. led.* and *sulph.*, or *ars. lach.* and *puls.*

For *acne rosacea:* 1) *Carb-an. kreos. rhus. veratr.* 2) *Ars. calc. carb-veg. mezer. ruta.* 3) *Aur-m. cann. caust. canth. cicut. laches. ledum. sepia.*

For *acne punctata* (*comedones, black pores*) most frequently: 1) *Bell. hep. natr. nitr-ac. sulph.* 2) *Natr-m. sabin. selen.*

ADIPOSIS: for adiposes of young men and girls, observation and symptoms point to the following remedies: 1) *Ant. calc. caps. ferr. puls. sulph.* 2) *Ars. baryt. cupr. lyc. veratr.*

AGUSTIA:

§ 1. The principal remedies are: 1) *Bell. lyc. natr-m. phosph. puls. sil.* 2) *Alum. amm-m. anac. calc. hep. hyos. kal. kreos. magn-m. n-vom. rhod. sec. sep. veratr.*

§ 2. For agustia from purely nervous causes, such as paralysis, the principal remedies are: *Bell. hyos. lyc. natr-m. n-vom. sep. veratr.*

For agustia attended with catarrh, &c., we use: 1) *N-vom. puls. sulph.* 2) *Alum. calc. hep. natr-m. rhod. sep.*

§ 3. Compare HEARING, HARDNESS OF, ANOSMIA, AMBLYOPIA, &c.

ALCOHOL, POISONING BY.—According to Hering, the principal remedies are: 1) Milk. 2) Mucilaginous drinks. 3) Caustic spirits of Ammonium, (one drop in a tumblerful of sugar-water, in teaspoonful doses). *Black coffee* is likewise useful, as well as *Nux-vom.* in homœopathic doses.

ALUM, POISONING BY, AND ILL EFFECTS OF, ABUSE OF, for poisoning by large doses of: 1) *Soap-water*, or, 2) *sugar-water*, until vomiting sets in; afterwards *Puls.* or *veratr.* for the remaining symptoms.

AMBLYOPIA, weakness or morbid alteration of sight; weakness of sight, from mere dim-sightedness to complete blindness may arise from so many causes, and may be attended with so many different morbid states of the organism, that there is scarcely a remedy which is not of advantage in the treatment of this affection. I have, therefore, noted only the most efficacious remedies for amblyopia, furnishing particular indications to serve as points of support, and to facilitate the selection of remedies for particular cases.

The principal remedies for amblyopia, are: 1) *Aur. bell. calc. caust. chin. cic. cin. dros. hyos. merc. natr-m. n-vom. phos. puls. rut. sep. sil. sulph. veratr.* 2) *Agar. cann. caps. con. croc. dig. dulc. euphr. guaj. kal. lach. lyc. magn. natr. nitr-ac. op. plumb. rhus. sec. spig. tart. zinc.*

For *amblyopia, simple weakness of sight:* 1) *Anac. bell. calc. caps. cin. croc. hyos. lyc. magn. puls. rut. sep.* and *sulph.* 2) *Cann. caust. natr. natr-m. phos. plumb.* &c.

For *amblyopia amaurotica (incipient amaurosis):* 1) *Aur. bell. calc. caps. caust. chin. cic. con. dros. dulc. hyos. merc. natr. natr-m. nitr-ac. op. phos. puls. rhus. sec. sep. sil. sulph. veratr.* 2) *Agar. caps. cin. dig. euphr. guaj. kal. lach. lyc. n-mosch.? plumb. zinc.* &c.

For *complete amaurosis,* provided it is not incurable, the same remedies should be used as for *amblyopia amaurotica,* the remedy depending not so much upon the *degree* of weakness, as upon the *totality of the symptoms.* Unless secondary symptoms should require other remedies, we may use: *Bellad. calc. merc. phosph. sep. sulph.* &c., though any other remedy may be used if indicated by the general symptoms.

For *erethic* amaurosis, principally: *Bell. calc. cic. con. hyos. merc. nitr-ac. op. phos. sep. sulph.* &c.

For *torpid* amaurosis: *Aur. caps. caust. chin. dros. dulc. natr. natr-m. op. phos.-ac. plumb. sec. veratr.* &c.

§ 2. As regards *external causes,* if the weakness should have been caused by *fine work,* give *Bell.* or *Ruta,* or perhaps, *Carb-v. calc.* and *spig.*

If by *debilitating causes, loss of animal fluids, sexual abuse,* &c., give *Chin.* or *cin.* or perhaps, 2) *Anac. calc. natr. natr-m. n-vom.* or *sulph.* or, 3) *Phos-ac. sep.*

If by DRINKING, *Chin. calc. lach. n-vom. op.* and *sulph.*

If by EXTERNAL INJURIES, BLOW ON THE HEAD, VIOLENT CONCUSSIONS, &c., 1) *Arn.* 2) *Con. euphr. rhus. rut.* or *staph.*

If by *old age,* principally: *Aur. bar. con. op. phos. sec.*

If by SCROPHULA: 1) *Bell. calc. chin. cin. dulc. merc. sulph.* 2) *Aur. euphr. hep. n-vom.* or *puls.* &c.

If by ARTHRITIC METASTASIS: *Ant. bell. merc. puls. rhus. spig. sulph.* &c.

If by RHEUMATIC CAUSES: 1) *Cham. euphr. lyc. merc. nux. puls. rhus. spig. sulph.* 2) *Caust. hep. lach.* &c.

If by SUPPRESSION OF SUPPURATION OF MUCOUS DISCHARGE: *Chin. euphr. hep. lyc. puls. sil. sulph.* &c.

If by SUPPRESSION OF HABITUAL DISCHARGES OF BLOOD, such as HÆMORRHOIDS, MENSES, &c.: *Bell. calc. lyc. n-vom. phos. puls. sep. sulph.* &c.

If by SUPPRESSION OF AN EXANTHEM: *Bell. calc. caust. lach. lyc. merc. sil. stram. sulph.* &c.

If by abuse of Mercury or some other metallic substance: 1) *Sulph.* 2) *Hep. nitr-ac. sil.* or, 3) *Aur. bell. carb-v. chin. lach. op. puls.* &c.

§ 3. As regards the *affections* which may *attend* amblyopia, if *nervous headache*, the principal remedies are: *Aur. bell. bry calc. hep. nitr-ac. n-vom. phos. puls. sep. sulph.* &c.

If CONGESTION OF BLOOD TO THE HEAD: *Aur. bell. calc. chin. hyos. n-vom. op. phos. sil. sulph.* &c.

If HEARING, and the EAR be AFFECTED: *Cic. nitr. ac. petr. phos. puls.* &c.

If by GASTRIC and ABDOMINAL AILMENTS: *Ant. calc. caps. chin. cocc. lyc. natr-m. n-vom. phos. puls. sulph.* &c.

If by UTERINE DERANGEMENTS: *Aur. bell. cic. cocc. con. magn. natr-m. n-vom. plat. phos. puls. rhus. sep. stram. sulph.* &c.

If by PULMONARY COMPLAINTS: *Calc. cann. hep. lach. lyc. natr-m. phos. sil. sulph.* &c.

If by DISEASES OF THE HEART: *Aur. calc. cann. dig. lach. phos. puls. sep. spig.* &c.

If by SPASMS, EPILEPSY, &c.: *Bell. lach. caust. cic. ign. hyos. lach. op. sil. stram. sulph.* &c.

§ 4. As regards *symptoms*, the remedy should be selected in accordance with the totality thereof, both the symptoms of the eye and those of the general organism. But as it would be impossible to enumerate those symptoms without repeating the pathogenesis of every remedy indicated, I must content myself with furnishing the following particular indications for the different remedies of the eyes, leaving to the practitioner the business of supplying omissions and modifying my indications agreeably to the general symptoms of the patient. Use:

AURUM: for black spots, or scintillations; half-sightedness, so that things appear to be cut off horizontally; tensive pain in the eyes.

BELLADONNA: for *dilated* or *insensible pupils; photophobia*, spasmodic motions of the eyes and eyelids, induced by the light impinging upon the retina; *scintillations* or mist, or *black spots or points before the eyes*, or spots of various colours, or silver-coloured; *hemeralopia, as soon as the sun is down;* diplopia; or the *objects appear red*, or inverted; stitches in the eyes, or *aching and distensive pains extending to the orbits* and forehead; red face.

CALCAREA: for *mistiness* of sight, gauze before the eyes, especially when reading, or after eating, with black motes before the eyes; extreme photophobia, with dazzling of the eyes by light; *dilated pupils;* pressure, or feeling of coldness in the eyes.

CAUSTICUM: for sudden and frequent loss of sight, with sensation as if a pellicle were stretched over the eyes; or dimsightedness as if looking through a cloth or mist; black threads or motes, scintillations; photophobia.

CHINA: for weak sight, the patient sees only the outlines of things near him; the letters look pale, are surrounded by white borders, blurred; dilated and not very sensible pupils; dimness of cornea as if the eyes were filled with smoke; scintillations or black motes; the eyes feel better after sleeping.

Cicuta: ***Frequent vanishing of sight***, as if by absence of mind, with *vertigo*, especially when walking; the objects seem to totter, and the letters to move when reading; diplopia; frequent obscuration of sight, alternating with hardness of hearing; blue margins around the eyes; photophobia, burning in the eyes; aching pain over the orbits.

Cina: for dimness of sight when reading, going off by wiping the eyes; dilated pupil; photophobia; pressure in the eyes, as if sand had got in, especially when reading.

Drosera: for frequent vanishing of sight, especially when reading, the letters look pale and blurred; photophobia, the eyes are dazzled by the light, or by the glare of fire; they are very dry; the nose is dry and stopped up; stitches in the eyes.

Hyoscyamus: for dilated pupils; frequent spasms of the eyes and eyelids; squinting; diplopia; hemeralopia; illusion of sight, as if things were red, or larger than they really are; aching, stupefying pains over the eyes.

Mercurius: for mistiness of sight; frequent, momentary loss of sight; black points; scintillations, black motes; *paroxysms of momentary blindness;* the letters seem to move when reading; *the eyes are very sensitive to the light, or the glare of fire;* cutting, stinging or aching pains in the eyes, especially when exerting the eyes; (dilated, or even insensible, or unequal pupils.)

Natrum mur.: for frequent obscuration of sight, especially when stooping, walking, reading, writing, &c.; dimsightedness as if through gauze or feathers; the letters look blurred; diplopia; half-sightedness; frequent, spasmodic closing of the lids; frequent lachrymation.

Nux vom.: for scintillations, or black or gray points, or flashes; *the eyes are very sensitive to light, especially early;* violent pressure in the eyes after using them ever so little; *red face;* dilated pupils; heaviness and frequent closing of the eyelids.

Phosphorus: for sudden *paroxysms of nyctalopia*, or *sensation as if things were covered with a gray veil;* the eyes are very *sensitive to the light*, or are dazzled by bright light; blackness or *black points or sparks;* aching pains in the eyes, orbits and forehead; frequent lachrymation, especially in the open air, and when exposed to the wind.

Pulsatilla: for frequent vanishing and obscuration of sight, with *paleness of sight*, and disposition to vomit; blindness at twilight, and sensation as if the eyes were bandaged; or mistiness of sight, or *sensation as i the dimness of sight could be removed by wiping*, particularly in the open air, or *in the evening*, or early on waking; diplopia, or paleness of sight; shining or flashing rings before the eyes; *photophobia*, with stitches in the eyes when the light impinges upon the retina; *frequent and copious lachrymation*, particularly *in the open air*, when exposed to wind and light; *contraction of the pupils*.

Ruta: for *mistiness of sight*, with complete obscuration at a distance; muscæ volitantes; aching or burning pains in the eyes on using them, particularly when reading; lachrymation in the open air.

•Sepia: for dimness of sight, particularly when reading or writing; contraction of pupils; *gauze, black spots or stripes before the eyes;* photophobia in the day-time; aching pain over the eyeball.

Silicea: for dimness of sight, as if looking through a gray cover; *paroxysms of sudden nyctalopia;* the letters look pale and blurred when reading; sparks and *black spots before the eyes; photophobia*, the light of day dazzles the eyes; *frequent lachrymation*, especially in the open air; stitches in the forehead which seem to strike through the eyes.

Sulphur: for *mistiness*, or *dimness of sight* as if *looking through black gauze or feather-dust;* frequent obscuration of sight, especially when reading; *photophobia*, especially from the *light of the sun*, and when the weather is warm and sultry; the eyes are dazzled by the light; *sudden paroxysms of nyctalopia;* scintillations and white spots, or motes and black points or stripes before the eyes; tearing burning pains in the head and eyes; *profuse lachrymation*, especially in the open air; or *great dryness* of the eyes, especially in the room; unequal or dilated and insensible pupils.

Veratrum: for hemeralopia; sparks and black spots before the eyes, particularly on rising from the bed, or from a chair; *profuse lachrymation*, with burning, cutting, and feeling of dryness; diplopia; photophobia, &c.

§ 5. The following remedies deserve particular consideration for particular symptoms:

Palesightedness: Dros. petr. sil.—Things look blue: Bell. lyc. stram. stront. sulph. zinc.—The eyes are dazzled by bright light: Bar. calc. caust. cic. dros. euphr graph. kal. merc n-vom. phos. phos-ac. sep. sil.—Periodical paroxysms of blindness: Calc. chel. chin dig. euphr. hyos. natr-m. n-vom. phos. puls. sep. sil. sulph.—Nyctalopia: Phos. sil. sulph.; acon. merc.; con. nitr. n-vom. phos. stram.—Hemeralopia: Bell. chinin ? hyos. merc. puls. stram. veratr.—Complete, *constant blindness: Bell. calc. caust.? chel.? cic.? con.? dig.? euphr.? hyos.? natr-m.? op.? phos.? puls.? sec.? sil. stram. sulph.*—Blindness with frequent desire to *wink: Croc. euphr. hep.*

petr. phos-ac. plat. staph.—Diplopia : Bell. cic. daph. dig. euph. hyos. lyc. natr-m. nitr-ac. oleand. puls. sec. stram sulph. veratr. —*Obscuration* (vanishing of sight): *Agar. aur. bell. bry calc. caust. cic. con. dig. dros. ferr. graph. hep. hyos. lyc. mang. merc. natr-m. nitr-ac. n-vom. oleand. phos. puls. sil. sulph.—Darkness* (gray black cover) before the eyes: *Agar. anac. aur. baryt. calc. caust. chin. chinin. con. euphr. magn-c. merc. natr. natr-m. phos. sep. sil.—Things look as if at a distance : Anac. carb-a. cic. natr-m. n-mosch. phos. stann. stram. sulph.—Coloured appearances before the eyes : Aur. bell. bor. camph. hyos. kal. n-vom. puls. spig. veratr.—Featherdust* before the eyes: *Calc. lyc. natr. natr-m. sulph.—Luminous* appearances (scintillations): *Aur. bell. bry. caust. croc. hyos. kal. lyc. natr. natr-m. n-vom. puls. spig. zinc.*—Black and *dark spots* before the eyes: *Amm-m. anac. aur. bar. bell. calc. caust. chin. chinin. kal. merc. natr-m. nitr-ac. phos. sep. sil.—Flying* spots and gauzes: *Acon. agar. am-m. bell. calc. chin. con. merc. nitr-ac. phos. sep. sil. stram. Luminous vibration : Amm. caust. cham. graph.—Gauze* or mist before the eyes: *Bell. calc. caust. chinin. croc. dros. ign. kreos. lyc. merc. natr-m. petr. phos. phos-ac. rut. sec. sep. sulph.*—Things look *yellow : Bell. canth. chin. dig. merc. sep.*—Things look *gray : Nitr-ac. n-vom. phos. sil. stram.*—Things look *larger* than they are: *Euph. hyos. natr-m. phos.—Half-sightedness: Aur. calc. caust. lyc. mur-ac. natr-m. sep.—Light* colours and appearances before the eyes: *Amm. bell. bor. calc. camph. hyos. kal. natr-m. n-vom. puls. sil. spig. valer.—Short-sightedness: Amm. calc. chin. con. cycl. euphr. hyos. lach. lyc. nitr-ac. petr. phos. phos-ac. puls. rut. sulph. sulph-ac. tart. valer.* —*Longsightedness : Calc. coff. con. dros. hyos. lyc. meph. natr. natr-m. n-vom. petr. sep. sil. sulph.—Dilated pupils : Acon. bell. calc. caps. chin. cic. cin. cocc. con. croc. cycl. guaj. hep. hyos. ign. ipec. led. lyc. nitr-ac. n-vom. op. sec. spig. squil. staph. stram. veratr. zinc.—Contracted pupils : Anac. arn. bell. camph. cham. chel. chin. cic. cocc. dig. ign. led. mez. mur-ac. phos. puls. rut. sep. sil. squill. sulph thuj. veratr. zinc.*—Colours as of the *rainbow : Bell. cic. kal. nitr. phos. phos-ac. stram. sulph.—Things look red : Bell. con. croc. dig. hep. hyos. spig. stront. sulph —Shadows* before the eyes: *Sen.*—Disposition to *squint : Alum. bell. hyos. puls.—Blackness of sight,* black colours before the eyes: *Bell. calc. chin. euphr. kal. magn-c. phos. sep. sil. stram.—Stripes* before the eyes: *Amm. bell. con. natr-m. puls. sep —Dimness of sight : Ambr. amm. anac. bar. bell. calc. cann. caust. chin. con. croc. euphr. hep. ign. kreos. lyc. merc. phos. puls. rut. sep. sil. sulph.—Things look inverted : Bell.*—Disposition to *wipe the eyes* all the time: *Carb-a. croc. lyc. natr. phos. puls.—The letters look blurred* when reading: *Bell. bry. chin. daph. dros. graph. hyos. lyc. natr-m. sen. sil. stram. viol-od.*

AMENIA: AMENORRHŒA, MENOSCHESIS, SUPPRESSION OF THE MENSES, and the AILMENTS INCIDENTAL THERETO:

§ 1. The best remedies are: 1) *Puls. sep. sulph.* 2) *Acon. bry. con. dulc. graph. kal. lyc. sil.* 3) *Amon. ars. bell. baryt. calc. caust. cham. coccul. cupr. ferr. natr-m. phosph.* 4) *Chin. jod. merc. n-mosch. op. plat. rhod. sabin. staph. stram. val. verat. zinc.*

§ 2. *Amenia* of young girls, that is, too long delay of the *first* menses, requires principally: 1) *Puls. sulph.*, or 2) *Caust. cocc. graph. kal. natr-m. petr. sep. veratr.*

Suppression of the menses in consequence of *a cold*, principally: 1) *N-mosch. puls.*, or 2) *Bell. dulc. sep. sulph.*,—or if occasioned by *fright* or *sudden emotions:* 1) *Acon. lyc.*, or 2) *Coff. op. veratr.*

For *feeble, though not entirely suppressed menses (menoschesis)*, give: *Calc. caust. con. graph. kal. lyc. magn. natr-m. phosph. puls. sil. sulph. veratr. zinc.*

§ 3. For amenia of *plethoric* individuals, use: *Acon., bell. bry. n-vom. op. plat. sabin.* or *sulph.*

For *debilitated* or *cachectic* individuals: *Ars. chin. con. graph. jod. natr-m. puls. sep. sulph.*

§ 4. Particular indications for the symptoms characterizing amenia:

ACONITUM: frequent congestion of blood to the head or chest, with palpitation of the heart; aching, pulsative or stitching pains in the head; redness of the face; full and hard pulse; frequent heat with thirst; disposition to be angry, &c.; is particularly suitable to young girls who lead a sedentary life.

ARSENICUM: great debility; pale, livid complexion with blue margins around the eyes; constant desire for sour things, coffee, or brandy; great craving for sexual intercourse; corrosive leucorrhœa; frequent paroxysms of fainting.

BRYONIA: amenorrhœa is attended with violent erethism of the circulation; frequent congestion of blood to the head or chest, with bleeding of the nose or dry cough; coldness, frequent shudderings which sometimes alternate with a dry or burning heat; constipation, belly-ache, and colic.

CALCAREA: frequent rush of blood to the head, vertigo, burning pains in the forehead, or throbbing and aching pain in the head; buzzing in the ears; belly-ache with a feeling of fulness in the hypochondria, and inability to wear tight clothes; colic, with pains down the thighs, especially at the time when the menses ought to appear; great languor, heaviness in the whole body, especially in the lower limbs.

CAUSTICUM: hysteric pains, colic, pains in the loins, abdominal spasms, yellowish complexion.

China: pale face with blue margins around the eyes; headache, especially at night; bellyache, particularly after dinner; bad digestion; emaciation; great debility with languor and heaviness of the lower limbs; sleeplessness or restless sleep, with anxious or fatiguing dreams; or: abdominal or pulmonary spasms; rush of blood to the head, with pulsations of the carotids; nymphomania; nervousness, great sensitiveness to the least noise, &c.

Cocculus: hysteric abdominal spasms at a time when the menses ought to appear, with pressure towards the chest, oppression, restlessness, anguish, sadness, moaning; great debility, which does not even allow the patient to talk; or: discharge of black blood in drops, attended with great nervous distress.

Conium: hysteric and chlorotic symptoms, flaccid and dry, or hard and painful breasts; great nervousness, involuntary laughing and weeping; great weakness after the least walk; anguish and sadness; abdominal spasms, distention of the abdomen, stitching pains, leucorrhœa, &c.

Cuprum: rush of blood to the head, with aching pain in the vertex; red face and eyes; or: pale face with blue margins around the eyes; frequent nausea with vomiting; abdominal spasms, or twitching of the limbs, with heaviness; palpitation of the heart, and spasms of the chest.

Ferrum: Great *nervousness* and *debility*, trembling of the limbs; emaciation, great *disposition to lie and sit*; rush of blood to the head, with throbbing pain, roaring, buzzing and prickling in the brain; pale, livid face, with blue margins around the eyes; or burning redness of the face, with red eyes; pressure in the stomach and head; great lassitude in the lower limbs, and other chlorotic affections.

Graphites: The menses appear occasionally, but are pale, and cease again shortly after; especially when *herpetic* or *erysipelatous eruptions* appear upon the skin; hysteric headache, nausea, pain in the chest, great debility; colic and hysteric spasms; leucorrhœa and sterility; hæmorrhoidal disposition.

Iodium: Frequent palpitation of the heart; pale face, sometimes alternating with redness; loss of breath on ascending an eminence; great nervousness, debility, especially in the lower limbs, and other chlorotic symptoms.

Kali carb.: very efficacious, particularly when attended with difficult breathing; palpitation of the heart; disposition to erysipelatous eruptions, and paleness of the face which sometimes alternates with great redness.

Lycopodium: Chlorotic symptoms, *disposition to sadness*, *melancholy*, and weeping; hysteric headache; sour vomiting and mouth; swelling of the feet, pains in the back and loins, colic; fainting fits; leucorrhœa; swelling and pressure in the umbilical region, and drawing or tensive pains through the whole body.

Mercurius: Rush of blood to the head; dry heat; orgasm of the circulation; leucorrhœa; œdematous swelling of the hands and feet, or of the face; pale face and sickly complexion; *great languor* and *debility*, with trembling and rushes of blood after the least exertion; irritable mood; sad, peevish, and whimsical.

Natrum: Frequent headache, hysteric or chlorotic symptoms; disposition to *melancholy*, with listlessness; great debility of body and mind, with heaviness in the limbs and aversion to motion; disposition to be angry and vehement.

Nux mosch.: *Suppression of the menses,* with spasms and other hysteric affections; disposition to sleep and faint away, with great nervousness, debility; complete exhaustion after the least exertion; pains in the loins; frequent water brash; fitful mood.

Opium: Suppression, with congestion of blood to the head, which feels heavy; redness and heat of the face, sopor and convulsive motions.

Pulsatilla: Amenorrhœa, especially *from a cold or getting wet;* or when attended with: frequent paroxysms of *hemicrania,* with stitching pains extending to the face and teeth; or aching pains over the forehead, with pressure on the vertex; pale complexion; vertigo with buzzing in the ears; *stitching toothache, the pains suddenly shifting from one side to the other;* frequent catarrh; difficult breathing, loss of breath and asthma after the least exertion; *palpitation of the heart; cold hands and feet,* frequently alternating with sudden heat; *disposition to mucous diarrhœa; leucorrhœa;* pains in the loins; oppressive weight in the abdomen; colic *with nausea* and *vomiting;* constant chilliness with yawning, stretching and great languor, especially in the lower limbs; *swelling of the feet;* especially suitable to females with blond hair, blue eyes, freckles in the face, *mild disposition* and *disposition to sadness* and *weeping.*

Sabina: When the menses, after flowing profusely at other times, cease, and are replaced by a thick fetid leucorrhœa.

Sepia: Ranks with *Puls.* for amenorrhœa with leucorrhœa; it is further indicated by frequent paroxysms of *hysteric* or *nervous headache; toothache,* with excessive sensitiveness of the dental nerves; delicate constitution; delicate and sensitive skin; *sallow complexion* or *dingy spots in the face;* nervous debility and great disposition to sweat; frequent alternation of chilliness and heat; *disposition to melancholy and weeping;* frequent paroxysms of catarrh; exposure to wet; pains in the limbs as if bruised; frequent colic and pains in the small of the back.

Sulphur: *Aching and tensive pain in the head, especially from the occiput to the neck;* or throbbing pains in the head, with congestion of blood, heat, digging, shocks, and *whizzing noise in the brain;* pale and sickly complexion, blue margins around the eyes, and red spots on the cheeks ; pimples on the forehead and around the mouth ; immoderate hunger, voracity ; general emaciation ; sour and burning eructations ; pressure, feeling of repletion and heaviness in the stomach, hypochondria, and abdomen ; hæmorrhoidal disposition ; *slimy diarrhœa ;* or constipation, with hard stools and frequent, ineffectual urging ; abdominal spasms ; *leucorrhœa ;* itching of the sexual organs ; hysteria, and chlorotic symptoms ; the limbs are liable to go to sleep ; asthma ; pains in the loins ; fainting fits ; *great disposition to take cold ;* nervous debility, great languor, *especially in the lower limbs,* and great *exhaustion after talking ;* irritable mood, disposition to be angry ; or sad and melancholy, frequent weeping.

Veratrum : Amenorrhœa with nervous headache, hysteric symptoms ; pale, livid face ; frequent nausea and vomiting ; cold hands, feet, and nose ; great weakness, with fainting turns ; sexual excitement, even nymphomania, and other forms of mania.

§ 5. See : Menstrual difficulties, Chlorosis, &c.

ANÆMIA.—The best remedies are : 1) *Ars. chin. puls. squill. staph. sulph.* 2) *Arn. bell. bry. calc. carb-v. chin. cin. con. ferr. hep. ign. kal. lyc. lach. merc. natr. natr-m. n-vom. phos. phos-ac. rhus. sep. sil. sulph. veratr.*

If it arise from *loss of blood,* or other fluids, give : 1) *Chin. n-vom. sulph. ;* or 2) *Calc. carb-v. cin. phos-ac. staph. sulph.*

If caused by *violent acute diseases,* use : *Calc. carb-v. chin. hep. kal. natr. natr-m. n-vom. veratr.*

See Chlorosis, Debility, Scurvy, &c.

ANASARCA.—Principal remedies : *Ars. bry. chin. dig. dulc. hell. merc.* and *sulph.,* or perhaps *Camph. convolv. lact. rhus. samb.* and *sol-nigr.*

For anasarca after cutaneous diseases, such as : *scarlatina, measles,* &c., we give with great effect, *hell.* and *ars. ;* in other cases the remedies have to be chosen in accordance with the symptoms. See Dropsy.

ANEURISM.—Best remedies, so far as known : *Carb-veg. lach.* and *lyc. ;* also : *Guaj. puls.* and *sulph.*—In some cases may be required : 1) *Calc. caust. graph. kali-carb.* 2) *Amb. arn. ars. ferr. natr-m. zinc.*

ANEURISM by anastomosis.—Yields to : *Carb-veg. caust. lycop. platin. thuj.*

ANGINA PECTORIS, NEURALGIA CORDIS.—One of the principal remedies seems to be *Hep.*, after which give: 2) *Ars. lach. samb. veratr.*, and 3) *Acon. aur. bell. caust. dig. phos. spong.*, and (according to Hartmann) *Angust. ipec.* and *sep.*

As regards the particular indications, we refer the reader to the remedies under ASTHMA, CONGESTIONS OF THE CHEST, SPASMS OF THE CHEST, SUFFOCATIVE CATARRH, and DISEASES OF THE HEART, and the symptoms of those remedies in HEMPEL'S " Jahr."

ANGUISH, PAROXYSMS OF.—Generally a mere symptom, though sometimes so prominent and distressing that it deserves a special treatment. Principal remedies: 1) *Acon. ars. aur. bell. cham. digit. merc. n-vom. puls. veratr.* 2) *Alum. anac. baryt. bryon. carb-an. carb-veg. coccul. cupr. graph. hyosc. ignat. lycop. nitr. nitr-ac. phosph. rhus. sepia. spigel. spong. sulph.*

See EMOTIONS, morbid, HYPOCHONDRIA, HYSTERIA.

ANOSMIA: The best remedies are: *Bell. calc. natr-m. n-vom. phosph. puls. sep. sil. sulph.*, or: *Alum. aur. caps. caust. hep. hyos. ipec. kal. lyc. magn-m. mez. nitr-ac. oleand. op. rhus. veratr.*

For loss of smell from *paralysis of the olfactory nerves*, we have principally: *Bell. caust. hyos. lyc. natr-m. n-vom. op. plumb. sep.*

For *catarrhal* anosmia: *Alum. calc. hep. mez. natr-m. n-vom. puls. sep. sil. sulph.*

Compare: NASITIS, CATARRH, &c., also: AMBLYOPIA; HEARING, HARDNESS OF, and the CAUSES and VARIETIES of these affections.

ANOREXIA.—§ 1. Though generally a mere symptom, yet it is sometimes a mere dislike to certain kinds of nourishment which can be treated with:

1) *Ant. arn. china. hepar. merc. n-vom. puls. rhus. sulph. tart.* 2) *Baryt. bryon. calc. cycl. natr-m. sepia. silic.* 3) *Ars. bell. canth. cicut. coccul. coni. ignat. lycop. natr-m. opi. plat. thuj. veratr.*

§ 2. For *independent* anorexia, or for anorexia remaining after gastric affections, we have: 1) *Ant. cyclam. sulph.* 2) *China. n-vom. puls. rhus. sepia. silic.*

For anorexia *accompanied with hunger*, use: 1) *China helleb. natr-m. rhus.* 2) *Bryon. calc. ignat. n-vom. opi. silic.* 3) *Ars. baryt. dulc. magnes-m. sulph-ac.*

For anorexia accompanied with complete *loathing of food*, give: 1) *Ipecac. puls. rhus.* 2) *Chin. ignat. n-vom.* 3) *Arn. bryon. coccul. natr-m.* 4) *Acon. bell. laches. mur-ac. sepia.*

§ 3. For *partial* anorexia, or aversion to *particular* kinds of nourishment, we have principally:

a) For aversion to *beer:* 1) *Bell. chin. cocc. n-vom.* 2) *Cham. stann. sulph.*—to *brandy: Ignat.*—to *wine: Ignat. laches. magn-aus. merc. sabad.*—to *milk: Bell. bryon. calc. carb-veg. cina. ignat. natr. puls. sepia. silic.*—to *coffee: Bell. bryon. cham. merc. natr-m. n-vom. rhus.*—to *drinks* generally: 1) *Bell. canth. hyosc. n-vom. stram.* 2) *Laches. natr-m.*

b) For aversion to *rye bread: Lycop. natr-m. n-vom. phos-ac. sulph.*—to *bread generally: Coni. lycop. natr-m. n-vom. phos-ac. puls.*—to *butter: China. carb-veg. merc.*—to *fat* and *fat things: Bryon. carb-an. carb-veg. helleb. hepar. natr-m. puls.*—to *meat* and *broth: Ignat. merc. mur-ac. nitr-ac. puls. silic. sulph.* 2) *Bell. calc. carb-veg. lycop. rhus. sabad. sepia.*—to *fish: Graph.*—to *vegetables: Helleb. magnes-c.*—to *warm, boiled food: Calc. graph. ignat. lycop. magnes-c. silic.*—to *solid food:* 1) *Bryon. staph. sulph.* 2) *Ferr. merc.*

c) For aversion to *sour things: Bell. cocc. fer. sabad. sulph.*,—to *sweets, sugar*, &c.: *Ars. caust. merc. nitr-ac. phosph. sulph. zinc.*

§ 4. For further indications, see: GASTRIC DERANGEMENT, STOMACH, DERANGEMENT OF; VOMITING, NAUSEA, &c.

ANTHRAX.—When caused by infection, the best remedy is *arsen.* unless *chin. silic.* and *rhus*, or *puls.* should be indicated.

The MALIGNANT PUSTULE generally yields to: *Ars. bell. rhus. silic.* or perhaps: *Chin. hyosc. mur-ac. sec. sep.*

The common *anthrax* or *carbuncle*, which is *not caused by infection*, generally requires *Silic.* or perhaps: *Hyosc. lyc.* or *nitr-ac.*—Sometimes *Arnica* is given with great effect at the commencement, after which *Nux-v.* completes the cure.

There is a kind of carbuncle which contains *lice;* this requires *Ars.* and *chin.*

ANTHROPHOBIA.—This kind of mania is best treated with: 1) *Baryt. hyos. lyc. natr. puls. rhus.* 2) *Acon. anac. aur. bell. cic. con. cupr. led. selen. stann.* 3) *Am-m. calc. mang. natr-m. nitr-ac. phosph. sulph.*

See: MENTAL DERANGEMENTS, and EMOTIONS, MORBID.

APHTHÆ.—The best remedies are: *Borax. merc. n-vom. sulph. sulph-ac.* &c.

See: STOMACACE.

APOPLEXIA.—The best remedies are: 1) *Arn. baryt. bell. cocc. lach. n-vom. op. puls.*, and then 2) *Acon. ant. coff. con. dig. hyos. ipec. merc. n-mosch. tart.*

§ 2) For *apoplexia sanguinea:* 1) *Arn. bell. lach. n-vom. op.*, or 2) *Acon. anth. baryt. coff. ipec. hyos. merc. puls.*
For *apoplexia serosa: Arn. ipec. dig. merc.;* or: *Baryt. cin. cocc. con.*
For *apoplexia nervosa:* 1) *Arn. bell. coff. hyos. stram.* 2) *Camph. laur.*

§ 3. For the *subsequent paralysis:* 1) *Arn. baryt. bell. cocc. lach. n-vom. rhus. stram. zinc.;* or 2) *Anac. calc. caust. con. dulc. natr-m. laur. phosph. plumb. ruta. sep. sil.*
For *hemiplegia*, particularly: *Alum. anac. caust. cocc. graph. kal. lach. phos-ac. sulph-ac.*

§ 4. For apoplexia of *drunkards*, give: *Lach. n-vom. op.;* or: *Baryt. coff. con. puls.*
For apoplexia of *old people: Baryt.*, or *Op.*, or *Con. dig. merc.* &c.
For apoplexia from *loss of blood*, or other debilitating causes: *Chin. ipec.*, or *Carb-veg. cocc. n-vom. puls. sep.*
For apoplexia from *overloading the stomach*: a few table-spoons of *black coffee*, or, if these should be insufficient: *Ipec. nux-v. or puls.*

§ 5. *Particular* indications:

Arnica: full and strong pulse, with *paralysis of the limbs* (especially on the left side); loss of consciousness and stupefaction, with stertorous breathing; sighing, *muttering*, involuntary *discharge of fæces and urine*, &c.

Baryta: for *paralysis of the tongue*, or the upper limbs (especially on the right side); the mouth is drawn to one side; disturbed consciousness, with *childish gesticulations* and inability to keep the body erect; *coma*, restlessness, moaning and muttering; circumscribed redness of the cheeks.

Belladonna: *Stupefaction, loss of consciousness* and speech, or convulsive movements of the limbs and muscles of the face; paralysis of the extremities, especially on the right side; *the mouth is drawn to one side;* paralysis of the tongue; ptyalism; *difficulty of swallowing*, or *entire inability to swallow;* (loss of sight;) *dilated pupils;* red, protruded eyes; *red and bloated face.*

Cocculus: The paroxysms are preceded and attended by vertigo, nausea; convulsive motions of the eyes; paralysis, especially of the *lower limbs*, with *insensibility*, &c.

Lachesis: Stupefaction and loss of consciousness, with *blue face* and convulsive movements, or *tremor of the extremities;* or paralysis, *especially of the left side;* the paroxysms are preceded by: frequent absence of mind, or vertigo, with rush of blood to the head.

NUX VOM.: Stupefaction, stertorous breathing and ptyalism; bleareyedness, dim eyes; *paralysis, especially of the lower limbs;* hanging down of the lower jaw; the paroxysms are preceded by: *vertigo with headache and buzzing in the ear*, or nausea with urging to vomit.

OPIUM: The paroxysms are preceded by: dulness of sense, vertigo and heaviness of the head, buzzing in the ears, hardness of hearing, staring look, sleeplessness, anxious dreams, or *frequent desire to sleep;* the paroxysm is attended by: *tetanic rigidity of the whole body; redness, bloatedness and heat of the face;* the head is *hot* and covered with sweat; red eyes, with dilated, *insensible pupils;* slow, *stertorous breathing; convulsive motions* and *trembling of the extremities*, foam at the mouth, &c.

PULSATILLA: For stupefaction and loss of consciousness, bloated and bluish-red face, loss of motion, *violent palpitation of the heart, almost complete suppression of the pulse*, and rattling breathing.

§ 6. For further indications see: CONGESTIONS OF THE HEAD, SOPOR, SPASMS, &c.

APPARENT DEATH: Put a few pellets of the specific remedy on the tongue of the patient, or administer the medicine by the rectum, not omitting the required mechanical means of cure; but never resort to bleeding.

If the asphyxia should have been occasioned by a *blow, fall,* &c., give *Arnica.* If the patient should have been bled before the exhibition of Arnica, give first *China,* (according to Hering), and then *Arnica*

If arising from suffocation, Hering recommends, for those who died by *suspension: Opium;* by *carbonic acid gas: Opium, acon.* or *bell.;* and by drowning: *Lachesis.*

For asphyxia from *congelation*, after the patient had been resuscitated by the usual means, give for the remaining symptoms: *Ars., carb-veg.;* or *Acon.* and *Bryo.*

For asphyxia by a *stroke of lightning*, give: *Nux vom.* The patient should at the same time be placed in recently dug soil, half sitting, half lying, and should be covered with it all over, except his face, which is to be turned towards the sun, until the first signs of life become apparent.

For *asphyxia* of new-born infants, we use: *Tart-emet. op. china,* (and *Acon. Hempel.*)

Compare: CAUSES and CONDITIONS.

ARTHRALGIA: Having said everything we had to say on the pathological character of the diseases belonging under this head, *rheumatism, gout, neuralgia,* &c., we here point out more particularly the parts to which the remedies have specific curative relations. This knowledge is not required in every case, but in many cases it is, since two or three remedies may correspond to the general state of the patient, and one of them only to the part affected.

§ 2. The remedies which are given for:—a) *arthralgia generally*, are: 1) *Agn. calc. caust. ferr. kal. led. lyc. mang. merc. natr-m. n-vom. puls. rhus. sep. stront. sulph.* 2) *Amb. amm. ant. arn. aur. bry. caps. carb-veg. coloc. dros. hell. hep. petr. phosph. rhod. ruta. sassap. sil. spig. stann. staph. sulph-ac. thuj. zinc.*

b) For pains in the *axillary joint:* 1) *Bry. calc. carb-veg. ferr. ign. kal. n-vom. puls. rhus. sep. staph. sulph. zinc.* 2) *Amb. arn. caps. caust. led lyc. merc. natr-m. petr. phosph. veratr.*

c) In the *elbow-joint:* 1) *Arg. bell calc. caust. kal. led. merc. rhus. sep. sulph.* 2) *Ant. bell. graph. lyc. mez. petr. phosph. puls. ruta. staph. veratr.*

d) In the *wrist-joint:* 1) *Amm. calc. caust. graph. kal. nitr. rhus. ruta. sep. sulph.* 2) *Alum. amm. carb-veg. euphr. hell. lach. led. mang. merc. natr-m. nitr-ac. puls. sabin. sil. stront.*

e) In the *finger-joints:* 1) *Agn. calc. carb-veg. caust. graph. hep. lyc. sep. spig. sulph.* 2) *Agn. aur. carb-an. cham. chin. colch. clem. cycl. graph. hell. ign. kal. lach. led. natr-m. nitr. petr. phosph. puls. rhus. sabin. sil. spong. staph. sulph.*

§ 3. a) For pains in the *hip* and *hip-joints:* 1) *Bell. bry. calc. carb-veg. caust. coloc. led. merc. rhus. sulph.* 2) *Ant. coccul. ferr. hell. ipec. kal. lyc. mez. natr-m. phosph. puls. rhod. sabad. sep. sil. stront. veratr.*

b) In the *knee* and *knee-joints:* 1) *Bry. calc. caust. chin. lach. led. natr-m. n-vom. petr. phosph. puls. rhus. sep. sil. sulph.* 2) *Alum. anac. ars. asa. carb-veg. coccul. con. ferr. graph. hell. hep. jod. kal. lyc. magn-c. merc. nitr-ac. rhod. ruta. spig. stann. staph. stront. veratr. zinc.*

c) In the *tarsal-joints:* 1) *Bry. caust. lyc. merc. natr-m. phosph. puls. rhus. ruta. sep. sulph.* 2) *Amb. ars. carb-an. dros. hep. ign. kal. kreos. led. natr. n-vom. oleand. spig. staph. zinc.*

d) In the *toe-joints:* 1) *Arn. caust. chin. kal. led. sabin. sep. sulph. zinc.* 2) *Aur. calc. cham. con. ferr. lyc. n-vom. rhus. sil.*

§ 4. a) For pains in the *upper arm:* 1) *Bry. coccul. ferr. sep. sulph.* 2) *Ars. asa. bell. chin. ign. magn-arct. mez. nitr. puls. stann. val.*

b) In the *fore-arm:* 1) *Calc. carb-veg. caust. lyc. merc. n-vom. rhus. sassap. sep. staph. sulph.* 2) *Arg. carb-an. chin. ferr.*

con. dulc. kal. mez. nitr. nitr-ac. phos-ac. rhod. spig. stront. thuja.

c) In the *hands:* 1) *Bell. bry. calc. carb-veg. lach. lyc. n-vom. rhod. sep. sulph.* 2) *Anac. amb. aur. caust. cham. chin. clem. cocc. ferr. graph. hep. hyos. kal. merc. mez. natr. natr-m. petr. phosph. rhus. sil. spig. spong. zinc.*

d) In the *fingers:* 1) *Amm. carb-veg. graph. hep. lyc. n-vom. phosph. puls. rhus. sil. sulph.* 2) *Amb. Amm-m. calc. caust. cycl. kal. lach. mang. merc. natr-m. nitr-ac. petr. phos-ac. rhod. sep. spig. staph. sulph-ac. thuja. veratr.*

§ 5. a) For pains in the *thighs:* 1) *Bry. calc. chin. hep. merc. petr. phos-ac. rhod. sep. sil. stann. sulph.* 2) *Arn. bell. caps. carb-veg. caust. coccul. coloc. graph. guaj. led. mez. natr-m. n-vom. oleand. plat. rhus. sassap. spig. spong. thuj.*

b) In the *legs:* 1) *Bell. bry. calc. caust. ferr. kal. lyc. n-vom. puls. sep. sil. staph.* 2) *Anac. asa. borax. con. graph. ign. merc. mez. phos ac. rhod. rhus. sulph.*

c) In the *tibia:* 1) *Asa. calc. lach. merc. mez. phosph. puls. sabin.* 2) *Agar. arn. bell. caust. con. dulc. ign. kal. lyc. mang. mur-ac. phos-ac. rhus. sep. sil.*

d) In the *calves:* 1) *Alum. ars. calc. cham. con. graph. lyc. natr. nitr-ac. puls. rhus. sep. staph. sulph. val.* 2) *Ant. bry. chin. coloc. euphr. ferr. ign. kal. magn-aust. natr-m. n-vom. sil. spig. stann. zinc.*

e) In the *tendo-achilles: Anac. ant. caust. mur-ac. natr. natr-m. puls. rhus. staph. sulph. zinc.*

§ 6. a) In the *feet:* 1) *Arn. bell. bry. camph. caust. lyc. puls. sep. sulph.* 2) *Ars. aur. baryt. ferr. graph. hep. kal. natr-m. nitr-ac. n-vom. phosph. rhod. rhus. ruta. sulph.*

b) In the *heels:* 1) *Amm-m. ant. arn. caust. graph. ign. led. lyc. magn-arct. natr. nitr-ac. puls. sabin. sep. sil. sulph.* 2) *Calc. coloc. con. magn-arct. merc. petr. rhod. rhus. spong.*

c) In the *dorsa of the feet:* 1) *Calc. camph. carb-an. caust. lyc. merc. puls. spig. thuj.* 2) *Anac. asa. bry. chin. colch. hep. ign. led. mur-ac. natr. n-vom. rhus. sassap. staph. sulph. zinc.*

d) In the *soles:* 1) *Amb. caust. graph. mur-ac. phosph. phos-ac. puls. spig. sulph.* 2) *Bell. bry. calc. chin. cupr. ign. led. lyc. natr. rhus. sil. tarax. zinc.*

e) In the *toes:* 1) *Arn. asa. caust. graph. sabin. sulph. thuja.* 2) *Agar. aur. carb-an. carb-veg. chin. kal. led. lyc. magn-arct. merc. phosph. phos-ac. plat. sep. sil. staph.*

f) In the *big toe:* 1) *Arn. ars. asa. bry. calc. caust. kal. plat. sabin. sil. sulph. zinc.* 2) *Amb. amm. amm-m. aur. coccul. cycl. led. magn-arct. natr. puls. rhus. sassap. sep. thuj.*

§ 7. For further particulars see : GOUT, RHEUMATISM, NEURALGIA, PAIN, PAROXYSMS OF, COXAGRA, GANITIS, &c.

ARTHRITIS.—The best remedies are : 1) *Acon. ant. ars. bell. bry. calc. caust. chin. cocc. coloc. ferr. guaj. hep. jod. led. mang. n-vom. phosph. phos-ac. puls. rhod. sabin. sass. sulph.* 2) *Canth. chel. cic. colch. con. daph. dulc. men. merc. stann. tart. thuj.* 3) *Arn. cin. ran-bulb. ran-sc. staph. chinin.*

§ 2. For *acute* arthritis : 1) *Acon. ant. ars. bell. bry. chin. ferr. hep. n-vom. puls.* 2) *Berb. canth. colch.*

For *chronic* arthritis : *Calc. caust. coloc. guaj. jod. mang. phos-ac. rhod. sass. sulph.*

For *erratic* arthritis : 1) *Arn. mang. n-mosch. n-vom. puls.;* or 2) *Asa. daph. plumb.* and *rhod.*

§ 3. *Arthritic nodosities* require : 1) *Calc. rhod.* 2) *Agn. ant. bry. calc. carb-veg. graph. led. lyc. n-vom. staph.;* or 3) *Aur. carb-an. dig. lyc. phosph. sabin. sep. sil. zinc.*

Arthritic contractions are frequently relieved by : 1) *Bry. caust. guaj. sulph.;* or 2) *Calc. coloc. rhus. sil. thuj.*

§ 4. For the *precursory symptoms of gout*, the same remedies are generally to be used that we use for the *gout itself.* The following remedies will generally answer : *Ant. bell. bry. n-vom.*

For recent *arthritic metastases*, the following are very useful : *Acon. bell. n-vom. sassap. sulph.*—In most cases the affected organs should be considered ; we refer the reader to the paragraphs on : *headache, ophthalmia, gastric derangement,* where the symptoms arising from arthritic causes will be found mentioned.

§ 5. For the *arthritic affections of drunkards,* we use : 1) *Acon. calc. n-vom. sulph.;* or 2) *Ars. chin. hep. jod. lach. led. puls.*

For arthritis of persons that indulge in *rich living : Ant. calc. jod. puls.* and *sulph.*

For that of persons working in the water : 1) *Calc. puls. sass. sulph.;* or 2) *Ant. ars. dulc. n-mosch.* and *rhus.*

§ 6. For particular indications see : *Rheumatic pains ;* and compare : *Causes, Pain, paroxysms of, Conditions, Periods of the day, Influence of the weather, Nourishment,* &c.

ARTHROCACE.—This inflammation of the terminal extremities of bones has been most successfully treated with : 1) *Coloc. phos-ac.;* or perhaps with : 2) *Calc. hep. sil. sulp.;* or 3) *Puls. rhus. zinc.*

ARSENIC, POISONING BY.—The antidotes are: 1) *Soap-water;* 2) *Albumen,* dissolved in water and used as a drink; 3) *Sugar-water;* 4) *Milk;* 5) *Sesquioxyde of iron. Vinegar* is useless; *oil* is hurtful.

After the first alarming symptoms have been removed, we give *Ipec.* After Ipec. we give *China,* especially when the patient is irritable, has a restless sleep and nightly febrile motions; or *Nux vom.* when the patient is worse in the daytime, particularly after sleeping, with constipation, or else with diarrhœic, slimy stools; or *Veratrum,* if after Ipec. frequent nausea remains, with vomiting and heat, or chilliness over the whole body, and great debility.

For the *eruptions, ophthalmia* and headache caused by wearing hats that have been worked with Arsenic, the best remedies are: 1) *Carb-veg. ferr.* 2) *China, hepar.*

The best remedies for the ill effects of Arsenic as a medicine, are: *Chin. ipec. n-vom. veratr.*

ASCITES.—The best remedies are: 1) *Ars. chin. hell. calc. merc. sulph.* 2) *Acon. bry cin. colch. dulc. euph. prun. sep.;* or 3) *Asa. colch. dig. led. lyc. puls. squill.*

Ascites from loss of blood by venesection, &c., yields to *China* as by a miracle.

In all other cases the selection of the remedy depends upon the exciting cause, and the pathological character of the disease, and the *general* symptoms of the remedy have to be carefully compared with the symptoms of the disease.

ASTHMA MILLARI ET WIGANDI.—The specific remedy for Asthma Millari, is, in most cases, *Sambucus.* In other cases, we give: *Acon. ars. ipec. lach. mosch.*

For the concealed Asthma Millari, the so-called *Asthma Wigandi,* we have principally: 1) *Acon. bellad. ipec. samb.* 2) *Ars. baryt. cham. chin. coff. cupr. lach. n-vom. op.*

For the particular symptoms, see: *Asthma spasmodicum,* and vol. i. of Hempel's Jahr.

ASTHMA SPASMODICUM, OR PERIODICUM, AND ASTHMA GENERALLY.—§ 1. The remedies are: 1) *Acon. ars. bell. bry. cupr. ferr. ipec. n-vom. phos. puls. samb. sulph.* 2) *Ambr. amm. aur. calc. carb-veg. cham. chin. coccul. dulc. lach. mosch. op. tart. veratr. zinc.* 3) *Ant. caust. coff. hyos. ign. kal. lyc. merc. nitr-ac. n-mosch. sep. sil. stann. stram.*

§ 2. The following remedies are the best to control an attack of asthma immediately: 1) *Lach.* 2) *Acon. ars. cham. ipec. mosch. op. samb. tart.;* or 3) *Bell. bry. chin. n-mosch. n-vom. puls.*

To remove the asthmatic disposition, we use: *Ant. ars. calc. n-vom. sulph.*; or *Amm. carb-veg. caust. cupr. ferr. graph. kali. lach. lyc. nitr-ac. phos. sep. sil. stann. zinc.*

§ 3. For asthma from *congestion of blood to the chest:* 1) *Acon. aur. bell. merc. n-vom. phos. spong. sulph.* 2) *Amm. calc. carb-veg. cupr. ferr. puls.*

For asthma attended with *menstrual irregularities:* 1) *Bell. coccul. cupr. merc. n-vom. puls. sulph.* 2) *Acon. phos. sep.*

For *flatulent asthma* (asthma from incarceration of flatulence in the abdomen): 1) *Carb-veg. cham. chin. n-vom. op. phos. sulph. zinc.* 2) *Ars. caps. hep. natr. veratr.*

For *asthma humidum or pituitosum* (asthma with accumulation of mucus in the bronchi or lungs): 1) *Ars. bry. calc. chin. cupr. dulc. ferr. graph. lach. phos. puls. sen. sep. stann. sulph.* 2) *Bar. bell. camph. con. hep. ipec. merc. n-vom. sil. tart. zinc.*

For the real *asthma spasmodicum*, the best remedies are: 1) *Bell. cocc. cupr. hyosc. lach. mosch., n-vom. samb. stram. sulph. tart. zinc.* 2) *Ant. ars. bry. caust. ferr. kali. lyc. op. sep. stann.*

§ 3. For asthma from inhaled dust, *stone-dust*, as takes place among sculptors, stone-cutters, &c., we employ: 1) *Calc. hep. sil. sulph.* 2) *Ars. bell. chin. ipec. n-vom. phos.*

For asthma caused by the *vapor of sulphur*, give *Pulsat.*;—by the *vapours of copper or arsenic:* 1) *Merc. hep. ipec.* 2) *Ars. camph.* or *cupr.*

For asthma from *a cold:* 1) *Acon. bell. bry. dulc. ipec.* 2) *Ars. cham. chin.*

For asthma caused by *an emotion: Acon. cham. coff. ign. n-vom. puls. veratr.*

If caused by *a suppressed catarrh:* 1) *Ars. ipec. n-vom.* 2) *Camph. carb-veg. chin. lach. puls. samb. tart.*

§ 4. For asthma of *children*, we generally find useful: 1) *Acon. ars. bell. cham. coff. ipec. mosch. n-mosch. n-vom op. samb. tart.* 2) *Camph. chin. cupr. hep. ign. lach. lyc. phos. puls. stram. sulph*

For asthma of *hysteric women:* 1) *Acon. bell. cham. coff. ign. mosch. n-mosch. n-vom. puls. stram.* 2) *Asa. aur. caust. con. cupr. ipec. lach. phos. stann. sulph.* &c.

For asthma of *old people:* 1) *Aur. bar. con. lach. op.* 2) *Ant. camph. carb-veg. caust. chin. sulph.*

§ 5. *Particular indications by the symptoms:*

Aconitum: 1) for sensitive individuals, young, plethoric girls leading a sedentary life, or when the paroxysms set in after the least emotion; 2) dyspnœa with inability to take a deep breath, accompanied with restlessness, heat and sweat; 3) *suffocative cough at night,* with barking and hoarse voice, spasmodic constriction of the throat and chest; *anxious, short* and difficult breathing, with open mouth; great anguish, with inability to utter a single word distinctly; or 4) for *asthma of adults,* caused by *rush of blood to the head,* with *vertigo, full* and *frequent pulse,* cough and bloody expectoration.

Arsenicum: *Acute* or *chronic asthma,* with difficult breathing, cough and accumulation of thick mucus in the chest; *shortness of breath,* particularly after a meal; oppression of the chest, and want of breath on walking fast, on ascending an eminence, or after any kind of exercise, even after laughing; *constriction of the chest and larynx,* with painful pressure on the lungs and in the pit of the stomach; anguish and suffocative paroxysms increased by the warmth of the room; *suffocative attacks,* especially *at night,* or *in the evening when in bed,* with panting and wheezing breathing, with the mouth open, *great anguish* as if the patient would die, and *cold sweat;* the paroxysms abate as soon as the patient begins to cough and throws off mucus, or a tenacious, viscid saliva in the shape of vesicles; the paroxysms come on again in rough weather, in the cold open air, or when the temperature of the air changes, and they may be caused by warm and tight clothes; *the paroxysms are accompanied by great debility;* or by paroxysms of pain and burning in the chest. (In acute asthma, *Arsen.* is frequently suitable after *Ipec.,* unless it had been given at the commencement of the attack.)

Belladonna: Suitable for children and women of an irritable constitution, and with disposition to spasms; *oppression of the chest* and *loss of breath,* tightness in the chest and *stitches under the sternum;* with *paroxysms of dry cough at night,* with catarrh, or moist cough and expectoration of mucus after a meal; *anxious sighing;* at times *deep,* at times *short* and *rapid breathing,* with open mouth, and great working of the chest; constriction of the larynx, with danger of suffocation on touching the larynx, and on turning the neck; uneasiness and *beating in the chest,* with palpitation of the heart; asthmatic paroxysms with loss of consciousness, relaxation of the muscles and involuntary discharge of urine and fæces.

Bryonia: *Difficult breathing* and loss of breath, particularly at night, and towards morning, with stitching colicky pains, urging to stool, inability to lie on the right side, pressure and tension in the chest and contractive sensation in cold air; frequent cough with pains in the hypochondria, tickling in the larynx, vomiting and expectoration, at first frothy, then thick and viscid; increased *difficulty of breathing,* when talking and during *any kind of exercise;* the patient feels relieved after expectorating or on rising from his recumbent posture; in the evening when in bed, the patient complains at times of palpitation of the heart, anguish and throbbing in the temples, with difficult, anxious and sighing breathing, with straining of the abdominal muscles and mingled with deep inspirations, or slow and deep breathing during exertions; frequent *stitches in the chest*, especially during an inspiration and when coughing, also during motion. (*Bry.* is frequently suitable after *Ipec.*, in acute asthma.)

CUPRUM: Suitable to children or hysteric individuals, especially after fright, chagrin, a cold, and before the appearance of the menses; with *spasmodic constriction of the chest, hiccough,* difficulty of breathing and talking; *hurried* breathing, stertorous and moaning, with convulsive straining of the abdominal muscles; *dyspnœa,* especially when walking and ascending an eminence, with desire to take deep breath; *short and spasmodic cough,* with dyspnœa, *suffocative fits* and *stridulous inspirations* when attempting to take deep breath; rattling in the chest as of mucus, expectoration of white and watery mucus; sensation of emptiness and faintness in the pit of the stomach, and painfulness of the pit on touching it; orgasm of the circulation with palpitation; red face covered with warm sweat; the symptoms are worse at the period of the menses.

FERRUM: Violent orgasm of the blood, *oppression of the chest,* with almost imperceptible movement of the thorax on taking breath, and greatly dilated nostrils during an expiration; *dyspnœa,* particularly at night or in the evening, in bed, in a recumbent posture, with the head low, or during rest generally, or from the least covering on the chest; the patient feels relieved after being uncovered, or after raising the trunk, or from taking ever so little physical or mental exercise; *suffocative fits,* in the evening, in bed, with warmth of the neck and trunk, the limbs being cold at the same time; spasmodic constriction of the chest, aggravated by motion; paroxysms of spasmodic cough with expectoration of tenacious and transparent mucus; expectoration of blood.

IPECACUANHA: Suitable to children and adults, for: Dyspnœa, nightly suffocative fits; *spasmodic constriction of the larynx, rattling of mucus in the chest;* dry and short cough, *great anguish* and fear of death, cries and restless running to and fro; *the face is alternately red and hot, or pale, cold and sunken;* anxious features; nausea with cold sweat on the forehead; the breathing is anxious, hurried and sighing, or short and as if through dust; tetanic rigidity of the body, with bluish redness in the face. *Ipec.* is generally first indicated in paroxysms of acute asthma; afterwards we give *Ars. bry.* or *nux-vom.*

NUX VOM.: Short or slow and stridulous breathing; anxious oppression of the chest, especially at night, early in the morning, and after eating; spasmodic constriction, especially of the lower part of the chest, with loss of breath in walking or talking, or in cold air and after every exercise; orthopnœa and nightly suffocative paroxysms, especially after midnight, preceded by anxious dreams; short cough, with difficult expectoration; expectoration of blood; the clothes feel unpleasant on the chest and hypochondria; distention, aching pain and anguish in the region under the heart and in the region of the hypochondria; tension and *pressure in the chest;* rush of blood to the chest, with orgasm of the blood; warmth, heat and palpitation of the heart; great anguish and distress in the whole body; the asthma is diminished in a recumbent posture, or by turning to the other side, or by raising the trunk.

Phosphorus: Noisy and panting breathing, dyspnœa, oppressed breathing and oppression of the chest, particularly in the evening and morning, or when sitting; *great, oppressive anxiety in the chest;* stridulous inspirations, in the evening on falling asleep; nightly suffocative paroxysms as if the lungs were paralyzed; *spasmodic constriction* of the chest; short cough, with either *salt,* or *sweetish,* or *blood-streaked* expectoration; stitching or pressure, heaviness, fulness and tension in the chest; *congestion of blood to the chest,* with ascension of heat in the throat, and *palpitation of the heart;* phthisicky disposition.

Pulsatilla: Especially for *children,* after suppression of rash, also for *hysteric* persons, after suppression of the menses or in consequence of cold, with *hurried, short* and superficial or rattling breathing; *arrest of breathing as if from the vapours of Sulphur;* oppression of the chest, loss of breath and *suffocative fits,* with anguish of death, *palpitation of the heart,* and spasmodic constriction of the larynx and chest, particularly at night and in the evening, in a horizontal posture; the asthmatic distress increases by motion, also by ascension of eminences, and by walking in the open air; short, barking cough with asthma, or copious expectoration of mucus, or blood-streaked expectoration; *spasmodic tension, sensation of fulness and pressure in the chest,* with internal heat and orgasm of the blood; stitches in the chest and sides.

Sambucus: Especially for *children,* when the following symptoms occur: *stridulous* and hurried breathing; oppression of the chest, with pressure in the stomach and nausea; pressure on the chest as from a load, with anguish and *danger of suffocation;* dyspnœa when lying; *nightly suffocative paroxysms, with spasmodic constriction of the chest,* sudden starting from sleep and cry; great anguish, trembling of the whole body, swollen, bluish hands and feet, heat of the whole body, mucous rattling in the chest, and inability to utter a single loud word; morbid sleep with the eyes and mouth half open; paroxysms of suffocative cough aud cries.

Sulphur: for chronic asthma, with difficulty of breathing, and painless oppression of the chest; frequent attacks of asthma in the day-time, even when talking; shortness of breath when walking in the open air; wheezing, mucous rattling, rhonchus in the chest; oppressed breathing and suffocative fits, especially at night; fulness and sensation of weariness in the chest; pressure in the chest as from a load, after eating ever so little; *burning* in the chest, with rush of blood and palpitation of the heart; suffocative cough, with spasmodic constriction of the chest and urging to vomit; difficult expectoration of whitish mucus, or copious, yellowish expectoration; blood-coloured saliva; *spasms in the chest*, with compressive sensation and pain in the sternum, bluish-red face, short breath and inability to speak.

§ 6. The following remedies may likewise be employed:

Ambra: suitable to children and scrofulous individuals with short, oppressed breathing, paroxysms of spasmodic cough with expectoration of mucus, wheezing in the air-passages, *pressure in the chest*, &c.

Ammonium: for *chronic* asthma, especially when attended with disposition to hydrothorax, with shortness of breath, especially on ascending an eminence; oppressed breathing and palpitation of the heart after the least exercise; congestion of blood to the chest and feeling of heaviness in the thorax.

Aurum: congestion of blood to the chest, with great oppression, and desire to take deep breath, especially at night and when walking in the open air; suffocative fits with spasmodic constriction of the chest, violent palpitation of the heart, bluish-red face, and falling down without consciousness.

Calcarea: for chronic asthma, with tight breathing and tension in the chest as if from rush of blood, relieved by raising the shoulders; desire to take deep breath and sensation as if the breath remained stopped between the scapulæ; the patient loses his breath by merely stooping; he is suffering with *dry* cough, especially *frequent at night.*

Carbo veg.: for spasmodic *flatulent* asthma, also for chronic asthma with disposition to *hydrothorax*, oppression and tight breathing; fulness, accumulation of mucus and anxious compression of the chest, heavy and short breathing, especially when walking; *pressure* and sensation of weariness in the chest, frequent attacks of spasmodic cough, &c.

Chamomilla: especially suitable to *children*, or for *suffocative fits*, with short, anxious breathing, *swelling of the pit of the stomach* and *hypochondria*, with uneasiness, screams and drawing-up of the legs; paroxysm of asthma after a fit of anger, or after taking cold.

CHINA: for difficult breathing and oppression, with inability to breathe with the head low; *wheezing during an inspiration; spasmodic cough* and nightly *suffocative fits*, as if from too much mucus in the throat, with difficult expectoration of a clear and thick mucus; *pressure in the chest* as if from rush of blood, with *violent palpitation of the heart;* sudden prostration; bloody expectoration.

COCCULUS: Suitable to hysteric females, or for rush of blood to the chest, with difficulty of breathing *as if the throat were constricted;* racking cough with oppression of the chest, especially at night; *spasmodic constriction of the chest*, especially on *one* side only; pressure in the chest and orgasm of the blood with anguish and palpitation of the heart; sensation of languor and emptiness in the chest.

DULCAMARA: For *humid asthma*, or for acute asthma *from a cold.*

LACHESIS: Suitable to persons suffering with hydrothorax, or of a large, *bloated, lymphatic* appearance, *shortness of breath after a meal*, during a walk and after exercising with the arms; tight breathing, dyspnœa and oppression of breathing, with *aggravation after eating; suffocative fits in a recumbent posture*, or when touching the neck; spasmodic constriction of the chest, obliging one to rise from bed and to sit with the trunk bent forwards; *slow and wheezing breathing;* desire to take deep breath, especially when sitting.

MOSCHUS: Suitable to hysteric individuals and to children, or for oppression of the chest and suffocative fits as if from the vapors of Sulphur, commencing with a desire to cough and getting worse until the patient despairs of getting over the paroxysm; *spasmodic constriction of the larynx and chest*, especially when feeling cold.

OPIUM: Congestion of blood to the chest, or pulmonary spasms, with deep, *stertorous*, rattling breathing; tightness of breath and *oppression*, with great anguish, tightness, and *spasmodic constriction* of the chest; *suffocative fits during sleep*, like nightmare; *suffocative cough* with bluish redness of the face.

SPONGIA: For pressure in the larynx as from a plug; *wheezing breathing*, or slow and deep breathing, as if from debility; mucous rattling; want of breath and *suffocative fits* after every exercise, with weariness, rush of blood to the chest and head, anguish and heat in the face; also for *asthmatic symptoms in consequence of goitre.*

STANNUM: For *asthma* and *oppression*, especially in the *evening* or *at night* when lying down, also in the day-time during every exercise, and frequently attended with anguish and desire to detach the clothes; oppression and mucous rattling in the chest; cough with *copious expectoration* of viscid or lumpy, clear or watery, yellowish, salt or *sweetish mucus.*

TARTARUS: Especially suitable to *old people*, also to *children*, or for anxious oppression, *difficulty of breathing* and shortness of breath, with desire to sit erect; *oppression* and *suffocative fits*, especially in the evening or in the morning, in bed; mucus and rattling in the chest; suffocative cough or congestion of blood to the chest, and palpitation of the heart.

VERATRUM: Suitable after *Chin., ars., ipec.*, especially for suffocative fits, even when sitting erect and during exercise; pains in the side; hollow cough; cold sweat, or cold face and cold limbs.

ZINCUM: For tight breathing and *oppression*, especially in the evening; shortness of breath after eating, from accumulation of flatulence; increase of asthma when the expectoration stops, decrease when it recommences.

See the Symptoms of these remedies in Vol. II. of *Hempel's Jahr*, and compare: CONGESTION OF BLOOD TO THE CHEST, CATARRH, PULMONARY PHTHISIS, &c.

ASTHMA THYMICUM (ASTHMA OF KOPP).—Remedies: 1) *Acon. bell. con. hep. ipec. merc. sen. spong. tart. veratr.* 2) *Amm. lach. phos. zinc.* 3) *Ambr. asa. aur. berb. cupr. ignat. ferr.*

For the *precursory symptoms: Acon. hep. ipec. sen. spong. tart.*

For the *cough: Bell. con. hep. merc. veratr.*

For the symptoms, we refer the reader to ASTHMA SPASMODICUM.

ATROPHY OF CHILDREN. — The best remedies for atrophy of *scrofulous* children are: *Sulph.*, followed by *Calcar.*; also: 1) *Ars. baryt. bell. chin. cin. n-vom. phos.* and *rhus.*, or also: 2) *Arn. cham. hep. jod. lach, magn. petr. phos.* and *puls.*

Particular indications:

ARSENICUM: Dry, parchment-like skin; hollow eyes with blue margins; the food is passed or vomited up undigested; *desire to drink frequently, but little at a time;* great restlessness and tossing to and fro, especially at night; short sleep, interrupted by *starting* and *convulsions;* œdematous swelling of the face; *greenish* or *brownish* diarrhœic stools with discharge of undigested food; weariness with constant desire to lie down; cold hands and feet; palpitation of the heart; nightsweats.

BARYTA: For *swelling of the cervical glands;* great physical debility; *constant desire to sleep;* bloated abdomen and face, pot-belliedness; *great laziness,* indisposition to work either with the mind or body; aversion to play; absence of mind; want of attention and weak memory.

BELLADONNA: Frequent colic, with involuntary stool; *whimsical and obstinate;* cough at night, with mucous rattling; swelling of the cervical glands; restless sleep or sleeplessness; aversion to exercise and open air; nervousness; especially suitable to children with premature intellect, blue margins and blond hairs.

CALCAREA: Great emaciation with a good appetite, *hollow, wrinkled face,* faint eyes, *swelling and induration of the mesenteric glands;* great debility with general weariness after the least exercise, and frequently with profuse sweat; frequent diarrhœa or *clayey stools;* dry, withered skin; dry hair; frequent palpitation of the heart; chills; pains in the small of the back; extreme nervous sensitiveness; aversion to exercise.

CHINA: Emaciation, especially of the hands and feet; œdematous swelling of the abdomen; *voraciousness;* diarrhœa, especially at night, with discharge of undigested food, or copious *whitish* and *papescent stools; copious sweats,* especially at night; idleness and listlessness; hollow, pale or livid face; stupefying, unrefreshing sleep; great debility and prostration.

CINA: Worm-affections, pale face, *wetting the bed,* and great *voracity.*

NUX VOM.: Yellowish, sallow complexion, bloated face, *obstinate constipation,* or alternate constipation and diarrhœa; large abdomen with flatulence; great hunger, desire to eat, with *frequent vomiting of the ingesta; constant desire to lie down;* aversion to open air; ill-humour, disposed to anger; nervousness.

PHOSPHORUS: Suitable to young girls with blond hair, blue eyes, delicate skin, slender stature, with cachectic cough, diarrhœa and frequent, exhausting sweats, great debility with orgasm of the blood, palpitation of the heart, or oppression of the chest after the least exercise.

RHUS TOX.: Great debility with constant disposition to lie down, pale face, hard and distended abdomen; great thirst; *slimy* or *bloody diarrhœa;* great appetite.

STAPHYSAGRIA: Large abdomen, voraciousness, and canine hunger; slow stool; *swelling of the submaxillary and cervical glands;* frequent or constant attacks of catarrh, with scurf in the nostrils; unhealthy, *readily-ulcerated skin; fetid night-sweats;* frequent boils

SULPHUR: In almost every case the treatment may commence with Sulphur; it should be given for the following symptoms: *hunger,* the patient sweats easily, *swelling of the inguinal glands,* or of the axillary and cervical glands; hard and distended abdomen; mucous rattling in the trachea; *fluent coryza, frequent, slimy diarrhœa,* or *obstinate constipation;* pressure on the chest; palpitation of the heart; pale colour of the skin, with bad looks, deep and hollow eyes; stitches in the chest and sides, &c.

Compare: HECTIC FEVER, PHTHISIS AND SCROFULA.

ATROPHY OF THE SPINAL MARROW (MARASMUS, TABES DORSALIS).

The following remedies are probably the most useful: 1) *N-vom. sulph.* 2) *Calc. carb-veg. caust. coccul. natr-m. phosph. phos-ac.* 3) *Chin.? staph.?*

I have treated 21 cases of this disease arising from *onanism*, accompanied with hypochondria, despondency, aversion to life, &c. The characteristic formication in the back was present in every case; I gave in every case a dose of *Nux vom.* 30, allowing it to act from 2 to 3 weeks, and then *Sulphur* 30, allowing it to act from 4 to 5 weeks. If unpleasant symptoms remain, I resort to *Calc. carb-veg. caust. phos-ac.*

China and *Staphys.* may prove useful in some cases.

For atrophy with *paralysis of the lower extremities*, the best remedies are: *Nux-v. sulph. nux-v. caust. nux-v. carb-veg. cocc. phos. rhus-tox.*, if given in this order and at long intervals. Constant change of remedies is exceedingly hurtful in this disease.

See: DEBILITY.

AWKWARDNESS.—If a natural defect, nothing can be done for it; if a morbid state, the following remedies may prove useful: *Bell. caps. carb-an. caust. coloc. graph. kal. lyc. natr-m. petr. sep. sil. sulph.*

BACK, SMALL OF THE, PAINS IN THE: Generally a mere symptom, especially in piles and uterine affections. The principal remedies are: 1) *Alum. amm. caust. kal. kreos. lach. natr-m. n-vom. puls. rhus. sep. sulph.* 2) *Amb. baryt. borax. calc. dulc. graph. lyc. natr. sil. veratr.* 3) *Arn. carb-an. cham. chin. coccul. ign. magn-m. merc. n-mosch. phosph. ruta. sabin. spong. zinc.*

BALANORRHŒA, or GONORRHŒA SPURIA.—If *syphilitic* or *sycosic*, the principal remedies are: *Merc. nitr-ac.*, or *thuj.*

In all other cases the following remedies will prove useful: 1) *N-vom. sep. sulph.*, or: 2) *Chin. merc. mez. nitr-ac. thuj.*

BLEPHAROPHTHALMIA.

The best remedies are: 1) *Acon. ant. ars. calc. bell. calc. cham. chin. euphr. hep. merc. n-vom. puls. sulph. veratr.* 2) *Alum. bar-c. bry. caust. cocc. dig. jod. kreos. lyc. natr. natr-m. phos-ac. rhus. sen. sep. spig. staph. thuj. zinc.*

§ 2. If the *external* surface of the lid be inflamed, give: *Acon. bell. hep.* and *sulph.*

If the *inner: Acon. ars. bell. hep. merc. n-vom. phos. puls rhus. sulph.*

For inflammation of the *margins* and *Meibomian glands: Bell. cham. euphr. hep. merc. n-vom. puls.*

For *styes: Puls.* or *staph.*, or *Am-c. calc.* or *ferr.*

For inflammation of the *upper lids:* 1) *Alum. bry. calc. caust. croc. hep. phos. puls. rhus. sep. spig. staph. sulph.* 2) *Bar. bell. cham. chel. con. cycl. ferr. lyc. merc. sil.*

For inflammation of the *lower lids:* 1) *Ars. bry. calc. dig. merc. natr-m. rhus. rut. sen. sep.* 2) *Alum. bell. caust.*

§ 3. For *acute* ophthalmia: *Acon. bell. cham. euphr. hep. merc. n-vom.* and *puls.*

For *chronic* ophthalmia: *Ant. ars. calc. chin.* and *sulph.*

§ 4 Particular indications:

Aconitum: The eyelids are *swollen, hard* and *red*, with *heat, burning* and *dryness;* or they are pale, shining and swollen, with burning and tensive pains; copious secretion of mucus in the eyes and nose; *extreme photophobia;* fever, with great heat and thirst, &c. (After *Acon.*, are frequently given: *Bell.*, *hep.* or *sulph.*)

Antimonium: Red swelling of the lids, with *gum* in the *canthi;* photophobia and stitches in the eyes.

Arsenicum: Inflammatory redness of the conjunctiva, with congestion of the vessels; great dryness of the lids, especially the edges, with spasmodic closing or nightly agglutination.

Belladonna: Swelling and redness of the lids, with burning and itching, constant agglutination, bleeding on opening the eyes, also attended with *eversion of the lids*, or with great paralytic weakness of the lids.

Calcarea: *Cutting*, burning or acute pains, especially *when reading*, with red, hard and big swelling, copious secretion of gum, and nightly agglutination; to be given especially when *Sulphur* does not seem to relieve the patient.

Chamomilla: Great dryness of the edges, or else copious secretion of mucus, with nightly agglutination, spasmodic closing, or great heaviness of the lids.

China: Frequent creeping on the inner surface of the lids, especially in the evening, with lachrymation.

Euphrasia: Ulceration of the margins, with itching in the day-time, and agglutination at night, with redness, swelling, photophobia and constant winking, coryza, headache, or heat about the head. (If *Euphr.* should be insufficient, *Nux vom.* and *puls.* will complete the cure.)

Hepar: Inflammatory redness of the lids, with *ulcerative* or *contusive pain on touching them;* nightly agglutination, or spasmodic closing of the eyelids. (This remedy is frequently suitable after *Acon.* or *merc.;* after *Hep.*, *Bell.* is frequently suitable.

Hyoscyamus: Spasmodic closing of the lids.

Mercurius: Hard lids as if contracted, with swelling, difficulty of opening the lids, cutting pains, ulcers on the margins, pustules on the conjunctiva, crusts around the eyes, eversion of the lids; stitching and burning pains, itching, or when there is no pain at all. (After *Merc.*, if insufficient, *Hep.* is frequently suitable.)

Nux vom.: Burning itching of the lids, especially the margins, or sore pain made worse by contact, agglutination of the lids, especially early in the morning; eye-gum in the canthi; catarrh, headache, or heat in the head. (*Nux vom.* is frequently suitable after *Euphrasia*, if this should not suffice to remove the inflammation.)

Pulsatilla: Inflammatory redness of the conjunctiva or the margins, copious secretion of mucus; trichiasis; *styes;* nightly agglutination; tensive or drawing pains (*Puls.* frequently effects a cure, if *Euph.* or *nux-vom.* should not suffice.)

Rhus tox.: Stiffness of the eyelids, as if paralyzed, with burning itching.

Sulphur: Inflammatory redness of the lids, with burning pains, secretion of mucus and eyegum; ulceration of the margins, pustules and ulcers around the eyes, &c. (*Acon.* is frequently suitable before *Sulphur*, and after *Sulph.*, *Calc.* is frequently suitable.)

Veratrum: Excessive dryness of the lids, lachrymation, difficulty of moving the lids, and great heat in the interior of the eyes.

§ 5. For further particulars, see: Ophthalmia, § 1—8, and the articles at the conclusion of that article.

BLEPHAROPLEGIA, paralysis of the eyelids.—The best remedies are: 1) *Bell. nitr-ac. sep. spig. stram. veratr. zinc.* 2) *Calc. cham. cocc. hyos. n-vom. op. phos. plumb. rhus.*

BLEPHAROSPASMUS.—Principal remedies: 1) *Bell. cham. croc. hep. hyos. merc. natr-m. staph. stram. sulph.* 2) *Ars. cocc. con. rhus. rut. sep. sil. viol-od.*

BLISTERS, bloody.—Best remedies: 1) *Ars. natr-m. sec.* 2) *Aur. bry. canth. sulph.*

BOILS.—Remedies: 1) *Arn. bell. hep. lyc. phos. sulph.* 2) *Alum. ant. calc. lach. led. merc. mur-ac. nitr-ac. n-mosch. n-vom. phos-ac. sec. sep. sil. staph. tart. thuj.*

Large boils require: 1) *Hep. lyc. nitr-ac. sil.* 2) *Hyos. natr. phos. tart.*

Small boils: 1) *Arn. bell. sulph.* 2) *Grat. magn-c. natr-m. zinc.*

If they mature *slowly*, give *Hepar;* if very much inflamed and painful, give *Bell.* or *merc.*

If *large* boils can be treated at the very commencement, *Calc.* sometimes eradicates the disposition.

If large boils threaten to become carbunculous, the best remedies are: 1) *Ars. bell. sil.* 2) *Caps. hyos. lach. rhus. sec. sil.*

For the disposition to boils, give: *Lyc. nux-v. phosph.* and *sulph.*

BONES, DISEASES OF: OSTITIS, EXOSTOSIS, CARIES, NECROSIS, and other diseases.

§ 1. The best remedies are: 1) *Ang. asa. aur. bell. calc. dulc. lyc. merc. mez. phosph. ruta. sep. sil. sulph.*, and likewise: 2) *Chin. hep. nitr-ac. phos-ac. rhus. staph.*

§ 2. Particular indications:

ANGUSTURA: For caries, particularly suitable to persons who have drank too much coffee, or have a morbid desire for coffee.

ASA: For *exostosis, caries,* and *necrosis*, especially of the extremities, also for softening of the bones.

AURUM: For *exostosis,* and other diseases of bones in consequence of *abuse of mercury*, especially for caries of the *nasal bones.*

BELLADONNA: For exostosis on the forehead, with caries of the palate, also for curvature of the back.

CALCAREA: For curvature of the spine and long bones; swelling of the joints; softening of bones; when the fontanelles remain open too long, and the skull is very large; for exostosis of the extremities; necrosis.

DULCAMARA: For exostosis, ulcers on the arm, in consequence of suppressed itch.

LYCOPODIUM: For exostosis, osteitis and caries, in scrofulous persons.

MERCURIUS: For exostosis, caries, pains in the bones as if broken, &c.

MEZEREUM: For exostosis on the arms and legs of scrofulous persons.

PHOSPHORUS: For exostosis of the skull, with tearing and boring pains, and swelling of the clavicle.

PULSATILLA: For curvature of the spine, with open fontanelles, in children.

RUTA: For pains in the bones as if broken, and disease of the periosteum, or even caries, in consequence of external injuries.

SEPIA: For exostosis and caries of the extremities.

SILICEA: For exostosis, caries, necrosis, delayed closing of the fontanelles, and for almost all diseases of bones. *Sil.* and *calc.* are the best remedies for diseases of bones.

SULPHUR: For curvature, softening, swelling, caries, and other diseases. *Sulphur* is suitable before *Calc.*

§ 3. a) For *interstitial distention* of the bones, give: 1) ***Asa. lyc.*** *merc. sil.* 2) *Calc. mez. phosph. phos-ac. sulph.*

b) For *necrosis:* 1) *Asa. calc. sil. sulph.* 2) *Ars. phosph. sabin. sec.*

c) For *ostitis:* 1) *Merc. sil. staph. sulph.* 2) *Asa. aur. calc. chin. lyc. nitr-ac. phosph. phos-ac. puls.*

d) For *softening:* 1) ***Asa.*** *calc. merc. sil.* ***sulph.*** 2) *Hep. lyc. mez. nitr-ac. phosph. puls. ruta. sep. staph.*

e) For *caries:* 1) *Asa. calc. lyc. merc. phos-ac. sil. sulph.* 2) *Ang. ars. aur. hep. mez. nitr-ac. rhus. ruta. sabin. spong. staph.*

f) For *swelling:* 1) *Asa. calc. lyc. merc. phos-ac. puls. sil. staph. sulph.* 2) *Aur. clem. daph. guaj. nitr-ac. phosph. rhus. ruta.*

g) For *fractures*, to promote the reunion of bones: *Asa. calc. lyc. nitr-ac. ruta. sil. sulph. symphitum officinale.*

h) For *curvatures:* 1) *Asa. calc. lyc. merc. puls. rhus. sil. sulph.* 2) *Bell. hep. nitr-ac. phosph. sep. staph.*

§ 4. a) For diseases of the *skull:* 1) *Aur calc. daphn. merc. phosph. phos-ac. puls.*

b) When the *fontanelles* remain open, and the infants have large heads: *Calc. puls. sil.*

c) For diseases of the *palatine bones: Aur. merc. mez. sil.*

d) For diseases of the *submaxillary bones: Cist. merc. sil.*

e) For diseases of the *nasal bones: Aur. calc. merc.*

f) For diseases of the *long bones:* 1) *Asa. calc. lyc. merc. phos-ac. sil. sulph.* 2) *Clem. daph. guaj. nitr-ac. phosph. puls. rhus. ruta.*

§. 5. *Remedies for particular pains:*

a) For *pains generally:* 1) *Asa. chin. lach. merc. phosph. phos-ac. puls. ruta. sabin. sil. staph.* 2) *Ars. aur. calc. coccul. cupr. cycl. ferr. kreos. lyc. mang. merc. mez. mur-ac. nitr-ac. sep. sulph.*

b) *Boring* pains: *Bell. calc. merc. puls. sep. sil. spig.*

c) *Burning: Asa. carb-veg. phosph. phos-ac. rhus. ruta. sulph.*

d) *Aching* pains: 1) *Arg. bell. cupr. sabin. staph.* 2) *Aur. bell. cycl. daph. guaj. hep. ign. kal. merc. mez. oleand. puls. rhus.*

e) Sensation as if the *flesh were beaten loose: Bry. dros. ign. kreos. nitr-ac. n-vom. rhus. sulph. thuj.*

f) *Beating* and pulsations: *Asa. calc. lyc. merc. mez. nitr. sabad. sil. sulph.*

g) *Creeping* pains: *Cham. plumb. sec. rhus.*

h) *Gnawing* or corrosive pains: ***Amm-m. canth. con. dros. lyc. mang. phosph. phos-ac. ruta. staph.***

i) *Tearing* pains: 1) ***Arg. baryt. carb. veg. chin. kal. merc. sabin. spig. staph.*** 2) ***Agar aur. bell. bry. caust. coccul. cupr. kal. lyc. merc. natr-m. nitr. phosph. phos-ac. ruta. zinc.***

k) *Scraping* and rasping pains: ***Asa. chin. puls. rhus. sabad. spig.***

l) *Cutting* pains: ***Anac. dig. sabad.***

m) *Stitching* pains: 1) ***Bell. calc. caust. dros. con. hell. merc. puls. sassap. sep.*** 2) ***Ars. asa. aur. chin. lach. mez. phosph. ruta.***

n) *Sore pains: **Con. graph. hep. ign. merc. phos-ac.***

o) Pain *as if broken : **Coccul. cupr. hep. magn-m. natr-m. puls. ruta. samb. sep. veratr.***

p) *Jerking* pains: 1) ***Asa. calc. chin. colch. lyc. natr-m. puls. rhus.***

§. 6. See: MERCURIAL DISEASE, RACHITIS, SCROPHULA, SYPHILIS, &c.

BRONCHITIS, CATARRHUS BRONCHIALIS.

§. 1. The best remedies are: ***Acon. bell. bry. cham. merc. n-vom. puls. rhus. sulph.*** 2) *Arn. ars. calc. caps. carb-veg. caust chin. cin. dros. dulc. euphr. hyos. ign. ipec. lach. phosph. phos-ac. seneg. sep. sil. spig. squill. stann. staph. veratr. verb.* 3) ***Bar-c. cann. con. ferr. hep. lyc. magn. mang. natr. natr-m. petr. sabad. sep. spong. squill. stram. tart.***

§. 2. For *ordinary* catarrh, with light cough and fever, we give with success: *Cham. merc. n-vom. puls. rhus. sulph.*

For violent and *dry* cough, give: 1) ***Bell. bry. cham. ign. n-vom. sulph.,*** or 2) *Acon. caps. cin. dros. hep. hyos. lach. lyc. merc. natr-m. phosph. rhus. spong.*

For *spasmodic* cough: ***Bell. bry. carb-veg. cin. dros. hep. hyos. ipec. merc. n-vom. puls. sulph.*** &c.

For *moist* cough, with copious expectoration: 1) ***Bry. carb-veg. dulc. euphr. merc. puls. sulph. tart.,*** or 2) ***Calc. caust. lyc seneg. sep. sil. stann.***

For catarrh with *hoarseness:* 1) ***Cham. dulc. merc. n-vom. puls. rhus. samb. sulph.,*** or 2) ***Ars. calc. carb-veg. dros. mang. natr. phosph. tart.***

For *fluent coryza : **Ars. dulc. euphr. ign. lach. merc. puls. sulph.***

§. 3. For *acute bronchitis,* give: 1) ***Acon. bell. bry. cham. dros. phosph. spong.,*** or 2) ***Ars. lyc. merc. n-vom. puls. squill. sulph.***

For *epidemic catarrh* or *grippe* (*influenza*) *:* 1) ***Acon. ars. bell. caust. merc. n-vom.,*** or 2) ***Arn. bry. camph. chin. ipec. phosph puls. sabad. seneg. sil. spig. squill. veratr.***

For *suffocative catarrh:* 1) *Ars. carb-veg. chin. ipec. lach. op.* or 2) *Bar-c. camph. graph. puls. samb. tart.*

For *chronic catarrh: Ars. bry. calc. carb-veg. caust. dulc. jod. lach. lyc. mang. natr. natr-m. petr. phosph. phos-ac. sil. stann. staph. sulph.*

Catarrhal affections consequent on *measles*, require: 1) *Bry. Carb-veg. cham. dros. hyos. ign. n-vom.*, or 2) *Acon. bell. cin. coff. dulc. sep.*

Catarrhal affections of *old people: Baryt. carb-veg. con. hyos. kreos. phosph. stann. sulph.*

Catarrhal affections *of children:* 1) *Acon. bell. cham. cin. coff. dros. ign. ipec. sulph.* — Catarrhal affections of *scrofulous* children, require: *Bell. calc.;* — of very *fat* children: *Ipec.* or *Calc.*

§. 4. Particular indications:

Aconite: Burning fever, with full, bounding pulse; rough, hoarse voice; painful sensitiveness of the affected part, with aggravation of the pain in breathing, coughing or talking; *short, dry cough with constant irritation* and painful titillation in the larynx and bronchi; oppressed breathing, with tension, soreness or stitches in the chest when coughing or breathing; violent, rough hollow cough at night, short and panting cough in the day-time; thirst, sleeplessness or restless sleep, with tossing about; burning headache, red face and eyes; or also when the cough is convulsive or hacking, with scanty expectoration of whitish and scanty mucus.

Belladonna: Dry cough with sore throat, coryza, fever in the afternoon and evening, dry and burning skin, frequent desire for cold drinks, without, however, drinking much; obstinacy and malice in children, with hurried respiration during sleep; or when the following symptoms occur: *spasmodic cough which does not allow one time to breathe;* racking cough, from intolerable titillation in the larynx, as if from dust or from some other foreign body; or dry, short, hollow, barking cough; the cough occurs at night, or in the afternoon or in the evening when in bed, and even during sleep, coming on again after the least motion; bruised pain in the nape of the neck when coughing, or headache as if the forehead would split; rheumatic pains in the chest; stitches in the sternum or hypochondria; mucous rattling in the chest; red face and headache; hoarseness and mucus in the chest; frequent sneezing, especially at the termination of a paroxysm.

Bryonia: Dry or moist cough, from titillation in the throat, or when the following symptoms occur: Spasmodic cough, suffocative cough, especially after midnight, or after eating and drinking, with vomiting of the ingesta; cough with *yellowish expectoration,* or expectoration of a dirty, reddish, or bloody mucus; *stitches in the side when coughing,* or pains in the chest and head as if these parts would split; great inclination to sweat; hoarseness, mucous rattling in, and painfulness of, the larynx, increased by smoking.

Chamomilla. Accumulation of tenacious mucus in the throat, with dry cough, *occasioned by constant titillation in the larynx and chest,* worse when talking; or cough evening and morning, or at night when in bed, and even during sleep, sometimes accompanied by suffocative fits; scanty expectoration of bitter mucus in the morning; or when the cough was caused by chagrin, or when children are attacked with it in consequence of their cries; or for hoarseness with coryza, dryness and burning in the throat, thirst; fever towards evening; ill humour, taciturnity, disposition to be angry and peevish.

Mercurius: *Roughness* and *hoarseness,* with burning and titillation in the larynx; *disposition to sweat,* but the sweat affording no relief; aggravation by the least draught of air; or when the following symptoms occur: *dry, racking cough,* especially in the evening, or at night, even during sleep, and occasioned by titillation and a feeling of dryness in the bronchi; cough with stinging pains in the chest; or with nausea, bleeding of the nose (in the case of children), pains in the head or chest, as if these parts would split, expectoration of blood, fluent coryza, hoarseness and mucous diarrhœa.

Nux vomica: Rough, dry and deep cough, occasioned by dryness of the larynx, with tension and pain in the larynx and bronchi; hoarseness and painful feeling of rawness in the throat; especially in the morning, or in the evening when in bed; accumulation of tenacious mucus in the throat, which the patient is not able to detach; dry coryza with dry mouth, hot and red cheeks, shivering or alternate chills and heat; constipation, painful heaviness in the forehead, ill humour, irritated spirits, obstinacy, &c.; or when the following symptoms are present: Convulsive, racking cough, occasioned by titillation in the throat, especially in the morning, or at night when in bed, or *after a meal,* or when occasioned by exercise, thinking or reading; oppression at night, or headache as if the skull would split; contusive pain in the epigastrium and pain in the hypochondria when coughing; or, for: cough with vomiting or with bleeding from the nose or mouth.

Pulsatilla: Hoarseness, aphonia; stitches and soreness of the throat and palate; coryza, with yellowish, greenish and fetid discharge; moist cough, with pain in the chest; chilliness and absence of thirst; or cough which is at first dry, then moist, with profuse expectoration of a salt, bitter, yellowish or whitish, or even bloody mucus; or racking cough, especially in the evening or at night in bed, worse when lying; with nausea, vomiting, suffocative sensation as if from the vapours of sulphur, and mucous rattle; painfulness of the abdomen, when coughing, as if bruised, or painful shocks in the arm, shoulder or back, or involuntary emission of urine.

Rhus toxicodendron: Hoarseness and roughness, soreness of the throat, frequent sneezing, considerable mucus in the nose without coryza, but with difficulty of breathing; or for: short and dry cough at night, occasioned by a titillation in the bronchi, with restlessness and shortness of breath, especially in the evening and before midnight; painful shocks in the head and chest, or tension or stitches in the chest; pain in the stomach or stitches in the loins; or when the cough gets worse in the cold air, and is less in warmth or during motion; or when the cough comes on in the morning on waking, or in the evening, with bitter taste in the mouth, or vomiting of the ingesta.

Sulphur: Hoarseness, aphonia, roughness and scraping in the throat, accumulation of mucus in the bronchi, fluent coryza, cough, soreness in the chest, chills, aggravation of the symptoms in cold and damp weather; or for: dry, racking cough, with nausea, vomiting and spasmodic constriction of the chest, especially in the evening, or at night when lying, or in the morning, or after a meal; or for: Cough with copious expectoration of thick, whitish or yellowish mucus, sometimes only in the day time, with dry cough at night; or obstinate, dry cough from titillation in the throat, stitches in the chest or head when coughing, stupefaction, obscuration of sight; feeling of fulness in the chest, oppression, mucous rattling, palpitation of the heart, and suffocative fits.

§. 5. The following remedies may likewise be used:

Arnica: Dry or moist cough, if excited by titillation in the larynx, especially in the morning, during sleep, with weeping and cries, or when it attacks children after crying much; or for moist cough, the patient being unable to throw off the loose mucus; and when the following symptoms are present: Aching and crampy pain in the head, as if the brain were strung together; stitches in the chest; pain in the loins and rheumatic pains in the limbs; frequent bleeding of the nose and mouth, or even bloody expectoration.

Arsenicum: Moist cough with difficult expectoration and tenacious mucus in the larynx and bronchi; or for: *dry, racking cough*, especially in the evening after lying down, or *at night*, excited by drink or cold air; attended with dyspnœa, or even *suffocative fits*, especially in the evening in bed; great languor, debility; hoarseness and coryza, with discharge of an acrid, corrosive mucus; rheumatic headache, with violent pains; the symptoms are worse at night and after a meal.

Calcarea: Frequent attacks of obstinate hoarseness; accumulation of tenacious mucus in the bronchi and larynx; dry, violent cough, with titillation as if from feather-dust in the throat, especially in the evening, in bed, or at night, during sleep; or moist cough, with mucous rattling, or with a thick, yellowish, fetid expectoration; pains and stitches in the side and chest; great languor, and sadness on account of one's ill health.

Capsicum: Hoarseness and *dry cough*, which is worse in the evening and at night, sometimes attended with nausea, wandering rheumatic pains, and headache as if the skull would split; pressure in the throat and ear; stitches in the chest or back, or pressure on the bladder, with stitches in that region; coryza, with stoppage of the nose and titillation in the nostrils.

Carbo veg: Obstinate hoarseness and roughness of voice, especially in the morning or evening, made worse by constant talking, or cold and damp weather; or *spasmodic cough*, either several paroxysms in the day-time, or only in the evening; or cough with profuse expectoration of greenish mucus; rheumatic pains in the chest or limbs; ulcerative pain, or scraping and titillation in the larynx.

Causticum: Violent, racking cough, especially at night, with pain in the throat and head; hoarseness, roughness and feebleness of the voice; mucous rattling; pain in the larynx and chest, as if raw; fluent coryza with headache; feeble appetite, nausea and vomiting of the ingesta; rheumatic pains in the limbs and facial bones; chill during every motion; heat at night, with palpitation of the heart; great debility of the lower limbs; aggravation of the symptoms in the open air; involuntary emission of urine during cough.

China: Hoarseness, rough and deep sound of the voice, owing to mucus adhering in the larynx; dry cough as if from the vapours of sulphur; or spasmodic suffocative cough at night, with bilious vomiting and difficult expectoration of viscid or whitish, and sometimes bloody mucus; the cough is excited by laughing, talking, breathing, and even by eating and drinking.

Cina: Suitable to children, when the cough is dry, or with scanty expectoration, with sudden starting during sleep as if in affright, want of breath, moaning, pale face or rough cough every evening, especially when the children are affected with worms; or when fluent coryza is present, with burning heat in the nostrils, and violent, and painful sneezing.

Drosera: Hoarseness with deep sound of the voice; dryness, roughness and scraping in the larynx, with accumulation of yellowish, gray or greenish mucus; dry, *spasmodic, racking* cough, especially at night or in the evening when in bed, frequently attended with nausea or vomiting of the ingesta, bleeding of the nose or mouth; paroxysms of suffocation or cough, excited by laughing or weeping, emotions, singing, tobacco-smoke, or drinking.

Dulcamara: Moist cough, especially after a cold, with hoarseness or bloody expectoration; or for panting, barking cough like whooping-cough, excited by a deep inspiration.

Euphrasia: Cough with violent catarrh attacking the eyes; cough which only exists in the day-time, with difficult expectoration, or only in the morning, with *copious expectoration* and tight breathing.

Hyoscyamus: Dry cough, worse at night and in a recumbent posture, less when sitting up; cough with titillation in the larynx or bronchi; or spasmodic cough, with red face and mucous rattling.

Ignatia: Dry and rough cough, with fluent coryza, headache, feeble voice; or short cough as if from feather-dust or the vapours of sulphur; the cough finally becomes spasmodic, especially suitable to patients who had suffered much grief; or when the catarrhal symptoms get worse after a meal, after going to bed, and in the morning, after rising.

Ipecacuanha: Especially suitable to children when they almost suffocate in consequence of the mucus, with rattling of mucus; or for spasmodic, suffocative cough, with bluish face and spasmodic rigidity of the body; contractive sensation and titillation in the larynx; or for dry cough, or cough with scanty expectoration of flat and unpleasant mucus, with nausea and vomiting of albuminous mucus, or with bleeding of the nose and mouth.

Lachesis: catarrhal cough and coryza, stinging pains in the head, stiff neck and distress in the chest; constant hoarseness, with sensation as if mucus adhered to the throat; the cough comes on at night during sleep, or in the evening when in bed, or after sleep, and is excited by a titillation in the larynx, or by the least pressure on the larynx; it is worse after eating, or when rising from a recumbent posture; the cough is attended with pains in the throat, eyes, ears and head.

Phosphorus: Hoarseness with cough, fever, and apprehension of death; roughness or complete extinction of voice; painful sensitiveness of the larynx; *dry* cough from tickling in the throat, with stitches in the larynx and soreness in the chest; the cough is excited by laughing, drinking, loud reading, or walking in the open air; or dry cough with expectoration of viscid or bloody mucus.

Phosphori acidum: Hoarseness, moist cough, from titillation in the pit of the stomach or throat-pit; the cough is dry in the evening, and in the morning it is attended with a whitish, or yellowish, or even purulent expectoration; with aching pains in the chest.

Sepia: Cough with copious expectoration of putrid, or salt mucus, of a yellow, greenish colour, or purulent, or even bloody, frequently only in the morning, or evening, with mucous rattling, weakness and soreness in the chest; or for dry, spasmodic cough, like whooping-cough, especially at night or in the evening in bed, with dyspnœa, nausea and vomiting of bile; especially suitable to scrofulous persons, or persons affected with herpes, or herpes in the joints.

Silicea: Obstinate cough, with copious, transparent or purulent expectoration; or racking cough, with sore throat and colic, or suffocative cough at night.

Squilla: Chronic catarrh, with profuse expectoration of a whitish and viscid mucus; the expectoration is at times easy, at others very hard.

Stannum: Copious expectoration of a yellowish or greenish mucus of a sweetish or salt taste; or dry, racking cough, especially in bed from evening till midnight, worse in the morning, and sometimes attended with nausea and vomiting of the ingesta.

Staphysagria: Cough with expectoration of a yellowish, viscid, purulent mucus, especially at night, ulcerative pain in the chest, or even bloody expectoration.

Veratrum: Hollow and deep cough, as if proceeding deep from the chest or abdomen; with colic, ptyalism, bluish face, involuntary emission of urine, violent pain in the side, difficult breathing and great debility; or stitches towards the abdominal ring, as if hernia would protrude.

Verbascum: Especially suitable to children, for dry and rough cough, especially in the evening and at night, during sleep, without waking the child.

Compare: *Catarrh, laryngitis, angina pectoris, pleuritis, pulmonary phthisis, asthma, croup, whooping-cough, influenza, cough, hoarseness,* &c.

BREASTS AND NIPPLES OF WOMEN.—The best remedies for *sore nipples* are: *Arn. sulph.*; or, *Calc. cham. ign. puls.*

Chamomilla: Inflamed or even ulcerated nipples; if the patient should have drank much chamomile-tea, give *Ign.* or *Puls.*, or perhaps, *Merc.* or *Sil.*

For simple soreness, use: *Arnica,* and if Arn. should not be sufficient, give *Sulph.* and *Calc.*

Beside these remedies, the following may be used: *Caust. graph. lyc. merc. n-vom. sep. sil.*

§ 2. For *inflammation of the breasts,* the best remedies are: *Bell. bry. carb-a. hep. merc. phos. sil. sulph.*

Belladonna: The breasts are swollen and hard, with *stitching* or tearing pains and erysipelatous redness, radiating from a central point. (Is frequently suitable in alternation with *Bryon.*)

Bryonia: The breasts are hard, rigid and turgid with milk,

with *tensive* or stitching pain in the swelling and burning heat on the outside; especially when febrile motions supervene. with heat, vascular orgasm, &c. (If *Bryon.* be insufficient, use *Bellad.*)

HEPAR: If suppuration should set in in spite of *Bell. bry.* and *Merc.*

MERCURIUS: If the inflammation yield neither to *Bell.* nor *Bryon.*, and the breasts remain hard and painful.

PHOSPHORUS: When *Hepar.* does not stop the suppurative process. The breasts are *ulcerated*, fistulous, the ulcers having hard and callous edges; or colliquative sweats and diarrhœa set in, with cough, feverish heat in the evening, circumscribed redness of the cheeks, and other symptoms of hectic fever.

SILICEA: Phosphorus being insufficient for suppuration of the nipples, fistulous ulcers, and symptoms of hectic fever.

§ 3. For *induration of the mammæ*, and nodosities in the breasts, give: 1) *Carb-a. con. sil.*; or, 2) *Clem. coloc. graph. lyc. merc. nitr-ac. ol-jec. phosph. puls. sep. sulph.*—If the disease should have been caused by a *blow*, *Arn. carbo-a.* and *con.* deserve a preference.

. For *cancer of the mammæ*, the principal remedies are: 1) *Ars. clem. sil.*; and also, 2) *Bell. con. hep.? kreos.?*

CALCULI RENALES.—Principal remedies: 1) *Lyc. sas-sap.* 2) *Ant. calc. natr-m. phosph. puls. ruta. sep. sil.* 3) *Alum. amm. amb. canth. chin. petr. thuja.*

CAMPHOR, ILL EFFECTS OF.—For poisoning with large doses: *black coffee* until vomiting sets in; afterwards *Opium* 30 in water, a teaspoonful every hour.

CANCER AND SCIRRHUS.—Best remedies: 1) *Ars. bell. con. n-vom. sep. sil. sulph.*; and perhaps, 2) *Aur. calc. carb-an. chin. clem. coloc. graph. lyc. merc. nitr-ac. phosph. puls. staph. thuj.*

For *open* cancer: 1) *Ars. con. sil.* and *sulph.* 2) *Aur. bell. calc. hep. lach. merc. nitr-ac. sep. staph.* and *thuj.*

For *Scirrhous* indurations: 1) *Bell. con. sep.* and *sil.*; and perhaps, 2) *Carb-an. carb-veg. cham. n-vom. phosph. staph.* and *sulph.*

Scirrhous or *cancerous* affections in consequence of *contusion* or *shock*, require *Con.* or *Staphys.*, or perhaps, *Arnica.*

See: *Cancer of the womb, face, and cancer of the other organs.*

CANCER OF THE EYES.—*Laurocer.* is the *only* remedy known for this affection. It is probable, however, that—1) *Bell. calc. con. sil.* 2) *Ars. hep. lyc. sep.* &c., are more specific.

CANCER OF THE NOSE.—Principal remedies: 1) *Ars. sil. sulph.* 2) *Aur. calc. carb-an. sep.*
See: CANCER AND ERUPTIONS IN THE FACE.

CANCER AND SCIRRHUS OF THE STOMACH.—The best remedies are: 1) *Ars. baryt. lyc. n-vom. phos. veratr.;* or, 2) *Con. ? sil. ? staph.? sulph.*
See: CANCER.

CANCER AND INDURATIONS OF THE UTERUS: *Carcinoma et Scirrhus uteri.*

§ 1. The best remedies are: 1) *Carb-an. graph. kreos.* 2) *Ars. aur. bell. chin. cic. clem. coccul. con. dulc. jod. magn-m. merc. nitr-ac. sep. sil. staph. thuj.*

§ 2. For *induration* (scirrhus) of the uterus, give: 1) *Carb-an.* 2) *Aur. bell. chin. magn-m. sep. staph.* 3) *Clem. coccul. con.;* also, *Rhus. phos.*

For *real cancer*, *Graph.* and *Kreasot.* have been used. The following remedies deserve consideration: 2) *Carb-an.* 3) *Ars. bell. chin. clem. merc. sep. sil.;* also, 4) *Lach. staph. sabin. phos. calc.* and *thuj.*

For the *phagedenic* (not cancerous) ulcers of the uterus and neck of the uterus, I have seen good effects from: 1) *Nitr-ac. thuj.* 2) *Ars. bell. chin. coccul. merc. sep.*

§ 3. Particular indications:

BELLADONNA: Frequent hæmorrhages of the uterus, with pressing towards the genital organs, violent pains in the small of the back, and excessive nervousness.

CONIUM: *Stitching* pains, especially when attended with nausea, vomiting, desire for various kinds of food, &c.

GRAPHITES: Hot and painful vagina: swelling of the lymphatic vessels and mucous follicles; the neck of the uterus is hard and swollen, with tuberculous nodes and cauliflower-excrescences great weight in the abdomen on rising, with fainting sort of weakness and aggravation of the pains; delaying menses, with aggravation of the pains shortly before and at the appearance of the menses; discharge of black, lumpy, fetid blood; stitches shooting through the abdomen as far as the thighs; *burning* and *stitching* pains; constipation; livid complexion; sad and anxious mood.

KREASOTUM: Stitches from the abdomen to the vagina; swelling of the labia and itching in the vagina; discharge of dark, lumpy menstrual blood, succeeded by discharge of an acrid, bloody ichor; pressing from above downwards, during and between the menses, &c.

§ 4. Compare: MENSTRUAL DIFFICULTIES, CANCEROUS ULCERS, and INDURATIONS.

CANTHARIDES, POISONING BY.—The best remedy for large doses is spirits of camphor in drop-doses, on sugar, one drop every ten or fifteen minutes. Use mucilaginous drinks and frictions with camphor.

For the ailments which frequently arise from abuse of Cantharides, *Acon.* and ***Puls.*** are frequently suitable.

CARDIALGIA, GASTRALGIA.

§ 1. The best remedies are: 1) ***Bell.*** *bry. calc.* ***carb-veg. cham.*** *chin.* ***cocc.*** *ign.* ***n-vom. puls. sulph.*** 2) ***Bism.*** *carb-an. caust. graph. grat. lach. lyc. magn-c. nitr-sp.* ***sil. stann. staph. stront.*** 3) ***Amm.*** *ant. coff. coloc. cupr. daph. euphorb. gran.? kal. kreos. natr. natr-m. n-mosch. sep.*

§ 2. For Cardialgia from *abuse of coffee: Cham. cocc. ign. n-vom.*

From abuse of *chamomile:* 1) *N-vom. puls.;* or, 2) ***Bell.*** *ign.*

From *emotions*, such as: anger, chagrin, &c.: *Cham. coloc.;* or, *n-vom. staph.*

From *debility, loss of animal fluids*, from *nursing, sweating*, abuse of *cathartics*, from the effects of a confinement, &c.: *Carb-veg. chin. cocc.*, or *nux-v.*

For Cardialgia of *drunkards*, or *debauchees: Carbo-veg. nux-v.*, or *calc. lach. sulph.*

§ 3. Cardialgia with sanguineous obstructions in the portal system: *Carb-veg.* or *nux-v.*

In the case of *hysteric* or *hypochondriac* individuals: *Calc. cocc. grat. ign. n-vom. magn-c. stann.* &c.

During the *menses: Cham. cocc. n-vom. puls.*—When the menses are too *feeble: Cocc. puls.*—When to profuse: *Calc.* or *lyc.*

For Cardialgia from *abuse of kitchen-salt: Nitr-sp.* or *carb-veg.*

§ 4. Particular indications:

BELLADONNA: When Chamomilla seems to be indicated, but is ineffectual; most generally suitable to females or delicate individuals, especially when the following symptoms are present: gnawing pressure, or spasmodic tension, obliging the patient to bend backwards, or to stop the breath, which alleviates the pain; the pains are brought on by eating; the pain is *so violent, that the patient loses his consciousness and faints away;* great thirst, with aggravation of the pains by drinking; slow and scanty stool; sleepless nights, sometimes a little sleep in the daytime.

BRYONIA: Pressure in the pit of the stomach as *from a stone*, especially during or immediately after a meal, with sensation of swelling in the region of the stomach; or contractive, pinching and cutting pains, abating by pressing upon the region of the stomach, or after several eructations; *aggravation of the pains by motion*, or when walking, *with stitches in the region of the stomach on making a false step;* constipation, pressure and compressive sensation in the temples, forehead and occiput, as if the skull would burst; relief is obtained by making pressure on the head or temples.

CALCAREA: Suitable to plethoric persons that are apt to bleed from the nose, or to females who menstruate profusely, or after *Belladonna* had been given with but partial effect; it is indicated by: Pressure in the stomach, compressive, crampy pains, or *clutching sensation in the region of the stomach*, with anxiety; aggravation of the pains at night, or *after a meal, frequently with vomiting of the ingesta*, acidity and nausea; painful sensitiveness of the region of the stomach when pressing upon it; *constipation* and *hæmorrhoidal distress*, or chronic looseness of the bowels; palpitation of the heart, &c.

CARBO VEG.: After *Nux-v.* had been given with partial effect, or when the following symptoms occur: *Painful, burning pressure, with anguish*, trembling and aggravation by contact, also at night and *after a meal*, especially after taking *flatulent food;* or spasmodic contractive pain, compelling the patient to bend double, with asthma and aggravation in a recumbent posture; heartburn; nausea; loathing of food, even when merely thinking of it; *frequent flatulence*, with oppression of the chest and *constipation*.

CHAMOMILLA: Distention of the epigastrium and hypochondria, with *pressure as from a stone;* oppression, short and difficult breathing; aggravation of the pains after a meal, or *at night*, with great *anguish and restlessness;* decrease of the pains by bending double, *instantaneous relief by coffee;* and when the following symptoms are present: Beating pain in the vertex, at night, obliging one to get out of bed; irritable, peevish mood. *Cham.* is frequently most suitable in alternation with *Coff.;* if it should be ineffectual, give *Bell.* instead.)

CHINA: Dyspeptic weakness, with *distention of and painful pressure in the region of the stomach, after eating or drinking ever so little;* acidity, heartburn, slimy or bilious passages; the pains get worse during rest, abate during motion; loss of appetite, aversion to food and drink; idleness; sleepiness; hypochondriac mood and *inability to work, especially after a meal;* slow stool; yellow, livid complexion; yellow appearance of the whites.

COCCULUS: After partial relief by *Nux-v.* or *Chamom.* Symptoms: Aching, contractive pains in the abdomen, passing off after discharge of flatulence ; the colic returns after eating, with nausea, water in the mouth and oppression of the chest; hard, delaying stool ; *ill, intractable mood*, taciturn.

IGNATIA : After partial relief by ***Pulsatilla***. Symptoms : ***Painful pressure as from a stone***, especially after eating or at night, in the region of the pylorus ; or sensation of weakness or emptiness in the pit of the stomach, with sensitiveness to contact, and burning in the stomach ; hiccough ; regurgitation of the ingesta ; aversion to food and drink, or to tobacco ; accumulation of mucus in the mouth, &c. ; suitable to persons who had been starving either from want or other causes.

NUX VOM.: *Contractive, aching* or *crampy pains*, with ***clutching*** or *clawing* sensation in the stomach ; the pressure of the clothes on the epigastrium feels unpleasant ; *the pains are worse after a meal*, after *taking coffee*, at night, or towards morning, or after rising ; sensation as if a band were tied round the chest, with pains extending to the back and kidneys ; the attack is attended with nausea, water in the mouth, heartburn, or even ***vomiting of the ingesta ;*** sour or foul taste in the mouth ; flatulent distention of the abdomen ; *constipation, hæmorrhoidal ailments, hypochondriac, peevish, quarrelsome mood*, with *vehement disposition ; hemicrania*, or aching pains in the forehead, with inability to work ; palpitation of the heart, with anguish. *Nux-v.* is generally suitable at the commencement of every case of cardialgia ; sometimes, however, an exacerbation of the symptoms takes place after every dose of Nux ; in such cases ***Puls. ign.***, or *Cham.* deserve a preference If *Nux-v.* should be without effect, though apparently indicated, *Cham.* or *Cocc.* should be tried.

PULSATILLA : *Stitching pains*, worse when walking or when making a wrong step ; or *crampy pains*, either before breakfast or *after a meal*, generally attended with nausea, or *vomiting of the ingesta ; absence of thirst*, except at the acme of the pains ; beating in the epigastrium, with anguish, or tension and compression in the region of the stomach ; soft, or liquid stools ; *aggravation of the pains in the evening*, with *chills which increase correspondingly with the pains ;* sour or bitter taste of the mouth or food ; sad and whining mood; bland temper.

SULPHUR : ***Pressure as from a stone***, particularly *after eating*, with nausea, water in the mouth, or vomiting ; also when the following symptoms are present : *acidity, heartburn, frequent regurgitation of the ingesta ;* aversion to fat food, rye-bread, sour things or sugar ; dulness of the head, with inability to think : the pressure of the clothes on the hypochondria is unpleasant, with distention of these parts ; disposition to piles or accumulation of mucus in the intestines; hypochondriac, whining mood, disposition to be vehement.

§ 5. The following remedies are sometimes useful:

BISMUTHUM: Aching pain, with feeling of heaviness and indescribable malaise in the stomach.

CARBO ANIMALIS: After partial relief by Carbo veg., *burning aching* pain, acidity, heartburn, mucus in the stomach, and constipation.

CAUSTICUM: Pressure, spasmodic contraction, and griping in the stomach, as if clawed; the hair stands on end as the pains increase, acidity and mucus in the stomach.

GRAPHITES: Crampy, spasmodic or clawing pains, or pressure with vomiting of the ingesta.

GRATIOLA: Pressure in the stomach, especially after a meal, with nausea, ineffectual attempts at eructations, constipation and hypochondriac mood.

LACHESIS: Aching pains which diminish immediately after a meal, but recommence again in a few hours, and are particularly violent after the siesta; dyspeptic weakness, flatulence and *constipation.*

LYCOPODIUM: Compressive pains as if the stomach were pressed together from both sides, less in the evening, but coming on again in the morning, *especially in the open air*, or after a meal.

MAGNESIA: Aching and contractive pains, with sour eructations.

NITRI SPIRITUS: Aching, contractive pains from eating too much salt, fulness in the stomach, after a meal, with sour or slimy vomiting; loss of appetite, heartburn and acidity.

SILICEA: *Aching pain in the stomach*, especially *after eating* or drinking rapidly, with mucus in the stomach and vomiting.

STANNUM: Obstinate cardialgia, with bitter eructations, canine hunger, diarrhœa, nausea, pale and sickly complexion.

STAPHYSAGRIA: Aching and tensive pain in the stomach, at times worse, at others better after eating, especially bread, with frequent nausea and constipation.

STRONTIANA: Aching in the stomach, especially after a meal, with fulness in the abdomen.

§ 6. For *pains in the stomach* with great *anguish* and oppression in the pit and region of the stomach: *Anac. ars. calc. carb-veg. cham. chin. graph. guaj. laur. lyc. natr-m. n-vom. op. puls. spig. stann. stram. sulph. thuj. veratr.*—Painfulness to contact, in the pit of the stomach: 1) *Ars. baryt. bry. calc. coloc. lyc. merc. natr. natr-m. n-vom. phosph. sil. spig. sulph. veratr.* 2) *Camph.*

cann. colch. dig. ferr. kal. magn-c. magn-m. phos-ac. plat. rhod. sep. stann.—*Boring* pains: *Amm. ars. caps. carb-an. natr. nitr. sep.*—*Burning* pains: 1) *Ars. camph. carb-veg. cic. dig. lach. n-vom. phosph. sep. sil. sulph.* 2) *Bry. dulc. hyos. lach. magn-c. merc. mez. mur-ac. natr. natr-m. zinc.*—*Aching* pains: *Ars. baryt. bell. bry. calc. carb-an. carb-veg. caust. cham. cic. dig. dulc. ferr. graph. hep. lach. lyc. merc. natr. natr-m. n-mosch. n-vom. phosph. rhus. sep. sil. stann. staph. sulph.*— *Ulcerative* pain: *Baryt. cann. carb-veg. con. hell. magn-c. magn-m. merc. rhus. stann.*—*Swelling* of the region of the stomach: *Amm. aur. calc. coff. hep. ipec. lyc. natr-m. petr. sulph.*—*Griping* and clawing in the stomach: 1) *Calc. carb-an. caust. magn-arct. natr-m. n-vom. phosph. puls. sil.* 2) *Arn. chin. coccul. graph. lyc. natr. nitr-ac. petr. stann. sulph. sulph-ac.*—*Feeling of coldness* in the stomach and pit of the stomach: *Alum. amm. baryt. caps. chin. colch. con. laur. natr-m. phosph. rhus. sulph. spong. zinc.*—*Beating* pains: *Bell. carb-veg. cic. dros. graph. kal. kreos. laur. lyc. magn-m. merc. mosch. mur-ac. natr-m. n-vom. puls. rhab. sep. sulph. tart. thuj. zinc.*—*Crampy* pains: See § 1.—*Creeping* pains:—*Alum. caust. colch. plat. puls. rhod. rhus.*—*Gnawing* pains: *Alum. amm. amm-m. ars. baryt. calc. carb-veg. graph. hep. lach. lyc. natr. nitr-ac. phosph. plat. puls. rhod. ruta. sil. sulph.*—*Tearing* pains: *Alum. amm. ars. baryt. carb-an. cupr. kreos. lyc. merc. n-vom. puls. ruta. sep. sulph.*—*Stitching* pains: 1) *Arn. bry. caust. colch. dig. lach. nitr-ac. rhus. sep.* 2) *Alum. amb. amm. baryt. calc. canth. carb-an. chin. con. cupr. graph. ign. magn-c. natr-m. phosph. sulph.*—*Feeling of fulness*: 1) *Chin. dig. kal. lach. lyc. n-mosch. n-vom. petr. phosph.* 2) *Acon. arn. asa. kal. merc. mez. staph.*—*Sore pain*: *Alum. baryt. bry. calc. chin. colch. con. hell. ign. kal. lach. magn-c. mang. mosch. nitr-ac. n-vom. ran. sabad. sep.*—*Constrictive*, contractive pains: 1) *Amm. carb-an. carb-veg. graph. magn-c. natr. natr-m. n-vom. sulph.* 2) *Alum. borax. chin. coccul. dig. guaj. kal. lyc. merc. natr-m. nitr-ac. petr. phosph. plumb. rhab. rhus. sep. sulph-ac.*

§ 7. Compare: VOMITING, STOMACH, *weakness of*, COLIC, PAIN, *paroxysms of*, CONDITIONS, CAUSES, &c.

CATARACT, GLAUCOMA, &c.—The best remedies for cataract are: 1) *Cann. caust. con. magn. phosph. puls. sil. sulph.* 2) *Amm. baryt. calc. chel. dig. euphr. hep. hyos. nitr-ac. op. ruta. seneg. spig. stram.*

For cataract from injury by a blow, &c., (*traumatic cataract*), the best remedy is said to be *Conium*, though we may likewise use: *Amm. euphr. puls.* and *ruta.*

Glaucoma, or bluė or green cataract, seems to require principally *Phosphorus.*

For *reticulated* cataract, give: *Caust.* and *Plumb.*

CATARRH, Coryza.

§. 1. Principal remedies: 1) *Amm. ars. cham. dulc. hep. lach. merc. n-vom. puls. sulph.* 2) *Bell. euphr. ign. ipec. lyc. natr. samb.* 3) *Alum. anac. bry. calc. carb-veg. caust. con. graph. natr-m. nitr-ac. sep. sil. zinc.*, &c.

§ 2. For the *precursory* symptoms, when the development of the catarrh seems to be delayed, with catarrhal affection of the frontal cavities, eyes, &c., use: 1) *Amm. calc. lach. n-vom. sulph.;* or, 2) *Caust. hep.* and *natr-m.*

For dry coryza, or catarrhal obstruction of the nose, use, together with the above-mentioned remedies: *Bry. ign. lyc. natr. natr-m. nitr-ac. phosph. plat. sil.*

Obstruction of the nose in the case of new-born infants, is generally relieved by *Nux-v.* or *Sambucus.*

For *fluent coryza,* discharge of mucus from the nose, give: 1) *Merc. puls. sulph.;* or, 2) *Ars. bell. cham. dulc. hep. ipec. lyc. merc. nitr-ac. sil.*

§ 3. The best remedies for *ordinary* catarrh, are: 1) *Merc. hep. bell. lach.;* or, 2) *Ars. dulc. n-vom. ipec.;* or, 3) *Cham. puls. sulph.;* or, 4) *Amm. bry. euphr. ign.*

For catarrh with *fever:* 1) *Merc. n-vom.;* or, 2) *Acon. ars. sabad. spig.*

For *chronic* catarrh, give: *Alum. anac. calc. carb-veg. caust. con. graph. lyc. natr. natr-m. nitr-ac. sep. sil. zinc.*—and the remedies indicated for "*Suppuration of the nose.*"

For the disposition to catarrh, the best remedies are: *Calc. graph. natr. puls. sil. sulph.* and the remedies indicated for "*Cold.*"

§ 4. For the consequences to *suppressed* catarrh, give: *Acon. ars. bell. bry. chin. cin. n-vom. puls. sulph.*

If the *head* be greatly affected, the best remedies are: 1) *Acon. bell. cham. chin. cin. n-vom. sulph.;* or, 2) *Ars. bell. carb-veg. lach. lyc. puls.*

If the *eyes* should be principally involved, use: 1) *Bell. cham. euphr. ign. lach. n-vom. puls.;* or, 2) *Hep. merc. sulph.*

For *asthmatic* complaints, use: 1) *Ars. ipec.;* or, 2) *Bry. n-vom.* or *sulph.*

And for *bronchitis: Acon. bry. merc. n-vom. puls. rhus.* or *sulph.*

§ 5. Particular indications:

Ammonium: *Stoppage of the nose, especially at night;* swelling and painful sensitiveness of the nostrils; discharge of blood from the nose on blowing it; *dryness of the nose;* painful eyes, lachrymation ; bleeding at the nose ; dry mouth, especially at night, &c.

Arsenicum: *Stoppage of the nose*, with copious discharge of a watery mucus, and burning in the nose, *with soreness of the adjacent parts;* sleepless nights; bleeding at the nose ; hoarseness; buzzing in the ears ; headache with beating in the forehead, and nausea ; *relief by warmth*, absence of thirst, or desire to drink all the time, but little at a time.

Dulcamara : Stoppage of the nose, with discharge which is suppressed by the least contact with cold air ; the symptoms are worse during rest, and abate during motion; bleeding at the nose; dryness of the mouth without thirst; rough and hoarse voice.

Chamomilla : Principally suitable to children, or after suppression of sweat, especially when the following symptoms occur : Ulcerated nostrils ; chapped lips ; great drowsiness, heaviness of the head with dulness ; *chills with thirst*. one cheek is red and the other pale ; acrid mucus from the nostrils (frequently suitable before or after *Puls.*)

Hepar : After partial relief by *Merc.*, in all cases of *ordinary catarrh*, or when the patient had been drugged with Mercury ; generally, when every breath of cold air causes a new attack of catarrh or headache ; or when the catarrh is confined to one nostril, and the headache gets worse by motion.

Lachesis : After partial effect of *Merc.* and *Hep.* Symptoms : *Copious discharge of watery mucus;* swelling and soreness of the nostrils and lips; scurf in the nostrils, lachrymation, frequent sneezing ; or when the catarrh remains undeveloped, with stoppage of the nose, buzzing in the ears, lachrymation, headache, ill-humour, inability to think ; especially after *Nux-v.*, if given without effect.

Mercurius: *Ordinary catarrh*, whether epidemic or not. Symptoms: Frequent sneezing, *copious discharge of watery saliva*, swelling, *redness* and *soreness of the nose*, with itching and pain in the nasal bones on pressing upon them ; *fetid smell of the nasal mucus;* painful heaviness in the forehead ; night-sweats ; chills or feverish heat ; great thirst ; pains in the limbs ; desire to be alone ; the symptoms are aggravated by warmth or cold. (Compare: *Bell. hep.* and *lach.*)

Nux vom: Suppression of the catarrhal discharge, with stoppage of the nose ; headache with *heaviness in the forehead*, or with stitching or tearing pains ; hot face, especially in the evening, with burning redness of the cheeks ; rigidity of the whole body; vexed mood, vehement ; the catarrh is fluent in the morning, dry in the evening or at night, with dry mouth, without much thirst; feeling of dryness in the chest; constipation or hard stools ; or *simultaneous stoppage of the nose*, and discharge of a *burning* and *corrosive mucus*, for which *Ars.* did no good. (Compare: *Ars. ipec.* and *lach.*)

PULSATILLA: Loss of appetite; loss of taste and smell; *discharge of a yellowish, green, thick and fetid mucus;* swelling of the nose; discharge of blood from the nose on blowing it; ulceration of the nostrils; frequent sneezing; photophobia; rough voice; dulness and *heaviness* of the head, especially in the evening and in a warm room, with obstruction of the nose; the symptoms are less in the open air; chills, especially in the evening, absence of thirst, whining mood. (Frequently suitable after or before *Cham.*)

SULPHUR: *Stoppage* and great dryness of the nose, or copious secretion of a thick, yellowish and purulent mucus; frequent sneezing; discharge of blood from the nose on blowing it; loss of smell; soreness and ulceration of the nostrils, &c. (Frequently suitable after *Puls.*)

§ 6. Of the other remedies, the following deserve consideration:

BELLADONNA: After partial effect of *Merc.* or *Hepar.*, the sense of smell is at times more, at others less keen than usual.

EUPHRASIA: Copious discharge of whitish mucus, with red eyes and lachrymation.

IGNATIA: Catarrh of nervous persons, with frontal headache and hysteric nervousness.

IPECACUANHA: After partial effect of *Ars.* and *Nux vom.:* for great debility, loss of appetite, nausea and vomiting.

LYCOPODIUM: *Stoppage of the nose, at night*, dull head, burning pain in the forehead.

NATRUM: The catarrh returns every other day; it is excited by the least draught of air, and does not yield to sweating.

SAMBUCUS: Suitable to new-born infants; the nose is obstructed by a tenacious, thick mucus, with sudden starting from sleep, as if suffocating.

§ 7. Compare COUGH, SUPPURATION OF THE NOSE, &c., and especially: MUCOUS MEMBRANES, DISEASES OF THE.

CATARRH, SUFFOCATIVE, ORTHOPNŒA PARALYTICA.—The best remedies are: 1) *Arsen. carb-veg. chin. ipec. lach. op.;* or, 2) *Baryt-c. camph. graph. puls. samb. tart.*

For suffocative catarrh with *accumulation of mucus in the bronchi*, give: 1) *Ars. camph. chin. ipec. tart.;* or, 2) *Carb-veg. graph. puls. samb.*

For *paralytic orthopnœa* (catarrh with paralytic state of the pulmonary nerves), give: 1) *Baryt-c. graph. lach. op.;* or, 2) *Ars. aur. carb-veg. chin.*

The best remedies for *children* are: *Acon. ipec. samb. tart.*

The best remedies for *old people:* 1) *Baryt. lach. op.;* or, 2) *Ars. aur. baryt-c. carb-veg. chin. con.*

For the more particular symptoms, see ASTHMA.

CATARRH OF THE BLADDER.—The best remedies are: 1) *Dulc. puls. sulph.*; or, 2) *Ant. calc. con. kal. n-vom. phos.* See CYSTITIS and ISCHURIA.

CATALEPSY, NYCTOBASIS, SOMNAMBULISM.

§ 1. These diseases are essentially related to each other. We include them in the same paragraph, in order to give the reader a chance, in case he should not discover suitable remedies for one form, to study the remedies of the other.

§ 2. For *catalepsy* we use principally: 1) *Cham. ipec. plat. stram.* 2) *Acon. agar. bell. cic. hyos. mosch. veratr.* 3) *Asa. camph. coloc. dros. ign. merc. op. petr.*

For *somnambulism*: 1) *Bry. natr-m. sil. sulph.* 2) *Petr. phos. rhab.*

For *natural clairvoyance*: *Phos.*; also: 1) *Acon. bry. cic. hyos. magn-arct.*; or, 2) *Agar. mosch. natr-m. sil. sulph. veratr.*

Compare: SPASMS, EMOTIONS, MORBID, and DREAMS.

CAUSES OF DISEASE.—A great many particular causes have been mentioned in special paragraphs. It may, however, be interesting to the reader to review the principal causes of disease under one head, as follows:

a) From *abuse of medicines*: (See the different drugs.)

b) From *sexual abuse*: 1) *Calc. chin. n-vom. phos-ac. sil. staph. sulph.* 2) *Arn. anac. carb-veg. con. merc. natr-m. phos. sep.* 3) *Agar. ars. cin. con. kal. natr. petr. phos. puls. sil. spig. thuj.*—(Compare: DEBILITY.)

c) From *bathing*: *Ant. ars. bell. calc. carb-veg. caust. nitr-ac. rhus. sassap. sep. sulph.*—(Compare: COLD.)

d) Inhalation of noxious *vapours*: (See VAPOURS.)

e) If from *congelation*: 1) *Acon. ars. bry. carb-veg. lach. nitr-ac. puls. sulph-ac.* 2) *Agar. camph. colch. petr. phos. sulph.*—(Compare: APPARENT DEATH.)

f) If from *being heated*: 1) *Acon. ant. bell. bry. camph. carb-veg. sil.* 2) *Caps. kal. natr-m. n-vom. op. thuj. zinc.*—(Compare: HEAT, ILL EFFECTS OF.)

g) From *weariness by walking*: *Arn. bry. cann. chin. coff. ferr. rhus. thuj. veratr.*—(Compare: WORN OUT.)

h) From violent *concussion of the body*: 1) *Arn. bry. cic. con. spig.* 2) *Acon. bell. calc. cin. hep. ign. n-vom. phos-ac. rhus ruta. sulph.*

i) From *riding in a carriage, swinging*, or some other passive motion: 1) *Ars. cocc. petr. sulph.* 2) *Colch. ferr. n-mosch. sep. sil.* 3) *Borax. carb-veg. colch. croc. graph. hep. ign. kal. natr. natr-m. phos. plat. selen. staph.*

k) From *mental exertion:* 1) *Bell. calc. lach. n-vom. puls. sulph.* 2) *Anac. arn. aur. cocc. colch. ign. lyc. natr-m. oleand. plat. sabad. sep. sil.*—(Compare: WORN OUT.)

l) From *emotions:* 1) *Acon. bell. bry. cham. coff. coloc. hyos. ign. lach. merc. n-vom. op. phos. phos-ac. plat. puls. staph. stram. veratr.* 2) *Ars. aur. calc. caust. cocc. coff. lyc. natr-m. nitr-ac. n-mosch. rhus. sep. sulph.*—(See: EMOTIONS.)

m) From hurtful food or drink.—(See STOMACH, WEAKNESS OF.)

n) From *poisonous things or animals.*—(See: POISONING.)

o) From *stings of insects.*—(See: STINGS OF INSECTS.)

p) From *physical exertions:* 1) *Acon. arn. bry. calc. chin. cocc. coff. merc. rhus. sil. veratr.* 2) *Alum. cann. lyc. natr-m. n-vom. ruta. sabin. sulph.*—(Compare: WORN OUT.)

q) From *derangement of the stomach:* 1) *Ant. arn. ipec. n-vom. puls.* 2) *Acon. ars. bry. carb-veg. chin. coff. hep. ign. natr. staph.* 3) *Calc. carb-veg. cham. hep. natr. natr-m. phos. sep. sil. sulph. veratr.*

r) From *watching:* 1) *Carb-veg. cocc. n-vom. puls.* 2) *Amb. bry. chin. ipec. natr. natr-m. phos-ac. ruta. sabin. selen. sep.*—(Compare: WORN OUT.)

s) From getting *wet by rain,* &c.: 1) *Calc. dulc. puls. sulph.* 2) *Ars. carb-veg. n-mosch. rhus. sassap.* 3) *Ars. bell. borax. bry. caust. colch. hep. lyc. phos. sep.*—(See: COLD.)

t) From *intoxication:* 1) *Ant. carb-veg. coff. n-vom. sulph.* 2) *Bell. bry. calc. chin. dulc. natr. nitr-ac. phos. phos-ac. rhus.*—(Compare: DRUNKARDS, DISEASES OF, and WORN OUT.)

u) From loss of *animal fluids, bloodletting,* &c.: 1) *Calc. carb-veg. chin. cin. lach. n-vom. phos-ac. sulph. veratr.* 2) *Ars. con. ferr. ign. kal. merc. natr. natr-m. phos. puls. sep. sil. spig. squill. staph.*—(Compare: DEBILITY.)

v) For ailments of *habitual drunkards:* 1) *Ars. bell. calc. chin. coff. hell. hyos. lach. merc. natr. n-vom. op. puls. sulph.* 2) *Agar. ant. carb-veg. cocc. ign. led. lyc. natr-m. n-mosch. ran. rhod. rhus. ruta. selen. sil. spig. stram. veratr.*—(See: DRUNKARDS, DISEASES OF.)

w) From *onanism:* 1) *N-vom. sulph.* 2) *Calc. carb-veg. chin. cocc. con. natr-m. n-mosch. phos. phos-ac. staph.* 2) *Anac. ant. cin. dulc. kal. lyc. merc. petr. phos. puls. sep. sil. spig. staph.*—(See: DEBILITY, ATROPHY OF THE SPINAL MARROW, SEXUAL INSTINCT, &c.

x) From *heat of the sun:* 1) *Ant. bell. camph. hyos. natr. puls.* 2) *Acon. agar. bry. euphr. lach. selen. sulph. val.*—(See: HEAT.)

y) From *stone-dust:* 1) *Calc. sil.* 2) *Lyc. natr. puls. sulph.*

z) From *suppression of habitual secretions or eruptions:* 1) *Acon. bell. bry. calc. chin. lyc. n-vom. puls. sulph.* 2) *Ars. carb-veg. caust. cham. dulc. graph. kal. lyc. phos. phos-ac. rhus. sep.*

sil. stram. 3) *Amb. amm. ant. arn. aur. baryt. cin. cocc. cupr. ferr. hep. hyos. ign. ipec. merc. mur-ac. natr. natr-m. nitr-ac. n-mosch. ran. seneg. spong.*—(See: SECRETIONS, SUPPRESSED.)

z a) From a *cold:* 1) *Acon. cham. coff. dulc. merc. n-vom. puls. sulph.* 2) *Ars. bell. bry. carb-veg. hyos. ipec. phos. rhus. sil. spig.* 3) *Calc. chin. coloc. con. graph. hep. lyc. mang. natr-m. nitr-ac. n-mosch. samb. sep. veratr.*—(See: COLD.)

z b) From *injuries:* 1) *Arn. cic. con. hep. lach. puls. rhus. sulph-ac.* 2) *Acon. amm. bry. calc. caust. cham. euphr. nitr-ac. n-vom. phos. ruta. sil. staph. sulph. zinc.* 3) *Alum. bell. borax. carb-veg. dulc. jod. petr. sil.*—(See: INJURIES.)

z c) From *washing* and *working in water:* 1) *Calc. n-mosch. puls. sassap. sulph.* 2) *Amm. ant. bell. carb-veg. dulc. merc. nitr-ac. rhus. sep. spig.*—(See: COLD.)

z d) From *suppression of fever and ague.*—(See: FEVERS, INTERMITTENT.)

CHAMOMILE, ILL EFFECTS OF.—The best remedies are: 1) *Acon. cocc. coff. ign. n-vom. puls.* 2) *Alum. borax. camph. coloc.*

ACONITUM: Fever with heat, and tearing or drawing pains, less during motion.

COCCULUS: Hysteric abdominal spasms, either recent or old ones aggravated.

COFFEA: Violent pains or feverish heat with great nervousness and excessive sensitiveness.

IGNATIA: Violent cramps and convulsions, or soreness in the folds, *Puls.* having proved ineffectual for the latter symptom.

NUX VOM: Old ailments are made worse, or cardialgia set in; *Coffea* being ineffectual.

PULSATILLA: Nausea with vomiting or diarrhœa, or soreness in the folds of infants.

CHEST, PAINS IN, DISTRESS IN THE.

This refers merely to the rheumatic pains in the chest, as the other pains are specially treated of under ASTHMA, ANGINA PECTORIS, CONGESTIONS OF THE CHEST, PLEURITIS, PNEUMONIA, &c.

Principal remedies: 1) *Acon. arn. bry. chin. n-vom. puls.*; or, 2) *Ars. bell. caust. carb-v. cham. colch. lach. merc. phos sulph. verat.*

FALSE PLEURISY (Pneumonia notha) requires *Arn.* or sometimes *Bry.*, or even *Acon.*, if the patient should be very restless and feverish.

If a metastasis of the rheumatism to the heart threaten to take place, *Hering* advises to give *Lach.*, after which *Caust.* and *Carb-v.* may be exhibited.

See: RHEUMATISM and PAIN, PAROXYSMS OF; also: CAUSES, PERIODS OF THE DAY, CONDITIONS.

CHILBLAINS.—The best remedies are: 1) *Agar. bell. nitr-ac. petr. phos. puls. sulph.*; or, 2) *Arn. carb-an. carb-veg. cham. chin. hyos. lyc. magn-aust. phos-ac. rhus. sulph-ac.*

For *inflamed* chilblains, give: *Ars. cham. lyc. nitr-ac. puls. sulph.*

For *blue-red and swollen* chilblains: *Arn. bell. kal. puls.*

For very *painful* ones: 1) *Hep.* 2) *Arn. nitr-ac. petr. phos-ac. puls. sep.*

CHILDREN, DISEASES OF, MORBI NEONATORUM.

§ 1. Many diseases of children having been mentioned in other articles, we here content ourselves with mentioning the acute or otherwise most important diseases under one head.

§ 2. *Asthmatic attacks* of infants, with spasms, danger of suffocation and bluish face, yield to *Ipec.*, and, if occurring during sleep, with screams, dry and husky cough, and anxiety, to: *Sambucus.* See: ASTHMA THYMICUM, and ASTHMA MILLARI.

Hardness and distention of the hypochondria and pit of the stomach, with shortness of breath, loss of breath, anguish and restlessness, tossing about, screams, drawing-up of the legs (*liver-grown*), yields to *Chamom.*

§ 3. For *ophthalmia neonatorum*, the best remedies are: (1 *Acon. cham. dulc. merc.*; or, 2) *Bell. bry. calc. n-vom. puls. sulph.*, &c.

(See: OPHTHALMIA.)

§ 4. For *hernia* of infants: *Aur. cham. n-vom. sulph. veratr.* —for *umbilical hernia*: *Nux-v.* or *sulph.*—for *inguinal hernia*: *Aur. cham. n-vom. sulph. veratr.*—These remedies should be given one at a time, and at long intervals.

§ 5. *Diarrhœa* of infants, from *acidity* in the primæ viæ, with colic and screams, tenesmus, and sour smell of the whole body, in spite of the greatest cleanliness, yields to *Rhubarb.*

If insufficient, if the colic be very violent, *Cham.* deserves a preference if the face should be very red, and *Bell.* if the face be pale.

If the pains be slight, with great debility and distention of the abdomen, and *Bell. cham. rhub.* have proved inefficient, give *Sulphur.*

Diarrhœa *from heat*, yields to a few doses of *Ipec.* or *Nux-vom.*

If the diarrhœa should set in whenever the weather grows hot, give *Bryon.*, to be followed, if insufficient, by *Carbo veg.*

If the diarrhœa should set in every time the weather cools off, give: *Dulcam.* or *Antim.*, if the tongue should be coated white.

(If the remedies which are here mentioned for diarrhœa, should prove insufficient, give *Aconite.*)

Arsen. is frequently useful, especially when the child becomes thin, feeble and pale.

Beside the above-mentioned remedies, the following have been mentioned: *Ferr. hep. jalap. magn. merc. n-vom. sulph-ac.*

§ 6. *Fevers* generally require: *Acon. cham. coff.*, or: *Bell. borax. ign. merc. n-vom.*

Aconitum: Great heat with thirst, especially when sleeplessness is present, or the sleep is restless, and the patients frequently start up from sleep, with anguish, cries, despondency; they cannot be quieted.

Chamomilla: Burning heat and redness of the skin, with frequent desire to drink; great restlessness, especially at night, with tossing about, anxiety, moaning; red face and cheeks, especially only *one* cheek; hot sweat about the head, even in the hairs; short, anxious breathing, mucous rattling; short, dry and panting cough, or convulsive twitching of the limbs.

Coffea: The fever is not very violent, but the nerves are irritated, with sleeplessness, restless sleep, and frequent, sudden starting and waking from sleep; fitful mood, alternately merry and whining.

§ 7. For the *spontaneous limping* of children, give first *Merc.*, then *Bell.*, or alternately.

If these remedies should be insufficient, give *Rhus tox.*, and then, according to the symptoms, *Calc.* or *Colocynth*, or one of the remedies mentioned under Coxagra and Coxarthrocace.

§ 8. For the rash of infants, a few doses of *Acon.* are generally sufficient; if *Acon.* should not suffice, give *Cham.*, and then *Sulphur*, if necessary.

§ 9. For the *gastric difficulties* of infants give: 1) *Bell. cham. ipec. merc. n-vom. puls.*; or, 2) *Bar-c. calc. hyos. lyc. magn. rhab. sulph.*

For *acidity* of the stomach, with sour vomiting or sour diarrhœa, the best remedies are: 1) *Bell. cham. rhab.*; or, 2) *Calc. magn. n-vom. puls.*

If the gastric symptoms denote a derangement of the stomach, *Ipec.* is the best remedy for the vomiting, especially when attended with diarrhœa; or *Puls.*, if *Ipec.* should be insufficient. For diarrhœa without vomiting, or mixed with undigested food, or if the child should have been weakened by cathartics, *China* is the best remedy. For vomiting with constipation, give *Nux-v.*

For chronic dyspepsia of children, or for weakness of the stomach with great tendency to be disturbed by the least indiscretion, we use: *Bar-c. calc. ipec. merc. n-vom. puls. sulph.*

§ 10. *Jaundice* of new-born infants generally yields to *Merc.*, or, if this be insufficient, to *China.*

§ 11. *Retention of urine* yields to *Camph.*, or to a few doses of *Acon.* or *Puls.*

§ 12. For *colic* the best remedies are: 1) *Borax. cham. cin. ipec. jalap. n-mosch. rhab. senn.*, or 2) *Acon. bell. calc. caust. cic. coff. sil. staph.* &c.— See *Colic.*

§ 13. *Convulsions* of children and infants require: 1) *Bell. cham. cin. coff. ign. ipec. merc. op.*, or 2) *Acon. caust. cupr. lach. n-vom. stann. sulph.*

Particular indications:

BELLADONNA: The paroxysms terminate in or alternate with coma; or the children suddenly wake as if in affright, with wild anxious and staring looks, as if they were afraid; dilated pupils; tetanic rigidity and icy coldness of the whole body, with burning heat of the hands and forehead; or, the children wet their beds frequently.

CHAMOMILLA: For convulsions of the extremities, with involuntary motions of the head, afterwards coma, with half-opened eyes and loss of consciousness; redness of one cheek and paleness of the other; sighing and frequent desire to drink (If *Cham.* should prove insufficient, give *Belladonna.*)

CINA: The children are affected with worms, or wet their beds frequently, with spasms in the chest, convulsions of the extremities, hard and distended abdomen, frequent itching of the nose, dry cough resembling whooping-cough, &c.

COFFEA: Suitable to feeble children, if they are frequently attacked with convulsions without any secondary symptoms.

IGNATIA: For convulsions from teething, or worms, or when the paroxysms recur every day at the same hour, with twitching of single muscles or extremities; the spasms are frequently succeeded or accompanied by heat or sweat; light sleep, with sudden starting; piercing cries and trembling of the whole body. (After *Ignat.*, *chamom.* is frequently suitable.)

IPECACUANHA: Between the paroxysms the children suffer with shortness of breath, nausea, vomiting and diarrhœa, with frequent spasmodic stretching of the limbs.

MERCURIUS: Hardness and distention of the abdomen, frequent eructations and ptyalism, or heat, sweat and great debility after the spasms.

OPIUM: The paroxysms are caused by fright, or are attended with trembling of the whole body, stretching of the extremities, piercing cries, coma and loss of consciousness, distention of the abdomen, constipation and retention of urine.

§ 14. *Muscular debility* of infants, in consequence of which they have great difficulty in learning to walk, yields to: 1) ***Bell. calc. caust. sil. sulph.***, or 2) ***Pinus-silvestris.***

§ 15. The best remedies for *acidity* or diarrhœa are: 1) ***Cham. rhab.***, or 2) *Bell. calc. sulph.*

§ 16. For *asphyxia* or apparent death of new-born infants, the best remedy, together with the necessary external manipulations, is one grain of *Tartar emetic* in 8 ounces of water, either as an injection, or in drop-doses, a few drops every 15 minutes.

If no change should take place in half an hour, give ***Opium***, if the face of the infant should be *blue*, or *China* if *pale.*

If the infant should show signs of life, give *Aconite* in case the face was blue or red, and *China* if pale.

§ 17. *Sleeplessness* of infants yields to *Coffea*, provided the nurse does not drink coffee; in this case give *Opium*, also when ***Coffea*** proves ineffectual, or the infant's face is red.

Sleeplessness with colic or screams yields to *Cham.*, or ***Jalap.***, or ***Rhub.***

For sleeplessness with restlessness and feverish heat, give ***Aconite.***

For sleeplessness after *weaning*, with constant cries for hours and even days, the best remedy is *Belladonna.*

§ 18. For *dry coryza* or *stoppage of the nose*, which prevents infants from breathing while nursing, the best remedy is *Nux v.*, or *Sambucus;* or to *Chamom.*, if the stoppage be attended with discharge of water from the nose; or to *Carb-veg.*, if the distress be worse in the evening; or to ***Dulc.***, if worse in the open air.

§ 19. For the *cries of new-born infants*, when *without any perceptible cause*, give *Bell.* or *Cham.*—If the child cries on account of headache or earache, give first *Cham.*, and then *Bell.*, provided *Cham.* is insufficient.

For colic, with the legs drawn up, and red face, *Cham.* is the best remedy; *Bell.* if the face be pale. If attended with sour diarrhœic stools and tenesmus, give *Rhubarb.* If these remedies should be without effect, try *Borax*, *Jalap*, *Ipec.* or *Senna.*

If *Chamomilla* should have been abused by the nurse or infant, give *Borax*, *Ignat.* or ***Puls.***

§ 20. For *aphthæ* or *thrush*, give *Mercury* and *Sulphur* in alternation. *Borax* and *Sulphuric acid* are likewise useful, the former particularly, if the urine smells like cat's urine, and is very acrid.

§ 21. For *stuttering*, the best remedies are: *Bell. euphras.*

merc. and *sulph.*, suitable mechanical exercises being instituted at the same time.

§ 22. For *constipation* of new-born infants, the remedies are: *Bry. nux-vom. opium.* If these remedies should be insufficient, give: *Alum. lyc. sulph. veratr.*

§ 23. For *soreness*, the best remedy is *Chamom.*, provided the nurse does not use chamomile-tea. In this case give *Borax, ign.* or *puls.*

If *Cham.* should prove insufficient, give *Borax*, or *Carb. veg.*, or *Mercury* if the skin of the infant be yellowish, and the parts be raw, or if the soreness extend behind the ears.

If all these remedies should prove ineffectual, *Sulph.* will be found useful, or *Silic.*, if *Sulph.* be not sufficient.

Caust. graph. lyc. sep. have likewise been recommended.

§ 24. The best remedies for the ailments incidental to *dentition*, are: 1) *Acon. bell. borax. calc. cham. coff. ign. merc. sulph.* or 2) *Ars. cin. ferr. magn. magn-m. n-vom. stann.*

For *sleeplessness*, give: *Coff.*, or *Acon. borax. cham.*

For *fever:* 1) *Acon. cham. coff. n-vom.*, or: 2) *Bell. borax. sil.*

For *restlessness* and *nervousness: Coff.*, or: *Acon. bell. borax. cham.*

For *constipation: Bry. magn-m. n-vom.*

For *diarrhœa:* 1) *Merc. sulph.*, or: 2) *Ars. calc. cham. coff. ferr. ipec. magn.*

For dry and spasmodic *cough: Cham. cin. n-vom.*

For *spasms* and *convulsions:* 1) *Bell. cham. cin. ign.*, or: 2) *Calc. stann. sulph.*

For *slow dentition*, give: *Sulph.* and *Calc.*, to aid the work of nature.

§ 25. For further particulars, we refer the reader to the special articles treating of these various diseases, and to ATROPHY, ANGINA, ECLAMPSIA, RHACHITIS, CRUSTA LACTEA, SCROFULA, WORM-AFFECTIONS, &c.

CHIRAGRA.—The best remedies are: 1) *Agn. ant. bry. caust. cocc. graph. led. lyc. n-vom. rhod. sulph.*, or: 2) *Aur. calc. carb-veg. dig. lach. phosph. ruta. sabin. sep. sil. zinc.*

For further particulars, see: ARTHRITIS.

CHLOROSIS.—The best remedies are: 1) *Bell. calc. coccul. ferr. lyc. nitr-ac. plat. puls. sulph.* 2) *Chin. con. dig. graph. hell. ign. kal. natr-m. n-vom. phos. plumb. sep. spig. staph. val.*, or: 3) *Ars. carb-v. caust. graph. phos-ac. sabin. sulph-ac. zinc.*

For further particulars, see: MENSTRUAL DIFFICULTIES and AMENIA.

CHOLERA and CHOLERINE.—The best remedies are: 1) *Ars. camph. cupr. ipec. sec. veratr.* 2) *Bell. canth. carb-v. cham. chin. cic. coloc. dulc. hyos. lach. laur. n-vom. op. phos-ac. sulph.*

§ 2. For *sporadic* cholera, during the summer heat, give: *Ars. cham. chin. coloc. dulc. ipec. merc. veratr.*

For *Asiatic* or *epidemic* cholera: 1) *Ars. camph. carb-v. cupr. ipec. sec. veratr.*, also: 2) *Bell. canth. cham. cic. laur. merc. n-vom. phos. phos-ac.*

For *cholerine*, or for diarrhœa during the cholera: *Phos. phos-ac.* and *sec.*

A species of cholera arising from *chagrin* or *anger*, requires: 1) *Cham.*, or 2) *Colocyn.*, if anger and chagrin were combined.

§ 3. For the *consequences* of cholera, the following remedies have been recommended: *Acon. bell. bry. canth. carb-v. chin. hyos. op. phos-ac. rhus. stram. sulph.*

If the *cerebral system* be involved: *Bell. lach. op.*, or: *Acon. hyos. stram.*

For *inflammatory* affections: *Acon.*

For *gastric* and *abdominal* affections: *Bell. bry. carb-v. merc. rhus. sulph.*

For *pulmonary* affections: *Acon. bell. bry. carb-v. rhus. sulph.*

For *general debility*: *China.*

For *debility of the intestinal canal*: *Phosph.* and *Sulph.*

For *typhoid* affections: *Bell. bry. carb-v. cocc. hyos. op phos-ac. rhus. stram.*

§ 4. Particular indications:

ARSENICUM: Violent pains in the stomach, with great anguish and burning in the epigastrium as if from hot coal; burning, unquenchable thirst, obliging one to drink frequently, but little at a time; constant nausea, *diarrhœa* and *violent vomiting* of watery, bilious or slimy, greenish, brownish or blackish substances; vomiting and diarrhœa come on again after drinking ever so little; *lips and tongue are dry, blackish and cracked;* the patient is unable to sleep, tosses about, moans, is apprehensive of approaching death; sudden prostration; hippocratic countenance, hollow cheeks, pointed nose, hollow and dim eyes; small, feeble, intermittent or tremulous pulse; tonic spasms in the fingers and toes; *icy coldness of the skin, and clammy sweat.*

CAMPHOR: At the commencement of the disease, when there is neither thirst, nor vomiting or diarrhœa; sudden prostration with wandering looks and hollow eyes; *bluish appearance and icy coldness of the face and hands, also coldness of the body;* disconsolate anguish, with fear of suffocation; the half stupified and insensible patient utters hoarse cries and moans, without complaining of any thing in particular; but, if asked, he complains of *burning pains in the stomach* and *throat*, with cramps in the calves and other muscles, and utters loud cries when one touches the pit of the stomach.—*Camphor* is seldom suitable when vomiting, diarrhœa and thirst have already set in, but it should never be given, except when the following symptoms are present: *Icy coldness* and *blueness of the limbs, face* and even *tongue*, with tonic and painful cramps in the extremities and calves, *dulness of sense, moaning, tetanus*, and *trismus*.

CUPRUM: Vomiting and diarrhœa, *convulsions of the extremities*, especially of the fingers and toes, sometimes with rolling of the eyeballs, great restlessness and coldness of the prominent parts of the face; aching pains in the pit of the stomach, getting worse by contact; *spasmodic colicky pains without vomiting*, or vomiting preceded by spasmodic constriction of the chest, arresting the breathing, or vomiting attended with violent pressure in the epigastrium; audible rolling, along the œsophagus, of the liquid which one swallows.

IPECACUANHA: Qualmishness in the stomach, chills proceeding from the stomach or bowels, or cold face and extremities; *when the vomiting is a prominent symptom*, or alternates with watery diarrhœa accompanied by colic; or yellowish diarrhœa without vomiting, but with cramps in the calves, fingers and toes; *Ipec.* is generally indicated by vomiting or diarrhœa at the commencement of the disease, or when the patient is otherwise improving.

For a violent attack, *Ipec.* is of no use. (Nor for a moderate attack: *Aconite* is the sole and real specific for every variety or form of cholera. HEMPEL.)

SECALE CORNUTUM: The vomiting is over, but the stools are not yet bilious, or there are still pains in the extremities; or for diarrhœic, brownish or flocculent and colourless stools with sudden prostration, icy coldness of the extremities, clean tongue or thinly coated with white mucus; the evacuations are preceded by vertigo, anguish, cramps in the calves, rumbling in the abdomen, and nausea.

VERATRUM: Principal remedy, when there are violent evacuations upwards and downwards; icy coldness of the body, great debility and cramps in the calves, vomiting, copious, watery, inodorous stools mixed with white flocks, pale face without any colour, blue margins around the eyes, deathly anguish in the features, cold tongue and breath; great oppressive anguish in the chest, giving the patient a desire to escape from his bed; violent colic, especially around the umbilicus, as if the abdomen would be torn open, the abdomen is sensitive to contact, with drawing and cramps in the fingers, wrinkled skin in the palms of the hand, retention of urine

§ 5. Belladonna: For typhoid symptoms, coma with half-opened or distorted eyes, grating of the teeth and distortion of the mouth, or great restlessness, desire to escape, stitches in the side or burning pains in the abdomen; burning heat and redness of the face, and desire for cold drinks; accelerated pulse which is more or less full, but not hard.

Cantharis: The urinary passages are principally involved, with violent burning in the hypogastrium, rumbling in the abdomen, bloody stools with tenesmus, heat in the abdomen, great restlessness, cerebral symptoms.

Carbo veg.: Incipient paralysis, with *complete collapse* of pulse, or with congestion of blood to the chest and head after cessation of the spasms, diarrhœa and vomiting, with oppression of the chest and coma; the cheeks are red and covered with clammy sweat.

Chamomilla: At the commencement of the disease, or in the precursory stage, especially when the following symptoms occur: The tongue is coated with yellow mucus, colic in the umbilical region, pressure from the region of the stomach to the heart, great anguish, cramp in the calves, watery diarrhœa and sour vomiting.

China: *Lienteria, vomiting of the ingesta*, painful oppression in the abdomen, after eating ever so little, with oppression of the chest and eructations affording relief; loss of appetite with sensation of repletion; hippocratic countenance; prostration unto fainting.

Cicuta: Little diarrhœa, but the vomiting alternates with violent, tonic spasms of the muscles of the chest and distortion of the eyes; or coma, with the eyes half open; heavy breathing, congestion of blood to the head and chest, vomiting or diarrhœa.

Colocynthis: Vomiting, first of the ingesta, afterwards of green substances, with violent colic, retention of urine, cramps in the calves, frequent, diarrhœic stools, which, with every new evacuation, become more colourless and watery.

Dulcamara: A species of cholera from taking cold drinks, with vomiting of the liquid, and of bilious, green or slimy and yellowish substances, frequent greenish stools, painful abdomen, with burning and retraction of the region of the stomach, great debility, collapsed pulse, cold extremities, burning thirst, great dulness of sense.

Hyoscyamus: Typhoid symptoms, after the vomiting, diarrhœa and coldness had ceased, with dulness of sense, wandering looks, red and hot face; *Bell.* having proved useless.

Lachesis: For typhoid symptoms, if *Bell.*, *hyoscyam.* or *opium* rove inefficient.

Laurocerasus: Rheumatic pains in the extremities, hardness

of hearing, cloudiness of the brain, distortion of features, and sensation of constriction in the throat when swallowing.

Nux vomica: Scanty diarrhœic stools, but *frequent urging and little or no discharge;* cardialgia, great debility, anguish in the pit of the stomach, aching pain in the occiput, and internal rather than external chilliness.

Opium: For stupor and coma which yield neither to *Hyoscyam.* nor *Bellad.;* these symptoms sometimes occur when the real cholera-symptoms have already ceased.

Phosphorus: Diarrhœa attended by violent thirst, rumbling in the abdomen and debility; the diarrhœa occurs during or after the cholera.

Phosphoric acid: Diarrhœa with pale face, dulness of the head, viscid tongue so that the finger adheres to it, rumbling in the abdomen, and green-whitish, watery and slimy stools, with diminished secretion of urine.

CINCHONA, ill effects of.

§ 1. The best remedies for these ailments are: 1) *Arn. ars. bell. calc. ferr. ipec. lach. merc. puls. veratr.;* or 2) *Caps. carb-v. cin. natr. natr-m. sep. sulph.*

Arnica: For rheumatic pains, heaviness, languor and bruised pain in all the extremities, drawing in the bones, sensitiveness of all the organs of sense, aggravation of the pains by motion, talking and noise.

Arsenicum: Ulcers on the extremities, dropsy or œdema of the feet, short cough and dyspnœa.

Belladonna: Congestion of blood to the head, with heat in the face, pains in the head, face and teeth; or for jaundice, when *Merc.* is insufficient.

Calcarea: Headache, otalgia, toothache, pain in the limbs, especially when these symptoms were occasioned in consequence of the suppression of fever and ague by large doses of Quinine, and *Puls.* proved insufficient.

Ferrum; For œdema of the feet.

Ipecacuanha: 6 pills in water, a tablespoonful 3 times a day, generally removes most of the symptoms.

Lachesis: For fever and ague which had been suppressed by large doses of Quinine; *Puls.* is inefficient.

Mercurius: For jaundice or other affections of the liver.

Pulsatilla: Otalgia, toothache, headache, pain in the limbs, after suppression of fever and ague.

Veratrum: Coldness of the body or limbs, with cold sweat, constipation or diarrhœa.

§ 2. For the consequences of suppressed fever and ague, give:

1) When the fever is actually suppressed: ***Arn. ars. bell. calc. carb-v.*** *cin. ferr. ipec. lach. merc. puls. sulph.*

2) When the fever still continues: 1) ***Ipec.***, and then: 2) ***Ars. carb-v.*** *lach. puls.;* or, but less frequently: 3) *Arn. cin. veratr.;* or finally: 4) *Calc. bell. merc. sulph.*

For further details, see: INTERMITTENT FEVER, HEPATITIS, LIENITIS, and the other diseases arising from abuse of *China.*

COFFEE, ILL EFFECTS OF.—The best remedies are: 1) ***Cham.*** *cocc. ign.* and *n-vom.* 2) ***Bell.*** *canth. carb-veg. caust. hep. ipec. lyc. merc. puls. rhus. sulph.*

Particular indications:

CHAMOMILLA: Headache and toothache; extreme sensitiveness to pain, with crying; *pains in the stomach, abating a little after taking coffee;* violent colic, great oppression in the pit of the stomach, with hard pain.

COCCULUS: Debility and sweat after every exercise, trembling of the limbs, sudden starting up during sleep as if in affright; flushes of heat; toothache when eating; sensation of emptiness in the head; colic; great sadness and anguish; aggravation of the symptoms in the open air, during motion, when eating or drinking, during sleep, or by tobacco-smoke.

IGNATIA: Headache, as if from a nail in the brain, or as if the forehead were pressed asunder, or for beating in the head *which is relieved by stooping;* debility; sensation of emptiness in the pit of the stomach; spasmodic colic; painfulness or going to sleep of the limbs; fitful mood; at times gay, at others sad.

NUX VOMICA: Sleeplessness, palpitation of the heart, extreme nervousness, hemicrania, or sensation as if a nail were driven into the brain, with aggravation of the pains on stooping or when walking, also in the open air; toothache, colic aggravated by coffee; extreme sensitiveness to the open air; lively and choleric temper.

For other affections, we refer the reader to the diseases of the special organs.

The chronic ailments arising from the abuse of coffee, are frequently relieved by ***Merc.*** or *Sulph.*, provided *Cham.*, ***Nux vom.*** or ***Ign.*** are not sufficient.

COLCHICUM, ILL EFFECTS OF.—Give: *Cocc. nux-v.* ***puls.***

COLD, ILL EFFECTS OF A.

§ 1. Principal remedies:—1. ***Acon. cham. coff. dulc. merc. n-vom. puls. sulph.*** 2) ***Ars. bell. bry. carb-veg. hyos.*** *ipec.* ***phos. rhus. sil.*** *spig.* 3) *Calc. chin. coloc. con. graph. hep. lyc. mang. natr-m. nitr-ac. n-mosch. samb. sep. veratr.*

§ 2. For *acute pains* occasioned by a cold, give: ***Acon. ars.***

bell. cham. coff. merc. n-vom. puls. samb. spig.—If *less acute: Dulc. chin. ipec. n-mosch.*

Obstinate, chronic ailments require, besides the above remedies: *Calc. carb-veg. graph. hep. lyc. mang. natr-m. nitr-ac. phos. sep. sil. sulph.*

§ 3. For colds *from exposure to wet*, or getting wet to the skin, give: 1) *Calc. dulc. puls. sulph.* 2) *Ars. carb-veg. n-mosch. rhus. sassap.* 3) *Ars. bell. bry. caust. colch. hep. lyc. phosph. sep.*

For a cold occasioned by *bathing*: 1) *Ant. calc. carb-veg. sulph.* 2) *Ars. bell. caust. nitr-ac. rhus. sassap. sep. sulph.*

By washing and working *in cold water*: 1) *Calc. n-mosch. puls. sassap. sulph.* 2) *Amm. ant. bell. carb-veg. dulc. merc. nitr-ac. rhus. sep. spig.*

By *profuse sweats*: *Acon. calc. carb-veg. chin. dulc. merc. phos-ac. rhus. sep.*

By the *head getting wet*: *Acon. baryt. bell. led. puls. sep.*

By the *feet getting wet*: 1) *Cupr. nitr-ac. puls. sep. sil.* 2) *Cham. merc. natr. rhus.*

By *taking cold on the stomach* in consequence of eating ice, fruit, acids, &c.: *Ars. carb-veg. puls.*

§ 4. For *suppression of sweat* or some other secretion by a cold, give: 1) *Bry. ipec.* 2) *Acon. ars. carb-veg. cham. dulc. merc. puls. rhus. sulph.*

For *suppression of coryza* by a cold: *Acon. ars. calc. chin. lach. n-vom. puls. sulph.*

For *derangement of the menses* by a cold: *Acon. bell. dulc. calc. chin. puls. sep. sil. sulph.*

See: "*Suppression of secretions.*"

§ 5. For the disposition to take cold, I recommend: 1) *Bell. calc. carb-veg. coff. dulc. nitr-ac. n-vom. puls. rhus. sil.* 2) *Acon. baryt. borax. graph. hyos. ign. lyc. magn-m. merc. natr. natr-m. petr. phos. sep. spig. sulph.*, giving the specific remedy at long intervals.

This remark applies to *sensitiveness to wind, weather, draught of air, warmth and cold.* If one is affected by every little *cold air*, take: *Bry. calc. carb-veg. cham. merc. rhus. veratr.*

If *cold weather is generally* hurtful, take: *Ars. baryt. bell. calc. camph. caps. caust. cocc. dulc. hell. n-mosch. n-vom. rhod. rhus. sabad.*

For great sensitiveness *to wind*: *Carb-veg. cham. lach. lyc. sulph.*

To *draughts* of air: *Acon. anac. bell. calc. cham. chin. sil. sulph.*

To *cool evening*-air: *Amm. carb-veg. merc. nitr-ac. sulph.*

To *rough weather*: *Bry. rhod. sil.*

To *damp* and *cold* weather: *Amm. borax. calc. carb-veg. dulc. lach. rhod. rhus. veratr.*

To *changes* of weather: *Calc. carb-veg. dulc. lach. merc. rhus. sil. sulph. veratr.*

If the weather change from cold to warm: *Carb-veg. lach. sulph.* are preferable; if from warm to cold: *Dulc. merc. rhus* or *veratr.*

Comp. §§ 5 and 6 of the article: "CONDITIONS."

§ 6, *Colds in spring*, generally require: *Carb-veg. lach. rhus. veratr.*

In *summer: Bell. bry. carb-veg. dulc.*, and if there should be thunder and lightning: *Bry. rhod. sep. sil.*

Cold in *autumn:* 1) *Dulc. merc. rhus. veratr.* 2) *Calc. bry. chin.*

In *winter:* 1) *Acon. bell. bry. dulc. rhod. rhus.* 2) *Cham. ipec. n-vom. sulph. veratr.*—in *dry* and cold weather: *Acon. bell. bry. cham. ipec. n-vom. sulph.*; in wet and cold weather: *Dulc. rhod. rhus. veratr.*

Compare: §§ 4 and 7 in the article: "CONDITIONS."

§ 7. Particular indications:

ACONITUM: Toothache, prosopalgia or other kinds of neuralgia with headache, congestion of blood to the head, buzzing in the ears, stiffness of the extremities, fever-heat, tossing about, anxiety, &c.

ANTIMONIUM: Headache, or gastric symptoms, loss of appetite, nausea, &c.

ARNICA: Pains in the limbs, rheumatic or gastric symptoms.

ARSENICUM: Asthmatic or gastric affections, with cardialgia.

BELLADONNA: Headache, dimness of sight, sore throat, gastric symptoms, coryza, feverish heat, &c.

BRYONIA: Spasmodic cough with nausea; pains in the limbs, diarrhœa, &c.

CALCAREA: Obstinate pains in the limbs, aggravated by every change in the weather, or working in the water.

CARB-VEG.: Hollow, obstinate cough, with vomiting; asthmatic affections; pains in the chest, &c.

CHAMOMILLA: Headache, toothache, otalgia or other kinds of painful neuralgia, restlessness, disposition to get angry, feverish heat, moist cough, painful colic and diarrhœa, &c. (especially suitable to children.)

COCCULUS: Gastric symptoms.

COFFEA: Headache or other nervous pains, with whining mood, toothache, sore throat, gastric symptoms, moist cough, painless diarrhœa, pains in the limbs, or fever.

HEPAR: Ophthalmia or toothache, or obstinate pains in the limbs.

IPECACUANHA: Gastric symptoms, nausea, spasmodic cough with vomiting, asthmatic affections, &c.

MERCURIUS: Pains in the limbs, sore throat, sore eyes, toothache, otalgia, painful diarrhœa, or even dysenteric stools.

NUX VOMICA: Fever, dry coryza, stoppage of the nose, dry cough, *constipation*, or dysenteric stools, or slimy, painful diarrhœa with tenesmus and scanty evacuations.

PHOSPHORI ACIDUM: Rheumatic pains, or cough, excited by the least cold weather.

PULSATILLA: Fluent coryza, moist cough, otalgia, fever, diarrhœa, &c., especially suitable to pregnant females.

RHUS-TOX.: Toothache or pains in the limbs.

SILICEA: Obstinate pains in the limbs, worse when the weather changes.

SULPHUR: Obstinate pains in the limbs; colic; slimy diarrhœa; profuse coryza; sore eyes; dimness of sight, otalgia, toothache, &c.

§ 8. Comp.: HEADACHE, OTALGIA, TOOTHACHE, RHEUMATISM, CONDITIONS, &c.

COLIC, ENTERALGIA, ABDOMINAL SPASMS.— Principal remedies: 1) *Bell. coloc. n-vom. puls.* 2) *Acon. ars. carb-v. cham. chin. cocc. coff. hyos. ign. lyc. merc. phos. sec. sulph.* 3) *Agn. alum. ant. arn. calc. caust. colch. cupr. ferr. ipec. kal. lach. magn-m. natr. natr-m. nitr-ac. n-mosch. op. plat. rhab. rut. sen. stann. veratr. zinc.*

§ 2. For spasmodic intussusception of the intestines (miserere, iliac passion): *Bry. n-vom. op. plumb. thuj.*

For *flatulent colic:* 1) *Bell. carb-v. cham. chin. cocc. n-vom. puls. sulph.* or 2) *Agn. colch. coloc. ferr. graph. lyc. natr. natr-m. nitr-ac. n-mosch. phos. veratr. zinc. magn-arct.*

For *hœmorrhoidal* colic: *Carb-v. coloc. lach. n-vom. puls. sulph.*

For *inflammatory* colic: 1) *Acon. bell. hyos. merc.* or 2) *Ars. bry. cham. lach. n-vom puls. sulph.* — Compare: "ENTERITIS."

For *spasmodic* colic: 1) *Bell. cham. cocc. coloc. hyos. ipec. magn. magn-m. n-vom. puls.* or 2) *Ars. coloc. cupr. ferr. kal. lach. phos. stann. sulph.*, &c.

For *worm* colic: 1) *Merc.*, or 2) *Cin. sulph.*, or 3) *Cic. ferr.* (*fil?*) *n-mosch. rut. sabad.* Compare: "WORMS."

For colic gastrica, hepatica, renalis, uterina, &c., see: CARDIALGIA, HEPATITIS, NEPHRALGIA, DISEASES OF THE UTERUS, &c.

§ 3. For colic from *derangement of the stomach* (gastric colic), give: 1) *Bell. n-vom. puls.;* or: 2) *Ars. acon. bry. carb-v. chin. coff. hep. sulph. tart.* Compare: "GASTRIC DERANGEMENT."

For colic from *chagrin* or *anger: Cham. coloc.* or *sulph.*

From some kind of injury, *blow, strain,* &c.: 1) *Arn. bry. rhus.*, or: 2) *Carb-v. lach.*

From *poisoning by lead: Opium,* or *bell.*, or *alum,* or *plat.*

From a *cold: Cham. chin. coloc. merc. n-vom.*,—from bathing: *Nux-vom.*,—from exposure to cold and wet: *Puls.*

See: DYSPEPSIA, CARDIALGIA, GASTROSIS, DIARRHŒA, &c.

§ 4. For the colic of *infants:* 1) *Cham. n-mosch. rhab.;* or: 2) *Acon. bell. calc. caust. cic. coff. sil. staph.;* or: 3) *Bor. cin. ipec. jal. senn.*

Of *pregnant* or *lying-in* females: *Arn. bell. bry. cham. hyos. lach. n-vom. puls. sep. veratr.*

Of *hysteric* females: 1) *Cocc. ign. ipec. magn-m. mosch. n-vom. stann. val.:* or: 2) *Ars. bell. bry. stram.*

Menstrual colic: *Bell. cham. carb-v. cocc. coff. n-vom. puls. sec. sulph zinc.*

Colic of *hypochondriacs: Calc. chin. grat. natr. natr-m. stann,* &c.

§ 5. Particular indications:

BELLADONNA: Pinching and drawing as if every thing would fall out below, with aggravation during motion; *pod-shaped protrusion of the colon,* with abatement of the pains on bending double or making pressure; or *clutching pains* in the abdomen, or spasmodic constriction in the abdomen with burning and pressure in the small of the back, and over the pubis; especially when the following symptoms are present: Thin, purulent stools, or congestion of blood to the head, with redness of the face, swelling of the veins of the head, and such violent pains that the patient becomes delirious. (After *Bell., Merc.* is sometimes suitable.)

COLOCYNTHIS: In most cases, especially for: *Violent,* cutting *constrictive or spasmodic* pains, with pinching, and griping; or cutting as if with knives; great sensitiveness and bruised feeling of the abdomen; distention of, or sensation of emptiness in the abdomen; the pains are *attended* with *cramps in the calves,* or chills and tearing in the lower limbs; also for *great anguish,* tossing about on account of the pain; no stool, or else diarrhœa and vomiting of bile, which recommences after the patient takes ever so little food; *the pains are relieved by coffee.* (It is supposed by some, but doubted by many and by myself, *Hempel,* that coffee should be given alternately with colocynth, to control the aggravation produced by the colocynth; this aggravation is a natural development of the disease, not an aggravation; after Colocynth, give *Causticum* for the remaining symptoms.)

NUX VOMICA: Obstinate *constipation,* or hard stool; pressure in the abdomen as *from a stone,* with rumbling and sensation of internal heat; pinching, drawing, *contractive* or *compressive* pains; pressure in the pit of the stomach, with distention of the abdomen and sensitiveness to contact; *distention* and *fulness, especially in the hypochondria*, with unpleasant sensation produced by the pressure of the clothes; cold hands and feet during the paroxysms, or even stupefaction unto loss of consciousness; cutting and flatulence deep in the abdomen; *sharp* and *hard* pressure over the *bladder* and *rectum*, as if the flatulence would press out by force, obliging the patient to bend double; aggravation by walking; relief by rest, sitting or lying; violent pains in the small of the back and loins, and violent headache.

Pulsatilla: Stinging pains; beating in the pit of the stomach; restlessness, heaviness and fulness in the abdomen, with *unpleasant distention;* contusive pain when touching it; rumbling, heat in the abdomen, causing anxiety; pinching, cutting, and tearing, especially in the epigastrium, with aggravation by contact; general heat with swelling of the veins of the hands and forehead; the clothes press upon the hypochondria; *the pains are worse* by *sitting* or *lying*, or in the *evening*, with *chills*, increasing with the pains; relief by walking; bruised pain in the loins when rising; nausea; diarrhœa; *pale face* with blue margins around the eyes; aching and tensive pain in the head.

§ 6. Aconitum: Colic, involving the bladder, with violent *cramp-pains*, contraction of the hypogastrium in the region of the bladder; constant but ineffectual urging to urinate; great *sensitiveness of the abdomen;* pains in the loins as if bruised; great anguish, restlessness, tossing about.

Arsenicum: Great pain with anxiety in the abdomen; violent cutting, or spasmodic, drawing, tearing or gnawing pains, frequently attended with *intolerable burning*, or with feeling of coldness in the abdomen; the pains set in especially *at night*, or after *eating* and *drinking;* nausea, or watery and bilious vomiting; constipation or diarrhœa; thirst, chill and *great debility*.

Carbo-veg.: Fulness and distention of the abdomen as if it would split, with rumbling, incarcerated flatulence, pinching, difficult breathing, rising of air; congestion of blood to the head, with aching pain; *slow action* of the bowels; heat in the abdomen, especially about the head; the pains set in even after the slightest meal.

Chamomilla: *Tearing, drawing* pains, with great uneasiness, obliging one to run to and fro; sensation as if the bowels were drawn up in a ball, or as if the whole abdomen were empty; loathing, *bitter vomiting* or *bilious diarrhœa;* pain in the loins as if bruised; *incarcerated flatulence*, with anguish, tension, *pressure* and *fulness* in the pit of the stomach and hypochondria, or with pressure towards the abdominal ring; blue margins around the eyes; alternate redness and paleness of the face; the pains appear at night, or in the morning at sunrise, or *after a meal.* (***Puls.*** is frequently suitable after *Cham.*)

CHINA: *Tympanitic* distention of the abdomen, with fulness, pressure as from a hard body, or spasmodic, constrictive pains, with incarceration of flatulence and pressure towards the hypochondria; the pains appear *at night*, or affect persons debilitated by sweating, depletions or other causes.

COCCULUS: Spasmodic constriction of the hypogastrium, with nausea, difficult breathing, copious flatulence, fulness and distention of the stomach and epigastrium, feeling of emptiness in the abdomen; tearing and burning in the bowels, with *compressive sensation* in the stomach; nausea, *constipation;* great anguish, nervousness, tendency to start.

COFFEA: *Excessive pains*, anguish and pressure in the epigastrium, great nervousness, restlessness, cries, grating of the teeth, convulsions, coldnesss of the limbs, moaning, suffocative fits.

HYOSCYAMUS: Spasmodic and cutting pains, vomiting, cries, headache, hard and sensitive abdomen.

IGNATIA: Nightly colic; splenetic stitches; incarcerated flatulence, with difficulty of passing them; relief by passing the flatulence; fulness and distention of the hypochondria; especially suitable to delicate females.

LYCOPODIUM: *Excessive accumulation of flatulence*, especially *after a meal*, with pressure in the stomach and epigastrium; fulness and distention of the abdomen and pit of the stomach; constipation, or scanty, hard stools.

MERCURIUS: Violent contractive pains, with hardness and distention of the abdomen, especially around the umbilicus; or tensive, burning or stinging pains; hiccough, canine hunger, aversion to sweet things; nausea and ptyalism; frequent urging to stool; or slimy diarrhœa; aggravation of the pains at night, especially after midnight; chill, with warm and red cheeks; great sensitiveness of the abdomen to contact; great prostration.

PHOSPHORUS: Flatulent colic, deep in the abdomen, worse when lying.

SECALE: In men: Colic with pain in the small of the back; tearing in the thighs; eructations and vomiting; or, in women, at the time of the menses: burning pain in the right side of the abdomen; constipation and cholera-pains in the abdomen; or: tearing colic, pale face, cold extremities, small and feeble pulse, cold sweat.

SULPHUR: Hæmorrhoidal colic, after ineffectual use of *Carbo-veg.* and *N-vom.;* also for bilious colic, if *Cham.* or *Coloc.* should prove ineffectual; or for *flatulent* colic, if not relieved by *Cham.*,

Cocc., *Nux-v.*, or *Carb-veg.;* or for *worm-colic*, if not entirely removed by *Merc.* or *Cina.*

§ 7. Give more especially:

a) For great *distention : Acon. arn. ars. bell. bry. carb-v. cham. chin. coccul. dig. graph. hyos. jod. kal. lach. magn-m. merc. mur-ac. natr. natr-m. n-mosch. n-vom. phos. rhus. sep. sil.*—For pains from flatulence: *Bell. calc. carb-v. caust. chin. chinin. con. graph. hep. ign. ipec. jod. kal. lyc. natr-m. nitr. nitr-ac. n-mosch. n-vom. phos. phos-ac. puls. sil. sulph. veratr.*— For *hardness* of the abdomen: *Anac. calc. caps. carb-v. graph. magn-m. n-mosch. petr. phos. plumb. sil.* — For excessive *flatulence : Agar. canth. carb-a. carb-v. caust. chin. graph. hell. kal. lyc. mang. merc. nitr-ac. oleand. phos. plumb. veratr.*

b) For *boring pains : Cin. coloc. sen. sep. tar.* —For *burning* in the abdomen: *Acon. ars. bell. canth. carb-v. cham. caust. lach. n-vom. phos. phos-ac. sec. sep. sil. veratr.* — For *aching* pains: *Bell. carb-v. caust. calc. lach. natr-m. n-vom. phos. sep. sulph.*— For *sensitiveness* of the abdomen: *Acon. amb. canth. carb-v. cham. coloc. graph. hep. hyos. lach. lyc. ..-v. puls. sulph. ther. thuj. veratr.* — For *bearing-down* pains: *Bell. dulc. lach. plat.* — For pains with pressure from *within outwards : Asa. bell. berb. con. lyc. prun. sulph. sulph-ac. zinc.* — For feeling of *heat* in the abdomen: *Bell. canth. carb-v. mez. phos. sil.* — For feeling of *hollowness* or emptiness: *Arn. coccul. coloc. hep. lach. mur-ac. phos. puls. sep. stann.*—For feeling of *coldness* in the abdomen : *Æth. ars. calc. chin. hell. kal. kreos. magn-arct. men. oleand. petr. phos. plumb. rut. sec. sep.* — For beating, *pulsative* pains: *Cann. caps. cin. kal. lach. lyc. sep. sulph-ac. tart.*— For *pinching* pains: *Bell. calc. carb-v. chin. lyc. merc. nitr-ac. n-vom. sil. sulph.* — For spasmodic, *crampy*, griping, constrictive pains: *Anac. asa. bell. calc. carb-v. cham. chin. chinin. coccul. coloc. hep. ipec. jod. lyc. magn-m. natr-m. n-vom. plat. puls. thuj.* — For pains which oblige one to bend *double : Bov. calc. carb-v. coloc. lyc. sulph.* — For *gnawing* pains: *Canth. oleand. rut. sen.* —For *tearing* pains: *Ars. bry. cham. ign. kal. lach. lyc. magn-m. sec. sulph.* — For *cutting* pains: *Ars. calc. coloc. con. lyc. merc. natr-m. nitr-ac. n-vom. petr. phos. sec. sep. sil. spong. sulph. veratr.*—For *stitching* pains: *Bell. calc. caust. cham. chin. con. lach merc. natr. nitr-ac. n-vom. sep. sulph* — For *shocks* in the abdomen: *Anac. arn. cann. con. croc. nitr. oleand. plat.* — For pains as if *sore* and *raw : Arn. ars. asar. bell calc. canth. carb-v. colch. con. hep. hyos. ipec. kal. n-vom. phos stann.*

c) For evening-exacerbations: *Amb. amm. ant. arn. bell. bov. bry. calc. caust. chin. con. dulc. hep ign. kal. lach. laur. lyc. magn-c. magn-m. mang. merc. mez. nitr-ac. phos. plat. puls. ran. rhus. sen. sep. stront. sulph. sulph-ac. val. zinc.* — For pains which are excited by the *cool evening air: Carb-veg. merc.* — For pains which are aggravated or excited by *contact: Acon. arn. ars. bell carb-v. cupr. hyos. lyc. merc. nitr-ac. n-vom. plumb. puls. sulph. veratr.* — By *motion: Asar. bell. bry. cann. dig. graph. kreos. ipec. magn-aust. merc. natr-m. n-vom. ther.* — Aggravation after a meal: *Ars. carb-v. cham. chin. coloc. graph. jod. kal. lyc. magn-c. natr. natr-m. nitr-ac. n-vom. phos. puls. rhus. sep. sil. sulph. zinc.* — For *nightly* pains: *Acon. arn. ars. bar. bry. calc. cham. chin. graph. hep. magn-m. merc. petr phos. puls. rhus. sep. sil. sulph.* — Aggravation by *drinking: Ars. n-vom. sulph.* —Amelioration by external *warmth: Alum. amm. ars. canth. natr. sil.*

d) For pains with great *anguish* and restlessness: *Ars. carb-v. cham. lyc. merc. mosch. n-vom. phos. puls. rhus. sep. sec. sulph. sulph-ac. verat.*—With *chilliness: Ars. colch. ferr. kal. magn-c. merc. puls.* —With pains *in the chest: Bell. caps. carb-v. lach. lyc. n-vom. phos. plumb. sulph.* — With pains in the small of the back: *Alum. amm. bar. calc. caust. cham. kal. kreos. magn-m. natr-m. n-vom. phos. sulph.* — With *diarrhœa: Ars. cham. coloc. merc. phos. puls. rhab. sulph. tart.* — With *constipation: Alum. bell. bry. calc. carb-v. lyc. natr-m. n-vom. op. plumb. sep. sulph.* — With nausea or *vomiting: Ant. ars. con. ipec. natr-m. n-vom. tart. veratr.* — With *eructations: Bell. bry. hep. lach.*

§ 8. For pains affecting principally the *epigastrium:* 1) *Arn. caust. cham. chin. coccul. ign. lyc. n-vom. puls.* 2) *Acon. amm. ant. bell. calad. calc. canth. chel. cin. coloc. kal. magn-arct. merc. phos. plumb. rhus. staph. sulph.*

The *umbilical* region: 1) *Bell. bry. coloc. chin. ipec. kreos. phos-ac. plumb. rhus. sulph. veratr.* 2) *Acon. amm-m. anac. cin. con. ign. n-mosch n-vom. plat. rhab. sep. sulph-ac. verb.*

The *abdomen:* 1) *Amb. bell. bry. carb-v. caust. chin. lyc. sep.* 2) *Arn. calc. caps. coccul. coloc ign. kal. merc. n-vom. phos. sil. spig. thuj.*

The *sides:* 1) *Asa. asar. bry. carb-v. chin. ign. sulph zinc.* 2) *Bell. calc. caust. cocc. led. lyc. natr. natr-m. n-vom. rhus. staph. tar. thuj.*

The abdominal *ring* and *inguinal* region: 1) *Aur. coccul. ign. lyc. magn-arct. n-vom. sulph. sulph-ac.* 2) *Alum. Amm-m. calc. cham. clem. coloc. magn-aust. rhus. sil. spig. thuj. veratr.*

The *abdomen generally:* 1) *Acon. ars. bell. carb-v. cham. chin. coccul coloc. coff. hyos. ign. lyc. merc n-vom. phos. puls. sec. sulph.* 2) *Agn alum. ant. arn. calc. caust. colch. cupr. ferr. ipec. kal. lach. magn-m. natr. natr-m. nitr-ac. n-mosch. op. plat. rhab. rut. sen. stann. veratr. zinc.*

COMPLEXION, MORBID ALTERATION OF THE COLOUR AND APPEARANCE OF THE FACE.—Though generally a mere symptom, yet the changes in the complexion frequently point to the proper remedy.

§ 1. a) For *pale* face, give: 1) ***Ars. bry. calc. carb-veg. chin. ferr. ipec. lach. phosph. puls. sep. spig. stann. tart. veratr.*** 2) *Alum. arn. camph. cin. hell. nitr-ac. n-mosch. phos-ac. rhus. samb sec.*

b) ***Red*** face: 1) ***Acon. ars. bell. cham. chin. coccul. hep. hyos. ign. jod. merc. n-mosch. op. rhus. stram. sulph.*** 2) *Chin. dulc. hyos. lach. puls. squill. tart. veratr.*

c) Paleness of *one*, and redness of the *other* cheek: ***Acon.*** *coloc. ign. n-vom. veratr.*

d) ***Red*** *cheeks:* 1) ***Acon. caps. cham. chin. ferr. lyc. merc. n-vom. phosph. puls. stann. sulph.*** 2) *Bry. cann. dros. dulc. jod. kal. stram.*

e) *Circumscribed* redness of the cheeks: 1) ***Acon. chin. lyc. phosph.*** 2) *Bry. calc. dros. dulc. jod. kal. kreos. lach. led. puls. samb. sep. stann. stram. sulph.*

f) Frequent *alteration* of colour, at times red, at others pale: 1) *Acon. bell. cham. cin. croc. ign. n-vom. phosph. plat. puls. veratr.* 2) *Alum. aur. caps. carb-an. chin. ferr. graph. hyos. magn-c. spig. squill. sulph-ac.*

g) *Blue-red* face: 1) *Acon. ang. cham. cupr. lach. puls.* 2) *Ars. aur. bell. bry. camph. con. hep. hyos. ign. ipec. merc. samb. spong. veratr.*

h) ***Bluish*** colour: 1) ***Ars. bell. hyos. op. veratr.*** 2) *Acon. ang. aur. bry. camph. cin. con. cupr. hep. lach. lyc. samb. spong. staph. tart.*

i) *brown-red* colour: 1) ***Bry. hyos. jod. nitr-ac. op. sep. staph. stram. sulph.*** 2) *Carb-veg. kreos. puls. sec.*

k) *Sallow, livid* colour: 1) ***Ars. chin. ferr. ipec. lach. lyc. merc. n-vom.*** 2) *Bry. carb-veg. croc. kreos. natr-m. nitr-ac. phosph. samb. sep. sil.*

l) *Gray* colour: *Carb-veg. kreos. lach. laur.*

m) *Greenish* colour: *Ars. carb-veg. veratr.*

§ 2) As respects *partial* colours, give:

a) For *blue margins* round the eyes: 1) ***Ars. chin. ipec. lyc. n-vom. phos-ac. rhus. sec. staph. veratr.*** 2) *Anac. coccul. cupr. ferr. hep. ign. phosph. sep. sulph.*—*yellow* margins: *Nitr-ac. n-vom. spig.*—*greenish: Ars. veratr.*

b) For borders around the nose, *yellowish*-looking: *Nux-v. sepia.*—for *yellow* saddle across the cheeks and nose: *Sep.*—for yellow nose and mouth: *Nux-v. sep.*—for yellow temples: ***Caust.***

c) For *bluish* mouth: *Cin. cupr. ferr. stann.*

d) For *spots* in the face: 1) *Ars. ferr. rhus. sabad. sil.* 2) *Calc. carb-an. colch. lyc. natr. samb. sulph. veratr.*

e) *Blue* spots: 1) *Ferr.* 2) *Cin. cupr. stann.*

f) *Yellow* spots: 1) *Colch. ferr. natr. sep.* 2) *Caust. nitr-ac. n-vom.*

g) *Red* spots: *Calc. lyc. rhus. sabad. samb. sil. sulph.*

h) *Black* points: 1) *Dros. graph. natr. nitr-ac. selen. sulph.* 2) *Bell. bry. calc. dig. hep. natr-m. sabad. sabin.*

i) *Shining* face, as from fat: 1) *Magn-c. natr-m. plumb. selen.* 2) *Bry. chin. merc. rhus. stram.*

§ 3. As respects other symptoms of the face, give:

a) For *sunken* face: 1) *Ars. chin. lach. n-vom. sec. sep. stann. veratr.* 2) *Anac. camph. cic. coloc. cupr. dros. ferr. lyc. phosph. phos-ac. staph. sulph.*

b) For sunken eyes, *hollow* looks: 1) *Ars. camph. chin. ferr. lach. phosph. phos-ac. sec. staph. sulph. veratr.* 2) *Anac. cic. coloc. cupr. cycl. dros. iod. kal. nitr-ac. oleand. puls. spong. stann.*

c) For *pointed nose*, collapse of features: *Ars. chin. n-vom. phos-ac. rhus. staph. veratr.*

d) For *hippocratic* face: 1) *Ars. chin. phosph. phos-ac. sec. veratr.* 2) *Canth. carb-veg. cupr. n-vom.*

e) For *altered* features: 1) *Ars. camph. chin. op. phos-ac. rhus. spig. stram. veratr.* 2) *Bell. canth. caust, cham. colch. graph. hell. lyc. oleand. sec.*

f) For *bloated* face: 1) *Acon. ars. bry. cham. chin. hyos. n-vom. op. phosph. puls. samb. spong. stram. sulph.* 2) *Arn. ars. bell. ferr. hell. ipec. kal. lach. rhus. sep. sil. spig. stann. veratr.*

g) For *bloatedness* around the eyes: *Ars. ferr. phosph. puls. rhab.*—*under* the eyes: 1) *Ars. chin. n-vom. phosph. veratr.* 2) *Bry. calc. sep.*—in the region of the glabella: *Kal.*—around the nose: *Calc.*

h) For *sickly* looks: 1) *Chin. n-vom. phosph. sulph.* 2) *Cin. clem. lach. puls.*

i) For *wrinkles: Calc. lyc. sep. stram.*—for wrinkles of the *forehead:* 1) *Cham. hell. lyc. sep. stram. sulph.* 2) *Amm. bry. graph. n-vom. rhab. rhus.*

k) For *distorted* features: 1) *Ars. bell. caust. cham. graph. hyos. ign. ipec. lach. n-vom. op. sec. stram. veratr.* 2) *Ang. camph. cic. coccul. cupr. hyos. lyc. merc. plat. puls. rhus. sil. spig. spong. squill.*

§ 4. For further details, see: ERUPTIONS IN THE FACE, SWELLING OF THE FACE, DISEASES OF THE NOSE, CANCER OF THE NOSE, &c

CONCUSSION OF THE BRAIN.—The best remedies for cerebral affections produced by concussion, fall, blow on the head, &c., are: 1) *Arn.* and *cic.;* or, 2) *Dig. ign. laur. petr. merc.* (See INJURIES.)

CONDITIONS OF AGGRAVATION, or AMELIORATION OF THE SYMPTOMS.

§ 1. There are practitioners who select a remedy principally with reference to the external conditions of the symptoms, such as: the time of day when they appear, the side of the body, head, chest, &c., where they appear, &c. This is evidently going too far, though it cannot be denied, that these external conditions have a general value in many cases, and facilitate the selection of a remedy, provided the practitioner is otherwise thoroughly acquainted with the essential points of our Materia Medica. To select a remedy with reference to these external conditions exclusively, might prove of great detriment to the patient.

§ 2. As regards the *time of day*, give:

a) When the pains occur or exacerbate principally in the *evening:* 1) *Amb. amm. amm-m. arn. ars. bell. bry. calc. caps. caust. colch. dulc. euphr. hell. hyos. lach. laur. mang. merc. nitr. nitr-ac. phosph. puls. ran-sc. sep. sulph-ac. thuj. zinc.* 2) *Ant. asa. borax. carb-an. carb-veg. cham. chin. cocc. con. croc. graph. guaj. hep. ign. kal. laur. led. lyc. magn-c. magn-m. mez. natr. natr-m. n-vom. petr. phos-ac. plat. rhod. rhus. seneg. sil. stann. staph. stront. sulph. tart.*

b) When in the evening, in bed, after lying down, or generally *before midnight:* 1) *Ars. bry. calc. carb-veg. graph. hep. lyc. merc. phosph. puls. rhus. selen. sep.* 2) *Alum. amm-m. arn. aur. calad. carb-an. caust. chin. cocc. dulc. ign. ipec. kal. lach. led. magn-c. magn-m. natr. natr-m. n-vom. phos-ac. ran. sassap. sil. stront. sulph. sulph-ac. tart. thuj. veratr.*

c) When *at night:* 1) *Acon. arn. ars. bell. calc. caps. cham. chin. cin. colch. con. dros. dulc. ferr. graph. hep. hyos. ign. magn-c. magn-m. mang. merc. natr-m. nitr-ac. phosph. puls. rhus. sep. sil. staph. stront. sulph. thuj.* 2) *Ant. aur. baryt. bry. camph. cann. canth. carb-an. carb-veg. caust. coff. croc. cupr. hell. jod. kal. kreos. lach. led. lyc. magn-arct. mez. natr. n-vom. plumb. ran. rhab. sabad. samb. sec. selen. spig. sulph-ac. tart. thuj.*

d) When *during sleep:* 1) *Alum. ars aur. bell. bry. cham. hep. lach. merc. mosch. nitr. nitr-ac. puls. samb. sep. sil. stram. sulph.* 2) *Acon. anac. arn. baryt. borax. calc. caust. chin. cin. con. dulc. graph. hyos. ign. kal. led. lyc. magn-art. mur-ac. natr. natr-m. n-vom. op. phosph. phos-ac. rhab. rhus. ruta. stann. thuj.*

e) When after midnight, or *early on waking: Alum. amb. amm-m. ars. bell. bry. calc. carb-veg. caust. con. graph. hep. kal. lach. lyc. nitr-ac. n-vom. op. petr. phosph. sep. sulph.* 2) *Amm. ant. arn. aur. calc. cann. canth. caps. carb-an. chin. croc. dros. ferr. ign. mang. merc. natr. natr-m. nitr. phos-ac. plat. ran. rhod. rhus. sabad. samb. sil. squill. staph. sulph-ac. thuj. veratr.*

f) When early in the *morning:* 1) *Amb. amm. amm-m. ant. ars. bry. calc. carb-veg. cin. croc. dros. guaj. ign. natr. natr-m. nitr. nitr-ac. n-vom. phosph. rhus. squill. sulph. veratr.* 2) *Acon. alum. anac. ant. aur. carb-an. coff. con. hep. kal. lach. lyc. magn-arct. magn-aust. petr. phos-ac. plat. puls. sabin. sep. sil. staph. sulph. tart. thuj.*

g) When in the *forenoon,* or after breakfast: 1) *Carb-veg. natr. natr-m. n-mosch. sep.* 2) *Amm. anac. ars. bry. calc. caust. cham. con. dig. graph. guaj. hep. kal. magn. nitr. nitr-ac. n-vom. phosph. phos-ac. rhus. sabad. sassap. sil. staph. sulph-ac. val. veratr.*

h) When in the *afternoon, after dinner:* 1) *Alum. asa. bell. lyc. nitr. nitr-ac. n-vom. phosph. puls. sil. thuj. zinc.* 2) *Amm. amm-m. ant. borax. calc. canth. cic. coloc. con. graph. ign. mosch. mur-ac. natr. natr-m. ran. sassap. selen. val.*

i) When the symptoms are worse *after sleep: Anac. calc. carb-veg. cocc. con. graph. lach. stann. staph. sulph. thuj.*

§ 3. As regards the period of *digestion,* give: a) When the symptoms which exist before breakfast are mitigated by the breakfast: *Baryt. calc. graph. hep. ign. jod. n-vom. petr. plat. rhus. sep. staph. sulph.*

b) When setting in or increasing *after breakfast: Amm-m. borax. bry. calc. carb-veg. caust. cham. con. graph. kal. lach. natr. natr-m. nitr. nitr-ac. n-vom. phosph. rhus. sep. sulph. thuj. zinc.*

c) When the symptoms which exist before a meal, are less *during* or *after* a meal: 1) *Amb. calc. cann. ferr. ign. jod. lach. natr. phosph. sabad. stront. zinc.* 2) *Alum. amb. anac. baryt. caps. chin. graph. laur. puls. rhus. sep. spig. sulph.*

d) When the pains come on *while eating:* 1) *Amm. baryt. carb-an. carb-veg. cocc. graph. hep. kal. lyc. natr-m. nitr-ac. phosph. puls. sep.* 2) *Amb. arn. borax. calc. caust. cham. cic. con. magn-m. n-vom. phos-ac. sil. sulph. veratr.*

e) When the pains come on or get worse *after eating:* 1) *Amm. anac. ars. bry. calc. carb-veg. caust. chin. con. kal. lach. lyc. natr. natr-m. nitr-ac. n-vom. phosph. sep. sil. sulph. zinc.* 2) *Amm-m. ant. borax. carb-an. cham. cin. cocc. hep. ign. natr. petr. phos-ac. puls. ran. squill. stann. sulph-ac. thuj.*

f) When the pains are caused by *drinking:* 1) *Ars. bell. canth. carb-veg. chin. cocc. ferr. natr. natr-m. n-vom. rhus. sil. veratr.* 2) *Acon. ant. arn. baryt. bry. caust. cin. coloc. con. hell. hep.*

hyos. ign. lach. nitr-ac. phosph. phos-ac. puls. sep. sil. stram. sulph. sulph-ac.

g) When the pains are caused or aggravated by *smoking:* 1) *Amb calc. ign. ipec. Lach. n-vom. phos. puls. spong. staph.* 2) *Acon. alum. anac. ant. arn. bry. carb-an. chin. cic. clem. cocc. euphr. magn-arct. natr. natr-m. petr. ruta. selen. sulph. sulph-ac.*

h) Compare under "STOMACH, WEAKNESS OF," the various kinds of nourishment.

§ 4. As regards *seasons and periods of the moon*, give:

a) For pains which *get worse* or *come on again* in *spring:* 1) *Carb-veg. lach. rhus. veratr.* 2) *Amb. aur. bell. calc. lyc. natr-m. puls.*

b) In *summer:* 1) *Bell. bry. carb-veg. dulc.* 2) *Lyc. natr. puls. rhod. sil.*

c) In *autumn:* 1) *Calc. colch. dulc. lach. merc. petr. rhod. rhus. veratr.* 2) *Aur. bry. chin.*

d) In *winter:* 1) *Acon. bell. bry. carb-veg. cham. colch. dulc. ipec. n-vom. petr. rhus. sulph. veratr.* 2) *Amm. aur. camph. merc. natr-m. n-mosch. phos. puls. rhod. sep.*

e) At a *change of the moon:* 1) *Alum. calc. sabad. sil.* 2) *Amm. caust. cupr. dulc. graph. lyc. natr. sep. sulph. thuj.*

f) At *new-moon:* 1) *Alum. amm. calc. caust. cupr. lyc. sabad. sep. sil.*

g) At *full-moon:* 1) *Alum. calc. graph. natr. sabad. sil. spong. sulph.*

h) At *increase of moon:* 1) *Alum. dulc. thuj.*

§ 5. As regards the influence of *air* and *wind*, give—

a) For the pains caused by *sultry* weather: 1) *Bry. rhod. sep. sil.* 2) *Carb-veg. caust. lach. merc. natr. natr-m. nitr-ac. n-vom. petr. phos.*

b) By *stormy* and windy weather: 1) *Bry. rhod. sil.* 2) *Carb-veg. chin. lach. lyc. mur-ac. n-mosch. n-vom. phos. puls. rhod. sil veratr.*

c) By *winds:* 1) *Carb-veg. cham. lach. lyc. sulph.* 2) *Acon. ars. aur. bell. chin. con. graph. mur-ac. n-vom. phos. plat. puls. sep. thuj.*

d) By *North-winds:* *Acon. caust. hep. n-vom. sep. sil.*

e) By *East-wind:* 1) *Acon. bry. carb-veg. hep. sil.* 2) *Caust. n-vom.*

f) By *South-wind:* *Bry. carb-veg. rhod. sil.*

g) By *West-wind:* *Calc. carb-veg. dulc. lach. rhod. rhus veratr.*

h) By a *draught of air:* 1) *Acon. anac. bell. calc. cham. chin. sil. sulph.* 2) *Caps. caust. graph. hep ign. kal. natr. n-vom. rhus. selen. sep.*

i) By *cool evening-air:* 1) *Amm. carb-veg. merc. nitr-ac. sulph.* 2) *Borax. mez. n-mosch. plat.*

k) By *open air* and during a walk: 1) ***Amm. calc. carb-an. caust. cham. cocc. coff. con. kal. lyc. natr. n-mosch. n-vom. sil. stram. sulph.*** 2) *Alum. bry. camph. carb-veg. chin. ferr. guaj. hep. ipec. lach. led. magn-aust. merc. natr-m. nitr-ac. petr. puls. rhus. selen. spig. sulph-ac. thuj. val. veratr.*

l) By confinement *in a room:* 1) ***Alum. asa. croc. magn-arct. magn-c. magn-m. n-vom. phos. puls. rhus. sabin.*** 2) *Acon. amb. anac. ant. asar. baryt. graph. hell. hep. ipec. lyc. mez. mosch. natr-m. op. plat. sassap. seneg. sep. spong. stront. thuj.*

§ 6. As regards *cold* and *dampness*, give:

a) For the pains caused by *cold weather:* 1) ***Ars. baryt. bell. calc. camph. caps. caust. cocc. dulc. hell. n-mosch. n-vom. rhod. rhus. sabad.*** 2) *Acon. amm. anac. aur. borax. carb-an. carb-veg. colch. hep. hyos. ign. kal. lach. lyc. mang. merc. mez. mosch. nitr-ac. phosph. phos-ac. sep. sil. spig. stront. sulph. sulph-ac. thuj.*

b) By *cold air:* 1) ***Bry. calc. carb-veg. cham. merc. rhus. veratr.*** 2) *Ars. aur. camph. caps. caust. cocc. colch. dulc. hell. lyc. n-mosch. phos. rhod. sep. stront.* 3) *Acon. amm. bell. carb-an. hep. kal. lach. mang. mez. mosch. nitr-ac. n-vom. phos-ac. sabad. spig. stront. sulph.*

c) By a *limb* becoming *cold: Bell. cham. hell. hep. puls. rhus. sep. sil.*

d) By *uncovering* a part: 1) ***Ars. aur. cocc. con. hep. kal. merc. mosch. n-vom. rhus. samb. squill. sil. stront.*** 2) *Arn. bry. camph. caust. cic. clem. colch. con. dulc. graph. hyos. magn-c. magn-m. natr. natr-m. n-mosch. phos. sabad. sep. staph.*

e) By *cold* and *damp* weather: 1) ***Amm. calc. carb-veg. dulc. lach. merc. n-mosch. rhod. rhus. veratr.*** 2) *Borax. carb-an. chin. colch. lyc. mang. nitr-ac. puls. ruta. sassap. sep. spig. sulph.*

f) By exposure to *wet:* 1) ***Ars. calc. colch. dulc. n-mosch. puls. rhus. sassap. sep.*** 2) *Bell. bry. hep. ipec. lach. lyc. phosph. sulph.*

g) By *working in the water*, or by *washing: Amm. ant. bell. calc. carb-veg. clem. merc. nitr-ac. n-mosch. phos. puls. rhus. sassap. sep. sulph.*

h) By every *change* of the *weather:* 1) ***Calc. carb-v. dulc. lach. merc. rhus. sil. sulph. veratr.*** 2) *Graph. mang. nitr-ac. n-vom. phos. puls. rhod.*

§ 7. As regards *warmth*, give:

a) For pains caused by a *change of temperature: Ars. carb-veg. dulc. n-vom. phos. puls. ran. rhus. sulph. veratr.*

b) By *warmth* generally: *Amb. ars. aur. camph. cann. carb-veg. dros. jod. led. natr-m. nitr-ac. phos. puls. rhus. sec. seneg. thuj.*

c) By *warm air* or warm weather: ***Ant. bry. carb-veg. cocc. colch.*** *jod. lach. lyc.* ***puls. sulph.***

d) By the *warmth* of the *bed :* 1) ***Ars. bell. carb-veg. cham. dros.*** *graph. led. lyc. merc.* ***puls. rhus. sabin. sulph. veratr.*** 2) ***Amb.*** *calc. caust. cocc. graph. kal. led. lyc. phos. phos-ac. spong.* ***thuj.***

e) By a *warm stove* in the room : ***Acon.*** *agn. alum.* ***anac. ant.*** *arn. cin. colch. croc. jod.* ***natr-m.*** *op. phos. plat.* ***puls. sabin. spong. sulph.*** *thuj.*

f) By the *action* of the *sun :* ***Agar. ant.*** *bell.* ***bry. camph. euphorb.*** *graph. lach. natr. puls. selen. sulph.* ***val.***

g) By wrapping a part up in *warm clothes :* ***Acon. borax. bry. calc.*** *ign. lyc. magn-arct. phos. puls. spig. sulph.* ***thuj. veratr.***

§ 8. As regards *mechanical pressure,* give:

a) For the pains caused by *pressure* upon the *affected part :* 1) *Agar. anac. baryt. bry. cin. hep. kal. lach. lyc. magn-c.* ***merc. plat. sil.*** 2) ***Ant.*** *arg. bell. calc. cann.* ***caps. carb-veg.*** *guaj.* ***magn-m.*** *mez. mur-ac. natr. natr-m. nitr-ac. n-vom. oleand.* ***phos-ac. ruta.*** *sep. val. zinc.*

b) By the *pressure of the clothes :* 1) ***Bry.*** *calc.* ***carb-veg. caust.*** *con. lach. lyc. merc. n-vom. puls. spong.* 2) ***Caps. hep. nitr-ac.*** *sassap. sep. stann. sulph. val.*

c) By mere *contact :* 1) *Ang. bell. bry. caps.* ***cham. chin. cin. cocc.*** *colch. cupr. hep. hyos. lyc. n-vom. puls.* ***ran. sabin. sep. spig.*** *staph. sulph. tart.* 2) ***Acon.*** *anac. arn. camph. cann.* ***carb-veg. caust.*** *euphorb. graph. kreos. hell. lach.* ***magn-c. magn-m. mez. natr-m.*** *nitr-ac. phos-ac. rhus. sil. stram. sulph. veratr.*

d) By *leaning* with the part on something : *Arn. bell.* ***carb-veg.*** *chin. con. hep. kal. nitr-ac. puls. rhab. rhus.* ***sep. sil. sulph. staph.*** *thuj. veratr.*

e) By *grasping* with the hands: *Amm. calc.* ***carb-veg. caust.*** *cham. chin. led. lyc. natr. natr-m. nitr-ac. plat. puls. sil.*

§ 9. As regards the different *positions of the body, give :*

a) For the pains caused by *raising one's self :* 1) *Acon.* ***arn. ars.*** *bell. bry. cocc. ign. natr. natr-m. n-vom. puls. rhus.* ***sulph.*** 2) ***Cham.*** *chin. con. lyc. op. veratr.*

b) By raising one's-self *from a recumbent posture :* ***Acon. bell. bry.*** *carb-veg. caust. cham. cocc. con. dulc. graph.* ***guaj.*** *hep.* ***ign.*** *lach. natr-m. nitr-ac. n-vom. oleand. petr. sep. sil.* ***val.*** *veratr.*

c) By rising *from a seat : Bell. bry. caps. carb-veg. caust. chin.* ***con.*** *ferr. lyc. mang. natr-m. nitr-ac. phosph. puls.* ***rhus.*** *ruta.* ***sil. staph.*** *sulph. tart. thuj. veratr.*

d) By *stretching* the affected part : *Alum. bry. calc. carb-an. carb-veg. caust. chin. con. hep. kal. mang. ruta. sep. sulph. thuj.*

e) By *stooping :* 1) *Acon. alum. baryt. bell. bry. calc. graph. hep. n-vom. petr. puls. sep. spig. thuj. val.* 2) *Amm. amm-m. arn.* ***cic. cocc. ipec. kal.*** *lach. lyc. merc.natr. natr-m. phosph.* ***rhus.sulph.***

f) By *standing* · *Agar. amm-m. aur. bry. caps. caust. cocc. con. mang. petr. phos-ac. plat. puls. sabad. sep. sil. stann. sulph. val. veratr.*

g) By *sitting:* 1) *Agar. amb. ars. asa. baryt. caps. cin. ferr. guaj. lach. magn-c. magn-m. natr. plat. puls. ruta. sep.* 2) *Acon. alum. anac. caust. chin. dulc. euphorb. graph. lyc. merc. natr-m. op. phos-ac. rhod. rhus. sulph. sulph-ac. tart. val. veratr.*

h) By *rest:* 1) *Agar. asa. aur. caps. con. dros. dulc. euphorb. ferr. lach. phos-ac. puls. rhod. rhus. samb. sulph. val.* 2) *Amm. amm-m. chin. coloc. kal. kreos. lyc. magn-c. magn-m. mosch. ruta. sabad. sil. stann.*

i) By *lying:* 1) *Amb. asa. caps. dros. mosch. natr-m. puls. rhus. samb. sep. verbasc.* 2) *Alum. assa. aur. carb-veg. chin. con. dulc. euphorb. ferr. lyc. mur-ac. natr. rhod. ruta. sil. val.*

k) By a *recumbent* posture: *Acon. amm. amm-m. ars. caust. cham. chin. coloc. cupr. ign. magn-m. merc. n-vom. phos. puls. rhus. sep. sil.*

l) By *lying* on one *side:* *Acon. ars. bry. calc. carb-an. cin. ferr. graph. hep. ign. kal. lyc. natr. phos. puls. rhus. sabad. sil. stann. sulph.*

m) By lying on the *right* side: *Amm-m. aur. borax. caust. kal. magn-m. merc. n-vom. puls. spong. stann.*

n) By lying on the *left* side: *Acon. amm. colch. kal. lyc. natr. natr-m. phos. puls. sep. sil. sulph. thuj.*

o) Lying on the *painless* side is more painful than lying on the affected side: *Amb. arn. bry. calc. caust. cham. coloc. ign. kal. magn-aust. puls. rhus. sep. stann.*

p) By *changing* one's position: *Caps. carb-veg. caust. con. lach. nitr-ac. phos. puls. ran.*

§ 10. As regards *motion*, give:

a) For the pains caused by motion generally: 1) *Arn. bell. bry. colch. dig. graph. hell. ipec. led. magn-aust. merc. natr-m. n-vom. phos. ran. spig. squill. staph.*

b) By moving the *affected* part: *Arn. bell. bry. caps. cham. chin. ferr. cocc. guaj. led. merc. mez. n-vom. puls. rhus. spig. staph. thuj.*

c) By *raising* the affected part: *Arn. bell. bry. chin. con. ferr. graph. kal. led. natr. puls. rhus. sil.*

d) By *turning* or bending the part: *Amm-m. arn. bell. bry. calc. chin. cic. hep. ign. kal. lyc. natr. natr-m. n-vom. puls. rhus. sep. sil. spig. spong. stann.*

e) By *riding* in a carriage, swinging, or other passive motions: 1) *Ars. cocc. petr. sulph.* 2) *Colch. ferr. n-mosch. sep. sil.* 3) *Borax, carb-veg. colch. croc. graph. hep. ign. kal. natr. natr-m. phos. plat. selen. staph.*

f) By *walking:* *Arn. bell. bry. calc. carb-veg. chin. colch.*

con. dig. graph. hell. hep. led. merc. natr-m. nitr-ac. n-vom. sassap. sep. squill. staph. sulph. sulph-ac. veratr.

g) By *running or walking fast : Arn. ars. aur. bry. calc. caust. ign. kal. natr-m. n-vom. rhus. seneg. sep. sil. sulph.*

h) By *riding* on horseback : *Ars. natr-m. sep. sulph-ac.*

i) By *ascending* an eminence : *Acon. alum. ars. aur. baryt. bry. calc. cann. merc. n-vom. petr. rhus. sep. spig. spong. stann. sulph. thuj.*

§ 11. As regards *fatiguing, concussive* motions, give :

a) For pains caused or aggravated by *concussion* generally: *Arn. bry. cic. con. hep. ign. n-vom. phos-ac. rhus. ruta. sulph-ac.*

b) By *stepping : Ant. arn. bell. bry. calc. caust. chin. con. graph. magn-m. merc. natr. natr-m. nitr-ac. n-vom. phos. ran. rhus. sep. sil. spig. sulph.*

c) By making a *false step : Arn. bry. cic. con. puls. rhus. spig.*

d) By bodily *exertions : Acon. arn. ars. bry. calc. chin. cocc. coff. lyc. merc. natr-m. rhus. ruta. sil. sulph. veratr.*

e) By *manual labour : Amm-m. merc. natr-m. nitr-ac. sil. veratr.*

f) By *laughing : Ars. bell. borax. carb-veg. chin. dros. kal. lac. mang. phos. stann.*

g) By *coughing : Acon. arn. ars. bell. bry. calc. carb-veg. dros. hep. ipec. natr-m. n-vom. phos. puls. sep. sulph. veratr.*

h) By *sneezing : Acon. amm-m. arn. ars. bell. borax. bry. carb-veg. chin. cin. lyc. merc. mez. mosch. n-vom. puls. rhus. sabad. sep. sil. spig.*

i) By *blowing* one's nose: *Arn. bry. calc. caust. merc. natr-m. n-vom. sep. spig. sulph.*

k) By *singing : Amm. dros. hep. stann. sulph.*

l) By *talking :* 1) *Anac. arn. ars. bell. calc. carb-veg. cocc. ign. natr. natr-m. n-vom. phos. rhus. sil. stann. sulph.* 2) *Acon. alum. amb. amm. aur. cann. chin. dulc. ferr. kal. magn-c. magn-m. phos-ac. plat. puls. rhus. selen. sil. veratr.*

§ 12. As regards the influence of *emotions* and *sensual impressions*, give :

a) For pains caused or aggravated by *emotions :* 1) *Acon. bell. bry. calc. cham. coloc. ign. lach. lyc. natr-m. n-vom. phos. phos-ac. puls. staph.* 2) *Ars. aur. caust. cocc. coff. hyos. nitr-ac. n-mosch. op. plat. rhus. sep. stram. sulph. veratr.*

b) By *solitude : Ars. con. dros. mez. phosph. sil. stram. zinc.*

c) By *company :* 1) *Baryt. hyos. lyc. natr. puls. rhus.* 2) *Amb.*

carb-an. carb-veg. con. magn-c. natr. petr. phos. plumb. sep. stann. stram. sulph.

d) By *mental exertions :* 1) *Bell. calc. ign. lach. natr-m. n-vom. puls. sep. sulph.* 2) *Amb. anac. arn. ars. aur. borax. cocc. lyc. natr. oleand. sabad. selen. sil. staph.*

e) By *reading :* 1) *Agn. aur. calc. cin. cocc. con. graph. lyc. natr-m. n-vom. phos. puls. sil.* 2) *Asa. bell. borax. bry. carb-veg. caust. chin. coff. dulc. ign. kal. natr. oleand. rhod. ruta. sabad. sulph. sulph-ac. verb.*

f) By *writing :* 1) *Asa. aur. calc. cin. ign. kal. natr-m. sep. sil. zinc.* 2. *Borax. bry. cann. carb-veg. chin. cocc. graph. hep. lyc. coccul. natr. n-vom. oleand. ran. rhod. rhus. ruta. sabin. spong. sulph. sulph-ac.*

g) By *bright light :* 1) *Acon. bell. calc. colch. con. graph. hyos. lyc. merc. phos. stram.* 2) *Arn. ars. bry. cham. chin. coff. euphr. hell hep. ign. natr. n-vom. phos-ac. puls. rhus. sep. sil. spig. sulph.*

h) By *noise*, &c.: 1) *Acon. arn. bell. calc. cham. coff. con. lyc. natr. n-vom. plat. sep. spig.* 2) *Ang. aur. bry. carb-an. chin. colch. ign. mang. petr. phos. phos-ac. puls. sil. zinc.*

i) By *strong odours :* 1) *Acon. aur. bell. cham. chin. coff. colch. graph. lyc. n-vom. phos.* 2) *Baryt. con. hep. ign. kal. phos-ac. selen. sep. sil.*

§ 14. Compare AMBLYOPIA, OPHTHALMIA, ACOUSTIA, HEADACHE, TOOTHACHE, FEVER, SLEEP, MORBID, CAUSES, &C.

CONDITIONS OF IMPROVEMENT.—Many of these conditions are, of course, the contrary of the conditions of aggravation ; all we have to do, therefore, is to point out the principal conditions of improvement in one series.

For pains which are relieved by *leaning* against something, give : *Bell. carb-veg. kal. merc. n-vom. rhus. staph.*

By *pressure* upon the part: 1) *Amm. amm-m. con. magn-m. mang. mur-ac. natr. phos-ac. stann.* 2) *Alum. anac. ars. aur. bry. cocc. dulc. graph. kal. phos. puls. rhus. sulph-ac.*

By *thinking* of the pain : *Camph.*

By *resting* the part upon something : *Alum. amm. hep. n-vom. phos. puls. ruta. staph. sulph.*

By *contact :* 1) *Asa. calc. mang. men. mur-ac. plumb.* 2) *Anac. bry. caust natr-m. phos. sulph. thuj.*

By *motion* (see : aggravation by rest.)

By *riding* in a carriage : *Graph. nitr-ac.*

By staying in the *open air.* (See : Aggravation in the room.)

By *walking :* 1) *Amm. amm-m. ars. dulc. ferr. magn-c. magn-m. mosch. plat. puls. rhus. sep. val.* 2) *Agar. alum. amb. ars.*

aur. caps. con. lyc. merc. mur-ac. nitr. sabad. samb. stann. sulph. veratr.

By *coffee : Ars. cham. coloc.*

By *external coldness.* (See : Aggravation by warmth.)

By *change of position : Ars. cham. ign. phos-ac. puls. val.*

By *lying* : *Alum. arn. ars. bry. canth. carb-an. cupr. lyc. magn-c. merc. natr-m. nitr-ac. n-mosch. n-vom. sabad. spig. spong. staph. stram. veratr.*

By a *recumbent posture : Bry. calc. carb-an. ign. kal. lyc. n-vom puls stann. sulph.*

By lying *on one side : Arn. ars. n-vom phos. sep.*

By lying on the *affected* side : *Amb. arn. bry. calc. caust. cham. coloc. ign. kal. magn-aust. puls. rhus. sep. stann.*

By *rest.* (See : Aggravation by motion.)

By *sleep : Calad. chin. colch. n-vom. phosph. puls. selen. sep.*

By *sitting : Acon. anac. bry. carb-an. carb-veg. coff. colch. mang. merc. natr-m. n-vom. petr. phos. phos-ac. rhus. squill. staph thuj.*

By *sunshine : Con. plat. stram. stront.*

By *standing : Ars. bell. calc. cocc. colch. graph. ipec. merc. mur-ac. phos. plumb.*

By staying *in the room.* (See : Aggravation in the open air.)

CONFINEMENT.—The principal remedies for the diseases of lying-in females are:

For *excessive* or too long *after-pains :* 1) *Arn. cham. coff.;* or, 2) *Calc. n-vom. puls.*—For *milk-fever :* 1) *Acon. coff.;* or, 2) *Arn. bell. bry. rhus.*—For *want of milk :* 1) *Calc. caust. puls.;* or, 2) *Acon. bell. bry. cham.*—For *suppressed secretion* of milk : *Acon. bell. bry. calc. cham. coff. merc. puls. rhus. sulph.*—For *galactorrhœa* and the consequences of weaning : *Bell. bry. calc. puls.* (See : NURSING.)

For *sore nipples :* 1) *Arn. sulph.;* or, 2) *Calc. cham. ign. puls.**—For *inflammation* or suppuration of the *mammæ : Bell. bry. merc. phos. sil. sulph.* (Compare : BREASTS.)

For *suppression* of the *lochia : Coloc. hyos. n-vom. plat. sec. veratr. zinc.*—For too *profuse* and too *long lasting* lochia : *Bry. calc. croc. hep. plat. puls. rhus. sec.*

For *phlegmasia alba dolens : 1) Arn. bell. rhus.;* or, 2) *Acon. ars. calc. jod. lach. n-vom. puls. sil. sulph.*

For *puerperal fever :* 1) *Acon. bell. bry. cham. n-vom. rhus.;* or, 2) *Coff. coloc. hyos. ipec. merc. puls. veratr.* (See : PUERPERAL FEVER.)

For the *emotions* of lying-in females : *Bell. plat. puls. sulph. veratr. zinc.*

* And especially *Graphites.*—HEMPEL.

For *convulsions*, eclampsia, &c.: 1) *Cycl. hyos. ign. plat.;* or, 2) *Bell. stram.* (Compare: SPASMS.)

For *debility:* 1) *Calc. kal.;* or, 2) *Chin. sulph.;* or, 3) *N-vom. phos-ac. veratr.* (Compare: DEBILITY.)

For *sleeplessness: Coffea.*

For *colic:* 1) *Bry. cham.;* or, 2) *Arn. bell. hyos. lach. n-vom. puls. sep. veratr.* (See: COLIC.)

For *diarrhœa:* 1) *Ant. dulc. hyos. rhab.* (Compare: DIARRHŒA.)

For *constipation; Bry. n-vom. op.* or *plat.* (Compare: CONSTIPATION.)

For the *falling off* of the *hair: Calc. lyc. natr-m. sulph.* (Compare: FALLING OFF OF THE HAIR.)

CONGESTIONS, SANGUINEOUS.—Principal remedies: 1) *Acon. arn. bell. bry. chin. ferr. hyos. merc. n-vom. op. phos. puls. sil. sulph.* 2) *Alum. amm. asa. aur. calc. carb-v. coff. graph. hep. kal. lyc. merc. mosch. natr. natr-m. nitr-ac. plumb. rhus. sep. spong. stram. sulph-ac. thuj. veratr.*

For particulars, see: CONGESTIONS OF THE ABDOMEN, CHEST, HEAD, &c.

CONGESTIONS OF THE ABDOMEN.—The best remedies are: 1) *Nux-v.* and *Sulph.;* or, 2) *Ars. caps. carb-v.;* or, 3) *Bell. bry. cham. merc. puls. rhus. veratr.*

ARSENICUM: Frequent, scanty, slimy, or watery stools, with great debility.

NUX VOM.: Suitable to persons who lead a sedentary life and are engaged in intellectual pursuits, &c.; especially for *constipation*, hard stools, pains in the loins as if the hips and back were broken and powerless; hard and tight abdomen.

CAPSICUM: Suitable to phlegmatic, lazy, clumsy, and sensitive people, especially when small, watery, or slimy stools are frequently present.

CARBO VEG.: Flatulence, slow action of the bowels, bad digestion and loss of appetite.

SULPHUR: Suitable to hypochondriac persons, especially after *Nux vom.*, even in the most obstinate cases.

See: HÆMORRHOIDS.

CONGESTIONS OF THE CHEST.—The best remedies are: *Acon. aur. bell. chin. merc. n-vom. phos. spong. sulph.*

ACONITUM: Violent pressure with palpitation of the heart, short breath, anguish, short and dry cough, disturbing the sleep, great heat and thirst.

AURUM: Great anguish with palpitation of the heart, oppression or real paroxysms of suffocation with sensation as if the chest were constricted, falling down without consciousness, and bluish complexion.

Belladonna: Great restlessness with beating in the chest, beating of the heart which is even felt in the head, oppression, heavy breathing, short cough disturbing sleep, internal heat and thirst.

China: When the congestion is caused by *debilitating losses*, with palpitation of the heart; heavy breathing, oppression, anguish; or when the breathing is impossible with the head low.

Mercurius: Anxious oppression and heavy breathing, with desire to take deep breath; heat and burning in the chest, palpitation of the heart, and cough with bloody expectoration.

Nux vom: Heat and burning in the chest, especially at night, with tossing about, anxiety, sleeplessness; or tensive pressure as from a weight, especially in the open air, with heavy breathing, and unpleasant pressure of the clothes upon the chest.

Phosphorus: Oppression and heaviness, tension and feeling of fulness in the chest; palpitation of the heart, anguish, and sensation of heat rising to the throat.

Spongia: Orgasm of the blood in the chest, after the least exertion, with dyspnœa, anguish, nausea, and fainting weakness.

Sulphur: Orgasm of the blood in the chest, with malaise, fainting, trembling of the arms, palpitation of the heart, heaviness, fulness and pressure in the chest, as from a weight, particularly when coughing; oppressed breathing, especially at night when lying.

Compare: Asthma.

CONGESTIONS OF THE HEAD.

§ 1. The best remedies are: 1) *Acon. arn. bell. bry. coff. merc. n-vom. op. puls. rhus. veratr.;* or, 2) *Cham. chin. dulc. ign. sil. sulph.;* or, 3) *Aur. cann. graph.*

§ 2. Persons who are fond of *spirits*, should take: *Nux vom.* or *puls.*, or *Opium, calc.* and *sulphur.* Persons leading a sedentary life, require: *Acon.*, or *Nux vom.* Girls at the age of pubescence: *Acon. bell.* or *puls.* Children during dentition: *Acon. coff.* or *cham.*

For congestion from great joy, give: *coff.* or *opium*,—from *fright* or *fear*, *opium*,—from violent *anger: Chamom.*, or perhaps *Bryon.* or *Nux-v.*,—and from suppressed anger, *Ignat.* For congestion from a fall, blow, or violent *concussion*, give: *Arn. cic. merc.*,—from *debilitating* losses: *Chin.* or *Calc. sulph. nux-v.* or *veratr.*—from the least *cold : Dulc.*,—from *lifting* heavy weights, or from injuries: *Rhus.* or *Calc.* Congestion from *constipation*, requires: *Bry. nux-v. opium.*, or *Merc.* or *Puls.*

The disposition to congestions of the head requires: *Calc. hep. sil.* or *sulph.*

§ 3. Particular indications.

ACONITUM: Beating and fulness in the head; frequent vertigo, especially when stooping; sensation as if the head would split, especially over the eyes, worse when stooping and coughing; scintillations and darkness before the eyes; buzzing in the ears; frequent fainting turns, palpitation, &c., or violent burning pains in the head, especially in the forehead, with red and bloated face, red eyes, paroxysms of rage or of being beside one's-self. (After *Acon.*, *Bell.* is frequently suitable.)

ARNICA: Heat in the head with chilliness of the remainder of the body; dull pressure in the brain, or burning beating, buzzing in the ears and vertigo, obscuration of sight, especially when rising from a recumbent posture.

BELLADONNA: Violent pressure in the forehead, or beating, burning and stitching pains in one side of the head; aggravation of the pains when walking, or during motion, when stooping, or by the least noise or light, with red and bloated face, red eyes, scintillations, darkness before the eyes, buzzing in the ears, diplopia, disposition to sleep; or for dull aching pains, deep in the brain, with pale, sickly complexion, loss of consciousness, delirium and muttering; or the pain appears after a meal, with languor, somnolence, painful stiffness of the nape of the neck, heavy tongue, and other apoplectic symptoms. (Is frequently suitable after *Aconite.*)

BRYONIA: Painful compressive sensation in both sides of the head, or as if everything would fall out at the forehead when stooping; nose bleeds without relief, burning eyes, lachrymation, constipation.

COFFEA: Lively temper, cerebral excitement, sleeplessness, heaviness of the head, increased congestion when talking; shining and red eyes.

MERCURIUS: Fulness in the head as if the forehead would split, or as if the head were bandaged, or when the symptoms are *worse at night*, with burning, tearing and stitching pains; the patient sweats readily and profusely. (Is frequently suitable after *Bell.* and *Opium.*)

NUX VOM.: Nervousness, with painful sensitiveness of the brain when walking or moving the head; pressure in the temples, remaining unchanged when lying or raising one's-self; dim eyes, with desire to close them without being able to sleep; great heaviness in the head, especially when moving the eyes, with sensation, when thinking, as if the head would split; aggravation of the symptoms in the morning, in the open air, or after a meal, and especially after taking coffee.

OPIUM: Violent congestion, with tearing pain, pressure in the forehead from within outward; throbbing in the temples; wandering look; thirst; dry mouth, sour eructations, nausea or vomiting

PULSATILLA: Exhausting pain on one side of the head; or the pain commences in the occiput, thence to the root of the nose, or vice versa; relief by tying a cloth round the head, or by pressure, or walking; aggravation by sitting; heaviness of the head; pale face with vertigo; whining mood; shivering, anguish, phlegmatic temperament, &c.

RHUS TOX.: The congestion is accompanied by burning, throbbing pains, with fulness in the head, aching, or creeping, vacillating sensation in the brain; the pains appear after eating.

VERATRUM: Shocks with pressure, or pains on one side, or sensation as if the brain were dashed to pieces; or contractive pain with astringent sensation in the throat; painful stiffness of the nape of the neck; copious secretion of watery urine, nausea, vomiting, &c.

Particular remedies for headache are:

a) When there is much *vertigo* or dizziness: 1) *Acon. arn. bell. bry. calc. caust. cic. con. lach. natr-m. nitr-ac. n-vom. phos. puls. rhus. sep. sil. sulph.* 2) *Amm. baryt. bruc. cann. carb-an. cham. chin. coccul. dig. hep. ign. kal. laur. lyc. petr. phos-ac. spig. stram. sulph-ac. tart. veratr.*

b) When the vertigo is so bad that one *falls down:* 1) *Bell. coccul. puls. rhus. sil.* 2) *Acon. chin. cic. con. graph. lach. phos-ac. rhus. sulph. zinc.*—that one falls *forward:* 1) *Cic. graph. sil.* 2) *Cupr. magn-c. magn-m. mang. natr-m. phos-ac. rhus. sabin. sassap. sulph.*—*backward:* 1) *Chin. phos-ac.* 2) *Kal. rhod. sassap.*—*sideways:* 1) *Con. sulph.* 2) *Acon. lach. sil. zinc.*—to the *left* side; 1) *Lach. zinc.* 2) *Dros. mez. n-mosch. sil.*—to the *right:* *Acon. ferr. sabad. sil.*

c) When there is much *heat* in the head: 1) *Acon. arn. bell. bry. carb-veg. chin. lach. merc. natr. natr-m. nitr-ac. sep. sil. sulph.*

d) When the head feels too *full:* 1) *Acon. bell. bry. calc. caps. chin. daph. graph. merc. phosph. sil. sulph.* 2) *Amm. carb-veg. chin. coff. petr. spong. sulph-ac.*

e) When it feels *heavy:* 1) *Arn. ars. bell. bry. calc. carb-veg. chin. merc. natr-m. n-vom. puls. rhus. sep. sil. stann. sulph.* 2) *Acon. amm. amm-m. camph. carb-an. cham. con. dulc. hell. kal. lach. laur. lyc. magn-c. magn-m. n-mosch. oleand. op. petr. phos. plumb. staph.*

§ 5. a) When the head feels *dull:* 1) *Anac. bell. calc. carb-veg. chin. hell. magn-aust. merc. natr-m. n-vom. op. petr. phos-ac. rhus. sep. sil. staph. sulph.* 2) *Acon. ars. bell. carb-an. cic.*

coccul. err. graph. hell. ign. kal. magn-c. natr. n-mosch. phos. puls. spig. staph. stram. thuj. zinc.

b) When it feels *cloudy*, with confusion of the senses, &c.: 1) *Acon. agar. bell. bry. cic. hell. hyos. laur. natr-m. op. stram. veratr.* 2) *Calc. cann. carb-veg. caust. cham. coccul. con. kal. magn-m. n-vom. phos-ac. puls. rhab. rhus. sil. veratr.*

c) When *stupefied:* 1) *Arn. bell. hell. hyos. laur. n-vom. op. phosph. phos-ac. plat. rhus. stram. veratr.* 2) *Ars. bry. calc. camph. cic. con. cupr. laur. natr-m. n-mosch. puls. rhab. sabad. sabin. stann. staph. sulph. verb.*

d) When there is *loss of consciousness:* 1) *Arn. bell. hyos. n-vom. op. phos-ac. plat. rhus. stram. veratr.* 2) *Baryt. camph. cic. cupr. hell. kal. mur-ac. natr-m. n-mosch. phosph. puls.*

§ 6. See: HEADACHE, APOPLEXY, CONGESTION, &c.

CONSTIPATION.

§ 1. This is a mere symptom, the cure of which requires a remedy corresponding to the totality of the symptoms characterizing a morbid state. For morbid states, where constipation is the principal symptom, the following are the best remedies: 1) *Bry. calc. cocc. lach. lyc. n-vom. op. plumb. sep. sil. staph. sulph. veratr.* 2) *Alum. bell. cann. canth. carb-veg. caust. con. graph. kal. kreos. merc. nitr-ac. phosph. plat. puls. sassap. stann. sulph-ac. zinc.*

§ 2. To obtain *immediate* relief, give: 1) *Bry. n-vom. op.* or, 2) *Cann. lach. merc. plat. puls. sulph. magn-arct.*

For *habitual* constipation, costiveness, use: *Bry. calc. caust. con. graph. lach. lyc. sep. sulph.*

§ 3. Constipation of persons who lead a *sedentary* life, requires: *Bry. n-vom. sulph.;* or, 2) *Lyc. op. plat.*

Constipation of *drunkards: Calc. lach. n-vom. op. sulph.*

Constipation resulting from the abuse of *cathartics*, or setting in after diarrhœa: 1) *N-vom. op.;* or, 2) *Ant. lach. ruta.*

Constipation of *old* people, or alternating with diarrhœa: 1) *Ant. op. phos.;* or, 2) *Bry. lach. rhus. ruta.*

Constipation of *pregnant* females: 1) *N-vom. op. sep.;* or, 2) *Alum. bry. lyc.*—and of *lying-in* females: *Ant. bry. n-vom. plat.*

Constipation of *infants* at the breast: 1) *Bry. n-vom. op.;* or, 2) *Alum. lyc. sulph. veratr.*

For constipation brought on by travelling in a *carriage: Plat.* or, *Alum. op. magn-arct.*

Constipation from *poisoning with lead*, requires: *Alum. op. plat.*

§ 4. For constipation with *ineffectual urging*, give: 1) *Caps. con. lach. lyc. merc. n-vom. sep. sulph.* 2) *Arn. bell. calc. carb-veg. caust. cocc. graph. ign. kal. natr. natr-m. nitr-ac. puls. sil. staph. veratr. zinc.*

Constipation *without the least desire:* 1) *Alum. chin. hep. kal. natr-m. n-vom. staph. thuj. veratr.* 2) *Anac. arn. bry. carb-veg. cocc. graph. ign. lyc. magn-m. natr. n-mosch. op. petr. rhod. ruta. sep. sil. staph. sulph.*

When the *fæces* are very *hard:* 1) *Amm. ant. bry. calc. carb-veg. con. guaj. lach. magn-m. op. plumb. sep. sil. sulph.* 2) *Alum. bry. carb-an. caust. guaj. kal. lyc. magn-arct. magn-c. merc. n-vom. petr. rhus. ruta. spong. staph. sulph-ac. thuj.*

When *lumpy*, like sheep's dung: 1) *Alum. magn-m. merc. op. sep. sil. sulph.* 2) *Amm. baryt. carb-an. caust. graph. kal. lach. mang. n-vom. petr. plumb. stann. sulph-ac. thuj. verb.*

When *too large:* 1) *Bry. calc. kal. magn-arct. n-vom.* 2) *Aur. graph. ign. magn-m. merc. stann. sulph-ac. thuj. veratr. zinc.*

When *very thin: Caust. graph. hyos. merc. mur-ac. natr. puls. sep. staph.*

When *too scanty*: 1) *Alum. arn. calc. graph. lyc. magn-m. natr. n-vom. sep. sil. sulph.* 2) *Ars. baryt. cham. chin. lach. ruta. stann. staph. zinc.*

§ 5. Particular indications:

Bryonia: Especially in summer, suitable to persons who are disposed to rheumatism, or when the constipation was caused by disordered stomach, with disposition to feel chilly, *congestion of blood to the head*, headache; irritable mood, disposition to be angry, taciturn; generally suitable to vehement individuals.

Lachesis: Obstinate constipation with pressure in the stomach, and ineffectual attempts at eructation.

Mercurius: The constipation is accompanied with bad taste in the mouth, painful gums, but no loss of appetite. (Give *Staphys.*, if *Merc.* should not suffice.)

Natrum muriaticum: Obstinate constipation, when all action of the bowels seems lost.

Nux vomica: Suitable to hypochondriac and hæmorrhoidal individuals; the constipation was caused by eating too much, or by deranging the stomach, &c. Symptoms: Loss of appetite, nausea, distention of the abdomen, with pressure and heaviness; heat, especially in the face; congestion of blood to the head, *headache;* inability to work; disturbed sleep, oppression, cardialgia, ill humour; *sensation as if the anus were closed or narrower than usual*, with frequent, ineffectual urging.

Opium; Sensation as if the anus were closed, but without any great urging; beating and sensation of heaviness in the abdomen;

cardialgia, dry mouth, loss of appetite, *congestion of blood to the head, headache, red face,* &c.

Platina: The patient is only able to pass small lumps, with tenesmus and creeping at the anus after every evacuation; chill with sensation of weakness in the abdomen; constrictive pain in the abdomen, with pressure, pain in the stomach and ineffectual attempts at eructation.

Pulsatilla: Corresponding to the symptoms of *Nux-v.*, when the patients are of a bland, phlegmatic disposition; or suitable for constipation produced by derangement of the stomach in consequence of eating too much fat; accompanied with chilliness, peevish and taciturn disposition.

Sepia: Suitable to females or to rheumatic individuals, or when *Sulphur* and *Nux-v.* are insufficient.

Sulphur: Habitual costiveness, especially suitable after *Nux-v.*, to hypochondriac and hæmorrhoidal individuals; *frequent but ineffectual urging to stool;* with incarceration of flatulence, malaise, distention of the abdomen, inability to perform any mental labour, &c.

§ 6. If these remedies should not prove sufficient, it will be necessary to select a remedy in accordance with the general state of the patient.

CONSTITUTION, AGE, SEX, AND TEMPERAMENT.

The following classification of remedies agreeably to constitution, sex, &c., is, of course, imperfect, and many remedies which have been omitted in the various paragraphs, may have to be supplied after a little more observation. Nevertheless, an intelligent physician will find the attempted classification of service, were it only to confirm the selection of a remedy, or to decide him in favour of one remedy among several doubtful ones.

§ 2. Premising all this, we will give the preference, as respects *age* and *sex:*

a) For the *male* sex, to: 1) *Acon. alum. aur. bry. canth. carb-veg. chin. clem. coff. coloc. dig. euphorb. graph. ign. kal. magn-arct. magn-m. merc. natr. natr-m. nitr-ac. n-vom. op. phos. rhus. sil. staph. sulph zinc.* 2) *Agar. alum. anac. ant. ars. baryt. caps. carb-an. caust. coloc. con. hep. lach. lyc. mosch. mur-ac. par. petr. phos-ac. plumb. puls. seneg. stann. sulph-ac. thuj. veratr.*

b) For the *female* sex, to: 1) *Acon. amb. amm-m. asa. bell. cham. chin. cic. con. croc. hyos. ign. magn-c. magn-m. mosch. n-mosch. plat. puls. rhus. sabin. sep. stann. val.* 2) *Alum. amm. arn. borax. calc. caust. cocc. ferr. graph. hell. hep. kal. lyc. merc. n-vom. phosph. ruta. sabad. sec. spig. stram. sulph. thuj. veratr. zinc.*

c) For *children:* 1) ***Acon. bell. bry. calc. cham. coff. hep. ign. ipec lyc. merc. n-mosch. rhab. sil. sulph.*** 2) ***Amb. ars. aur. baryt. borax. bry. canth. chin. cin. dros. hep. magn-c. n-vom. puls. rhus. ruta. spong. stann. staph. sulph-ac. veratr. viol-tr.***

d) For *young* people: *Acon. bell. bry. lach.* and many others.

e) For *old* people: *Amb. aur baryt. con. op. sec.*

§ 3. As respects *constitution:*

a) For *blond* persons of *lax* fibre, to: *Bell. calc. caps. cham. clem. con. coccul. dig. graph. hyos. lach. lyc. merc. rhus. sil. sulph.*

b) For *dark-complexioned,* with *rigid* fibre: *Acon. anac. arn. ars. bry. kal. natr-m. nitr-ac. n-vom. plat. puls. sep. staph. sulph.*

c) For *bilious* individuals: 1) *Acon. bry. cham. chin. coccul. merc. n-vom. puls.* 2) *Ant. ars. asa. asar. cann. coloc. daphn. dig. ign. ipec. lach. sec. staph. sulph. tart.*

d) For *nervous* persons: 1) *Acon. baryt. bell. chin. coff. con. cupr. ign. magn-arct. merc. natr. n-vom. phos. plat. puls. sil. stann. sulph. val. viol-od.* 2) *Alum. ars. carb-veg. cham. dig. graph. hep. hyos. laur. lyc. natr-m. n-mosch. phos-ac. rhus. sabin. sep. stram. teucr.*

e) For *plethoric* individuals. See: PLETHORA.

f) For *lymphatic* individuals: 1) *Bell. calc. carb-veg. chin. lyc. merc. natr-m. nitr-ac. phos. puls. sep. sil. sulph.* 2) *Amm. arn. ars. baryt. dulc. ferr. graph. kal. petr. rhus. thuj.*

g) For *bloated,* spongy persons: *Amm. ant. ars. asa. bell. calc. caps. cupr. ferr. hell. kal. lach. merc. puls. rhus. seneg. spig. sulph.*

h) For *slender* individuals: *Amb. n-vom. phos. sep.*

i) For *thin,* lean subjects: 1) *Amb. ars. bry. chin. graph. lach. merc. natr-m. n-vom. stann. sulph.* 2) *Ant. baryt. cham. clem. cupr. ferr. ign. ipec. lyc. merc. nitr-ac. phos. plumb. puls. sec. sil. staph. veratr.*

k) For *fat,* large persons: *Ant. bell. calc. caps. cupr. ferr. graph. lyc. puls. sulph.*

l) For *weakly, cachectic* individuals: 1) *Arn. calc. chin. natr-m. n-vom. phos-ac. sulph. veratr.* 2) *Ars. carb-veg. lach. merc. phos. sec. sep.* &c.

§ 4. As respects *temperament* and *disposition:*

a) For *choleric,* vehement individuals: *Acon. ars. aur. bry. carb-veg. caust. hep. kal. lyc. magn-aust. natr-m. nitr-ac. n-vom. phos. plat. sep. sulph.*

b) For *bland* dispositions: *Amb. bell. calad. cic. coccul. ign. lyc. magn-arct. puls. sil. sulph.*

c) For *phlegmatic* individuals: *Bell. caps. chin. lach. merc. natr. natr-m. mez. puls. seneg.*

d) For *lively* dispositions: *Acon. ars. cham. nitr-ac. n-vom.* &c.

e) For *melancholy* persons: *Acon. aur. bell. bry. calc. chin. graph. ign. lyc. natr-m. plat. puls. rhus. stram. sulph. veratr.*

f) For *sensitive* people: *Ars. ant. calc. canth. coff. con. cupr. ign. lach. lyc. n-vom. phos. plat. sabad.*

CONTRACTION OF MUSCLES, Induration.

The principal remedies for this affection, which is generally connected with rheumatic or arthritic ailments, are: 1) *Amm. amm-m. caust. coloc. graph. lach. natr. natr-m. puls. rhus. sep. sulph.* 2) *Baryt. carb-an. carb-veg. con. lyc. n-vom.*

See: Gout and Rheumatism.

COPPER, ill effects of, or Verdigris.

For poisoning with large doses, Hering recommends: 1) *Albumen*, either with or without water; 2) *Sugar*, or *Sugar-water*; 3) *Milk*; 4) *Mucilaginous* drinks: 5) Iron *filings* dissolved in vinegar, and mixed with gum-water.

The subsequent dynamic affections require: 1) *Hep. n-vom.*; or, 2) *Aur. bell. chin. cocc. dulc. ipec. merc.*

CORNS.

§ 1. The principal remedies, which, indeed, do not always cure, but palliate the pain, are: 1) *Ant. calc. sep. sil.* 2) *Amm. carb-an. ign. petr. lyc. nitr-ac. sulph.*

§ 2. a) For *boring* pains, give: *Borax. caust. natr. phos.*

b) For *burning* pains: *Calc. ign. magn-arct. petr. phos-ac. sep. sil. sulph.*

c) For *aching* pains: *Ant. graph. bry. phos. sep.*

d) For *inflammation*: *Lyc. sep sil.*

e) For *tearing* pains: *Bry. lyc. magn-m. natr. sep. sil. sulph.*

f) For *stitching* pains: *Ant. bry. calc. lyc. natr. natr-m. rhus. sep. sil. sulph. thuj.*

g) For *pain* generally: *Bry. calc. lyc. n-vom. phos. rhus. sep. sil. sulph.*

h) For *soreness*: *Amb. graph. ign. lyc. magn-arct. n-vom. rhus. sep.*

§ 3. See: Skin, induration, thickening of the.

CORNEA, diseases of the.—Principal remedies: 1) *Calc.*

cann. con. euphr. puls. sulph. 2) *Ars. aur. chel. chin. cin. hep. lach. magn-c. merc. natr. nitr-ac. ruta. seneg. sep. sil. spig.*

For *specks*, give : 1) *Cann. euphr. hep. nitr-ac. seneg. sil.* 2) *Ars. calc. cin. ruta. sep. spig* 3) *Aur. con.*

For *ulcers* and *cicatrices :* 1) *Euphr. hep. sil.* 2) *Ars. calc. lach. merc. natr.*

For *obscuration* of the cornea : 1) *Cann. euphr. magn-c. puls. sulph.* 2) *Calc. chel. chin. nitr-ac.*

Compare : OPHTHALMIA.

COUGH.

§ 1. Cough being, generally speaking, a mere symptom, it seems impossible to furnish precise instructions for the treatment of every species of cough. Nevertheless, it may not be superfluous to mention the principal remedies for cough, provided the practitioner selects his remedy in accordance with the general symptoms of the patient.

The principal remedies for cough, are : 1) *Acon. ars. bell. bry. calc. carb-veg. hep. ipec. lyc. n-vom. phos. puls. sep. stann. sulph.* 2) *Cham. chin. cin. con. dros. dulc. hep. hyos. ign. kal. led. lach. lyc. rhus. sil. spong.* 3) *Arn. caps. caust. euphr. op. phos-ac. squill. stann. staph. veratr. verb.*

§ 2. For *catarrhal* cough : 1) *Acon. bell. bry. cham. merc. n-vom. puls. rhus. sulph.;* or, 2) *Arn. ars. calc. caps. caust. chin. cin. dros. dulc. euphr. hyos. ign. ipec. lach. phos. phos-ac. sep. sil. spig. squill. stann. staph. veratr. verb.*

For *nervous* and *spasmodic* cough : 1) *Bell. bry. carb-veg. cin. cupr. dros. hep. hyos. ipec. merc. n-vom. puls. sulph.;* or, 2) *Amb. chin. con. ferr. jod. lact. nitr-ac. sil. magn-arct.*

For cough accompanied with *vomiting* or *nausea*, give : *Bry. carb-veg. dros. ferr. ipec. n-vom. phos-ac. puls. sep. sulph. tart. veratr.*

For cough attended with *suffocative paroxysms : Bry. cham. chin. dros. hep. ipec. lach. op. samb. spig. sulph. tart. magn-arct.*

§ 3. a) For *dry* cough without expectoration : 1) *Acon. bell. bry. cham. coff. hep. hyos. ign. ipec. lach. n-vom. petr. phos. sep. spong. sulph.* 2) *Ant. arn. ars. calc. carb-veg. caust. chin. cin. coff. cupr. dros. hep. jod. kreos. lach. lyc. merc. nitr-ac. n-mosch. plat. puls. rhus. seneg. spig. squill. stann. staph.*

b) For *loose* cough with expectoration : 1) *Ars. bry. calc. chin. jod. lyc. phos. puls. seneg. sep. sil. squill. stann. sulph.* 2) *Acon. alum. anac. dros. ferr. kal. phos-ac. ruta. spong. staph. thuj. veratr.*

c) For cough loose in the *day-time*, dry *at night : Ars. calc. cham. graph. n-vom. puls. sabad. sil. sulph.*

d) For cough with expectoration *only in the morning :* 1) *Alum. amm. bry. calc. carb-veg. ferr. hep. magn-c. mang. natr-m. phos. puls. sep. squill. sulph-ac.* 2) *Bell. kal. led. lyc. mur-ac. natr. nitr-ac. phos-ac. sil.*

e) Expectoration *only in the evening :* 1) *Arn. cin. graph.* 2) *Calc. kal. lyc. mur-ac. nitr. n-vom. phos. ruta. sep. stann.*

f) Expectoration *only at night : Bell. calc. caust. hep. led. lyc. sep.*

g) When it is impossible to throw off the detached substance : *Amb. arn. caust. kal. sep.*

§ 4. a) For *bloody* expectoration : 1) *Acon. arn. bry. calc. ferr. ipec. lyc. nitr-ac. phos. sulph.* 2) *Ars. bell. chin. con. croc. dros. dulc. hep. hyos. laur. led. merc. nitr. rhus. sabin. sec. sep. sil. squill. sulph-ac.*

b) For blood-streaked expectoration, or *mucus mixed with blood :* 1) *Ars. bry. chin. ferr. phos. sabin. sep.* 2) *Acon. arn. bell. borax. jod. ipec. laur. lyc. magn-c. op. sulph-ac. zinc.*

c) For *purulent* expectoration : 1) *Calc. carb-veg. chin. con. kal. lyc. natr. nitr. phos. sep. sil. staph. sulph.* 2) *Ars. bell. carb-an. dros. ferr. hep. merc. nitr-ac. phos-ac. puls. rhus. stann.*

d) For *jelly-like* expectoration, or resembling boiled starch, &c. *Arg. baryt. chin. dig. ferr. laur.*

e) *Frothy* expectoration : *Ars. ferr. op. phos. puls. sec. sil.*

f) *Mucous* expectoration : 1) *Ars. bry. calc. chin. lyc. phos. puls. stann. sulph.* 2) *Amm. arg. baryt. bell. carb-veg. cin. dulc. jod. kreos. lach. magn-m. nitr-ac. n-mosch. ruta. staph. thuj.*

g) *Fetid* expectoration : 1) *Calc. natr. sil. sulph.* 2) *Ars. con. graph. guaj. lyc. magn-m. nitr-ac. phos-ac. sep. stann.*

h) *Watery* expectoration, or of thin mucus : *Arg. carb-veg. cham. chin. ferr. graph. lach. lyc. magn-c. merc. stann. sulph.*

i) *Tenacious* expectoration : 1) *Ant. ars. bell. bov. carb-veg. seneg. sil.* 2) *Alum anac. cann. cham. chin dulc. ferr. jod. kal. magn-c. magn-m. lach. merc. mez. phos-ac. rhus. spong. zinc.*

§ 5. a) *Yellow* expectoration : 1) *Bry. calc. carb-veg. dros. kreos. phos. puls. stann. staph. thuj.* 2) *Acon. amm-m. ars. lyc. mang. merc. natr. nitr-ac. ruta. sep. spong.*

b) *Gray* expectoration : 1) *Amb. ars. lyc. sep.* 2) *Anac. arg. chin. kreos. lach. magn-m. n-vom. thuj.*

c) *Greenish* expectoration : 1) *Ars. carb-veg. magn-c. lyc. puls. stann.* 2) *Borax. colch. led. mang. natr. phosph. sil. thuj.*

d) *Reddish*, not bloody expectoration : *Bry. squill.*

e) *Blackish* expectoration : *Chin. lyc. n-vom. rhus.*

f) *Whitish* expectoration: 1) *Arg. carb-veg. kreos. lyc. phos. sep. sulph.* 2) *Acon. amm-m. carb-an. chin. cin. cupr. ferr. rhus. sil.*

§ 6. a) For *bitter* expectoration: 1) *Ars. cham. merc. n-vom. puls.* 2) *Arn. bry. canth. dros nitr-ac. sep.*

b) *Foul* expectoration : *Arn. bell. carb-veg. cham. con. cupr. ferr. puls. sep. stann.*

c) *Salt* expectoration : 1) *Ars. lyc. natr. phos. puls. sep.* 2) *Alum. amb. baryt. calc. chin. dros. graph. magn-c. magn-m. merc. n-vom. samb. sil. sulph.*

d) *Sour* expectoration: 1) *Calc. n-vom. phos.* 2) *Bell. cham. chin. hep. kal. magn-m. plumb. puls. sulph.*

e) *Musty* expectoration : *Borax.*

f) For expectoration tasting like old *catarrhal* mucus : *Bell. puls. sulph.*

g) For *sweetish* expectoration : 1) *Calc. phos.* 2) *Kreos. kal. lach. magn-c. n-vom. puls. samb. squill stann. sulph.*

h) For expectoration tasting like *tobacco : Puls.*

i) For expectoration having an *offensive* taste : 1) *Ars. dros. merc. puls.* 2) *Calc. ferr. ipec. lach. natr-m. sep.*

k) For other kinds of taste, compare TASTE.

§ 7. a) For *racking*, exhausting cough, give : 1) *Lach. merc. n-vom. puls. stann. sulph.* 2) *Anac. carb-veg. hyos. ign. lyc. sil.* 3) *Ars. caust. chin. con. cupr. graph. kal. ipec. phosph. rhus.*

b) For *suffocative* cough: 1) *Ars. cupr. ipec. op. sil. tart.* 2) *Carb-an. carb-veg. caust. cin. con. hep. lach. magn-arct. n-mosch. n-vom. puls. sep. spig.*

c) For *hollow*, barking cough : 1) *Bell. dros. hep. nitr-ac. spong. staph.* 2) *Caust. cin. ign. kreos. phos. samb. spig.*

d) For *hoarse* deep cough : 1) *Carb-veg. cin. hep. ign. merc. n-vom. stann.* 2) *Acon. amb. ars. carb-an. caust. hep. kreos. lyc. nitr-ac. samb. veratr.*

e) For panting *wheezing* cough : 1) *Cin. dros.* 2) *Bell. carb-veg. con. cupr. dulc. hyos. ipec. phos. puls. spong. veratr.* 3) *Acon. amb. chin. kreos. lyc. rhus.*

f) For *titillating* cough : 1) *Acon. ars. cham. jod. ipec. lach. natr-m. n-vom. phos. puls. sep. staph.* 2) *Amm. bell. carb-an. caust. con. nitr. sil. spong. stann. veratr.*

g) For *spasmodic* cough: 1) *Amb. bry. carb-veg. cin. ferr. hyos. ipec. magn-arct. n-vom. puls.* 2) *Acon. bell. calc. chin. con. dros. ign. kal. kreos. merc. natr-m. sep. sil.*

h) For short, *hacking* cough : 1) *Acon. ars. coff. lach. merc. natr-m. n-vom. sulph.* 2) *Alum. bry. caust. chin. graph. hep.*

ign. kreos. ***lyc.*** ***nitr. nitr-ac.*** *rhus.* ***sep. spong. squill. stann. sulph-ac.***

i) For cough as if from the *vapours* of *sulphur* or from *feather dust* in the throat: 1) *Ars. chin. ign. puls.* 2) *Amm. calc. cin. teucr.*

§ 8. a) For cough coming on *in the evening*, give: 1) ***Ars.*** *calc. caps. carb-an. carb-veg. dros. hep. kreos. merc. natr-m. nitr-ac. petr. puls. stann.* 2) *Amm. con. kal. lach. lyc.*

b) *At night in bed*, or after lying down: 1) *Acon.* ***amm. ars.*** *baryt. bell. calc. caps. cham. dros graph. hyos. kal. merc. natr-m. n-vom. petr. puls. sep. sil.* 2) *Anac. arn. carb-an. carb-veg. caust. chin. coccul. coff. colch. hep. ipec. kreos. lyc. magn-arct. magn-m. phos. puls. sulph.*

c) In the *morning: Alum. ars. bry. caust. chin. jod. lyc. natr-m. n-vom. puls. rhus. sil. sulph.*

d) *After a meal: Ars. bry. calc. carb-veg. chin. hep. lach. n-vom. phos. puls sil. staph. sulph.*

e) *After drinking: Acon. ars. bry. chin. dros. hep. lach. phos. squill.*

f) In the *open air:* 1) *Ars. nitr. phos. sulph. sulph-ac.* 2) *Alum. ipec. magn-arct. rhus. seneg.*

g) In *the cold*, in cold air, or after taking a cold drink: 1) *Amm-m. caust. hep. phos. sil. squill.* 2) *Carb-veg. dulc. nitr-ac. sabad. sep.*

h) *During exercise:* 1) *Ars. bry. chin. dros ferr. lach. n-vom. phos. sil. stann.* 2) *Hep. natr-m.*

i) When *laughing*, talking, singing, reading, &c.: 1) *Chin. lach. n-vom. phos. stann.* 2) *Anac. baryt caust. dros. mang. merc. mur-ac. natr-m. sil.*

k) When *lying*, going off again when raising one's-self or rising from a seat: 1) *Hyos. mez. puls. sabad. sulph.* 2) *Con. ipec. nitr-ac. phos. sep. sil.*

§ 9. a) For cough affecting the head, and causing pain in the head, give: 1) *Bell. bry. calc. caust. natr-m. n-vom. sulph.* 2) *Alum. amb. anac. caps. carb-veg. hep. lach. lyc. merc. phos. sep. squill.*

b) Cough with pain in the throat: 1) *Acon. carb-veg. hep. kal. merc. natr-m. n-vom. phos. spong.* 2) *Ars. calc. caust. chin. lyc. nitr-ac.*

c) Cough affecting the *chest:* 1) *Acon. bell. bry. lyc. phos. puls. sulph.* 2) *Amm. arn ars. borax. calc. carb-veg. caust. dros. kal. mang. merc. nitr. nitr-ac. petr. sep. squill.*

d) Cough with pain in the region of the stomach and hypochondria: 1) *Bry dros. lach. n-vom. phos.* 2) *Amb. amm. ars. hep. lyc. nitr-ac. sep. sulph.*

e) Cough with *pains in the side:* 1) *Acon. bry. squill. phosph. sulph.* 2) *Amb. chin. veratr.*

f) Cough with *pressure on the bladder*, and causing the urine to spirt out: 1) *Caust. natr-m. phos. squill. zinc.* 2) *Ant. caps. colch. kreos. puls. staph. sulph.*

g) Cough with *retching* and *vomiting:* 1) *Bry. carb-veg. dros. hep. ipec. lach. n-vom. rhus. sulph. tart.* 2) *Calc. chin. kreos. natr-m. rhus. sep. sil.*

h) Cough with *arrest* or *difficulty of breathing:* 1) *Ars. cupr. ipec. op. sil. tart.* 2) *Acon. bell. carb-an. carb-veg. cin. con. hep. kreos. lach. magn-arct. natr-m. n-mosch. n-vom. puls. sep. sil. spig.*

i) Cough with pressure through the abdominal ring, as if *hernia* would *protrude:* 1) *Magn-arct. n-vom. sulph.* 2) *Cocc. natr-m. sil. veratr.*

k) Cough with *red* or blue *face:* *Acon. bell. cin. con. cupr. ipec. kal. n-vom. op. sil.*

§ 10. Compare: Asthma, Croup, Angina pectoris, Pleuritis, Whooping-cough, Influenza, Bronchitis, Laryngitis, Pneumonia, Pulmonary phthisis, &c.

CRAMP IN THE CALVES.—Although a mere symptom, yet it is sometimes so distressing that it requires a special treatment.

The principal remedies are: 1) *Cham. cupr. rhus. sulph. veratr.* 2) *Calc. camph. caust. coloc. euphr. lyc. natr. natr-m. nitr-ac. sec. sep. sil.* 3) *Alum. amb. anac. chin. con. ferr. graph. ign. magn-aust. natr-m. n-vom. phos. puls. spig. stann. staph.*

CROUP, Angina membranacea.

§ 1. The best remedies are: *Acon. spong.* and *hep.*, in water, a tablespoonful every hour or half hour.

Aconitum: During the inflammatory period, should be continued as long as the following symptoms are present: Great nervous and vascular excitement, burning heat with thirst, *dry* and *short cough, short* and *hurried*, but not yet wheezing or sawing respiration.

Spongia: The above symptoms are less, but the characteristic symptoms of croup remain or these symptoms exist from the commencement, with *rough, crowing*, and *barking cough*, or dry cough, with difficult expectoration of scanty mucus; *slow, loud, wheezing* and *sawing breathing*, or *suffocative fits* with inability to breathe, except with the head bent backwards.

Hepar: The cough has become less after the use of Spongia,

but the air-passages remain clogged with mucus; or the *croup symptoms* are attended with *rattling of mucus* from the commencement, the *cough is moist*, with little difficulty of breathing and slight nervous or vascular excitement.

§ 2. For the *rough* and *barking* cough which sometimes sets in a few days previous to the attack of croup, give: *Cham. chin. cin. dros. hyos. n-vom. veratr.*

For croup with *paralytic* state of the lungs, give: *Tart.*

Croup with *Asthma Millari*, requires: *Samb.* or *Moschus.*

In desperate cases, when *Acon. hep.* and *spong.* remain ineffectual, give: 1) *Mosch. phos.*; or, 2) *Cham. cupr. lach.*

For *laryngitis*, hoarseness and catarrhal affections remaining after croup, give: 1) *Hep. phos.*; or, 2) *Arn. bell. carb-v. dros.*

For the *disposition* to croup: *Lyc.* or *Phosphorus* has been recommended.

CYANOSIS.—*Digit.* is said to have cured this disease.—*Lachesis* has been recommended. It is incurable when depending upon an organic affection of the heart.

For *symptomatic* cyanosis, not depending upon an organic affection (as in cholera, &c.,) I recommend: 1) *Acon. camph. carb-v. cupr. dig. lach. op. veratr.* 2) *Arn. ars. aur. bell. merc. natr-m. n-vom. phos. puls. rhus. samb. sec. sil. spong.*

CYSTITIS, Inflammation of the bladder.

The best remedies are: 1) *Acon. camph. cann. canth. dig. n-vom. puls.*; or, 2) *Calc. graph. hyos. kal. lyc. mez. sep. sulph.*

Aconitum: Violent fever with thirst, frequent and violent urging to urinate, with no discharge or only a few drops of dark, red and turbid or *bloody* urine; painfulness of the region of the bladder when touching it, with increase of the pains during micturition. (After *Acon.* give *Cann.*)

Camphora: When the disease is caused by abuse of Cantharides, in whatever shape they may have been used; or for complete suppression of urine, slow and thin stream, burning in the urethra and bladder.

Cannabis: Frequently after Aconite, for complete suppression of urine, or for urging to urinate especially at night, with burning pain; or drops of *bloody* urine.

Cantharides: Violent, but ineffectual urging to urinate, with drop-discharge of a saturated, dark urine, stinging and burning pains in the region of the bladder, before and after micturition, or cutting pains from the kidneys to the bladder; the abdomen is distended and painful to contact, especially in the region of the bladder.

DIGITALIS: The neck of the bladder is principally affected, with retention of urine and constrictive pain in the bladder, or frequent and painful urging to urinate, with discharge of a few drops of dark-red and turbid urine.

DULCAMARA: For chronic affections of the bladder, constant urging to urinate, painful pressing-down in the region of the bladder and urethra; drop-discharge of urine with *mucous sediment* or mixed with bloody lumps. (After *Dulc.*, *kal.* or *phos.* is sometimes suitable.)

KALI CARB: Violent cutting and tearing in the bladder, neck of the bladder and urethra; less urine and fiery, with a good deal of ineffectual urging. (Is frequently suitable after *Dulc.*)

NUX VOM.: Frequent urging to urinate, with violent pains during and after micturition, which is very scanty; burning pain in the urethra, bladder and kidneys; contractive pain in the urethra after urinating; is suitable to patients who use a good deal of spirits, or who suffer with hæmorrhoids.

PHOSPHORUS: Retention of urine as if there were an obstacle in the urethra, with pain in the abdomen when the last drops are discharged; contractive pain in the bladder, or stitches from the neck of the bladder to the anus. (Is frequently suitable after *Dulc.*)

PULSATILLA: The urging to urinate is attended by aching, burning and cutting pains in the region of the bladder; heat and redness of this region, and sometimes complete suppression of urine; or scanty, painful discharge of slimy urine, or of bloody urine, with purulent sediment.

SULPHUR: In obstinate cases, the urine is mixed with mucous or blood, *burning in the urethra during micturition.* (After *Sulph.*, *Calc.* is frequently suitable, especially when the disease is caused by suppression of hæmorrhoids; if the burning pains do not yield to Calc., give *Ars.* or *Carbo-veg.*)

See: HÆMATURIA, URINARY DIFFICULTIES, ISCHURIA, NEPHRITIS, and NEPHRALGIA.

CYSTOPLEGIA.

Principal remedies: *Ars. dulc. lach.*; or, *Acon. bell. cic. hyos. lach. lauroc. magn-aust.*

CYSTOSPASMUS, SPASM OF THE BLADDER.

The best remedies are: *Asa. caps. clem. phos-ac. puls. sassap. sep. ter.*

DEADNESS of single parts, a mere symptom, which, in conjunction with other symptoms, frequently points to: 1) *Calcar.*

chelid. coni. lycop. n-vom. phos. puls. rhus. secal. sulph. 2) *Antim. merc. natr-m. silic. stann. thuj. zinc.*, &c.

DEBILITY, Asthenia.

§ 1. In many cases a mere symptom, which disappears with the general disease. Sometimes, however, it arises from *loss of animal fluids*, *sexual excesses*, and violent *acute* diseases, and requires special treatment.

§ 2. For debility *from loss of animal fluids*, give: *China*, and if this should be insufficient: 1) *Calc. carb-veg. cin. lach. n-vom. phos-ac. sulph. veratr.*; or, 2) *Nitr-ac. sulph-ac.*

§ 3. For debility from *sexual excesses* without onanism, give: *China*; chronic debility requires: 1) *Calc. n-vom. phos-ac. sil. staph. sulph.*; or, 2) *Anac. arn. carb-veg con. merc. natr-m. phos.* and *sep.*

Calc. is indicated when an embrace causes languor, trembling of the extremities, weariness, pain in the head.

Staphysagria: when the patient worries about his ailments, and is affected with asthma after an embrace, and with hypochondriac mood.

§ 4. *Onanism* generally requires *Nux vom.*, then *Sulph.* and *Calc.*, provided *Phos-ac.* or *Staphys.* is not sufficient. Frequently we give with success: *Carb-veg. cin. cocc. con. natr-m. n-mosch.* and *phos.* China is of very little use.

To eradicate the vice, give: *Sulph. calc.*; or, *Chin. cocc. merc. phos.*; or, *Ant. carb-veg. plat. puls.*

For debility in consequence of *acute diseases*, give: 1) *Chin. hep. sil. veratr.*; or, 2) *Calc. kal. natr-m. phos-ac. sulph.*

For debility from *blood-letting*: *Chin. phos-ac. sulph-ac.*

Debility from *growing too fast*, requires: *Phos-ac.*

That of *old* people: *Aur. baryt. chin. con. op.*

For *hysteric debility*, see: Hysteria.

DEBILITY, nervous; or, excessive nervous excitement, requires: 1) *Acon. chamomilla, chin. coff. n-vom. puls. magn-arct.* 2) *Asar. hep. ign. nitr-ac. teucr. val. veratr.*

If caused by *study*, *watching*, or a *sedentary* life, give: 1) *N-vom. sulph.*; or, 2) *Calc. carb-veg. cocc. lach. puls. magn-arct.*

If caused by *abuse of Mercury*: *Carb-veg. cham. hep. nitr-ac. puls.*

If by *narcotics*: *Cham. coff. merc. n-vom.*, &c.

If by *abuse of coffee*: *Cham. ign. merc. n-vom. sulph.*

If by abuse of *wine* or *spirits*: *Acon. bell. coff. n-vom. puls. sulph.*

Symptomatic indications:

Aconitum: Suitable to young people (especially young girls) when plethoric and leading a sedentary life, or for extreme sensitiveness to pain, sleeplessness, tossing about, extreme sensitiveness of sight and hearing, *red cheeks*, tendency of blood to the head, *palpitation of the heart*, &c.

Chamomilla: Sensitiveness to pain, disposition to faint when suffering ever so little; disconsolate, tossing about, moaning and lamenting; irritable, quarrelsome mood, alternate paleness and redness; or one cheek *pale* and *cold*, the *other warm* and *red*, &c.

China: Great debility with trembling, aversion to physical or mental labour; excessive *nervous* sensitiveness; sensitiveness to draughts of air, sleeplessness from thoughts crowding upon one's mind, or remaining awake late at night; heavy dreams, causing anxiety even after waking, disposition to sweat, hypochondriac mood.

Coffea: Sleeplessness, mental excitement, ill humour, or excessive mirthfulness and liveliness; extreme sensitiveness to pain.

Nux vom.: Irritable, nervous sensitiveness of all the organs of sense, tendency to start, anguish, disposition to lie down, aversion to open air and exercise, peevish mood, vehement, disposed to be angry.

Pulsatilla: Corresponds to the symptoms of Nux, but more suitable to females or people of bland disposition.

Magn. arct.: Nervousness, trembling, distention of the abdomen, anguish, nervous debility.

DEGLUTITION, DIFFICULT, Dysphagia.

§ 1. Principal remedies: 1) *Bell. canth. caust. hyos. lach. merc. n-vom. puls. sil. stram.* 2) *Acon. alum. amm. ant. ars. aur. calc. cham. cic. cocc. con. cupr. dros. ign. kal. laur. lyc. merc. n-vom. op. rhus.*

§ 2. If caused by inflammation, give: *Acon. bell. canth. cham. ign. merc. n-vom. puls.;* and the other remedies indicated for *sore throat*.

If caused by *spasms* of the fauces: 1) *Bell. canth. hyos. lach. stram.* 2) *Alum. ars. cic. coccul. con. ign. laur. lyc. merc. n-vom. op. veratr.*

If caused by *paralysis* of the muscles: 1) *Caust. con. graph. lach. sil.* 2) *Ars. bell. carb-veg. cocc. cupr. hyos. ipec. kal. laur.? n-mosch.? n-vom.? op. plumb. puls.? rhus.?*

§ 3. See: Pharyngitis, Spasms, Paralysis, &c.

DELIRIUM.

§ 1. Delirium is a mere symptom, though of great importance in selecting a remedy. For delirium *without fever*, or *mania*, see : MENTAL DERANGEMENT : delirium *with fever* or violent cerebral irritation, requires : 1) *Bell. hyos. op. stram. veratr.* 2) *Acon. aur. bry. cupr. lach. lyc. n-vom. phos. sulph.* 3) *Arn. ars. calc. canth. cham. cin. ign. kal. puls. rhus. sec. spong.*

§ 2. Particular indications :

a) For *anxious, frightful* or *frightening* delirium, give : 1) *Acon. bell. hyos. op. puls. sil. stram.* 2) *Anac. calc. hep. n-vom. phos. veratr.*

b) Delirium *with fancies :* 1) *Bell. stram. sulph.* 2) *Cham. hyos. op. sep. sil. spong.* 3) *Graph.*

c) Delirium with *desire to escape*, jumping up from bed : 1) *Bell. bry.* 2) *Acon. coloc. op.*

d) *Loquacious* delirium : 1) *Bell. rhus. stram. veratr.* 2) *Lach. op.*

e) Delirium with *visions, phantasmata*, &c. : 1) *Bell. hyos. op. stram.* 2) *Ars. n-vom puls. sulph.* 3) *Calc. camph. carb-veg. dros. hell. hep. nitr-ac. plat.*

f) *Merry* delirium : 1) *Bell.* 2) *Acon. op. sulph. veratr.*

g) *Muttering* delirium : 1) *Bell. hyos. stram.* 2) *N-vom.*

h) Delirium with *illusions of space.: Bell. bry. lach. veratr.*

i) *Religious* delirium : 1) *Bell. puls. stram. veratr.* 2) *Aur. croc. lach. sulph.*

k) Delirium with *screams : Plat. puls. stram.*

l) Delirium with talking about *dead people :* 1) *Bell. n-vom. op.* 2) *Ars. canth. hep.*

m) *Sad, whining* delirium : *Acon. bell. puls.*

n) *Furibond* delirium : *Acon. bell. op. plumb. veratr.*

§ 3. Compare : FEVER, MENTAL DERANGEMENT, MORBID SLEEP, and DREAMS.

DIABETES, DIABETES MELLITUS.—Principal remedies : *Carb-veg. led. natr-m. phos-ac. ;* of the last remedy we know only four cases of cure of certain urinary affections with discharge of milky urine, which, in diabetes, sometimes alternates with watery and colourless urine.

Try also : *Aur. carb-veg. meph. merc. mur-ac. nitr-ac. phos. sulph. ;* and compare : SECRETION OF URINE, URINARY DIFFICULTIES, DISEASES OF THE KIDNEYS, &c.

DIAPHRAGMITIS, INFLAMMATION OF DIAPHRAGHM.

The following remedies have been recommended : *Acon. amb.*

ars. cham. cann. coccul. colch. dros. laur. n-mosch. n-vom. phos. puls. sep. spig. veratr.

DIARRHŒA.

§ 1. Principal remedies : 1) *Ars. cham. chin. dulc. ferr. ipec. merc. puls. rhab. sec. sulph.;* or, 2) *Ant. bry. calc. caps coloc. n-vom. phos. phos-ac. rhus. ;* or, 3) *Arn. bell. berb. carb-veg. cupr. graph. hep. hyos. lach. magn. nitr-ac. n-mosch. petr. sep. veratr.*

§ 2. *Painless* diarrhœa : *Ferr. ;* or, *Chin. cinn.*

Diarrhœa with *colic : Ars. bry. cham. coloc. hep. merc. nitr-ac. puls. rhab. rhus. sulph.*

With *tenesmus : Ars. caps. hep ipec. lach. merc. n-vom. rhab. rhus. sulph.*

With *vomiting : Ars. bell. ipec.;* or, *Cham. coloc. dulc. ferr.*, &c. (Compare : CHOLERA.)

With discharge of *undigested* food (lienteria) : *Chin. ferr. ;* or, *Ars. bry. n-vom*

Colliquative diarrhœa : *Ars. chin. ipec. veratr. ;* or, *N-mosch. phos phos-ac. sec.*

For *bilious, slimy* diarrhœa, see : GASTRIC DERANGEMENT.

Chronic diarrhœa requires : *Calc. chin. ferr. graph. hep. lach. nitr-ac. petr. phos. phos-ac. sep. sulph.*

For disposition to diarrhœa, give : *Calc. graph. kreos. natr-m. nitr-ac. phos. sulph.*

§ 3. Diarrhœa in *consequence of an exanthem*, such as measles, scarlatina, smallpox, &c., requires : *Ars. chin. merc. phos-ac. puls. sulph.*

Diarrhœa from a *cold* : 1) *Bell. bry. cham. dulc. merc n-mosch. veratr. ;* or, 2) *Caust. chin. natr. n-vom. op. puls. sulp.*—From a cold in *summer, fall*, or *winter : Ars. dulc. ;* or, *Bry. merc.*—From a *cold drink : Ars. carb-veg. n-mosch. puls.*

Diarrhœa from violent *emotions, fright*, sudden *joy :* 1) *Ant. coff. op. veratr. ;* or, 2) *Acon. puls.*—From *depressing emotions*, such as *grief : Ign.* or *Phos-ac.*—From *chagrin* or *anger : Cham.* or *Coloc.*

Diarrhœa from *deranged stomach*, or *irregular living : Ant. coff. ipec. puls. n-vom.*—From *revelling : Carb-veg. n-vom.*—From drinking *milk : Bry. sulph. ;* or, *Lyc. natr. sep.*—From the use of *acids* or *fruits : Ars. lach. puls. ;* or, *Chin. ? rhod. ?*

Diarrhœa from *abuse of cathartics* or *calomel : Hep. ;* or, *Carb-veg. chin. nitr-ac.*—From abuse of *magnesia : Puls. rhab.*—From abuse of *rhubarb : Cham. merc. puls. ;* or, *Coloc. n-vom.*—From abuse of *tobacco : Cham. puls.*

§ 4. Diarrhœa of *enfeebled* individuals, requires: *Chin. ferr. n-mosch. phos. phos-ac. sec.*

That of *consumptive persons: Calc. chin. ferr. phos.*

Of *scrofulous* persons: *Calc. dulc. lyc. sep. sil. sulph.;* or, *Ars. bar-c. chin.*

Of *old* people: *Ars. bry. phos. sec.*

Of *pregnant* females: *Ant. dulc. hyos. lyc. petr. phos. sep. sulph.*—And of *lying-in* females: *Ant. dulc. hyos. rhab.*

Of *children: Ant. cham. ferr. hyos. ipec. jalap. magn. merc n-mosch. rhab. sulph. sulph-ac.*—During *dentition: Ars. calc. cham. coff. ferr. ipec. magn. merc. sulph.*

Particular indications.

Arsenicum: *Watery* or *slimy*, whitish, greenish or *brownish* evacuations, especially *at night*, after midnight, or towards morning, or after eating, or *drinking;* with colic, burning or tearing pains in the abdomen; *violent thirst;* loss of appetite with nausea or vomiting; emaciation; debility; sleeplessness, anguish at night; distention of the abdomen; cold limbs; pale face with sunken cheeks; hollow eyes and blue margins around the same.

Chamomilla: *Watery, bilious* or *slimy diarrhœa* of *yellowish*, whitish or *greenish* colour, almost like *stirred eggs;* discharge of undigested food; rumbling in the abdomen; loss of appetite, thirst, coated tongue; tearing or cutting pain in the bowels, fulness in the pit of the stomach; distended abdomen; frequent eructations with nausea or *bilious* vomiting; bitter mouth; and, in children: screams, restlessness, tossing about, constant desire to be carried, &c.

China: Copious watery, *brownish* evacuations, mixed with undigested food; especially at *night*, or after a meal; with violent, aching, constrictive and spasmodic colic, or no pain at all; great weakness in the abdomen; rumbling, eructations, burning pains about the anus; loss of appetite, thirst and complete prostration.

Dulcamara: Liquid greenish or *yellowish*, slimy or *bilious* stools; *nightly* evacuations, with colic, especially in the umbilical region; loss of appetite, thirst; *nausea* or real vomiting; pale face, languor and restlessness.

Ferrum: *Nightly* diarrhœa, or after *eating* and *drinking*, easy painless stools, discharge of watery substances mixed with undigested food; pale face; emaciation, distended abdomen, without flatulence; thirst; canine hunger alternating with loss of appetite; cardialgia; spasmodic pains in the back and anus.

Ipecacuanha: *Watery* or *slimy* diarrhœa, of a *bilious, whitish* or *greenish* colour, with nausea, vomiting of yellowish, whitish or greenish mucus; tearing or cutting colic, with screams (in children), tossing about; accumulation of mucus in the mouth;

distention of the abdomen ; debility with constant desire to be lying down ; pale face with blue margins around the eyes ; chilliness, ill and vehement humour.

MERCURIUS: *Watery*, slimy, *frothy* or *bilious* or *bloody* stools, especially at night, of a *greenish*, whitish or yellowish colour ; the stools look like stirred eggs ; frequent tenesmus, burning, itching and soreness of the anus ; frequent *colic ;* heartburn, nausea and eructations ; *chills* and *shivering ;* cold sweat, trembling and great languor.

PULSATILLA : *Slimy*, bilious or watery diarrhœa of a whitish, yellowish or *greenish* colour, or changeable colour ; papescent stools ; or liquid, fetid stools with soreness of the anus ; with bitter mouth, white-coated tongue, nausea, disagreeable eructations or slimy and bitter vomiting ; colic, especially at night.

RHUBARB : The stools have a *sour* smell, they are liquid, slimy, as if fermented, with pale face, ptyalism, colic, frequent urging and tenesmus ; or copious evacuations with vomiting and great debility ; or, in children, when the diarrhœa is accompanied with screams and restlessness, the children toss about and draw up their legs. (If Rhubarb should be insufficient, *Chamom.* will frequently effect a cure, especially if the pains be very violent.)

SECALE : *Painless* evacuations, with debility ; watery, yellowish or *greenish* stools, which are discharged rapidly, *with great force* and even *involuntarily ;* discharge of undigested food ; colic, especially at night ; slime on the tongue ; pappy taste, frequent rumbling, flatulence, and fulness of the abdomen.

SULPHUR : Frequent evacuations, especially *at night*, with colic, tenesmus, distention of the abdomen, heavy breathing, chilliness and debility ; *slimy*, or watery, frothy, or putrid stools, *whitish* or *greenish ;* discharge of undigested, *sour* or bloody substances ; the diarrhœa sets in again after the least cold ; *emaciation*, &c.

§ 6. We may likewise use :

ANTIMONIUM : Watery diarrhœa with deranged stomach ; white-coated tongue, loss of appetite, eructations and nausea.

BRYONIA : In summer, especially when the diarrhœa was caused by cold drinks, or by anger and chagrin, and *Cham.* proved insufficient.

CALCAREA : Frequently after *Sulphur*, for chronic diarrhœa, especially suitable to scrofulous children, with debility, emaciation, pale face and great appetite.

CAPSICUM : Slimy diarrhœa, with tenesmus and burning at the anus.

COLOCYNTHIS : Bilious or watery diarrhœa, with violent, spasmodic, colicky pains, especially when caused by anger or chagrin, *Cham.* being insufficient.

NUX VOM.: Frequent, scanty evacuations of watery, *slimy*, whitish or greenish substances, with colic and tenesmus.

PHOSPHORUS: Chronic diarrhœa, painless, and gradual loss of strength.

PHOSPHORI ACIDUM: Watery or slimy diarrhœa, with discharge of undigested substances, or involuntary stools.

RHUS TOX.: Diarrhœa, especially *at night*, with tearing in the limbs, headache and colic, worse after eating or drinking.

VERATRUM: *Painless*, brownish or greenish, watery or papescent diarrhœa, with *much rumbling*, feeling *of coldness in the abdomen*, and more or less disposition to debility.

§ 7. In general, use:

a) For *bloody* stools: 1) *Ars. canth. chin. ipec. merc. n-vom. puls. rhus. sep. sulph.* 2) *Arn. asar. bry. calc. caps. carb-veg. dros. ferr. hep. lyc. nitr-ac. phos. sil. sulph-ac.*

b) *Papescent:* 1) *Ant. chin. lach. phos-ac. rhab. rhod. sil. sulph.* 2) *Bell. calc. cin. mez. natr. phos.*

c) *Purulent:* 1) *Arn. canth. lach. merc. sil.* 2) *Bell. calc. kal. puls. sep. sulph.*

d) *Putrid:* 1) *Ars. carb-veg. chin. n-mosch. n-vom. sulph.* 2) *Coccul graph. ipec. nitr-ac. sec. sep.*

e) *Flocculent:* 1) *Ars. veratr.* 2) *Ipec.*

f) *Bilious:* 1) *Cham. chin. merc. phos. sulph.* 2) *Ars. cin. coloc. dulc. ipec. n-vom. veratr.* (Compare: GREEN and YELLOW.)

g) *Yellow:* 1) *Ars. chin. coccul. dulc. ipec. petr. rhus.* 2) *Calc. cham. coloc. merc. petr.*

h) *Gray, ash-coloured: Dig. merc. phos-ac.* (Compare: WHITISH.

i) *Green:* 1) *Cham. merc. puls. phos. sulph.* 2) *Ars. dulc. ipec. sep. stann.*

k) *Fæcal: Ars. cham. cin. merc. mur-ac. rhab.*

l) *Sour:* 1) *Calc. graph. hep. merc. rhab. sulph.* 2) *Cham. magn-c. natr. sep.*

m) *Acrid, corroding:* 1) *Ars. cham. chin. ferr. merc. n-vom. puls. sulph. veratr.* 2) *Ant. dulc. graph. ign. kal. lach. phos.*

n) *Frothy:* 1) *Chin. coloc. rhus.* 2) *Calc. magn-c. merc. sulph.*

o) *Slimy:* 1) *Asar. bell. borax. caps. cham. chin. merc. n-vom. phos. puls. sulph.* 2) *Ars. carb-veg. coloc. graph. hell. ign. ipec. petr. phos-ac. rhab. rhus. ruta. sec. sep. tart.*

p) *Black:* 1) *Ars. camph. chin. ipec. squill. sulph-ac. veratr.* 2) *Cupr. merc. stram. sulph. sulph-ac.*

q) *Fetid, cadaverous:* 1) *Ars. carb-veg. chin. puls. sil. sulph.* 2) *Ars. calc. cham. guaj. merc. nitr-ac. n-vom. sep. squill. sulph-ac.*

r) *Undigested:* 1) *Chin. phos-ac.* 2) *Arn. ars. ferr. oleand.* 3) *Asar. bry. calc. cham. con. lach. merc. n-vom. sulph.*

s) *Involuntary:* 1) *Arn. bell. chin. hyos. op. phos. phos-ac. rhus. sec. veratr.* 2) *Ars. calc. carb-veg. cin. mur-ac. natr-m. sulph.*

t) *Watery:* 1) *Cham. chin. ferr. hell. ipec. n-vom. phos. phos-ac. puls. sec.* 2) *Acon. ars. calc dig. natr-m. petr. sulph. veratr.*

u) *Watery* stools: 1) *Calc. cham. chin. dig. hep. merc. puls. rhus-t. sulph.* 2) *Acon. ars caust. cin. ign. lach. nux-v. phos. phos-ac. spong. veratr.*

v) Stools like *stirred eggs:* 1) *Cham. merc. puls. rhus-t.* 2) *Lach. nux-mosch. sulph-ac. viol-tr.*

§ 8. Compare: CHOLERA, VOMITING, GASTRIC DERANGEMENT, LIENTERIA, DYSENTERY, WORM-AFFECTIONS, &c.

DISTENTION OF THE ABDOMEN, AND FLATULENCE.

The best remedies are: 1) *Asa. chin. n-vom. puls. sulph.* 2) *Bell. carb-v. cham. cocc.;* or, 3) *Agn. calc-ph. caps. colch. coloc. ferr. graph. lyc. natr. natr-m. nitr-ac. n-mosch. phos. veratr. zinc. magn-arct.*

If arising from the use of *flatulent food*, give: 1) *China.*, or: 2) *Bry. lyc. petr.* 3) *Calc. kal. puls. sep. veratr.*

If after taking a *drink:* 1) *N-vom.;* or, 2) *Chin. cocc. ferr. veratr.*

After using *pork* or *fat:* 1) *Chin. colch. puls.;* or, 2) *Carb-v. colch. natr-m.*

In particular, give:

a) For *copious* flatulence: *Agar. carb-v. chin. graph. kal. lach. lyc. nitr-ac. n-vom. phos. phos-ac. plumb. staph. sulph.*—For *distress* from flatulence: *Caps. carb-v. chin. chinin. lach. n-mosch. n-vom. phos. puls. sulph.*—For *incarcerated* flatulence: *Carb-a. carb-v. caust. chin. con. graph. hep. jod. kal. lach. lyc. natr. natr-m. nitr. nitr-ac. n-vom. phos. sil. sulph.*—For pains occurring *early* in the morning: *Alum. asa. bar. carb-a. caust cham. magn-arct. natr-m. nitr-ac. n-vom. phos.*—For *rumbling:* *Agar. ant. arn. bry. canth. carb-v. caust. chin. hell. ign. lyc. natr-m. n-vom. phos. phos-ac. puls. sassap. sep. sulph. veratr.*

b) For *copious discharge* of flatulence: *Agar. canth. carb-a. carb-v. caust. chin. graph. hell kal. lyc. mang. merc. nitr-ac. oleand. phos. plumb. veratr.*—For discharge of *inodorous* flatulence: *Amb bell. carb-v. lyc.*—Of *fetid* flatulence: *Arn. ars. asa. calc carb-v. chin. graph. plumb. puls. sil. sulph.*—*Foul-smelling* flatulence: *Arn. ars. carb-v. ign. oleand. puls. sulph.*—For flatulence smelling like *rotten eggs:* *Arn. coff. sulph. tart.*

teucr. sulph.—For *warm, humid* flatulence: *Carb-v. chin.*—*Hot* flatulence: *Acon. cham. phos. staph. zinc.*—*Cold*: *Con.*—Smelling like *garlic*: *Agar. asa. mosch. phos.*—*Sour*-smelling: *Arn. calc. cham. graph. hep. magn-c. merc. natr. natr-m. rhab. sep. sulph.*—*Noisy* flatulence: *Lach. merc. squill. teucr. zinc.*

DREAD OF AIR, EXTREME SENSITIVENESS TO THE OPEN AIR. Though generally a mere symptom, yet it points principally to the following remedies: 1) *Calc. carb-an. caust. cham. cocc. coff. ign. kal. mez. natr. n-vom petr. puls. rhus. sil.* 2) *Amm. bell. bry. chin. con. guaj. hep. lyc. magn-aust. merc. mosch. nitr-ac. n-mosch. phos. sep. spig. sulph. sulph-ac.* 3) *Ars. cin. ferr. ipec. lach. phos-ac. ruta. staph. thuj.*

DROPSY.

§ 1. The best remedies are: 1) *Ars chin. dig. dulc. hell. kal. led. lyc. merc. sulph.* 2) *Bry. camph. canth. convolv. ferr. lact. phos. prun. rhus. samb. sol-nigr. squill.* 3) *Ant. baryt. chel. con. hyos. sabad. sabin.*

§ 2. Dropsy in consequence of *suppression of exanthemata,* requires: *Ars. dig. hell. rhus. sulph.*

From suppression of *intermittent fevers*: *Ars. dulc. ferr. merc. sol-nigr.* and *sulph.*

From *loss of blood* or *animal fluids*: *Chin. ferr. merc.* and *sulph.*

Dropsy of *drunkards*: *Ars. chin. hell. led. rhus.* and *sulph.*

Dropsy from *abuse of Mercury*: *Chin. dulc. hell.* and *sulph.*

§ 3. Particular indications:

ARSENICUM: Anasarca, ascites and œdema of the lower extremities, more especially when the skin, and particularly the face, look *livid,* pale or *greenish;* great debility and prostration; tongue dry and red; thirst very great; asthma with symptoms of suffocation when lying on the back; cold extremities, tearing pains in the back, small of the back and limbs.

BRYONIA: Anasarca and œdema of the feet, especially when the swelling increases in the day-time and decreases in the evening.

CAMPHORA: Anasarca, with red urine and thick sediment.

CANTHARIS: Dropsy from atony of the urinary passages, with ischuria, tenesmus of the neck of the bladder, pains in the limbs, chronic coryza. &c.

CHINA: Anasarca and ascites, especially in old people. Suitable for organic affections of the liver and spleen, although *Ars.* and *Ferr.* concur in this case.

CONVOLVULUS: Œdema, dropsy, with constipation, distress in the abdomen, and debility.

DIGITALIS: Ascites, anasarca, hydrothorax, when there are organic affections of the heart, and a hurried pulse.

HELLEBORUS: Anasarca, ascites, hydrothorax, &c., acute dropsy, especially for: great debility, vapour, feverish symptoms, stitching pains in the limbs, diarrhœa, suppression of urine, &c.

KALI: Ascites, dropsy, of old people.

LACTUCA: Anasarca with great swelling of the feet, abdomen and eyelids.

LEDUM: Dropsy, with pains in the limbs, and dry skin.

MERCURIUS: Ascites, hydrothorax, acute or chronic anasarca, sometimes accompanied with affections of the liver, oppression on the chest, general heat and sweat; constant short and racking cough; anguish, &c.

PHOSPHORUS: Dropsy, œdema of the hands, feet and face.

PRUNUS: Ascites and dropsy.

RHUS, SAMBUCUS, and SOLANUM NIGRUM: Anasarca.

§ 4. Compare: ANASARCA, ASCITES, HYDROTHORAX, HYDROCEPHALUS, HYDROCELE, &c.

DROPSY OF THE JOINTS, HYDRARTHRUS—Is frequently cured by *Sulphur.*, or by: *Ant. ars. bry. calc. jod. kal. lyc. puls. rhus. sil. sulph.*

DRUNKARDS, DISEASES OF, AND ILL EFFECTS OF SPIRITS GENERALLY.

§ 1. The best remedies are: 1) *Acon. ant. ars. bell. calc. carb-v. chin. coff. hyos. lach. merc. natr. n-vom. op. puls. stram. sulph.* 2) *Agar. arn. coccul. dig. ign. led. lyc. natr-m. n-mosch. ran. rhod. rhus. rut. selen. sil. spig. veratr. zinc.*

§ 2. For *intoxication* itself, the best remedies are said to be: *Acon. bell. coff. op.*

For the *consequences of revelling* at night, and of intoxication, give: 1) *Ant. carb-v. coff. n-vom. sulph.;* or, 2) *Bell. bry. calc. chin. dulc. natr. nitr-ac. phos. phos-ac. rhus.*

For the *chronic* consequences of *drinking: Ars. bell. calc. chin. coff. hell. hyos. lach. merc. natr. n-vom. puls. sulph.*

For *delirium tremens: Ars. bell. calc.. coff. dig. hyos. n-vom. op. stram.*

For the *disposition* to drink: *Ars. calc. lach. merc. sulph. sulph-ac.*

§ 3. As regards symptoms, give:

ACONITUM: When drinking wine is followed by: *feverish heat,* tendency of blood to the head, red face and eyes, and even loss of reason.

ANTIMONIUM: Gastric affections in consequence of revelling, nausea, loathing, loss of appetite, &c., *Carb-veg.* being insufficient.

ARSENICUM: Mental derangement, anguish which drives one to and fro, fear of thieves, ghosts, and solitude, with desire to hide one's-self, trembling of the limbs, &c.

BELLADONNA: Loss of reason, delirium, visions of mice, rats, &c., red and bloated face, tongue coated, aversion to meat, sleeplessness, stammering speech with constant smile, dry feeling in the throat, with difficult deglutition, violent thirst, paroxysms of violent fever, &c.

CALCAREA: Delirium, visions of fire, murder, rats and mice, neither *Bell.* nor *Stram.* being sufficient.

CARB VEG.: Aching or throbbing pain in the head, in consequence of a debauch, relief in the open air; nausea without desire to vomit; liquid, thin stools.

CHINA: Debility of drunkards, especially when dropsy is setting in.

COFFEA: Great excitement of feeling, (especially in children), with excessive mirthfulness, *sleeplessness*, nausea and even vomiting; or headache after intoxication, with sensation as if a nail were sticking in the brain, *Nux vom.* being insufficient. *Coffea* has likewise removed the trembling of the hands of drunkards.

HYOSCYAMUS: Epileptic convulsions in consequence of drinking; sleeplessness with constant tossing about; delirium with visions as if persecuted, and with desire to escape; tremor of the limbs, &c.

LACHESIS: Debility and tremor of the hands, especially when the patient finds it hard to correct himself.

MERCURIUS: Debility of drunkards who abuse coffee, *Nux-v.* and *Sulph.* having proved fruitless.

NATRUM: Debility and dyspepsia of drunkards.

NUX VOMICA: Hemicrania after intoxication, with sensation as if a nail had been driven into the brain; aggravation in the open air, by walking, motion, thinking and stooping; nausea with desire to vomit and straining; *constipation*, or else small, slimy stools, with tenesmus; vertigo; red eyes, with gum in the canthi; photophobia; hacking cough, &c.; or, in confirmed drunkards: for tendency of blood to the head, cloudiness or loss of consciousness, delirium, frightful visions, and desire to escape; great anxiety driving the patient to and fro; sometimes with cold and damp hands, feet and face; nausea, *waterbrash*, vomiting of food or *bitter substances;* sleeplessness or half sleep, with sudden *startings as if in affright;* anxious dreams; constipation, or else diarrhœic, scanty stools; tremor of the limbs, debility, &c. Suitable to drunkards who indulge in abuse of coffee.

OPIUM: Comatose sleep with stertorous breathing, or anxious delirium, with visions of mice and scorpions, &c.; fear, desire to escape, or dreams from which the patient wakes as soon as he is spoken to with a loud voice; constipation, troublesome breathing, general sweat, epileptic convulsions and spasms; *trembling of the extremities*, lock-jaw, twitching of the muscles of the face and mouth, staring look; dark-red face, &c.

PULSATILLA: Derangement of the stomach, cloudiness, heaviness in the forehead, relief in the open air; nausea, especially after eating or drinking; *sour eructations*, coated tongue, &c.; especially when the wine was sulphurated.

STRAMONIUM: Suitable to habitual drunkards; anguish driving one to and fro; taciturn; wandering look, fear, desire to escape; epileptic convulsions, rage; *red, hot*, and *bloated face;* visions, illusions of fact, (such as, that the half of the body is cut off, &c.)

SULPHUR: Trembling, dropsical and other affections of drunkards, especially when they indulge in abuse of coffee.

DYSENTERY, BLOODY FLUX.

§ 1. Principal remedies: 1) *Acon. ars. merc. rhus. sulph.* 2) *Bry. carb-v. cham. chin. coloc. ipec. n-vom. puls.;* or, 3) *Bell. caps. colch. dulc. gran. hep. kreos. lach. nitr-ac. n-mosch. staph.*

§ 2. Particular indications.

ACONITUM: For dysentery when the days are warm and the nights cool; rheumatic pains in the head, nape of the neck and shoulders; or violent chills, heat and thirst (If *Aconite* should not be enough, give: *Cham. merc. nux-v.*, or *Puls.*)

ARSENICUM: Putrid stools, involuntary stools, debility, fetid urine, bad odour from the mouth, stupefied state, red or blue spots on the skin. (If *Ars.* should not be sufficient, give *Carb-v.* or *Nux-v.*)

BRYONIA: Frequently after *Acon.*, especially during hot summers, and for dysentery from taking cold drinks.

CARBO VEG.: When *Ars.* is insufficient to remove the putrid symptoms, when the patient's breath is cold, and he complains of burning pains. (If, after *Carbo veg.*, the stools should continue putrid, give *China.*)

CHAMOMILLA: Frequently after *Aconite*, especially when there are great heat, thirst, rheumatic pains in the head, and great restlessness.

CHINA: When both *Ars.* and *Carbo veg.* are insufficient to remove the putrid symptoms, or for dysentery in *marshy* districts, especially when the symptoms are *intermittent.*

COLOCYNTHIS: One of the principal remedies for dysentery, next to *Merc.*, especially when the patient complains of: spasmodic colic obliging one to bend double, with great restlessness; evacuations of bloody mucus; fulness and pressure in the abdomen, tympanitic distention, chills proceeding from the abdomen, white-coated tongue.

IPECACUANHA: Suitable for fall-dysenteries (bilious dysenteries), especially after giving *Aconite*, or when the patient complains of: violent tenesmus and colic, with *bilious stools*, afterwards *bloody* mucus. (If *Ipec.* should be insufficient, *Coloc.* will frequently help.)

MERCURIUS: Specifically indicated by: *violent tenesmus previous to, and still more after stool*, as if the bowels would be pressed out, with frequent discharge of pure blood, or bloody, green mucus like stirred eggs; screams during stool (in children); violent colic; nausea, eructations, *chilliness* and *shuddering;* cold sweat on the forehead; great exhaustion and trembling of the extremities.

NUX VOMICA: Frequent, small stools, with tenesmus and discharge of bloody mucus; violent cutting in the umbilical region; great heat and thirst; especially after *Aconite* or *Bryonia*, for dysentery occurring during the summer-heat, or when the evacuations have still a putrid smell, and *Ars.* did not remove this.

PULSATILLA: Nothing but blood-streaked mucus is passed; pappy taste in the mouth, white-coated tongue; desire to vomit or else vomiting of mucus, frequent chills, especially towards evening, difficult breathing and whining mood.

RHUS TOX.: Involuntary stools at night, without stools or tenesmus.

SULPHUR: In desperate cases, for: difficult breathing, *blood-streaked mucus stools*, frequent urging to stool, *violent tenesmus, especially at night*, suitable to persons who suffer with hæmorrhoids.

§ 3. See: DIARRHŒA.

EARS, HERPES OF THE.

§ 1. The *herpes* or *scurfs* on or behind the ears, require principally: 1) *Graph. hep. merc. oleand. petr. sulph.;* or, 2) *Ant. baryt. calc. cic. kal. lach. lyc. mez. phos. puls. sep. sil. staph.*

§ 2. Give more particularly:

For eruption *near* or *on the ears:* 1) *Baryt. calc. cic. sulph.* 2) *Ant. kal. petr. phos. puls. sep. sil.*

For *scurfs behind* the ears: *Baryt. calc. graph. hep. lyc. mez. oleand. puls. sep. staph.*

For *scurfy* eruption : *Graph. hep. lach. lyc. puls. staph.*
For *soreness : Graph. kal. lach. merc. petr. sulph.*
For *humour : Calc. graph. lyc. oleand. petr.*
For *ulcerated eruption :* 1) *Amm. carb-v. merc. puls. ruta. spong.* 2) *Alum. kal. stann.*
For *itching* of the parts : *Amm. anac. baryt. lyc. puls. sulph.*
For *swelling* of the ear : *Anac. calc. kal. lyc. merc. puls. sep.*
For *fetid* smell of the ears : *Aur. carb-veg. graph. hep. oleand.*

§ 3. Compare : Eruptions, Herpes, Scaldhead, Ostitis, &c.

ECCHYMOSIS, sugillatio.

Principal remedies : 1) *Arn. bry. con. lach. n-vom. rhus. rut. sulph-ac.* 2) *Ars. berb. calc. cham. chin. dulc. ferr. laur. par. plumb. sec. sulph.*
If caused by *injuries*, give : 1) *Arn.* 2) *Bry. con. rhus. rut. sulph-ac.*
Sanguineous spots or *petechiæ*, such as occur in putrid typhus, require : *Ars. bry. rhus.*
For *morbus maculosus Werlhofii*, the principal remedy is ***Bry.*** Besides, we may have to use in complicated cases : *Led. phos. sil. stram.*
The *cadaverous spots* of old people, require principally : 1) ***Con.*** 2) *Ars. bar. lach. op.*

ECZEMA.

Principal remedies : 1) *Acon. bell. dulc. merc. phos.* 2) ***Ars.*** *aur. carb-v. clem. con. petr. rhus. sulph.*
For eczema *with fever*, give : 1) *Acon. bell. dulc.* 2) ***Petr.*** *phos.*
Chronic eczema requires : *Clem. dulc. merc. petr. phosph. sulph.*
Mercurial eczema : 1) *Chin. hep. sulph.* 2) *Acon. bell. dig.*
Eczema *solare* (caused by the action of the sun) : 1) *Acon. bell. camph.* ; or, 2) *Clem. hyos.*
Impetiginous eczema : *Carb-v. con. rhus. zinc.*
Compare : Eruptions, Exanthemata, Herpes.

EMACIATION.—Though a mere symptom, yet it points principally to : 1) *Ars. calc. china. graph. lycop. natr-m. stann. staph.* 2) *Ambr. baryt. bryon. cham. clem. coccul. cupr. ferr. guaj. ign jod. ipecac. laches. nitr-ac. n-vom. petr. phos. phos-ac. plumb. puls. secal. silic. veratr.*
Compare : Atrophy, Phthisis, Marasmus, &c.

EMOTIONS, ILL EFFECTS OF.

§ 1. Principal remedies: 1) *Acon. aur. bell. bry. cham. coff. coloc. hyos. ign. lach. merc. n-vom. op. phos. phos-ac. plat. puls. staph. veratr.* 2) *Ars. calc. caust. coccul. cupr. lyc. natr-m. rhus. sep. stram. sulph.*

§ 2. For the consequences of *anguish, fright, fear,* give: 1) *Acon. ign. op. puls.* 2) *Bell. caust. coff. hyos. lach. n-vom. samb. veratr.*

Of excessive *joy:* 1) *Coff. op. puls.* 2) *Acon. caust. croc.*

Of *grief:* 1) *Ign. phos-ac. staph.* 2) *Ars. coloc. graph. hyos. lach. lyc. n-vom. veratr.*

Of *homesickness:* 1) *Caps. merc. phos-ac.* 2. *Aur. carb-an. caust. staph.*

Of *unhappy love:* 1) *Hyos. ign. phos-ac.* 2) *Aur. caust. coff. hell. n-vom. staph.*

Of *jealousy:* 1) *Hyos.* 2) *Ign. lach. n-vom. phos-ac. staph.*

Of *mortification, insults:* 1) *Bell. coloc. ign. plat. puls. staph.* 2) *Aur. cham. natr-m. phos-ac. seneg.*

Of *chagrin* and *contradiction:* 1) *Acon. bry. cham. coloc. ign. n-vom. plat. staph.* 2) *Ars. bell. coff. phos. puls.*—And when accompanied with *indignation: Coloc. staph.*

Of *violent anger: Acon. bry. cham. n-vom. phos.*

§ 3. Particular indications.

ACONITUM: Headache, feverish heat, tendency of the blood to the head, and constant fear, especially in children; or when *Opium* had not been given at the onset for fright.

BELLADONNA: Loss of consciousness, or constant anxiety with fear, weeping, howling, and malice (in children); also when *Acon.* and *Op.* had proved insufficient for the consequences of fright.

BRYONIA: Chilliness and shuddering over the whole body, great tendency to vehement anger, loss of appetite, nausea, vomiting and bilious state in consequence of anger.

CAPSICUM: For sleeplessness caused by homesickness, with heat and redness of the cheeks.

CHAMOMILLA: For the following consequences of anger: Bitter taste in the mouth, nausea, disposition to start and vomiting of bilious matter; *cutting colic;* diarrhœa; *pressure in the stomach and pit of the stomach;* headache; fever with heat, thirst, red face and eyes, anguish and restlessness; jaundice; cough; palpitation of the heart; shortness of breath; asthma, suffocative fits; or, in children, convulsions and asthma, or derangement of the stomach in consequence of eating or drinking after anger.

COFFEA: Nervous excitement in consequence of great joy, with trembling, disposition to faint, especially in females and children;

or if the patient took chamomile-tea immediately after a fit of anger.

Colocynthis: When the consequences of *chagrin* or *mortification* are: Spasmodic-colic, cramp in the calves, nausea, bitter taste with vomiting, sleeplessness, &c.

Hepar: When children, after a fit of anger, weep constantly without one being able to quiet them, and *Bellad.* did not help.

Hyoscyamus: In consequence of fear: Stupefaction and apathy; inability to swallow, convulsions, sudden starting or involuntary laughing during sleep, desire to escape, &c. And, when, in consequence of *unhappy* love, the patient feels jealous, runs about restlessly, &c.

Ignatia: For the consequences of *fright, mortification, chagrin, grief*, especially after losing a friend, relative, or the consequences of *unhappy love*, or for: deep, gnawing, irresistible grief, vomiting, gastric symptoms, headache, vertigo, pale face, or even convulsions or epilepsy, especially in children, in consequence of fright or fear.

Mercurius: Recent or inveterate consequences of *fright* or *mortification*, also *home-sickness*, and for: great anguish, trembling and restlessness, sudden starting from sleep, orgasm of the blood on making the least effort, sleeplessness, inability to bear the warmth of the bed; great nervousness, quarrelsome mood; the patient complains of every body and even his own family; desire to escape, constant shivering, night-sweats.

Nux vom.: For the consequences of *anger*, with general chilliness, and when *Bryonia* proved insufficient, or if the patient had taken chamomile-tea directly after the fit of anger, or had eaten or drank any thing else, and if *Chamom.* had not removed the ill effects entirely.

Opium: To be used immediately after a paroxysm of *joy* or *fear*, especially for: Pains in the forehead, stupefaction or loss of consciousness, heat and sweat about the head, with coldness of the rest of the body, tendency of blood to the head, eructations or sour vomiting, great anguish, heaviness in the abdomen; *diarrhœa*, or involuntary stools; pressure on the chest and difficulty of breathing; *fainting fits, paroxyms of spasm* or even *epilepsy;* trembling, cries or sopor with stertorous breathing; spasmodic rigidity of the whole body; internal heat with coldness of the body, cold sweat, &c.

Phosphoric acid: For the consequences of *deep grief, unhappy love, homesickness*, or in all cases where *Ignat.* is not sufficient, especially when the patient is taciturn, dull, listless; when the hair falls out or turns gray; hectic fever with profuse sweat in the morning; constant desire to sleep, &c.

Platina: When *anger* or *mortification* is followed by: Indifference, alternate sadness and laughter; pride with contempt of others; great anguish and dread of death; in females, the urinary passages are involved.

Pulsatilla: Diarrhœa with heat in the abdomen and cold limbs, in consequence of *fear;* or for the consequences of *anger,* in persons of a bland disposition; or when the patient took chamomile-tea directly after the anger; and when *Cham.* was not sufficient.

Sambucus: When *fright* or *fear* occasion: Coldness of the whole body, trembling, convulsive twitchings; oppression of the chest; sopor with stertorous breathing; *Opium* was not sufficient.

Staphysagria: For the consequences of *anger,* especially for: Indignation and ill-humour, the patient pushes violently away from him what is near him; ill-humour, restlessness, fear;—or when *deep grief* occasions: sadness with disposition to take every thing in bad part, great dread of the future, sleep in the daytime, and sleeplessness at night; falling off of the hair; feeble and faint voice; hypochondriac mood.

Veratrum: When *fright* or *fear* occasioned: diarrhœa, or involuntary evacuations from the bowels, with coldness of the whole abdomen.

§ 4. Give more particularly:

a) For *jaundice: Cham. merc. chin.*—for *convulsions: Bell. cham. ign. hyos. op. samb.*—for *tetanic spasms: Bell. op. ign.*—for epileptic attacks: *Ign. op. (bell. lach. caust.)*—for great *debility* with trembling: *Merc. op. phos-ac. veratr.*—for *fainting fits: Coff. op. veratr.*—for *spasmadic* pains: *Coloc.*—for *nervous* excitement: *Acon. coff. magn-arct. merc. n-vom.*—for *vascular* orgasm: *Acon. coff. merc.*

b) When there is *fever: Acon. bry. cham. n-vom.*—*chills* and *shuddering: Bry. merc. puls.*—*coldness* of the body: *Op. puls. samb. veratr.*—*heat* and *redness* of the cheeks: *Caps. ign. acon.*—*night-sweats: Merc. phos-ac.*—*hectic fever: Ign. phos-ac. staph.*

c) For *sleeplessness: Acon. coff. merc. caps. coloc. staph.*—*Sopor: Op. samb. (phos-ac. staph.)*

d) For *melancholy* and *sadness: Aur. ign. phos-ac. plat. staph.*—for constant *weeping* and *lamenting: Bell. hep.*—for constant *cries: Bell. op.*—*constant anxiety* and *fear: Acon. bėll. cham. merc. plat. staph.*—*mental derangement: Bell. hyos. lach. op. stram. veratr.*—*indifference, dulness, apathy: Hell. hyos. phos-ac.*—constant *indignation: Coloc. staph.*

e) *Loss of consciousness* and *stupefaction: Bell. hyos. nux-v. op.*—*tendency of blood* to the head, and headache: *Acon. bell.*

coff. ign. merc. n-vom. op.—*falling off* of the hair, or when the hair turns *gray: Phos-ac. staph.*

f) *Loss of appetite*, nausea, vomiting: *Bry. cham. coloc. ign. n-vom. op. puls.*—*bilious* ailments: *Acon. bry. cham. coloc. ign. n-vom.*—*pains* in the *stomach: Cham. nux-v. puls.*—*colic* and *diarrhœa: Cham. puls. veratr.* — *involuntary stools: Op. veratr.*

g) *Pains* in the *chest, asthma*, &c.: *Aur. bell. cham. n-vom. op. samb.*—violent *palpitation* of the *heart: Acon. cham. hep. op. puls.*

Compare: Emotions, morbid, Mental derangement, Melancholy, &c.

EMOTIONS, MORBID.

§ 1. Having mentioned the remedies, which require to be used for the different varieties of mental diseases, in the articles on: Mental derangement, Clairvoyance, Hydrophobia, Weak memory, Hypochondria, Imbecility, Melancholia, &c., it remains for us now to exhibit in one series the remedies which are proposed for the various symptoms that characterize mental diseases.

The principal remedies for those diseases are: 1) *Aur. bell. hyos. ign. lach. lyc. op. phos. phos-ac. plat. puls. sep. stram. veratr.* 2) *Acon. anac. ars. calc. cann. caust. cham. coccul. con. graph. hell. merc. natr. natr-m. n-vom. op. rhus. sil. sulph.* 3) *Ant. baryt. bry. cann. canth. chin. cin. coff. cupr. hep. rhus. stann. staph.*

§ 2. Use more particularly:

a) For *anguish*, anxiety: 1) *Ars. puls. veratr.* 2) *Acon. arn. bell. bry. calc. carb-v. cham. graph. ign. lyc. merc. n-vom. phos. rhus. samb. spig. spong. sulph.*—For *fear* and apprehensions: *Acon. anac. ars. baryt. bell. bry. calc. caust. cic. coccul. graph. hep. hyos. lach. merc. n-vom. op. sulph-ac. veratr.*—For *uneasiness* as if from a bad conscience: *Alum. amm. ars. aur. carb-veg. caust. cin. coccul. con. cycl. dig. ferr. graph. hyos. merc. n-vom. puls. sil. stram. sulph. veratr.*—For *anxiety* driving one from one place to another: *Acon. ars. aur. bell. bry. canth. carb-v. coloc. cupr. dros. graph. hyos. merc. n-vom. op. plat. puls. sep. spig. staph. stram. veratr.*

b) For *vexed* mood: 1) *Ars. calc. caust. cham. ign. kal. lyc. merc. nitr-ac. n-vom. phos. puls. sep. sulph.* 2) *Acon. alum. aur. bell. bry. chin. con. graph. hep. lach. natr. natr-m petr. phos. phos-ac. plat. sil. staph. zinc.*—For *irritable* vexed mood: 1) *Ars. bry. carb-v. caust. con. natr-m. nitr-ac. phos. puls. staph. sulph.* 2) *Arn. aur. bell. cham. chin. coccul. hep. ign. lyc. merc. natr.*

petr. phos-ac. plat. sep. spig.—For disposition to be *angry :* 1) *Aur. bry carb-v. cham. caust. hep. nitr-ac. n-vom. phos. sulph.* 2) *Arn. ars. caps. chin. croc. graph. lyc. magn-aust. natr. natr-m. petr. sep. sil.*

c) For *suspicion* and distrust: 1) *Baryt. caust. cic. hyos. lyc. puls.* 2) *Anac. ant. aur. bell. cham. dros. hell. lach. merc. op. ruta. sulph-ac.*—For *anthropophobia :* 1) *Amb. baryt. hyos. natr. puls. rhus.* 2) *Bell. cic. con. cupr. lyc. selen.*

d) For *nervous* excitement: 1) *Acon. arn. aur. bell. calc. cham. coff. magn-arct. merc. phos. val.* 2) *Asar. bry. carb-veg. chin. ferr. hep. hyos. lyc. natr-m. sep. sulph. teucr. veratr.*—For great *tendency* to *start :* *Acon. bell. borax. calc. carb-veg. caust. cham. coccul. con. natr-m. petr. phos. sil. sulph.*

e) For *malice :* 1) *Anac. bell. hyos. lach. lyc. n-vom. stram. veratr.* 2) *Ars. caps. cupr. natr. natr-m. petr. phos. plat. sec.*—For disposition to *swear : Anac. veratr.*—Disposition to *kill* somebody: *Ars. chin. hep. lach. stram.*—For disposition to commit *acts of violence :* 1) *Bell. hyos. stram. veratr.* 2) *Anac. ars. baryt. chin. coccul. cupr. hep. lach. lyc. mosch. natr. n-vom. plat.*—For *vindictive* mood: *Agar. anac. aur. lach.*—For *artful* disposition: *Cupr. lach. n-vom.*

f) For bold, *audacious* disposition: 1) *Ign. magn-arct. op.* 2) *Acon. agar. merc. sulph.*

g) For *obstinacy*, headstrongness: *Bell. calc. ign. kal. lyc. nitr-ac. n-vom. sil. sulph.*—For *quarrelsome* mood: 1) *Ars. caps. chin. ign. lach. merc. natr-m. veratr.* 2) *Arn. aur. bell. caust. cham. hyos. lach. lyc. mosch. n-vom. petr. sep. staph.*

h) For abundance of *fancies* and *fixed ideas :* 1) *Bell. coccul. ign. phos-ac. sabad. stram. sulph.* 2) *Acon. amb. cic. hell. hyos. lyc. merc. n-vom. op. phos. plat. puls. rhus. sec. sil. val. veratr.*—For *hypochondriac* ideas and apprehensions: 1) *Calc. chin. natr. n-vom. sulph.* 2) *Anac. aur. con. grat. lach. mosch. natr-m. phos. phos-ac. sep. staph.* 3) *Ars. caust. chin. graph. hell. hep. lyc. nitr-ac. n-mosch. petr. puls. rhus. val.*

i) For *serious* mood: *Alum. aur. bell. caust. cham. euphorb. hell. hyos. ign. led. merc. n-mosch. n-vom. phos-ac. puls. spig. stann.*—For *silent*, taciturn mood: *Aur. bell. caps. caust. cham. euphorb. hell. hyos. ign. ipec. lyc. n-vom. phos-ac. plat. puls. stann.*—For want of disposition to *talk :* 1) *Amb. bell. bry. ign. lach. n-vom. phos-ac. puls. stann.* 2) *Alum. calc. chin. coloc. cycl. hell. natr-m. plat. sulph.*

k) For *indifference*, apathy, listlessness: 1) *Ars. bell. calc. ign. phos. phos-ac. puls. sep. sil. staph.* 2) *Arn. cham. chin. coccul. con. merc. natr-m. nitr-ac. plat.*

l) For *vehement, angry* mood: 1) *Bry. carb-veg. caust. hep.*

lyc. natr-m. n-vom. sep. 2) ***Anac. aur.*** *dros. kal. lach. mosch. nitr-ac. petr. phos. plat. sulph.*

m) For *greedy desire* to possess a thing: 1) *Ars. bry. puls.* 2) *Calc lyc. sep.*

n) For *moaning, weeping*, lamenting: *Acon. ars. bell. bry. calc. cham. cin. coff. graph. hyos. ign. lyc. natr-m. n-vom. plat. puls. sep. stram. sulph. veratr.*

o) For merry mood, singing, whistling, dancing, &c.: 1) *Bell. coff. croc. lach. lyc. natr-m. op. plat. stram. veratr.* 2) *Aur. cann. carb-an. cic. hyos. natr. spong. zinc.*

p) For *despondency* and despair: *Acon. aur. calc. caust. con. graph. ign. lach. lyc. merc. natr. natr-m. nitr-ac. puls. rhus. sep. sil. stann. sulph. veratr.*—For being *tired of life*: *Amb. amm. ars. aur. bell. chin. lach. natr. natr-m. nitr-ac. phos. plat. rhus. sep. sil. staph. sulph. sulph-ac. thuj.*—For desire of *suicide*: 1) *Ars. aur. n-vom. puls.* 2) *Alum. ant. bell. carb-veg. chin. dros. hep. hyos. mez. rhus. sec. sep. spig. stram. tart.*

q) For *illusions* of *fancy*: 1) *Bell. stram.* 2) *Anac. lach. natr-m. op. puls. sil. sulph.* 3) *Acon. ars. bry. calc. canth. carb-veg. cham. dulc. hell. hep. kal. magn-m. merc. natr. nitr-ac. n-vom. phos. plat.*

r) For *religious* mania: 1) *Bell. hyos. lach. puls. stram. sulph.* 2) *Ars. aur. croc. lyc. selen.*

s) For *bland*, tender turn of mind: *Coccul. croc. ign. lyc. magn-arct. mosch. puls. sil.*

t) For *pride*, vanity, &c. 1) *Lyc. plat. stram. veratr.* 2) *Alum. arn. caust. chin. cupr. hyos. ipec. lach. par. phos.*

u) For *sadness*, melancholy, &c.: 1) *Ars. aur. bell. ign. lach. puls. sulph.* 2) *Acon. bry. calc. caust. cham. coccul. con. graph. hell. hyos. lyc. merc. natr-m. n-vom. petr. plat. rhus. sep. sil. staph. stram. sulph. veratr.*

v) For *amorous* disposition: 1) *Ant. hyos. veratr.* 2) *Graph. ign. lach. lyc. merc. natr-m. n-vom. plat. puls. sil. stram.*—For *lasciviousness*: 1) *Canth. hyos. phos. stram. veratr.* 2) *Chin. lach. lyc. merc. natr-m. n-mosch. n-vom. plat. puls.*

w) For *mania, craziness*, &c.: 1) *Acon. bell. calc. hyos. lach. n-vom. op. plat. stram. veratr.* 2) *Agar. anac. ant. arn. ars. cann. canth. caust. cic. coccul. coloc. con. croc. cupr. dig. dulc. ign. lyc. merc. natr. n-mosch. oleand. par. phos. plumb. puls. rhus. sec. sep. sil. sulph. zinc.*—For *rage*: 1) *Bell. canth. hyos. lyc. stram. veratr.* 2) *Agar. ars. camph. cann. coccul. croc. cupr. lach. merc. plumb. sec.*

x) For *fitful* mood: 1) *Acon. alum. bell. croc. ferr. ign. plat. stram. sulph-ac. zinc.* 2) *Aur. cann. caps. carb-an. caust. chin. coccul. cycl. ferr. graph. hyos. kal. lyc. magn-arct. natr-m. sep. val.*

§ 3. Compare: WEAK MEMORY, MENTAL DERANGEMENT, CLAIRVOYANCE, HYDROPHOBIA, HYPOCHONDRIA, MELANCHOLIA, &c.

ENTERITIS, INFLAMMATION OF THE BOWELS.—Give first a few doses of *Aconite*, to reduce the inflammation, after which, *Lach. bell.* or *merc.* will complete the cure.

In obstinate cases use: 1) *Ars. bry. hyos. n-vom.*; or, 2) *Ant. canth. cham. chin. coloc. ipec. nitr-ac. phos. puls. rhus. sec. squill. sulph.*, in accordance with the symptoms.

Compare: FEVERS, INFLAMMATORY, GASTRITIS, GASTRIC DERANGEMENT, CHOLERA, COLIC, DIARRHŒA, &c.

EPILEPSY.

Principal remedies: 1) *Bell. calc. caust. cic. cin. hyos. lach. op. stram. sulph.* 2) *Ars. camph. cham. coccul. ign. ipec. kal. lyc. natr-m. nitr-ac. n-vom. plumb. sep. sil.* 3) *Agar. con. plumb. stann.*

For particular indications see: SPASMS.

EPISTAXIS.

§ 1. Principal remedies: 1) *Acon. arn. bell. bry. chin. croc. merc. n-vom. puls. rhus. sulph.* 2) *Amb. cann. carb-v. cin. ferr. gran. kreos. led. sabin. sec. sep. sil.*, &c.

For *hæmorrhage* from the nose: 1) *Acon. chin.* 2) *Arn. bell. chin. merc. puls. rhus. sec.*

§ 2. If caused by *tendency of blood* to the head, give: 1) *Acon. bell. chin. croc. con.*; or, 2) *Alum. cham. graph. rhus.*

If occurring during a *cold*: *Ars.* or *Puls.*

If affecting children who have *worms*: *Cin.* or *Merc.*

For females who *menstruate scantily*: *Puls.* or *Sec.* or *Sep.* —If the menses be too *profuse*, give: *Acon. calc. croc. sabin.*— With *amenorrhœa*: *Bry. puls.* or *sep.*

For *debilitated* persons, in consequence of loss of blood, &c.: 1) *Chin.* or *sec.*; or, 2) *Carb-v. cin. ferr.*

If in consequence of being *stimulated* by spirits: *N-vom.*, or *Acon. bell. bry.*

If caused by *bodily exertions*: *Rhus. arn.*, or, *Bry. calc. puls. sulph.*

Epistaxis after a *blow, contusion*, requires: *Arn.*

§ 3. For the *disposition* to epistaxis, give: *Calc. carb-v. sep. sil.* or *sulph.*

Compare: HÆMORRHAGES, CONGESTIONS OF THE HEAD, CA-

TARRH, MENSTRUAL DIFFICULTIES, DEBILITY, HEAT, ILL EFFECTS OF, WORN OUT, INJURIES, &c.

ERGOTISM, RAPHANIA.—If caused by the use of spurred rye : *Solan-nigr.* is a specific.—Besides, we may require : *Acon. bell. colch. hyos. op. plat. stram. rhus.;* or, especially when gangrene sets in : *Ars. chin. euphorb. sil.*

ERUPTIONS, CUTANEOUS.—The size of this work only allows us to offer a condensed series of the principal symptoms, though it will be found sufficient to answer all ordinary demands.

Give for:

a) *Itching* eruptions: *Agar. ant. ars. bry. caust. cham. clem. kal. lach. merc. mez. nitr-ac. oleand. ran. rhus. sep. staph. sulph. veratr.—Biting : Amm-m. bry. calc. caust. euph. lach. led. lyc. mez. natr-m. oleand. phos-ac. puls. ran-sc. sulph.—Burning : Ambr. ars. bell. bry. caps. carb-v. caust. con. hep. kreos. lyc. merc. mez. ran. rhus. sil. staph. sulph. viol-tr.—Stinging-itching : Acon. ars. bar. bell. bry. clem. con. dros. hep. led. merc. nitr-ac. puls. ran. rhus. sep. sulph.*

b) *Painless* eruptions : *Amb. hell. hyos. lyc. stram. sulph.—Painful : Ant. arn. bell. chin. clem. cupr. dulc. hep. lyc. magn-m. phos-ac. puls. sep. sil. veratr.—Tearing* and painful : *Calc. lyc. mez. sep sil. staph. sulph.—Tensive* and painful : *Arn. bar. caust. con. phos. puls. rhus. sulph.*—Painful as if *sore* or *ulcerated : Alum. amm-m. arg. aur. bry. calc. caust. cic. colch. dros. graph. hep. kal. mang. merc. natr-m. nitr-ac. petr. phos. phos-ac. puls. rhus. sep. sil. staph. sulph. veratr. zinc.*

c) *Blue-coloured* eruptions : *Ars. bell. con. lach. ran. rhus.—Transparent : Cin. merc. ran. — Yellowish : Agar. ars. cic. euph. kreos. merc. natr. nitr-ac. sep.—Purple-coloured : Acon. bell.—Rose-coloured : Alum. natr-phos. sil.—Scarlet-coloured : Amm. ars. bell. croc. euph. hyos. merc. phos.—Blackish : Ars. bell. bry. lach. rhus. sec. sil.—Whitish : Agar. ars. bry. ipec. phos. sulph. thuj. val. zinc.*—With *white tips : Ant. puls. tart.*

d) *Readily bleeding : Calc. dulc. merc. sulph.—Blood-blisters : Ars. bry. natr-m. sec. sulph.—Gangrenous : Ars. bell. camph. carb-v. lach. mur-ac. ran. sabin. sec. sil.—Purulent : Ars. cic. clem. dulc. hep. lyc. magn-m merc. petr. rhus. sep. staph. tart. zinc.—Humid : Bov. calc. carb-v. cic. clem. graph. hep. kal. kreos. merc. nitr-ac. petr. rhus. sel. sep. staph. viol-tr.—Spreading : Ars. bor. calc. caust. cham. clem. con. graph. hep. kal. magn-c. merc. natr. nitr-ac. petr. rhus. sep. sil. squill. staph. sulph. viol-tr.—Scurfy : Alum. ant. ars bar. bell. bov. calc. carb-a. chel. cic. clem. coloc. con. dulc. graph. hell. hep. kal. lyc.*

merc. natr-m. oleand. ***puls*** *ran.* ***rhus. sassap.*** *sep.* ***sil.*** *staph.* ***sulph.*** *viol-tr.—Dry : Bar. bov. calc. carb-v. cupr. dulc. led. magn-c. merc. mez. petr. phos. sassap. sep. sil. staph. veratr. viol-tr. zinc.*

e) *Peeling off : Acon. amm. amm-m. bell. clem. cupr. led. merc. mez. phos. sep. sil. staph.—Scaly : Agar. amm-m. aur. cic. clem. dulc. led. magn-c. merc. oleand. phos. sulph.—Horny : Ant. graph. ran.—Cracked : Alum. calc. cham. cycl. hep. lach. merc. petr. puls. rhus. sassap. sep. sulph.*

f) Fine eruptions, with a *fine grain : Bry. carb-v. graph. hep. merc. phos-ac. sulph.—Grit-shaped : Graph. hep. natr-m.—Millet-shaped : Agar. ars. led. val.—Clustered : Agar. calc. ran. rhus. veratr.—Zone*-shaped : *Ars. graph. merc. puls. rhus. sil. sulph.—Grape*-shaped : *Calc. rhus. staph. veratr.—Confluent : Agar. cic. hyos. phos-ac. tart. val.*

g) *Pimple*-shaped : *Acon. ant. ars. bell. bry. caust. cham. dulc. graph. hell. hep. kal. merc. natr-m. nitr-ac. oleand. phos. phos ac. puls. rhus. sassap. sep. spong. staph. sulph. tart. thuj.—Vesicular : Amm-m. ant. ars. bell. bry. canth. caust. chin. clem. graph. hep. kal. lach. phos. ran. ran-sc. rhus. sulph.—Papular : Alum. ant. calc. caust. dulc. graph. hep. lach. lyc. mez. natr-m. puls. rhus. sep. sil. staph. veratr.—Pustulous : Ant. arn. ars. bell. hyos. merc. nitr-ac. puls. rhus. sil. staph. sulph. tart.*

h) Eruptions which only appear on *covered parts : Led. thuj.* —On *hairy* parts : *Kal. lyc. merc. natr-m. nitr-ac. phos-ac. rhus.*

§ 2. Compare : Blood-blisters, Variola, Herpes, Maculæ, Rash, Eruptions in the face, Scaldhead, Measles, Crusta lactea, Rubeolæ, Erysipelas, Scarlatina, &c.

ERUPTIONS IN THE FACE, Herpes, Spots, Ulcers.

§ 1. Principal remedies : 1) *Ars. aur. baryt. calc. carb-v. cic. dulc. graph. hep. led. lyc. magn-m. natr-m. nitr-ac. phos-ac. rhus. sep. sulph.* 2) *Amm. ant. bov. bry. caust. con. kreos. lach. sassap. sil. staph. veratr.*

§ 2. As regards simple *maculæ* and *pimples*, give :

a) For *freckles (ephelides) : Alum. ant. calc. dulc. graph. lyc. mur-ac. puls. sep. sulph.*

b) For *acne :* 1) *Ars. bell. calc. carb-v. hep. lach. sulph.* 2) *Aur. cann. canth. carb-an. caust. cic. kreos. led. natr. nitr-ac. n-vom. phos-ac. puls. rhus. ruta. sep. veratr.*

c) For *acne simplex* in young people, and especially high-livers : 1) *Bell. hep. led. n-vom. sulph.* 2) *Ars. calc. carb-v. lach. n-vom. phos-ac. puls.*

d) For *acne of drunkards: Kreos. led. n-vom.—Ars. lach. puls.*

e) For *acne rosacea:* 1) *Ars. carb-an. kreos. rhus. ruta. veratr.* 2) *Aur. calc. cann. canth. carb-v. caust. cic. led. lach. sep.*

f) *Acne punctata* (black pores, comedones): 1) *Graph. natr. nitr-ac. selen. sulph.* 2) *Bell. bry. calc. dig. dros. hep. natr-m. sabin.*

§ 3. As regards *herpes in the face*, give:

a) For *impetigo facialis* (humid scurf in the face): 1) *Calc. graph. sulph.* 2) *Ars. cic. lyc. rhus. sep.*

b) For *crusta lactea:* 1) *Rhus.* 2) *Calc. sulph.* 3) *Ars. baryt. cic. graph. lyc. merc. sassap.* (*Viol-tr. ? ? ?*)

c) For *scrofulous* (eruption from teething): 1) *Merc. sulph.* 2) *Calc. graph. rhus. sep.*

d) For *herpes furfuraceus:* 1) *Ars. bry. cic. sulph.* 2) *Anac. merc. thuj.*

e) For *lupus* or *impetigo rodens*, or *herpes exedens scrophulosus:* 1) *Ars. bell. hep. merc. sep. sil. staph. sulph.* 2) *Cic. graph. natr-m. nitr-ac.*

f) *Lupus* of the *wing of the nose, herpes exedens idiopathicus:* 1) *Staph.* 2) *Ars. ? aur. ? calc ? sep. ? sil. ? sulph. ?*

g) *Psoriasis facialis:* 1) *Calc. graph. lyc. sep. sulph.*

h) *Ulcerated corners of the mouth:* 1) *Amm. bell. calc. caust. graph. hep. ign. kreos. merc. natr-m. sil.* 2) *Ant. arn. natr. nitr-ac. phos. sep. sulph. veratr.*

i) *Mentagra* (*herpes of the chin*): 1) *Ant. cic. graph. sulph.* 2) *Carb-v. ? clem. ? dulc. ? kreos. ? merc. ? sassap. ? sep. ?*

k) *Crusta serpiginosa:* 1) *Ars. cic. graph. merc. sassap.* (2. *Calc. baryt. lyc. rhus.* (*Viol-tr. ?*)

§ 4. As regards *ulcers* of the *face* and *lips*, give:

a) For *cancerous ulcers:* 1) *Ars. bell. sil. sulph.* 2) *Clem. con. hep. merc.*

b) *Scrophulous* ulcers*:* 1) *Bell. hep. merc. sep. sil. staph. sulph.* 2) *Cic. ? graph. ? natr-m. ? nitr-ac. ? sulph-ac. ?*

§ 5. And lastly, give, as a general rule:

a) For *eruptions* on the *forehead: Ant. bell. caust. hep. kreos. led. natr-m. phos. phos-ac. rhus. sep. sil. staph. sulph.*

b) On the *temples: Alum. ant. bell. carb-v. caust. lyc. mur-ac. natr-m. sulph. thuj.*

c) Around the *eyes: Ars. con. hep. merc. staph. sulph.*

d) In the *eyebrows: Caust. kal. natr-m. selen. staph.*

e) On the *cheeks: Ant. bell. calc. caust. kreos. lach. natr. natr-m. phos. rhus. sep. sil. staph. veratr.*

f) On the *nose: Alum. aur. carb-an. carb-v. caust. graph. merc. natr. natr-m. nitr-ac. phos-ac. sep. sil. sulph.*

g) *Around the nose : Ant. caust. natr. rhus. sep. sil. sulph.*

h) On *mouth* and *lips : Ars. bry. calc. caust. kreos. natr-m. n-vom. rhus. sep. sil. staph. sulph.*

i) In the *corner* of the *mouth : Ant. amm. arn. bell. calc. caust. graph. hep. ign. kreos. merc. natr. natr-m. nitr-ac. phos. sep. sulph. veratr.*

k) On the *chin : Ant. bell. caust. con. graph. hep. kal. kreos. lyc. merc. natr-m. rhus. sep. sil. sulph. veratr.*

§ 6. Compare: ERUPTIONS, HERPES, MACULÆ, ULCERS, &c.

ERUPTIONS, HERPETIC.

Principal remedies: 1) *Ars. bov. calc. clem. con. dulc. graph. lyc. merc. oleand. rhus. sassap. sep. sil. sulph.* 2) *Bry. carb-v. caust. cin. hep. kreos. led. natr. natr-m. petr. ran. staph. zinc.*

§ 2. Use more particularly :

a) For *herpes phlyctænoides* s. *miliaris :* 1) *Acon. bell. rhus. sil. sulph.* 2) *Ars. bov. calc. lyc. merc. sep.*

b) For *herpes exedens* s. *phagedenicus, impetigo rodens, lupus :* 1) *Ars. graph. rhus. sil. sulph.* 2) *Alum. calc. cic. clem. con. merc. sep.*

c) *Herpes furfuraceus, pityriasis :* 1) *Ars. bry. calc. kreos. sil. sulph.* 2) *Dulc. graph. lyc. sep. sulph.* 3) *Anac. cic. lach. led. merc. natr-m. thuj.*

d) *Herpes crustaceus, impetigo :* 1) *Calc. lyc. sulph.* 2) *Con. graph. rhus.* 3) *Ars. cic. dulc. lach. merc. sep. sulph.*

e) *Herpes circinnatus :* 1) *Sep.* 2) *Natr. natr-m.* 3) *Calc.? caust.? sulph.?*

f) *Herpes squamosus, psoriasis :* 1) *Ars. clem. dulc. led. magn-c. merc. phos. rhus. sep. sulph.* 2) *Calc. caust. lyc. graph.*

g) *Psoriasis inveterata, herpetic rhagades :* 1) *Graph. lyc. sep. sulph.* 2) *Calc. hep. merc. puls. rhus. sil.*

h) *Lichen :* 1) *Coccul.? dulc.?* 2) *Acon? bry.? cic.? lyc.? mur-ac.? sulph?*

§ 3. As regards subjective symptoms, give :

a) For *burning* of the herpes: 1) *Ars. carb-v. caust. merc. rhus. sulph.* 2) *Calc. lyc. hep. puls. sep. staph.*

b) *Itching :* 1) *Ars. calc. caust. clem. merc. rhus. sep. sulph.* 2) *Bov. con. graph. nitr-ac. oleand. ran. sil. staph.*

c) *Stinging* or *tearing* pain of the eruption : *Calc. clem. lyc. merc. nitr-ac. puls. rhus. sep. sil. sulph.*

§ 4. Give more particularly:

a) For *yellowish*, brown-yellow *herpes: Merc. lyc. natr. sep.*

b) *Red: Cic. clem. dulc. lyc. magn-c. merc. staph.*

c) *Whitish: Ars. bry. graph. lyc. zinc.*

§ 5. a) *Impetigo*, humid herpes: 1) *Calc. dulc. graph. kreos. lyc. merc. rhus. sep.* 2) *Alum. bov. carb-v. caust. phos-ac. staph. sulph.*

b) *Dry* herpes: 1) *Dulc. led. merc. phos. sep. sil. veratr.* 2) *Baryt. bov. calc. clem. kreos. phos-ac. staph. sulph.*

c) *Suppurating:* 1) *Cic. clem. merc. rhus. sep.* 2) *Dulc. lyc. natr. sulph.*

d) *Readily bleeding: Ars. carb-v. lyc. merc. phos. phos-ac. sil. sulph.*

§ 6. For *local* herpes see: *Eruptions* in the *face*, on the *lips, chin, pudendum*, &c.

Compare: Eruptions, Maculæ, Ulcers, &c.

ERYSIPELAS.

§ 1. Principal remedies: 1) *Acon. bell. graph. lach. merc. puls. rhus.* 2) *Arn. ars. bry. calc. camph. canth. carb-an. cham. clem. hep. nitr-ac. phosph. plumb. sil. sulph.* 3) *Amm. carb-veg. chin. croc. euphorb. hyos. jod. kal. lyc. sep. stram. thuj.*

§ 2. For *simple* erysipelas, give: *Acon. bell. hep. lach.*

For erysipelas *fugax:* 1) *Bell. rhus.* 2) *Graph. puls.*

For *phlegmonous* erysipelas: 1) *Bell. graph. hep. merc. puls. rhus.* 2) *Acon. calc. chin. kal. lyc. nitr-ac. phosph. sulph. thuj.*

For *scarlet-coloured:* 1) *Amm. bell. hyos. merc. phosph.* 2) *Acon. ars. bry. croc. lach. stram. sulph.*

For *vesicular* erysipelas: 1) *Rhus.* 2) *Graph.* 3) *Ars. bell. hep. lach.*

For *zona:* 1) *Rhus.* 2) *Graph. puls.* 3) *Ars. merc. sil. sulph.*

§ 3. For *secondary* erysipelas, with œdematous swellings, give: 1) *Rhus;* or, 2) *Ars. chin. kal. merc. sulph.*

For herpetic erysipelas, with large, ulcerated surfaces: 1) *Clem. rhus.* 2) *Ars. graph. merc. sil. sulph.*

For *gangrenous* erysipelas: 1) *Ars. carb-veg.* 2) *Bell. camph. chin. lach. sabin. sec.*

§ 4. Compare: Swelling, Gangrene, Erysipelas in the face, Zona, Scarlatina, &c.

ERYSIPELAS FACIEI.—Principal remedies: 1) *Bell. lach. rhus.* 2) *Cham. graph. hep. puls. sulph.*; or, 3) *Acon. camph. canth. carb-an. carb-veg. euphorb. sep. stram.*

Belladonna: For delirium, stitching headache, furious look, violent thirst, dry tongue, parched lips and other symptoms pointing to an approaching metastasis to the meningeal membranes.

Lachesis: From the first, or when the cerebral affection did not yield to *Bell.*—After *Lach*, *Hep.* and *merc.* are sometimes indicated.

Rhus-tox.: For *vesicular* erysipelas, or erysipelas of the scalp, generally a specific.

Compare: Erysipelas, Swelling of the cheeks.

ERYTHRIASIS.—*Acon.*, given to the mother, is a specific remedy.

EXANTHEMATA, ACUTE.

§ 1. The principal remedies for acute exanthemata, (*variola, measles, rubeolæ, scarlatina, purple-rash*, &c.,) are:

1) *Acon. bell. bry. coff. merc. phosph. puls. sulph.* 2) *Ars. amm. baryt. chin. lach. hell. rhus. stram.*

§ 2. For the previous *inflammatory* fever, give: 1) *Acon.* 2) *Bell. bry. coff.*, and, in general, the remedies indicated for *inflammatory* fever.

§ 3. For the *eruption itself*, see the respective heads: Rash, Measles, Variola, Scarlatina, Varicella, Rubeolæ, &c.

As regards the appearance of the eruption, give:

For *maculæ*: *Acon. amm. bell. bry. phosph. puls.*

For *rash*: *Acon. bry. ipec. rhus. val.*

For *suppurating* eruption: 1) *Bell. merc. rhus.* 2) *Ars. ant. puls. sulph. tart.* 3) *Hyos.*

For *gangrenous* eruption: 1) *Ars. carb-veg.* 2) *Bell. hyos. lach. rhus. sec. sil.*

For *erysipelatous* eruptions: 1) *Bell. rhus.* 2) *Amm. euphorb. phosph.* 3) *Camph. carb-veg. graph.*

§ 4. *Suppression* of eruption by a cold or other causes, requires: 1) *Ars. bry. phosph. puls. stram. sulph.* 2) *Bell. caust. hell. phos-ac. op.*

If the suppression be attended with *metastasis to the brain*, give: 1) *Bell hell. stram.* 2) *Ars. arn. phos-ac. puls.*

If succeeded by *distress of breathing* and pain in the chest: *Bry. phosph. sulph.*

§ 5. *Secondary affections* require:

a) *Catarrhal* affections: *Bry. carb-veg. dros. dulc. hyos. ign. n-vom. sep.*

b) Affections of the *ear* and *sense of hearing: Bell. carb-veg. colch. hep. lyc. men. merc. nitr-ac. phosph. puls. sulph.*

c) *Diarrhœa: Chin. merc. puls. sulph. veratr.*

d) *Dropsy:* 1) *Ars. hell. dig.* 2) *Arn. bell. phos-ac. seneg. sulph.*

§ 6. Compare: VARIOLA, MEASLES, SCARLATINA, &c.

EXCRESCENCES, FUNGOUS. — Principal remedies: 1) *Ars. carb-an. carb-veg. phosph. sep. sil. sulph.* 2) *Ant. bell. calc. clem. con. kreos. lach. lyc. merc. nitr-ac. staph.* 3) *N-vom.? petr.? rhus.? sabin.? tart.? thuj.?*

For *fungus hæmatodes:* 1) *Ars. carb-an. phosph.* **sil.** 2) *Carb-veg. lach. lyc. merc. nitr-ac. sulph.* 3) *Calc.? clem.? kreos.? n-vom.? rhus.? sabin.? sep.? staph.? tart.? thuj.?* The principal remedies are: *Calc.* and *phosph.* at long intervals.

For *fungus medullaris:* 1) *Bell. carb-an. phosph thuj.* 2) *Sil.? sulph.?*

For *fungus articulorum:* 1) *Ant. kreos. lach. sil.* 2) *Ars. jod. lyc. phosph. staph.* 3) *Clem.? petr.? rhus.? sabin.? sulph.?*

EXERCISE, DREAD OF.—A mere symptom which, in conjunction with other symptoms, generally points to: 1) *Ars. bell. chin. lach. natr. natr-m. n-vom. sulph. tart.* 2) *Acon. calad. caps. chel. dulc. hell. hyos. ign. jod. merc. mez. mur-ac. rut. thuj.*

EXHALATION, DEFICIENT.—A symptom which, with the other symptoms that exist with it, generally points to:

1) *Acon. bell. calc. cham. chin. colch. dulc. graph. kal. led. lyc. n-mosch. phos. sen. sil. sulph.* 2) *Amm. arn. ars. cann. caust. coff. hep. hyos. jod. ipec. lach. magn-c. mur-ac. natr. nitr-ac. phos-ac. plat. puls. rhus. sabad. sec. sep. staph. verb. viol-od.*

EYES, CONTRACTION OF.—Principal remedies: 1) *Agar.?* 2) *Ant. arn. canth. croc. crotal. squill.* — See OPHTHALMIA.

EYES, NEURALGIC PAINS IN THE.

§ 1. For true *neuralgic* pains, give: 1) *Bell. chin. hyos. spig.* 2) *Asar. caust. guaj. hep. par. phos-ac. plumb. thuj.*

§ 2. As regards the *pains*, with or without inflammation, give:

a) For sensation as if the eyeballs were *too large: Bell. spig.*

—*Asar. caust. guaj. hep. hyos. natr. natr-m. op. par. phos-ac. plumb. sen. tar. thuj.*

b) For pains which increase by *contact: Bell. chin. hell. hep. sulph.*—By *motion: Arn. ars. bell. bry. calc. cham. chin. hep. led magn-aust. natr-m. n-vom. phos. ran. spig. sulph.*—For *boring* pains: *Bis. calc. hep. kal. natr-m. spig. thuj.*—*Burning* pains: *Acon. ars. asar. bell. bry. calc. carb-v. coloc. croc. crotal. euphr. lach. lyc. magn-m. merc. n-vom. phos. phos-ac. rhus. sep. spong. sulph.*—Aggravation by *turning the eyes: Acon. bry. caps. cupr. lyc. n-vom. puls. rhus. sep. sil. spig.*—For *aching* pains: *Arn. bar. bell. bry. calc. carb-v. caust. chin. cin. cupr. graph. ign. lach. lyc. merc. nitr-ac. n-vom. ol-an. puls. rhus. rut. sabad. sep. spig. staph. sulph. veratr. zinc.*—Sensation as of a *thread* being *drawn* through the eyes: *Bry. ign. lach. mur-ac. par. plat. valer.*—Sensation as of a *foreign body (sand* or *dust): Acon. bell. bry. calc. carb-v. chin. cin. con. graph. ign. merc. natr-m. nitr-ac. phos. puls. spig. sulph. sulph-ac. thuj.*—*Pressing-down* pains: *Aur. cann. hell. oleand. par. puls.*—Pressure from *within outward: Acon. asar. bell. bry. cann. canth. caust. con. dros. guaj. ign. led. magn-arct. n-vom. par. puls. ran. rhus. spig. val.*—*Stitches* from *within outward: Calc. cocc. dros. natr. sil. sulph.*—*Pressure* from *without inward: Agar. anac. aur. bis. chin. phos-ac. spig. zinc.*—*Stitches* from *without inward: Arn. bell. phos.*—*Feeling of coldness in the eyes: Alum. amm. berb. calc. con. kal. lyc. magn-arct. par. plat.*—*Beating* pains: *Acon. ars. bell. bry. calc. (cham. cocc.) ign. magn-aust. (phos.) petr.*—*Pinching* pains: *Croc. nitr-ac.*—*Bone-pains* in the cavities: *Aur. hep. merc. natr-m. nitr-ac. phos. phos-ac rhus. staph. sulph.*—*Tearing* pains: *Ars. bell. bry. (cham. chin. colch. con.) kal. led. lyc. magn-c. (merc.) n-vom. (puls.) sen. sil. sulph. zinc.*—*Scraping* pains: *Ars. lyc. puls. rhus.*—*Cutting* in the eyes: *Bell. calc. canth. coloc. kal lyc. merc. mur-ac. puls. rhus. spig. sulph. veratr.*—Pains as if *sore* or *excoriated: Alum. arn. bar. bry. carb-v. croc. euphr. jod. kal. lyc. magn-aust. natr-m. nitr-ac. n-vom. phos. sep. sil. staph. sulph.*—*Feeling of heaviness* in the eyes: *Bell. calc. natr. plat. sep.*—*Tension* in the eyes: *Acon. aur. calc. led. lyc. natr-m. phos. sulph-ac.*—*Stitching* pains: *Ars. bell. bry. calc. coloc. con. dig. euphr. graph. hep. lyc. merc. nitr-ac. phos. puls. sen. sep. spig. thuj. val. veratr.*—Feeling as if *bruised: Arn. bry. chin. cupr. hep. lyc. n-vom. rhus. sulph. veratr.*

For further details, see: PAIN, PAROXYSMS OF, and CONDITIONS.

EYES, SUPPURATION OF.—Remedies: 1) *Caust. euphr. kreos. nitr-ac.* 2) *Bell. bry. graph.*

Compare: OPHTHALMIA.

FALLING OFF OF THE HAIR, Allopecia.

§ 1. Principal remedies: 1) *Calc. hep. graph. kal. lyc. nitr-ac. phos-ac. sil. sulph.* 2) *Aur. bar-c. carb-v. caust. chin. kal. magn. merc. natr-m. sep. staph. zinc.*

§ 2. Falling off of the hair after *severe acute diseases,* requires: 1) *Lyc. hep. sil.;* or, 2) *Calc. carb-v. natr-m. phos-ac.* and *sulph.*—To *lying-in females* give: *Calc. lyc. natr-m. sulph.*

If caused by *loss of animal fluids,* (depletion, excesses, &c.) give: *Chin. ferr.;* and, if caused by frequent sweats, give: *Merc.*

If caused by *long grief,* give: *Phos-ac.* or *staph.;* or, *Caust. graph. ign. lach.*

If caused by *nervous* or *hysteric* headache, give: 1) *Hep. nitr-ac.* 2) *Ant. calc. sil. sulph.;* or, 3) *Aur. phos. sep.*

If caused by *abuse of Mercury,* give: *Hep.* or *carbo-v.;* and if by *abuse of China,* give: *Bell.* or *hep.*

§ 3. As regards the condition of the *scalp* and *hair,* give for *sensitiveness of the scalp: Calc. bar-c. carb-v. chin. hep. natr-m. sil. sulph.*

For violent *itching* of the *scalp,* especially if in consequence of old *suppressed eruptions,* give: *Graph. kal. lyc. sil. sulph.*

For *scales* on the head: *Calc. graph. magn. staph.*

For the *disposition* of the hair to turn *gray,* give: *Graph. lyc. phos-ac. sulph-ac.*

For great *dryness* of the hair: *Calc. kal. phos-ac.*

When the hair is frequently covered with *viscid sweat: Chin. merc.*

§ 4. Moreover,—a) When the hair falls off on the *sides* of the head: 1) *Graph. phos.* 2) *Kal.? zinc.?*

b) On the *sinciput: Ars. natr-m. phos.*

c) On the *vertex: Baryt. graph. lyc. sep. zinc.*

d) On the *occiput:* 1) *Carb-v. phos. sil.* 2) *Petr.?*

e) On the *temples: Calc. kal. lyc. natr-m.*

f) For some places getting *bald:* 1) *Canth. phos.* 2) *Jod.*

g) Behind the *ears: Phos.*

§ 5. For falling off of the hair on other parts of the body:

a) In the eyebrows: *Agar. bell. caust. kal.*

b) *Whiskers: Calc. graph. natr-m.*

c) *Moustaches: Kal. natr-m. plumb.*

d) On the *mons veneris: Natr. natr-m. rhus.*

§ 6. Compare: Scaldhead, Nails, Itching of the skin, &c.

FEBRIS HELODES, Sudor anglicus.—Hahnemann recommends *Samb.*—The best remedies in my own practice have proved to be *Acon.* and *Bry.*; the former sometimes breaks the disease in a few hours.

FEVER, CATARRHAL AND RHEUMATIC.

§ 1. The principal remedies are: 1) *Acon. ars. bell. bry. caust. cham. chin. dulc. merc. n-vom. puls. rhus. sulph.*; also, 2) *Arn. camph. coff. ipec. phos. sabad. sang. sil. spig. squill. stann. veratr.*

§ 2. For violent *acute* fever, give: 1) *Acon. bell. bry. cham.*; or, 2) *Ars. coff. ign. merc. puls. rhus. squill.*

If the fever should be *light*, or if it *abate*, use: 1) *Chin. dulc. n-vom. puls. rhus.*; or, 2) *Arn. ipec. phos. seneg. veratr.*

For *profuse* sweats without relief: *Bry. chin. merc. sulph.*

For *violent* pains: 1) *Acon. ars. cham. coff. ign.*; or, 2) *Merc. puls. sulph.*

§ 3. For *catarrhal* ailments after fever: 1) *Sulph. phos. seneg. stann.*; or, 2) *Ars. bry. dulc. merc. puls. sil. squill.*

For *rheumatic affections*: 1) *Caust. chin. phos. sil. sulph.*; or, 2) *Hep. lach.*

§ 4. Compare: Bronchitis, Rheumatism, Sore Throat, Headache, Ophthalmia, Cough, Toothache, &c.

See likewise: Inflammatory fever, Gastric fever, Typhus, &c.; also: Pleuritis, Influenza, Angina pectoris, &c.

FEVER, GASTRIC AND BILIOUS.

§ 1. Principal remedies: 1) *Acon. bell. bry. cham. cocc. ipec. merc. n-vom. puls.* 2) *Ant. coloc. dig. rhus. squill. tart. veratr.* or, 3) *Daph. gran.? sulph.*

§ 2. As regards the *varieties* of fever, give:

When the gastric symptoms are predominant: 1) *Ipec. n-vom. puls.*; or, 2) *Ant. bry. cham. cocc. dig. rhus. sulph. tart. veratr.*; or, 3) *Bell. daph. squill.*

When the *bilious* symptoms: 1) *Acon. bry. cham. chin. cocc. n-vom. puls.*; or, 2) *Ars. coloc. daph. dig. gran.? ipec. sulph.*

When the *mucous* symptoms: 1) *Bell. chin. dig. merc. puls. rhus.*; or, 2) *Ars. cham. cin. dulc. ipec. n-vom. rhab. spig. sulph.*

When *worm* symptoms are predominant, give: 1) *Cic. cin. merc sil. spig. sulph.*; or, 2) *Acon. dig. hyos. n-vom. sabad. stann. stram. teucr. val.*

§ 3. According to the character of these fevers, give :

When *inflammatory* (*inflammatory gastric fever*) *: Bell. bry. cham. merc. puls. tart.*—*Aconite* is only indicated when bilious symptoms are present, never by purely gastric symptoms.

When the character of the fever is *typhoid*, use : 1) *Bell. bry. cocc. rhus. veratr.; or*, 2) *Ars. carb-v. chin, hyos.*, &c.

When *putrid*, use : *Ars. carb-v. chin. merc. mur-ac. phos-ac. rhus. sulph. sulph-ac.*

See : INFLAMMATORY FEVER, TYPHUS.

§ 4. As respects causes, give :

a) For gastric fever arising from *indigestion :* 1) *Ipec. puls.* ; or, 2) *Ant. bry. n-vom. sulph. tart.*

b) From a *cold : Acon. bell. bry. cham. ipec. merc. n-vom. puls. sulph.*

c) From swallowing *cold water, ice* or *acids :* 1) *Ars. puls.* ; or, 2) *Natr-m. sulph. sulph-ac. lach.*

d) From *chagrin* or *anger ;* 1) *Cham. coloc.;* or, 2) *Acon. bry. chin. n-vom. staph.*—If the patient had used much chamomile-tea, give *Puls.*

§ 5. Particular indications :

ACONITE : When bilious symptoms prevail, such as : Yellow coating on the tongue, bitter taste in the mouth and of food and drink, except water; burning thirst; bitter eructations, bitter, greenish or slimy vomiting, (vomiting of ascarides) ; distention of the hypochondria; painfulness of the region of the liver, with stitches and pressure ; *suppressed* stool, or small frequent stools with tenesmus ; *red, scanty* urine ; *dry heat* with full frequent pulse, sleeplessness and restlessness; moaning, quarrelsome, vehement disposition. (Compare : *Bry. cham.*)

BELLADONNA : The tongue is coated yellowish or white, thick coating ; aversion to drink and food, sour taste of the mouth and rye-bread; vomiting of sour, bitter or slimy substances; slimy diarrhœa ; dry heat, especially about the head, with thirst, alternating with chills ; anguish, restlessness, suspicious or whimsical mood, violent headache as if every thing would fall out at the forehead; dry mouth ; difficult deglutition ; sopor in the day-time, sleepless nights, &c. (Compare : *Cham.* and *Merc.*)

BRYONIA : Dry, brownish-yellow tongue ; putrid smell from the mouth ; bitter taste, especially after sleeping, or pappy, insipid or foul taste ; great desire for wine, sour drinks, or coffee, with aversion to solid food ; nausea, accumulation of mucus in the stomach, frequent desire to vomit, or real vomiting of bile, especially after drinking ; stitches in the head, in the pit of the stomach or side, in the extremities, especially when coughing or walking ; pressure and tension in the pit of the stomach, especially after eating; constipation: watery, clear or yellowish urine with yellowish sediment; violent heat, with burning thirst, or chilliness and shuddering over the whole body, with redness (and heat) of the face; vehement disposition; great debility; dulness of the head with vertigo, &c. (Compare: *Acon. cham. nux-vom.*)

CHAMOMILLA: Red and chapped or yellowish-coated tongue; bitter taste of the mouth and food; fetid smell from the mouth; loss of appetite, nausea, or bitter or sour eructations and vomiting; great anguish, tension and pressure in the region of the stomach, hypochondria, and especially in the pit of the stomach; flatulent colic with tearing pains and distention of the abdomen; constipation, or diarrhœic, greenish stools, or sour diarrhœic stools mixed with fæcal matter and mucus resembling stirred eggs; yellowish urine with flocculent sediment; hemicrania; pains in the limbs; great nervousness with restlessness and moaning, or vehement disposition; asthma; heat, especially of the face and eyes, with red cheeks (sometimes only of one cheek), or heat mixed with shivering and the hair standing on end; sleeplessness with restlessness, or restless sleep with anxious dreams, starting, &c. (Compare: *Acon. bell. nux-v. puls.*)

COCCULUS: Yellow-coated tongue; loathing of food; dry mouth, with or without thirst; fetid eructations and desire to vomit; painful fulness of the stomach, with difficult breathing; constipation, or soft stools with burning at the anus; great debility, with sweat on taking the least exercise; headache, especially in the forehead, with vertigo, &c. (This remedy is frequently suitable after abuse of *Chamomile.*)

IPECACUANHA: Yellow coating on the tongue, with dry mouth; loathing of food (especially greasy things), with desire to vomit; fetid odour from the mouth; bitter taste in the mouth, and of food); nausea, with regurgitation of the ingesta, and vomiting of undigested food; pressure and painful fulness in the pit of the stomach; colic; diarrhœic, yellowish stools, or fetid, putrid stools; pale, yellowish colour of the skin; headache, especially in the forehead; febrile heat with thirst or shiverings. (Compare: *Nux-v.* and *Puls.*)

MERCURIUS: Moist tongue, coated white or yellowish; dry and burning lips, nauseous, foul or bitter taste; nausea with desire to vomit, or vomiting of mucus and bitter substances; painfulness of the hypochondria, pit of the stomach, or around the umbilicus, especially at night, with anguish and restlessness; sleepy in the day-time, *wakeful at night;* peevish, irritable mood; chills alternating with heat; *burning* thirst, sometimes with aversion to beverage, &c. (Compare: *Bell.*)

NUX VOM: Dry and white, or yellowish-coated tongue, especially towards the root; burning thirst with burning in the throat; bitter or foul taste, bitter eructations, constant nausea, especially in the open air; desire to vomit, or vomiting of undigested food; cardialgia with aching pain; painful pressure and tension in the whole region of the stomach and hypochondria; spasmodic colic with pinching and rumbling in the umbilical region; constipation with frequent but ineffectual urging to stool, or with small, diarrhœic, slimy or watery stools; aching pain in the forehead, with vertigo; angry, vehement, peevish, hypochondriac mood; great debility and languor; red and hot, or yellowish and livid face; heat, mixed with chills or shuddering; bruised feeling in the limbs; aggravation of the symptoms towards morning, &c. (Compare: *Acon. bry. cham. ipec.* and *puls.*)

Pulsatilla: Whitish mucus coating on the tongue; flat, pappy or bitter taste, especially after swallowing; eructations tasting of the food which one had just eaten, or bitter eructations; aversion to food, especially to fat and meat, with desire for sour or spirituous drinks; waterbrash; regurgitation of the ingesta; nausea, great desire to vomit; vomiting of slimy and whitish, bitter and greenish substances, or sour substances; vomiting of undigested food; pressure in the pit of the stomach, with difficult breathing; constipation, or diarrhœic, white, slimy, or bilious and greenish stools; or stools resembling stirred eggs; hemicrania; frequent chills with absence of thirst; or dry heat and thirst; alternate pale and red face, or one cheek is red and the other pale; sad mood, with whining, moaning, and restlessness. (Compare: *Cham. ipec.* and *nux-vom.*)

§ 6. We may likewise use:

Antimonium: In consequence of indigestion, with loss of appetite, loathing of food, nausea and desire to vomit; these ailments neither yield to *Ipec.* nor *Puls.*

Colocynthis: Indigestion with the following symptoms: Bilious fever with cardialgia, spasmodic colic and diarrhœic stools which come on again after eating ever so little; cramps in the calves, &c.; *Cham. bry. nux-v.* or *puls.* were unable to effect a change.

Digitalis: Nausea early on rising; bitter taste in the mouth, thirst, slimy vomiting, diarrhœic stools and great debility.

Rhus tox.: Great debility, delirium, putrid diarrhœa, dry tongue, thirst, and typhoid symptoms.

Squilla: The disease is accompanied with pleuritic stitches, and neither *Acon.* nor *Bry.* helps.

Tartarus: In children, especially when catarrhal symptoms occur at the same time, with loose cough, profuse secretion of mucus, and difficulty of breathing.

Veratrum: Great debility after an evacuation, with fainting turns; yellowish colour of the skin; dry tongue or tongue coated yellowish or brownish, &c.

§ 7. For more details, see: Gastric derangements, Inflammatory fever, Typhus, Catarrhal fever, &c.

FEVER, HECTIC.

§ 1. Principal remedies: *Ars. calc. chin. cocc. ipec. phos. phos-ac. sil. sulph.;* also, *Bell. con. cupr. dig. hell. ign. jod. kal. lach. lyc. merc. n-vom. puls. sep. stann. staph. veratr. zinc.*

§ 2. For *slow nervous fever,* give: *Ars. chin. cocc. merc. mosch. n-vom. phos-ac. staph. veratr.*

Hectic fevers attended with local chronic inflammations, suppurations, &c., require the remedies which correspond to the respective organic affections, principally: 1) *Ars. calc. chin. cocc ipec. phos. sil. sulph.;* or, 2) *Bell. canth. hep. lach. lyc. merc. puls.*

Hectic fevers caused by *emotions,* long *grief, homesickness,* &c., require: *Phos-ac. staph.;* or, *Ign. lach. merc.,* and even *Ars. graph.*

If caused by debilitating loss of animal fluids, by depletion, sexual excesses, &c., give: 1) *Chin. n-vom. phos-ac. sulph.;* or, 2) *Calc. cin. lach, staph.,* &c.

If coming after severe *acute* diseases, such as *typhus, cholera,* &c., give: 1) *Cocc. hell. hyos. phos-ac.;* or, 2) *Ars. chin. veratr.*

Hectic fevers may likewise result from dyscrasia (scrophula, syphilis, &c.), or from abuse of medicinal substances, or from slow poisoning, in which case give the antidotes indicated under these respective heads.

§ 3. Particular indications.

Arsenicum: Great emaciation with debility and palpitation of the heart; night-sweats, with hot and dry skin in the day-time; *thirst,* obliging one to drink frequently, but little at one time; restless sleep, unrefreshing, disturbed by sudden starting; constant desire to lie down; irritable and strange mood; loss of appetite, with weak digestion, &c.

Calcarea: Constant heat with little thirst, or frequent paroxysms of flushes of heat, with anguish and palpitation of the heart, or constant shuddering, especially in the evening, with red cheeks; withering, dry skin; emaciation, debility with listlessness; loss of appetite; paroxysms of anguish, in the evening; dry and short cough; great desire to be magnetised; great prostration after talking; sweat breaking out easily; great apprehensions about one's health; slow, weak digestion; night-sweats, &c.

CHINA: Pale complexion and sunken cheeks and eyes; great listlessness; dry and flaccid skin; sleeplessness, or restless sleep, unrefreshing, with anxious dreams; loss of appetite with desire for dainties; or great hunger, even voracious, with weak digestion; ill-humour, malaise, distended abdomen and other ailments after eating; frequent sweats, especially at night; frequent diarrhœic stools, even with discharge of undigested food.

COCCULUS: Great debility and trembling after the least exertion; frequent flushes of heat, especially in the face; blue margins around the eyes; dry mouth; loss of appetite; oppression of the chest with orgasm of the blood, and anguish; great *sadness;* sudden starting from sleep, and anxious dreams; frequent nausea; sweat easily breaks out during motion; bland temper.

IPECACUANHA: Dry and extremely troublesome heat, especially in the evening, with thirst; great restlessness, burning in the palms of the hands and night-sweats; parchment-like skin; *desire for dainties* only; very listless; out of breath after the least motion, &c.

PHOSPHORUS: Dry cough with short and oppressed breathing; chilliness towards evening, followed by dry heat; *debilitating diarrhœa;* exhausting *clammy night-sweats;* emaciation, debility, &c.

PHOSPHORIC ACID: Sad, oppressed mood; taciturn, listless; the hair turns gray; febrile heat in the evening, with anguish and accelerated pulse; debilitating sweats, in the morning, &c.

SILICEA: Pale, livid complexion, dry, short cough; emaciation; loss of appetite; shortness of breath; debility, especially in the joints; febrile heat in the evening or morning, &c.

SULPHUR: Febrile heat, especially towards evening, with sharply circumscribed redness of the cheeks (especially the left cheek); dry skin, with thirst; thin, pale face; dry or diarrhœic and slimy stools; short, oppressed breathing; palpitation of the heart; sweat towards morning; debility, tired feeling in the limbs, with heaviness, dry cough, &c.

Compare: PLUMONARY PHTHISIS, LARYNGEAL PHTHISIS, TUBERCLES, &c.

FEVERS, INFLAMMATORY, SYNOCHA, SYNOCHUS, &c.

§ 1. The principal remedies for inflammatory fevers, or acute fevers with local inflammations, are: 1) *Acon. bell. bry. hyos. merc. n-vom. phos. puls. rhus.* 2) *Ars. cann. cham. kal. lyc. nitr. sulph. veratr.* 3) *Chin. chinin. coccul. coloc. coff. hep. ipec. lach. mez. natr-m. nitr-ac. op. phos. sec. sep.*

§ 2. For *simple synochal fevers we use :* 1) *Acon.* 2) *Bell. bry.* 3) *Ars. cham. hyos. merc. puls. rhus. sulph.*

If they assume a typhoid character, with symptoms of cerebral irritation, the following remedies are required: 1) *Bell. bry. hyos. op. rhus.* ; or, 2) *Cham. coccul. n-vom. phos-ac. stram.*, and others.

See: TYPHUS, also: TYPHUS PUTRIDUS.

§ 3. If these fevers should be attended by symptoms of *meningitis, pleurisy, pneumonia,* violent *pains* in the *stomach, enteritis,* &c., *acute cutaneous eruptions, vomiting, diarrhœa,* &c., give the remedies indicated under these respective heads.

In every local inflammation, no matter what organ is affected, *Aconite* is the principal remedy when the fever is violent, with thirst, dry, burning heat, and a hard (full or not full) pulse; *Acon.* should be continued until the inflammatory pulse is subdued. Very sensitive persons sometimes require the alternate use of *Coffea* and *Acon.*

§ 5. Particular indications.

ACONITUM: *Burning heat,* sometimes preceded by chills or shuddering; burning *thirst;* dry and *burning skin;* bloated, *hot* and *red* face, or *red spots* on the cheeks; or *redness of face* which alternates with *paleness* especially when the patient raises himself; red, inflamed and painful eyes; sleeplessness; restlessness, *agonizing tossing about,* sometimes attended with anguish, dread of death, screams; full and *hard* or *subdued* pulse; violent stitching, or aching and beating pain in the head; vertigo on raising the head; nightly delirium; dry lips and mouth; clean and moist tongue; hurried, stuttering speech; dark-red urine; oppression of the chest, with short, anxious, hurried breathing; stitches in the chest or sides; short cough; *palpitation* of the heart; pains in the limbs. (Compare: *Bell. bry. cham.*)

BELLADONNA: Internal and external heat with *dark-red face and eyes;* burning thirst, with aversion to drink, or constant desire to drink without ability to do so; moist (and clammy) skin; *sleepiness in the day-time, sleepless at night;* or restless sleep with *sudden starting,* twitching of the limbs, *loss of consciousness,* muttering, grasping at flocks, or screams and convulsions, or *furibond delirium,* frightful visions, desire to escape from bed; obstinate and malicious; *hot head;* violent headache, especially in the forehead, as if every thing would issue through the forehead; *dilated pupils;* furious and wandering look; *photophobia;* dry mouth and lips; *ulcerated corners* of the mouth; hurried and indistinct speech; *sore throat* with difficulty of swallowing; cough with headache and redness of the face; scanty, yellow urine ; stitching pains in the limbs ; *red spots* on the skin. (Compare: *Acon. cham. merc.*)

Bryonia: Great heat or chill with chattering of teeth, either one or the other symptom attended with *redness* and *heat* of the *head* and *face; nightsweat*, especially towards morning; unquenchable thirst, sometimes followed by vomiting; drowsiness, with sudden starting, screams and delirium, as soon as the patient closes his eyes; *delirium* day and *night;* irritable mood, or apprehensions on account of his illness, dread of death; taciturn; restless, tossing about, grasping at flocks; *great* and *general debility;* hard, full and hurried pulse; stupefying headache, with vertigo on raising the head; dulness of hearing and sight; dry lips; pressure in the pit of the stomach; constipation; dry cough, with pain in the pit of the stomach; stitches in the chest or side; tearing or stitching pains in the limbs. (Compare: *Acon. bell. cham. nux-vom.*)

Chamomilla: Internal and external heat, sometimes preceded by chill; or heat in the face and eyes, with red cheeks or only one cheek being red; burning thirst, with burning from the mouth to the stomach; sleeplessness, with restlessness and tossing about; or sleep with anxious dreams and sudden starting; great restlessness and anguish; hemicrania; vertigo on raising the head, with darkness or scintillations before the eyes and fainting turns; red and cracked tongue; *bitter taste* in the mouth and of the food; sour or bitter eructations and vomiting; *anguish*, tension and pressure in the region of the stomach and hypochondria; colic and diarrhœa; hot, burning urine; tearing in the limbs, face and head; fetid breath; distress of breathing, and orthopnœa. (Compare: *Acon. bell. nux-vom.*)

Mercurius: Chills alternating with heat, red skin, *burning thirst*, sometimes with aversion to drink; frequent full pulse; stitching and aching pains in the head; red, bloated face; vertigo on raising one's-self; dry and burning lips; moist tongue or coated white or yellowish; painful sensitiveness in the region of the hypochondria, epigastrium and umbilicus; great anguish, tossing about, sleeplessness; sleepy in the day-time; peevish and disposed to be vehement. (Compare: *Bell.*)

Nux vom.: Heat, especially in the face, sometimes mixed with shuddering; dry and burning skin; hard, frequent pulse; great debility and fainting turns; anguish with palpitation of the heart and dread of death; extreme nervousness; sleeplessness or comatose sleep; headache worse on stooping; vertigo on stooping; hot, *red* face, sometimes accompanied with chilliness of the body; dull, dim, red eyes; *dry* and *white* tongue; thirst with burning in the throat; aching pain in the stomach and region of the stomach; constipation; bruised feeling in the limbs; vehement, irritable mood. (Compare: *Bry.* and *Cham.*)

§ 6. Of other remedies, use:

ARSENICUM: For burning heat at night, with burning in the veins; sleeplessness with great restlessness and tossing about; anguish, with despair and dread of death; great *debility* and necessity to lie down.

CHINA: Heat, dry mouth, parched and burning lips, red face, delirium, chill as soon as the patient uncovers himself ever so little; debility and pains in the limbs.

COFFEA: Suitable to children: for great restlessness, tossing about, nervousness, screams, weeping.

HYOSCYAMUS: Violent delirium, sleeplessness from nervous excitement, subsultus tendinum, grasping at flocks; red and hot face; red, staring and sparkling eyes.

LYCOPODIUM: Circumscribed redness of the cheeks, cerebral irritation, debility, dry and red tongue; constipation, ill humour after sleeping, screams, headstrongness and grumbling.

PULSATILLA: Dry heat at night, especially in the face, with heat and redness of one cheek; delirium; whining mood; no thirst, or else unquenchable thirst; tongue covered with white mucus; painfulness of the pit of the stomach; bitter taste, diarrhœic, slimy stools.

RHUS-T.: Great heat, anguish, dry skin, stupefying headache, delirium with desire to escape; red, burning face; red, dry and rough tongue; debility; grasping at flocks.

SULPHUR: Frequently useful for the ailments remaining after the use of *Acon. bell.* or *bry.*

Compare: GASTRIC FEVER, BILIOUS FEVER, HECTIC FEVER, TYPHUS, and all the local inflammations.

FEVER PUERPERAL.

The best remedies are: 1) *Acon. bell. bry. cham. coff. coloc. n-vom. rhus.*; or, 2) *Arn. ars. hyos. ipec. lam. merc. plat. puls. sec. stram. veratr.*

ACONITUM: Violent fever, with dry and burning heat, violent, burning thirst and desire for cold drinks; red and hot face, short breath, difficult and sighing breathing; distended abdomen and sensitive to contact; periodical cutting pains through the whole abdomen; scanty, bleeding and fetid lochia. (After *Acon.* use *Bell.* or *bry.*)

BELLADONNA: Distended abdomen, with stitching and digging pains; violent spasmodic colic, as if part of the intestines were grasped with claws, or painful pressing downwards towards the sexual organs; the abdomen is sensitive to contact; chills in some parts, heat in others, or else burning heat, especially about the face and head, with red face and eyes; aching in the forehead, with throbbing of the carotids; dry mouth with red tongue and thirst; difficult deglutition with spasms of the fauces; sleeplessness with tossing about; or sopor, with furibond delirium or other cerebral symptoms; the lochia are scanty, watery and slimy; or metrorrhagia, with coagulated, fetid blood; the breasts are swollen and inflamed or else flaccid and without milk; constipation, or diarrhœic, slimy stools. (If *Bell.* be insufficient, try *Hyoscyam.*)

Bryonia: Distended abdomen, sensitive to contact and motion; constipation; stitching pains in the abdomen, worse by pressure; violent fever, with burning heat of the whole abdomen; burning thirst with desire for cold drinks; irritable temper, vehement, or apprehensive dread of the future, fears about one's recovery.

Chamomilla: The breasts are flaccid and empty, with metastasis of the milk to the abdominal organs and whitish diarrhœa; rather scanty lochia; distended abdomen, sensitive to contact; colic-like labour-pains; general heat with red face, and great thirst; aggravation at night, with subsequent sweat; great restlessness; impatience, nervousness; especially indicated when the fever was caused by a fit of anger, or by a cold.

Coffea: Great nervousness and sensitiveness to the least pain.

Colocynthis: *Cham.* having been insufficient, and the disease being caused by violent chagrin, there is: delirium alternating with sopor; hot head, red face, glistening eyes, dry heat, hard, full and hurried pulse.

Nux vomica: Sudden suppression of the lochia; feeling of heaviness and burning in the sexual organs and abdomen; or else the lochia are too profuse, with violent pains in the small of the back; ischuria and burning when urinating; constipation; nausea, desire to vomit, or actual vomiting; red face; rheumatic or spasmodic pains in the thighs and legs, with going to sleep of these parts; dullness of the head, or beating and pressure in the head, with vertigo, obscuration of sight, ringing in the ears, and fainting turns.

Rhus tox.: Great nervousness, the least contradiction aggravates the symptoms, the white lochia again assume a bloody tinge, with discharge of clots of blood.

Compare: Peritonitis, Metritis, Inflammatory Fevers, Typhus, Diseases of lying-in females, &c.

FEVERS, INTERMITTENT.

§ 1. Principal remedies: 1) *Ars. chin. ign. ipec. lach. natr-m. n-vom. puls. rhus. sulph.* 2) *Acon. ant. arn. bell. bry. calc.*

caps. carb-veg. cham. cin. ferr. op. veratr, 3) *Canth. cocc. coff. dros. hep. hyos. men. merc. mez. n-mosch. sabad. samb. sep. staph. thuj. val.* 4) *Ang. cupr. hell. kal. lam. phosph.*

§ 2 a) For *marsh-intermittent* fevers: 1) *Ars. chin. ipec.* 2) *Arn. carb-veg. cin. ferr. natr-m. rhus. veratr.*

b) For fevers prevailing in *damp* and *cold* seasons: *Calc. carb-veg. chin. lach. n-mosch. puls. rhus. sulph. veratr.*

c) For fevers prevailing in *spring* and *summer*, or in the warm seasons generally: 1) *Ars. bell. calc. caps. cin. ipec. lach. sulph. veratr.* 2) *Ant. bry. carb-veg. natr-m. n-vom. puls. thuj.*

d) For the *fall*-intermittent: *Bry. chin. n-vom. rhus. veratr.*

e) For *mismanaged* intermittent fevers, by large doses of Quinine: 1) *Arn. ars. bell. ferr. ipec. lach. puls. veratr.* 2) *Calc. caps. carb-veg. cin. merc. natr-m. n-mosch. n-vom. sep. sulph.*

§ 3. a) For fevers with *simple type*: 1) *Arn. ars. bell. bry. carb-veg. chin. cin. hyos. ign. ipec. natr-m. n-vom. puls. rhus. sulph. veratr.* 2) *Acon. ant. calc. caps. cham. cocc. coff. dros. ferr. hep. men. merc. mez. n-mosch. op. sabad. samb. sep. staph. thuj. val.*

b) For fevers with *double* type: *Ars. bell. chin. dulc. graph. n-mosch. puls. rhus. stram.*

c) For *quotidian* fevers: 1) *Acon. ars. bell. bry. caps. carb-veg. chin. cic. ign. ipec. lach. lyc. natr-m. n-vom. puls. rhus. stram. sulph. veratr.* 2) *Alum. calc. con. diad. graph. petr. sabad. veratr.*

d) For *tertian* fevers: 1) *Ars. bell. bry. canth. carb veg. chin. ipec. n-vom. puls. rhus.* 2) *Ant. arn. calc. caps. cham. cic. dros. dulc. lach. lyc mez. natr-m. n-mosch. n-vom. rhus. sabad. staph. veratr.*

e) For *quartan* fevers: 1) *Ars. puls. veratr.* 2) *Acon. arn. carb-veg. clem. hyos. ign. jod. lyc. n-mosch. puls. sabad.*

f) For fevers that come on *every fortnight*: *Ars.*

g) *Every year*: *Ars. carb-veg. lach.*

§ 4. As regards the *period* when the fever sets in, give:

a) For *evening*-fevers: 1) *Arn. ars. bell. bry. carb-veg. lach. nitr-ac. puls. rhus. sulph.* 2) *Acon. alum. calc. carb-an. carb-veg. dulc. graph. ign. ipec. led. lyc. merc. n-vom. petr. sabad. sep. staph.*

b) For *night*-fevers: 1) *Bell. carb-veg. cham. merc. n-vom. rhus. veratr.* 2) *Amm-m. ars. baryt. borax. calc. caps. carb-an. caust. hell. hep. nitr-ac. phos-ph. puls. sep. squill. staph. stram. sulph. thuj.*

c) For *morning*-fevers: 1) *Arn. bell. bry. calc. cham. lach. natr-m. n-vom. sabad. staph. veratr.* 2) *Ars. carb-veg. chin.*

con. graph. guaj. hep. lyc. merc. nitr-ac. sep. sil. spig. spong. sulph. zinc.

§ 5. As regards the relation of the *stages*, give:

a) For fevers where the *chill* and *coldness* prevail either entirely or partially: 1) ***Bry. canth. caps. chin. n-vom. puls. sabad. veratr.*** 2) ***Coff.*** *diad. hyos. ipec. petr. phosph. ruta. staph.*

b) When there is only *chill* and *heat*, but no sweat: 1) ***Arn. ars.*** *bell. bry. carb-veg.* ***cham.*** *dulc ign. ipec. nitr-ac. n-vom.* ***rhus.*** *sulph.* 2) ***Acon.*** *caps.* ***carb-an.*** *hell. lyc. merc.* ***phosph.*** ***phos-ac. puls.*** *sabad. sep. spig. sulph. tart. val.*

c) When there is only *chilliness* and *sweat*, but no heat: 1) ***Caust.*** *magn-aust. puls. rhus. veratr.* 2) ***Amm-m.*** *ars. bry. carb-am. lyc. sabad. sulph. thuj.*

d) For mere *heat*, with little or no chill and sweat: 1) ***Acon.*** *bell. bry. ipec n-vom. sabad. sil. val. veratr.* 2) ***Ars.*** *calc.* ***coff.*** *coloc. dulc. lach. lyc op. phosph. puls. staph. sulph.*

e) For *heat* and *sweat* without chill: 1) ***Ars.*** *caps.* ***carb-veg.*** *cham. coff. led. n-vom. op. phosph. rhus. stram.* 2) ***Acon.*** ***amm-m*** *bell. bry. carb-an. chin. cin. hell. hep. ign. ipec.* ***puls. sabad.*** *spig. staph. tart. val. veratr.*

f) When the sweat prevails: 1) ***Bell.*** *bry. calc. chin.* ***hep.*** *merc. rhus. samb. sep. sulph. veratr.* 2) ***Acon.*** *ars.* ***carb-veg.*** *graph. natr-m. puls.*

g) When *chill*, *heat* and *sweat* exist in the same degree: 1) ***Acon.*** *ars. bell. bry. caps. cham. graph. ign. ipec. rhus. sabad. spong. veratr.* 2) ***Chin.*** *cin. hell. hep. lyc. magn-aust.* ***nitr-ac.*** *n-vom. phosph. puls. sabin. staph. sulph.*

§ 6. As regards the *succession of the symptoms*, give:

a) When the chill comes first, then the heat: 1) ***Acon. arn.*** *bell. cin. hep. natr-m. n-vom. puls. rhus. spig. sulph.* 2) ***Bry.*** *caps carb-veg. chin. dros. hyos. ign. ipec. natr-m. nitr.* ***petr.*** *phosph. phos-ac. sabad. veratr.*

b) When the heat comes first, then the chill: 1) ***Bry. calc.*** *caps. n-vom. sulph.* 2) ***Bell. lyc.*** *puls. sep. staph.*

c) When *heat* and *chilliness alternate*: 1) ***Ars.*** *bry. calc.* ***chin.*** ***merc.*** *n-vom.* 2) ***Asar.*** *baryt. bell. cocc. lyc. natr-m.* ***phosph.*** ***phos-ac.*** *sabad. sil. spig. sulph. veratr.*

d) When heat and chilliness exist *simultaneously*: 1) ***Acon.*** ***ars.*** *bell. calc. cham. hell. ign. merc. n-vom. puls.* ***rhus. sep.*** 2) *Anac. asar. bry. chin. ipec. lyc. nitr-ac. oleand. rhab.* ***sabad.*** ***spig.*** *sulph. veratr.*—***External heat***, internal chill: *Acon. ars. bell. calc. coff. ign. lach. lyc. men. nitr. n-vom. phosph. sep. sil. squill.* ***sulph.***—***Internal heat***, external chill: *Arn. bry. chin. hell.* ***merc.*** ***mosch.*** *phos-ac.* ***puls.*** *rhus. sabad. spong. stann. veratr.*

e) ***Sweat*** and ***chill*** coming on ***simultaneously***: 1) ***Lyc. puls.***

sabad. sulph. 2) *Ars. calc. led. n-vom. thuj.*—Sweat *after the chill*, no heat: 1) *Carb-an. caust. lyc. rhus. thuj. veratr.* 2) *Bry. caps. lyc. magn-aust. sabad.*

f) *Sweat* and *heat* together: 1) *Bell. caps. cham. hep. n-vom. op. rhus.* 2) *Acon. bry. chin. cin. hell. ign. ipec. merc. phosph. sabad. spig. staph. val. veratr.*

g) Sweat *after the heat:* 1) *Ars. cham. ign. ipec. rhus. veratr.* 2) *Bry. carb-veg. chin. cin. coff. graph. hep. lyc. nitr-ac. op. puls. spong. staph. sulph.*

§ 7. As regards the *thirst*, give:

a) For thirst *before the paroxysm: Arn. chin. puls.—during the chill:* 1) *Acon. bry. caps. carb-veg. cham. cin. ign. natr-m. n-vom. rhus. veratr.* 2) *Ant. arn. ars. calc. chin. hep. ipec. kal. natr. sulph.—After the chill* or *before the heat: Ars. chin. dros. puls. sabad. thuj.*

b) *Thirst* and *heat together:* 1) *Acon. bell. bry. calc. cham. hep. hyos. lach. merc. natr-m. rhus. sec. sulph.* 2) *Caps. chin. n-vom. puls. sil. val. veratr.—No thirst* during the heat: 1) *Ars. camph. caps. carb-veg. chel. chin. hell. ign. ipec. men merc. n-mosch. sabad.* 2) *Bell. lach. n-vom. puls. rhus. samb. sep. spig. sulph. veratr.*

c) Thirst *after the heat: Amm-m. chin. n-vom. op. puls. tart.*—Thirst *during sweat: Ars cham. chin. hep merc. natr. natr-m. puls. rhus. stram. veratr.*—Thirst *after the sweat: Lyc n-vom. sabad.*

§ 8. As regards *secondary symptoms*, give:

a) For *pains* in the *limbs: Ars. chin hell. ign. natr-m n-vom rhod. rhus. veratr.*—For great *debility: Ars chin. ferr. hyos lach. lyc. merc. natr-m. n-vom. phos-ac. rhus.*—For *dropsical* symptoms: *Ars. chin. ferr hell stram.*—For *sopor* or drowsiness: *Bell. carb-veg. hell. hyos. lach op. puls. rhus. tart.*—For great *nervous* and *mental excitement: Acon. ars. bell. bry. cham. coff. ign. lyc. n-vom. puls.*—For *tendency of blood* to the head (with vertigo, delirium, stupor, &c.): *Acon bell bry. camph. carb-veg. coloc. hyos. lach. n-vom op. puls. rhus. stram. val.—Violent headache: Arn. ars. bell. chin. ign. lach. lyc. mez. natr-m. n-vom. phos. puls. rhod rhus. sep. spig.*—*Gastric* symptoms: *Ant. ars. asa. bell. bry. cham. chin. dig. ign. ipec. natr-m. n-vom. puls. stram. sulph. tart.—Diarrhœa: Arn. ars. cham. chin. coloc. ipec. phos. phos-ac. puls. rhus. veratr—Constipation: Ars. bry. calc. lyc. natr-m. n-vom. veratr.—Liver-complaint: Ars. chin. merc. n-vom.—Affections of the spleen: Ars. cap. cham. chin. mez. n-vom.—Catarrhal symptoms* (cough, &c.): *Acon. bell. bry. chin. con. hep. kreos. lach. merc. n-vom. puls. rhus. sa-*

bad. spig. sulph.—*Oppression* of the chest, and distress of breathing: *Acon. ant. arn. ars. bry. chin. ferr. hep. ipec. lach. n-vom. phos. puls. sep. sulph.*

And when these secondary symptoms set in principally *before* the *paroxysm*, give: 1) *Arn. ars. carb-v. chin. ipec. natr-m. puls. rhus.* 2) *Bell. calc. cin. hep. ign. n-vom. phos. spong. sulph.*

If *during the chill:* 1) *Ars. bry. caps. chin. hep. ign. natr-m. n-vom. puls. rhus. veratr.* 2) *Arn. calc. carb-v. cin. hell. ipec. lach. merc. mez. n-mosch. sabad. sep.*

If *during the heat:* 1) *Acon. ars. bell. carb-v. cham. ign. natr-m. n-vom. op. puls. rhus.* 2) *Bry. calc. caps. chin. coff. dros. hyos. ipec. lach. merc. op. phos-ac. sep. sil. sulph. veratr.*

If *during the sweat: Acon. ars bry. cham. lach. merc. natr. n-vom. op. phos. puls. rhus. sep. sulph. veratr. zinc.*

If *after* the paroxysm *is over: Ars. bry. carb-v. cic. coff. ign. lach. lyc. n-vom. plumb. puls. rhus. sabad. sil.*

§ 9. As regards the *pulse* (a very imperfect indication in fever and ague) give:

a) For *intermittent* pulse: *Ars. chin. dig. lach. merc. natr-m. nitr-ac. n-vom. op. phos-ac. sec.*—For apparently wanting, *imperceptible* pulse: *Acon. ars. carb-v. con. cupr. hyos. op. sec. sil. stram. tart. veratr.*—*Hard* pulse: *Acon. bell. bry. canth. hyos. jod. n-vom. phos. plumb. stram. sulph.*—*Small* pulse: *Acon. ars. bell. camph. canth. clem. cupr. dig. hyos. lach. laur. merc. n-vom. op. phos. plumb. sec. sil. stram. veratr.*—*Slow* pulse: *Bell. camph. chin. con. cupr. dig. laur. merc. op. phos. plumb. puls. rhod. rhus. samb. sec. veratr.*—*Hurried* pulse: *Acon. ars. bell. bry. coloc. hyos. jod. merc. phos. puls. sec. sil. spong. sulph.*—*Irregular* pulse: *Acon. ant. ars. bry. chin. dig. hep. kal. lach. merc. natr-m. nitr-ac. phos-ac. rhus. sec. spig. stram. val.*—*Full* pulse: *Acon. bell. bry. camph. coloc. ferr. hyos. lach. n-vom. op. phos. puls. samb. sec. sep. spong. stram. sulph. tart.*—*Soft* pulse: *Carb-v. chin. cupr. jod. plumb. stram veratr.*—*Tremulous* pulse: *Ars. cic. con. merc. rhus. spig. stram. tart.*

§ 10. Symptomatic indications.

Arsenicum: Chill and heat set in simultaneously, or alternate with each other, or internal chilliness and external heat, or *vice versa;* also: burning heat, as if boiling water were flowing through the veins; no sweat, or sweat long after the heat and especially at the commencement of sleep; or *little heat and chilliness*, and when the chill is accompanied with: pains in the limbs, anguish, uneasiness, flushes of heat when talking or stirring ever so little; oppression of the chest, pulmonary spasms, headache, &c.; during the heat: Restlessness, pressure in the forehead, vertigo or even delirium; during the sweat: buzzing in the ears; after or during the fever, generally: *great debility*, vertigo, painfulness of the liver or spleen; nausea; disposition to vomit, *violent pains in the stomach;* ulcerated corners of the mouth, bitter mouth, trembling, great anguish in the præcordial region, lameness of the extremities, or *violent pains;* tendency to dropsy. (Compare: *Chin. ferr. ipec. veratr.*)

CHINA: Nausea, canine hunger, headache, anguish, palpitation of the heart or other ailment previous to the paroxysm: *Thirst, generally before or after the chill and heat*, or *during the sweat*, or during the whole of the paroxysm, or during the apyrexia; chill alternating with heat, or the heat sets in long after the chill; *no thirst, tendency of blood to the head*, headache, pale face during the chill, dry and burning mouth and lips, *red face* and canine hunger during the heat; great debility during or after the paroxysm; *uneasy sleep, yellow complexion;* drowsy after a meal, pains in the liver and spleen, bilious or dropsical symptoms, painfulness or swelling of the liver and spleen, &c.

IGNATIA: Thirst only during the chill; chill moderated by external heat; external heat with partial *internal shuddering;* nausea and vomiting; pale colour of the skin and pains in the back during the chill; *no thirst*, headache, vertigo, delirium, *pale face*, or else alternately *pale* and *red*, or only one cheek red, during the heat; headache, pain in the pit of the stomach; great languor, deep sleep with stertorous breathing, after or during the fever; eruption on the lips and in the corners of the mouth, nettle-rash, &c.

IPECACUANHA: Much chilliness with little heat, or much heat and little chilliness; the chill is increased by external heat; no thirst or but little during the chill, violent thirst during the heat; previous to or between the paroxysms: nausea, vomiting and other *gastric symptoms*, with clean or coated tongue and oppression of the chest.—Even if *Ipec.* should not be exactly indicated, yet it is very apt to effect a favourable change, so that *Arn. chin. ign. nux v.*, or *Ars. carb-veg.* or *cin.* will complete the cure.

LACHESIS: Chills after a meal or in the afternoon, with violent pains in the limbs and pleuritic stitches, oppression of the chest and convulsive motions; *violent headache* during the heat; delirium, burning thirst, red face, restlessness, internal shudderings during the heat, livid complexion, *debility*, prostration between the paroxysms, *heat, especially at night;* sweat after the heat, the fever is easily excited by eating sour things.

NATRUM MURIATICUM: Constant chilliness; heat with stupefaction, obscuration of sight, vertigo, red face; violent headache during the heat, bone-pains, yellowish complexion, debility, *ulcerated corners of the mouth*, thirst during the chill and especially during the heat; *dry tongue;* painful sensitiveness of the pit of the stomach to contact; bitter taste and no appetite.

Nux vomica; Great debility from the commencement, then chill and heat; or heat first, then chill; or external heat and internal chill, or *vice versa;* constant desire to be covered, even during the heat and sweat; during the chill, the skin, hands, feet and face are blue; cold, or pleuritic stitches, stitches in the abdomen, pains in the back and small of the back, or drawing in the limbs; during the heat: headache, buzzing in the ears, distress in the chest, *heat about the head and face, red cheeks and thirst* during the chill and heat; gastric or bilious symptoms, vertigo, anguish and constipation. Is frequently suitable after *Ipec*. (Compare *Ars. bry. chin. ign.* and *puls.*)

Pulsatilla: No thirst during the fever, or thirst only during the heat; or chill and heat simultaneously, with thirst; aggravation in the afternoon and evening; headache, anguish and oppression during the chill; during the heat: red and bloated face, sweat in the face, shuddering as soon as the patient uncovers himself, or only red cheeks; or, between the paroxysms: *gastric or bilious symptoms*, bitter mouth, slimy, bilious or sour vomiting, diarrhœa or constipation, oppression of the chest, moist cough or headache. Is frequently suitable after *Lachesis*, or when the fever comes on again after overloading the stomach ever so little. (Compare *Cin. ign nux-v.*, or *Ant.* and *cham.*)

Rhus tox.: Chill and heat together, the paroxysms generally in the evening or at night, sweat after midnight or towards morning; *during the chill:* pains in the limbs, headache, vertigo, toothache; during or between the paroxysms: convulsive twitching of the limbs, nettle-rash, colic, diarrhœa and gastric affections; jaundice, sleeplessness with tossing about, thirst at night, palpitation of the heart with anguish and pressure in the pit of the stomach. (Compare *Ars. ign. nux-v. puls.*)

§ 11. Moreover, we require to use:

Aconitum: For violent heat and chill; heat, especially about the head and face, with red cheeks; anguish, palpitation of the heart, pleuritic stitches; whining, lamenting mood, ill humour, or sadness, despondency, dread of death.

Antimonium: Little thirst, coated tongue, bitter taste in the mouth, eructations, nausea, loathing, vomiting, and other gastric ailments, colic, tension and pressure in the region of the stomach, constipation or diarrhœa.

Arnica: Chill in the evening; thirst, even before the chill; bone-pains before the attack; during the fever: constant desire to change one's position; apathy; pains in the stomach, no appetite, aversion to meat during the apyrexia; yellow colour of the skin, bitter taste in the mouth, listlessness. Suitable after *Ipec.*

Belladonna: Violent headache with stupefaction; much heat and slight chill, or vice versa; *some parts are cold*, others warm; heat with red face and throbbing of the carotids; no thirst, or else a good deal; irritable, whining mood.

Bryonia: *Coldness prevails, chill*, with red cheeks, heat about the head, and yawning; or the *heat prevails*, with subsequent chilliness, or pleuritic stitches; *headache* and *vertigo* during the heat (or before the chill), *coated tongue;* bitter taste, aversion to food, nausea, desire to vomit, or vomiting; *a good deal of thirst*, constipation or diarrhœa.

Calcarea: Heat in the face, then chill; or heat in the face with cold hands; or alternate chill and heat; or external chill with internal heat; vertigo; heaviness of the head and limbs; stretching, pains in the small of the back, restlessness.

Capsicum: Thirst during the chill, or during the whole fever chill, then burning heat; *much mucus in the mouth, throat and stomach;* diarrhœa, with slimy and burning evacuations; ill humour, anguish and stupefaction, increasing with the chill.

Carbo veg.: Chill in the evening or at night; thirst only during the chill; copious sweat with subsequent chill; rheumatic pain in the teeth and limbs before or during the fever; vertigo, nausea, and red face during the heat.

Chamomilla: Pressure in the pit of the stomach, hot sweat on the forehead; despair, tossing about, or bilious vomiting, diarrhœa and colic: *thirst*, heat and sweat prevailing.

Cina: Vomiting and canine hunger before, during or after the paroxysms; thirst only during the chill or heat; pale face during the whole of the paroxysm; frequent tickling in the nose; *dilated pupils;* emaciation.

Ferrum: Chill with thirst and headache, orgasm of the blood, swelling of the cutaneous veins; tendency of the blood to the head; œdema of the face, especially around the eyes; vomiting of the ingesta; short breath, debility.

Opium: Sleep during the heat and even chill; stertorous breathing with the mouth open; convulsive twitchings; warm sweat; suppression of the secretions. Suitable to old people and children.

Veratrum: External chill and cold sweat, or internal heat with dark-red urine, delirium and red face; or chill with nausea, vertigo, pains in the small of the back and back; or chill, alternating with heat; constipation; or vomiting with diarrhœa; thirst during the chill and heat.

§ 12. Consider moreover:

CANTHARIS: When the urinary passages are involved.

COCCULUS: Nervousness, spasmodic symptoms, cardialgia, constipation.

COFFEA: Very sensitive and nervous, even with mild fever; heat with thirst, red face, lively mood; sweat with thirst, soft stools or diarrhœa; colic with shuddering, restlessness, tossing about.

DROSERA: Violent chilliness with cold face; icy-cold hands and feet; nausea, bilious vomiting; headache, spasmodic cough during the heat; gastric symptoms during the apyrexia.

HEPAR: Fever with coryza, cough, distress in the chest; or chill with thirst, preceded by bitter taste, followed by heat and sleep.

HYOSCYAMUS: Chills or heat, cough at night, or even epileptic attacks.

MENYANTHES: Chill, shuddering, chilliness in the abdomen.

MERCURIUS: Heat and chill; heat with anguish and thirst; *sour* or *fetid sweat*, with palpitation of the heart.

MEZEREUM: Chill, coldness, especially of the hands and feet, or violent heat; *great thirst;* headache, pale face; painfulness, swelling and hardness of the spleen; debility, sensitiveness to cold air.

NUX MOSCHATA: Little thirst during the heat, *desire to sleep*, white tongue, rattling, bloody expectoration.

SABADILLA: *Chill* with little thirst, or no thirst; dry, spasmodic cough, tearing pains in the bones during the chill; delirium, sleep, stretching during the heat.

SAMBUCUS: Sweat, or great heat, without thirst.

SEPIA: Chill with thirst, pains in the limbs, icy cold hands and feet, deadness of the fingers.

STAPHYSAGRIA: Fever in the evening, with chill, scorbutic affections and nocturnal heat.

SULPHUR: Fever from suppressed itch, with chills every evening, heat and sweat towards morning; fever with palpitation of the heart, violent thirst, even before the chill.

THUJA: Chill with cold trembling, externally and internally with or without thirst; then sweat without previous heat.

VALERIANA: No chill, but great heat and thirst, and dullnes of the head.

FEVER, YELLOW.—We know of one case cured by *Crotalus.*—(*Aconite* is probably the only specific for this disease "Hempel.")—Try: 1) *Arn. ars. carb-veg.* 2) *Amm. bry. rhus.* 3) *Bell. chin. ipec. merc. n-vom.*

FISH-POISON, ICHTYOTOXICON.—For poisoning with muscles, "Hering" recommends powdered charcoal with molasses or sugar-water; afterwards smell of camphor, and drink *black coffee.*

For *poisoning with fish*, take powdered charcoal mixed with brandy; if this, and *black coffee*, should not be sufficient, drink sugar-water, very sweet.—If this should not help, drink a quantity of *half vinegar and water.*

If this poisoning should be followed by scarlet-redness on the skin, with swelling of the face and hands, sore throat, &c., take *Bell.* or *cap.*

FISTULA LACHRYMALIS.—Principal remedies: 1) *Bell. calc. chel. puls ruta.* 2) *Bry. natr. natr-m. petr. phosph. sil. stann. staph. sulph.*

Compare: ULCERS and OPHTHALMIA.

FISTULA RECTI.—Give: *Calc. caust. sil.* and *sulph.*—Compare: ULCERS, FISTULOUS.

FISTULA URINARIA. — Give: *Ars. calc. carb-an. sil. sulph.*

Compare: ULCERS, GONORRHŒA, and URINARY DIFFICULTIES.

FONTANELLES, OF INFANTS, RETARDED CLOSING OF.—Give *Calc.* or *sil. sulph.*

FORMICATION.—Generally arising from paralysis of the nerves which ramify through the affected part. Principal remedies: 1) *Baryt. carb-veg. rhodod. secal. sulph.* 2) *Aur. borax. lycop. magnes-m. natr. phos-ac. platin. sabad. staph.* 3) *Cann. lauroc. mur-ac. phosph. rhus. silic. zinc.*

FUNGUS ARTICULORUM.—Principal remedies for this deposit in the cellular tissue, are: 1) *Ant. sil.* 2) *Ars. con. kreos. jod. lach. lyc. petr. phosph. staph. sulph.*

GANGRENE.—§ 1. Principal remedies: 1) *Ars. chin. lach. sil.* 2) *Asa. bell. euph. hell. plumb. sabin. sec. squill.* 3) *Acon. con. merc. ran. sulph sulph-ac. tart.*

§ 2. For *humid* gangrene: *Chin. hell. squill.*

Hot gangrene: 1) *Sabin. sec.* 2) *Ars. bell. mur-ac.*

Cold gangrene: 1) *Ars. asa. chin. squill. sec.* 2) *Bell. con. euph. lach merc. plumb. ran. sil. sulph. sulph-ac. tart.*

§ 3. *Gangræna senilis:* 1) *Sec.* 2) *Chin. con. plumb.*

§ 4. *Gangrenous* or black variola, requires: 1) *Ars. carb-v.* 2) *Bell. hyos. lach. rhus. sec. sil.*; or, 3) *Ant. mur-ac. sep.*

Gangrenous blisters : 1) ***Ars. bell. camph. lach. ran. sabin. sec.*** 2) *Acon. carb-v. mur-ac. phos.*

Carbuncles : 1) ***Ars. bell. sil.*** 2) ***Caps. hyos. rhus. sec. tart.*** (Compare : ANTHRAX.)

GASTRITIS.

§ 1. True gastritis is characterized by the following symptoms: Continuous violent pain in the region of the stomach, aggravated by contact, by moving the abdominal muscles, and by introducing ever so little food or drink into the stomach, with painful sensitiveness, distention, heat or throbbing in the epigastrium ; vomiting of the ingesta ; great anguish, cold hands and feet, great debility, spasms and other consensual nervous symptoms ; acute gastritis is almost always accompanied by violent inflammatory fever.

Principal remedies : 1) ***Acon. ars. bell. bry. chel. hyos. ipec. n-vom. puls. veratr.*** ; or, 2) ***Ant. canth. euphorb. ran. stram.*** ; and perhaps, 3) ***Asa. baryt. bar-m.? camph. cann.? colch. coloc cupr. dig. hell. laur.? mez.? nitr. phosph. sabad. sec. squill. tereb.?***

§ 2. Particular indications :

ACONITUM : Inflammatory fever, with great pain ; the disease is caused by taking cold, or by taking a cold drink while heated.

ANTIMONIUM : Caused by derangement of the stomach, with frequent vomiting, the tongue is coated with white or yellow mucus.

ARSENICUM : Frequently in alternation with ***Aconite***, especially when the disease is caused by a cold on the stomach, by eating ice, &c. ; or with ***sudden prostration***, pale, hippocratic face, cold extremities, &c. ; ***Veratr.*** being insufficient.

BELLADONNA : Cerebral symptoms, dullness, loss of consciousness, delirium. ***Hyoscya.*** being fruitless.

BRYONIA : Frequently after ***Acon*** or ***Ipec.***, especially when the disease was caused by taking a cold drink while heated.

HYOSCYAMUS : Dropsical or cerebral symptoms, apathy, loss of consciousness, or delirium ; the patient is insensible to the danger of his situation.

IPECACUANHA : A good deal of vomiting, with violent pains ; the disease is caused by derangement of the stomach, or by taking a cold drink, ***Acon.*** being insufficient.

NUX VOM. : The same causes as last-named, ***Acon. bry. ipec.*** or *ars.* being insufficient.

PULSATILLA : Caused by gastric impurities, or by eating ice, ***Ars*** and *ipec.* being insufficient.

VERATRUM : When the disease is characterized by : Excessive

coldness of the extremities, sudden prostration, pale and hippocratic face.

§ 3. Compare: INFLAMMATORY FEVERS, CHOLERA, GASTRIC DERANGEMENT, and: WEAK STOMACH and CARDIALGIA.

GASTRIC DERANGEMENT, GASTROSIS.

§ 1. Principal remedies: 1) *Acon. ant. arn. ars. bell. bry. cham. cocc. ipec. merc. n-vom. puls.* 2) *Caps. carb-veg. chin. coff. coloc. dig. hep. rhab. rhus. squill. tart. veratr.* 3) *Asa. asar. berb.? calc. cann. cic. cin. colch. con. cupr. daph. dros. ign. lach. lyc. magn-m. natr. natr-m. nitr-ac. petr. phos. rhab. sec. sep. sil. stann. sulph-ac. tarax.*

§ 2. For acidity, *sour eructations*, &c.: 1) *N-vom. puls. sulph.;* or, 2) *Bell. calc. caps. carb-veg. cham. chin. con. phosph. sep. staph. sulph-ac.*

For *bilious* state, (bitter taste, eructations or vomiting): 1) *Acon. bry. cham. chin. cocc. merc. n-vom. puls. sep. veratr.* 2) *Ant. ars. asa. asar. cann. coloc. daph. dig. gran.? ign. ipec. lach. sec. staph. sulph. tart.*

For *pituitous* symptoms (with mucous coating of the tongue, slimy taste and vomiting): 1) *Bell. caps. chin. ipec. merc. n-vom. puls. sulph. veratr.;* or, 2) *Ars. carb-veg. cham. cin. dulc. petr. rhab. rhus. spig.*

For *saburral* symptoms (spoiled taste, nausea, loss of appetite): 1) *Ipec. n-vom. puls.;* or, 2) *Ant. arn. ars. bell. bry. carb-veg. cham. coff. hep. merc. tart. veratr.*

§ 3. For *gastric complaints of children:* 1) *Bell. cham. ipec. merc. n-vom. puls.;* or, 2) *Bar-c. calc. hyos. lyc. magn-c. sulph.*

For gastric symptoms occasioned by *derangements* of the stomach: 1) *Ant. arn. ipec. n-vom. puls.;* or, 2) *Acon. ars. bry. carb-v. chin. coff. hep. sulph. tart.*, &c.

By abuse of *spirits:* 1) *Carb-veg. n-vom.;* 2) *Ant. coff. ipec. puls.*—By abuse of *coffee:* 1) *Cocc. ign. n-vom.* 2) *Cham. merc. puls. rhus. sulph.;*—of *tobacco:* *Cocc. ipec. merc. n-vom. puls. staph.;*—of *acids:* 1) *Acon. ars. carb-veg. hep.;* or, 2) *Lach. natr-m. sulph. sulph-ac.?*

By abuse of *chamomile:* *Puls.* or *nux-v.;*—of *rhubarb:* *Puls.;* —of *mercury:* *Carb-veg. chin. hep.* or *sulph.*

By *getting heated:* *Bry.* or *sil.;*—by a *cold:* *Ars. bell. cham. cocc. dulc. ipec.;*—by *ice, fruit,* &c.: *Ars. puls. carb-veg.*

By *external injuries*, such as: a blow upon the stomach, or by *straining*, &c.: 1) *Arn. bry. rhus.;* or, 2) *Puls. ruta.*

By *nervous excitement, excessive watching* or studying, &c.: 1) *Arn. n-vom. puls. sulph.* 2) *Carb-veg. cocc. ipec. veratr.;* or, 3) *Calc. lach.?*

By *loss of animal fluids*, nursing, vomiting, abuse of cathartics: 1) *Chin. carb-veg. ruta.* 2) *Calc. lach. n-vom. sulph.*

By *emotions*, anger, chagrin, grief, &c.: 1) *Cham. coloc.* 2) *Acon. bry. chin. n-vom. puls.*

Compare: INDIGESTION, CAUSES, &c.

Particular symptomatic indications:

ACONITUM: Yellow coating on the tongue, bitter taste in the mouth and of food and drink, except water; excessive nausea; *bitter eructations;* violent but ineffectual urging to vomit, or *bitter, greenish* or *slimy vomiting;* distention and swelling of the hypochondria, with painful sensitiveness of the region of the liver; no stool, or small, frequent stools with tenesmus; beating or stitching pain in the head, worse when talking.

ANTIMONIUM: Indigestion, with the following symptoms: Frequent hiccough, loss of appetite, loathing, tongue coated or covered with blisters, dry mouth; or else: accumulation of saliva or mucus in the mouth; thirst, at night; nausea, desire to vomit, increased by drinking wine; *eructations smelling and tasting of the ingesta,* or with a fetid smell; vomiting of the ingesta or of slimy and bilious substances; painfulness of the stomach to the touch, with painful feeling of fullness; colic and frequent flatulence; diarrhœa or constipation; dull headache, worse when smoking or going up stairs. (After *Ant.*, *Bry.* is sometimes suitable.)

ARNICA: Gastric symptoms occasioned by external injuries, *watching*, mental exertions, &c.; generally for: Great nervousness with dry or yellow-coated tongue; putrid, bitter or sour taste; bad smell from the mouth; desire for acids; aversion to smoking; eructations tasting of putrid eggs; urging to vomit; flatulent distention, especially after a meal; heaviness of the whole body; giving way of the knees; vertigo, dulness of the head, aching pain with heat in the brain, and stupefaction. (After *Arn.*, are sometimes suitable *Nux v.* and *cham.*)

ARSENICUM: Acrid, bitter eructations; dry tongue with violent thirst, and desire to drink frequently, but little at a time; salt or bitter taste, nausea, vomiting of the ingesta, or of bilious, brownish or greenish substances; colic, or burning pains in the stomach and abdomen, with chilliness and anguish, or violent, burning pressure at a small spot in the stomach; great sensitiveness of the region of the stomach to contact; great debility, desire to lie down; no stool, or else watery, greenish, brownish or yellowish diarrhœa with tenesmus; the vomiting or diarrhœa comes on again after drinking and after every motion of the body.

BELLADONNA: Whitish, yellowish, or thickly-coated tongue; aversion to drink and food; sour taste of rye-bread; vomiting of food or of sour, bitter or slimy substances; sometimes with constant nausea, dry mouth or thirst; headache, in the sinciput, as if every thing would fall out at the forehead, with throbbing of the temporal arteries; no stool, or slimy diarrhœa.

BRYONIA: Especially in summer and hot and damp weather; for: dry tongue, coated white or yellow, and covered with blisters; thirst day and night, with sensation of dryness in the mouth and throat; putrid smell from the mouth; *bitter taste*, especially on waking, or pappy, flat, foul taste; aversion to solid food, with desire for wine, acids or coffee; frequent, ineffectual attempts at vomiting; or else: bilious vomiting, especially after drinking; tension and fullness in the region of the stomach, especially after eating; constipation; dullness of the head with vertigo, or burning, oppressive or distensive pain in the head, worse after drinking; chilliness and shuddering.

CHAMOMILLA: Red and cracked tongue, or coated yellow; bitter taste in the mouth, and of food; fetid odour from the mouth; loss of appetite, nausea, or eructations and greenish, bitter or sour vomiting; great and oppressive anxiety, tension and pressure in the pit of the stomach, hypochondria and epigastrium; constipation, or greenish, diarrhœic stools; or sour diarrhœa, or discharge of fæcal matter and mucus, resembling *stirred eggs* in appearance; restless sleep, with tossing about and frequent waking; pain and fullness in the head; hot and red face; red and burning eyes; sensitive, suspicious temper. (If the patient should have made excessive use of chamomile-tea, give *Cocc.* and *puls.*)

COCCULUS: Yellow-coated tongue, loathing of food; dry mouth with or without thirst; fetid eructations, nausea and desire to vomit, especially when talking, after sleeping, when eating, or during motion, particularly riding in a carriage; painful fullness in the region of the stomach, with laboured breathing; constipation, or soft stools, with burning at the anus; debility, with sweat during the least exercise; aching in the forehead, with vertigo.

IPECACUANHA: Clean tongue, or thickly coated with a yellowish mucus, dry mouth; loathing of food, especially fat food, with desire to vomit; violent, ineffectual straining, or else vomiting of the ingesta or of slimy substances, easy but with great force; fetid smell from the mouth, bitter taste in the mouth and of food; violent pains, pressure and fullness in the region of the stomach; colic and diarrhœic stools of yellowish colour or fetid, putrid smell; chilliness or shuddering over the whole body; pale, yellowish complexion; aching in the forehead, or sensation as if all the bones of the skull were broken; sometimes nettlerash.

MERCURIUS: Moist tongue, or coated white or yellowish;

dry, burning lips, offensive, foul and bitter taste; nausea, desire to vomit, or bilious, mucous vomiting; painful sensitiveness of the epigastrium and abdomen, especially at night, with anguish and restlessness; drowsy in the day-time, sleepless at night; sometimes aversion to drink. (Is frequently suitable after *Bell.*)

Nux vom.: Dry and white tongue, or yellowish towards the root; no thirst, or else burning thirst with heartburn; accumulation of albuminous mucus or of water in the mouth, bitter or foul taste in the mouth, or else the food tastes flat; *bitter eructations*, constant nausea, especially in the open air; desire to vomit, or vomiting of the ingesta; cardialgia; painful pressure and tension in the epigastrium and hypochondria; constipation, with frequent but ineffectual urging to stool; or small, diarrhœic, slimy or watery stools; dullness of the head, with vertigo; heaviness, especially in the occiput; ringing in the ears, rheumatic pains in the teeth and limbs; worn-out feeling, inability to think; restless, quarrelsome, vehement disposition; hot and red, or yellowish and sallow face. (After *Nux-v.*, *Cham.* is frequently suitable.)

Pulsatilla: Tongue coated with whitish mucus; foul, pappy or bitter taste, especially after swallowing; bitter taste of food, especially of bread; bitter, sour or putrid eructations, or tasting of the ingesta; aversion to food, especially warm (boiled food), also to fat and meat, with desire for acids or spirits; acidity in the stomach; excessive mucus in the stomach; *regurgitation of the ingesta;* excessive nausea, desire to vomit, especially after eating and drinking, or with evening-exacerbations; vomiting of food, or mucus, or bitter and sour vomiting (especially at night); hard, distended abdomen, with flatulence, rumbling; slow stool, or slimy and bilious diarrhœa; hemicrania, tearing or darting; chilliness with languor and drawing through the whole body; ill humour; taciturn, vehement without reason, especially when the patients are habitually of a bland and obliging disposition.

§ 5. Use likewise:

Capsicum: Suitable to phlegmatic, clumsy individuals, or to suspicious persons who take every thing in bad part, with mucous evacuations, heartburn, burning in the stomach and at the anus during every stool.

Carbo veg.: No appetite, malaise, or even vomiting of food after the least meal, frequently with acidity in the stomach; pains in the stomach when pressing on the pit; great sensitiveness to cold or hot, dry or damp weather; heaviness and dulness of the head, with debility.

China: No appetite, loathing of food and drink, as if one had eaten enough; frequent eructations, or regurgitation and vomiting of the ingesta; painful distended abdomen, with pressure around the umbilicus; frequent discharge of fetid flatulence; lienteria; chilliness and shuddering after drinking.

COFFEA: Gastric symptoms accompanied by great nervousness and by sleeplessness.

COLOCYNTHIS: Cardialgia, vomiting or diarrhœa after eating ever so little; spasmodic colic; cramp in the calves.

DIGITALIS: Nausea, especially on waking in the morning, with bitter taste in the mouth; thirst, vomiting of mucus; diarrhœa and debility.

HEPAR: Aching in the stomach, with nausea, eructations, desire to vomit, or slimy, bilious or sour vomiting and heartburn; colic and constipation; or else diarrhœic, slimy stools.

RHUBARB: Pappy taste, aversion to solid food or coffee; nausea with colic, or diarrhœic, *sour stools*, or slimy and brownish stools.

RHUS TOX.: Gastric symptoms, especially at night, with colic, aching pain in the stomach, dry and bitter mouth, nausea and desire to vomit.

SQUILLS: Gastric symptoms accompanied by pleuritic stitches, *Acon.* and *bry.* being insufficient.

TARTARUS: Constant nausea with desire to vomit; great anxiety, or violent ineffectual urging to vomit; or else: slimy vomiting and diarrhœa.

VERATRUM: Dry tongue, or else coated yellowish or brownish, bilious vomiting and diarrhœa, debility, fainting fits after stool.

§ 6. Compare: LOSS OF APPETITE, MALACIA. COATED TONGUE, VOMITING, HEARTBURN; STOMACH, DERANGEMENT OF; COLIC, DIARRHŒA, GASTRIC FEVERS, &C.

GASTROENTERITIS.—For the treatment, we refer the reader to GASTRITIS and ENTERITIS.

GLANDS, DISEASES OF.

§ 1. Principal remedies: 1) *Amm. aur. bar-c. bell. calc. carb-veg. cham. cist. con. dulc. hep. lyc. merc. nitr-ac. sil. spong. staph. sulph.* 2) *Alum. bov. canth. carb-an. graph. jod. kal. mang. ol-jec. plumb. sabin.*

§ 2 Particular indications:

AMMONIUM CARB.: Swelling of the cervical glands, with itching eruptions of the face and body.

AURUM: Swelling and suppuration of the inguinal glands in consequence of syphilis, or abuse of mercury.

BARYTA: Swelling, inflammation and induration of the cervical glands, especially when there is dry scurf on the head and in the face.

BELLADONNA: Inflammatory swelling of the glands and lymphatic vessels, forming red and shining strings or cords, with lumps; heat of the affected parts, tensive and stitching pains; also for swelling, suppuration or induration of the inguinal or cervical glands, and for cold swellings.—After *Bell.* are frequently suitable: *Dulc. hep. merc. rhus-t.;* or *Calc. nux-v.* and *sulph.*

BRYONIA: Swelling of the cutaneous glands, forming small, hard knots under the skin

CALCAREA: Swelling and induration of the submaxillary, axillary and inguinal glands, also of the cervical, parotid and facial glands, especially when there is otorrhœa and hard hearing.—Also for *cold swellings* and swelling of the mesenteric glands. *Calc.* is frequently suitable after *Sulph.*

CARB. VEG.: Induration of the axillary glands, and lumps in the breasts.

CHAMOMILLA: Inflammatory and painful swelling of the submaxillary and cervical glands, and for induration of the mammæ of new-born infants.

CISTUS: Swelling and suppuration of the submaxillary glands, with caries of the jaws.

DULCAMARA: Cold swelling, also for inflammation and induration of the inguinal and cervical glands, with tensive pain.—*Dulc.* is frequently indicated after *Bell.* or *merc.*

GRAPHITES: Scrofulous swelling of the cervical glands.

HEPAR: Suppuration of the axillary and inguinal glands, especially when much mercury had been used.

IODIUM: Scrofulous or arthritic induration of the *inguinal*, cervical or axillary glands.

MERCURIUS: Cold swellings, inflammation, swelling or suppuration of the submaxillary, axillary, inguinal or parotid glands, especially in scrofulous or syphilitic individuals.—After *Merc.* are frequently suitable: *Dulc. bell. hep.*, or *rhus-t.*

NITRI AC.: Inflammatory swelling or suppuration of the inguinal or axillary glands, especially after abuse of mercury, or in syphilitic subjects.

NUX VOM.: Inflammation of the lymphatic vessels, with heat and shining redness, hardness and painfulness.—*Nux-v.* is frequently suitable after *Bell.*

SILICEA: Scrofulous induration and swelling of the cervical, parotid, axillary and inguinal glands, with or without inflammation.

SPONGIA: Scrofulous swelling and induration of the cervical glands.

SULPHUR: Swelling, induration and suppuration of the inguinal, axillary and submaxillary glands, also of the cervical and even cutaneous glands, either from scrofula or in consequence of some cutaneous disease, such as scarlatina, &c., or from abuse of mercury.*

§ 2. Give more particularly:

a) For *inflammatory* swelling: 1) ***Bell. merc. phosph. sil.*** 2) *Acon. baryt. camph. cham. graph. hep. nitr-ac. n-vom.* ***puls. staph.*** *sulph. thuj.* 3) *Arn. carb-an. carb-veg. lyc. rhus.*

b) *Cold* swellings: 1) *Ars. bell. calc. cocc. con. merc.* 2) ***Asa. dulc.*** *lach.*

c) *Hard* swellings: *Baryt. bry. calc. con. phosph. puls.* ***rhus. sulph.***

d) *Painful* swellings: *Aur. bell. carb-an. chin. jod. puls.* ***sil. sulph.***

e) *Painless* swellings: *Calc. con. dulc. phos-ac. sep. sulph.*

§ 3. Also:

a) For *suppurating* glands: *Bell. calc. cist. hep. merc.* ***nitr-ac.*** *sil. sulph.*—*Aur. lach. sep.*

b) *Ulcerated* glands: *Ars. phosph. sil.*—*Bell. con. hep.* ***lach. sulph.*** *thuj.*

c) *Indurated* glands: *Baryt. bell. calc. carb-an. clem.* ***con. graph.*** *lyc. sulph.*—*Carb-veg. cham. chin. magn-m. rhus. spong.*

§ 4. Compare: INFLAMMATION, SWELLINGS, SUPPURATION, ULCERS, &c.

GLANDERS, POISON OF.—The best remedies, according to Hering, are: 1) *Ars. phos-ac.* 2) *Calc. sulph.*

GOITRE, STRUMA.—Principal remedies: 1) ***Jod. spong.*** 2) *Amb. amm. calc. caust. hep. lyc. natr. natr-m. spong. staph;* and perhaps, 3) *Carb-an. con. dig. kal. magn-c. merc.* ***petr. phos-ac.*** *plat. sil. sulph.*

GONITIS, INFLAMMATION OF THE KNEE.—For *lymphatic* or *scrofulous* swelling of the knee: *Calc.* or *sulph.;* or, 2) ***Arn. ars.*** *ferr. jod. lyc. sil.*

Arthritic swelling requires: *Arn. bry. chin. cocc. lyc.* ***n-vom. sulph.***

For *suppuration:* 1) ***Merc. sil.;*** or, 2) *Bell. hep. sulph.*

For *serous effusion* (*hydrarthrus*): 1) ***Sulph.;*** or, 2) ***Calc.*** *jod. merc. sil.;* or, 3) *Con. dig.*

For *white* swelling, (or *phlegmasia alba dolens*): 1) ***Bry. lyc.*** 2) *Ant. ars. puls. rhus. sabin. sulph.* 3) *Bell. calc.* ***chin.*** *jod. merc. rhus. sep. sil.*

* *Rhus tox.* is a most important remedy for glandular swellings.—HEMPEL.

See: Arthritis, Suppuration, Tumor, Dropsy, Scrophula, &c.

GONORRHŒA.

§ 1. For inflammatory gonorrhœa the best remedy is *Cannabis* 30, 3 pellets, only one dose, allowing it to act about a week. This is better than the tincture, and will produce a favourable change, provided the patient keeps *perfectly quiet.* After the inflammatory symptoms have been subdued, give *Merc.* or *sulph.*, either alone or alternately; *Merc.* for a greenish and purulent, *Sulph.* for a whitish, serous, and painless discharge.

Cantharides are indicated by violent inflammation, suppression of urine, priapism, painful erections, &c.; or *Petrosel.*, when the ischuria does neither yield to *Merc.* nor *sulph.*

Acon., in water, is sometimes excellent for violent pains.

§ 3. The best remedies for secondary gonorrhœa, especially when it had been mismanaged with large doses of *Copaiva* or *Cubebs*, are *Sulph.* and *Merc.;* or: *Caps. ferr. natr-m. nitr-ac. n-vom. sep. thuj.*—*Caps.* is indicated by a whitish, thick discharge like cream, with burning during micturition; if *Caps.* should be insufficient, give *Ferr.* or *nux-vom.*—For *strictures*, give: 1) *Clem. petr. sulph.* 2) *Dig. dulc. puls. rhus.*

§ 4. *Figwarts* require: *Nitr-ac. thuj.* or *cinnab.; Merc.* and *sulph.* sometimes effect a cure.

For *gonorrhœa* and *chancre* combined, give *Merc.*

§ 5. The following remedies have likewise been recommended: *Agn. con. cop. cub. dulc. hep. led. lyc. merc-c. mez. petr. sabin. selen.*—*Agnus* is suitable when the sexual instinct has become extinct or greatly diminished, and when there is a whitish serous gleet, without pain.

For the consequence of suppressed gonorrhœa, see: Rheumatism in the extremities, Orchitis, Ophthalmia, &c.*

GROWING, ill effects of.

The best remedy is *Phos-ac.*, not only for the pains in the limbs, but also for the bodily and mental languor of which so many young people complain when growing too fast.

GUMS, DISEASES OF THE.

§ 1. Principal remedies: 1) *Amm. amm-m. bell. borax. carb-v. chin. hep. merc. mur-ac. natr-m. nitr-ac. n-vom. phos-ac. rhus.*

* See Hartmann's work on the homœopathic treatment of disease, vol. iv. Published by W. Radde, 322 Broadway, New-York. Edited by Chs. J. Hempel, M D.

staph. sulph. 2) ***Ars.*** *baryt. calc. caps.* ***carb-an.*** *caust.* ***dulc*** *graph. kal. kreos. phos. puls. ruta. sep sulph-ac. thuj.*

§ 2. For *swelling* and *inflammation* of the gums: 1) ***Bell*** *calc. caust. cham. chin. cist. graph. hep. merc. n-vom. phos-ac. sep. staph. sulph.*; or, 2) *Amm. amm-m. baryt. borax. natr-m. nitr-ac. phos. sil.*

For the *liability* to *bleed*: *Ars. calc. carb-v. cist. merc. natr-m. nitr-ac. phos. phos-ac. sil. staph. sulph.*

For *ulceration*: *Alum. calc.* ***carb-v.*** *kal. lyc. merc. natr-m. staph. sulph-ac.*

For *abscesses* and *fistulæ*: *Calc. sil. staph. sulph.*; or, *Caust. lyc.? natr-m petr.? canth.?*

For *fleshy excrescences*: ***Staph.*** *thuj.*

For *looseness* of the teeth: 1) *Carb-v. cist. merc. phos-ac.* 2) *Ant. natr. phos. rhus. sep.*

For *scorbutic affections*: 1) *Caps. carb-v. merc. natr-m. nitr-ac. staph. sulph.*; or, 2) *Amm. amm-m. ars. bry. caust. dulc. kal. kreos. mur-ac. sep.*, &c.

§ 3. For *mercurial* symptoms: ***Carb-v.*** *chin.*; or, ***Hep.*** *nitr-ac. staph.*, &c.

Ill effects of salt require: *Carb-v.* or *nitr. sp.*

Persons who lead a sedentary life, and are corpulent and phlegmatic, require: 1) *Caps.* 2) *Bell. calc. merc. sulph.*; thin and lively persons, on the contrary: ***Nux-v.***; or, *Carb-v. chin. natr-m.*

HÆMATEMESIS, VOMITING OF BLOOD.

Principal remedies: 1) *Acon. arn. ferr. hyos. ipec. n-vom. phos.* 2) *Amm. bell. bry. canth. carb-v. caust. chin. lac. lyc. mez. mill. plumb. puls. sulph. veratr.*

See: VOMITING and STOMACH, DERANGEMENT OF.

HÆMORRHOIDS.

Principal remedies: 1) *Acon. ant. ars. bell. calc. carb-v. caps. cham. ign. mur-ac. n-vom. puls. sulph.*; or, 2) *Amb. amm-c. amm-m. anac. berb.? caust. chin. coloc. graph. kal. lach. nitr-ac. petr. rhus. sep.*

§ 2. *Hæmorrhoidal colic* requires: ***Carb-v.*** *coloc. lach.. n-vom. puls. sulph.*

Itching of the *anus*: *Acon. n-vom. sulph.*

Inflammation of hæmorrhoidal tumors: *Acon. cham. puls.*; or, *Ars. mur-ac. n-vom. sulph.*

Hæmorrhage: 1) *Acon. bell. ipec. phos.* 2) *Calc. chin. sulph.*

Anomalous pains and diseases arising from the suppression of an habitual hæmorrhoidal discharge: 1) *N-vom. sulph.*; or, 2) *Calc. carb-v. puls.*

Mucous hæmorrhoids: 1) *Ant. caps. carb-v. puls. sulph.*; or, 2) *Borax. ign. lach. merc.*

Hæmorrhoidal disposition: 1) *N-vom. sulph.*; or, 2) *Calc. carb-v. caust. graph. lach. petr.*, &c.

§ 3. Particular indications:

Aconitum: Bleeding piles, with stitches and pressure in the anus, feeling of repletion in the abdomen, with tension, pressure and colicky pains; pains in the small of the back, as if the back or the os-sacrum were broken.

Antimonium: Copious secretion of a light-yellow mucus, with burning, creeping, itching or even smarting at the anus. (Is frequently suitable in alternation with *Puls.*)

Arsenicum: Burning discharge of blood, with burning and stitching pains in the tumors; heat and restlessness, burning in all the veins, or great debility. (Is frequently suitable in alternation with *Carb-v.*)

Belladonna: Bleeding piles, with violent pains in the small of the back, as if the back would break. (If *Bell.* should not be sufficient, give *Hep.*)

Calcarea: After *Sulph.*, if this should be insufficient or if it should have been abused; for frequent bleeding of the piles, or for suppression of habitual bleeding.

Capsicum: The tumors are very large, with discharge of blood or bloody mucus from the rectum, burning pains at the anus; painful drawing in the small of the back and back; colic.

Carbo veg.: Large bluish tumors, with stitching pains in the small of the back, stiffness of the back, burning and tearing in the limbs; constipation, with burning stools and discharge of blood; frequent tendency of the blood to the head, bleeding of the nose, flatulence, slow action of the bowels, &c., also for copious and burning discharge of mucus from the rectum.

Chamomilla: Flowing piles, with compressive pains in the abdomen, frequent urging to stool, occasional burning and corrosive diarrhœic stools; tearing pains in the small of the back, especially at night; or painful and ulcerated rhagades of the anus.

Ignatia: Violent stitches in the rectum, itching and creeping at the anus, copious discharge of blood, prolapsus recti during stool, or sore, contractive pain of the rectum, with frequent, ineffectual stools and discharges of blood-streaked mucus.

Muriatic ac.: The hæmorrhoidal tumors are inflamed, swollen, bluish, with swelling of the anus, sore pains, violent stitches and great sensitiveness to contact.

NUX VOMICA : Blind and flowing, or irregular piles, especially suitable to persons who lead a sedentary life or use too much coffee or spirits; also suitable to pregnant females or persons affected with worms, &c.; generally for: stitching, burning or itching of the anus; stitches and shocks in the small of the back, with bruised pain so that the patient is unable to raise himself; *frequent constipation with ineffectual urging to stool*, and with sensation as if the anus were *closed or constricted;* frequent tendency of the blood to the head or abdomen, with distention of the epigastrium and hypochondria; heaviness of the head, inability to think, vertigo; ischuria, suppression of urine; discharge of blood and mucus from the anus.

SULPHUR : If *Nux* should be insufficient, especially for alternate constipation and discharges of blood-streaked mucus; feeling of soreness at the anus, with itching and stitches; frequent tendency of the blood to the head; palpitation of the heart; the vascular system is easily excited, throbbing in the whole abdomen, with anguish and oppression, after the least emotion; weak digestion; dysuria; bleeding, burning and frequent protrusion of the hæmorrhoidal tumors. (*Sulph.* is best given in alternation with *Nux-v.*; these two remedies in alternation are sufficient in most cases to effect a cure.)

§ 4. See: COLIC, CONSTIPATION, CONGESTIONS OF THE ABDOMEN, &c.

HÆMORRHOIDS OF THE BLADDER.

Principal remedies: 1) *N.-vom. puls. sulph.* 2) *Acon. ars. bor. calc. carb-v. graph. lach. merc. sab.*

Compare: CATARRH OF THE BLADDER, CYSTITIS, and URINARY DIFFICULTIES.

HÆMORRHAGES.

§ 1. Principal remedies: 1) *Acon. arn. bell. calc. chin. croc. ferr. ipec. merc. nitr-ac. n-vom. phos. puls. sabin. sep. sulph.* 2) *Ant. ars. cann. caps. carb-a. carb-v. cham. cupr. dros. hyos. jod. kal. lach. led. lyc. nitr. plumb. puls. rhus. sec. sil. stram. sulph-ac. zinc.*

§ 2. For *active* hæmorrhages of young plethoric subjects, give: *Acon. bell.* 2) *Croc. ferr. hyos. puls.* 3) *Arn. calc. cham. chin. ipec. kal. lyc. merc. nitr-ac. n-vom. phos. rhus. sabin. sep. stram. sulph.*

Passive hæmorrhage, of persons who have been weakened by depletions or loss of animal fluids, requires: *China.* We may consider moreover: *Ars. carb-v. ferr. ipec. phos-ac. puls. rhus. sec. sep. staph. sulph.*

§ 3. For *arterial* hæmorrhage, give: 1) *Acon. bell. dulc. hyos. sabin.* 2) *Arn. calc. carb-v. ferr. ipec. led. magn-aust. merc. phos. rhus. sec.*

For *dark-red, venous* hæmorrhage: 1) *Cham. croc. n-vom. puls. sep.* 2) *Amm. ant. arn. lach. magn-c. nitr-ac. n-mosch. phos-ac. sulph.*

§ 4. If the blood be *brown*, use: 1) *Bry. carb-v.* 2) *Calc. con. puls rhus.*

For *acrid* blood: 1) *Canth. kal. nitr. sil.* 2) *Amm. ars. carb-kal. rhus. sulph. sulph-ac. zinc.*

Coagulated blood: 1) *Bell. cham. plat. rhus.* 2) *Arn. chin. croc. ferr. hyos. ign. ipec. merc. nitr-ac. n-vom. phos-ac. sabin. sec. sep. stram.*

Fetid blood: 1) *Bell. bry. carb-a. sabin.* 2) *Caust. cham. chin. croc. ign. kal. merc. phos. plat. sec. sil. sulph.*

Tenacious, viscous blood: *Croc. cupr. magn-c. sec.*

§ 5. See: Hæmorrhage from the respective organs.

HÆMORRHAGE FROM THE ANUS.

See: *Hæmorrhoids.*—If caused by injuries of the anus or rectum, give: *Acon. arnic. china. croc. phos. sulph. sulph-ac.*

HÆMORRHAGE FROM THE EYES.

Principal remedies: 1) *Bellad. carb-v. cham. n-vom.* 2) *Arnic. calc crotal. euphras. ruta. seneg.*

Bloody sweat: Bell. calc. n-vom. seneg.

Ecchymosis: 1) *Arn. bell. calc. n-vom. seneg.* 2) *Cham. crotal. plumb. ruta.*

HÆMORRHAGE FROM THE LUNGS, HÆMOPTYSIS.

Principal remedies: 1) *Acon. arn. chin. ferr. ipec. nitr-ac. phos. puls. sulp.* 2) *Ars. bell. carb-v. dros. dulc. hyos. ign. n-vom. op. rhus.* 3) *Amm. bry. cocc. coff. con. croc. cupr. kal. kreos. lach. led. lyc. merc. mill. sep. sulph-ac.*

§ 2. For *spitting* of blood: 1) *Arn. bell. bry. carb-v. chin. dulc. lach. merc. nitr-ac. puls. rhus. sil. staph. sulph.* 2) *Amm. ars. bry. con. cupr. kal. led. lyc. nitr-ac. sep. sulph. sulph-ac.*

For real *hæmorrhage*, loss of large quantities of blood, give: 1) *Acon. arn. bell. carb-v. chin. dulc. ferr. hyos. ipec. n-vom. op. phos. puls. rhus.* 2) *Ars. croc. ign. led. mill. sulph. sulph-ac.*

In *severe* cases, with imminent danger, give: *Acon. chin. ipec. op.*

After-ailments require: 1) *Carb-v. chin.* 2) *Ars. coff. ign. sulph.*

Preventive remedies: *Ars. n-vom. sulph.*, alternately, at *long intervals, one dose* only.

§ 3. Particular indications.

ACONITUM: The paroxysm is preceded by: Orgasmus sanguinis in the chest, with feeling of fulness and burning pain; palpitation of the heart, anguish, restlessness, aggravation on lying down; pale face, expression of anguish in the countenance; copious discharge of blood from time to time, even when coughing but very little. (After *Acon.* are sometimes suitable: *Ars.* and *Ipec.*)

ARNICA: The hæmorrhage is caused by mechanical injury, fall, blow on the breast or back; or for: slight expectoration of black and coagulated blood, with heavy breathing, stitching, burning and contraction in the chest, palpitation of the heart, great heat in the abdomen, and fainting fits; or for: discharge of bright-red, frothy blood, mixed with mucus and coagulated lumps; tickling under the sternum; stitching in the head and bruised pain in the region of the ribs when coughing. (In traumatic hæmorrhage it may sometimes be necessary to give a dose of *Acon.* previous to *Arn.*)

ARSENICUM: If *Aconite* be insufficient, and for: Great anguish with palpitation of the heart, sleeplessness, dry, burning heat, and restlessness driving one out of bed; also after *Chin. arn. ferr.* in violent hæmorrhages,—or after *Hyoscyam.*, in the blood-spitting of drunkards.—After *Ars.* are sometimes suitable: *Ipec. nux-v. sulph.*, especially in chronic hæmorrhage.

BELLADONNA: Constant tickling in the throat, with desire to cough and aggravation of the hæmorrhage by coughing; sensation as if the chest were filled with blood, with aching or stitching pains which are made worse by motion.

CARBO VEG.: Violent, burning pains in the chest, even after the hæmorrhage; in general suitable to persons who are very sensitive to changes of weather or who suffer with mercurial symptoms.

CHINA: Bloody expectoration during violent cough which was first hollow, dry and painful, with taste of blood in the mouth; alternate shiverings and flushes of heat; great debility with constant desire to lie down; frequent sweats; trembling, obscuration of sight or dulness of the head.—Or after great loss of blood, the patient being pale and cold, with fainting fits and convulsive twitching of the hands and facial muscles. (After *Chin.* are frequently suitable, especially for the last-mentioned symptoms, *Ferr.* or *Arn.*, also *Ars.*)

DULCAMARA: Constant titillation in the larynx, with desire to cough; expectoration of bright-red blood, with aggravation during rest; the hæmorrhage is caused by a cold or a loose cough which had existed for some time previous.

FERRUM: Scanty expectoration of pure bright-red blood during a slight paroxysm of cough, with pains between the scapulæ, heavy breath, especially at night; inability to sit; relief by motion, but frequent desire to lie down, and great debility after talking. (Is suitable to thin persons, of yellowish colour of the skin, and whose sleep is frequently disturbed:—also after *China* in severe cases.)

HYOSCYAMUS: The discharge of blood is preceded by a dry cough, especially at night, obliging the patient to get up; frequent sudden starting from sleep; also suitable to drunkards, particularly if *Op.* and *Nux-v.* should not be sufficient. (In such a case, *Ars.* is sometimes suitable after Hyoscyamus.)

IGNATIA: For debility after the arrest of the hæmorrhage, with disposition to be vehement and vexed.

IPECACUANHA: If, after *Acon.*, there remain: Taste of blood in the mouth, frequent hacking with expectoration of blood-streaked mucus, nausea and debility; also after the incomplete action of *Ars.*, the paroxysm recurring.

NUX VOM: After *Ipec.* or *Ars.* (and, in drunkards, after *Op.*) for: Tickling in the chest, with cough distressing the head; aggravation towards morning, especially in persons of a lively and choleric temperament; or when the hæmorrhage is occasioned by suppression of the hæmorrhoidal flux, by a fit of anger or by a cold. (In the latter case *Sulph.* is frequently suitable after *Nux-v.*; *Hyos.* and *Ars.* are especially suitable to drunkards.)

OPIUM: Suitable to persons who are addicted to drinking, in severe cases; or for: discharge of a thick, frothy blood; the cough is aggravated by swallowing; oppression or heavy breathing and anguish; burning at the heart, tremor of the arms, and feeble voice: anxious sleep with sudden starting; coldness, especially of the extremities, or heat, especially in the chest or other parts of the trunk. (After *Op.*, *Nux-v.* is frequently suitable.)

PULSATILLA: In obstinate cases, discharge of black and coagulated blood; anguish and shuddering, especially at night; debility, pains especially in the lower part of the chest; qualmishness or empty feeling in the pit of the stomach; suitable to timorous, phlegmatic and readily-weeping individuals: or for hæmorrhage from suppression of the menses. (In this case *Cocc.* is sometimes suitable.)

RHUS TOX.: Bright-red blood, aggravation of the symptoms from chagrin or the least emotions; disposition to be angry, uneasy and timid mood; tickling in the chest.

SULPHUR: Frequently suitab'e after *Nux*, to persons affected with piles, or after *Ars.* to prevent relapses.

See: HÆMORRHAGES, PNEUMONIA, PULMONARY PHTHISIS, COUGH, &c.

HÆMORRHAGE FROM THE MOUTH.

— Principal remedies: *Arn. bell. chin. dros. ferr. kreos. led. lyc.*

See: HÆMORRHAGE and EPISTAXIS.

HÆMORRHAGE FROM THE UTERUS, METRORRHAGIA and MENORRHAGIA.

§ 1. For *metrorrhagia* or *hæmorrhage*, give: 1) *Arn. bell. bry. cham. chin. cinnam. croc. ferr. hyos. ipec. plat. puls. sabin. sec. sep.*; or 2) *Acon. calc. carb-an. ign. magn-m. natr-m. n-vom. phosph. sil. sulph. veratr.*; or 3) *Cann. jod. rat. ruta.*

§ 2. For *active* hæmorrhage, in plethoric persons, give: 1) *Acon. bell. bry. calc. cham. ferr. n-vom. plat. sabin. sulph.*; or 2) *Arn. croc. hyos. ign. ipec. phosph. sil. veratr.*

For *passive* hæmorrhage, in debilitated, cachectic subjects: 1) *Chin. croc. puls. sec. sep. sulph.*; or 2) *Carb-veg. n-vom. ipec. phosph. ruta.? veratr.*

For *menorrhagia*: *Acon. bell. bry. calc. cham. ign. ipec. magn-m. natr-m. n-vom. phosph. plat. sec. sep. sil. sulph. veratr.*

For hæmorrhage *during pregnancy*, or *after confinement* or a *miscarriage*: 1) *Bell. cham. croc. ferr. plat. sabin.*; or 2) *Arn. bry. cinnam. hyos. ipec.*

Hæmorrhages at the *critical age*, require: *Puls.*, or *Bell. lach.*

§ 3. Particular indications:

ARNICA: Hæmorrhage in consequence of missing a step, straining, by *lifting a heavy weight*, especially in pregnant females, provided *cinnam.* had been ineffectual.

BELLADONNA: The blood is neither bright nor dark; violent aching and tensive pains in the abdomen; constrictive or distensive sensation; painful pressure over the sexual organs as if every thing would fall through them, with pain in the loins as if the os-sacrum would break.

BRYONIA: Frequently after *Croc.*, if ineffectual, or for profuse discharge of a dark-red blood, with violent, aching pains in the loins, distensive pain in the temples, violent pressure in the abdomen, nausea, vertigo and fainting fits.

CHAMOMILLA: Discharge of a dark-red, or black, fetid blood, with lumps, the discharge taking place by fits and starts; with labour-like pains in the abdomen; great thirst, cold limbs, pale face, debility and even fainting fits, obscuration of sight and buzzing in the ears.

CHINA: Paroxysmal discharges of blood, with spasmodic pains in the uterus; colic; frequent urging to urinate, and painful tension in the abdomen; or suitable to persons who have lost much blood, even in *severe* cases, with heaviness of the head, vertigo, vanishing of the senses, sopor, fainting fits, cold extremities, pale or bluish face and hands. with convulsive jerks across the abdomen.

CINNAMONUM: Suitable to pregnant or lying-in females, after straining, missing a step, or some other exertion. (Give *Arn.* if *Cham.* be insufficient.)

CROCUS: *Black*, glutinous, *lumpy* blood, *Cham. chin. ferr.* being insufficient; or for: *Bounding* and *turning in the abdomen as if of something alive;* yellowish, sallow complexion; debility with vertigo, dim eyes, fainting turns; sadness, and great anxiety and restlessness.

HYOSCYAMUS: Labour-like pains, with drawing in the loins, kidneys and extremities; heat through the whole body, with full and quick pulse. swelling of the veins of the hands or face, great restlessness; increased liveliness, trembling through the whole body; or: the extremities go to sleep, with dulness, obscuration of sight, delirium, subsultus tendinum or convulsive twitching of the limbs alternating with tetanic rigidity of the extremities.

FERRUM: Copious discharge of partly fluid, and partly black and coagulated blood, with pains in the loins and labour-like colic; violent vascular excitement, with headache, vertigo, glowing-red face, full and hard pulse. (After *Ferr.*, *Chin.* is frequently suitable.)

IPECACUANHA: Suitable to pregnant females, or after parturition, with copious and uninterrupted discharge of fluid and bright-red blood; cutting pain in the umbilical region; violent pressure over the uterus and rectum, with shuddering and chilliness, heat about the head, debility, pale face, nausea and constant desire to lie down.

PLATINA: Thick and dark blood, not coagulated, with drawing pains in the loins extending to the inguinal region, and causing a sensation as if all the inner parts would be drawn down, or great sexual excitement.

PULSATILLA: The hæmorrhage ceases for a short time and then recommences with redoubled force. the blood being black, mixed with coagulated lumps; labour-like pains; suitable to pregnant females and females at the critical period, or after parturition, or when the placenta adheres.

SABINA: After parturition, or miscarriage, with black, dark, lumpy blood; pains in the abdomen and loins, like labour-pains; great debility or rheumatic pains in the extremities or head.

SECALE: After parturition or miscarriage, suitable to debilitated and cachectic persons; with cold extremities, pale or sallow face, small and almost suppressed pulse, anxiety, dread of death.

SEPIA: Induration of the neck of the uterus, with spasmodic

colic, painful pressure over the sexual organs, and transitory stitches through the parts.

HEADACHE, CEPHALALGIA.

§ 1. Sometimes symptomatic, but in many cases *idiopathic*, or constituting the most prominent symptom in the group. For such headache the principal remedies are: 1) *Acon. ant. bell. bry. calc. caps. cham. chin. coff. coloc. ign. merc. n-vom. puls. rhus. sep. sil. sulph. veratr.* 2) *Arn. ars. aur. carb-veg. cin. cocc. dulc. hep. ipec. lyc. op. plat.* 3) *Amm. amm-m. asar. clem. con. ferr. graph. guaj. hyos. kal. lach. mosch. natr-m. petr. phosph.*

§ 2. As regards the *pathological* varieties, give for *arthritic* headache: 1) *Bell. bry. coloc. ign. ipec. n-vom. sep. veratr.*, or 2) *Arn. ars. aur. caps. caust. cin. mang. nitr-ac. petr. phosph. puls. sabin. zinc.*

For *catarrhal* headache: 1) *Acon. cham. chin. cin. merc. n-vom. sulph.*; or 2) *Ars. bell. carb-veg. ign. lach. lyc. puls.*

For headache from *congestion of blood to the head*: 1) *Acon. arn. bell. bry. coff. merc. op. puls. rhus. veratr.*, or 2) *Cham. chin. cin. cocc. dulc. hep. ign. nitr-ac. sil. sulph.*; or 3) *Alum. amm-c. con. lach. led.*

For *gastric* headache: 1) *Ant. ipec. n-vom. puls. sulph.*; or 2) *Arn. berb.? bry. carb-veg. cocc. n-mosch.*; and if *constipation* should be the principal cause: *Bry. coff. magn-c. n-vom. op.* or *veratr.*

For *hysteric* headache: 1) *Aur. cocc. hep. ign. magn. magn-m. mosch. nitr-ac. phosph. plat. sep. val. veratr.*; or 2) *Caps. cham. lach. rhus. ruta.*

For *nervous* headache, *megrim*: 1) *Calc. chin. coloc. puls. sep.* 2) *Bry. caps. ign. ipec. n-vom. rhus. veratr.* 3) *Acon. arn. ars. bell. cham. chin. cic. coff. hep. nitr-ac. petr. sil. sulph.*; or, 4) *Agar. asar. caust. con. graph. hyos. mang. mosch. natr-m. phosph. plat. sabin. spig. zinc.*

For *rheumatic* headache: 1) *Acon. cham. chin. lyc. merc. nitr-ac. n-vom. puls. spig. sulph*; or 2) *Bell. bry. chin. ign. phosph.*; or 3) *Caust. lach. led. magn-m.*

§ 3. For the headache to which *females* are liable, give: *Acon. ars. bell. bry. calc. chin. cocc. coloc. dulc. magn-m. n-vom. puls. plat. spig. veratr.*

For *nervous*, sensitive persons: *Acon. cham. chin. coff. ign. ipec. spig. veratr.*

For *children*: *Acon. bell. caps. cham. coff. ign. ipec.*

§ 4. As regards *external causes*, give for headache from

abuse of *coffee :* 1) ***Cham. ign. n-vom.*** 2) ***Bell. caust. coccul. hep.*** *lyc. merc. puls.*

From *heat* or *getting heated*: 1) ***Acon. bell.*** *bry.* or ***Carb-veg.;*** or 2) ***Amm.*** *calc. baryt. caps. ign. ipec. sil.*

From *nightly revelling* or abuse of *spirits :* 1) ***Carb-veg. n-vom.;*** or 2) ***Ant.*** *ars. bell. bry. calc. chin. coff. ipec.* ***nitr-ac.*** *phosph. puls. rhus. sulph.*

From excessive *studying, exertions, &c. :* 1) ***N-vom. sulph.;*** or 2) ***Aur.*** *calc. lach. natr. natr-m. puls. sil.* ; or 3) ***Anac. graph. lyc.*** *magn. phosph. magn-arct.*

From *grief : Ign. staph.* or *phosph-ac.*

From *chagrin* or *anger :* 1) *Cham. n-vom. ;* or 2) ***Coloc. lyc. magn-c.*** *natr-m. petr. phosph. plat. rhus. staph.*

From *external injuries, blows* on the head, *fall, concussion of the brain :* 1) *Arn. cic.* 2) ***Merc.*** *petr. rhus.*, &c. ;—and from *straining :* 1) *Calc. rhus. ;* 2) ***Amb.*** *arn. bry. natr.* ***phos-ac. sil.***

From the influence of *metallic* substances, give *Sulph.*, as the principal remedy ; or, if principally from the influence of *copper*, give *Hepar ;* or if from abuse of ***Mercury***, give : 1) ***Carb-veg. chin. puls.*** 2) ***Aur.*** *hep.* ***nitr-ac. sulph.***

Headache from *cold*, requires : 1) ***Acon.*** *bell. bry. calc.* ***cham. dulc. n-vom*** ;. or, 2) *Ant. chin. coloc. puls.*—From *draught* of air : *Acon. bell. chin. coloc. n-vom.*—From *bathing : Ant. calc.* or *puls.* ;—and from a *cold drink :* 1) *Acon. bell.* 2) *Ars.* ***natr. puls.***—Headache from bad *weather*, requires : *Bry. carb-veg.* ***n-vom.*** or *rhod.*

Headache from *smoking* or abuse of *snuff*, requires: *Acon.* ***ant.*** or *Ign.*

From long *watching :* 1) ***Cocc. n-vom.*** or ***puls.*** 2) ***Bry. calc.*** *chin. sulph.*

Compare : Causes.

§ 5. Particular indications:

Aconitum : *Violent, stupefying, compressive,* or *contractive* pains, especially over the root of the nose ; great heaviness and feeling of fulness in the forehead and temples, as if the head would burst ; *burning pains through the brain,* or *drawing pains* in one side of the head ; headache with buzzing in the ears and coryza, or with desire to vomit ; moaning, lamenting, dread of death, excessive sensitiveness to noise or motion ; pale and cold, or else *red* and *bloated face* with *red eyes ;* strong, full and quick, or small and even intermittent pulse ; sensation as if the hair were pulled, or as if a ball were rising into the brain, spreading a coolness ; aggravation by motion, when talking, raising one's self and drinking ; relief in the open air. (After *Acon.* are frequently suitable : *Bell. bry.* or *cham.*)

Antimonium : When, in consequence of derangement of the

stomach, indigestion, cold, or suppressed eruption, the following symptoms make their appearance: pain in the forehead, as if it would break, or boring, crampy, dull (and tearing) pains, especially in the forehead, temples or vertex; aggravation on going up-stairs; relief in the open air; falling off of the hair; nausea, loathing, loss of appetite, eructations, desire to vomit. (This medicine is frequently suitable after *Puls.*)

BELLADONNA: Great fullness and violent aching pains, or *pains as if the head would split, or as if every thing would issue through the forehead or one side;* pains over the eyes and nose, or semi-lateral, drawing, tearing or stitching pains; wavering shocks and *undulations in the head, as of water,* with sensation as if the skull were too thin; violent throbbing of the temporal arteries, and swelling of the veins of the head; the headache sets in every afternoon and lasts until morning; it gets worse by motion, especially by moving the eyes, or by ascending an eminence, by contact, in the open air, or in a draught of air, or at night in the warm bed; *Bell.* is particularly suitable when the headache is accompanied by *vertigo,* stupefaction, *red* and *bloated face, red eyes;* excessive *sensitiveness to noise, light, shock* or *contact;* ill humour; moaning, desire to remain in bed, buzzing in the ears, obscuration of sight. (After *Bell.* are frequently suitable: *Hep. merc.* or *plat.*)

BRYONIA: Distensive pressure or compressive sensation in the head, with feeling of fulness as if everything would issue through the forehead; beating, jerking or drawing pains and *stitches in the head,* especially on one side, or from the orbital bones to the temple; burning pain in the forehead, or heat in the head; headache with vomiting, nausea, and desire to lie down; the headache sets in every day after dinner, or early in the morning on waking and first opening one's eyes; aggravation by walking, stooping, and by contact; vehement, quarrelsome disposition; frequent chills. After *Bry.* are frequently suitable *Rhus-t.,* or *Nux-vom*

CALCAREA: Stupefying, aching, beating or hammering pains, or hemicrania with nausea, eructations and desire to lie down; or boring in the forehead as if the head would split; heat or feeling of *coldness* in the head; cloudiness and dullness of the head as if in a vice; the headache sets in every morning on waking; aggravation by mental labour, spirits, bodily exertions, motion, stooping, chagrin, &c.; falling off of the hair. (*Calc.* is particularly suitable after *Sulph.* or *nitr-ac.* After *Calc.* are frequently suitable *Lyc nitr-ac.* or *sil.*

CAPSICUM: Semi-lateral, stitching and aching pains, with nausea, vomiting and weak memory, or pains as if the skull would split: the pains get worse by moving the head or eyes, by walking, in the open air and in cold; especially suitable to phlegmatic, indolent persons of suspicious disposition, or to headstrong, clumsy people, afraid of exercise or the open air, with frequent chills, especially after drinking.

CHAMOMILLA: Suitable to children and to persons who are driven to despair by the least pain; for tearing and jerking in one side of the head (down to the jaws); stitching, heaviness or painful beating in the head; one cheek is red, the other pale; hot sweat about the head, even the hair; bloated face, painful eyes; catarrhal state of the throat or bronchi, or bitter, foul taste in the mouth, &c. (*Cham.* is suitable after *Acon.* or *coff.*; after *Cham.* are frequently suitable: *Bell.* and *puls.*)

CHINA: Suitable to persons who are sensitive to pain, especially for: *aching pains* at night that prevent sleep, or piercing, jerking pains in the forehead as if the contents would issue through it; boring in the vertex, with contusive pain in the brain; or jerking. tearing, and sensation as if the skull would split; aggravation by contact, reflection, conversation, open air, motion, draughts of air and wind; the hairy scalp and the hair are very sensitive to contact; or suitable to persons of a peevish, dissatisfied disposition; or to obstinate, disobedient children that are fond of dainties, of pale complexion, with flushes of heat and redness, loquacity and restlessness at night. (Is suitable after *Coff.* and *caps.*)

COFFEA: *Pain as if a nail were driven into the head*, or as if the brain were torn or bruised; sensitiveness to noise, music, and to pain; which appears intolerable, with despair, screams, weeping, restlessness and great anguish, chilliness, aversion to the open air; especially suitable to persons who do not use coffee, or to persons, who take a momentary dislike to coffee, though they are otherwise fond of it; the headache is caused by thinking, chagrin, a cold, &c. (Is frequently suitable after *Acon.* or *cham.*; or before *Ign. nux-v.* or *puls.*)

COLOCYNTHIS: Violent semi-lateral, tearing, drawing pains, or *crampy* aching pains, with nausea and vomiting; *compressive* sensation in the forehead, worse when stooping or lying on the back; the headache sets in every afternoon or evening, with great anguish and restlessness, obliging one to leave the bed; violent pain, extorting cries from the patient; sweat smelling like urine; copious watery urine during the pains, or scanty, fetid urine between the paroxysms.

IGNATIA: Aching pains over the nose; *worse or better when stooping*, or jerking and beating, pressing *as if the parts would split*, or boring stitches deep in the brain; tearing in the forehead, and sensation as if a nail had been driven into the brain, with nausea, obscuration of sight, photophobia. pale face, copious and watery urine; momentary disappearance of the pains by a change of position; they come on again after eating, in the evening after lying down, or early after rising; aggravation by coffee, brandy, tobacco and strong odours; tendency to start, fitful mood, taciturn and sad. (Is frequently suitable after *Cham. puls* or *nux-vom.*.)

Mercurius: Feeling of fulness as if the skull would split, or as if the head were tied up with a bandage; *tearing*, burning or *stitching* and boring pains, or semilateral tearing down to the teeth and neck, with *stitches in the ears;* violent aggravation at night, *by the warmth of the bed*, also by contact, hot and cold things; constant night-sweat, but without relief.

Nux vomica: Pain as from a nail driven into the brain, or stitching pains with nausea and sour vomiting; stitches and pressure in one side of the head, worse towards morning, driving the patient out of his senses; excessive sensitiveness of the brain to motion and walking; heaviness of the head, especially when moving the eyes, thinking, *with sensation as if the skull would split;* whizzing in the head, with vertigo, or with shocks when walking; *contusive pain in the brain; headache every morning on waking, after eating, in the open air*, when stooping, or during motion, even when merely moving the eyes; the pains come on again after *drinking coffee*, with aversion to coffee; pale, worn out look; constipation, with tendency of the blood to the head; irritable, vehement disposition, or lively, sanguine temper, &c. (Compare *Bry. cham. coff. ign.* and *puls.*)

Pulsatilla: Tearing pains, worse towards evening; or beating stitches, early after rising and in the evening after lying down; semilateral tearing pains, shocks and stitches, with vertigo, desire to vomit; heaviness in the head; obscuration of sight; photophobia; whizzing, tearing, darting or jerking in the ears; *pale face*, whining mood, loss of appetite, *no thirst*, chill, anguish, paroxysms of bleeding at the nose; *palpitation of the heart;* aggravation in the evening, also *during rest*, and especially when sitting; relief in the open air, decrease of the headache by pressing or bandaging the head; bland temper, or else cold and phlegmatic.

Rhus tox.: Tearing, stitching pains, extending to the ears, root of the nose, malar bones and jaws, with painfulness of the teeth and gums; burning or beating pains; fullness and oppressive heaviness of the head; headache immediately after a meal; desire to be quiet and lie down; the pains are excited again by the least chagrin, or by walking in the open air; *wavering of the brain when stepping*, and *creeping in the head.* (Is frequently suitable after *Bryonia.*)

Sepia: Stitching and boring pains, extorting cries from the patient, with nausea and vomiting; headache every morning;

semilateral tearing and drawing in the head; pressure and drawing in the occiput; photophobia, with inability to open one's eyes; constipation; sexual desire; aversion to food; tendency of the blood to the head, with heaviness and confusion; pressure over the eyes, when looking at bright day-light; feeling of coldness about the head.

Silicea: Beating pains with heat and tendency of the blood to the head; headache every morning or afternoon; aggravation by mental labour, talking or stooping; pains at night from the nape of the neck to the vertex; sensation as if the head would split, and as if the brain would issue through the forehead and eyes; semilateral stitching or tearing pains, extending to the nose and face; tumours on the head; frequent sweat about the head; great sensitiveness of the scalp; falling off of the hair. (Is frequently suitable after *Hep.* or *Lyc.*)

Sulphur: Fullness, pressure and heaviness of the head, especially forehead; or pressure as if the head would split; tearing, stitching, drawing or jerking pains, especially *on one side;* or beating and painful bubbling in the head, with heat and tendency of the blood to the head; roaring in the head; aching pain over the eyes, obliging one to knit one's brow or to close one's eyes; or headache with dim sight, inability to think, nausea and desire to vomit; headache every week, or every morning or night; or in the evening in bed, or after a meal; aggravation by thinking, in the open air, by walking; great sensitiveness of the scalp to contact; falling off of the hair.

Veratrum: Maddening pains; semilateral beating with pressure, or constriction in the brain, with constriction of the throat; sensation as if the brain were bruised; pains in the stomach; painful rigidity of the nape of the neck; copious discharge of clear urine; nausea, vomiting, &c.; great debility even unto fainting, with great *malaise* on raising one's-self from a recumbent posture; chilliness and cold sweat over the whole body; thirst; diarrhœic stools, or else constipation with tendency of blood to the head.

§ 6. Besides, we may use:

Arnica: For pains over one eye with greenish vomiting; crampy compression in the forehead, as if the brain were compressed and indurated; heat in the head, with coldness of the rest of the body.

Arsenicum: Semilateral. beating pains, with nausea, buzzing in the ears, &c., periodically, especially after a *meal,* or in the morning, or at night, or in the evening, in bed, with weeping and moaning; the pains sometimes become maddening; painfulness of the scalp; cold applications relieve the pain.

AURUM: Bruised pains, especially early in the morning, or during mental labour, so that the ideas frequently become confused; roaring in the head, in hysteric females.

CARB-VEG.: Aching or beating pains over the eyes, or in the whole head. commencing at the nape of the neck; the pains set in especially in the evening or after a meal, with tendency of the blood to the head, and heat in the head.

CHINA: Tearing, drawing or oppressive pains, as from a load on the head, worse in the open air and when reading or thinking; with coryza.

COCCULUS: Headache with *feeling of emptiness* in the head, or with bilious vomiting.

DULCAMARA: Oppressive, stupefying pain in the forehead, with stoppage of the nose; or boring and burning in the forehead, with digging in the brain; aggravation during motion, even when talking, with heaviness in the head.

HEPAR: Pain as from a nail in the brain; violent boring in the head, or nightly pains as if the forehead would be pulled out, with painful tumours on the head.

IPECACUANHA: Headache with nausea; sensation extending to the tongue as if the brain were bruised; vomiting or desire to vomit.

LYCOPODIUM: Headache with disposition to faint and great restlessness; or tearing headache, especially in the afternoon or at night; pains extending to the eyes and nose, even teeth, with desire to lie down.

OPIUM: Tendency of blood to the head, with constipation, violent, tearing pains, or tensive pressure through the whole brain, with beating or great heaviness in the head; unsteady look, thirst, dry mouth, sour eructations, desire to vomit, &c.

PLATINA: Violent, crampy pains, especially over the root of the nose, with heat and redness of the face, restlessness, whining mood, roaring in the head as of water, with coldness in the ears, eyes and one side of the face; scintillations, illusions of sight, objects appearing smaller than they really are. (Is frequently suitable after *Bell.*)

§ 7. Use more particularly:

a) For *pressing* pains *as if the skull would split:* 1) *Bell. bry. chin. natr-m. n-vom. puls. sep. sil. sulph.* 2) *Acon. amm. ant. baryt. calc. caps. caust. graph. magn-arct. merc. mez. natr. plat. phos. phos-ac. rhus. spig. spong. staph. stront.*

b) For *aching* pains: 1) *Anac. arn. bell. calc. carb-an. carb-veg. chin. coccul. ign. kal. lyc. natr-m. n-vom. phosph. sep. stann. sulph.* 2) *Acon. ars. asa. aur. bry. caust. cham. cic. dig. dulc. ferr. ipec lach mez. natr. petr. plat.*

c) For *tensive* pains: 1) ***Arn. asa. bell. caust. lyc. n-vom. puls. sil.*** *stront.* ***sulph.*** 2) ***Ars.*** *cann.* ***carb-an.*** *carb-veg. clem.* ***graph.*** *magn-arct.* ***mosch.*** *natr. natr-m. nitr. petr. spig.* ***stann. tart.*** *veratr.*

d) For *crampy*, pinching, spasmodic pains: 1) *Acon.* ***arn. calc.*** ***carb-veg.*** *coloc. ign. phos-ac. plat.* ***stram.*** 2) *Amb. ang.* ***chin.*** *colch. mez.* ***mosch.*** *n-mosch. n-vom. petr. sep. stann. zinc.*

e) For *compressive* pains: 1) *Arn. bry. carb-veg. chin.* ***cocc.*** *hell. lyc. men. mosch. natr-m. n-mosch. phos-ac. plat. sil. spig.* ***staph. tart.*** 2) *Acon. alum. anac. calc. caust. cic. con. dulc. graph. magn-arct. nitr-ac. oleand. sep. staph. sulph-ac.*

f) For *constrictive, contractive* pains: 1) *Anac. asa. carb-veg. chin. cocc. graph. laur. merc. natr-m. nitr. petr. phosph. plat. puls.* 2) *Acon. camph. cann. hyos. ipec. lach. mosch. petr.* ***phos-ac.*** *stann. sulph-ac. val. veratr.*

g) For pain as if *tied up with a bandage* or surrounded with a tight band: *Cycl. jod. laur. merc. nitr-ac. sassap. stann. sulph.*

§ 8. a) For *boring*, digging-up pains: 1) *Calc. dulc. hep.* ***puls. sep.*** 2) *Amm. amm-m. bell. cocc. ign. laur. magn-c. merc. mez. phos-ac. plat. sabin. spig. stann. staph. zinc.*

b) For *beating*, hammering, pulsative pains: 1) *Acon.* ***ars.*** *bell. calc. carb-veg. ferr. ign. kreos. lach. natr-m. phosph.* ***puls. sep.*** *sil. stram. sulph.* 2) *Borax. bry. cham. cocc. dros. euphr. kal. laur. led. mang. nitr-ac. op. oleand. petr. plat. sabad. seneg.* ***squill.***

c) For pain as if a *nail* or *plug* were driven into the brain: 1) *Anac. arn. hep. ign. magn-arct. n-vom. plat. sulph-ac.* 2) ***Asa*** *carb-veg. cocc. coff. dulc. hell. kreos. natr-m. oleand. rhus. thuj.*

d) For *tearing* or drawing pains: 1) *Arn. ars. bell. calc.* ***chin.*** *con. ign. lach. merc. natr-m nitr-ac. n-vom. puls. sep. sil.* ***sulph.*** 2) *Amb. aur. bry. caps. carb-an. carb-veg. cham. natr. phosph. spig. staph.*

e) *Stitching* pains: 1) *Acon. bell. bry canth. caust. con. ign. merc. natr. petr. puls. rhus. sep. sil. stann. sulph.* 2) ***Alum. arn.*** *asa. calc. chel. chin. lach. laur. magn-c. natr-m. n-vom.* ***selen. staph.***

f) *Sore* or *ulcerative* pains: 1) ***Amm.*** *ars. carb-veg.* ***caust. chin.*** *ign. lyc. magn-c. mez. natr-m. n-vom. phosph. sep.* ***sulph. zinc.*** 2) *Acon. borax. kreos. lach. magn-arct. mang.* ***oleand.*** ***rhus.*** *sabad. sabin. stront.*

g) Pain as if *bruised*, torn or dashed to pieces: 1) *Aur.* ***bell.*** *camph. chin. con. hell. ign. n-vom. puls. veratr.* 2) *Alum.* ***am-m. ars.*** *carb-an. caust. coff. con. euphr. hep. ipec. merc. mur-ac. phosph. phosph-ac. rhus. sep. stann. sulph. zinc.*

h) *Darting, jerking* pains: 1) ***Amb. arn. bell. calc. chin.***

ign. kal. ***magn-aust. nitr-ac.*** *puls. sep.* ***sil.*** 2) ***Anac. caust. graph.*** *lyc.* ***n-vom.*** *petr.* ***phosph.*** *phos-ac. plumb. sulph.*

§ 9. a) *Feeling of coldness* in the head or on the vertex: 1) *Bell. calc. phosph. sep. sulph. Veratr.* 2) *Acon. arn. dulc. mosch.*

b) *Burning* in the head: 1) *Acon. bell. bry. eug. merc. n-vom. phosph. sabad. sep.* 2) *Amm. arg. arn. carb-veg. caust. cocc. dulc. graph. hell. kal. mur-ac. phos-ac. rhus. spig. stann. sulph-ac. veratr.*

c) *Roaring, buzzing* in the head: 1) *Aur. calc. graph. lach. plat. puls. staph. sulph. zinc.* 2) *Acon. baryt. carb-veg. caust. cocc. dulc. graph. hell. kal. mur-ac. phos-ac. rhus. spig. stann. sulph-ac. veratr.*

d) sensation as if the brain were *loose, moving,* falling against the skull: 1) *Acon. bell. chin. sep. sulph.* 2) *Acon. ars. baryt. bry. calc. carb-an. cic. coff. kal. lyc. magn-s. phos-ac. plat. puls. rhus. spig.*

e) Wavering (*swashing*) in the head, as of water: 1) *Bell. dig. amm. asa. aur. carb-an. hep. hyos. lach. magn-m. n-vom. rhus. spig. squill.*

f) *Creeping* sensation as of something alive: 1) *Arn. colch. hyos. laur. magn-aust. plat. puls. rhus.* 2) *Acon. baryt. canth. cic. cocc. cupr. petr. phosph. phos-ac. sil. sulph.*

g) Sensation as if a ball were *rising* into the head: *Acon. ign. lach. plumb. sep.*

h) Sensation as if a *current of air* were *passing through the head,* or as if wind were blowing upon one: *Aur. colch. magn-aust. puls. sabin. zinc.*

§ 10. a) For pains from *above downwards,* pressure, stitches from above downwards: 1) *Carb-veg. caust. ferr. magn-arct. puls. sulph.* 2) *Amb. cin. con. cupr. mur-ac. nitr-ac. n-vom. phos-ac. plat. rhus. spig. spong. tart. veratr.*

b) Pains from *below upwards:* 1) *Bell. caust. cham.* 2) *Phos-ac. rhus. sep. sil. staph.*

c) From *within outwards:* 1) *Asa. bell. bry. calc. chin. con. dulc. merc. mez. phosph. rhus. sep. sil. spig. spong. stann. sulph. val.* 2) *Acon. alum. carb-veg. dros. ign. lach. lyc. magn-arct. magn-m. mur-ac. natr. natr-m. n-mosch. n-vom. phos-ac. rhod. sabad. samb. staph. verb.*

d) From *without inwards:* 1) *Anac. arn. calc. canth. laur. plat.* 2) *Coccul. dulc. hell. ign. plumb. sabin. spig. stann. staph. sulph-ac.*

e) Pains seated at a *small spot:* 1) *Acon. bry. lyc.* 2) *Amb. anac. dulc. eug. ferr. graph. hep. laur. led. mosch. n-mosch. plat. sep. spig. squill. staph.*

f) *external* pains, in the integuments of the skull: 1) *Acon. arn. bell. calc. chin. lyc. merc. mez. n-vom. rhus. staph.* 2) *Alum. carb-veg. caust. graph. guaj. hep. nitr-ac. phosph. puls. ruta. sep. spig. sulph. thuj. veratr.*

§ 11. a) *Forehead* and *sinciput* are principally affected: 1) *Acon. amm. ars. bell. calc. chin. cocc. dulc. ign. kreos. lyc. natr-m. n-mosch. n-vom. phosph. plat. sabad. stann. sulph.* 2) *Alum. arn. caps. carb-veg. ferr. hep. ipec. lach. magn-c. magn-m. merc. mez. natr. nitr-ac. puls. spig. thuj.*

b) The *temporal* region: 1) *Bell. calc. natr-m. plat.* 2) *Acon. alum. anac. chin. kal. kreos. magn-c. mang. n-mosch. petr. puls. sabin. sulph-ac.*

c) The *sides* of the head: 1) *Acon. bry. natr-m. phos-ac.* 2) *Asa. canth. graph. guaj. kal. laur. lyc magn-arct. magn-aust. magn-c magn-m. mang. plat. puls. sulph. thuj. veratr.*

d) *Semilateral* pains: 1) *Ars. calc. chin. cic. coloc. ign. merc. n-vom. puls. sep* 2) *Agar. alum. amm-m. anac. asa cin. dulc. kal. mang. mez. mur-ac. phosph. phos-ac. plat. sabad. sabin. sassap. spig. staph. sulph-ac. verb.*

e) *Left side: Ant. arn. asa. asar. calc. chin. colch. coloc. dros lach. merc. mez. nitr ac. n-mosch. rhod. selen. sil. spig. sulph zinc.*

f) *Right side: Acon. alum. calc. caust. dros. ferr. hep. ign. lyc. mosch. plumb. ruta. sabad. sabin. sil.*

g) *Vertex* and *upper head:* 1) *Agn. calc. caust. con. lach. lyc. nitr-ac. phosph. spig.* 2) *Acon. amb. anac. carb-an. cocc. cupr. natr. natr-m. n-mosch. phosph. sep. sil. staph. sulph. veratr.*

h) *Occiput:* 1) *Acon calc. carb-veg. ign. kal. nitr-ac. petr. rhus sep. sulph.* 2) *Amb. carb-an. colch. magn-m. mez. mosch. natr. n-vom. sil. thuj.*

§ 12. a) The *eyes* are involved, or the pains extend to the eyes: 1) *Acon. baryt. bell. bry. calc. coccul. hep. lach. natr. natr-m. n-vom. puls. selen. sep. sil.* 2) *Ars. borax carb-veg. caust. cic ign. kreos. nitr phosph phos-ac. spong. sulph-ac.*

b) The *region of the ears* is principally affected, or the pains extend to the ears: 1) *Canth. lyc. merc. mosch. mur-ac. puls. rhus. sep. sulph.* 2) *Anac. alum. arn. borax. calc. caps. caust. con. ign. natr. natr-m. nitr. phosph.*

c) The pains are seated over *the root of the nose*, or extend down to the nose: 1) *Acon. hep n-vom. phosph. rhus.* 2) *Ars. ign. lach. lyc. merc. mez. mosch. stann.*

d) They affect the *face:* 1) *Acon. hep. rhus. sil.* 2) *Amb. bry. calc. carb-veg. cin. dros. graph. kreos. lach. natr-m. nitr. n-vom. petr. phosph. spong. sulph. thuj.*

e) They cause *heat* and *redness* of the face: ***Acon. bell. ign. lach.*** *natr-m. n-vom. phosph. plat. sil.* ***sulph.***

f) They extend to the *teeth:* 1) ***lach.*** *lyc.* ***puls. rhus. sep.*** 2) *Calc. carb-veg. caust. ign. kreos. magn-c. merc.* ***sulph.***

g) The *nape* of the neck is involved, or the pains extend to the nape of the neck: ***Baryt. bell. carb-veg. caust.*** *con. graph.* ***kal. lyc. puls. sabin.***

§ 13. a) The pains attack the *understanding* and impede thought: *Acon. amb aur. bell. bry. calc. carb-an. caust. cocc.* ***hell.*** *kal. lach. magn-c. natr. n-vom. op. petr. phosph. puls* ***rhus. sil. sulph.***

b) They cause *vertigo* or dizziness: 1) *Acon. bell. bry.* ***calc. carb-an.*** *caust. lach. n-vom. phosph puls.* 2) *Anac. chin. cocc. con. hell. magn-m. mur-ac. natr. natr-m. nitr-ac. rhus. sep.*

c) *Dimness* or *weakness* of sight: *Acon. arn. bell. calc.* ***cham. cic.*** *hyos. ign. n-vom. puls. sil. stram.*

d) *roaring* in the ears: *Acon. ars. borax. chin. n-vom. puls.* ***rhus. staph.*** *thuj.*

e) *Nausea* or vomiting: 1) ***Amm.*** *arn.* ***bell.*** *bry.* ***carb-veg.*** *coloc.* ***ipec.*** *lach. nitr-ac. n-vom. puls. sep. sulph.* 2) *Alum. calc. chin. cocc. con. dulc. ign. kal. magn-c. natr-m. phosph. stann. veratr.*

f) They *oblige* one to *lie down:* 1) *Bry. calc. con.* ***n-vom. phos-ac.*** *puls. rhus.* ***selen. sep.*** 2) ***Alum. amm.*** *anac.* ***bell. graph. kal.*** *magn-m. natr-m. nitr-ac. oleand. op. petr. sil. stann. sulph.*

§ 14. a) The pains occur principally *in the evening:* 1) *Alum.* ***carb-an.*** *carb-veg. laur. lyc. magn-c. magn-m. phosph. puls. sulph.* 2) *Coloc. hep. merc. mur-ac. nitr. nitr-ac. n-vom. petr.* ***rhus. sep. sil.*** *val.*

b) *At night* or *in the evening in bed :* 1) ***Bell.*** *chin. hep. lach. lyc. puls. sil. sulph.* 2) *Alum. ars. magn-c. merc. natr. nitr-ac. op.* ***sassap.*** *sepia.*

c) In the morning *on waking :* 1) *Bry. calc.* ***kal.*** *lyc.* ***natr-m. n-vom.*** *sulph.* 2) ***Baryt.*** *bell.* ***cham.*** *chin. coff. con. hep. ign. ipec.* ***lach.*** *magn-c. magn-m.* ***nitr-ac.*** *phosph. puls. thuj.*

d) In the *morning* generally: 1) *Bry. calc. caust. chin. hep.* ***kal. lach.*** *lyc. natr-m. n-vom. petr. phosph. phos-ac. sep. sil. sulph.* 2) *Amm. amm-m. ars. aur. baryt. bell. carb-an. con. jod. lyc.* ***magn-c.*** *magn-m. mang. mur-ac. natr. nitr. nitr-ac. n-mosch.* ***puls.*** *thuj.*

e) *After a meal:* 1) *Amm. ars. bry. carb-an. carb-veg. n-vom.* ***phosph.*** *puls. rhus. sulph.* 2) *Alum. arn. baryt. calc. canth.* ***caust. chin.*** *cin. coff. con. graph. ign. kal. lach. lyc. magn-c. magn-m.* ***natr.*** *nitr. nitr-ac. puls.*

f) In consequence of *mental labour* (reading, writing, thinking

&c.): 1) ***Calc. chin. natr. n-vom. puls. sil.*** 2) ***Arn. aur. carb-veg. caust.*** *cin. cocc. coff. ign. lyc. natr-m. petr. phosph. sep. sulph.*

g) Worse in the *open air*, better in a room: 1) *calc. caust. chin. coff. con. rhus. spig. sulph.* 2) *Bell. ferr. hell. hep. magn-arct. mang. merc. mur-ac. n-vom. petr. puls. staph. sulph. sulph-ac.*

h) *Worse in a room*, better in the open air: 1) *Alum. amm. arn. asar. bov. carb-an. magn-c. magn-m. phosph. puls. sabin.* 2) *Acon. ant. arn. hell. sep. sulph.*

§. 15. Compare: CONGESTIONS OF THE HEAD, PAINS, PAROXYSMS OF, CAUSES, CONDITIONS, &c.

HEAD, LARGE, OF CHILDREN.—The best remedies for this affection and the retarded closing of the fontanelles, are: *Calc. sil. sulph.* (See: SCROPHULA.)

HEAD, MORBID CONDITION OF, in consequence of mental exertions.—Principal remedies: 1) *N-vom. sulph.;* or: 2) *Aur. calc. colch. lach. mosch. natr. natr-m. puls. sil.;* or: 3) *Amm. amb. bell. cham. cic. dig. jod. laur. led. nitr. n-mosch. phosph. sep. spong. sulph-ac. val. zinc.*

See: WORN OUT, WEAK MEMORY, EMOTIONS, MORBID.

HEARING, DEFECTIVE, DYSÆCIA, &C.

§ 1. The principal remedies for this affection are: 1) *Bell. calc. caust. graph. hyos. lach. led. lyc. mang. merc. nitr-ac. op. petr. phosph. puls. sil. sulph.* 2) *Amm. anac. asa. aur. coff. con. hep. kal. magn-c. mur-ac. natr. natr-m. n-vom. phos-ac. sec. staph. veratr.* 3) *Amb. ant. ars. carb-veg. cic. coccul. dros. jod. laur. oleand. plumb. rhus. ruta. stram.*

§ 2. If caused by *congestion of blood*, with buzzing, &c., give: 1) *Aur. bell. caust. graph. merc. phosph. puls. sil. sulph.;* or: 2) *Anac. bry. calc. lyc. mur-ac. n-vom. sep. spig.*

For *nervous* deafness, from *paralysis* of the auditory nerves: 1) *Bell. caust. hyos. n-vom. petr. phosph. phos-ac. puls. sil.;* or: 2) *Anac. calc. coccul. con. graph. lyc. mur-ac. nitr-ac. op. veratr.*

For *catarrhal* or *rheumatic* deafness, in consequence of a *cold* in the head, or of the whole body, give: 1) *Acon. ars. bell. cham. hep. led. merc.* and *puls.;* or: 2) *Calc. caust. coff. lach. nitr-ac. sulph.*

§ 3. If caused by *suppression* of *herpes* or other cutaneous eruptions: *Sulph.*, or *Ant.*, or: *Caust. graph.* or *Lach.* ? &c. See: CAUSES: SUPPRESSED ERUPTIONS.

If a sequel to some acute exanthem, measles, scarlatina, &c.: 1) *Bell. merc. men. phosph. puls. sulph.;* or: 2) *Carb. veg. phosph.*—Deafness caused by *measles,* requires: *Puls., Carb. veg.;* by *scarlatina: Bell.* or *Hep.;* and by *variola: Merc.* or *Sulph.*

If caused by suppression of fever and ague, give: 1) *Calc. puls.;* or: 2) *Carb-veg. hep. n-vom. sulph.*

If by *abuse* of *mercury*: 1) *Asa. nitr-ac. staph.;* or: 2) *Aur. carb-veg.? chin.? hep. petr. sulph.*

If by *swelling* or *hypertrophy* of the *tonsils,* give: *Aur. merc. nitr-ac. staph.*

If by *typhoid* diseases: *Arn. phosph. phos-ac. veratr.*

If by *suppression* of an habitual *discharge from the ears* or nose: 1) *Hep lach. led.;* or: 2) *Bell. merc. puls.*

§ 4. Particular symptomatic indications:

Belladonna: Tendency of blood to the head, with buzzing in the ears, scintillations, pressing pain in the forehead from within outwards, especially in young. plethoric, large individuals; also in scrofulous subjects, with a fine, delicate skin, red and white cheeks; also after apoplexy, meningitis, typhus, &c

Calcarea: Deafness as if the ears were closed; frequent buzzing, rolling or ringing, singing and musical sounds in the ears; or frequent beating and heat in the ears; *constant dryness* of the ears, or purulent discharge; aching pain in the forehead, &c.

Causticum: Sensation as if the ears were stopped up, with buzzing and roaring in the head; *loud reverberation of sounds and of one's own words in the ears;* otorrhœa, rheumatic pains in the ears and extremities; extreme sensitiveness to cold winds, &c.

Graphites: *Great dryness* in the ears, or purulent discharge; hard hearing, which sometimes ceases while riding in a carriage; singing, whizzing and ringing, or buzzing and thundering *reports in the ears,* especially at night, or sensation as if air were penetrating into the eustachian tube; herpes and crusts around the ears and on other parts of the body.

Hyoscyamus: Hard hearing as if stupefied, especially after apoplexy, if *Bell.* proves ineffectual.

Lachesis: *Dry* ears, with hard and pale, or white and pappy cerumen; painful beating, cracking or whizzing, rolling and *drumming* in the ears, with reverberation of the sounds; soreness and crusts around the ears, &c. (Frequently suitable after *Caust.*

Ledum: The ears feel as if closed, with whizzing in the ears; dullness and stupefaction of the head on the affected side, feeling of stiffness in the scalp, and after suppression of otorrhœa or of coryza or catarrh of the eyes.

LYCOPODIUM: Roaring and whizzing in the ears, or cracking as of air-vesicles; sensation as if hot blood were tending towards the ears; humid scurf in the region of the ear, or on the ears.

MERCURIUS: Stoppage of the ears discontinuing when swallowing or blowing one's nose; loud reverberation of all the sounds in the ear; ringing, buzzing and whizzing, especially in the evening, or purulent otorrhœa with ulceration of the ears; rheumatic pains in the ears or head, or in the teeth; *great tendency to sweat*, &c.

MANGANUM: Frequent otalgia, with tearing and stitching extending to the tympanum; ulcerative pain in the ears; whizzing and rushing in the ears, especially after stooping; *report*, when swallowing or blowing one's nose; hard hearing as if the ear were stopped up, the ear opening when blowing one's nose; the deafness increases or decreases according as the weather is fair or bad.

NITRI ACIDUM: Dry ears, or discharge of cerumen; stoppage of the ears, with roaring, beating and detonations; frequent toothache, with scorbutic affection of the gums; stitches in the teeth and ears.

OPIUM: Suitable after apoplexy, or to patients who are liable to epileptic fits; or in alternation with *Bell.* or *Hyoscyam.*

PETROLEUM: Painful dryness of the inner ear, or discharge of blood and pus; ringing, or rumbling and roaring in the ears; herpes and soreness on or near the ears; frequent toothache with swollen cheek; bleeding of the gums, pressing pains in the occiput, from within outwards, &c. (Is frequently suitable after *Nitr-ac.*)

PHOSPHORUS: Hard hearing, especially deep to the human voice, with loud reverberation of the sounds, especially *words*, in the ears, extending to the inner head; tendency of blood to the ears, with beating and throbbing; dry feeling, or discharge of cerumen.

PULSATILLA: Hard, black or liquid cerumen, with discharge; stitching pains in the ears, or discharge of pus or blood; the ears are stopped with roaring and whizzing, or beating, murmuring, ringing or chirping; especially suitable to persons of a bland disposition, or to females who are liable to leucorrhœa and other irregularities of the urinary system.

SILICEA: Discharge of cerumen; stoppage, passing off with a report, or when blowing the nose; deafness, especially to the human voice, also without noise in the ears, or also with ringing, gurgling and fluttering; the deafness is worse when the moon changes, especially at full or new moon; deafness, alternating with extreme sensitiveness of hearing; crusts behind the ears.

Sulphur: Deafness, especially to the human voice; frequent stoppage of the ears, especially when eating or blowing one's nose; also *on one side only;* murmuring or undulating sensation in the ears as if caused by water, or whizzing and roaring; tendency of blood to the head; disposition to coryza or other blennorrhœas, discharge of the ears, &c.

§ 5. Use more particularly, for *roaring* and *whizzing* in the ears: 1) *Acon. bell. caust. chin. con. graph. lyc. merc. nitr-ac. n-vom. petr. puls. sep. sulph.* 2) *Anac. alum. amb. amm. baryt. borax. bry. calc. carb-veg. cham. croc. hep. kal. lach. natr-m. op. phosph. plat. spig. therid.*

Buzzing: Amm. bell. caust. con. graph. hyos. jod. natr-m. puls. sulph.

Thundering, rumbling: Amm-m. calc. caust. graph. plat.

Ringing and singing: 1) *Bell. calc. caust. chin. graph. kal. lyc. men. natr-m. n-vom. puls.* 2) *Amm. baryt. borax. chel. con. petr. sil. sulph.*

Fluttering (as of a bird): *Aur. bell. calc. caust. graph. petr. puls. sil. spig. sulph.*

Ringing, as of bells: *Amb. calc. con. led. natr-m. sil.*

Cracking, when chewing or moving the jaw: *Baryt. calc. graph. kal. men. natr-m. nitr-ac. petr.*

Frequent *reports: Graph. kal. mang. natr. sil. staph. zinc.*

§ 6. For deafness to the *human voice: Ars. phosph. sil. sulph.*

For sensation of *stoppage:* 1) *Bry. con. lyc. mang. merc. puls. sil. spig.* 2) *Calc. caust. graph. kal. jod. lach. men. nitr-ac. petr. sep sulph.*

Sensation as if *closed* by something in front: 1) *Calc. nitr-ac. sulph.* 2) *Acon. ant. carb-veg. chin. coccul. hyos. led. men. phosph. spig.*

For occasional alternation with great *sensitiveness* of hearing: *Aur. bell. calc. coff. lyc. sep. spig.*

§ 7. Comp.: Excessive *irritation* of the sense of hearing, Eruptions on the ears, Hæmorrhage from the ears, Otorrhœa, Cerumen, Pains in the ears, &c.

Thinking practitioners, who endeavour to reason from analogy, may find useful indications under Amblyopia.

HEARING, excessive irritation of.— Principal remedies: 1) *Arn. aur. bell. bry. coff. lach. lyc. natr. phos-ac. sep. spig.* 2) *Acon. calc. cham. chin. con. graph. merc. n-vom. petr. phosph. puls. sulph.*

For sensitiveness to *noise*, give: 1) *Acon. bell. bry. cham. coff. ign. lyc. n-vom.* 2) *Ang. arn. borax. calc. colch. con. ipec. natr. phos-ac. plat. puls. sep. spig.*

To *music*: 1) *Bry. natr. phos-ac. sep.* 2) *Acon. amb. cham. lyc. n-vom. phosph. puls.*

Comp.: NERVOUS IRRITATION, DEBILITY, &c.

HEARTBURN, ERUCTATIONS, REGURGITATION, &c.

§ 1. Principal remedies: 1) *Arn. bry. calc. carb-veg. con. ign. lyc. merc. natr-m. n-vom. phos. rhus. sep. sulph. veratr.* 2) *Amm. arn. carb-an. caust. cocc. graph. natr. sil. staph. tart. val.* 3) *Alum. amb. ant. bell. cann. canth. caps. chin. cin. croc. cycl. dros. graph. kal. mez. natr. nitr-ac. petr. ran. rhod. sabad. sassap. stan. sulph-ac. thuj.*

§ 2. For *frequent rising of air*, give: 1) *Arn. bell. bry. carb-veg. caust. cocc. con. hep. kal. lach. merc. natr. natr-m. n-vom. phosph. puls. rhus. ruta. sep. staph. sulph. veratr.* 2) *Alum. amb. amm-m. ant. calc. carb-an. chin. dulc. graph. ign. lyc. mur-ac. petr. sabad. sassap. sil. spong. stann. sulph-ac. thuj. val. verb.*

Painful *eructations* require: *Coccul. n-vom. petr. phosph. sabad. sep.*— *Ineffectual urging* to eructate: *Amb. carb-an. caust. cocc. con. graph. hyos. ign. kal. magn-arct. magn-c. n-vom. phos. plumb. puls. rhus. sulph. zinc.*

Eructations *tasting of the ingesta*: *Amb. amm. ant. carb-an. carb-veg. caust. chin. con. lyc. natr-m. phosph. puls. sil.*

§ 3. *Regurgitation* of food; 1) *Arn. bry. carb-veg. graph. n-vom. phosph. puls. sassap. sulph. sulph-ac. tart.* 2) *Ant. bell. calc. can. con. dros. hep. ign. lyc. merc. natr-m. plumb. staph. veratr. zinc.*

Regurgitation of *undigested* food: 1) *Bry. cham. con. ign. lach. phosph.* 2) *Amm-m. camph. magn-m. mez. sulph.*

§ 4. *Sour* eructations or regurgitation: 1) *Calc. cham. chin. lyc. n-vom. phosph. sulph.* 2) *Amm. ars. bell. caust. ferr. graph. ign. ipec. kal. natr-m. phos-ac. puls. sassap. stann. thuj. veratr.*

Pyrosis, heartburn: 1) *Amm. calc. chin. can. croc. lyc. natr-m. n-vom. sulph.* 2) *Caps. carb-an. carb-veg. caust. dulc. graph. hep. ign. jod. kal. merc. nitr-ac. phosph. puls. sabad. sep. sil. staph. sulph-ac.*

Waterbrash: 1) *Ars. calc. carb-veg. lyc. natr-m. nitr-ac. n-vom. phosph. sep. sulph.* 2) *Baryt. bell. caust. cupr. dros. graph. hep. ipec. led. natr. petr. rhus. sabad. sil. staph. veratr.*

§ 5. Comp.: GASTRIC DERANGEMENT, WEAK STOMACH, DERANGEMENT OF THE STOMACH, &c.

HEART, DISEASES OF :

§ 1. The best remedies are: 1) *Acon. calc. natr-m. puls. sep. spig. sulph.* 2) *Arn. ars. aur. cann. caust. dig. lach. phosph. spong.;* or 3) *Amb. asa. bell. con. cupr. kreos. mang. mosch. natr. n-mosch. n-vom. rhus.*

§ 2. For *carditis* use: 1) *Acon. bry. cann. caust. lach. puls.;* or 2) *Ars. cocc. spig.*

For acute *rheumatism* of the heart: 1) *Acon. caust. lach.;* or, 2) *Ars. bry. puls. spig.*

For *aneurism:* 1) *Carb-veg. lach. lyc.;* or 2) *Calc. caust. graph. guaj. puls. rhus. spig.;* or 3) *Amb. arn. ars. ferr. natr-m. zinc.*

For *hypertrophy: Ars.? jod.? phosph.? spong.?*

For *polypi* of the heart: 1) *Lach.;* or 2) *Calc.? staph.?*

§ 3. For *palpitation:* 1) *Acon. calc. chin. jod. lyc. merc. natr-m. phosph. puls. sep. spig. sulph.* 2) *Alum. ars. aur. bell. bry. caust. cocc. coff. ign. kal. lach. n-vom. petr. phos-ac. ruta. thuj. veratr.*

For palpitation from *plethora* or *rush of blood: Acon. aur. bell. coff. ferr. lach. n-vom. op. phosph. sulph.*

In the case of *nervous* or *hysteric* individuals: *Asa. cham. cocc. coff. lach. n-vom. puls. veratr.*

After *emotions: Acon. cham. coff. ign. n-vom. op. veratr.*— After *chagrin: Acon. cham. ign. n-vom.*— After a *fright: Op.* or *Coff.*—After sudden *joy: Acon.* or *Coff.*—After great *fear* or anguish: *Veratr.*

After debilitating *loss of fluids:* 1) *Chin.;* or 2) *N-vom. phos-ac. sulph*

After *suppression* of *eruptions*, or old ulcers, &c.: *Ars. caust. lach. sulph.*

According to several practical observations communicated to me by a friend and colleague, *Bromine* 30 (and even higher) is an excellent remedy for many diseases of the heart, and also *polypi of the heart;* and *Ars.* and *Kalic.* are excellent remedies for *dropsy of the pericardium* and *pericarditis.*

§ 4. Compare: CONGESTION OF THE CHEST, EMOTIONS, PLETHORA, &c.

HEATED, ILL EFFECTS OF GETTING, in consequence of exertions, exposure to the heat of the sun, &c.

§ 1. The best remedies are: 1) *Acon. ant. bell. bry. camph. carb-veg. sil.;* or: 2) *Op. thuj. zinc.*

§ 2. Particular indications:

ACONITUM: For the consequences of a *stroke of the sun*, or of excessive *heat of the stove*, especially when the patient had been sleeping in the sun or near the hot stove.

ANTIMONIUM: One is unable to bear the heat of the sun, or is exhausted by doing the least work in the sun, with night-sweat, constant desire to sleep, gastric symptoms, &c., and in general, if *Bryon.* should not be sufficient to remove these symptoms.

BELLADONNA: *Aconite* being insufficient, and especially for: headache, with feeling of fullness, and sensation as if every thing would issue through the forehead; worse when stooping, moving or by the least emotion; great anguish and restlessness, rage, or great irritation of the cerebral nerves, or great fearfulness, tendency to start, and dread of the things *around and near one;* disposition to weep and scream.

BRYONIA: Painful feeling of fulness in the head; loss of appetite, or *loathing*, vomiting and diarrhœa; milk is indigestible; mobility and trembling; the pressure of the clothes on the hypochondria is troublesome; vehement disposition, fits of anger; dread of the future.

CAMPHOR: *Acon.* or *Bell.* being insufficient to remove the effects of heat.

CARBO VEG.: Every exposure to heat causes headache, or heaviness, pulsative pains and pressure over the eyes; pain in the eyes, whenever the patient endeavours to look at a thing.

SILICEA: The heat causes nausea or other gastric ailments, for which *Ant.* and *Bry.* are insufficient.

§ 3. For the *weariness* which one often experiences in heavy sultry weather, give: 1) *Bry. carb-veg. n-vom. rhod. sil.;* or 2) *Caust. lach. natr. natr-m. nitr-ac. petr. phosph.*

§ 4. Comp.: SEASONS and WEATHER, WORN OUT, DEBILITY, &c.

HEMERALOPIA.—The best remedies for this kind of blindness, which commences at twilight, are: 1) *Bell. veratr.;* or, 2) *Merc. hyos. puls. stram.*

See: Amblyopia, for particular indications.

HEPAR SULPHURIS, ILL EFFECTS OF.

For poisoning with large doses: 1) *Vinegar diluted with water*, or *citric acid;* 2) Mucilaginous drinks and the like, or *injections.*

For secondary ailments and the consequences of medicinal abuse of Hepar, give: 1) *Bell.;* or, 2) *Cham. sil.* 3) *Alum. ign. graph.*

HERNIA.

§ 1. The best remedies for the cure of hernia, are: 1) *Amm-m. aur. cocc. lyc. magn-c. n-vom. sil. sulph-ac. veratr.* 2) *Cham. clem. magn-arct. nitr-ac. rhus. sil. sulph.*

Hernia of *little children*, occasioned by constant screaming, requires: *Aur. cocc. n-vom. nitr-ac.* or *veratr.*

§ 2. *Incarceration* of hernia is generally cured, without operation, by: 1) *Acon. n-vom. op. sulph.;* or, 2) *Ars. bell. lach. veratr.*

Aconitum: Violent *inflammation* of the parts, with burning pains in the abdomen as from hot coal, extreme sensitiveness to contact, nausea, *bitter, bilious vomiting*, anguish and cold sweat; in most cases relief is obtained by one dose, which may be followed by a second dose in one hour; but if no relief sets in after the third dose, give *Sulphur*. (See below.)

Nux vom.: The swelling is less painful or sensitive to contact, and the vomiting is less violent, but there is great difficulty of breathing; the incarceration is caused by a cold, exposure to heat, by a fit of anger or by chagrin, or also by irregular living, &c. (May be repeated every two hours.)

Opium: If no relief is obtained after the second dose of Nux, or if the following symptoms occur from the commencement: Red face; distended, hard abdomen, putrid eructations or vomiting of fæcal matter. (Repeat every fifteen minutes until relieved.)

If the vomiting should be attended by cold sweat and coldness of the extremities, *Veratr.* deserves a preference; and if no improvement takes place after the second dose, give *Bell.*

Sulphur: If *Aconite* remains without effect, or if the bilious vomiting should change to *sour*. If, after giving the Sulphur, the patient should go to sleep, do not disturb him for some hours at least.

If gangrenous symptoms should set in, give *Lach.;* or *Ars.* if Lach. should not suffice.

HEPATITIS, inflammation of the liver, with other diseases.

§ 1. Principal remedies: 1) *Acon. bell. bry. cham. chin. lach. merc. n-vom. puls. sulph.* 2) *Aur. calc. kal. lyc. magn-m. natr. natr-m. nitr-ac.* 3) *Alum. amb. amm-c. cann. canth. n-mosch.* 4) *Cic. dig. magn-m. mang. nitr. petr. ran.*

§ 2. *Acute* hepatitis requires: 1) *Acon.* 2) *Bell. merc. n-vom.;* or, 3) *Bry. cham. chin. lach. puls. sulph.*

Aconitum: Violent, inflammatory fever, with stitches in the region of the liver, intolerable pains, moaning, tossing about, anguish and dread of death.

Belladonna: Aching pains extending to the chest and shoulder; distention in the pit of the stomach ; tension in the region of the stomach ; laboured and anxious breathing ; congestion of blood to the head ; obscuration of sight ; vertigo with fainting ; burning thirst; anxious tossing about and sleeplessness (Is frequently suitable after *Acon.*, in alternation with *Merc.* or *Lach.*)

Bryonia: Aching pains, with tension in the hypochondria, yellow-coated tongue, *violent oppression of the chest*, with hurried, anxious breathing, constipation, aggravation of the pains by motion.

Chamomilla: Dull aching pains, not aggravated *either by pressure or motion, or breathing ;* pressure in the stomach, tension in the hypochondria, oppression of the chest; *yellow colour of the skin*, yellow-coated tongue, bitter taste in the mouth, and paroxysms of anguish.

China: Aggravation every other day, with stitching and aching pains, swelling and hardness of the region of the liver and stomach ; headache, bitter taste in the mouth, and yellow-coated tongue.

Lachesis: *Merc.* or *Bell.* being insufficient, or alternately with either, suitable to drunkards.

Mercurius: *Bell.* being insufficient, especially for aching pains which do not allow one to lie on the right side ; bitter taste in the mouth ; loss of appetite, thirst ; constant chills, *very yellow colour of the skin and eyes.* (After *Merc.*, *Lach.* is frequently suitable.)

Nux vom.: Stitching or beating pains, with excessive sensitiveness of the region of the liver to contact ; bitter and sour taste, desire to vomit or vomiting ; pressure in the hypochondria and region of the stomach, with short breath ; thirst, red urine, headache, vertigo and paroxysms of anguish. (After *Nux-v.*, *Sulph.* is frequently suitable.)

Pulsatilla: Frequent attacks of anguish, especially at night, with diarrhœic, greenish and slimy stools ; desire to vomit ; bitter taste in the mouth, yellow-coated tongue ; oppressed chest ; tension in the hypochondria and pressure in the stomach.

Sulphur: Frequently after *Nux-v.*, especially when the stitching pains continue ; or when the above-mentioned remedies are ineffectual, or produce only a partial improvement.

§ 3. The best remedies for *chronic* affections of the liver are: 1) *N-vom. sulph.;* or, 2) *Aur. lach. lyc. magn-m. natr.;* or, 3) *Alum. amb. calc. chin. sil.;* or, 4) *Chel. ign. jod.*

For *swelling* or *induration* of the liver: 1) *Ars. calc. chin. n-vom. sulph.;* or, 2) *Caps. graph. lyc. magn-m. merc. natr-m. n-mosch. puls.*

For *abscesses:* *Lach.* or *Sil.;* or: *Bell.? merc.? hep.?*

For affections of the liver resulting from *mismanaged* or *suppressed fever and ague:* 1) *N-vom. sulph.* 2) *Calc. caps. lach. natr-m. puls.*

For *bilious calculi* in the liver, I recommend: *Calc. hep. lach. sil. sulph.*

HERPES PUSTULOSUS, Ecthyma.—Not to be confounded with *rupia*, the primitive form of ecthyma being *pustulous*, that of rupia *vesicular;* the ecthyma-pustules, at their base, are more inflamed, harder and more firmly seated, than in rupia. (See: Rupia, Rhypia.)

However, rupia and ecthyma being closely related to each other, externally at least, the same remedies will probably do for either eruption. Ecthyma seems to require more particularly: *Ars. merc. rhus. sulph.;* or, *Borax. cham. staph.*

See: Rupia and Herpes.

HERPES OF THE SEXUAL ORGANS, HERPES PRÆPUTIALIS, &c.

§ 1. For true *herpes præputialis* (spots on the prepuce): *Aur. hep. nitr-ac. phos-ac.*—Besides: *Dulc. sep. sulph.*

Itching of the pudendum requires: 1) *Calc. carb-v. con. kal. lyc. natr-m. sep. sil. sulph.* 2) *Amm. graph. kreos. magn-c. nitr-ac. staph.*

Itching and *herpes* of the *scrotum.* 1) *Dulc. petr. natr-m. nitr-ac. sulph.* 2) *Amb. coccul. rhod. thuj.*

Itching and humour of *the anus:* 1) *Merc. nitr-ac. sep. sulph. thuj.* 2) *Bar. calc. zinc.*

See: Herpes, Vagina, swelling of, Phimosis, &c.

HERPES SQUAMOSUS, Psoriasis.

§ 1. Principal remedies: 1) *Ars. calc. cic. clem. dulc. led. lyc. merc. sep. sulph.* 2) *Bry. caust. graph. mur-ac. nitr-ac. oleand. petr. phos. rhus. thuj.* 3) *Aur.? cupr.? magn-c.? sassap.? zinc.?*

§ 2. For psoriasis *infantilis:* *Calc. cic. lyc. merc. sulph.*

Psoriasis *inveterata :* 1) *Clem. sulph.* 2) *Calc. merc. petr. rhus. sep.*

Psoriasis *syphilitica : Merc.*, or, if much Mercury should have been used: 1) *Clem. sassap. sulph.* 2) *Lyc. n-jugl. nitr-ac. thuj.*

§ 3. Psoriasis *labialis*, with cracked, ulcerated lips: 1) *Merc. natr-m.* 2) *Calc. graph mez. nitr-ac. phos. sep. sil.*

Psoriasis *facialis :* 1) *Calc. sulph.* 2) *Graph. lyc. sep.* 3) *Cic. led. merc. oleand.*

Psoriasis *palmaris :* 1) *Mur-ac. sulph-ac. zinc.* 2) *Aur. calc. graph. hep. merc. petr. sassap. sil. sulph.*

Psoriasis *scrotalis : Petr. nitr-ac. thuj.*

§ 4. See : HERPES.

HICCOUGH, SINGULTUS.

Generally a mere symptom, though sometimes very troublesome, and then pointing to the following remedies: 1) *Acon. amm-m. bell. bry. cupr. hyos. ign. magn-m. n-mosch. n-vom puls. stram. sulph.* 2) *Agar. ars. baryt. borax. calc. carb-v. cocc. coff. cupr. graph. lach. led. lyc. merc. mur-ac. natr-m. nitr-ac. ruta. sep. sil. spong. staph. veratr.*

HOARSENESS, RAUCEDO, APHONIA.

§ 1. Principal remedies: 1) *Carb-v. dros. mang. phos. spong.* 2) *Bell. bry. caps. caust. cham. dulc. hep. merc. natr. n-vom. petr. puls. rhus. samb. sil. sulph.* 3) *Amb. calc. chin. graph. natr-m. seneg. stann. veratr.*

§ 2. *Catarrhal* hoarseness requires: 1) *Cham. carb-v. dulc. merc. n-vom. puls. rhus. samb. sulph.*; or, 2) *Bell. calc. caps. dros. hep. mang. natr. phos. tart.*

Chronic hoarseness: 1) *Carb-v. caust. hep. mang. petr. phos. sil. sulph.*; or, 2) *Dros. dulc. rhus.*

Aphonia (loss of voice) : *Ant. bell. caust. merc. phos. sulph.*

§ 3. Hoarseness in consequence of *measles : Bell. bry. carb-v. cham. dros. dulc. sulph.*

In consequence of *croup :* 1) *Hep. phos.*; or, 2) *Bell. carb-v. dros.*

Of *bronchial catarrh : Carb-v. caust. dros. mang. phos. rhus. sil. sulph.*

Of a *cold : Bell. carb-v. dulc. sulph.*; and if aggravated by every return of cold and damp weather: *Carb-v.* and *Sulph.*

§ 4. As regards *affections of the voice*, give :

a) For *monotonous* sound of voice, without modulation: ***Dros.*** *graph. spong. stram.*

b) For high, fine, *shrill* voice: ***Bell. cupr. stann. stram.***

c) *Hollow*, dull voice, as if from the grave: 1) ***Bell. caust.*** *dros. phos. samb. spong. veratr.* 2) *Camph. carb-v. hep. ipec. stann. veratr.*

d) For *croaking voice*: *Acon. cin. ruta.*

e) *Crowing* voice: *Cupr stram.*

f) *Loss of voice*: 1) *Baryt. bell. carb-veg. caust. phos.* 2) *Ant. dros. hep. lach. merc. natr-m. plat. puls. spong. sulph. veratr.*

g) *Nasal* voice: 1) *Aur. bell. lach. lyc. merc. phos-ac.* 2) *Alum. bry. staph.*

h) *Rough*, hoarse voice: 1) *Carb-v. dros. mang. phos. spong.* 2) *Bell. bry. caps. caust. cham. dulc. hep. merc. natr. n-vom. petr. puls. rhus. samb. sil. sulph.* 3) *Amb. calc. chin. graph. natr-m. seneg. stann. veratr.*

i) *Feeble*, low voice: 1) *Ant. canth. caust. hep. sec. veratr.* 2) *Bell. carb-v. chin. lyc. op. spong. staph.*

k) *Deep* bass-voice: 1) *Chin. dros. sulph.* 2) *Anac. jod. laur. par.*

l) *Insonorous* voice: *Agn. dros. spong.*

m) *Falsetto* voice, not pure: 1) *Caust. graph. merc. spong.* 2) *Baryt. camph. chin. croc. nitr-ac. n-mosch. sabad.*

n) Voice that *gives out*: *Dros. spong.*

o) *Hissing voice*: *Caust. phos.*

§ 5. Compare: BRONCHIAL CATARRH, COUGH, SPEECH, DEFICIENT, &c.

HOME-SICKNESS, NOSTALGIA.

Principal remedies: 1) *Caps. merc. phos-ac.*; or, 2) *Aur. carb-an. ign.*

CAPSICUM: Red cheeks, weeping and sleeplessness.

MERCURIUS: Anguish, trembling and restlessness, especially at night, sleeplessness; vexed mood, causing one to complain of every body; desire to escape, &c.

PHOSPHORI ACIDUM: Taciturn; dull mood, hectic fever with drowsiness and morning-sweat.

HONEY, ILL EFFECTS OF POISONOUS.

According to Hering, the principal remedy is *Camph.*, by olfaction and as a liniment; then: drink *black coffee* or *tea*, as hot as you can bear it.

HUNGER, CANINE.

§ 1. Principal remedies: 1) *Calc. chin. cin. jod. lyc. petr. phos. sil. spig. staph. sulph. veratr.* 2) *Con. graph. hep. kal. natr-m. n-vom. sabad. sep.* 3) *Bry. coccul. hyos. lach. magn-m. merc. rhus. squill.*

§ 2. The desire to eat much, gluttonous, requires: 1) *Chin. cin. lyc. merc. petr. staph.* 2) *Calc. natr-m. sil. sulph. veratr.*

If this hunger should set in during recovery after violent acute diseases, after debilitating loss of animal fluids or blood, or after other debilitating causes, give: 1) *Chin. veratr.*; or, 2) *Calc. natr-m. sil. sulph.*

§ 3. Sudden hunger, inducing fainting unless satisfied, requires 1) *Calc. chin. cin. hyos. merc. sabad. sil. spig.* 2) *Con. magn-m. natr-m. n-vom. petr. sep.*

When the food is readily thrown up again: 1) *Bry. n-vom. phos. puls. sil. sulph.* 2) *Calc. cin. hyos. lyc. natr-m.*

When passed *undigested* as soon as taken into the stomach: 1) *Chin. phos. veratr.* 2) *Bry. calc. con. merc. sulph.*

§ 4. If affecting *pregnant females*: *Con. magn-m. natr-m. n-vom. petr. sep.*

If persons who are affected with *worms*: *Hyos. merc. sabad. sil. spig.*

§ 5. Compare: WEAK STOMACH, GASTRIC DERANGEMENT, MALARIA, &c.

HYDROCEPHALUS ACUTUS.

§ 1. Principal remedies: 1) *Acon. bell.* 2) *Bry. hell. sulph.* 3) *Ars. cin. con. dig. lach. merc. op. stram.*

Acute hydrocephalus requires: 1) *Acon. bell.*; or, 2) *Bry. hell. sulph.*

Chronic: *Hell. ars. sulph.*

Particular indications:

ACONITUM: Violent vascular and nervous excitement as in all inflammatory fevers; (see: *Meningitis*).

BELLADONNA: After *Acon.*, the fever having abated, but without discontinuance of the disease (See: *Meningitis.*)

BRYONIA: *Acon.* and *Bell.* being insufficient, or for: Face red, almost brown-red; the eyes roll about in their sockets; at times closed, at others wide open; dry lips; dry, yellow-brown coated tongue; distended abdomen; no stool; scanty urine, or burning while passing it; quick, moaning breathing; dry, hot skin over the whole body; thirst, with hasty swallowing of the liquid.

HELLEBORUS: *Bryonia* being insufficient, or for: Moderate fever; feeble, not very quick, soft and irregular pulse; laboured breathing occasionally with deep sighs; complete apathy; inability to raise one's-self alone; the patient frequently moves his trembling hands to his head; constant relapsing of the head on raising the trunk; frequent rubbing at the nose; the eyes are half-opened with the pupils turned sideways or upwards, and convulsive movements of the lips; dilated pupils; wrinkled forehead and covered with cold sweat; no desire for any thing but drink, swallowing it greedily and in large quantities, and moving the mouth constantly as if chewing, both before and after drinking; easily angry, striking about, unwilling to have any body near him, and getting the more angry the more kindly he is spoken to; pale and bloated face; stupor; starting frequently, with screams and howling; the nostrils become dirty and dry; dropping of the lower jaw.

SULPHUR: Smelling of it, if *Helleborus* should do no good.

(*Digitalis* is an excellent remedy for hydrocephalus, in alternation with *Acon.*, *Helleborus*, &c. *Hempel.*)

HYDROPHOBIA.—Doctor Hering advises first to apply heat at a distance, and to continue this proceeding until chills set in, after which the application of heat is to be renewed three or four times a day, until the wound is healed without leaving a cicatrix with discoloration.

At the same time the patient is to take a dose of *Bell.* or *Lach.*, as often as the wound becomes worse, or a dose of *Hydrophobin*, and this treatment is to be continued until the wound is perfectly healed.

If, after the lapse of seven or eight days, a little vesicle should show itself under the tongue, accompanied with febrile motions, it should be opened with a pointed knife, and the mouth should be rinsed with salt-water.

If the rage should have actually broken out without any thing having been done for it previously, give: *Bell.* or *lach.*, or *canth.*, *hyoscyam.* and *merc.*, or *stram. veratr.* (See: MENTAL DERANGEMENT, and PHARYNGITIS.)

HYDROPHOBIA, SPURIOUS, DREAD OF WATER, symptomatic hydrophobia.

This disease requires: *Amm. calc. nitr-ac. sassap. sep. sulph.*

The following remedies may likewise be considered, though I have no evidence of their curative powers in this disease: 1) *N-mosch. puls.* 2) *Amm. ant. bell. carb-veg. dulc. merc. rhus. spig.*, &c.

HYDROTHORAX.—Principal remedies: 1) *Am-c. ars. bry.*

carb-v. dig. hell. kal. lach. merc. spig; or, 2) *Aur. calc. dulc. lyc. sen. squill. stann*

For symptoms, see: ASTHMA; PNEUMONIA; PULMONARY PHTHISIS; HEART, DISEASES OF; CATARRH, SUFFOCATIVE, &c.

HYPEROITIS, INFLAMMATION OF THE PALATE.—Principal remedies: 1) *Baryt. bar-m. bell. calc. lach. merc. n-vom.;* or, 2) *Acon. aur. chin. coff. sil.*

Inflammation of the *velum*, requires: *Acon. bell. coff. merc. n-vom.*

Inflammation of the *palate:* 1) *Calc. chin. n-vom.;* or, 2) *Bar-c. bar-m. lach. merc.;* or, 3) *Aur. bell. sil.*

Ulceration or *caries* of the palate: 1) *Aur. lach. merc. sil.;* or, 2) *Baryt. calc.*, &c. (See: BONES, DISEASES OF.)

If caused by *abuse of mercury*, give: 1) *Aur. lach;* or, 2) *Bell. bar-m. calc. sil.*, &c. Compare: SORE THROAT, STOMACACE.

HYPOCHONDRIA.

§ 1. The principal remedies for this condition of the mind are: 1) *Nux-v.* and then *Sulph.;* or, 2) *Calc.* and then *Chin.* and *Natr.;* or, 3) *Anac. aur. con. grat. lach. mosch. natr-m. phos. phos-ac. sep. staph.*

If caused by *sexual abuse*, loss of animal fluids or other debilitating causes, give: 1) *Calc. chin. nux-v.* and *sulph.;* or, 2) *Anac. con. natr-m. phos-ac. sep.* and *staph.*

If caused by derangement of the abdominal functions, sedentary mode of life, &c., give: 1) *Nux-v.* and *sulph.;* or, 2) *Aur. calc. lach. natr.* and *sil.*

§ 2. Symptomatic indications, as far as possible.

CALCAREA: Lowness of spirits, with disposition to weep; paroxysms of anguish, with orgasmus sanguinis, palpitation of the heart, shocks in the region of the heart; despair about one's health; apprehensions of illness, misfortune, infectious diseases, insanity, &c.; dread of death; excessive sensitiveness of all the organs of sense; malaise, aversion to work, inability to think or to perform any mental labour, &c. (Compare: *Sulphur.*)

CHINA: Languor, mental dullness; or excessive sensitiveness of all the organs of sense; mental distress; discouragement; *fixed idea that he is unhappy* and persecuted by enemies; headache, or boring pain in the vertex; *weak* digestion, with distention of the abdomen, ill humour, indolence after eating; sleeplessness on account of ideas crowding upon his mind, or restless, unrefreshing sleep, *with anxious dreams, tormenting the patient even after he wakes*, &c.

NATRUM: Lowness of spirits, weeping and lamenting on account of the future; *desire to be alone;* aversion to life; ill-humour; disposition to vehemence; inability to perform any mental work; headache; want of appetite, feeble digestion, ill humour, and a number of bodily and mental ailments after a meal, and after the least irregularity, &c.

NUX VOM.: Ill humour, despondency, *aversion to life, disposition to vehemence;* indisposition to work, or to perform any mental labour; fatigue of the mind after the least mental exertion; unrefreshing sleep, *aggravation of the distress in the morning;* dullness of the head, with aching pains, or sensation as if a pin were sticking in the brain; aversion to the open air, *constant desire to lie down*, with great exhaustion after walking; painfulness and distention in the region of the hypochondria, epigastrium and pit of the stomach; constipation, slow action of the bowels, hæmorrhoidal disposition, &c. (*Sulph.* is frequently suitable after *Nux.*)

SULPHUR: Lowness of spirits, painful anxiety of mind; solicitude on account of one's affairs, health, salvation; fixed ideas; paroxysms of anxiety, with impatience, restlessness, vehement disposition; *bodily* and *mental indolence;* absence of mind, irresoluteness; dullness of the head, with inability to perform any mental labour; exhaustion after the least mental exertion; headache, especially on the vertex; fullness and pressure in the pit and region of the stomach; *constipation*, hæmorrhoidal disposition: disposition to feel very unhappy, &c. (*Calc.* is frequently suitable after *Sulph.*)

§ 3. Use moreover:

ANACARDIUM: For sadness, desire to be alone; dread of the future, despondency, fear of approaching death, &c.

AURUM: Great restlessness, dread of death, whining mood, painfully anxious state of the mind; *inability to reflect*, with headache after making the least mental exertion, as if the brain were dashed to pieces, &c.

CONIUM: Listlessness, dread of company and death at the same time, &c.

GRATIOLA: Peevish, capricious, constipation, oppression of the stomach after a meal, &c.

LACHESIS: Uneasy about one's health; idea that one is hated by one's own family; inability to perform any mental or physical labour, &c.

MOSCHUS: The patient complains without knowing what ails him, with anguish, palpitation, &c.

NATRUM MUR.: When *Natr.* is insufficient, though it seems to be indicated.

PHOSPHORUS: Sadness, alternating with mirth and laughter;

uneasy about one's health; paroxysms of anguish, when alone, or in stormy weather, with timorous disposition, &c.

PHOSPHORI ACID.: Dread of the future, brooding over one's condition, *taciturn*, &c.

SEPIA: Anxious about one's health, feels indifferent even to his own family; aversion to one's own affairs; desponding, weary of life.

STAPHYSAGRIA: Listless, sad, dreading the future; *sad distressing thoughts about one's illness;* aversion to mental or physical labour; *inability to think*, &c.

§ 4. Compare: MENTAL DERANGEMENT; MELANCHOLY, HYSTERIA, EMOTIONS, MORBID.

HYSTERIA.—Principal remedies: 1) *Agn. aur. bell. calc. caust. cic. cocc. con. grat. ign. lach. mosch. n-mosch. n-vom. phosph. plat. puls. sep. sil. stram. sulph. veratr.;* or, 2) *Anac. ars. asa. bry. cham. chin. jod. natr-m. nitr-ac. stann. staph. stram. val. viol-od.*

Compare: HYPOCHONDRIA; EMOTIONS, MORBID; HEADACHE, HYSTERIC; COLIC; FAINTING, &c.

JAUNDICE.—*Merc.* is the principal remedy, provided the patient had not abused it previously, in which case *China* should be given. *China* may likewise be given alternately with *Merc.* In obstinate cases, when *Merc.* and *China* are insufficient, *Hep. sulph.* or *lach.* should be tried, either alone, or in alternation with *mercury*.

For jaundice caused by a fit of *chagrin* or *anger*, give: *Cham. nux-v.*, or *lach. sulph.*

For jaundice from *abuse of China*, give: *Merc.;* or, *bell. calc. nux-v.*—from *abuse of Merc.: Chin. hep. lach. sulph.;*—from *abuse of Rhubarb: Cham.* or *merc.*

Try moreover: *Acon. ars. calc. carb-veg. dig.;* or, *Nitr-ac. puls. rhus-t.*

ICHTHYOSIS. — *Coloc. hep.* and *plumb.* have been recommended.

ILEUS, MISERERE, &c.—The characteristic symptoms of this affection is: Vomiting of fæcal matter and urine. If caused by intussusception of the intestines, give: *Op. plumb. thuj.:* or, *Cocc.? nux-v.? sulph.?*

If caused by *inflammation*, or by some *internal* swelling, give: *Bry. sulph.;* or, if fever should be present: *Acon.*—Perhaps *Bell. lach. merc.* may be required. See: ENTERITIS and HERNIA.

IMBECILITY, IDIOCY.—Principal remedies: *Bell. hell. hyos. lach. op. sulph.;* or, *Anac. croc. n-mosch.*
See: EMOTIONS, MORBID.

IMPETIGO, HERPES CRUSTACEUS.

§ 1. Principal remedies: 1) *Lyc. sulph.* 2) *Alum. ars. baryt. calc. cic. clem. dulc. graph. hep. lach. merc. oleand. rhus. sil. staph.*

§ 2. For impetigo *scabida: Lyc. sulph.*
Impetigo *sparsa* (scattered): *Cic. lach. sulph.*
Impetigo *rodens* (spreading and corrosive): *Ars. calc. cic. rhus. sep. sulph.*

§ 3. For scurfs *around the eyes:* 1) *Ars. hep. merc. sulph.* 2) *Calc. oleand. petr. sil. staph.*
Scurfs *around the mouth: Ars. calc. graph. kreos. rhus. sep. sil. staph.*
Scurfs *on the nipples: Ars. cham. hep. graph. lyc. sulph.*

INDOLENCE, INDISPOSITION TO MOVE, &c.—Principal remedies: 1) *Acon. ars. caps. chin. guaj. lach. natr. natr-m. n-vom. sep.* 2) *Alum. baryt. bell. bry. chell. cocc. dulc. hell. ign. jod. mez. mur-ac. op. puls. ruta. tart. thuj.*
Indolence with *heaviness,* require: 1) *Natr. natr-m. phosph. stann* 2) *Asa. calc. chin. dig. ign. kal. mez. nitr-ac. phos-ac. rhab. sec. sep. sil. spong.*

INDURATIONS.

§ 1. Principal remedies: 1) *Bell. carb-an. carb-veg. con. lach. rhus. sep. sil. spong. sulph.* 2) *Agn. alum. baryt. bov. bry. can. cham. clem. dulc. jod. kal. magn-m. phosph. plumb. ran. staph.* 3) *Arn. calc. chin. graph. lach. lyc. petr. phos-ac. puls. squill.*

§ 2. *Inflammatory* indurations (after inflammations): 1) *Bell. carb-veg. chin. clem. lach. magn-m. rhus. sep. sulph.* 2) *Agn. arn. baryt. bov. bry. calc. cham. con. dulc. graph. jod. lyc. puls. sep. sil. staph.*
Scirrhous indurations: *Bell. carb-an. carb-veg. cham. clem. con. magn. magn-m. n-vom. phosph. sep. sil. staph. sulph.*
§ 3. Compare: GLANDS, DISEASES OF, and CANCER.

INDURATION OF THE SKIN, CALLOSITIES, &c.—Principal remedies: 1) *Ars. clem. graph. rhus. sep.* 2) *Ant. chin. dulc. lach. ran. sil.*
Hard *callosities* require: 1) *Ant. graph. ran. sep. sil.* 2) *Dulc. lach. rhus. sulph. thuj.*
Horny indurations: *Ant. graph. ran. sulph.*

When the *hard pieces* of skin become *detached:* 1) *Graph. natr. sep.* 2) *Amm. ant. borax. clem. ran. sil. sulph*

INFLAMMATION.—§ 1. The principal specific for inflammation is *Aconite,* though this is not the only remedy. Aconite is principally indicated by fever, hard and accelerated pulse, dry skin, &c.; in short, by the so-called *sthenic* inflammations of the old school.

§ 2. *Sulphur* is the principal remedy for *chronic* inflammations, though only remedial when indicated by the totality of the symptoms.

See: INFLAMMATORY FEVERS.

INFLUENZA, GRIPPE.

§ 1. Principal remedies: 1) *Acon. ars. bell. caust. merc. n-vom.* 2) *Arn. bry. camph. chin. ipec. phosph. puls. sabad. sen. sil. spig. squill. veratr.*

§ 2. ACONITUM: Inflammatory symptoms, pleuritic stitches and inflammation of the chest; or for *dry,* violent and racking cough, with or without oppression, stitches in the chest or sides; also for rheumatic symptoms, with bronchial catarrh and sore throat.

ARSENICUM: Rheumatic headache with violent pains, fluent coryza and discharge of corrosive mucus; or for: Great debility with aggravation at night or after a meal; spasmodic cough with desire to vomit, or with vomiting and expectoration of watery mucus; running of the eyes; inflamed eyes with ulcers on the cornea and excessive photophobia. (For this last symptom, *Bell.* or *Lach.* is sometimes indicated.)

BELLADONNA: Spasmodic cough, or excessive aggravation of the headache by talking, bright light, walking and other motions; or when the meningeal membranes are involved, with burning heat, restlessness, delirium and convulsions.

CAUSTICUM: Rheumatic pains in the limbs, and chills, aggravation by motion; pains in the malar bones and jaws; dry, violent cough, worse at night, with heat of the whole body; sensation in the chest as if raw and excoriated; constipation, loss of appetite, and nausea, or even vomiting of the ingesta.

MERCURIUS: *Rheumatic pains in the head,* face, *ears, teeth* and extremities, with sore throat; pleuritic stitches, inflammation of the chest, with dry, violent,, racking, unceasing cough, not allowing the patient to utter a single word; dry or *fluent coryza;* frequent bleeding at the nose; constipation or *mucous* or *bilious diarrhœa;* chill or heat with profuse sweat.

17

NUX VOMICA: Rough and hollow cough, with mucous rattling or thick expectoration; violent headache as if the brain were bruised; heaviness of the head, vertigo, pains in the loins, constipation, loss of appetite, *nausea* and desire to vomit; thirst; sleeplessness or restless sleep, with anxious dreams; stitches or pain in the chest as if raw.

§ 3. Use besides:

ARNICA: Inflammatory symptoms with spurious pleurisy, rheumatic pains in the limbs, crampy headache or bleeding at the nose, and hæmoptysis.

BRYONIA: Rheumatic pains in the limbs and chest, not allowing one to move.

CAMPHORA: Catarrhal asthma with excessive accumulation of mucus in the bronchi, suffocative fits, and dry and cold skin.

CHINA: Debility after the influenza, with loss of appetite and heat without thirst.

IPECACUANHA: Paroxysms of cough accompanied by violent urging to vomit and vomiting of mucus.

PHOSPHORUS: The bronchial and laryngeal affection is so intense that the voice becomes altered from the pain, and speech is almost impossible.

PULSATILLA: Cough day and night, especially when lying, with mucous distress in the bowels, and diarrhœa.

SABADILLA: Fluent coryza, dulness of the head, gray-dingy colour of the skin, dull cough with vomiting or spitting of blood, especially when lying down; aggravation of the symptoms in the cold, also towards noon, and still more towards evening; red spots in the face or on the chest.

SENEGA: Constant tickling and burning in the larynx and throat, with danger of suffocation when lying.

SILICEA: For catarrhal disposition left after an attack of influenza.

SPIGELIA: Influenza accompanied by prosopalgia.

SQUILLA: Moist cough from the commencement, with mucous expectoration.

STANNUM: Cough dry at first, then moist, with copious expectoration, or when the influenza threatens to assume a phthisicky character.

VERATRUM: Influenza accompanied with symptoms of sporadic cholera, with few catarrhal symptoms, but great debility.

Compare: CATARRH, BRONCHIAL CATARRH, COUGH.

INSECTS, STINGS OF.—*Acon. arn. bell.* or *merc.* generally procure prompt relief.

If the sting should suddenly cause fever and inflammation, give *Aconite*, and cause the patient to smell of *Camphor*.

If the *tongue* be stung by a bee, give *Aconite*, and then *Arn.*

If no relief should be obtained, give *Bell.* in water, and afterwards *Mercury* if the *Bell.* should cease to act.

For stings in the *eye*, give *Acon.* and *Arn.*

INSENSIBILITY TO EXTERNAL PHYSICAL IMPRESSIONS.—If this condition should exist during illness to such an extent that no remedy seems to affect the patient, give: 1) *Carb-veg. laur. oleand. op. phosph-ac.* 2) *Anac. bell. camph. carb-an. hyos. lach. stram. sulph.*

IODIUM, ILL EFFECTS OF.—For poisoning with large doses, give: 1) *Starch* mixed with water; 2) *Wheat-flour;* 3) *Mucilaginous drinks.*

For *secondary* affections, or drug-symptoms, give: *Bell.*, then *Phosphorus;* or: *Ars. chin. coff. hep. spong. sulph.*

IRON, ILL EFFECTS OF.—Principal remedies: 1) *Chin. hep. puls.;* or: 2) *Arn. ars. bell. ipec. merc. veratr.*

ISCHIAS, COXALGIA, COXARTHROCACE.

§ 1. Principal remedies: 1) *Bell. bry. calc. colch. coloc. hep. merc. puls. rhus. sulph.;* or: 2) *Ant. arg. arn. ars. asa. aur. canth. cham. dig. graph. kreos. lach. lyc. n-vom. sep. staph.*

§ 2. Genuine *coxalgia* seems to require: 1) *Bry. calc. caust. led. rhus.;* 2) *Ant. bell. colch. coloc. lach. merc. n-vom. puls. sep. sulph.*

Nervous coxalgia (ischias): 1) *Puls.* 2) *Arn. bell. coloc. lyc. rhus. sep.*

Coxarthrocace: Coloc. phos-ac.; or: *Calc. hep. sil. sulph zinc.*

Luxatio or *claudicatio spontanea* (involuntary limping): *Merc.* and *Bell.*, alternately, every few days a dose; or: *Calc. coloc. lyc. puls. rhus. sulph. zinc.*

§ 3. See: COXARTHROCACE, GOUT, NEURALGIA, RHEUMATISM, PAIN, PAROXYSMS OF, &c.

ISCHURIA.—*Spasmodic* ischuria requires: 1) *N-vom. op. puls.;* or: 2) *Aur. canth. con. dig. hyos. lach. rhus. veratr.*

Compare: URINARY DIFFICULTIES.

For ischuria *paralytica*, give: *Ars. dulc. hyos.*, &c.

See: URINARY DIFFICULTIES.

ITCH, SCABIES.

§ 1. Principal remedies: 1) *Merc.* and *sulph.;* 2) *Carb-veg. caust. clem. hep. lach. lyc. rhus. sep. veratr.;* or: *Dulc. natr. phos-ac. squill.*

§ 2. For *dry* itch, give *Merc.* and *Sulph.* alternately every 4, 6 or 8 days, until an improvement takes place, or the symptoms change; these new symptoms generally indicate: *Carb-veg.* or *Hep.*, provided it is the *dry* itch, or *Causticum*, if a few pustules should have supervened. The symptoms which remain after *Carb-veg.* or *Hep.*, frequently yield to *Sep.* or *Veratr.*

§ 3. For *pustulous* itch give first *Sulph.* and *Lyc.* alternately as above. If the itch should become drier, give *Carb-veg.* or *Merc.* Give *Caust.* once a day, if *Sulph.* or *Lyc.* remain without effect. If *Caust.* should not produce a change in 2 or 3 days, give a dose of *Mercury* every 48 hours.

If ulcers should form, give *Clem.* or *Rhus-t.;* if the pustules should change to large vesicles of a yellowish or bluish colour, give *Lach.*

§ 4. Itch mismanaged by *Sulphur-ointment*, requires *Merc.* or *Caust.;* or: *Calc. dulc. nitr-ac. puls. selen. sep.*—If mismanaged by the *Sulphur* and *Mercurial-ointment*, give: *Chin.* and *Caust.* alternately, and then the above-mentioned remedies.

The so-called baker's itch requires: 1) *Sulph. lyc;* or: 2) *Calc. dulc. rhus.* and *graph.*

§ 5. Other eruptions are easily confounded with the itch. Impetigo, eczema, &c., exactly resembling the itch, may be gradually developed by uncleanliness, vermin; and the only difference between these eruptions and the itch is, that the acarus, this only true pathognomonic characteristic of the itch, is wanting in the former.

For acarous itch, *Sulph.* is undoubtedly the principal specific, though it seems by no means impossible that *Caust. merc.*, &c., might cause such an alteration in the cutaneous exhalations as would lead to the destruction of the acarus, which I regard as the cause, not the effect, of the itch. I know of a young man who contracted an eruption in consequence of having slept in an unclean bed on a journey, and who removed it by a wash of tobacco-juice and vinegar.

This *acarous* itch admits of a mere external treatment, with the Sulphur-ointment, without exposing the patient to the danger of contracting secondary diseases. Of course I do not wish to be understood as if I would sanction the treatment, by external applications, of the various itch-like eruptions where the acarus is not present. These are the eruptions to which Hahnemann's psora-doctrine should be applied, and the suppression of which, by salves and washes, will induce the various secondary affections enumerated by Hahnemann and Autenrieth.

The proper way, therefore, would be to distinguish, 1) *Scabies acarosa*, which can be treated externally without danger, provided the acarus is the cause, not the effect of the disease; 2) *Scabies impetiginosa, eczematica*, &c., dynamic diseases requiring a purely internal treatment.

As regards symptoms, I recommend for eruptions seated in the folds of joints, and especially on the hands and between the fingers, if characterized by *itching* :

a) Generally: 1) *Sulph.* 2) *Carb-veg. caust. merc. selen. sep. sulph.* 3) *Ant. ars. lach. veratr.* 4) *Coloc. dulc. cupr. kreos. mang. phos-ac. squill. tart. zinc.*

b) For eruptions *readily bleeding :* 1) *Merc.* 2) *Calc. dulc. sulph.*

c) *Dry* and *rash-like* eruptions : 1) *Carb-veg. merc. sep. sil. sulph.* 2) *Calc. caust. cupr. dulc. led. veratr.*

d) *Humid* eruptions: 1) *Carb-veg. graph. lyc. sulph.* 2) *Caust. clem. kreos. sep. staph.*

e) *Pustulous* eruptions : 1) *Caust. kreos. merc. sep. sulph.* 2) *Ant. squill.*

§ 6. See ERUPTIONS and HERPES.*

ITCHING OF THE ANUS.—*Aconite* is an excellent remedy, especially if the skin be inflamed; we may likewise try: *Merc. nitri-ac. sepia. sulph. thuja.*, and: *Baryt. calc. zinc.* at long intervals. See: HERPES, ITCHING OF THE SKIN, HÆMORRHOIDS, WORM-AFFECTIONS.

ITCHING OF THE SKIN, PRURITUS, PRURIGO SIMPLEX.

§ 1. This itching may depend upon a variety of causes, of which the principal are: 1) *a simple irritation* of the skin, by sweat, &c. 2) A so-called *humour* characterized by a very fine vesicular eruption.

§ 2. For *simple itching*, in the evening while undressing, or after having got warm in bed or by exercise, give: 1) *Bry. n-vom. op. puls. rhus. sil. sulph.* 2) *Coccul. oleand.*

* An excellent means of removing inveterate itch, is the hydropathic treatment. I know of a case that had been treated homœopathically for a whole year, here and in Europe, without the least success, and finally yielded completely to hydropathic treatment (at Brattleborough) in the short space of five weeks. *Hempel.*

The *acrid humour* about the anus, sexual organs, &c., (*prurigo*) requires: 1) *Calc. merc. nitr-ac. sep. sulph.* 2) *Carb-veg. con. natr-m. sil.* 3) *Alum. amb. amm. baryt. caust. coccul. graph. lyc. phosph. rhus. thuj.*

§ 3. For *itching of the anus,* give: 1) *Alum. amm. calc. carb-veg. caust. lyc. nitr-ac. sep. sulph.* 2) *Baryt. kal. phosph. sil. thuj. zinc.*

Itching of the *scrotum:* 1) *Nitr-ac. petr. sulph.* 2) *Amb. carb-veg. caust. coccul. graph. lyc. thuj.*

Itching of the *pudendum:* 1) *Calc. carb-veg. con. natr-m. sep. sil. sulph.* 2) *Alum. amb. amm. merc. nitr-ac. rhus.*

§ 4. Compare: Herpes of the sexual organs and anus, and: Eruptions, herpes.

LABOUR.—§ 1. The best remedies to facilitate labour or to remove dynamic difficulties, are: 1) *Cham. coff. n-vom. n-mosch. op. puls. sec.;* or: 2) *Acon. bell. calc.*

§ 2. *Spasmodic* pains require: 1) *Coff. n-vom.;* or: 2) *Bell. cham. n-mosch. puls.*

Coffea: For *violent* pains, driving the patient to despair: if *Coffea* should not help, give *Acon.*

Nux vom.: Pains without actual labour, with constant urging to go to stool or to urinate.

If *Nux* should not suffice, give: 1) *Cham.* or *bell.;* or: 2) *Nux-mosch.* or *puls.*

§ 3. *Deficient* pains, require: *Op. puls. sec.*

Opium: Sudden cessation of pains in plethoric, robust females, in consequence of fright or some other emotion, with tendency of blood to the head, red and bloated face, and sopor.

Pulsatilla: When in females of a good constitution, the pains do not set in, or *spasmodic distress* sets in, or the uterus remains inactive.

Secale corn.: Deficient pains in enfeebled, cachectic females, or exhausted by loss of blood, no matter whether spasmodic pains or no pains at all are present. Secale is eminently suitable for these symptoms, but dangerous in most other cases.

§ 4. If the placenta should not be expelled readily, or should adhere to the uterus, give: *Puls.* or *sec.* If *puls.* should not be sufficient, or if there should be: tendency of the blood to the head, red face, glistening eyes, dryness of the skin and vagina, great anguish and restlessness, *Bell.* is the best remedy.

§ 5. Violent and long-lasting after-pains require: 1) *Arn. cham. coff.*; or: 2) *Calc. n-vom. puls.*

§ 6. *Convulsions* or *spasms* during labour, require: 1) *Hyos ign.*; or: 2) *Bell. cham. cic.*

Injuries of the sexual parts, in consequence of painful labour, require *Arn.*, bathing the parts with 10 drops in 8 ounces of water.

For *metrorrhagia*, use: 1) *Croc. plat.*, or: 2) *Bell. cham. ferr. sabin.*

Compare: CONFINEMENT.

LAGOPHTHALMUS, PARALYSIS OF THE EYELIDS.—Principal remedies: 1) *Bell. nitr-ac. sep. spig. stram. veratr. zinc.* 2) *Calc. cham. cocc. hyos. n-vom. op. phos. plumb. rhus.*

LARYNGITIS, and LARYNGEAL PHTHISIS.—Principal remedies: 1) *Acon. ars. carb-veg. caust. dros. hep. lach. merc. phosph. spong.*; or, 2) *Calc. cham. cist. jod. ipec. led. mang. nitr.? nitr-ac. seneg. stann.*

Acute laryngitis requires: 1) *Acon. hep. spong.*; or, 2) *Cham. dros. lach. merc. ipec. phosph. seneg.*

Chronic laryngitis, *phthisis* of *the larynx*: 1) *Ars. calc. carb. veg. caust. cist. phosph.*; or, 2) *Dros. hep. jod. kreos. led. mang. nitr-ac.*

See: HOARSENESS, COUGH, BRONCHITIS, CROUP, PHARYNGITIS, &c.; also: TRACHEITIS.

LASSITUDE or DEBILITY FROM BODILY OR MENTAL EXERTIONS.—§. 1. Principal remedies: *Acon. arn. bry. calc. carb-veg. chin. cocc. coff. ipec. merc. n-vom. puls. rhus. silic. veratr.*—*Ang. n. mosch.*

§. 2. If worn out by *bodily exertions*, take: *Acon. arn. bry. calc. chin. coccul. coff. merc. rhus. silic.* and *veratr.*

If by frequent *watching*: *Carb-v. coccul. n-vom. puls.*

If by *excessive study*: *Bell. calc. lach. n-vom. puls.* and *sulph.*

If by *sedentary* habits: *N-vom.* and *sulph.*

§. 3. Particular indications:

ACONITUM: Full and hurried pulse, in consequence of some heating kind of work, with panting breathing, shortness of breath, cough, *pleuritic stitches* and pains in the limbs.

ARNICA: If the stitches in the side continue in spite of the *Acon.*, or if, after a fatiguing journey on foot, a pain is experienced in all the limbs as if bruised and broken, especially the muscles, with swelling and painfulness of the feet.

Belladonna: Headache and cerebral irritation caused by excessive study.

Bryonia: *Acon.* being insufficient, and even *Arnica* not relieving the stitches in the side.

Calcarea: Exhausted by the least exertion, even a mere conversation, or when the least mental exertion causes a headache.

Carbo veg.: For the tired feeling after nightly revelling, especially for *oppressive* or *throbbing headache, less in the open air;* nausea without any other symptoms; liquid, pale stool.

China: After a bodily exertion, with profuse sweat, especially suitable to persons that have been exhausted by frequent sweats and other debilitating causes.

Cocculus: For the consequences of fatiguing work, or long *watching* at night, generally for great prostration after the least work or watching: also for trembling and feeling of emptiness in the head, heat in the face, blue margins around the eyes, dry mouth, aversion to food, attack of nausea even unto fainting, feeling of repletion in the stomach, oppression of the chest, aggravation in the open air, or by conversation and coffee, great sadness, sudden starting during sleep and anxious dreams.

Coffea: Worn out by bodily exertions, and want of proper nourishment.

Ipecacuanha: Headache from long-continued watching; loathing, disposition to vomit, and when the patient is obliged to continue his watching some time longer.

Mercurius: For the consequences of some heating labour, rush of blood after the least exertion, tendency of the blood to the head, chest or face.

Nux vomica: For the consequences of *watching, study,* or *sedentary life,* generally suitable to persons that have been in the habit of stimulating themselves by *coffee, wine* or other spirituous *drinks;* or for headache with tendency of the blood to the head; cloudiness, heaviness in the forehead when moving the eyes, and painful concussion of the brain by every step one makes; pale and sunken face, or livid complexion, gastric ailments, disposition to vomit, slow action of the abdominal organs; cough and nervous toothache; aggravation in the open air; aversion to motion and walking; excessive nervousness; shuddering, weariness, hypochondria and ill humour; animated and choleric disposition.

Pulsatilla: Worn out by study or watching, especially in the case of females; the head feels cloudy as when intoxicated, or the brain feels empty and the head light, or the head feels heavy, with photophobia; *relief in the open air;* bland disposition.

Rhus tox.: Painfulness of the joints after carrying or lifting heavy weight, or after any other fatiguing work, especially when commencing to move or while resting one's-self.

Silicea: Shortness of breath in consequence of running, with aggravation when walking or ascending an eminence; cough, mucous expectoration, &c.

Sulphur: When sedentary habits, excessive study or watching cause: fatigue of the head, hypochondriac mood, gastric ailments, bad digestion and constipation, *Nux v.* being insufficient.

Veratrum: Debility in consequence of bodily exertion, the least work fatigues one unto fainting.

See: Debility, and Watching at night.

LAUGHTER, SPASMODIC, Hysteric.—Principal remedies: 1) *Alum. bell. calc. con. croc. cupr. hyos. n-mosch. phosph. stram.* 2) *Acon. anac. asa. cic. natr-m. plat. veratr.*

P. S. For *Risus sardonius*, frequently a dangerous symptom in severe cerebral affections, are proposed: *Ran-sc. zinc-ox.*

LEAD, ill effects of.—§. 1. Poisoning with large doses requires: 1) *Sulphate of Magnesia*, dissolved in water, as a drink; 2) *Sulphate of potash;* 3) *Soap-water;* 4) *Albumen;* 5) *Milk;* 6) *Mucilaginous drinks*, or *injections.*

§ 2. The subsequent dynamic ailments require: *Alum. bell. n-vom. op. plat.*—These remedies likewise remove the drug-symptoms occasioned by lead.

LEPRA.—*Hering* recommends: *Alum. ars. carb-a. carb-v. caust. graph. natr. petr. phos. sep. sil. sulph.*

For the *spots* and *tumours* of leprous patients, give: *Alum. natr.* and *sil.*

LEUCORRHŒA, fluor albus, whites.

§ 1. This affection depends upon an inflammatory irritation of the vaginal mucous membrane, or upon some more deep-seated affection of the uterus. In the former case, even if the disease should be very obstinate and malignant, the following remedies should be used principally: 1) *Calc. merc. puls. sep. sulph.* 2) *Alum. amb. amm. carb-an. carb-veg. chin. cocc. con. graph. kal. kreos. lyc. magn-c. magn-m. mez. natr. natr-m. phosph. ruta. sabin. sil. stann. zinc.* 3) *Acon. agn. bov. cann. caust. dros. hep. jod. nitr-ac. n-vom. petr. phos-ac. sulph-ac.*

§ 2. As regards symptoms, give: a) For *bloody mucus*, like serum: *Baryt. calc. carb. veg. chin. cocc. con. kreos. nitr-ac. sep. sulph-ac.*—*Bluish* mucus: *Amb.*—*Brown: Amm. m. cocc. nitr-ac.*

—*Thick:* *Ars. borax. carb-veg. con. magn-m. natr. natr-m. puls. sep.*—*Thin watery:* *Alum. amm. carb-an. carb-veg. graph. magn-c. magn-m. puls. sil. sulph.*—*Purulent:* *Chin. cocc. ign. con. merc. nitr-ac. sep.*—*Albuminous:* *Amm-m. borax. bov. mez. petr. plat.*—*Yellow:* *Ars. carb-an. carb-veg. cham. kal. kreos. natr. phos-ac. sabin. sep. stann. sulph.*—*Greenish:* *Carb-veg. lach. merc. natr-m. nitr-ac. sep.*—*Milky:* *Amm. calc. carb-veg. con. lyc. phosph. puls. sabin. sep. sil. sulph-ac.*—*Slimy:* *Amb. amm. calc. carb-veg. chin. con. magn-c. merc. mez. natr. natr-m. nitr-ac. phosph. puls. sassap. sep. stann. tart. thuj. zinc.*—*Fetid:* *Caps. kreos. natr. nitr-ac. n-vom. sabin. sep.*

b) For *burning* leucorrhœa: *Alum. amm. calc. carb-an. con. kreos. puls. sulph-ac.*—*Smarting, Itching:* *Calc. cham. con. ferr. lach. merc. phosph. sep. sil. sulph.*—*Corrosive*, acrid: *Alum. amm. ars. borax. carb-veg. cham. con. ign. kreos. merc. natr-m. phosph. puls. ran. ruta. sep. sil. sulph. sulph-ac.*

c) For leucorrhœa *preceding the menses:* *Baryt. calc. carb-veg. chin. graph. kreos. lach. phosph. puls. sep. sulph. zinc.*—*During the menses*, or in *their stead:* *Alum. chin. cocc. lach. puls. zinc.*—*After the menses:* *Alum. graph. kreos. nitr-ac. phos-ac. puls. ruta. sil. sulph.*

d) For leucorrhœa accompanied with abdominal spasms or *colic:* *Caust. con. dros. lyc. magn-c. magn-m. puls. sep. sil. sulph. zinc.*—With *pains* in the *small* of *the back:* *Baryt. caust. con. graph. kreos.*—With *great debility:* *Natr-m.*—With *yellow complexion:* *Chin. ferr. natr-m. sep.*—With *pale face:* *Ars. graph. kreos. puls. sep.*

§ 3. Comp.: Amenia and Menstrual Irregularities.

LICE-MALADY, Phthiriasis.

§ 1. For lice on the head and other parts of the body, the best remedy is cleanliness and regular habits. If lice should have formed, use:

For *lice on the head:* Frequent washing with vinegar, mixed with part of a solution of one spoonful of tobacco-juice in a tumblerful of water, or snuff in the place of the juice. If the scalp should not be sound, or if the children are very small, it is best to use the vinegar without tobacco-juice. The same mode of washing should be adopted for lice on other parts of the body.

Tobacco-juice is likewise the best remedy for *lice of the sexual organs*, either in the shape of a wash of equal parts of tobacco-juice and vinegar, or of an ointment made of snuff and lard. If the use of tobacco should induce unpleasant symptoms, diarrhœa, vomiting, &c., *Puls.* will remove them very speedily.

If the *lice* should have got into one's *clothes*, these have to be heated in an oven; nothing else will clean them.

§ 2. Spontaneous generation of lice in the skin or in boils and tumours on the skin, requires: 1) *Ars. chin. staph.*; or 2) *Merc. sulph.*; or 3) *Lach.? magn-arct.? oleand.? sabad.?*—These remedies deserve confirmation.

LICHEN.—Principal remedies: *Acon. bry. cic. cocc. dulc. lyc. mur-ac. natr-m. sulph.*

Lichen *simplex*: 1) *Coccul. dulc.* 2) *Acon. bry. puls.*

Lichen *agrius*: *Cic. lyc. mur-ac. sulph.*

Lichen *strofulus*: *Cic. caust. cham. merc. sulph.*—*Graph. rhus.*

Try likewise: *Agar. amm. ars. calc. carb-veg. con. phos-ac. staph. stront.*

LIENITIS, Splenitis, and other affections of the spleen.—Principal remedies: 1) *Agn. arn. bry. caps. chin. ign. n-vom. sulph.*; or 2) *Acon. ferr. jod. mez.?*

Acute lienitis requires principally: *China*; also: *Acon. arn. ars. bry. n. vom.*—*Acon.* when there is inflammatory fever.

Arnica: *China* being insufficient, especially for aching, stitching pains arresting the breathing, or for typhoid symptoms, with languor, listlessness, dullness of sense; the patient does not think that he is very sick.

Arsenicum: Frequent bloody diarrhœic stools, with burning, great debility; or when the disease assumes an intermittent character, and *China* is insufficient.

Bryonia: The swelling continuing after giving *Chin.*, *Ars.* or *Nux. v.*, with stitching pains in the region of the spleen during motion.

China: After *Acon.*, or even from the commencement, for aching, stitching pains, or when the disease has an intermittent character.

Nux vomica: After *Chin.* or *Ars.*, the swelling and the aching pain in the stomach continuing, and the general state of the patient being the same.

For *constipation, swelling* and *induration* of *the spleen*, give: *Ars. caps. chin. ign. sulph.*; or *Jod. mez.?*

LITHIASIS, Gravel.

§ 1. Principal remedies: 1) *Lyc. sassap.* 2) *Ant. calc. cann. n-vom. petr. phosph. ruta. sep. sil. zinc.* 3) *Alum. amb. amm. arn. canth. chin. lach. natr-m. nitr-ac. n-mosch. thuj. uv.*

§. 2. For *stone in the bladder: Cann. sassap. uv.*
For *gravel:* 1) *Lyc. sassap.* 2) *Ant. calc. phosph. ruta. sil. zinc.*

§ 3. See SECRETION OF URINE and URINARY DIFFICULTIES.

LOCK-JAW, TRISMUS.—A mere symptom, though indicating principally: 1) *Camph. hyos. ign. veratr.* 2) *Lach. merc. plat. sil.* 3) *Acon. ang. camph. hydroc. cal. laur. merc. mosch. n-vom. plumb. phosph.*

LOVE, UNHAPPY, ILL EFFECTS OF:—Generally removed by: 1) *Aur. hyos. ign. phos-ac. staph.* 2) *Lach. puls. sulph.*
Melancholy, weeping, religious mania: *Aur. puls. sulph.*
Jealousy: Hyos. lach. n-vom.
Grief: Ign., or: *Phos-ac. staph.*
Hectic fever: Phos-ac. staph., or: *Puls.*

LUMBAGO.—Principal remedies: *Bry. nux-v. puls. rhus-t. sulph.*—See RHEUMATISM, PAINS IN THE SMALL OF THE BACK, and PAINS IN THE BACK.

LUPIÆ.
Principal remedies: 1) *Calc. daph. graph. kal.;* and 2) *Hep. nitr-ac. sil. sulph.*
I have so far cured every case of *lupia* with one dose of *Calcarea* 30, allowing it to act 7 or 8 weeks. The swelling generally commences to diminish in the 4th to the 7th week.
For *Steatoma* the principal remedy seems to be *Bar-c.*
For *Ganglia: Sil.*, or sometimes: *Amm.* or *phos.*

MACULÆ, EPHELIDES, PURPURA, &c.

§ 1. Principal remedies: 1) *Bry. lyc. natr. phosph. sep. sulph.* 2) *Alum. ant. ars. calc. carb-veg. con. graph. hyos. lach. merc. n-vom. nitr-ac. oleand. sabad. staph. sulph-ac.*

§. 2. For *Ephelides* (*freckles*): 1) *Lyc. phosph. sulph. veratr.* 2) *Amm. ant. calc. dulc. graph. natr. nitr-ac. puls.*
Hepatic spots: 1) *Lyc. merc. nitr-ac. sep. sulph.* 2) *Ant. carb-veg. con. dulc. hyos. lach. natr. n-vom. phosph.*
Furfuraceous spots (ptyriasis): *Ars. alum. bry. lyc. phosph. sep.;* and when these spots are seated on the head or along the border of the hairy scalp: *Ars.* and *alum.*, or: *Calc. graph. oleand. staph.*
Spots of *pregnant* females yield to: *Sep.* or *con.*

Moles (nævi) to: 1) *Carb-veg. sulph.* 2) *Calc. graph. sulph-ac.*

§. 3. *Blue-red* spots require: *Bell. phosph.*

Bloody spots: 1) *Ars. bry. rhus.* 2) *Hyos. led. phosph. sec. sulph-ac.* (See: PETECHIA.)

Brown-red: 1) *Nitr. ac. phosphor.* 2) *Cann.*

Yellow: Arn. ferr. petr. phosph. sulph.

Greenish: Arn. con. sep.

Copper-coloured: Ars. carb-an. kreos. mez. rhus. ruta. veratr.

Red: 1) *Carb-veg. lyc. merc. nitr-ac. phosph. sep.* 2) *Arn. con. kal. sulph. sulph-ac.*—If growing pale in the cold: *Sabad.*

Spots as if by *contusion, shock, blow:* 1) *Con.* 2) *Arn. sulph-ac.*—(See PETECHIÆ.)

Scarlet: 1) *Amm. bell. merc. phosph.* 2) *Croc. euphorb. hyos. sulph.*

Violet: Phos. veratr.

Black: Ars. lach. rhus. sec.

Wine-coloured: Coccul. sep.

White: see § 4.

§ 4. *White leprous spots:* 1) *Ars. sil.* 2) *Alum. phosph. sep. sulph.*—*Rose-coloured: Natr. phosph. sil.*

Syphilitic (copper-coloured, violet): *Merc. nitr-ac.*

§ 5. See PETECHIÆ, ECCHYMOSES, PURPURA, &c.

MAGNESIA, ILL EFFECTS OF.—The principal antidotes of this medicine when given in too large quantities, are: *Ars. cham. coff. coloc. n-vom. puls. rhab.*

ARSENICUM: For violent, burning pains, worse at night and compelling one to leave the bed.

CHAMOMILLA: Violent colic with or without diarrhœa.

COFFEA: Sleeplessness and nervous excitement.

COLOCYNTH: Excessive spasmodic pains, constipation or slow stool.

NUX VOM.: Obstinate constipation, or constipation with colic, *Colocynth* having proved ineffectual.

PULSATILLA: Spasmodic colic with leucorrhœa, or watery diarrhœa with colic, after *Rhubarb* had been tried without effect.

RHUBARB: Watery, sour diarrhœa with colic and tenesmus.

MALACIA, desire for strange or exceptional things.

a) Desire for *beer: Acon. caust. coccul. merc. natr. n-vom. petrol. puls. sulph.*—For *brandy: Ars. china. hepar. n-vom. opi. selen. sepia. sulph.*—*Wine: Acon. bryon. calc. cicut. hepar. laches. sepia. staph. sulph.*—*Spirits* generally: *Hepar. puls. sulph. sulph-*

ac.—Refreshing things: *Caust. coccul. phosph. phos-ac. puls. rhab. sabin. valer.—Coffee: Angust. ars. aur. bryon. carb-veg. coni. —Milk: Ars. bovist. merc. rhus. sabad. silic. staph.*

b) *Fat: Nux-v. nitr-ac.—Herrings: Nitr-ac. veratr.—Smoked* things: *Caust.—Meat: Helleb. magnes-carb. sulph.—Vegetables: Alum. magnes-c.—Oysters: Laches.—Cucumbers: Ant. veratr. —Sourkrout: Carb. an. cham.—Flour: Sabad.—Warm* food: *Cycl. ferr. lyc.—Bread: Ars. bell. natr. natr-m. puls.—Liquids: Bryon. ferr. merc. staph. sulph.*

c) *Bitter* things: *Dig. natr-m.—Salt* things: *Carb-veg. caust. coni. mephid. veratr.—Sour* things: *Ant. arn. ars. borax. bryon. cham. hepar. ignat. kali. phosph. puls. sepia. squill. stram. sulph. veratr.—Sweet, dainties: Amm. baryt. china. ipecac. kali. lycop. magnes-m. natr. rhab. rhus. sabad. sulph.—Juicy* things: *Phos-ac.—Fruit: Alum. ignat. magnes-c. sulph-ac. veratr.*

d) Desire for *clay*, chalk, lime: *Nitr-ac. nux-v.*—For *charcoal: Cicut. con.*

Comp.: Gastric derangement, Weak stomach, &c.

MAMMÆ and NIPPLES:—§. 1. The best remedies for sore nipples are: *Arn. sulph.*, or *Calc. cham. ign. puls.*

Chamomilla is suitable for inflamed or ulcerated nipples, provided the patient had not previously used it to excess; in which case, *Ign.* or *Puls.*, or perhaps *Merc.* and *Sil.*, are the best remedies.

For simple soreness, use *Arn.;* and if this should not be sufficient, *Sulph. calc.*

Afterwards we may require to use: *Caust. graph. lyc. merc. n-vom. sep. sil.*

§. 2. For *mastitis*, give: *Bell. bry. carb-a. hep. merc. phos. sil. sulph.*

Belladonna: The breasts are swollen and hard, with stitching and tearing pains, and erysipelatous redness radiating from a central point. (Acts well in alternation with *Bry.*)

Bryonia: The breasts are hard, rigid, turgescent, with *tensive* or stitching pains in the swelling, and burning heat on the outside, especially when there are febrile motions, heat, vascular irritation, &c. (If *Bry.* be insufficient, try *Bell.*)

Hepar: When suppuration has set in, in spite of *Bell.*, *Bry.*, &c.

Mercurius: *Bell.* and *Bry.* being insufficient, hard and painful lumps continuing to form in the breasts.

Phosphorus: Ulceration of the breasts, fistulous passages with hard and callous edges, or colliquative sweat and diarrhœa, with suspicious cough, feverish heat in the evening, circumscribed redness of the cheeks, and other symptoms of hectic fever.

SILICEA: *Phosphorus* being unable to arrest the suppuration of the nipples, with fistulous ulcers and symptoms of hectic fever.

§. 3. The principal remedies for *induration* and *lumps* of the breasts, are: 1) *Carb-a. con. sil.*; or 2) *Clem. coloc. graph. lyc. merc. nitr-ac. ol-jec. phos. puls. sep. sulph.*—If caused by a *blow* or *shock*, give: *Arn. carb-a. con.*

Cancer of the mammæ requires: 1) *Ars. clem. sil.*; or 2) *Bell. con. hep.? kreos.?*

MANIA OF SUICIDE.—Principal remedies: 1) *Ars. aur. n-vom. puls.* 2) *Alum. amb. amm. bell. lach. nitr-ac. plat. sep.* 3) *Ant. carb-veg. chin. dros. hep. hyos. mez. rhus. sec. spig. stram. tart.*

For disposition to *hang* or *choke* one's-self, give *Ars.*—to *drown* one's-self: *Bell. dros. hyos. puls. sec.*—to *shoot* one's-self: *Ant. carb-veg.*

When accompanied with great *dread* of *death*: *Alum. chin. nitr-ac. plat. rhus.*—When the mania is caused by excessive *anguish* or *fear*: 1) *Aur. n-vom. puls.* 2) *Bell. caust. chin. dros. hep. plat. rhus. spong. staph.*—When by *sadness*, melancholy, &c.: 1) *Aur. lach.* 2) *Carb-veg. hep. plat. ruta. spong. sulph. sulph-ac.* —When by despair: *Amb. carb-veg. hyos. lach. natr. sep.*

MARASMUS SENILIS.—Principal remedies: *Baryt. con. op. phosph. sec.*

Purpura senilis requires: 1) *Con.* 2) *Ars. bry. rhus. sec. sulph-ac.* 3) *Lach.? op.? baryt.?*

MEASLES, MORBILLI.

§ 1. Principal remedies; 1) *Acon. puls.*; or: 2) *Bell. bry. chin. phosph. sulph.*

§ 2. To facilitate the eruption and to abbreviate the precursory stage, give *Acon.* or *puls.*, or even *coffea*, if the patients should be very restless, sleepless, and should be beside themselves and toss about.

Photophobia is frequently relieved by *Bellad.* if *acon.* and *puls.* should not be sufficient.

The *cough* sometimes requires a dose of *Coff.* or *hep.* after *acon.*; real pulmonary catarrh or inflammation of the chest sometimes requires *Bry.*

§ 3. If the eruption should recede, give: 1 *Bry. puls. phosph*; or: 2) *Ars. bell. caust. hell.* and *sulph.*

The *cerebral symptoms* require: 1) *Bell. stram.*; or: 2) *Ars. hell, puls.*

The *pulmonary* symptoms: *Bry. phosph.* or ***Sulph.***

Typhoid, putrid symptoms: 1) ***Phosph. puls. sulph.***; 2) ***Ars.*** *carb-veg. mur-ac. phos-ac. sulph-ac.*

§ 4. For the sequelæ of measles, give: *Bry. carb-veg. cham. chin. dros. dulc. hyos. ign. nux. rhus. sep. stram. sulph.*

The *catarrhal affections*, such as: *Cough, hoarseness, sore throat, &c.* require: *Bry. carb. veg. cham. con. dros. dulc. hyos. ign. n-vom. sep. sulph.*—If the cough should be dry and *hollow*, give: *Cham. ign. n-vom.*—If *spasmodic*: 1) *Bell. cin. hyos.*; or: 2) *Carb-veg. dros.*; or: 3) *Canth. cupr. dig. ipec.*

The *mucous diarrhœic* stools require: *Chin. merc. puls. sulph.*

Otitis and *otorrhœa*: 1) *Puls.* 2) *Carb-veg.*; or 3) *Colch. lyc. men. merc. nitr-ac. sulph.*

Parotitis yields to *Arn.* or *Rhus-t.*, and the *white rash* to *Nux-v.*

§ 5. Particular indications:

Aconitum: Vertigo, *red* and *painful* eyes, with *photophobia;* coryza; sore throat with hoarseness and dry, hollow, hacking cough; stitches in the sides and chest; sleeplessness or little sleep with vivid dreams, and sudden starting; *dry heat* all over, with red and hot face, or bloated face; bleeding at the nose; frequent urging to urinate; vomiting, or colic also with diarrhœa.

Belladonna: Swelling of the parotid glands, with ptyalism; sore throat with difficult deglutition and painful stitches when swallowing; hoarseness and dry cough which fatigues the chest, with oppression and suffocative fits; dry heat with violent aching in the forehead, delirium and convulsive twitching of the limbs; *violent thirst;* anguish and restlessness with nervousness and sleeplessness.

Bryonia: *Rheumatic* pains in the limbs, with dry cough and stitches in the chest when breathing or coughing.

China: Violent colic with unquenchable thirst.

Phosphorus: *Typhoid symptoms*, with loss of consciousness; watery diarrhœa; tongue coated with dirty, thick mucus; *black lips;* debility; or dry cough with desire to vomit, or vomiting.

Pulsatilla: In almost every stage of the disease, and in most cases, even with putrid and typhoid symptoms; and for: *inflammation* of the *inner and outer* ear, with or without discharge; also for dry mouth without thirst, short and dry cough, stitches in the chest, &c.

Stramonium: Delirium with frightful visions of cats, mice, &c; desire to hide one's-self; spasmodic symptoms in the pharynx, and difficulty of swallowing.

Sulphur: Ophthalmia with scanty eruption; or: violent

otalgia, with purulent discharge; hardness of hearing, tearing and beating in the head; pain in the limbs, and lameness; or when typhoid symptoms are present, with moist cough, and purulent discharge.

§. 6. Apply moreover:

Arsenicum: Retrocession of the eruption; sallow complexion, with blue or greenish-brown stripes; crusts around the mouth; bloated face, pale or red; burning, beating pains in the eyes with photophobia; typhoid symptoms; vomiting, diarrhœa.

Bryonia: Very useful after *Aconite*, in *inflammatory* measles, with ophthalmia, constipation, inflammation of the chest, or pleurisy; brings the eruption out again if it should have disappeared.

China: Abdominal ailments, with *frequent stools;* emaciation; pale face; *debility* and no *fever.*

Ipecacuanha: Gastric symptoms with violent fever; short and dry cough, hurried breathing, *coated tongue, nausea,* vomiting, mental uneasiness.

Pulsatilla: Disposition to catarrhal affections of the mouth and bronchial passages.—Facilitates the breaking out.

§ 7. Compare: Inflammatory Fevers, Exanthemata, Rubeola, Scarlatina, &c.

MELANCHOLIA.

§ 1. Principal remedies: 1) *Ars aur. bell. ign. lach. puls. sulph.;* or 2) *Calc. caust. cocc. con. graph. hell. hyos. lyc. merc. nair-m. n-vom. petr. sil. stram. veratr.*

For *black* melancholy: 1) *Ars. aur. lach. n-vom.;* or 2) *Ant. anac. calc. graph. merc. sulph.*

For *silent* melancholy: 1) *Cocc. hell. ign. lyc. phos-ac. puls. sil. veratr.;* or 2) *Con. petr. sulph.,* &c.

For *religious* melancholy: *Aur. bell. lach. lyc. puls. sulph.*

§ 2. Particular indications.

Arsenicum: Periodical attacks of *anguish* and *restlessness*, restless moving about, inability to remain quiet in bed or to sit still; the anguish sets in at night, or in the evening at twilight; disposition to weep: fixed idea that one has offended every body, or cannot lead a happy life; *fear*, with disposition to kill one's-self, or excessive *fear of death;* oppressive and compressive sensation in the pit of the stomach; hot and red face, &c.

Aurum: Violent præcordial anguish, weeping, praying, palpitation of the heart, aversion to life, desire to kill one's-self; disposition to despair of one's-self and of the respect of others, and to consider every thing from the worst side; inability to perform mental labour, even the least; frequent buzzing in the ears and headache; bruised pain of the brain after every mental labour; affections of the liver, &c.

Belladonna: Great anguish, especially at the approach of persons; disposition to attack people, followed by tears of repentance; or restless, gloomy and whining moods, with listlessness and indifference; amorous paroxysms; spasms in the throat and urinary passages; excited sexual instinct, &c.

Ignatia: Taciturn, staring look; *grief, indifference* to every thing; anguish, palpitation of the heart; disposition to cry; desire to be alone; debility; frequent sighing; sallow, sunken face; falling off of the hair, &c.

Lachesis: Anguish and restlessness, inducing the patient to go out into the open air; low spirits with longing to give one's-self up to grief, to despair of one's salvation; frequent sighing; followed by relief, &c.

Pulsatilla: Great tendency to start; anguish with desire to drown one's-self; sleeplessness with anguish, or restless sleep with anxious dreams; anxious contractive sensation in the chest, especially in the evening or at night, with asthma and suffocative fits; despair of salvation, with constant praying; great disposition to weep, or to sit still with folded hands, &c.

Sulphur: Anguish with apprehension about one's fate, domestic affairs, salvation; disposition to sit still and listlessly, or to despair and escape; fear, anguish whining mood, praying and complaining of impious thoughts that crowd upon one; pale face; *great listlessness*, &c.

§ 3. See: Mental derangement; Emotions, morbid; Home-sickness; Hypochondria, &c.

MEMORY, WEAK, inability to think.

§ 1 Principal remedies: *Aur. arn. calc. carb-veg. chin. lach. merc. natr. natr-m. n-vom. puls. rhus. sil. staph. sulph. veratr.*

§ 2. If caused by *debilitating loss of animal fluids*, give: *Chin. nux-vom.* and *sulph.* (Compare: Debility.)

If caused by *excessive studying* or *mental labour*, give: 1) *N-vom.* and *sulph.*; or, 2) *Aur. calc. lach. natr. natr-m. puls. sil.* (Compare: Lassitude.)

If caused by *external injuries*, as a blow, fall on the head, &c., give *Arn.*; or perhaps: *Cic. merc. rhus.*

If by *abuse of spirits*: *Nux-v.*; or, *Calc. lach. op. merc. puls. sulph.*

Compare: Drunkards, diseases of.

If caused by *violent emotions, fright, grief, anger*, &c.: 1) *Acon. staph.*; or, 2) *Phos-ac. op.*, &c.

Compare: Emotions.

If caused by exposure to *wet* or *dampness*, give: 1) ***Carb-veg.*** *rhus. veratr.*; or, 2) *Calc. puls. sil.*

If by *congestion* of blood to the head: *Chin. merc.* ***rhus.*** *sulph.*

§ 3. Use moreover:

For general *morbid state* of the head: 1) *Aur. bell.* ***calc.*** *hyos. lach. lyc. n-vom. op. phos-ac. puls. sep. stram. sulph. veratr.* 2) *Acon. anac. caust. chin. coccul. hell. hep. ign. merc. natr. natr-m. phosph. plat. rhus. sil. staph.*

For *weak memory*: 1) *Anac. bell. hyos. lach. lyc. natr-m. n-mosch. rhus. staph. sulph.* 2) *Alum. bry. calc. con. cycl.* ***graph.*** *hell. hep. oleand. petr. sil. stram. veratr. zinc.*

For *loss of memory*: *Anac. bell, bry. con. hep. hyos.* ***natr-m.*** *op. petr. puls. sil. stram. veratr.*

For *difficult comprehension*: *Amb. calc. con. cycl. hell. ign. lyc. merc. natr. natr-m. n-mosch. oleand. op. phos-ac. rhus. sep. staph. stram. thuj.*

For *slow* flow of ideas: *Alum. amm. aur. calc. carb-veg. hyos. lach. lyc. natr-m. n-mosch. n-vom. op. petr. phos-ac. rhus. sep. sil. staph.*

For *loss* of ideas: *Alum. amm. caust. hell. hyos. lach. natr. natr-m. nitr-ac. oleand. staph. thuj. veratr.*

For *dullness of sense, idiocy*, &c.: *Alum. bell. calc.* ***hell.*** *hyos. natr. natr-m. oleand. op. phos-ac. sep. staph. stram. sulph.*

§ 4. Compare: MENTAL DERANGEMENT; EMOTIONS, MORBID; HEADACHE, &c.

MENINGITIS, ENCEPHALITIS.

§ 1. These two affections have been arranged under one head, because their symptoms are almost alike.

The best remedy for meningitis is *Bell.*, which is sometimes to be preceded by *Acon.* In some cases, we have to give: 2) *Bry. hyos. op stram. sulph.*; or, 3) *Camph. canth. cin. coccul. cupr. dig. hell. hyos. lach. merc.*

§ 2. Meningitis of *children* may, beside *Bellad.*, require: *Acon. cin. hell. lach. merc.*

Meningitis caused by a *stroke of the sun*, requires: *Bell.* or *camph.*, also *lach.*

Compare: CAUSES.

If caused by *congelation* or a mere *cold* in the head, give: *Acon. bry.*, or *Ars. hyosc.*

Meningitis from *suppression of erysipelas*, or some other *eruption*, such as *scarlatina*, requires: *Bell.* or *rhus-t.*, or ***Lach.***

merc. or *phosph.;* and if caused by suppression of otorrhœa, give *Puls* or *sulph.*

If meningitis threaten to pass into hydrocephalus, give: 1) *Bell. bry. hell.;* or 2) *Arn. dig. cin. con. hyos. op. stram.*

See: HYDROCEPHALUS.

§ 3. Symptomatic indications:

ACONITUM: Inflammatory fever, delirium, violent burning pains through the whole brain, especially in the forehead; red and bloated face, red eyes, &c.

BELLADONNA: Boring with the *head into the pillow; sensitiveness to light* and *noise;* or for: Violent burning and stitching pains in the head; red, sparkling eyes, with furious look; red and bloated face; sopor, with distorted and half-opened eyes; *heat in the head,* with violent throbbing of the carotids; swelling of the veins of the head; loss of consciousness and speech, or muttering, violent delirium; convulsive movements of the limbs; spasmodic constriction of the throat with difficult deglutition and other hydrophobic symptoms; vomiting, involuntary discharge of urine and fæces, &c.

BRYONIA: Chills, red face, heat about the head, and great thirst; constant sopor, with delirium; sudden starting from sleep, screams and cold sweat on the forehead; burning and aching pains in the head, or stitches shooting through the brain.

CINA: *Vomiting, with clean tongue,* or discharge of worms by the mouth or rectum.

HYOSCYAMUS: Stupor, loss of consciousness; delirium, the patient talking about his domestic affairs; singing, muttering, smiling, grasping at flocks, sudden starting, &c.

OPIUM: *Lethargy,* stertorous breathing with the eyes half closed; and stupefaction after waking; frequent vomiting; complete listlessness and dullness of sense, the patient not desiring nor complaining of any thing.

STRAMONIUM: The sleep is almost natural, with twitching of the limbs, moaning, tossing about, absence of mind after waking; or: Staring look; slow and shy retreating, or desire to escape, with screams; *frightful visions;* feverish heat, red face and moist skin.

MENSTRUAL DIFFICULTIES, SPASMS, COLIC, DIFFICULT MENSTRUATION, MOLIMINA.

§ 1. Principal remedies: 1) *Bell. bry. calc. cocc. coff. graph. ign. n-vom. phos. plat. puls. sec. sep. sulph. veratr.* 2) *Acon. amm. amm-m. carb-veg. caust. cupr. kal. kreos. lach. lyc. magn-c. magn-m merc. natr-m. n-mosch. petr. sil zinc.* 3) *Baryt. borax. cham. chel. con. phos-ac. sabin. stram. tabac.*

Particular indications :

BELLADONNA : Colic before the menses, with great languor, loss of appetite and obscuration of sight ; or the menses are accompanied by sweat on the chest at night, frequent yawning, chills, colic ; præcordial anguish, burning thirst, pains in the loins and spasmodic pains in the back ; *pressing-down* in the abdomen, as if the contents would push through the sexual parts, with heaviness as from a stone ; the limbs go to sleep while sitting, with pressure on the rectum ; tendency of the blood to the chest and head, with beating pains, heat about the head, red and bloated face ; suitable to young, plethoric subjects.

BRYONIA : Tendency of the blood to the chest or head, with short cough and frequently bleeding ; leucorrhœa, rheumatic pains in the limbs ; aching or burning pain in the stomach ; pressure and fullness in the epigastrium ; chilliness or frequent shuddering ; constipation.

CALCAREA : Tendency of the blood to the head, with stupefaction and vertigo ; or tearing, boring headache, made worse by an emotion or by a change of weather ; *leucorrhœa*, colic, pain in the back and spasmodic pains in the small of the back ; violent colicky pains ; loss of appetite ; asthmatic ailments ; toothache, nausea, or vomiting.

CHAMOMILLA : Violent colic after profuse and premature menses, with great sensitiveness of the abdomen to contact, as if the inner parts were ulcerated ; pains in the small of the back and abdominal spasms of the worst kind, with diarrhœic, greenish or whitish stools ; nausea, eructations, desire to vomit, yellow-coated tongue, and bitter taste in the mouth ; especially suitable when the blood is of a dark colour, clotty, and when there are fainting fits with thirst, cold limbs, pale and worn-out appearance.

COCCULUS : Premature menses, with abdominal spasms, or feeble menses, with leucorrhœa between the menses ; or discharge of a few drops of black, coagulated blood, with aching colicky pains, flatulence, nausea unto fainting, laming weakness, oppression and spasms of the chest, anguish and convulsive motions of the extremities ; or reddish leucorrhœa in the place of the menses, mixed with purulent and blood-streaked serum.

COFFEA : Excessively painful and violent paroxysms of colic, with excessive discharge of blood, profuse secretion of mucus, voluptuous itching and excessive sexual excitement.

GRAPHITES : The menses are too scanty and short, the blood being thick and black or watery and pale ; *colic* and *abdominal spasms*, headache, nausea, pains in the chest, bronchial catarrh or coryza ; great debility, rheumatic pains in the limbs ; œdematous swelling of the feet and legs ; *herpes* or toothache with swelling of the cheeks.

IGNATIA: Premature and profuse menses, with thick, clotty blood; *spasmodic colic;* painful heaviness in the head, photophobia, anguish, palpitation of the heart and great debility unto fainting.

NUX VOMICA: *Premature*, profuse and long-lasting menses, preceded by drawing pains in the nape of the neck; or for: uterine spasms with aching pain in the hypogastrium down to the thighs; nausea with fainting, especially in the morning; languor, chill, rheumatic pains in the limbs; pains in the small of the back as if bruised; constipation with ineffectual urging; frequent pressure on the bladder, without result; sensation as if the abdomen would burst; tendency of the blood to the head, with vertigo and headache; irritable, quarrelsome mood, or restless and *beside herself*.

PHOSPHORUS: Scanty menses, preceded by leucorrhœa, whining mood, colicky pains and cutting as if with knives, vomiting of bile, mucus and food; or the menses delay at first, and then appear so much more profusely and last so much longer, accompanied with great debility, blue margins around the eyes, emaciation and restlessness; or stitching headache, bruised pain in the limbs, palpitation of the heart, spitting of blood, chills, and swelling of the gums or cheek.

PLATINA: The menses are *too profuse* and last too long, or they appear too early, with discharge of black and slimy blood; leucorrhœa before and after the menses; *spasmodic colic* with painful pressure over the *sexual parts;* frequent desire to urinate; constipation or hard stools; colic; loss of appetite; frequent paroxysms of vertigo or anguish with restlessness and weeping; discharge of black and thick blood; sleepless nights; short breath and suspicious mood.

PULSATILLA: *Delaying* menses, with discharge of black and coagulated or pale and watery blood; or for: colic, abdominal spasms, pains in the liver, cardialgia, pains in the small of the back, nausea, desire to vomit, or *sour* and *slimy vomiting;* megrim; vertigo; *chilliness* with pale face; a good deal of urging on the rectum and bladder; *leucorrhœa;* whining mood, or anguish; sadness and melancholy.

SECALE: The menses are too scanty or last too long, with tearing or cutting colicky pains; *cold extremities;* pale face, cold sweat; great *debility;* small and almost suppressed pulse.

SEPIA: *Profuse* or not very scanty menses, with leucorrhœa, spasmodic colic and pressure over the sexual organs, headache, rigidity of the limbs, toothache and melancholy.

SULPHUR: Premature and profuse menses, or scanty menses with discharge of pale blood; or when the menses are preceded, accompanied or succeeded by: *colicky pains, abdominal spasms, headache, tendency of the blood to the head, bleeding at the nose, pains in the small of the back;* great restlessness and anguish; toothache; heartburn; cardialgia, itching of the pudendum and leucorrhœa; asthmatic complaints; cough, or epileptic convulsions.

§ 3. Use more particularly:

When the pains occur in young girls who have not yet menstruated, at a period when the menses ought to appear: 1) ***Puls. sulph.***; or, 2) *Caust. cocc. graph. kal. natr-m. sep. veratr.*

For *premature* menses: 1) ***Amb. amm. calc. carb-v. ipec kreos.*** *kal. natr-m. n-vom. phos. plat. rhus. sabin. sep.* ***sil. sulph-ac.*** 2) *Amm-m. cham. cin. coccul. con. croc. ign. ruta. sec.* ***sulph-ac.***

Delaying menses: 1) ***Caust. con. cupr. dulc. graph. jod. kal.*** *lyc. magn-c. natr-m. puls. sep. sil. sulph.* 2) *Dros. hep. lach.*

Too *short: Amm. baryt. dulc. graph. lach. natr-m. phos. puls. sulph.*

Too *long: Chin. cupr. kreos. lyc. natr. n-vom. phos. plat. puls. sec. sulph-ac.*

Too *scanty:* 1) *Alum. amm. carb-v. caust. con. graph.* ***kal.*** *lach. magn-c. natr-m. puls. sil. sulph.* 2) *Coccul. dulc. ferr. lyc. merc. phos. ruta. sabad. sassap. sep. staph.*

Too *profuse:* 1) *Acon. ars. bell. calc. carb-v. chin. ferr.* ***ipec.*** *natr-m. n-vom. phos. plat. sabin. sec. sil. stram. sulph-ac.* 2) *Bry. cham. cin. hyos. ign. lyc. merc. nitr-ac. ruta.* ***samb. sep.*** *sulph.*

When the menses are about to cease, at the *critical* period: 1) *Lach. puls.* 2) *Caust. coccul con. graph. kal. lyc.* ***natr-m.*** *ruta. sep. sulph.*

§ 4. When the menses are *too pale, too watery:* 1) ***Bell.*** *calc. carb-v. cocc. ferr. graph. lyc.* ***nitr-ac.*** *plat. puls. sulph.* 2) *Ars. chin. con. hell. kal. natr-m. n-vom. phos. plumb.* ***sep.*** *spig.*

Brown blood: *Bry. calc. carb-v. rhus.*

Thick blood: 1) *Croc. cupr. plat. sulph.* 2) *Arn.* ***n-mosch.*** *puls.*

Dark, black blood: 1) *Bell. bry. cham. croc. n-vom. puls.* ***sulph.*** 2) *Amm. ant. kreos. lach. magn-c. nitr-ac. sep.*

Bright-red blood: *Bell. calc. carb-v. dulc. ferr. hyos.* ***nitr-ac.*** *sabin. sulph.*

Lumpy coagulated blood: *Amm. bell. cham. chin. coccul. ferr. hyos. ign. magn-c. magn-m. nitr-ac. plat. puls. rhus.* ***sabin.*** *stram.*

Corrosive blood: ***Amm. carb-v. kal. natr. nitr. sassap. sil.*** *sulph.*

Fetid blood : *Bell. bry. carb-an. carb-v. caust. cham. croc. kal. phos. sabin. sil.*

§ 5. When the menses are attended with *congestion of blood* to the head, vertigo : *Caust. jod. merc. phos. veratr.*

With *headache :* 1) *Carb-v. lyc. natr-m. n-vom. sulph.* 2) *Calc. cupr. graph. hyos. magn-c. magn-m. phos. sep. veratr.*

When the *eyes* are affected : *Calc. magn-c. merc. puls. sil. sulph.*

When the *cheeks* are *swollen : Graph. phos. sep.*

With *toothache :* 1) *Baryt. calc. carb-v. kal. magn-c. sep.* 2) *Amm. graph. natr-m. phos. sulph-ac.*

With *nausea* or vomiting: 1) *Amm. carb-v. lyc. n-vom. puls. veratr.* 2) *Caps. hyos. magn-c. phos. sulph.*

With *colic* or abdominal spasms : *Bell. calc. cham. coccul. coff. con. graph. n-vom. phos. plat. puls. sec. sep. sulph.*

With *diarrhœa :* 1) *Graph. sil. veratr.* 2) *Alum. amm. caust. kreos. magn-c.*

With *distress of breathing : Cocc. graph. lach. puls. sep.*

With *palpitation* of the heart : *Alum. cupr. ign. jod. nitr-ac. phos. sep. spong.*

With pains in the *back and small of the back : Amm. amm-m. calc. caust. graph. kal. lach. magn-c. magn-m. n-vom. phos. plat. sep.*

With *pains* in the *limbs : Bry. graph. sep. veratr.*

With *spasms :* 1) *Acon. cham. coccul. coff. cupr. ign. plat. puls.* 2) *Bry. con. chin. graph. magn-m. natr-m. n-vom.*

With great *debility*, languor, fainting: *Caust. graph. ign. magn-c. n-vom. puls. sep.*

With *derangements* of the *mental* or *emotive sphere : Acon. cham. hyos. natr-m. stram. veratr.*

§ 6. When the distress sets in shortly *before* the *appearance* of the menses : 1) *Baryt. calc. carb-v. cham. coccul. cupr. iach. lyc. merc. phos. puls. sep. sulph. veratr.* 2) *Amm. asar. con. dulc. natr-m. phos-ac. plat. sil.*

When *during* the menses : 1) *Amm. amm-m. calc. carb-v. cham. con. graph. hyos. kal. kreos. lach. phos. puls. sep.* 2) *Alum. ars. borax. bry. calc. chin. cocc. coff. ign. lyc. magn-c. magn-m. merc. natr-m. n-vom. plat. sil. sulph. veratr. zinc.*

When *after* the menses : 1) *Borax. graph. kreos. lyc. natr-m. n-vom. phos-ac. plat. ruta. stram.* 2) *Alum. ars. calc. con. magn-c. phos. sep. sil.*

§ 7. Compare : Uterus, diseases of, Hæmorrhage from the uterus, Colic, Amenia, Leucorrhœa, &c.

MENTAL DERANGEMENT, INSANITY, MANIA, RAGE, &c.

§ 1. Principal remedies: 1) *Acon. bell. calc. hyos. lach. n-vom. op. plat. stram. veratr.* 2) *Anac. arn. ars. canth. cupr. lyc. puls. sil. sulph.* 3) *Agar. ant. cann. caust. cic. coccul. con. coloc. croc. dig. dulc. ign. merc. natr. n-mosch. oleand. par. phos. plumb. rhus. sec. sep. zinc.*

§ 2. If caused by depressing emotions, such as: *grief, mortification, chagrin, anger,* &c., give: 1) *Ign. phos-ac. staph.;* or, 2) *Bell. hyos. n-vom. plat.,* &c.

See: EMOTIONS.

If by *excessive study,* use: 1) *Lach. plat. stram.* 2) *N-vom. op. sulph.;* or, 3) *Bell. hyos. veratr.*

Compare: *Lassitude* by mental labour.

If connected with *religious fancies,* give: 1) *Bell. hyos. lach. puls. stram. sulph. veratr.;* or, 2) *Ars aur. croc. lyc. selen.*

For *delirium tremens:* 1) *N-vom. op.* 2) *Ars. hell.;* or, 3) *Bell. calc. hyos. lach. stram.;* or, perhaps, *Puls. merc. sulph.*

Compare: *Drunkards, diseases of.*

Mental derangement of *females,* if caused by irregularity of the sexual function, requires: 1) *Acon. bell. plat. puls. stram. veratr.;* or, 2) *Cupr. lach. merc. sulph.*

Compare: *Menstrual irregularities, Sexual instinct,* &c.

§ 3. Symptomatic indications:

ACONITUM: *Fear* and *presentiment of approaching death;* desire to escape from home or from one's bed; *gloomy, taciturn;* paroxysms of anguish and convulsions; *cold sweats; tendency of the blood* to the chest or head; *palpitation of the heart* and oppressive anxiety; delirium, the patient weeping and laughing alternately, &c.

BELLADONNA: Great anguish, with restlessness and apprehensions; the patient becomes unconscious in such a manner that he knows his family only by hearing them talk; frightful visions of *ghosts,* devils, soldiers, war, oxen, with desire to escape or hide himself; distrustful, diffident mood, or quarrelsome, or desire to spit, *beat, bite,* to tear every thing, or to *tear out his teeth;* screams, howls, &c. Conversation with dead people; dread of death; desire to be alone, aversion to talk, taciturn; ill humour, disposed to be vehement and peevish, or moaning and praying; *foolish gesticulations; wild eyes;* with fixed, *furious look; bloated face;* great desire to look at the sun or fire; froth and foam at the mouth; stuttering speech; *burning thirst,* or *aversion to drink, with difficult deglutition;* sudden starting, twitching; *trembling of the extremities,* especially the hands; sleepless, restless, &c.

Calcarea: Delirium, talking of murder, fire, rats and mice; or for: ill will, obstinacy, ill humour, taciturn mood, trembling of the limbs, &c.

Hyoscyamus: Rage, alternating *with epileptic spasms;* sleepless, delirious, loquacious; *anguish* and fear, especially at night, with dread of being betrayed or poisoned; desire to escape; visions of dead persons; *jealousy;* rage, with desire *to beat and kill; foolish gesticulations;* delirium, talking about his affairs, *trembling of the limbs*, &c.

Lachesis: *Loquacious*, jumping rapidly from one subject to another; ecstasy, unto crying; distrust, suspicion; *jealousy*, pride, presentiment of death; *doubt of salvation*, &c.

Nux vom.: Anguish and restlessness, with desire to leave one's house and wander about the fields; loss of consciousness, delirium, frightful visions, irrational acts and speeches; pale and bloated or red and hot face; tendency of the blood to the head, stuttering, *trembling of the limbs;* dull and *heavy head*, fullness and indolence of the body; pressure, heaviness and pressing in the pit of the stomach, in the region of the stomach and hypochondria; desire to vomit, vomiting of bile and food; *constipation* or watery diarrhœa; sleeplessness with sudden starting, &c.

Opium; Coma, loss of consciousness; rage with strange or fixed fancies, the patient imagines that he is outside of his own body; frightful visions of mice, scorpions, &c., *convulsive motions* and trembling; anguish, rage, inability to go to sleep, with bloated and flatulent abdomen; tendency of the blood to the head with red face, &c.

Platina: Delirium, talking of past things, singing, laughing, weeping, dancing, making faces and gestures; obstinate, or irritable and quarrelsome, with desire to reproach others with their faults; *despising others, and thinking much of one's-self;* excessive sexual excitement; constipation; *anguish*, with palpitation of the heart and fear of death; frightful visions, with fear, fixed ideas, the patient fancies that every body he sees is a demon, &c.

Stramonium: Stupefaction, with great anxiety and restlessness, or *loss of consciousness*, so that he no longer recognises his own family; fixed ideas, the patient imagines that his body is broken, &c.; *delirium, with frightful visions, fear*, desire to escape, or praying, the patient looking devout and exhibiting religious attitudes; or very *loquacious*, lascivious, or assuming all sorts of manners, an important look, conversing with spirits, dancing, laughing, beating about, or ridiculous gestures, alternating with expressions of sadness and melancholy; or *indomitable rage*, with desire to bite, spit, cut down and kill; *desire for light and company*, aggravation when alone and in the dark, and at the pe riod of the fall-equinox; *red and bloated face,* with an insipid friendly look, &c.

VERATRUM: Anguish and restlessness, fear and tendency to start; despondency; *very* taciturn, swearing and cursing on every occasion; desire to reproach others with their faults; loss of consciousness, with singing, whistling, laughing, *lascivious* thoughts, desire to wander about out of doors; irrational and proud ideas; disposition to assert that he is suffering with imaginary ailments; religious delirium, &c.

§ 4. Of other remedies, use:

ANACARDIUM: For strong disposition to laugh at serious things, and to be serious in the presence of things that are really ludicrous; constant contradiction with one's-self; want of moral and religious sentiment, even with disposition to swear and curse; fixed idea that he is possessed of the devil, &c.

ARNICA: Foolish mirth, with great levity of manners, wanton and malicious, headstrong, quarrelsome, &c.

ARSENICUM: Excessive anguish and irresoluteness; *fear of ghosts, thieves* and *solitude,* with desire to hide one's-self; aversion to conversation, with desire to censure.

CANTHARIS: Rage with screams, beating and howling; the paroxysms come on again, at the sight of water, or if water should get into his throat; *great sexual excitement, and excitement of the parts;* great thirst, aversion to drink, with difficult deglution, &c.

CUPRUM: Deficient moral force; fixed idea that one is doing some imaginary work; singing, or malicious and peevish disposition; *wild, red* and *inflamed eyes during the paroxysms;* weeping and anguish, or ludicrous gestures and desire to hide himself; *sweat after the paroxysm,* &c.

LYCOPODIUM: Rage, attended with desire to blame others, and arrogant manners.

PULSATILLA: The patient is quiet, with folded arms, he moans, says that nothing ails him, is stupefied, delirious at night, with frightful visions, fear, desire to hide himself, &c.

SILICEA: Fixed ideas, for instance: the patient counts pins, is afraid of them, collects them from every part of the room; taciturn, listless; anguish, aversion to work; *aggravation* at *full moon.*

SULPHUR: Fixed idea that he possesses beautiful things and an abundance of every thing, with confusion of ideas, such as: mistaking a hat for a bonnet, old rags for beautiful cloths, &c.

§ 5. Use more particularly:

a) For mental derangement with anxiety, *fear, frightful visions* and thoughts: 1) *Bell. hyos. op. stram.* 2) *Ars. calc. cupr. lyc. n-vom. op. sulph. veratr.*

b) For *restlessness*, obliging one to leave the house or bed, and *wander* about: 1) *Bell. hyos. n-vom. op. stram. veratr.* 2) *Acon. ars. bry. canth. coloc. cupr.*

c) For *praying*, begging, moaning, weeping: 1) *Ars. bell. merc. puls. stram.* 2) *Acon. ign. mosch. natr-m. sulph.*

d) For religious *praying*, kneeling and other religious acts: 1) *Bell. hyos. lach. puls. stram. sulph. veratr.* 2) *Ars. aur. croc. lyc. selen.*

e) For disposition to *curse*, swear, quarrel, &c.: 1) *Anac. bell. hyos. lyc. stram. veratr.* 2) *Acon. ars. cupr. natr-m. n-vom.*

f) For *rage*, acts of violence, biting, spitting, tearing, beating: 1) *Bell. canth. hyos. lyc. stram. veratr.* 2) *Agar. ars. camph. cann. coccul. croc. cupr. lach. merc. plumb. sec.*

g) For mania as if *possessed of the devil*: *Anac. hyos.*

h) For *illusions of fancy, visions*, seeing of ghosts, &c.: 1) *Bell. stram.* 2) *Anac. lach. natr-m. op. puls. sil. sulph.*

i) For *erroneous* fancies, *fixed ideas*, &c.: 1) *Bell. coccul. ign. phos-ac. sabad. stram. sulph.* 2) *Acon. amb. cic. hell. hyos. lyc. merc. n-vom. op. phos. plat. puls. rhus. sec. sil. val. veratr.*

k) For *false* representations, such as: that one is sick, &c.: *Bell. veratr.*

l) For *crazy mirthfulness*, singing, whistling, dancing, warbling, &c.: 1) *Bell. coff. croc. natr. op. stram. veratr.* 2) *Aur. cann. cic. hyos. phosph. phos-ac. plat.*

m) For *ludicrous* gestures and acts: 1) *Bell. hyos. merc. stram.* 2) *Cic. cupr. n-mosch.*

n) For *gesticulating* all the time: 1) *Bell. hyos. mosch. stram.* 2) *Ars. cic. n-mosch. puls. sep. veratr.*

o) For performing all sorts of crazy actions, as if one were *very busy*: 1) *Bell. merc. stram.* 2) *Camph. cupr. op. sec. sulph. veratr.*

p) For *loquacity*: 1) *Bell. hyos. stram.* 2) *Acon. ars. camph. n-vom. n-mosch. lach.*

q) For *lascivious* speeches and acts: 1) *Hyos. phos. stram. veratr.* 2) *Bell. n-mosch.*

r) For *amorous* craziness: 1) *Ant. hyos. veratr.* 2) *Aur. ign. phos-ac.*

§ 6. See: EMOTIONS, MORBID, and comp.: MELANCHOLY, and all those BODILY ailments with which deranged persons are apt to be affected.

MERCURY, ILL EFFECTS OF.

§ 1. Poisoning with *corrosive sublimate*, requires (according to Hering): 1) *Albumen*, dissolved in water, as a drink; 2) *su-*

gar-water; 3) *milk;* 4) *starch,* mixed with water, or book-binder's paste.—*Albumen* and *sugar-water* are the principal remedies, which may be used in alternation.

§ 2. *Secondary affections* require the usual antidotes for the drug-symptoms of Mercury, the principal of which is: ***Hepar,*** in water, a teaspoonful night and morning; especially for: headache at night, *falling off of the hair, painful nodes* on *the head;* inflamed, red eyes, with painful sensitiveness of the nose when pressing upon it; scurfs around the mouth; ptyalism and *ulcerated gums;* swelling of the tonsils and cervical glands; swelling and ulceration of the inguinal and axillary glands; diarrhœic stools with tenesmus; inflammation of the skin, and *disposition to ulcerate,* &c.

After ***Hep.*** give ***Bell.*** or *nitr-ac.*—If symptoms remain after *Nitr-ac.*, give a dose of *Sulphur* for one or two weeks; after *Sulphur, Calc.* does good service.

The ill effects of *Mercury* and *Sulphur* together, require ***Bell.*** *puls.*, or even *mercurius.*

§ 3. As regards symptoms and chronic affections, give:

For affection of the *mouth* and *gums, ptyalism,* &c.: 1) *Carb-veg. dulc. hep. nitr-ac. staph. sulph.*; or, 2) *Chin. jod. natr-m.*

For *sore throat:* 1) *Bell. carb-veg. hep. lach. staph. sulph.;* or, 2) *Arg. lyc. nitr-ac. thuj.*

For nervous *debility:* 1) *Chin. hep. lach.;* or, 2) *Carb-veg. nitr-ac.*

For nervous *excitement: Carb-veg. cham. hep. nitr-ac. puls.*

For *excessive sensitiveness* to changes in weather, to cold, &c.: *Carb-veg. chin.*

For *rheumatic* pains: 1) *Carb-veg. chin. dulc. guaj. hep. lach. phos-ac. sassap. puls. sulph.;* or, 2) *Arn. bell. calc. cham. lyc.*

For affections of the *bones, exostoses, caries,* &c.: 1) *Aur. phos-ac.;* or, 2) *Asa. calc. dulc. lach. lyc. nitr-ac. sil. sulph.*

For affections of *glands, buboes,* &c.: *Aur. carb-veg. dulc. nitr-ac. sil.*

For *ulcers: Aur. bell. carb-veg. hep. lach. nitr-ac. sass. sil. sulph. thuj.*

For *dropsical* symptoms: *Chin. dulc. hell. sulph.*

§ 4. See: MERCURIAL AILMENTS under: HEADACHE, OPHTHALMIA, TOOTHACHE, COLIC, DIARRHŒA, &c.

METRITIS.—Principal remedies: 1) *Acon. bell. cham. coff. merc. n-vom.;* 2) *Bry. canth. chin. ign. lach. plat. puls. rhus. sec.*

ACONITUM: *Violent fever*, especially when the disease was caused by *fright* during confinement, or during the catamenia, or if abuse had been made of chamomile.

BELLADONNA: When the disease occurs during confinement, with suppression of the lochia, or adhesion of the placenta; or: heaviness, drawing and pressure in the hypogastrium, as if every thing would press through the vagina, with burning stitches, pain in the small of the back as if bruised and broken; and stitching pains in the hip-joint, not allowing the parts to be touched or moved.

CHAMOMILLA: After confinement, when the disease is caused by a fit of *chagrin* or *anger*, with copious secretion of the lochia and discharge of a black, clotty blood. If abuse of chamomile should have contributed to the development of the disease, give: *Acon. ign. n-vom. puls.*

COFFEA: The disease is caused by a sudden joy, either during the menses or during confinement.

MERCURIUS: The pains in the uterus are stitching, aching or boring, with little heat, but frequent sweats or chills.

NUX VOM.: Violent aching pains in the hypogastrium, aggravated by pressure and contact; violent pains in the loins; constipation or hard stools; retention of urine, dysuria or ischuria; swelling of the os-tincæ, with contusive pain and stitches in the abdomen; aggravation towards morning.

See: PUERPERAL FEVER; and compare: UTERUS, DISEASES OF.

MEZEREUM, ILL EFFECTS OF.—Principal remedies: *Bry. merc. rhus.*

MERCURIUS: When the bones or the parts of the inner mouth are affected.

BRYONIA: The joints are principally affected, in which case it should be given in alternation with *Rhus-t.*

MISCARRIAGE.—Principal remedies: 1) *Bell. calc. carb-v. croc. cham. ferr. ipec. lyc. n-vom. sabin. sec. sep. sil. sulph. zinc.* 2) *Asar. bryon. cannab. canth. chin. croc. cic. hyosc. n-mosch. plumb. puls. ruta.*

For the *disposition* to miscarriage, give: 1) *Calc. carb-veg. ferr. lyc. sab. sep. sulph. zinc.* 2) *Asar. cann. cocc. kreos. n-mosch. plumb. puls. ruta. sil.*

CALCAREA: Suitable to *plethoric* persons, with profuse and premature menses, disposition to leucorrhœa, painful nipples, tendency of the blood to the head, colic, pains in the loins, varices of the sexual organs.

CARBO VEG.: Pale, or premature and profuse menses, with

varices of the sexual organs; frequent headache, pains in the loins, abdominal spasms, &c.

FERRUM: Suitable to chlorotic females, with leucorrhœa, when the menses are suppressed; or to plethoric females, with great vascular action, red face, full and strong pulse, premature and profuse menses.

LYCOPODIUM: The menses are too profuse and last too long, with itching, burning, and varices of the sexual organs; dryness of the vagina, disposition to melancholy, with sadness and weeping; leucorrhœa, frequent headache and pains in the loins, fainting fits, &c.

SABINA: Suitable to *plethoric* persons, with profuse and too long menses; the miscarriage generally takes place in the third month of pregnancy.

SEPIA: Leucorrhœa, with soreness, eruption and itching of the sexual parts: scanty or premature menses, with weeping, melancholy, headache and toothache; frequent attacks of megrim; feeble constitution; tender and sensitive skin; gray colour of the skin, with brownish or yellowish spots in the face; slender waist, nervous debility, disposition to sweat; frequent colic, disposition to catarrh.

SULPHUR: *Premature* and *profuse*, or scanty and delaying menses, with leucorrhœa, itching, burning and soreness of the parts; eruption or herpes on the skin; hæmorrhoidal disposition; disposition to catarrh or other blennorrhœas; nervous debility, with loss of appetite; great languor, especially in the lower limbs; frequent headache, with tendency of the blood to the head, &c.

Compare: AMENORRHŒA, and DYSMENORRHŒA.

§ 3. The *precursory* or *first* symptoms of miscarriage, indicate: 1) *Arn. bell. bry. cham. hyosc. ipec. n-vom. sabin. sec.* 2) *Cann. chin. cin. cocc. n-mosch. plat. puls. rhus. ruta.*

ARNICA: Is indicated, if labour-pains set in in consequence of a shock, motion, or some other external injury, with the discharge of blood or serous mucus.

BELLADONNA: For violent aching or tensive pains through the whole body, with sensation of constriction or distention, pains in the loins as if broken, bearing-down and congestion to the sexual organs, with or without discharge of blood.

BRYONIA: Violent pains with obstinate constipation, tendency of the blood to the head, dry mouth and thirst, particularly if *Nux vom.* should have been ineffectual against this condition.

CHAMOMILLA: Violent cutting pains from the loins to the abdomen, with frequent desire to urinate or go to stool; discharge of blood from the vagina, with discharge of coagula; heaviness in the whole abdomen, frequent yawning, cnills and shuddering; great restlessness and convulsive motions of the limbs.

Hyoscyamus: Alternately *clonic* and *tonic* spasms, with loss of consciousness and discharge of a bright-red blood, especially during the spasmodic paroxysms.

Ipecacuanha: For spasms with consciousness, especially when accompanied with cutting pains around the umbilicus, with pressure towards the sexual organs, and with discharge of blood. If *Ipec.* should be insufficient, *Plat.*, or even *Cina*, is frequently indicated.

Nux vom.: Obstinate constipation, with congestion of blood to the womb, especially suitable to patients who have indulged in stimulating drinks, such as: wine, coffee, &c.

Sabina: The precursory symptoms of miscarriage set in in the first period of pregnancy; or at any other period, when pressing and drawing pains from the loins to the pudendum are present; discharge of blood from the vagina; relaxed and soft abdomen; constant urging to stool with diarrhœa, or desire to vomit, or vomiting, even of the ingesta; fever with shivering and heat.

Secale: Suitable to enfeebled and cachectic females, with disposition to passive hæmorrhage, spasmodic affections, &c., or when the uterus is in a state of atony, or affected with organic diseases.

§ 4. For the consequences of miscarriage, such as: *metrorrhagia*, *metritis*, &c., see these heads.

MOLES, Nævi. — Principal remedies: 1) *Calc. carb-veg. sulph.* 2) *Graph. sulph-ac.* 3) *Caust.? lyc.? nitr-ac.? petr.? phos-ac.? plat.? sil.? thuj.?*

MUCOUS DERANGEMENT, diseases of the mucous membranes. — § 1. Principal remedies: 1) *Alum. ars. bell. bry. calc. caps. carb-veg. caust. chin. dulc. hep. lyc. merc. mez. n-vom. phosph. puls. rhus. seneg. stann. sulph.* 2) *Acon. amm-m. ant. borax. carb-an. cham. dig. dros. euphr. graph. hyos. ign. kal. magn-c. natr-m. nitr-ac. plumb. sep. sil. spig. spong. staph. sulph-ac.* 3) *Cann. canth. cin. cocc. colch. guaj. jod. lach. magn-m. natr. petr. thuj. zinc.*

§ 2. Use more particularly:

a) For *inflammation* of the mucous membranes, without, or only with *serous secretion:* 1) *Acon. ars. bry. cann. canth. merc. mez. n-vom. phosph. sil. spong. sulph.* 2) *Borax. cham. dros. hyos. ign. ipec. kreos. petr. puls. sep. squill. staph.*

b) For chronic *blennorrhœas* and increased but not inflammatory secretion: 1) *Calc. caps. chin. dulc. euphr. merc. natr-m. phosph. puls. seneg. sep. stann. sulph.* 2) *Alum. ars. borax. canth. carb-an. carb-veg. caust. cham. dig. dros. graph. hep. hyos. ign. lyc. magn-c. mez. nitr-ac. n-vom. petr. rhus. sil. spig. staph. sulph-ac.*

c) For *disorganizations* of the mucous membranes (thickening, interstitial distention, &c.): 1) *Calc. caust. con. dulc. merc. mez. natr-m. petr. phosph. puls. sil. sulph.* 2) *Alum. ars. bell. carb-veg. chin. euphr. graph. lyc. seneg. sep. stann. staph.*

d) For *ulceration:* 1) *Ars. asa. bell. calc. carb-veg. caust. merc. nitr-ac. phosph. puls. sil. sulph.* 2) *Aur. canth. chin. con. dros. dulc. hep. kreos. lach. lyc. petr. rhus. staph. thuj. zinc.*

§ 3. As regards the *nature* of the secretions, give:

a) For *bloody* (blood-streaked, or with specks of blood): 1) *Acon. ars. bell. chin. ferr. jod. merc. n-vom. puls. sep. sil.* 2) *Baryt. canth. carb-veg. caust. cocc. dros. kreos. lyc. natr-m. nitr-ac. phosph. sabin. sulph. sulph-ac. thuj. zinc.*

b) For *thick mucus:* 1) *Alum. amm-m. baryt. calc. carb-veg. magn-m. natr. natr-m. phosph. puls. sil. stann. staph. sulph.* 2) *Acon. alum. ars. borax. kreos. ruta. spong.*

c) *Thin mucus,* watery: 1) *Ars. carb-veg. cham. graph. lach. magn-m. merc. puls. rhus. sulph.* 2) *Amm. amm-m. carb-an. chin. magn-arct. mez. mur-ac. n-vom. sep. sil. squill.*

d) *Purulent:* 1) *Ars. asa. bell calc. carb-veg. caust. merc. nitr-ac. phosph. puls. sil. sulph.* 2) *Aur. cann. canth. chin. con. dros. dulc. hep. kal. kreos. lach. magn-m. natr. phos-ac. rhus. sep. stann. staph. zinc.*

e) *Albuminous: Amm-m. borax. mez. petr. plat.—Jelly-like,* or like boiled starch: *Arg. hell. laur. rhus. sabin. selen.—Milky:* 1) *Calc. puls. sil.* 2) *Carb-veg. con. ferr. lyc. phosph. sabin. sep. sulph-ac.*

f) *Tenacious,* viscid: 1) *Ars. bell. cann. cham. cist. hep. merc. mez. phosph. phos-ac. samb. seneg. stann. sulph.* 2) *Alum. borax. carb-an. carb-veg. caust. kal. plat. sep. spong.—Fibrinous: Alum. seneg.—Lumpy,* flocculent: *Agar. amb. kal. kreos. magn-c. merc. phosph. sabad. sabin. sep. sil. sulph. thuj.—Indurated,* in hard pieces: *Bry. con. natr. phosph. sep. sil. sulph.*

g) *Corrosive,* acrid: 1) *Alum. amm. amm-m. ars. borax. merc. natr-m. phosph. puls. sep. sil. sulph.* 2) *Carb-veg. cham. ferr. ign. kreos. mez. nitr-ac. ruta. sulph-ac.*

§ 4. As regards *colour,* give:

a) For *blue-coloured: Amb. ars. cupr.*

b) *Brownish: Amm-m. ars. bell. borax. carb-v. nitr-ac. sulph.*

c) *Flesh-coloured: Alum. cocc. kreos. merc. nitr-ac. sabin.*

d) *Yellow:* 1) *Ant. bell. bry. calc. carb-veg. kreos. lyc. n...*

nitr-ac. n-vom. phosph. puls. sep. sil. stann. sulph. 2) *Acon. alum. ars. cann. canth. cham. cic. graph. hep. kal. natr-m. sabin. selen. stann. staph. thuj.*

e) *Gray-coloured:* 1) *Amb. arg. ars. lyc. sep. sil. thuj.* 2) *Anac. carb-an. caust. chin. kreos. lach. magn-m. merc.*

f) *Greenish:* 1) *Carb-veg. dros. led. lyc. magn-c. merc. phosph. puls. stann. sulph.* 2) *Ars. ferr. kreos. natr. sep. thuj.*

g) *Whitish:* 1) *Asar. bell. calc. colch. merc. phosph. puls. sil.* 2) *Carb-veg. con. ferr. lyc. phosph. sep. sulph-ac.*

§ 5. As regards *colour* or *taste*, give:

a) For *bad* secretions (badly smelling or foul tasting): 1) *Ars. calc. led. merc. natr. puls. sep. stann. sulph.* 2) *Aur. bell. con. dros. ferr. graph. guaj. hep. ipec. lach. magn-m. natr-m. nitr-ac. n-vom. phos-ac. sabin.*

b) For *foul*, putrid smell or taste: 1) *Ars. calc. hep. merc. natr. puls. sil stann. sulph.* 2) *Bell. con. cupr. ferr. graph. kreos. mur-ac. nitr-ac. sep.*

c) For *metallic* taste: *Calc. cupr. ipec. n-vom. rhus.*

d) For *salt* taste: 1) *Ars. baryt. graph. lyc. natr. petr. phosph. puls. sep. sil.* 2) *Calc. carb-veg. chin. dros. graph. rhus. samb. stann. sulph. zinc.*

e) For *sourish* taste or smell: 1) *Calc. chin. graph. hep. kal. magn-m. merc. natr. natr-m. n-vom. phosph. plumb. puls. sep. sulph.*

f) For *musty* taste or smell: *Borax. carb-veg.*

g) For smell or taste as of old *catarrhal mucus: Bell. ign. n-vom. phosph. puls. sulph.*

h) For *sweetish* taste: *Asar. calc. dig. kreos. lach. magn-c. merc. n-vom. phosph. plumb. puls. samb. stann. sulph.*

§ 6. Compare COUGH (expectoration), WHITES, SUPPURATIONS, &c.

MUSCLES, CONTRACTION, INDURATION OF: See *Contraction*, &c.

MUSHROOM, NOXIOUS, ILL EFFECTS OF.—For poisoning: 1) Powdered charcoal mixed in water; 2) Smelling of *spiritus nitri dulcis.*—For the secondary diseases: 1) *Coff. puls.* 2) *Acon. n-vom.*

MYELITIS.—The principal remedy for *all acute cases* is *Dulcamara*, to be preceded by *Aconite*, on account of the fever.

If *Dulc.* should fail, select: 1) *Bell. bry. coccul. n-vom. rhus.*; or, 2) *Ars. calc. caust. dig. ign. puls. veratr.*

In a case of chronic inflammation of the upper portion of the spinal marrow, with apparently incipient softening, and paralysis and atrophy of one arm, I have used *Caust.* and *staphysagria* with great benefit, also *Dulc.* and *lach.*

MYOPIA.—Principal remedies: 1) *Amm. anac. carb-veg. con. nitr-ac. petr. phosph. phos-ac. puls. sulph.*
For myopia in consequence of *ophthalmia: Puls.* and *sulph.*
For myopia from *abuse of mercury:* 1) *Carb.veg. nitr-ac. sulph.;* or, 2) *Puls.*
Myopia in consequence of *typhus* or debilitating loss of animal fluids, requires: *Phos-ac.*

NAILS, DISEASES OF THE.—§ 1. Principal remedies: 1) *Graph. sil. sulph.* 2) *Alum. ant. ars. calc. caust. con. hep. lach. magn-aust. merc. natr-m. nitr-ac. n-vom. puls. ran. sabad. sep. squill.*

§ 2. For *panaritia* (an inflammation of the skin, tendons, and their sheaths, or of the periosteum,) use: 1) *Sil. sulph.* 2) *Hep. lach.* 3) *Alum. calc. kal. merc. nitr-ac. petr. puls. sep.*
If these ulcers should have been occasioned by a *splinter* or the *prick* of a pin, use: 1) *Nitr-ac. sil.* 2) *Hep. lach. petr. sulph.*
For *onychia*, a panaritium under the nail, *Hep.* is almost specific, after which *Lach.* acts well; and, if ulceration should have set in, *Silicea* or *sulph.*
In phlegmonous inflammation between the skin and the sheaths of the tendons, it is well to give first *Sulph.*, and if this should not prevent suppuration, *Hep.*, which sometimes opens the abscess in a few hours.
Inflammations of the tendinous sheaths and synovial membranes first require *Sulph.*, then *Silic.*, if no change should take place in 24 hours.
If the *periosteum* should have been involved, *Sil.* is the principal remedy; otherwise try *Calc.* or *sulph.* in alternation with *Sil.*

§ 3. Use more particularly:
a) For breaking, peeling-off and splitting of the nails: 1) *Graph. sil. squill. sulph.* 2) *Alum. merc. sep.*—For *thickening, curvature,* roughness of the nails, use: 1) *Graph. sabad. sil. sulph.* 2) *Alum. calc. merc. sep.*—For *growing into the flesh:* 1) *Graph. magn-aust. sulph.* 2) *Kal. sil.*—For *falling off: Ant. ars. hell. merc. squill. sec. sep. thuj.*—For *hang-nails:* 1) *Natr-m. rhus. sulph.* 2) *Calc. lyc. merc. sabad. stann.*
b) For *painfulness* and sensitiveness: 1) *Caust. graph. magn-aust. n-vom. sep. sil.* 2) *Amm-m. natr-m. puls. rhus. sulph.*
c) For *discoloured* nails: *Ant. ars. graph. mur-ac. nitr-ac. sep. sulph* -For *blue-coloured: Aur. chel. chin. dig. lyc. natr-m.*

n-vom. sil.—For *spotted:* 1) *Nitr-ac. sil.* 2) *Alum. ars. natr-m. sulph.*—For *yellow-coloured:* 1) *Amb. con. sep.* 2) *Chin. merc. nitr-ac. n-vom. sil. spig.*—For *white spots: Nitr-ac. sil.*

NARCOTISM, ILL EFFECTS OF NARCOTIC SUBSTANCES.—Poisoning with large doses requires: 1) Large quantities of *black coffee;* 2) Vinegar mixed with water.

The remaining ailments yield to: 1) *Bell. carb-veg. cham. coff. lach. merc. n-vom. op. puls.* 2) *Amm. ars. caust. graph. hyos. ipec. lyc. natr-m. rhus. sep. sulph. kal.*

Compare: DRUNKARDS, DISEASES OF: OPIUM, and the other narcotic substances mentioned in this work.

NEPHRITIS and NEPHRALGIA, and other AFFECTIONS OF THE KIDNEYS.—The best remedies, so far as known, are: 1) *Bell. cann. canth. nux-v. puls.*, and perhaps also in some cases: *Alum. berb. colch. hep. lyc. sass.*

BELLADONNA: Is principally indicated by stitching pains in the kidneys, extending along the ureter as far as the bladder, with periodical aggravation, great anguish and colicky pains. (If *Bell.* should not suffice, try *Hep.*)

CANNABIS: Drawing pains from the kidneys to the pubic bones, with anguish and malaise.

CANTHARIS: Stitching, tearing and cutting pains, with painful discharge of only a few drops of urine, or with complete suppression of urine, or when the urine is mixed with blood.

NUX VOMICA: When the disease was caused by suppression of piles, or congestion of blood to the abdomen, with tension, distention and pressure in the region of the kidneys.

PULSATILLA: When the disease is accompanied with amenorrhœa or scanty menses, in females of a delicate constitution, and bland, phlegmatic disposition, or when the urine is bloody and deposits a purulent sediment.

Compare: CYSTITIS, URINARY DIFFICULTIES, URETRORRHAGIA, RETENTION OF URINE, and SECRETION OF URINE.

NETTLE-RASH, URTICARIA.—Principal remedies: 1) *Calc. caust. dulc. hep. lyc. rhus.* 2) *Acon. ant. ars. bell. bry. carb-veg. con. clem. cop. ign. mez. natr-m. n-vom. petr. puls. sep. sulph. urt. verat.*

Acute nettle-rash requires: 1) *Acon. bry. dulc. rhus. urt.;* and *chronic* nettle-rash: *Calc. lyc.*, or, *Ars. carb-veg. caust. lyc. petr. rhus. sulph. urt.*

For *essera* we have: *Cop. puls.*

NIGHTMARE, INCUBUS.—Give:

ACONITE to children and females, for: Feverish heat, thirst, palpitation of the heart, orgasmus sanguinis, oppression of the chest, anguish, and restlessness.

NUX VOM.: The paroxysms are caused by spirits, beer, copious meals, sedentary life, &c.

OPIUM: Severe paroxysms with suppressed breathing, half-opened eyes, open mouth, stertorous breathing, rattling, anxious features, cold sweat in the face, twitchings and convulsive motions of the extremities, &c.

PULSATILLA: Stertorous inspirations; anxious, sad dreams with weeping; lying on one's back, with the arms stretched above the head, or with the hands laid cross-wise on the abdomen, and the feet drawn up: suitable to females; or for dreams about *black beasts.*

SULPHUR: Light, unrefreshing sleep, with aching or beating pains in the head, dreams about fire, the arms stretched above the head, the eyes sometimes half open.

Try moreover: 1) *Amm. bryon. coni. hepar. phosph. ruta. sil. valer.* 2) *Alum. cinnab. coni. guaj. natr. natr-m.*, &c.

NITRATE OF SILVER, POISONING WITH.

First swallow large quantities of *salt water*, then mucilaginous drinks.

NOMA, CANCER AQUATICUS.

I know of one case that was greatly benefited by *Sulph. calc. sil.*, given in this order. The physician was induced to this selection of remedies by the scrofulous constitution of the child and his parents. This is another proof that the remedies ought not to be selected with reference to *one* pathological symptom, but in accordance with the general state and constitution of the patient.

NOSE, SUPPURATION OF.—Fetid, inflammatory ulceration of the Schneiderian membrane, *Ozæna.*

§ 1. Principal remedies: *Alum. amm. asa. aur. bry. calc. carb-v. caust. con. graph. kal. lach. lyc. magn-c. magn-m. merc. natr. nitr-ac. puls. sil. sulph. thuj.*

§ 2. For *chronic* stoppage of the nose: 1) *Bry. calc. caust. con. graph. natr. natr-m. nitr-ac. phos. sil. sulph.* 2) *Alum. amb. anac. ant. aur. carb-an. carb-v. kal. lach. lyc. magn-c. magn-m. mur-ac. n-vom. petr. puls. rhod. sep. spig. staph. thuj.*

For *ulceration, rhagades* and *scurfs* of the nostrils: *Alum. aur. Borax. calc. cic. graph. lach. lyc. merc. nitr-ac. puls. sulph.*

For *purulent* discharge, or ozæna in the narrower sense: 1) *Aur. merc.;* or, 2) *Alum. asa. calc. cic. con. lach. puls. sulph.*

For *syphilitic* ozæna, *Merc.* is the principal remedy; if *Merc.* should have been abused by the patient, give: 1) *Aur.* 2) *Asa. hep. lach. nitr-ac. sulph. thuj.*

§ 3. Compare: NOSE, SWELLING OF, CATARRH, &c.

NOSE, SWELLING OF, AND INFLAMMATION OF THE EXTERNAL NOSE.

§ 1. Principal remedies: *Arn. ars. asa. aur. bell. bry. calc. hep. merc. natr-m. phos. puls. sep. sulph. zinc.*

§ 2. If caused by a *blow, contusion, fall,* &c., *Arn.* is the best remedy.

If by *abuse of Mercury,* give: *Asa. aur. bell. hep. lach.? sulph.*

If by *hard drinking:* 1) *Ars. calc. puls. sulph.;* or, 2) *Bell. hep. lach. merc.*

To *scrofulous* patients give: 1) *Asa. aur. calc. hep. merc. puls. sulph.;* or, 2) *Bry. lach. phos.*

§ 3. For *red* and *painful* swelling of the nose, give: 1) *Bell. hep. merc.;* or, 2) *Alum. bry. calc. phos. rhus. sulph.*

If the *tip* be red, give: *Carb-an. nitr-ac. rhus.*

Red spots require: *Phos-ac. sil.*

Copper-redness: 1) *Ars. carb-an. veratr.* 2) *Calc. caun. carb-v. kreos. mez. rhus. ruta.*

§ 4. When the swelling is accompanied by *black pores:* 1) *Graph. natr. selen. sulph.* 2) *Bry. calc. natr-m. sabin.*

When by *scurf* on the tip: 1) *Carb-v. natr-m. sep. sil.* 2) *Carb-an. nitr-ac.*

When by *old warts: Caust.*

§ 5. Compare: NOSE, SUPPURATION OF, CANCER OF THE NOSE, ERUPTIONS IN THE FACE, CATARRH, &c.

NURSING, LACTATION.

§ 1. Principal remedies for the ailments incident to nursing: 1) *Bell. calc. cham. merc. puls. sep. sil.* 2) *Acon. bry. carb-v. chin. con. dulc. kal. n-vom. phos. phos-ac. rhab. rhus. staph. zinc.* 3) *Ars. borax. carb-an. cin. graph. ign. ipec. lach. lyc. natr-m. samb. stann.*

§ 2. For *deficiency of milk:* 1) *Agn. calc. caust. dulc. puls. rhus. zinc.* 2) *Acon. bell. bry. cham. chin. cocc. jod. merc. n-mosch. sep. sulph.*

If this deficiency be caused by *want of vital action* (in the breasts or the organisms generally), give: *Calc. caust. puls. rhus.*

If the secretion of milk should be prevented by an *excess of vital action* in the breasts, with tension, redness and throbbing in these parts, and if considerable milk fever should be present, give: 1) *Acon. bry. cham.*; or, 2) *Bell. merc.*

Lumps or *nodes* in the breasts, require: 1) *Dulc.*; or, 2) *Agn. bell. cham. rhus.*

If the deficiency of milk depend upon some unknown cause, and no particular remedy be indicated, try: 1) *Dulc.* 2) *Agn. calc. zinc.*

§ 3. *Milk-fever*, if medical interference should be at all necessary, requires: *Acon.* or *Coff.*, alone or alternately.

If these remedies be insufficient, try: *Bell. bry.*; or, *rhus.*

Arn. is sometimes useful, especially when, in consequence of hard labour, the sexual parts have been injured.

§ 4. For the *retrocession of the milk*, give: 1) *Bell. bry. dulc. puls.* 2) *Acon. calc. cham. coff. merc. rhus. sulph.*

If this retrocession should be caused by *violent emotions*, give: 1) *Bry. cham. coff.* 2) *Acon. bell.*

If by a *cold*: 1) *Bell. cham. dulc. puls.*; or, 2) *Acon. merc. sulph.*

A *metastasis* to the abdominal organs, requires: *Bell. bry. puls. rhus.*

The *chronic* consequences of the retrocession of the milk, require: *Rhus-t.*; or, *Calc. dulc. lach. merc. puls. sulph.*

§ 5. *Bad, thin* milk, or if the infant refuse to take it, give the mother: 1) *Cham. cin. merc. sil.* 2) *Borax. carb-an. lach. n-vom. puls. rhab. samb.*

BORAX: The milk coagulates readily; if Borax be insufficient, give *Lach.*

SILICEA: The child throws up after nursing and refuses the breast.

§ 6. *Puls.* is the best remedy to arrest the secretion of milk after *weaning* the child, or to prevent the secondary ailments of weaning. *Bell. bry. calc.* are likewise useful.

Galactorrhœa requires *Calc.*, especially when the breasts are turgid with milk. Try moreover: *Bell. borax. bry. rhus.*; or, *Chin. con. phos. puls. stram.*

§ 7. Compare: MAMMÆ.

NYCTALOPIA.

Principal remedies for sudden paroxysms of blindness in the day-time: 1) *Acon. merc. sil. sulph.* 2) *Con. nitr. n-vom. phos. stram.*

Compare: AMBLYOPIA.

ŒDEMA OF THE FEET.—Principal remedies, provided no organic diseases are present: *Ars. chin. ferr. kal. lyc. merc. phos. puls. rhus-t. sulph.*

If caused by *loss of blood*, give *Chin.* or *Ars.* and *Ferr.*

If caused by *abuse of China*, give: *Ferr.* or *Ars.*, or, perhaps, *Puls. sulph.*

ŒSOPHAGITIS.—Principal remedies. 1) *Arn. ars. bell. cocc merc. mez. rhus.* 2) *Asa. carb-v. euphorb. laur. sabad. sec.*

Compare: SORE THROAT, DEGLUTITION, DIFFICULT, PHARYNGITIS, &c.

OPHTHALMIA.—§ 1. Principal remedies: 1) *Acon. ars. bell. calc. cham. euphras. hepar. ignat. merc. n-vom. puls. sulph.* 2) *Ant. arn. bryon. caust. china. coloc. digit. dulc. ferr. graph. hyosc. laches. nitr-ac. petrol. rhus. sepia. spigel. sulph-ac. veratr.* 3) *Alum. aur. baryt. borax. cannab. canth. clem. coni. led. lycop. natr-m. phosph. silic. staph. thuj.*

§ 2. For *acute* ophthalmia the first remedy is *Acon.;* after which a dose of *Bell.* is generally sufficient to cure the disease. The following remedies can likewise be used: 1) *Cham. dulc. euphr. ign. merc. n-vom. puls.* 2) *Ant. arn. bor. canth. lach. nitr-ac. spig. sulph-ac. veratr.*

Chronic ophthalmia requires, beside the above-mentioned remedies, *Sulphur*, and: 1) *Alum. ars. bor calc. euphr. hep. lach. lyc. nitr-ac. spig. phosph. sil. thuj.* 2) *Ant. bar. caust. chin. col. dig. dulc. ferr. graph. hyos. petr. rhus. sep. veratr.*

§ 3. As regards the pathological character of ophthalmia, give for *arthritic* ophthalmia: 1) *Acon. bell. col. spig.* 2) *Ars. cham. dig. hep. merc. n-vom. rhus.* 3) *Berb. colch. led. lyc.*

Comp.: ARTHRITIC AILMENTS.

For *catarrhal* ophthalmia: 1) *Acon. ars. bell. cham. euphr. hep. ign. n-vom. puls.* 2) *Dig. euph. merc. sulph.*

Rheumatic: 1) *Acon. bell. bry. cham. euphr. ign. merc. n-vom. puls. rhus. sulph. veratr.* 2) *Bell. led. lyc. spig.*

Scrofulous: 1) *Ars. bell. calc. dulc. hep. ign. merc. n-vom. puls. rhus. sulph.* 2) *Caust. chin. ferr. graph. petr. sep.* 3) *Aur. bar. cann. cham. con. dig. euphr. jod. lyc. magn-c. natr-m.*

Syphilitic: 1) *Merc. nitr-ac. thuj.* 2) *Aur.? lyc.? phosph.?*

Gonorrhœal, in consequence of suppressed gonorrhœa: 1) *Acon. puls.* 2) *Nitr-ac. merc. thuj. sulph.*

Purulent ophthalmia of new-born infants: 1) *Acon. bell. cham. euphr. merc. sulph.* 2) *Calc. dulc. puls. rhus.* 3) *Bor. bry. n-vom.*

Contagious, egyptic ophthalmia: 1) *Acon? bell.? calc.? euphr.? merc.? nitr-ac.? sulph.?* 2) *Phos.? staph.? thuj.?*

Scorbutic: 1) *Amm. amm-m.? caust.? carb-veg.? merc.? mur-ac.? staph.? sulph.?* 2) *Canth.? cist.? hep.? natr-m.? nitr-ac.? n-vom.?*

§ 4. As regards *external causes*, give for ophthalmia caused by a *cold*: *Acon. ars. bell. calc. cham. dulc. hep. n-vom. puls. sulph.*

By *external injuries*: 1) *Acon. arn. calc. sil. sulph.* 2) *Euphr. nitr-ac. petr. puls. rut. sulph-ac.*

By *straining* the eyes in doing fine work: *Bell. carb-veg. rut. spig.*

By *abuse* of Mercury: 1) *Bell. hep. nitr-ac. puls. sulph.* 2) *Dulc. chin. lach. lyc. staph. thuj.*

After *exanthems* (measles, scarlatina, smallpox): *Bell. Bry. cham. hep. hyos. merc. nitr-ac. puls. rhus. sulph.*

After *suppression of eruptions* generally: *Alum. ars. carb-v. caust. graph. lach. natr-m. sel. sep. sulph. zinc.*

§ 5. Symptomatic indications:

Aconitum: For acute ophthalmia, especially if the following symptoms should be present: *Red eyes*, with dark redness of the vessels; intolerable, burning, stitching or aching pains, especially when moving the eyes; *photophobia;* copious *lachrymation* and bleareyedness, or great dryness of the eyelids. (After *Acon.* are frequently suitable: *Ant. bell.* or *hep.*)

Arsenicum: For *burning pains* as from hot coal; or aching and stitching pains, aggravated by light or motion of the eyes; violent pains obliging one to lie down, or intolerable pains, with anguish, obliging the patient to rise from bed; congested eyes; corrosive lachrymation; nightly agglutination; photophobia; *specks and ulcers on the cornea.*

Belladonna: Vivid redness of the sclerotica, burning and corrosive lachrymation, or great dryness of the eyes, with painful sensitiveness to the light; aching pains around the eyes or deep in the eyes, or stitching pains in the eyes and head; aggravation by moving the eyes; dilatation of the pupils; violent catarrh with cough ; or violent *headache with vertigo, stupefaction,* sparks or black spots before the eyes ; or obscuration of sight, or *specks* and *ulcers* on the cornea, &c. (*Bell.* is frequently suitable after *Acon. hep.* or *merc.*)

CALCAREA : Violent aching or stinging pains with itching ; or burning and cutting pains aggravated by reading or candle-light ; redness of the sclerotica, lachrymation, *specks* and *ulcers on the cornea ; photophobia ;* mistiness of sight or as if spots were hovering before the eyes, *especially when using the eyes.* (*Calc.* is frequently suitable after *Sulph.* or *Dulc.*)

CHAMOMILLA : Red eyes, with aching pains when moving them or shaking the head ; or stinging, aching and burning pains, as if heat were rushing out of the eyes ; red and swollen eyelids, with copious secretion of mucus and nightly agglutination ; great dryness of the eyes. The pains are intolerable, &c.

EUPHRASIA : Aching pain in the eyes, redness of the sclerotica ; inflammation of the cornea, with vesicles, or specks and ulcers on the cornea ; *copious secretion of mucus and tears ;* swelling of the eyelids ; frequent desire to wink ; rash around the eyes, or coryza and headache ; *photophobia,* flickering of the light.

HEPAR S. : Redness of the eyes and eyelids, with soreness when touched ; spasmodic closing of the eyelids ; difficulty of moving the eyes ; photophobia, especially in the evening ; the sight is at times dim and obscured, at others clear ; pressure in the eyeball, as if it would start out of the head ; specks and ulcers on the cornea and pimples around the eyes and eyelids ; copious lachrymation, nightly agglutination. (*Hep.* is frequently suitable after *Bell.* and *Merc.*)

IGNATIA : The eyes are not so much red as painful, with sensation as of sand in the eyes ; copious lachrymation, especially from the light of the sun ; nightly agglutination ; *photophobia ;* mistiness of sight ; fluent coryza or headache.

MERCURIUS : *Cutting* pains or pressure as if from sand in the eyes, especially after *using the eyes,* or in the evening and in bed ; or tearing, itching and stinging, especially in the open air ; copious lachrymation, especially in the evening ; excessive sensitiveness of the eyes to the glare of fire or to light ; vesicles and pimples on the sclerotica ; ulcers on the cornea ; *pustules* and scurfs around the eyes and on the margins of the lids ; mistiness of sight ; the inflammation is brought on again by the least cold. (*Merc.* is frequently suitable after *Bell.*)

NUX VOM. : The canthi are redder than the eyes ; ecchymosis and softening of the sclerotica ; burning pains and pressure in the eyes as if from sand ; lachrymation ; photophobia, especially in the morning; nightly agglutination; the inflammation is attended with nightly headache, catarrh with stoppage of the nose; aggravation in the morning on waking, or after a meal, or in the evening in bed.

PULSATILLA: Pressure as if from sand, or *tearing, stitching*, cutting and boring pains in the eyes; redness of the eyes and eyelids with copious secretion of mucus; *copious lachrymation*, especially in the cold air, wind, and when exposed to the light of day; great dryness of the eyelids, especially in the evening; burning and corrosive lachrymation; nightly agglutination; *œdematous swelling of the eyelids* or around the eyes; photophobia, with stitches in the eyes; aggravation towards evening. (***Puls.*** is suitable at the commencement of scrofulous ophthalmia, previous to *Ferr.*; or after *Acon.* in rheumatic ophthalmia.)

SULPHUR: Pressure as if from sand, or itching and burning in the eyes and eyelids, with aggravation on moving the eyes or exposing them to the light of the sun; redness of the eyes and eyelids; inflammation of the iris, with distorted pupil; dimness of the cornea as if covered with dust, or *specks, vesicles* and *ulcers* on the cornea: pustules, ulcers and scurfs around the eyes and on the lids; lachrymation, especially in the open air; or *dryness* of the eyes, especially in the room; photophobia, with closing of the lids; mistiness of sight, scintillations, &c. (*Sulph.* is frequently suitable after *Acon.*, or *Merc.* and *Puls.*;—after *Sulph.*, *Calc.* is most suitable.)

§ 6. Try moreover:

ANTIMONIUM: For red eyelids, with eye-gum in the canthi, photophobia and stinging pains.

ARNICA: Difficult and painful motion of the eyelids and eyes, as if excoriated; dilated pupils, sensitiveness to light; red and swollen eyelids and eyes.

BRYONIA: Red eyes with burning pains and pressure, as if from sand, with aggravation in the evening or at night; swollen eyelids with pains in the head, when opening the eyes. (***Bry.*** is frequently suitable after ***Puls.***, in rheumatic ophthalmia.)

CAUSTICUM: Swelling and ulceration of the eyelids, with nightly agglutination; pressure or burning pains in the eyes.

CHINA: Aggravation towards evening, with pressure as if from sand in the eyes; photophobia; frontal headache; hot and red, or dim and faint eyes, as if filled with smoke in the orbits.

COLOCYNTHIS: Violent burning and cutting extending far back in the head and nose, with great anguish and restlessness.

DIGITALIS: Redness of the eyes and conjunctiva; stitches through the eyes; lachrymation, increased by light and cold; photophobia; obstruction and dryness of the nose.

DULCAMARA: Aching pain when reading; dimness of sight, scintillations, aggravation by rest.

FERRUM: The eyes become weak and moist after using them ever so little; or they become red, with burning pains and styes.

GRAPHITES: Ulcers on the cornea, photophobia, swollen lids, agglutination.

LACHESIS: Dry eyes, photophobia, lancinations, dimness of sight.

NITRI ACIDUM: Pressure and stitches in the eyes; lachrymation especially when reading; yellow rings round the eyes; specks on the cornea; swelling of the eyelids and suppuration of the eyes.*

PETROLEUM: Burning, stitching or pressure over the root of the nose, and swelling of the nose, with discharge of pus.

RHUS TOX.: *Bry.* being insufficient, with burning and stitching and copious lachrymation, nightly agglutination and erysipelatous swelling of the eyelids, with photophobia.

SEPIA: Photophobia, catarrh, nightly agglutination, pustules on the eyeball; aching pains.

SPIGELIA: Aching, stitching or boring pains, penetrating into the orbits and head, with sensation as if the eyeballs were too large; excruciating pains.

SULPHURIS-AC.: Burning pains, with photophobia, lachrymation, especially when reading, difficulty of opening the lids.

VERATRUM: Tearing pains, with violent headache, photophobia, heat and feeling of dryness in the eyes.

§ 7. Use more particularly:

a) For *evening-exacerbation:* 1) *Amm. amm-m. asar. bell. calc. carb-a. caust. euphr. hyos. lach. lyc. merc. natr-m. nitr-ac. phos. puls. sep. sulph-ac.*—*Night-exacerbation: Acon. arn. ars. cham. chin. croc. euphr. hep. hyos. ign. kal. lyc. merc. natr-m. nitr-ac. n-vom. sep. staph. sulph.*—*Morning*-exacerbation: *Acon. amm-m. calc. carb-v. euphr. graph. ign. natr-m. nitr. nitr-ac. n-vom. petr. phosph. phos-ac. sep. sil. sulph. sulph-ac.*—Exacerbation *after eating: Bry. calc. caust. lyc. natr-m. n-vom. phos. puls. sep. sil. sulph.*

b) For *congestion of the vessels: Acon. ars. bell. ign. lach. merc. phos-ac. spig. sulph.*—*Interstitial distention of the sclerotica: Bell. sen. sulph.*—*Eruption around the eyes,* accompanying the inflammation: *Bell. euphr. merc. nitr-ac. sen. sep.*

* Specifically suitable for syphilitic ophthalmia.—*Hempel.*

spong. staph. sulph. thuj.—*Bloody spots* and sweat: *Arn. bell. calc. carb-v. cham. crotal. n-vom. plumb. rut. sen.*—*Suppuration: Bell. bry. caust. euphr. graph. hep. kreos. merc. nitr-ac. puls. sulph.*—*Twitching* of the lids: *Bell. calc. carb-v. caust. croc. kreos. lyc. n-vom. sulph.*—*Worse in the open air: Acon. amm-m. bell. bry. calc. caust. lyc. merc. natr-m. nitr-ac. n-vom. phos. puls. rut. sen. sep. sil. staph. sulph. sulph-ac. thuj.*—*Yellow colour* of the sclerotica: *Acon. ant. ars. bell. cham. chin. dig. ign. merc. n-vom. phosph. puls. sulph.*—*Styes: Con. ferr. graph. puls. rhus. sen. sep. staph. sulph.*—*Swelling* of the affected parts: *Acon. bell. bry. calc. cham. dig. euphr. guaj. ign. merc. n-vom. puls. rhus. sen. sep. sulph. thuj.* —Ophthalmia with *ulcers on the cornea: Ars. calc. euphr. hep. lach. merc. sil. sulph.*—*Heat and burning* of the eyes: *Acon. ars. bell. bry. calc. carb-v. croc. euphr. lach. lyc. merc. n-vom. phos. sep. sulph.*—*Itching* of the eyes: *Alum. bar. bell. bry. calc. caust. ign. merc. natr-m. n-vom. puls. sil. sulph.*—*Spasm* of the eyes: *Bell. cham. croc. hep. hyos. merc. natr-m. rut. sil. staph.*—*Photophobia: Acon. amm. amm-m. ars. bar. bell. bry. calc. cham. croc. euphr. graph. hep. hyos. ign. lyc. merc. n-vom. phos. rhus. sil. spig. sulph.*—*Blepharoplegia: Bell. nitr-ac. sep. spig. veratr.*—*Ectropium: Bell. merc.*—*Closing* of the lids: *Ars. bell. cham. croc. hep. hyos. merc. natr-m. nitr-ac. phos. rhus. sep. staph. sulph.*—*Redness* of the parts: *Acon. ant. arn. ars. bell. bry. calc. cham. chin. euphr. graph. ign. lach. merc. nitr-ac. n-vom. phos. puls. sep. sil. spig. spong. sulph.*—Sensation as of *sand in the eyes: Bell. bry. calc. carb-v. chin. ferr. graph. hyos. ign. merc. nitr-ac. phosph. puls. sulph. sulph-ac.* —*Halo around the light: Alum. bell. calc. dig. phos. puls. rut. sep. staph. sulph.*—*Blennorrhœa: Bell. dig. euphr. graph. merc. puls. sen. sulph.*—*Lachrymation: Acon. alum. arn. ars. bell. bry. calc. dig. euphr. graph. hep. ign. lach. lyc. natr-m. nitr-ac. n-vom. petr. phos. puls. rhus. rut. sil. spig. staph. sulph. thuj.*—*Dryness: Acon. ars. bar. bry. lyc. n-vom. puls. staph. sulph. veratr.*—*Varicose swellings: Carb-v. puls.*—*Contraction of the lids: Agar. ant. arn. canth. croc.*—*Indurations: Bry. spig. staph. thuj.*—*Nightly agglutination: Ars. alum. bar. bell. bry. calc. carb-v. caust. cham. croc. dig. euphr. graph. hep. ign. lyc. merc. natr-m. n-vom. phos. puls. rhus. ruta. sep. sil. spig. staph. sulph. thuj.*

c) The *whole* eye being affected: *Acon. arn. bell. calc. caust. cham. croc. dig. euphr. hep. ign. lyc. merc. natr-m. n-vom. phos. puls. rhus. sep. spig. sulph.*—The *conjunctiva: Acon. ars. bell. dig. euphr. merc. puls. sulph.*—For *pains in the orbits: Bell. calc. chin. hyos. plat. spig.*—The *cornea* being particularly diseased: *Ars. bell. calc. chin. euphr. hep. lach. merc. nitr-ac. rut.*

sen. sep. sil. spig. sulph.—The *lids: Acon. ant. arn. ars. bell. bry. calc caust. cham. croc. dig. graph. hep. lyc. merc. nitr-ac. n-vom. puls. rhus. sep. spig. sulph.*—*The canthi being principally affected: Alum. aur. bell. bry. calc. carb-v. caust. euphr. natr-m. n-vom. phos. puls. sep. sil. staph. sulph. thuj.*—*The external canthus: Bar. bry. calc. hep. ign. natr-m. n-vom. sep. sulph.*—*Inner canthus: Alum. aur. bell. bry. calc. carb-v. caust. euphr. n-vom. petr. phos. puls. rut. sil. staph. sulph.*

§ 8. Compare: HÆMORRHAGE FROM THE EYES, RUNNING OF THE EYES, BLEPHAROPHLEGIA, BLEPHAROSPASMUS, BLEPHAROPHTHALMITIS, PAINS IN THE EYES, AMBLYOPIA, DISEASES OF THE CORNEA, &c.

OPIUM AND LAUDANUM, ILL EFFECTS OF.

The best remedy for poisoning with large doses, is: 1) *Black coffee*; or, 2) *Vinegar*.—If consciousness should have returned, a few doses of *Ipec.* will be found very useful. If any ailments should remain after *Ipec.*, give *Nux-vom. merc.* or *bell.*

The last mentioned remedies are excellent antidotes against the drug-symptoms occasioned by the medicinal abuse of *Opium*.

ORCHITIS, OSCHEOCELE, HÆMATOCELE, SARCOCELE, &c., inflammation and swelling of the testes.

§ 1. Principal remedies: 1) *Arn. aur. clem. nitr-ac. puls.*; or, 2) *Ars. con. lyc. merc. natr. n-vom. spong. staph. zinc.*

§ 2. Orchitis caused by *contusion*, *shock*, *blow*, &c., requires: 1) *Arn. puls.*; or, 2) *Con. zinc.*

By *suppression of gonorrhœa*: 1) *Merc. puls.*; or, 2) *Aur. clem. nitr-ac.*

By metastasis of *parotitis*: *Merc.*, *puls.*, or *n-vom.*

§ 3. Erysipelatous orchitis, as affects *chimney-sweeps*, requires: *Ars.* or *Merc.*

§ 4. *Chronic induration* of the testes (sarcocele) frequently yields to: *Agn. arg. aur. bar-m. clem. con. graph. lyc. rhod. sulph.*

Hæmatocele: See the remedies for *contusion*, &c.

Hydrocele: Give: *Graph. puls. sil. rhod. sulph.*—Scrofulous persons require: *Silicea.*

Oscheocele or *scrotal hernia* has been treated most successfully with *Magn-mur.* and *Nux-v.*

See: HERNIA.

OTALGIA, PAINS IN THE EARS.

§ 1. Principal remedies: 1) *Bell. cham. merc. puls. sulph.;* or, 2) *Arn. chin. dulc. hep. n-vom. plat. spig.;* or, 3) *Ant. borax. bry. calc. magn-c. phos-ac.*

Inflammatory otalgia requires: 1) *Bell. merc. n-vom. puls.;* or, 2) *Borax. bry. calc. magn-c.*

Rheumatic otalgia: 1) *Bell. merc. puls.;* or, 2) *Arn. chin. hep. n-vom.*, &c.

Otalgia caused by a *cold* or by sudden suppression of some secretion, requires: 1) *Cham. chin. dulc.;* or, 2) *Merc. puls.* or *sulph.*

§ 2. Particular indications:

BELLADONNA: Stitches in and behind the ears; digging and boring pains, *tearing* and *stitches* extending to the throat, with ringing, buzzing and roaring in the ears; extreme sensitiveness to noise; painful state of the head and eyes, also with photophobia; red and hot face; tendency of the blood to the head.

CHAMOMILLA: *Lancinations*, or tensive and drawing pains extending to the lobe of the ear; dry ears or as if stopped up; great sensitiveness to noise, especially to music; excessive sensitiveness to pain; suspicious, ill humour, and disposition to get angry without sufficient cause.

MERCURIUS: Stitching, deep-seated pains, or tearing extending to the cheeks and teeth, with *chilly feeling in the ears; the pains are aggravated in bed;* or spasmodic pains with inflammatory redness of the ears; discharge of cerumen; profuse sweat, affording no relief.

PULSATILLA: Darting, tearing pains, as *if something would penetrate through the ears; the outer ear is red, hot and swollen;* or stitching and tearing pains affecting the whole side of the head, and almost depriving the patient of his reason; suitable to chilly individuals disposed to cry, and especially to females.

SULPHUR: Drawing, tearing or stitching pains extending to the head and throat; burning heat through the ears; extreme sensitiveness to noise, the patient being nauseated even by the slightest musical sounds; especially suitable to persons that are subject to catarrh or tendency of the blood to the head.

§ 3. Use likewise:

ARNICA: In the case of sensitive, nervous individuals, when the pain is brought on again by the least cause, with pressure and stitches in and behind the ears, tearing, internal heat and great sensitiveness to noise.

CHINA: The tearing pains are felt more externally, are *aggra-*

vated by contact, with redness of the ear, stitches in the ear and ringing of the ears. (Is frequently suitable after *Arn.*)

DULCAMARA: The pains are aggravated at night, during rest, with nausea.

HEPAR: Frequently after *Bell.*, when this remedy is insufficient, and the patient complains of stitches in the ears, when blowing his nose, and of beating, throbbing and roaring.

NUX VOMICA: Suitable to persons of a lively, choleric disposition, for: *tearing, stitching pains*, extorting cries, or extending to the forehead and temples, with *tearing* in the facial bones; aggravation in the morning, or in the evening in bed.

PLATINA: Violent crampy pains, shocks, rumbling and detonations in the ears, which feel cold, numb, and as if dead, with creeping extending to the face.

SPIGELIA: Painful aching, as if a large nail were sticking in the ear; with aching and tearing pains in the facial bones.

§ 4. Use more particularly:

For *throbbing* pains in the ear: 1) *Acon. calc. magn-m. natr. nitr-ac. phos. sep. sil.* 2) *Acon. bell. caust. cham. chin. graph. kal. puls. rhus. sulph:*

For *tearing* pains: 1) *Bell. cham. colch. con. merc. n-vom. puls. zinc.* 2) *Acon. alum. amb. arn. caps. kal. lyc. spig. sulph.*

For pains as if the ear would be *torn out: Bell. merc. puls.*

For *stitching pains:* 1) *Bell. calc. cham. con. dros. kal. merc. nitr-ac. n-vom. puls. sulph.* 2) *Alum. baryt. canth. caust. chin. ign. magn-m. men. natr. natr-m. nitr. phos-ac. plumb. ran. sassap. sil. spig. staph. zinc.*

For *stitches through the ear:* 1) *Con. kal. sil. spong.* 2) *Alum. amm-m. mang. natr.*

For crampy, *dragging* pains: 1) *Bell. cham. dros. n-vom. puls. sulph.* 2) *Amb. arn. dulc. mur-ac. n-mosch. phos. plat. sabad. spig. spong. stann. thuj.*

§ 5. Compare: PROSOPALGIA, HEADACHE, PAIN, PAROXYSMS OF, CONDITIONS, CAUSES, TOOTHACHE, &c.

OTITIS, INFLAMMATION OF THE EAR.

§ 1. For *acute* internal otitis, *Puls.* is, in most cases, a specific remedy. *Bell.* deserves a preference when the brain is affected, with great anguish, vomiting, coldness of the extremities, delirium, &c.

For the subsequent ailments, which do not yield to *Bell.* or

Puls., try: 1) *Merc. n-vom. sulph.*; or, 2) *Borax. bry. calc. cham. magn-c.*

§ 2. For *chronic internal* otitis, see: OTORRHŒA.

§ 3. For *external* otitis, *Puls.* is likewise the chief remedy; or: 2) *Bell. borax. calc. magn-c. merc. rhus. sil. sulph.*

If the ears should be *swollen*, try: 1) *Borax. merc. puls. rhus. sil.* 2) *Calc. kal. lyc. nitr-ac. sep.*

If *ulcerated*: *Merc. puls. ruta. spong.*

If *itching*: *Amm. puls. rhus. sulph.*

§ 4. Compare: OTALGIA, HERPES ON THE EAR, OTORRHŒA, &c.

OTORRHŒA.

§ 1. Principal remedies: 1) *Merc. puls. sulph.* 2) *Calc. carb-v. caust. con. lach. lyc. nitr-ac. petr. sil.* 3) *Alum. anac. asa. aur. carb-an. cham. cist. colch. gran. kal. lyc. men. natr-m. phos.*

§ 2. Discharge of *cerumen* requires: 1) *Con. merc.* 2) *Kal. lyc. natr-m. nitr-ac. puls.*; or, 3) *Amm-m. anac. phos.*

Catarrhal or *mucous* otorrhœa: 1) *Merc. puls. sulph.*; or, 2) *Bell. calc. carb-v. hep. lyc. natr-m. phos. sulph.*

Purulent otorrhœa: 1) *Bell. hep. merc. puls. sil.*; or, 2) *Asa. calc. caust. lach. nitr-ac. petr*; or, 3) *Amm. aur. borax. carb-v. cist. kal. lyc. natr-m.*

Scrofulous otorrhœa, with ulceration of the concha: *Hep. lyc. merc. puls. sulph.*

Bloody discharge: 1) *Merc. puls.*; or, 2) *Bell. calc. cist. con. graph. lach. lyc. nitr-ac. rhus. sep. sil. sulph.*

§ 3. *Obstinate* otorrhœa, after acute *otitis*, requires: *Merc. puls. sulph.*

Otorrhœa in consequence of some *acute exanthem*, such as: *Scarlatina, measles, variola*, &c., requires: *Bell. colch. hep. lyc. merc. men.*, or *Carb-veg.*

If caused by *abuse of mercury*, give: *Aur. asa. hep. nitr-ac. sil. sulph.*

If *caries* should be present: *Aur. nitr-ac. sil.*

If caused by abuse of *sulphur*: *Puls.* or *merc.*

§ 4. To remove the consequences of *suppressed* otorrhœa, give: 1) *Bell. merc. puls.*; or, 2) *Bry. dulc. n-vom.*

If this suppression should be followed by *swelling* of the cervical or *parotid* glands, give: *Bell. merc. puls.*

If by *headache* or *fever*: *Bell.*, or *bry.*; and if the discharge should have been arrested by a *cold*, give: *Dulc.* or *merc.*

If *orchitis* should set in, give: *Merc. puls.*, or *Aur. n-vom. zinc.*

§ 5. Discharge of *diseased cerumen*, requires: *Amm-m. calc. con. lach. merc. selen. sep. sil. thuj.*

Red cerumen, like blood: *Con.*

Cerumen like *pap*: *Lach.*

§ 6. Compare: HEARING, DEFICIENT; OTITIS; OTALGIA, &c.

OVARIES, DISEASES OF.—Principal remedies: 1) *Bell. lach. merc.* 2) *Con. chin. dulc. plat. sabin.* 3) *Acon. ars. amb. ant. canth. staph.*

In a case of *acute* inflammation of an old indurated ovary, which had been treated with salves, &c., by the best old school physicians, a dose of *Con.* 30, in water, a teaspoonful every three hours, was sufficient to remove not only the imminent danger, but the inflammation itself, so that, in eight days, the patient was able to walk several miles without inconvenience. It is now seven years since this case occurred, and the patient has remained well so far; the induration, however, never disappeared.

Dr. Hering saw good effects from *Lach.*, and then *Plat.*, in a case of *induration* and *suppuration* of an ovary.

For *dropsy* of the ovaries, *Dulc.* and *sab.* have been recommended by *American* physicians.

PAIN, PAROXYSMS OF; NEURALGIÆ; ARTHRITIC AND RHEUMATIC PAINS.

§ 1. Principal remedies: 1) *Acon. arn. ars. bry. cham. chin. coff. hep. ign. merc. n-vom. puls. rhus. veratr.* 2) *Bell. caps. colch. coloc. con. kal. magn-c. mez. phosph. ruta. sep. spig. stann. staph. thuj. val. verb.* 3) *Agn. alum. anac. ant arg. asa. asar. aur. baryt. calc. canth. caust. cocc ferr. graph. hyos. led. magn-aust. natr. natr-m. phosph. rhod. sabin. sassap. spong. stront. sulph zinc.*

§ 2. Pains of *irritable*, *nervous* persons, require: 1) *Acon. ars. bry. cham. chin. coff. hep. ign. merc. n-vom. val. veratr.* 2) *Asar. aur. canth. cocc. ferr. magn-arct. phosph. puls. rhus. sil. staph.*

If affecting *rheumatic* individuals, give: 1) *Acon. arn. bell. bry. cham. merc. n-vom. phosph. puls. rhus.* 2) *Ant. ars. carb-veg. caust. chin. colch. ferr. ign. lach. lyc. rhod. ruta. sassap. sep. sulph. thuj. veratr.*

If *arthritic*: 1) *Acon. bell. bry. colch. kal. merc. phosph. rhod.*

rhus. sabin. spong. staph. 2) *Agn. arg. baryt. calc. caust. chin. cocc. ferr. graph. n-vom. puls. sassap. sep. stann. sulph. thuj.*

If persons who have used *much mercury:* 1) *Arn. carb-veg. cham. chin. hep. puls.* 2) *Arg. bell. dulc. calc. guaj. lach. lyc. mez. phos-ac. sassap. sulph.*

If persons who have indulged in the excessive *use of coffee:* 1) *Cham. coff. ign. n-vom.* 2) *Bell. canth. caust. cocc. hep. merc. puls. sulph.*

If *plethoric* individuals: 1) *Acon. arn. bell. ferr. hyos. merc. natr-m. n-vom. puls.* 2) *Aur. bry. calc. chin. lyc. nitr-ac. phosph. sep. sulph.*

§ 3. Symptomatic indications:

Aconitum: *Intolerable pains,* especially at night, stitching or throbbing; fever-heat, sighing, lamenting, inconsolable, anxious, or with dread of death; thirst, *red cheeks,* small and hurried pulse, great sensitiveness of the whole nervous system, especially of the organs of sight and hearing; sleeplessness, with tossing about.

Arnica: Creeping in the affected parts, with restlessness, obliging one to move them constantly; aggravation by the least exertions, and even by the least noise.

Arsenicum: The pains are burning or tearing, setting in principally at night or during sleep, or driving the patient to despair; attended with: great anguish, debility, obliging one to lie down; intermission; feeling of coldness in the affected part; aggravation during rest, after working, or in the evening, in bed, or after eating; relief by external warmth.

Belladonna: Stitching, burning pains, aggravated by motion, light or noise, also by the least concussion, or even by the stepping of other people in the room; the paroxysms set in every day, after noon, and last until midnight; aggravation by a draught of air, warmth of the bed, &c.

Bryonia: Aching, or drawing and tearing, or stitching pains, or as if an ulcer were under the skin; aggravation by moving the body, relief by moving the affected part; irritable, vehement disposition; disposition to rheumatism, &c.

Chamomilla: Jerking, tearing, and beating pains, with sensation of rigidity in the affected parts; excessive sensitiveness to pain; extreme debility, even unto fainting, after the first paroxysm of pain; bloated face, or one cheek is pale, the other red; hot sweat about the head, even in the hairs, with restlessness, cries, weeping, and irritable, quarrelsome mood.

China: Extreme sensitiveness of the skin; aggravation by the least touch; sensation of rigidity and laming weakness in the affected parts, attended with aching pains, ill humour, dissatisfied temper, sensual disposition, pale face, with frequent flushes and warmth, very loquacious or restless at night. *China* is frequently very useful after *Coffea*.

Coffea: Intolerable pains, whining mood, the patient is beside himself, with restless tossing about, cries and great anguish; shuddering in the open air; excessive sensitiveness of all the organs of sense, and especially sight; cannot bear the least noise. (After *Coff.* are frequently suitable: *Nux-vom. ign. chin.*, or *puls.)*

Hepar: Pains as if sore, or from subcutaneous ulceration, aggravated by contact; fainting turn when the least paroxysm of pain occurs, especially in the evening.

Ignatia: Tearing pains or pressure from within outwards, or stitching boring; pale face, watery urine; momentary relief by changing one's position; the pains come on again after eating, in the evening after lying down, or early after rising; changeable mood with tendency to start; or sad, taciturn mood; bland, sensitive temper.

Mercurius: Suitable to persons that are disposed to rheumatism, with night-sweats, tearing and stitching pains; aggravation at night; feeling of coldness in the affected parts, debility and orgasmus sanguinis on making the least exertion; pale face, or flushes on the face, or red spots on the cheeks.

Nux vomica: Suitable to persons who are addicted to the use of spirits or coffee, of a lively, choleric temper and red face; or suitable to people who lead a sedentary life; for drawing or jerking pains setting in in the morning, in bed, after eating, or in the evening, aggravated by open and cold air, reading or meditating.

Pulsatilla: Tearing, or stitching and beating pains, only on *one* side, worse after *retiring in the evening*, or early in the morning, also during rest and when sitting; relief in the open air; suitable to females and individuals of a bland, timid and quiet temper, with pale complexion and disposition to feel chilly.

Rhus tox.: Creeping and burning pains, or drawing-stitching; or pains as if from subcutaneous ulceration; aggravation during rest and in the open air; relief by motion and warmth; quiet disposition, disposition to melancholy and sadness, or paroxysms of anguish.

Veratrum: Violent pains inducing delirium and frenzy for a short time; or pains with debility, even unto fainting; *cold sweat*, general coldness of the body, with thirst; aggravation in bed, and at night, or towards morning; relief on rising and walking.

§ 4. Use more particularly:

a) When there is: great *nervous* and *muscular* excitement, with feverish heat, red cheeks, &c.: 1) *Acon. cham. chin. coff. ign. merc. val.* 2) *Arn. ars. bell. bry. canth. n-vom. puls. rhus.*

b) When great *debility*, chilliness and coldness: 1) *Ars. veratr.* 2) *Arn. chin. hep. merc. n-vom. puls.*

c) When the *affected* parts become very *thin, emaciated:* 1) *Caust. staph.* 2) *Ars. carb-veg. graph. led. mez. natr-m. plumb. puls. sil.*

d) When they sweat readily: *Bell. calc. cham. chin. graph. merc. natr-m. n-vom. phosph. puls. rhod. sep. sulph.*

§ 5. a) For sensation as if the affected part would be *stretched, enlarged,* widened: *Bell. bry. carb-veg. chin. dulc. hyos. ign. laur. merc. n-vom. oleand. op. puls. rhus. sep. spig. staph. sulph-ac.*

b) For painful *tension* in the affected part: 1) *Asa. bell. bry. caust. lyc. natr-m. n-vom. puls. stront. sulph.* 2) *Arg. arn. ars. aur. calc. coloc. con. kal. magn-m. mang. merc. mez. mosch. nitr-ac. phosph. plat. rhod. rhus. sep. stann. veratr. zinc.*

c) For feeling of *fullness:* 1) *Acon. arn. bell. bry. carb-veg. chin. merc. mosch. phosph. rhus. sil. sulph.* 2) *Amm. amm-m. asa. calc. caps. cham. coff. con. graph. hell. kal. lyc. magn-c. magn-m. natr. natr-m. n-vom. petr. puls. sep. spong. sulph-ac.*

d) For sensation as if every thing would *issue through the affected part* (forwards, upwards, or downwards): 1) *Acon. bell. bry. caust. cham. chin. cocc. kal. lach. lyc. magn-arct. magn-m. mosch. natr. n-vom. plat. puls. sep. sil. sulph. sulph-ac.* 2) *Alum. amm. amm-m. aur. calc. cann. con. croc. magn-c. phosph. phos-ac. spig. spong. staph. stront. thuj.*

e) As if the part would *fly to pieces:* 1) *Bell. bry. calc. caust. con. ign. lach. merc. natr-m. puls. sep. sil. spig. sulph.* 2) *Acon. amm. ant. baryt. caps. carb-an. carb-veg. chin. con. graph. hep. kal. magn-arct. merc. mez. natr. n-vom. oleand. petr. phosph. ran. sabin. spong. staph. thuj.*

§ 6. a) For *compressive* pains, as if in a vice: *Alum. bell. cocc. hell. ign. ipec. magn-c. mosch. natr-m. n-vom. plat. spig. spong. sulph. sulph-ac.*

b) Sensation as if the part were tied up *with a band: Anac. aur. bell. chin. con. graph. ign. merc. natr-m. nitr-ac. n-vom. phosph. plat. puls. sassap. sulph.*

c) Sensation *as if the clothes were too tight,* as if they pressed upon the affected part: 1) *Bry. calc. carb-veg. caust. kreos. lach. lyc. merc. n-vom. sulph.* 2) *Amm. caps. carb-an. nitr-ac. puls. sassap. sep. sil. spong. stann.*

d) For *sensation of heaviness* in the affected part: 1) *Acon. bell. calc. carb-veg. chin. magn-arct. merc. natr-m. n-vom.*

phosph. puls. rhus. sep. sil. stann. sulph. 2) *Alum. amm. amm-m. arn. ars. baryt. bry. carb-an. cham. con. dulc. kreos. lach. lyc. magn-c. magn-m. mur-ac. natr. n-mosch. op. petr. plumb. sabad. sabin. spig. spong. staph. thuj. veratr.*

§ 7. a) For *aching* pains: 1) *Arn. bell. calc. carb-veg. caust. chin. cupr. ign. lyc. n-vom. phosph. sep. stann. staph. sulph. zinc.* 2) *Acon. alum. amb. amm-m. anac. ars. aur. carb-an. cocc. cupr. ign. magn-arct. merc. natr. natr-m. phos-ac. plat. ruta. sassap. veratr.*

b) Pressure as if a *plug* or *nail* had been driven in: 1) *Arn. hep. ign. n-vom. oleand. plat. ruta. sulph-ac.* 2) *Acon. anac. ant. asa. carb-veg. cocc. coff. dulc. hell. lyc. magn-arct. natr-m. rhus. ruta. spig. spong. sulph. thuj.*

c) *Boring* pains: 1) *Bell. calc. dulc. hep. merc. natr-m. puls. ran-sc. sep. spig.* 2) *Acon. ang. ant. arg. aur. carb-an. carb-veg. caust. cin. cocc. hell. ign. kal. laur. magn-c. magn-m. merc. mosch. rhod. sil. stann. staph. thuj. zinc.*

d) *Digging* pains: 1) *Amm-m. arn. bell. cin. dulc. mang. n-mosch. rhod. sep. spig. stann.* 2) *Acon. asa. bry. calc. carb-an. cin. cocc. con. kal. magn-m. natr. natr-m. nitr-ac. phosph. phos-ac. plat. rhod. rhus. ruta. seneg. sulph. val.*

e) Sensation as if a ball were ascending in, or adhering to certain parts: *Acon. ign. lach. natr-m. plumb. sep. sil.*

§ 8. a) For *constrictive* sensation in the affected parts: 1) *Alum. anac. bell. chin. graph. ign. natr-m. nitr-ac. n-vom. plat. plumb. puls. rhus. sulph.* 2) *Acon. aur. calc. canth. cocc. con. dig. dros. ipec. lyc. mosch. n-mosch. phosph. phos-ac. sassap. sep. stann. sulph. sulph-ac. thuj. veratr.*

b) *Griping, grasping,* clawing: 1) *Calc. carb-an. carb-veg. caust. ign. n-vom. phosph. puls. sil. sulph.* 2) *Amm. bell. coloc. graph. hep. lyc. magn-m. merc. natr. natr-m. stann. stront.*

c) *Dragging* pains: 1) *Arn. bell. calc. merc. n-vom. puls. rhus. sulph.* 2) *Amb. ars. cham. colch. mez. natr. natr-m. nitr-ac. phosph. plat. rhab. sep. staph. veratr.*

d) Sensation as if the part were *too short*, or *contracted:* 1) *Amm. amm-m. baryt. caust. coloc. con. graph. lach. natr. natr-m. phosph. puls. rhus. sep. sulph.* 2) *Alum. arn. asa. bell. bry. carb-an. lyc. magn-c. magn-m. merc. mez. nitr-ac. n-vom. oleand. phos-ac. plat. rhod. seneg. stann. stront. zinc.*

e) *Crampy, spasmodic* pains: 1) *Amb. calc. carb-veg. coloc. ign. oleand. phos-ac. plat.* 2) *Acon. anac. ang. arn. ars. bell. carb-an. caust. chin. cin. cocc. con. graph. kal. lyc. magn-c. magn-m. mez. natr. natr-m. n-vom. phosph. puls. rhod. sep. stann. staph. sulph.*

f) For actual *cramp :* 1) *Anac. ang. bell. calc. caust. cin coloc. graph. lyc. merc. plat. rhus. sep.* 2) *Agar. amb. ars. asa. camph. cann. cocc. con. dulc. ign. kal. magn-arct. mez. nitr-ac. n-vom. petr. phosph. sec. spig. stann. sulph. thuj.*

g) For *contraction* of the parts: 1) *Calc. caust. coloc. graph. guaj. lyc. merc. rhus. sec. sil.* 2) *Anac. carb-an. caps. chin. cic. cin. ferr. hyos. lach. merc. n-vom. op. phosph. plat. sol-nig. stram. tart.*

§ 9. a) For *benumbing* pains, with feeling of *numbness* in the affected parts: 1) *Acon. bry. cham. cocc. con. lyc. n-vom. oleand. plat. puls. rhus. sulph.* 2) *Amm. anac. ars. asa. bell. calc. carb-an. caust. chin. hell. hyos. ign. merc. mosch. op. phosph. phos-ac. sec. sep. stram.*

b) For *laming* pains: 1) *Aur. caps. carb-veg. cham. chin. cin. cocc. colch. n-vom. puls. rhus. sabad. sabin. staph.* 2) *Acon. bell. bry. caust. ign. magn-arct. natr-m. phosph. rhod. sil. veratr.*

c) Pains as if *bruised :* 1) *Arn. chin. cocc. hep. ign. natr. natr-m. n-vom. puls. rhus. ruta. sep. sulph. veratr.* 2) *Arg. aur. bry. calc. camph. carb-veg. caust. con. dros. ferr. magn-c. magn-m. merc. nitr-ac. phosph. phos-ac. sil. stann. thuj.*

d) Sensation as if the flesh were *beaten loose* on the bones: *Bry. canth. ign. led. merc. mosch. natr-m. nitr-ac. n-vom. rhus. staph. sulph. thuj.*

e) Sensation of *contusion, blow,* &c.: 1) *Arn. cic. cin. con. dros. lach. oleand. plat. puls. ruta.* 2) *Acon. alum. amm. caust. ign. kal. natr. natr-m. n-mosch. phosph. plumb. rhus. sulph.*

f) Pain as if *strained* or *sprained :* 1) *Arn. bry. calc. caust. ign. natr-m. petr. phosph. puls. rhod. rhus. sulph.* 2) *Amb. amm. carb-veg. graph. lach. nitr. n-vom. ruta. sep. spig. stann. thuj.*

§ 10. a) For *tearing* pains: 1) *Acon. arn. bell. bry. caust. chin. ign. kal. lyc. merc. n-vom puls. rhod. rhus. sil. stront. sulph. zinc.* 2) *Alum. amb. arg. calc. caps. carb-veg. ferr. led. natr. natr-m. nitr. phosph. phos-ac. sassap. sep. thuj. val.*

b) *Cutting* pains: 1) *Bell. calc. canth. coloc. dros. kal. lyc. merc. natr. phos-ac. rhus. sil. sulph-ac.* 2) *Alum. caust. chin. con. dulc. graph. hyos. ign. mur-ac. nitr-ac. n-vom. phosph. puls. sep. spig. staph. sulph.*

c) *Stitching* pains: 1) *Acon. asa. bell. bry. calc. canth. chin. guaj. ign. merc. nitr-ac. phosph. puls. rhus. sep. spig. staph. sulph. thuj.* 2) *Amm. amm-m. arn. ars. caust. cocc. colch. con. dros. graph. hell. kal. magn-c. magn-m. natr-m. n-vom. sabad. sassap. sil. spong. sulph-ac. verb.*

d) *Shocks* or *jerks :* 1) *Amb. calc. cic. colch. ign. magn-arct. n-mosch. n-vom. phosph. plat. puls. sep. sil. spig. stann. sulph. sulph-ac.* 2) *Anac. arn. ars. bell. cann. cham. lyc. magn-c. mez. petr. rhus. spong. tart.*

e) *Twitching, jerking* pains: 1) *Asa. calc. caust. chin. colch. cupr. graph. ign. kal. natr-m. nitr-ac. n-vom. puls. rhus. sil. sulph.* 2) *Alum. anac. aur. bell. bry. cin. clem. con. graph. lyc. magn-aust. merc. phos-ac. sep. spig. stann. val.*

§ 11. a) *Gnawing*, corrosive, scraping pains: 1) *Alum. ars. asa. baryt. bell. calc. canth. caust. cham. con. cupr. dros. kal. kreos. lach. lyc. mang. natr-m. phosph. phos-ac. plat. puls. ran-sc. rhus. ruta. sabad. spig. staph.*

b) *Tingling* in the parts: 1) *Acon. arn. bell. caps. chin. colch. kal. phos-ac. plat. puls. sec. sep. solan-nig. spig. sulph.* 2) *Alum. ars. caust. croc. euphr. ign. magn-aust. merc. natr. natr-m. n-vom. sabad. zinc.*

c) *Creeping: Alum. arn. aur. bell. calc. kal. nitr-ac. n-vom. rhod. rhus. sec. sep. staph. sulph. thuj.*

d) *Going to sleep of the parts:* 1) *Calc. carb-an. carb-veg. chin. cocc. croc. graph. kal. lyc. merc. petr. phos-ac. puls. rhus. sep. sil. sulph.* 2) *Amb. arg. baryt. caps. cham. con. guaj. hyos. ign. magn-arct. magn-aust. magn-m. natr-m. n-vom. phosph. rhod. stram. sulph. thuj. veratr.*

e) Sensation as if *wind were blowing* on the parts, or as if a current of air were passing through: *Aur. colch. graph. magn-aust. oleand. puls. rhus. sabin. spig. stram. zinc.*

f) *Feeling of coldness* in the parts: *Ars. calc. camph. carb-veg. chin. colch. dros. ipec. laur. lyc. magn-aust. merc. mez. natr. natr-m. nitr. n-vom. phosph. phos-ac. sep. sulph. veratr.*

§ 12. a) For *burning* pains: 1) *Acon. ars. bell. bry. canth. carb-veg. caust. euphorb. graph. merc. n-vom. phosph. phos-ac. rhus. sabad. sep. stann. sulph.* 2) *Arn. calc. chin. kal. lach lyc. mez. petr plumb. rhod. ruta. sabin. sil. veratr.*

b) *Beating*, throbbing, pulsative, hammering pains: 1) *Acon. amm-m. ars. bell. calc. carb-veg. cham. cocc. ferr. ign. kal. magn-aust. natr-m. phosph. puls. sep. sil. sulph. tart.* 2) *Alum. asa. bry. cann. caps. kreos. lach. lyc. magn-c. magn-m. nitr-ac. petr rhod. rhus. ruta. sabad. stram. veratr.*

c) Pains as from *subcutaneous ulceration:* 1) *Amm-m. bry. caust. kal. lach. phosph. puls. ran. rhus. sil.* 2) *Cann. caust. cham. cic. graph. ign. mang. merc. mur-ac. natr-m. nitr-ac. phosph. thuj. zinc.*

d) Pain as if *burnt: Baryt. bell. bry. caust. hyos. ign. lach. magn-m. n-vom. phosph. puls, sep. sulph-ac.*

e) *Sore* and *smarting* pain: 1) *Arg. canth. cic. graph. hep. ign. mez. n-vom. plat. sep. sulph-ac. zinc.* 2) *Alum. arn. bry. calc. caust. cin. kal. kreos. lyc. merc. natr-m. nitr-ac. phosph. puls. ran. rhus. sil. stann. staph. sulph.*

§ 13. a) For pains striking, *from above downwards : Acon. agar. baryt. hell. bry. canth. caps. carb-veg. caust. chin. cin. ferr. graph. kal. kreos. lyc. magn-arct. magn-aust. merc. natr. natr-m. nitr-ac. n-vom. phos-ac. puls. sabin. sassap. sep. sulph. val. veratr. zinc.*

b) From *below upwards : Acon. alum. anac. arn. ars. bell. calc. carb-veg. caust. cham. chin. colch. con. dulc. euphr. magn-arct. magn-c. merc. natr. natr-m. nitr-ac. n-vom. puls. rhus. samb. sep. spong. stront. sulph. thuj. val.*

c) From *within outwards :* 1) *Arg. asa. bell. bry. chin. con. rhus, spig. spong. stann. sulph. val.* 2) *Acon. alum. calc. dros. dulc. ign. lyc. magn-arct. magn-aust. merc. mez. mur-ac. natr. natr-m. n-vom. phosph. phos-ac. sabad. sep. sil. staph.*

d) From *without inwards :* 1) *Anac. arn. calc. canth. ign. kal. plat. spig. staph. zinc.* 2) *Bell. calc. cann. caust. cocc. dulc. hell. laur. mez. nitr-ac. oleand. plumb. rhus. sabin. sulph-ac.*

e) For *semilateral* pains: 1) *Alum. asa. calc. cocc. coloc. dulc. graph. kal. magn-arct. magn-aust. mang. mez. n-vom. oleand. phos-ac. plat. puls. sassap. spig. staph. sulph-ac. verb.* 2) *Agar. amb. anac. arg. ars. canth. carb-veg. caust. chin. cic. cin. guaj. ign. lach. merc. mur-ac. phosph. rhus. sabad. sassap. stann. zinc.*

f) Pains, felt *cross-wise*, right shoulder, left foot, &c.: *Agar. calc. mang. nitr-ac. sil. val.*

g) *Left side :* 1) *Calc. chin. coloc. lach. merc. petr. phosph. sulph.* 2) *Arn. asa. asar. colch. cupr. graph. hep. lyc. mez. nitr-ac. phosph. rhod. sep. spig. sulph-ac. thuj.*

h) *Right side :* 1) *Amm. amm-m. canth. caust. sabad. stront. zinc.* 2) *Agar. alum. calc. dros. ign. lyc. mosch. ruta. sabin.*

i) *Erratic* pains: 1) *Arn. chin. daph. n-mosch. puls. rhod. sulph.* 2) *Ars. asa. bell. con. ign. jod. mang. sabin. sassap. sec. sep. val. zinc.*

§ 14. See: CONDITIONS, CAUSES, RHEUMATISM, GOUT, &c.

PARALYSIS.—Principal remedies: 1) *Caust. cocc. n-vom. rhus.* 2) *Arn. baryt. bell. bry. dulc. ferr. lach. led. lyc. oleand. ruta. sil. stann. sulph. zinc.*

§ 1. For paralysis in consequence of *apoplexy*, give: 1) *Arn. bar-c. bell. n-vom. stann. zinc.* 2) *Anac. con. lach. laur. stram.*

In consequence of *loss of animal fluids*, &c., give: *Chin. ferr. sulph.*

If caused by *rheumatism*, give: 1) *Arn. ferr. ruta.;* or, 2) *Bry. caust. lyc. sulph.*

If by *suppression* or *retrocession of an eruption*, or some other morbid secretion: *Caust. sulph.*

§ 2. Paralysis of the *eyelids*, requires: 1) *Sep. spig. veratr.* 2) *Bell. nitr-ac. stram. zinc.* 3) *Coccul. op. plumb. rhus.*

Paralysis of the *facial muscles*: *Caust. graph. op.*

Paralysis of the *pharynx*, organs of deglutition: 1) *Caust. lach. sil.* 2) *Ars.? bell.? ipec.? kal.? plumb.? puls.? n-mosch.?*

Of the *tongue* and the organs of speech: 1) *Bell. caust. dulc. hyos. lach.* 2) *Acon. hydroc. op. stram.*

Of the *upper extremities*: 1) *Calc. chin. coccul. n-vom. rhus. sep.* 2) *Acon. bell. lyc. nitr. veratr.*

Of the *hands*: 1) *Ferr. ruta. sil.* 2) *Amb. cupr. natr-m.*

Of the *fingers*: 1) *Calc.* 2) *Magn-c. phosph.*

Of the *legs*: *Bell. bry. chin. cocc. n-vom. rhus. veratr.*—Of the *feet*: *Ars. chin. oleand. plumb.*

Of the *thighs*: *Acon. aur. chel. cocc. sulph.*

PARALYSIS OF THE LUNGS, ORTHOPNŒA PARALYTICA, SUFFOCATIVE CATARRH, &c.

§ 1. Principal remedies: 1) *Ars. carb-veg. chin. ipec. lach. op.* 2) *Acon. baryt. camph. graph. puls. samb. tart.* 3) *Aur. bell. bry. cham. con. dros. hep. hyos. ign. magn-arct. merc. n-vom. op. phosph. spong. sulph. veratr.*

§ 2. If of a *catarrhal* nature, or caused by excessive accumulation of mucus in the bronchi, give: 1) *Ars. camph. chin. ipec. tart.* 2) *Dros. hep. merc. phosph. puls. spong. sulph. veratr.*

If of a *congestive* nature, caused by congestion of blood to the lungs, give: 1) *Acon. bell. bry. chin. ipec. phosph. samb.* 2) *Ars. aur. cham. n-vom. op. spong. sulph.*

Purely *nervous* paralysis requires: 1) *Baryt. graph. hyos. lach. n-vom. op.* 2) *Ars. aur. carb-veg. chin. magn-arct.*

§ 3. To *children* give: 1) *Acon. ipec. samb. tart.* 2) *Bell. cham. hep. ign. merc. sulph.*

To *old* people: 1) *Baryt. lach. op.* 2) *Ars. aur. carb-veg. chin. con. phosph. veratr.*

§ 4. See: ASTHMA, CONGESTIONS OF THE CHEST, BRONCHITIS, COUGH, PNEUMONIA, &c.

PAROTITIS.

The best remedy for *acute* parotitis is *Merc.*, in most cases a specific, though *Aurum* is sometimes indicated.

Erysipelatous inflammation or metastasis to the brain, with

disappearance of the swelling, stupor and delirium, requires ***Bell.***, or ***Hyoscyam.*** if ***Bell.*** should not be sufficient.

In case Mercury should have been abused previously, or in case it should not be sufficient, or the swelling should commence to harden, with *hectic* fever, &c. *Carbo-veg.* is indicated. This remedy is generally indicated when the patient is very hoarse, and there is a metastasis to the stomach.

If ***Carbo-veg.*** should not be sufficient for the hectic fever, ***Cocculus*** will be found to be of great service.

In obstinate cases, consider: 1) *Kal. rhus.* 2) *Amm. aur. calc. cham. con.*

Comp.: SORE THROAT.

PEMPHIGUS.—Both *chronic* and *acute* pemphigus require: 1) *Bell. dulc. rhus. sep.* 2) *Canth. hep. ran.*

Compare vesicular erysipelas, which is so much like pemphigus that the same remedies may perhaps be employed for either.

We have no written evidence of the treatment of this disease; nevertheless, the remedies which have been recommended by Hahnemann, for phagedenic blisters, or the so-called Fressblasen, (spreading and corrosive blisters) may be tried for pompholix, though these blisters seem to be of the class of ecthyma rather than pompholix.

PERITONITIS.— Principal remedies: 1) *Acon. bell. bry. cham.;* or 2) *Coff. coloc. hyos. n-vom. rhus.*

Comp.: ENTERITIS, METRITIS, PUERPERAL FEVER, INTERMITTENT FEVER, &c.

PETECHIÆ, MORBUS MACULOSUS.

Petechiæ which occur in typhus putridus, require: *Ars. bry. rhus.*

Morbus maculosus *Werlhofii* yielded in my practice to ***Bry.*** in every instance.

We may try, moreover: *Arn. bell. berb. hyos. lach. led. n-vom. phos. rut. sec. sil. stram. sulph-ac.*

PHARYNGITIS, with inflammation of the velum and uvula. —Principal remedies: 1) *Acon. alum. bell. canth. hyos. lach. merc. n-vom. puls. stram.;* or 2) *Ars. calc. dulc. ign. veratr.*

For *simple*, uncomplicated inflammation, give: *Acon. bell. canth. lach. merc.*

Inflammation with *spasmodic* constriction of the fauces, requires: 1) *Bell. hyos. lach. stram. veratr.;* or 2) *Alum. ars. cic. cocc. ign. laur. lyc. merc. n-vom. op.*

For sensation as of a foreign body in the throat, give: 1) *Ars. ign. merc. n-vom. puls.;* or 2) *Bell. lach. sulph.*

If the inflammation should extend to the velum, give: *Acon. bell. coff. merc. n-vom.*

Inflammation of the *uvula* requires in most cases: 1) *Bell. coff. merc. n-vom.;* or 2) *Calc. seneg. sulph.*

Compare: SORE THROAT.

PHAGEDENIC BULLÆ (blisters) OF HAHNEMANN. —A kind of spreading, ulcerated blisters on the buttocks, feet, heels, toes, hands and fingers, always *isolated,* and distinguished from pompholix by the absence of those mucous derangements of the stomach, intestinal canal, or other functional derangements, which are generally said to accompany pompholix. Principal remedies: 1) *Cham. graph petr. sil.* 2) *Ars. bor. calc. caust. clem. hep. kal. magn-c. merc. natr. nitr-ac. rhus-t. sep. squill. sulph.*

PHIMOSIS, paraphimosis and inflammation of the prepuce. If caused by syphilis, give *Mercurius,* or *Nitr-ac. sep. thuj.* Phimosis with *gonorrhœa,* requires: *Cann. merc. sulph.*

Phimosis from friction or some other mechanical cause, requires *Arn.,* and, if inflammation should be present, give *Acon.,* then *Arn.,* and, if *Arn.* should not be sufficient, try *Rhus-t.* or *Euphrasia.*

If caused by *uncleanliness, Acon.* or *Merc.* or *Sulph.* will be found sufficient.

If by *chemical* or *poisonous* substances, &c., give: *Acon. bell. bry. camph.*

Suppuration requires *Merc.* or *Caps.* or *Hep.,* and subsequent *indurations: Lach.* or *Sulph.* or *Sep.*

For threatening *gangrene,* give: *Ars.* or *Lach.* or *Canth.*

To *little children,* give: *Acon.* or *Merc.* or *Calc.* and *Sulph.*

PHOSPHORUS, ILL EFFECTS OF.—Complete poisoning requires: 1) according to *Hering,* vomiting as speedily as possible; if necessary, excite it by tobacco or mustard; 2) *black coffee,* in large quantities; 3) *water* mixed with common *Magnesia.*—Oil and fat things are hurtful, milk likewise.

If symptoms remain, use: 1) *N-vom.* 2) *Alum. bell. sulph.*

PHOTOPHOBIA.—Principal remedies: 1) *Bell. con. euphr. ign. puls. staph. veratr.* 2) *Acon. ars. calc. hep. merc. n-vom. phosph. rhus. sulph. veratr.*

BELLADONNA: Halo of various colours around the flame; red spots, mist or darkness before the eyes, diplopia and decrease of sight.

CINA: Suitable to scrofulous children, that wet their beds frequently, and to onanists.

CONIUM: Pale redness of the eyeball, with congested vessels of the conjunctiva, suitable to scrofulous subjects.

EUPHRASIA: Headache, the light of the candle seeming to be dark and to flicker.

IGNATIA: Pressure in the eyes, with lachrymation, and without any other perceptible symptoms.

PULSATILLA: Bright circles around the candle-light, with dimness of sight as if through mist, or as if through something that can be rubbed off; diplopia, or obscuration of sight.

STAPHYSAGRIA: Blackness or scintillations before one's eyes, or flames, especially at night, or halos around the candle-light; with dimness of sight.

VERATRUM: Black motes or sparks before the eyes, with diplopia.

Comp.: OPHTHALMIA and AMBLYOPIA.

PLAGUE, ORIENTAL.—The best remedies seem to be: 1) *Ars. bell. carb-veg. chin. rhus.* 2) *Bry. hep. lach. sil. sulph.*

PLETHORA.—Such a thing as too much blood does not exist. and the symptoms which seemed to point to an excess of blood, frequently yield as by magic to: 1) *Acon. bell. ferr. hyos. merc. n-vom. phos. puls. sulph.* 2) *Arn. aur. bry. calc. chin. croc. dig. graph. lyc. natr-m. nitr. nitr-ac. rhus. sep. stram. thuj.*, to be chosen in every case in accordance with the symptoms.

PLEURITIS, PLEURISY.—The principal remedy is *Acon.*, a few pellets in water, a tablespoonful every 2 or 3 hours. After *Acon.*, if the improvement should not continue, give *Bry.*, as above; and if sensitiveness to the weather should still remain, give *Sulphur* after *Bry.*—Complicated cases may require: *Chin. kal. lach. n-vom. squill.*; and perhaps: *Arn. gran.?*

Comp: PNEUMONIA and the other AFFECTIONS of the CHEST.

PLICA POLONICA.—The principal remedies seem to be: *Vinca. borax. lyc. natr-m.*

PNEUMONIA.

§ 1. Principal remedies: 1) *Acon. bry. cann. chin. phosph. rhus. squill. sulph.* 2) *Bell. lach. merc. puls. seneg. sulph.*; or 3) *Ars. bell. canth. nitr. n-vom. op. phos-ac. sabad. sep. tart. veratr.*

§ 2. The principal remedy, in the first stage, is *Acon.*, after which *Bry.* may be given, to be continued until the breathing is easier and the expectoration looks better.

If weakness of the chest, oppression and cough should remain after *Bry.*, give *Phosph.* or *Sulph.;* or *Chin. lach. lyc. sil.*

§ 3. If *hepatization* should already exist before the hom. physician is called, *Acon.* and *Bry.* may still be of great use; but the principal remedy is *Sulph.*, a few pellets in a tumblerful of water, a tablespoonful every 3 hours.

Lach. lyc. phosph. are likewise very useful at times, even after *Sulph.* (Jahr proposes to give only one dose, and to allow it to act for weeks! *Hempel*)

§ 4. For *asthenic* pneumonia (pneumonia notha) as we see it in old people, with danger of paralysis of the lungs, the principal remedy is likewise *Acon.;* after which, if another paroxysm should set in, *Mercury* should be given.

Bell. should be given after *Merc.*, if a spasmodic constriction of the chest, with dry hacking cough should remain; or *Cham.*, if the breathing continue wheezing. (After *Cham. n-vom.* is frequently suitable.)

If no change should take place after *Merc*, give *Ipec.*, especially if the breathing be anxious and hurried; or *Veratr.*, if the extremities be cold, with constriction of the chest and great anxiety; or *Ars.*, if the patient sink more and more, with suffocative paroxysms.

§ 5. *Typhoid* pneumonia first requires *Op.*, then sometimes *Arn.*

If no change should occur after these two remedies, give *Veratr.*, or *Ars.*, if the debility and rattling increase.

Bry. and *Rhus-t.; Ipec.* and *Ars.*, or *Veratr.* and *Ars. alternately*, are likewise useful.

If the improvement should not continue, give *Sulph.* and then again one of the former remedies which seemed to be most beneficial.

Bed-sores, especially if *gangrenous*, require *Chin.* and *Ars.*

For *obscuration of sight* give *Bell;* and if the strength should continue to fail, *Natrum-m.* is sometimes useful.

§ 6. If symptoms of *incipient phthisis* should set in after pneumonia, or if the inflammation should threaten to become *chronic*, and if the existence of *tubercles* should have to be suspected, give 1) *Sulphur;* or: 2) *Amm. lach. lyc. phosph.;* or, 3) *Ars. aur. calc. hep. kal. nitr. nitr-ac. ol-jec. stann. sulph-ac.*

If *purulent expectoration* should remain after pneumonia, give: 1) *Chin. ferr. hep. lach. lyc. merc. sulph.;* or, 2) *Dros. dulc. laur. led. puls.;* or 3) *Bell.? hyos.? phos-ac.?*

§ 7. Particular indications for other remedies:

ARNICA: If the disease be caused by some external injury.

ARSENICUM: Fetid and dingy-green expectoration, pointing to approaching gangrene, *China* or *Lach.* being insufficient.

CANNABIS: Pneumonia accompanied with diseases of the heart or the larger vessels; or with greenish vomiting and delirium.

CAPSICUM: Pneumonia with bronchial catarrh or bronchitis, suitable to phlegmatic, indolent and suspicious persons.

CHINA: If the patient had lost much blood either by depletion or hæmorrhage; or bilious symptoms or symptoms of incipient gangrene being present.

MERCURIUS: Pneumonia and bronchitis, especially when the patients are disposed to blennorrhœa, or when there is profuse expectoration of viscid, bloody mucus.

NUX VOM.: Bronchial symptoms being present, or when the patients are addicted to drinking, or suffer with piles.

PHOSPHORUS: Pneumonia accompanied with bronchial catarrh and dry cough, or for inflammations which occur during the course of tuberculous phthisis. (In the last-mentioned case *Kal.* and *Lyc.* will prove useful.)

PULSATILLA: Pneumonia after measles, or in consequence of an obstinate bronchial catarrh, or suppressed menses.

SQUILLS: Pneumonia attended with gastric symptoms, or after it had been treated by bleeding, *Chin.* being insufficient; or when a profuse expectoration of mucus was present from the commencement.

§ 8. Compare: CONGESTIONS OF THE CHEST, PLEURITIS, ASTHMA, BRONCHITIS, COUGH, PULMONARY PHTHISIS, &c.

PODAGRA.

Principal remedies: 1) *Acon. sulph.* 2) *Arn. ars. bry. calc. sabin. sulph.* 3) *Amb. amm. asa. coccul. kal. led. sil. thuj. zinc.*

See: GOUT.

POISON, ADIPIC.—This dreadful poison sometimes develops itself in badly kept sausages or other pork. According to *Hering*, a beverage composed of equal portions of *vinegar and water*, to be taken in large quantities, is the best antidote. It may likewise be employed as a wash or gargle.

Instead of vinegar lemon-juice may be employed; and, if the patient should desire, these acids may be used alternately with sugar, *black coffee*, or fresh *black tea*.

If the dryness of the throat should continue after using these remedies, and if even slimy injections should not procure an evacuation from the bowels, give *Bry.*, and continue it as long as the symptoms continue to be unfavourable.

The ailments which remain after *Bry.*, sometimes yield to *Phos-ac.;* and, if *paralysis* or *consumption* should set in, give *Ars.* or *Kreos.*

POISONING, TOXICATION.

§ 1. We refer the reader to Dr. *Hering's* treatise on "*Poisons,*" from which the principal items contained in this work about poisons and their antidotes have been borrowed.

§ 2. In treating a case of poisoning, two things are required: 1) *Removal of the exciting cause;* and, 2) *Treatment of the disease occasioned by the poisoning.*

This treatment is to be conducted in every case agreeably to the principles of the New School.

The removal of the poisonous substances should be effected by the simplest and most innocent method, either with the finger, or, if this should be impossible, as in the case of poisons that had been swallowed, we recommend the following means suggested by *Hahnemann* and *Hering:*

1) Excite *vomiting* or *stool* by the simplest means, copious administration of *tepid water, irritating the fauces* by means of a *feather* or something-similar; placing on the tongue a pinch of *salt, snuff,* or *mustard;* or, if neither of these means should be sufficient, resort to *injections of tobacco-smoke.*

2) *Neutralize the poison* by means of: The *white of an egg, vinegar,* or *lemon-juice, coffee, camphor, milk, oil, soap, mucilaginous drinks, tea, wine, sugar;* or, in some cases: *ammoniacal gas, iron-rust, charcoal, kitchen-salt, epsom-salt, sweet-almond oil, spiritus nitr., dulc., potash,* boiled *starch,* &c.

§ 3. Particular indications:

WHITE OF AN EGG, dissolved in a sufficient quantity of water, and used as a drink, especially for: Metallic substances, such as, quicksilver, corrosive sublimate, verdigris, tin, lead, and sulphuric acid; when the patient complains of violent pains in the stomach or abdomen, with tenesmus, or diarrhœa and pains at the anus.

VINEGAR: Antidotes poisoning with alkaline substances; but is hurtful in cases of poisoning with mineral acids, corrosive vegetable substances, Arsenic, and a large quantity of salts. In many cases it removes the ill effects of *Aconite, Opium, narcotic substances, poisonous mushrooms, belladonna, carbonic-acid gas, hepar sulphuris, poisonous muscles* and *fish,* and even of *adipic acid.* The vinegar may be drank or administered by the rectum, alternately with mucilaginous substances. The vinegar should be as pure as possible. Crab-vinegar is, of itself, poisonous.

COFFEE: *Strong black coffee,* the beans being little roasted, and drank as hot as possible. Indispensable for a large number of poisons, especially when causing *drowsiness, intoxication, loss of consciousness*, or *mental derangement, delirium*, &c., in general, antidoting narcotic substances, such as: *Opium, nux-vom., belladonna, narcotic mushrooms, poisonous sumach, bitter almonds, prussic acid* and all those substances containing it, *Bell., colocynth, valer., cicuta* and *cham.* In case of poisoning with *Antimony, Phosphor.* and *Phosphoric acid*, coffee is no less indispensable.

Camphor: Principal antidote of all vegetable substances, especially such as have a *corrosive* effect, or when *vomiting* and *diarrhœa, pale face, cold extremities* and *loss of consciousness* are present. Camphor is a specific remedy for the ill effects of poisoning insects, especially *cantharides*, whether administered internally or externally. Likewise for the effects of so-called *worm-medicines, tobacco, bitter almonds*, and other fruits containing *prussic acid.* It is likewise useful for the secondary affections remaining after poisoning with *acids, salts, metals, phosphorus*, poisonous mushrooms, &c., after the poisonous substance itself had been removed from the stomach by means of vomiting, &c.

Milk: Less useful than is supposed. To procure an artificial covering or envelop for the poison, mucilaginous substances are to be preferred. *Fat milk* (or *cream*) is suitable in all cases where *oil* is, and hurtful where oil is. Curdled or sour milk is suitable or not suitable in all cases where vinegar is or is not.

Olive oil: Less useful than is believed. It is of no use in cases of metallic poisoning, and even hurtful in cases of poisoning with Arsenic. It is very bad for the ill effects of *Canthar.* This remark applies to poisoning with any other insect, or if the poison should have got into one's eye. Oil may be used to facilitate the extraction of insects from the ear in case they should have got into it. Oil is most suitable for poisoning with corrosive acids, such as: *nitric acid, sulphuric acid*, &c. It is sometimes useful in cases of poisoning with alkalies, to be administered alternately with vinegar, and in cases of poisoning with mushrooms.

Mucilaginous substances, drinks, or injections of mucilaginous substances, should be resorted to in cases of poisoning with alkalies, especially when administered alternately with vinegar.

Soap, *common castile soap*, dissolved in four times its bulk of hot water and drunk, is one of the best remedies in many cases of poisoning. It may be drank by the cupful,—a cupful every two, three, or four minutes, in all cases where the white of an egg is indicated but does not produce sufficient relief. Soap is particularly useful in all cases of poisoning with metallic substances, especially *Arsenic, lead*, &c. Likewise for poisoning with corrosive acids, such as: *Sulphuric acid, nitric acid*, &c., with

22*

alum, corrosive vegetable substances, castor oil, &c. Soap is hurtful in cases of poisoning with alkalies, such as: *Lye, nitrate of silver, potash, soda, oleum tartari, ammonium muriaticum,* (Salmiac) *ammonium carbonicum, caustic* or *burnt lime, barytes,* &c.

SUGAR, or sugar-water, one of the best remedies in many cases. In case of poisoning with mineral acids or *alkalies,* it is best to resort at once to the specific antidote, though sugar is not hurtful. In cases of poisoning with *metallic substances,* various kinds of *paint, verdigris, copper, sulphate of copper, alum,* &c., sugar is preferable to every other remedy, and not till the patient has been relieved by the sugar, administer the *white of an egg* or soap-water alternately with sugar. Sugar is likewise an excellent antidote in cases of poisoning with *arsenic* or *corrosive vegetable substances.*

§ 4. Of the other antidotes, use:

AMMONIACAL GAS: For *alcohol, bitter almonds, prussic acid.*

IRON-RUST: For *Arsenic.*

EPSOM-SALTS: For *alkaline poisons.*

CHARCOAL: For *foul fish, foul meat, poisonous mushrooms, poisoning muscles,* &c.

KITCHEN-SALT: For *nitrate of silver* and *poisonous wounds.*

MAGNESIA: For *acids.*

SWEET-ALMOND OIL: For *acids.*

POTASH: For *acids.*

STARCH: For *iodine.*

SPIRITS OF NITRE: For *alkaline poisons* and *animal substances.*

TEA: For *adipic acid* and *poisonous honey.*

WINE: For *noxious vapours* and *poisonous mushrooms.*

§ 5. The first thing we have to do, in treating a case of poisoning, is to remove the poison by vomiting, and then to administer suitable antidotes.

If we should not be able to ascertain what kind of poison had been swallowed, we should first administer the white of an egg; and, if there should be stupefaction, *coffee.*

If we should know that the poison is:

a) A metallic substance, we have to give: first the *white of an egg, sugar-water, soap-water,* and afterwards, for the remaining ailments: *Sulph.,* which is a real antidote to metals.

b) If *acids* and *corrosive substances,* give: 1) *Soap-water;* 2) *Magnesia* dissolved in water; 3) *Chalk-water;* 4) *Alkalies* or *potash* dissolved in water, taking a tablespoonful as long as the vomiting continues. Afterwards mucilaginous drinks, and alternately *Coff.* and *Op.* as homœopathic antidotes.

As regards the remaining ailments, give *Puls.* for sulphuric acid; *Bry.* for muriatic acid; *Acon.* for the other acids, and especially crab-apple vinegar. If the skin should have been corroded by poisons, apply soap-water, or a watery solution of *Caust.;* and if corrosive substances should have got into the eyes, apply *sweet almond-oil*, or *fresh unsalt-butter.*

c) For *alkaline substances:* 1) *Vinegar and water* in large quantities; 2) *Lemon-juice*, or acids from other fruits, diluted with much water; 3) *Sour milk;* 4) *Mucilaginous drinks*, or injections. *Vinegar* is hurtful in cases of poisoning with Barytes; but epsom-salt dissolved in water, renders good service; afterwards, *Camph.* or *Nitr. spir.* The secondary effects of poisoning with potash, require: *Coff.* or *Carb-v.;* and those of poisoning with spirits of Ammonia, *Hep.*

d) For the inhalation of *noxious vapours:* Sprinkle the patient with *vinegar and water*, or let him inhale the *vapours of a solution of chlore;* afterwards, after the return of consciousness, give *black coffee*, or a few doses of *Op.* or *Bell.*

(See: VAPOURS.)

e) For *vegetable poisons:* 1) *Camphor*, by olfaction, or sometimes a drop of the spirits of camphor on sugar; 2) *Black coffee* or *vinegar*, especially for narcotic vegetable juices. The best antidotes for corrosive vegetable juices, are soap-water and milk.

f) For *animal poisons:* See the single poisons, such as: *Cantharides, adipic poison, stings of insects, fish-poison, poisonous honey*, &c.—For *toad-poison*, or similar poisons, if they should have got into the stomach, give powdered charcoal, stirred up with oil or milk; or let the patient smell of the sweet spirits of nitre, if bad symptoms should set in, and afterward give *Ars.*— If a poison of this kind should have got into the eye, give *Acon.*

§ 6. As regards the *wounds* or bites inflicted by poisonous animals, *Hering* proposes the following mode of treatment: For the *bites of poisonous serpents, mad dogs*, or other poisonous animals, apply *heat at a distance*, for which purpose any thing may be used which is handy at the time: a red-hot iron, incandescent piece of coal, or even a burning cigar; hold this as near as possible without burning the skin. The heat should be kept up uniformly, and should be concentrated upon the wound exclusively. The edges of the wound should be covered over with *oil* or *fat*, and this should be repeated as often as the skin gets dry. If no oil or fat can be had, use *soap*, or even saliva. Wipe off carefully every thing which is discharged from the wound. Continue the application of heat until the patient feels chilly and stretches himself; if this should take place too speedily, continue to apply the heat for about an hour, or until the effects of the poison commence to disappear.

§ 7. At the same time administer internal remedies. In the case of a serpent's bite, give the patient a swallow of salt-water from time to time, or a pinch of salt or powder, or a few pieces of garlic.

If, nevertheless, dangerous symptoms should set in, give a tablespoonful of wine or brandy every 2 or 3 minutes; continue this until the symptoms abate, and repeat the brandy at every return of a paroxysm.

If the stitching pains should increase in violence, and be felt nearer the heart; if the wound, at the same time, should be bluish, checkered like marble and swollen, with vomiting, vertigo and diarrhœa, give *Ars.* 30, and another dose in half an hour, if the symptoms should continue to get worse, or only in 3 hours, if they should remain unchanged; if an improvement should set in after the first dose, do not repeat the medicine until the symptoms get worse again.

If *Ars.*, even if repeated, should have no effect, give *Bell.* In some cases *Senega* may be tried. The chronic sequelæ of the bite of a serpent require: *Phos-ac.* and *Merc.*

§ 8. If the bite should have been inflicted by a mad dog, apply *heat at a distance* as above, and for the remaining treatment see: HYDROPHOBIA.

If the bite should proceed from a man or animal which is not mad, but *furious*, give *Hydrophobin;* which is recommended by *Hering*.

§ 9. Wounds which have become poisonous in consequence of decayed animal matter or pus having got into them, require *Ars.*

To guard against unpleasant consequences in case we should have to touch decayed animal substances, poisonous wounds or ulcers, or men and animals infected with contagious diseases, we should hold our hands for ten or fifteen minutes near as strong a heat as can be borne, and afterwards wash them with soap. The use of *Chlore* in such cases is well known.

POLYPI.—Principal remedies: 1) *Calc.* 2) *Phosph. puls. staph.* 3) *Con. merc. sil. thuj.* 4) *Amb. ant. ars. aur. graph. hep. lyc. mez. petr. phos-ac. sep. sulph. sulph-ac. teucr.*

Mucous growths seem to require: 1) *Calc. merc. puls.* 2) *Hep. mez. sulph. teucr.*

Fibrous growths: 1) *Calc. staph.* 2) *Ars. petr. phosph. sep. sil. sulph. thuj.*

It should not be forgotten, that, if we wish to treat polypi successfully, we should allow a dose of the appropriate remedy to act 6 or 8 weeks.

POLYPUS OF THE BLADDER.—In regard to this disease, we possess the record of only one case, successfully treated with *Calc.*—Perhaps we might try : *Staphys.*; or: *Con. merc. phosph. puls. sil. thuj.*

I ought to remind my readers of my previous remarks about the long action of *Calc.* I have always found, that one dose of *Calc.*, if allowed to act, will remove the polypus (from the nose or uterus) in from 4 to 7 weeks ; whereas a repetition of the dose, even from the same solution, was attended with unpleasant consequences.

POLYPUS OF THE EAR.—Try : ***Calc.*** and ***Staphys.***
See : POLYPI.

POLYPUS OF THE NOSE.—Principal remedies: ***Puls.;*** f insufficient, give *Calc.*—*Teucr.* is of little use.—Try : ***Phosph.*** *staph. sep. sil.*

POT-BELLIED.—If the patients be *children,* see : ATROPHY of scrofulous children.

If *young girls,* at the age of pubescence, give ***Lach.***

If *old females,* or females who have borne many children, give 1) *Sepia* ; or, 2) *Bell. calc.? chin.? n-vom.? plat.*

PREGNANCY.

§ 1. Principal remedies for the morbid states incident to pregnancy :

a) For *convulsions* and *spasms :* 1) ***Bell. cham. cic. hyos. ign.;*** or, 2) *Cocc. ipec. mosch. plat. stram. veratr.*

b) For affections of the *emotive sphere :* 1) ***Bell. puls.;*** or 2) *Acon. cupr. lach. merc. plat. stram. veratr.*

c) For *headache :* 1) ***Bell. bry. cocc. n-vom. puls. plat. veratr.;*** or, 2) *Acon. calc. magn. sep. sulph.*

d) For the *yellow* or *brown spots* in the face : *Con. ferr. nitr-ac sep.*

e) For *toothache :* 1) ***Magn. n-mosch. n-vom. puls.;*** or, 2) *Alum. bell. calc. hyos. rhus. staph.*

f) For *bulimy : Magn-m. natr-m. n-vom. petr. sep.*

g) For *affections of the stomach,* such as: *Nausea, vomiting,* &c.: 1) ***Con. ipec. n-vom. puls.;*** or, 2) *Acon. ars. ferr. kreos. lach. magn-m. natr-m. n-mosch. petr. phosph. sep. veratr.*

h) For *colic:* 1) *Arn. bry. cham. n-vom. puls. sep.;* or, 2) *Bell. hyos. lach. veratr.*

i) For *constipation:* 1) *Bry. n-vom.;* or, 2) *Alum. lyc. op. sep.*

k) For *diarrhœa:* 1) *Ant. phosph. sep. sulph.;* or, 2) *Dulc. hyos. lyc. petr.*

l) For *ischuria* and *dysuria:* 1) *Cocc. phos-ac. puls.;* or, 2) *Con. n-vom. sulph.*

m) For *varices:* 1) *Lyc.* 2) *Carb-veg. puls.*

PRESBYOPIA.—Principal remedies: 1) *Calc. dros. sep. sil. sulph.;* or, 2) *Carb-an. coff. con. hyos. lyc. meph. natr. natr-m. petr.*

See: AMBLYOPIA.

PROLAPSUS OF THE RECTUM.—Principal remedies: *Ign. nux-v. merc. sulph.;* and perhaps, to remove the disposition to this affection: *Ars. calc. lyc. ruta. sep.*

Prolapsus of the rectum in *children,* requires: *Ign.* or *n-vom.*

PROLAPSUS UTERI et VAGINÆ.—Principal remedies so far as known: *Aur. bell. n-vom. sep.;* or perhaps: *Calc. gran.? kreos. merc. n-mosch.? stann.?*

Prolapsus of the *uterus* requires: *Aur. bell. calc. n-vom. sep. stann.*

Of the *vagina:* *Kreos. merc. n-vom.*

Recent prolapsus, of about a fortnight's duration, yields to one dose of *Nux-v.* 30, in 24 hours, provided the patient remains quiet in bed for 24 hours.

PROSOPALGIA.

§ 1. Principal remedies: 1) *Acon. bell. caust. coloc. con. hep. lyc. merc. mez. n-vom. phosph. plat. spig. staph.;* or, 2) *Bry. calc. caps. chin. lyc. puls. rhus. sil. stann. sulph. thuj. veratr.;* or, 3) *Actæa. agar. arn. ars. ant. bar-c. cham. coff. kal. kal-chl.? magn.? magn-m.?* &c.

§ 2. *Inflammatory* prosopalgia requires: 1) *Acon. arn. bry. phosph. staph. sulph.;* or, 2) *Bar-c. bell. lach. merc. plat. thuj. veratr.*

Rheumatic: 1) *Acon. caust. chin. merc. mez. phosph. puls. spig. sulph. thuj.;* or, 2) *Arn. bry. hep. lach. magn. n-vom. veratr.*

Arthritic: *Caust. coloc. merc. n-vom. rhus. spig.,* &c.

Nervous: 1) *Spig.* 2) *Bell. caps. lyc. plat. spig. magn-arct.* or, 3) *Hyos. lach. magn. n-vom.,* &c.

If caused by *abuse of Mercury: Aur. carb-veg. chin. hep. sulph.* See: MERCURIAL AFFECTIONS.

§ 3. Prosopalgia of plethoric persons is frequently removed by: 1) *Acon. Bell.;* or, 2) *Calc. chin. lach. phosph. plat.*

Of *nervous* persons, by: *Bell. lach. lyc. plat. spig.*

§ 4. Symptomatic indications:

ACONITUM: Red and hot face, with pain on *one side*, creeping or as from an ulcer; swelling of the cheek or jaws; fever-heat, thirst; violent pains with restlessness and anguish, &c.

BELLADONNA: The pain follows the course of the infra-orbital nerve, and is easily excited by friction; or for tearing, stitching pains in the bones, jaws or malar bones; in many cases rigidity of the nape of the neck; spasms of the eyelids; convulsive twitching of the facial muscles and distortion of the mouth; hot and red face, &c.

CAUSTICUM: Tensive or beating pains in the facial bones, especially under the eyes, with a sort of lameness of the facial muscles; or drawing pains in the jaws, so that the patient is unable to open his jaws; rheumatic pains in the limbs, buzzing in the ears, &c.

COLOCYNTHIS: Tearing and stitching pains, affecting principally the *left side* of the face, and extending to the head, temples, nose, ear and teeth, with swelling of the face, aggravation *by touching the parts ever so slightly*, &c.

CONIUM: The pains set in at night; tearing or stitching.

HEPAR: Pains in the malar bones, worse when touching the parts, extending to the ears and temples.

LYCOPODIUM: Pains commencing with a feeling of coldness, especially in the right side of the face, worse at night or in the evening.

MERCURIUS: Tearing or stitching pains, affecting one whole side of the head, from the temple to the teeth, *worse at night in the warm bed*, with ptyalism, lachrymation, sweat in the face or about the head, sleeplessness, &c.

MEZEREUM: Spasmodic, stupefying pains affecting the left malar bone, and extending to the eye, temple, ear, teeth, throat and shoulder, worse after taking any thing warm or on coming out of the open air and entering a room.

NUX VOM.: Tearing and drawing pains extending to the inner ear, with swelling of the cheeks; *red face* or *cheek*, (or *one only*) or yellowish tinge, especially around the nose and mouth; *creeping* in the face with twitching of the muscles; aggravation by mental labour, wine, coffee, &c.

PHOSPHORUS: Tearing pains, especially on the left side, with itching and tension of the skin of the face; swelling and paleness of the face; aggravation by moving the facial muscles when eating, talking, &c., or by the slightest touch; pains from the jaws to the root of the nose or the inner ear; congestion of blood to the head, with vertigo; buzzing in the ears, &c.

PLATINA: Tingling pains, with feeling of coldness and numbness in the affected side; or for cramp-pain and tensive pressure in the malar bones; aggravation in the evening and during rest; whining mood; red face, thirst, &c.

SPIGELIA: Jerking tearing, *burning* and pressure in the malar bones; violent pains, not allowing either to touch or move the part, with shining swelling of the affected side, or with anguish of heart and great restlessness.

STAPHYSAGRIA: Aching, beating pains from the teeth to the eye, or stitching, burning, drawing, cutting or tearing pains, with sensation of swelling in the affected side, spasmodic weeping, cold hands and cold sweat in the face.

§ 5. Use more particularly:

a) For *distensive* pains: *Bell. ign. phos. plat. spig.*

b) *Burning* pains: *Bell. cham. coloc. graph. ign. phos. phos-ac. rhus. samb. spig. veratr.*

c) *Aching* pains: *Bell. chin. mez. rhus. par. spig. stann. staph.*

d) *Crampy* pains: *Mez. nitr-ac. par. plat. stann. thuj.*

e) *Beating: Acon. bell. merc. plat. staph.*

f) *Tingling: Nux-v. plat.*

g) *Tearing: Alum. carb-v. chin. coloc. con. hep. lyc. merc. nitr-ac. n-vom. phos. rhus. spig. staph.*

h) *Cutting:* 1) *Bell. staph.* 2) *Calc. coloc. rhus.*

i) *Stitching: Alum. ars. bell. coloc. con. graph. lyc. merc. rhus. sil. staph. sulph.*

k) *Tensive: Aur. baryt. caust. coloc. hep. par. phos. rhus.*

l) Pains with feeling of *numbness* in the affected parts: *Mez. plat.*

m) *Digging* pains: *Coloc. plat.*

n) *Drawing* pains: *Ars. carb-v. hep. kal. rhus. sil. stann.*

o) *Jerking* pains: *Chin. n-vom. phos. spig. thuj.*

§ 6. For pains worse:

a) By *contact: Actaea. chin. dros. hep. phos. spig.*

b) By *motion*, talking, chewing: *Actaea. bell. bry. calc. mez. natr-m. nitr-ac. n-vom. phos. spig. staph.*

c) For pains on *one* side only: *Acon. actaea. bell. coloc. con. dros. mez. natr-m. n-vom. phos. plat. puls. spig. stann. staph.*

d) Pains on the *left* side: 1) *Coloc. graph. lach. staph. sulph.* 2) *Acon. calc. con. nitr-ac. n-vom. spig. verat.*

e) *Right* side: *Bell. bry. con. rhus. spig.*

f) Worse in the *evening:* 1) *Bell. con. lach. mez. nitr-ac. phos. plat. puls.* 2) *Acon. bry. calc. coloc. kal. rhus. stann.*

g) *Nightly* pains: 1) *Acon. con. merc. nitr-ac. sil.* 2) *Bell. bry. calc. cin. dros. kal. lach. mez. natr-m. phos. puls. rhus. spig. staph. thuj.*

h) Worse after *eating:* 1) *Bry. calc. con. kal. natr-m. n-vom. phos. sil.* 2) *Nitr-ac. puls. rhus.*

§ 7. See: HEADACHE, TOOTHACHE, PAIN, PAROXYSMS OF, CAUSES, CONDITIONS, &c.

PROSTATITIS.

The principal remedies, so far, are: *Puls.* and *Thuja.* We may likewise try: *Agn. aur. cann. canth.? jod. merc. spong.? sulph.?*

If caused by *gonorrhœa*, give, above all, *Puls.* and *Thuja.*

PRUSSIC ACID, POISONING WITH.

Resort to: 1) *Spirits of ammonia*, which the patient should smell of, or dissolve a few drops in a tumblerful of water, and give it in teaspoonful doses; 2) *Black coffee* by the mouth and rectum; 3) *Vapours of vinegar* or *Camphor.*

Subsequent secondary ailments require: *Coff. ipec. nux-v.*

The same mode of treatment applies to poisoning with *bitter almonds* or *laurocerasus.*

PSOITIS.

Principal remedies: *Acon. bry. n-vom. puls. rhus. staph.*

See: RHEUMATISM and PAIN, PAROXYSMS OF.

For *suppuration*, see: ABSCESS, and INFLAMMATORY TUMOUR.

PTYALISM.

Principal remedies: 1) *Bell. calc. canth. colc. dulc. euphorb. hep. jod. lach. merc. nitr-ac. op. sulph.* 2) *Alum. amb. ant. arg. baryt. bry. caust. cham. chin. dros. graph. hell. hyos. ign. ipec. lyc. natr-m. puls. seneg. sep. staph. stram. sulph-ac. veratr.*

If caused by *abuse of Mercury*, give: *Bell. chin. dulc. hep. jod. lach. nitr-ac. op. sulph.*

See: STOMACACE.

PULMONARY PHTHISIS.

§ 1. Principal remedies: 1) *Calc. kal. lyc. phos. puls. stann.* 2) *Ars. chin. dros. ferr. jod. lach. nitr. nitr-ac. sep. sil. sulph.* 3) *Bry. carb-v. con. dulc. hep. kreos. laur. led. merc. natr-m.*

phos-ac. samb. 4) *Amm. amm-m. ırn. bell. dig. guaj. hyos. n-mosch. n-vom. seneg. spong. zinc.*

Acute phthisis (*florida*) in consequence of violent and badly treated pneumonia, or of violent pneumorrhagia, requires: 1) *Lyc.* 2) *Ferr. hep. lach. merc. sulph.*; or, 3) *Dros. dulc. laur. led. puls.*

Suppuration of the lungs in consequence of *abuse of mercury*, requires principally: 1) *Carb-v. guaj. hep. lach. nitr-ac. sulph.*; or, 2) *Calc.? chin.? dulc.? lyc.? sil.?*

Phthisis of *stone-cutters*: 1) *Calc. hep. lyc. sil.*; or, 2) *Lach.? sulph.?*

§ 3. For *tuberculous* phthisis, try: 1) *Calc. kal. lyc. phosph. puls. stann.* 2) *Ars. carb-v. hep. lach. merc. nitr-ac. samb. sil sulph.*; or, 3) *Amm. arn. bell. bry. dulc. hyos. natr. natr-m. nitr. n-mosch.*

In the first stage, the tubercles being still *crude* or commencing to inflame and soften, give: 1) *Amm. calc. carb-v. lyc. phos. nitr-ac. sulph.*; or, 2) *Acon. arn. ars. bell. dulc. ferr. hyos. kal. merc. nitr. stann. sulph-ac.*

In the second stage, with purulent expectoration, give: 1) *Calc. kal. lyc. phos. puls. sep. sil. sulph.* 2) *Carb-v. chin. con. dros. ferr. lach. merc. natr. nitr. nitr-ac. phos-ac. rhus. stann.* 3) *Dulc. hep. guaj. laur. samb. zinc.*

Phthisis mucosa, with copious expectoration of tuberculous phthisis, requires: 1) *Dulc. hep. lach. merc. seneg. sep. stann. sulph.*; or, 2) *Ars. calc. carb-v. chin. crot. dig. lyc. phos. puls. sil. zinc.*

§ 4. Symptomatic indications:

ACONITUM: Frequent congestion of blood to the chest, with short cough, hæmoptysis and disposition to pneumonia.

AMMONIUM: Slimy and bloody expectoration, with violent oppression of the chest and short breathing.

BELLADONNA: Suitable to scrofulous children, with cough at night, shortness of breathing and mucous rattling; or suitable to young girls at the age of pubescence. (After *Bell.* are frequently suitable: *Hep. lach. phos.* or *sil.*)

CALCAREA: An excellent remedy in the second stage after *Sulph.* or *Nitr-ac.* refuse to act, or even in the first stage, suitable to plethoric young people that are affected with congestions of blood, bleeding of the nose, &c.; also to young girls with profuse and too frequent menstruation. (After *Calc.*, *Lyc.* or *Sil.* or *Nitr-ac.* is frequently suitable.)

CARBO VEG.: Violent, spasmodic cough, at times dry and painful, at others purulent, slimy and mixed with tuberculous substances.

CHINA: Suitable to patients that have frequently been attacked with pneumorrhagia, or have been debilitated by bleeding. (After *Chin.*, *Ferrum* is frequently suitable.)

DULCAMARA: When there is great disposition to take cold, or when the disease originates in frequent colds.

FERRUM: When the disease occurred in consequence of pneumonia or a neglected catarrh, and is attended by heavy breathing and vomiting of food or lienteria. (In this latter case *China* is excellent.)

HEPAR: Suitable to children or scrofulous young people, in the first stage of the disease, frequently after *Bell.* or alternately with *Merc.* or *Sil.*

KALI CARB.: Excellent for incipient or developed phthisis, especially after *Nitr-ac.* or *Sil.*, or when the children look bloated over the eyes and between the eyebrows.

LACHESIS: After or alternately with: *Bell. hep. sil.*

LYCOPODIUM: For hectic fever with cough and purulent expectoration in consequence of violent or neglected pneumonia; or for incipient or even fully developed tuberculous phthisis, bloody or purulent expectoration. (Suitable after or alternately with: *Calc. sil. phos.*)

NITRI-AC.: At the commencement of the disease, before using Kali, suitable to persons with brown hair, yellowish complexion, and disposed to diarrhœa.

PHOSPHORUS: Suitable to thin, blond, slender individuals, or to children and delicate girls, with dry, short cough, short breath, striking thinness, *bloated appearance under the eyes*, disposition to diarrhœa or sweat, &c. (Suitable after *Bell.* or alternately with *Lyc. sil.*)

SAMBUCUS: The disease is accompanied by profuse, colliquative sweats, or frequent paroxysms of asthma. (Is frequently suitable after, or in alternation with *Ars.*)

SILICEA: Almost the same symptoms as those for *Phosphorus* in most cases of incipient or confirmed phthisis, especially after: *Lyc. phos. hep.* or *calc.*

STANNUM: This remedy is not indicated by a decidedly purulent expectoration; but more than any other remedy by mucous expectoration in the first stage of consumption, or when a neglected catarrh threatens to pass into phthisis.

SULPHUR: For pulmonary suppression after violent pneumonia, also for tuberculous phthisis in the second stage, even for incipient tuberculosis, provided the inflammatory symptoms had been removed by other remedies, (such as: *Acon. phos.*), and a dose is allowed to act for several weeks.

§ 5. It may be proper here to repeat, that the remedy must be well chosen, otherwise it might produce a dangerous irritation and even inflammation of crude tubercles. The medicine should not be repeated unless we are sure that it is the proper remedy, and that the first dose has ceased to act.

§ 6. Compare: *Asthma*, *Congestions* of the chest, *Bronchitis*, *Cough*, *Pneumonia*, &c.

PURPLE-RASH.

Principal remedies: 1) *Acon. coff.* 2) *Bell. sulph.*

If the disease should be complicated with scarlatina, give: *Dulc.*

See: Inflammatory fevers and Exanthems, and compare: Variola, Rash, Measles, Scarlatina.

RANULA.

Principal remedies: *Calc. merc. thuj.*—perhaps also, *Ambra.*

RASH, miliaria.

Principal remedies: *Acon. ars. bell. bry. cham. ipec. puls. sulph.*

If the *breaking out* should be accompanied with great anguish, give *Ars.*

Lying-in women require principally: *Bry.* or *Ipec.*; ano *children: Acon. bell. bry. cham. ipec.*

If sudden retrocession or slow development of the eruption should be followed by asthmatic complaints, gastric symptoms and fainting turns, give *Ipec.*

Miliaria alba requires principally: *Ars. bry.*, and perhaps, *Bell. val.*

See: Purple and Scarlet-rash.

RETENTION OF URINE, ischuria.—*Spasmodic* ischuria: 1) *N-vom. op. puls.*; or, 2) *Aur. canth. con. dig. hyos. lach. rhus. veratr.*

Comp.: Urinary difficulties.

Inflammatory ischuria: *Acon. cann. canth. n-vom. puls.*, &c.

Comp.: Cystitis and Urinary difficulties.

Paralytic ischuria: Ars. dulc. hyos., &c.

Comp.: Urinary difficulties.

RHACHITIS, rickets.—Principal remedies: 1) *Asa. bell. calc. lyc. merc. puls. sil. staph. sulph.*; and, 2) *Mez. nitr-ac. petr. phosph. phos-ac. rhus.*

For *curvature* of the spine : *Bell. calc. puls. sil. sulph.*

For curvature of the *long bones* and *swelling of the joints : Asa. calc. sil. sulph.*

For too *large size* of the head, the fontanelles remaining open : *Calc. puls. sil.*

See : SCROPHULA and BONES, DISEASES OF.

RHAGADES.

§ 1. Principal remedies : 1) *Alum. calc. hep. lyc. merc. petr. puls. rhus. sep. sulph.* 2) *Arn. aur. cham. cycl. lach. mang. natr-m. nitr-ac. sassap. sil. zinc.*

§ 2. Rhagades of the *hands*, from *working in water :* 1) *Calc. hep. sep. sulph.* 2) *Alum. ant. cham. merc. rhus. sassap.*

Chapping in *cold weather : Petr. sulph.*

§ 3. Hæmorrhoidal rhagades at the *anus*, require : 1) *Agn. arn. cham. graph.* 2) *Hep. rhus. sassap. sulph.*

Rhagades of the *lips : Arn. ars. caps. cham. ign. merc. natr-m. puls. sulph.*

Of the *alæ nasi : Merc. sil.*

Of the *prepuce : Arn. merc. sep. sil. sulph. thuj.*

§ 4. Deep, *bleeding* rhagades, require : 1) *Cham. merc. sil.* 2) *Calc. graph. lach. nitr-ac. petr. staph. sulph.*

The principal remedy for syphilitic rhagades of the hands, or between the toes, is *Merc.;* if the patient should have had much Mercury, give : *Aur. carb-veg. lach. nitr-ac. sassap. sep. sulph.;* nevertheless, *Merc.* will be found indispensable, provided the rhagades are not exclusively mercurial.

Comp.: ULCERS, SUPPURATIONS, SORENESS OF THE SKIN.

RHEUMATISM.

§ 1. Principal remedies : 1) *Acon. bell. bry. cham. merc. n-vom. phosph. puls. rhus.* 2) *Ant. ars. carb-veg. caust. chin. colch. ferr. hep. ign. lach. lyc. n-mosch. rhod. ruta. sassap. sep. sulph. thuj. veratr.* 3) *Camph. cann. canth. coloc. cupr. euphr. kreos. magn-c. mez. nitr-ac. ran. spig. squill. stann. tart. val.*

§ 2. For *acute* rheumatism : *Acon. arn. ars. bell. bry. cham. chin. colch. dulc. ign. merc. n-vom. puls.* and *rhus.*

Chronic rheumatism : *Caust. clem. hep. lach. lyc. phosph. sulph. veratr.;* or *: Bry. dulc. ign. merc. n-vom. puls. rhus. thuj.*

Rheumatism and *swelling* of joints : *Acon. ant. arn. bell. bry. chin. clem. hep. n-vom. rhus. sulph.*

Rheumatism with *curvature* and *stiffness* of the affected part :

1) *Ant. bry. caust. guaj. lach. sulph.* 2) *Amm-m. coloc. graph. lyc. natr-m. n-vom. rhus. sep.*

Rheumatism with *lameness:* 1) *Arn. chin. ferr. ruta.;* or, 2) *Cin. coccul. hell. plumb. sassap. staph.*

Erratic rheumatic pains: 1) *Bry. n-mosch. n-vom. puls.; or,* 2) *Arn. ars. asa. bell. daph. mang. plumb. rhod. sabin. sassap. sep. sulph. val.*

§ 3. Rheumatism in consequence of *gonorrhœa:* 1) *Clem. sassap. thuj.;* or, 2) *Daph. lyc.* and *sulph.*

If caused by *abuse* of *Mercury:* 1) *Carb-veg. chin. guaj. lyc. sassap. sulph.,* or: 2) *Arg. arn. bell. calc. cham. chin. guaj. hep. lach. lyc. mez. phos-ac. puls.*

Pains coming on after taking the *least cold,* require: *Acon. arn. bry. calc. dulc. merc. phos-ac. sulph.*

If caused by *bad weather,* give: 1) *Calc. dulc. n-mosch. rhod. rhus. veratr.;* or: 2) *Amm. ant. carb-an. carb-veg. lach. lyc. mang. merc. nitr-ac. puls. sep. spig. stront. sulph.*

If by a *change* of *weather: Bry. calc. carb-veg. dulc. graph. lach. mang. merc. n-mosch. phosph. rhod. rhus. sil. sulph. veratr.*

If by being *in the water,* or by exposure to *wet* and *damp* weather: 1) *Calc. n-mosch. puls. rhus sassap. sep.* 2) *Bell. borax. bry. carb-veg. caust. colch. dulc. hep. lyc. sulph.*

If by exposure to the *cold* in winter; 1) *Ars. bry.* or *n-vom.* 2) *Carb-veg. colch. nitr-ac. phosph. puls. sulph-ac.*

§ 4. Symptomatic indications:

Aconitum: Tearing or *stitching* pains, less when sitting, *intolerable* at night, with complaints and reproaches; red and shining swelling of the affected part, and excessive sensitiveness to contact and motion; *aggravation* or *return of the pains* by wine or *other heating causes,* also by emotions; *high fever,* with dry heat, thirst, redness of cheeks, or alternation of redness and paleness of the face.

Arnica: Pains as if sprained or contused, feeling of lameness and tingling in the affected parts, or hard, red and shining swelling; *violent pains* in the affected part, with sensation as if resting upon something very hard; aggravation by moving the affected part (*Arn.* is suitable, after or before: *Chin. ars. ferr.* or *rhus.*)

Belladonna: *Stitching, burning* pains, worse at night and by motion, swelling of the affected part, with shining, widely spreading redness; violent fever, with throbbing of the carotid arteries, congestion of blood to the head, red face and eyes. (*Bell.* is frequently suitable after: *Acon. cham. merc.* or *puls.*)

Bryonia: Tensive and *tearing* pains, with stitching in the affected part *as often as it is moved;* or pains which have no certain locality, and affect the muscles rather than the bones; red and shining, or pale and tensive swelling, or stiffness of the affected part; aggravation at night and during the least motion; general sweat or *chilliness* and *shuddering*, or fever-heat with headache, *bilious* or gastric symptoms; vexed mood, or anger. (Frequently after *Acon.* or *Rhus-t.*)

Chamomilla: Drawing or tearing pains, with sensation of numbness or lameness in the affected part; the pains are continuous and get worse at night; *fever* with *burning heat* in the affected part, preceded by shuddering; hot sweat about the head, even in the hair; *redness*, of *one* cheek only, generally; great restlessness, *tossing about*, or chill; desire to be in bed. (Suitable after or before *Bell. puls.* or *ign.*)

Mercurius: Stitching, burning or tearing pains, worse in *cold and damp weather*, in *bed*, at night or toward morning; *œdema* of the affected parts; the pains are principally felt in the joints or bones; feeling of coldness in the affected parts; *copious sweat, affording no relief.* (Is frequently suitable after *Bell. bry. chin. dulc.* or *lach.*)

Nux-vom.: *Tensive, jerking* or *pulling* pains, especially in the back, loins, chest or joints, with pale, tensive swelling; *numbness* or lameness of the affected muscles, with spasms or twitchings in the muscles; aversion to the open air and great sensitiveness to cold; gastric symptoms; constipation, shuddering with trembling and aggravation of the symptoms. (Rarely suitable at the commencement, but frequently after: *Acon. cham. ign.* or *arn.*)

Pulsatilla: Drawing, tearing and jerking pains, worse *at night* or in the evening in bed; also by the warmth of the room, or by attempting to change a position which the patient had been in for a long time; or pains *which shift* rapidly from one *joint to the other;* sensation of numbness or lameness in the affected parts, or stitches and feeling of coldness at every change of weather; relief by uncovering the part or in the open air; pale face and chills, increasing with the pains. (Frequently suitable after: *Cham. ign.* or *arn.*)

Rhus-tox.: Tearing and burning or tensive pains, or pain as if sprained, with sensation of lameness and creeping in the affected parts; rigidity or red and shining swelling of the joints, with stitches when touched; aggravation during rest and in bad weather. (Suitable after *Arn.* or *Bry.*)

§ 5. Use likewise:

Arsenicum: For burning, tearing pains, worse at night, and in the *cold*, abating by the application of warmth.

Causticum: The pains are worse in the open air, in the room

and bed; or with lameness, stiffness and curvature of the affected part.

CHINA: Pains which are made worse by motion, with lameness of the affected parts, profuse sweat, &c.,

COLCHICUM: Paroxysms of tearing, stitching or drawing pain in the affected part through to the bone; lameness of the affected part; tearing in *warm weather*, with stitches in the limbs, when the weather is cold; the pains are worse from evening till morning, *sometimes intolerable in the evening;* nightly heat with thirst; nervousness; yellow spots in the face; loss of appetite with loathing of the smell rather than taste of the food; diminished, dark, brown urine.

DULCAMARA: The pains set in at night and during rest, with little fever.

FERRUM: For rheumatic lameness of the shoulder.

IGNATIA: Pains as if contused or sprained, or sensation as if the flesh were *loose on the bones in consequence of blows;* the pains are worse at night, diminished by a change of position.

LACHESIS: Chronic rheumatism, alternately with *Hepar;* or stiffness and curvature of the affected parts.

LYCOPODIUM: Drawing and tearing pains, worse at night and during rest; painful rigidity of the muscles and joints, with sensation of numbness in the affected part. (Suitable after: *Rhus. calc. puls.* or *nux-mosch.*)

NUX-MOSCH.: Wandering, aching or drawing pains, worse during rest, or in the open and cold air.

PHOSPHORUS: Tearing, drawing and tensive pains, setting in when taking the least cold, with headache, vertigo, oppression of the chest, &c.

RHODODENDRON: The pains are worse during rest, excited by rough, damp, windy weather.

RUTA: Rheumatic lameness of the wrist or tarsal joint.

SEPIA: Rheumatic affections in persons of a slender form, especially suitable to females with a delicate skin and complexion.

SULPHUR: Chronic rheumatism, and secondary ailments of acute rheumatism. (Frequently after: *Acon. bell. bry. merc.* or *puls.*)

THUJA: Tearing and beating pains, as from subcutaneous ulceration, with coldness and feeling of numbness in the affected parts, worse during rest and in bed.

VERATRUM: Pains as if bruised, worse in bed and bad weather, less when walking, with weakness and trembling of the affected part.

§ 6. Comp.: GOUT, PAIN, PAROXYSMS OF, CONDITIONS, CAUSES, WEATHER, &c.

RUPIA s. RHYPIA.

§ 1. Names have caused an immense confusion in the department of cutaneous diseases. *Samuel Plumbe*, Schœnlein and others, confound *rupia* and *ecthyma; Hebra* applies the name rupia only to syphilitic herpes with pyramidal crusts; *Bateman*, who distinguishes R. simplex and R. proeminens, understands by it an eruption very similar to ecthyma with which other authors have either confounded rupia, or who, in its higher forms, have classed it with the corroding and spreading ulcers. According to Bateman, the primitive form of rupia is vesicular, never pustulous, as that of ecthyma, though it is very difficult to distinguish these eruptions from each other, when more developed, except perhaps by the fact that the crusts of rupia are broader and less firmly adhering than those of ecthyma. *Hebra's* rupia is the syphilitic form with conical scurfs, and is the same as *Bateman's* rupia proeminens; whereas *Bateman's* rupia simplex is identical with the so-called phagedenic blister of *Hahnemann* and a kind of phagedenic ulcers of older writers.

§ 2. According to these distinctions, we propose for *rupia*, or rupia (*Schœnlein*), one or more of the following remedies, or of those which have been indicated for ecthyma.

b) For *rupia simplex* (*Bateman*), (the ulcus phagedenicum of some authors, or the bulla phagedenica of Hahnemann: 1) *Ars. cham. graph. petr. sil.* 2) *Borax. calc. clem. hep. natr. nitr-ac. rhus. sep. squill. staph.*

c) For the rupia of *Hebra* (rupia syphilitica or rupia proëminens of Bateman) *Mercurius*. This is not always sufficient; in one case I had to give: *Alum. nitr-ac. clem. thuj. sassap.*, then *Sulph.*, and lastly another dose of *Merc.*, which effected a permanent and thorough cure.

§ 3. See: HERPES, ULCERS, HERPES, PUSTULOSUS, and SYPHILIS.

RUBEOLÆ.—This disease is intermediate between scarlatina and measles, the symptoms of the mucous membranes being like those of scarlatina and the eruption itself resembling measles.

The principal remedies are: *Acon. bell. n-vom. puls.*

See: EXANTHEMATA, MEASLES and SCARLATINA.

RUNNING OF THE EYES—Blennorrhœa oculorum, Ophthalmo-blennorrhœa.

Principal remedies: 1) *Dig. euphr. graph. puls. sen.* 2) *Alum. amm. calc. caust. chin. euphr. guaj. hep. lyc. nitr-ac. sil. spig. sulph. thuj.*

For frequent *lachrymation*, give: 1) *Acon. bell. calc. euphr. kreos. puls. rut. sil. spig. staph. sulph.* 2) *Alum. ars. bry dig graph. hep. ign. kal. lach. lyc. merc. natr-m. n-vom. phos. phos-ac. rhus. spong. staph. thuj.*

Bleareyedness, lippitudo: 1) *Acon. euphr. merc. puls.* 2) *Rhus. spig.* 3) *Gran.? par.?*

RUSH OF BLOOD.

Complained of by plethoric, debilitated, hypochondriac or nervous individuals; the principal remedies are: 1) *Acon. aur. calc. hep. kal. kreos. lyc. phos. sep. sulph.* 2) *Amb. amm. arn. bell. bry. carb-v. caust. croc. chin. ferr. jod. natr-m. n-vom. op. petr. phos-ac. rhus. samb. sassap. sen. sil. stann. thuj.*

Rush of blood of *plethoric* individuals requires: 1) *Acon. aur. bell. calc. lyc. phos. sep. sulph.* 2) *Arn. bry. chin. ferr. natr-m. n-vom. rhus. thuj.*

Of *nervous*, very irritable individuals: 1) *Acon. arn. bell. chin. n-vom.* 2) *Amb. aur. calc. ferr. lyc. petr. samb.*

SAFFRON, ILL EFFECTS OF.

The best antidote, according to *Hering*, is *black coffee*, to be drank until vomiting sets in, and for the secondary diseases: *Opium.*

Chronic secondary affections require: *Acon. bell. plat. puls.*

SAL AMMONIAC, and NITRE, POISONING WITH.

Tepid water with unsalt butter, to be drank until vomiting sets in; afterwards mucilaginous drinks in large quantity.

Secondary ailments require: *Nitr-sp. coff. n-vom.*

SALT, ILL EFFECTS OF.

Principal remedy: *Nitri-sp.* After this: *Ars. carb-v. lyc. merc. n-vom. puls.*

SASSAPARILLA, ILL EFFECTS OF.

Hering recommends *Bell.* or *Merc.;* we may try moreover: *Amm. cham. lyc. sulph.*

SCARLATINA, Scarlet-fever.

§ 1. The principal remedy is *Bell.*, unless we should have to give: 2) *Acon. am. ars. bar. camph. carb-v. lach. merc. phosph. sulph.;* or, 3) *Con. coff. ipec. phos-ac. rhus.*

§ 2. For the fever in the precursory stage, give: *Acon.*

The *sore throat* requires, next to *Bell.*, *Baryt.* and *Merc.*

Gangrenous sore throat: 1) *Amm. ars. carb-v.;* or, 2) *Lach.* or *sulph.*

The *vomiting* requires *Acon.* or *Ars.*, if *Bell.* should not stop it; for the *tenesmus* and the *ischuria* give *Con.*, and for the *pulmonary spasms Ipec.*, provided *Bell* is insufficient.

The *sleeplessness* frequently yields to *Acon.* or *Coff.*

§ 3. For *retrocession* of the eruption, the best remedies are: *Bry. phos. phos-ac. sulph.*—If cerebral symptoms with coma should have set in, give *Op.;* or, *Bell.* if the patient should start as soon as he closes his eyes.

For the *parotitis* which sometimes sets in after the disease, give: *Bell. carb-v. phos. rhus. sil.;* or, *Merc.*

§ 4. The *dropsical* symptoms after scarlatina, require: *Arn. ars. bell. dig. hell phos-ac. seneg.*

Hydrocephalus: Arn. bell. hell. phos-ac.

Hydrothorax: 1) *Ars. hell. seneg.;* or, 2) *Arn. dig.*

Ascites: Dig. hell.

Anasarca: Ars. hell. or *bar-m.*

§ 5. *Parotitis* or *otorrhœa* in consequence of scarlatina, requires: *Bell. hep. puls.;* or, *Colch. lyc. men. merc. nitr-ac.;* or, if *caries* of the ossicula aurium should have set in: *Aur. calc. natr-m.* or *sil.*

§ 6. The principal remedies for scarlet-rash, are: *Acon.* and *Coff.;* or, *Sulph.* and *Bell.*, if *Acon.* or *Coff.* should not be sufficient.

For a combination of scarlatina and scarlet-rash, *Dulc.* has proved efficient.

§ 7. Particular indications:

Aconitum: Frequent colic, with bilious vomiting; violent fever, with dry heat; frequent, full and hurried pulse; congestion of blood to the head, with bloated face, vertigo and stupefaction, or delirium; or drowsiness with sudden starting from sleep; dry, short, painful cough; bleeding of the nose or spitting of blood; angina faucium.

Belladonna: Violent inflammation of the throat and tonsils, with stitching pains and spasmodic contraction; inability to swallow liquids, which frequently return by the nostrils; suffocative sensation on touching the pharynx or turning the head; violent thirst, with or without dread of water; inflamed and painful eyes, with photophobia; violent pressure in the forehead, as if the eyes would be pressed out, or tearing and stitching in the head; vertigo with obscuration of sight; red and dry tongue; sleeplessness, with nervousness ; frightful visions on closing the eyes ; sudden starting from sleep and jumping up.

MERCURIUS: Inflammation and swelling of the tonsils, ptyalism, ulcers in the mouth, swelling of the inguinal glands, &c.

PHOSPHORUS: Dry and hard tongue and lips, which are covered with blackish crusts ; loss of *speech* and *hearing*, difficult deglutition ; inability to retain the urine ; *falling off of the hair.*

RHUS TOX.: When the eruption becomes vesicular, with sopor, sudden starting from sleep, restlessness, ischuria and great thirst.

SULPHUR: Cerebral affection not yielding to *Bell.*, with *sopor*, sudden starting, distortion of the eyes; constant delirium, bloated and shining-red face ; stopped nose; dry, cracked, red tongue, covered with a brownish mucus ; thirst and difficulty of swallowing.

§ 8. Try moreover:

ARSENICUM: For complete prostration, sudden emaciation, nightly fever, with burning heat ; burning-hot face ; distorted features ; cold hands and no thirst ; *gangrenous* inflammation of the throat ; restless and sleepless ; fetid ulcers. Suitable for dropsy after scarlatina.

CAPSICUM: Very red face, and alternately pale ; swollen and chapped lips ; burning blisters in the mouth and on the tongue ; slimy saliva ; *sore throat;* painful deglutition, with fullness and compression in the throat ; painful pressure in the palate and velum, during deglutition ; sensation of contraction and spasm in the throat ; tickling and roughness in the fauces, with sneezing, hoarseness and hacking cough ; *accumulation of thick mucus* in the *nose* and *throat.*

MURIATIC ACID: Malignant scarlatina with dark redness of the cheeks ; bluish colour of the throat, red and dim eyes ; irregular, faint eruption becoming dark-red, mixed with petechiæ ; ulceration of the tonsils and adjoining parts ; fetid breath ; corrosive discharge from the nose, with soreness and blisters round the nose and lips.

SULPHURIS ACIDUM: Pale face, sudden prostration ; frequent chills, stitching pains in the throat, with swelling extending to the submaxillary glands ; bluish-red spots covered with a pellicle and with suppuration underneath ; imperfect, dark eruption with petechiæ.

See: EXANTHEMS, ERYSIPELAS, PURPLE-RASH, SORE THROAT, &c.

SCROPHULOSIS.

§ 1. Principal remedies: 1) *Ars. asa. baryt. bell. calc. cin. con.*

hep. jod. lyc. merc. rhus. sil. sulph. 2) *Aur. mur. carb-an. carb-v. cist. dulc. graph. lach. kreos. pin. staph.* 3) *Amb. amm. aur. bar-m. bry. chin. cocc. ferr. ign. magn-c. mez. mur-ac. natr. natr-m. nitr-ac. n-vom. phos. petr. puls. ran. rhab. sep. veratr.*

§ 2. At the commencement of the disease, when the children have great *difficulty* in *learning to walk*, give: *Bell. calc. sil. sulph.*, and perhaps in some cases: *Ars. chin. cin. ferr. lyc. magn. pin. puls. rhab. sep.*

In the *second period*, when the glands are affected: 1) *Baryt. bell. calc. cist. con. dulc. hep. lyc. merc. nitr-ac. phos. rhus. sil. staph. sulph.* 2) *Ars. bry. carb-an. clem. graph. kal. natr. n-vom. puls.*

The *cutaneous affections* (*eruptions, herpes, ulcers,* &c.,) require: 1) *Aur. baryt. calc. cist. clem. con. dulc. hep. lyc. merc. mur-ac. rhus. sil. sulph.* 2) *Canth. kal. mez. nitr-ac. ol-jec. petr. ranunc.*

Affections of the *bones*: 1) *Aur. calc. cist. lyc. merc. phos. phos-ac. puls. sil. sulph.* 2) *Asa. bell. hep. mez. nitr-ac. rhus. ruta. sep. staph.*

Scrofulous enlargement of the abdomen of children: *Sulph.*; then *Calc.*; or: *Ars. baryt. bell. chin. cin. lyc. n-vom. puls. rhus.*

§ 3. Particular indications, which, however, must necessarily be incomplete on account of the great variety of the symptoms:

Arsenicum: *Atrophy*, emaciation, swelling of the cervical glands, and hard, distended abdomen; bloated face; diarrhœa; debility, with constant desire to lie down; *pale and bloated*; herpes, scurfy eruptions and ulcers; ophthalmia; scurfs on the hairy scalp; cancerous affections, &c.

Asa: Exostosis, caries; curvature of the bones; glandular swellings; otorrhœa; ophthalmia; ulcers of the nose, or nasitis with swelling, &c.

Baryta: *Atrophy*; swelling and induration of the cervical glands; bloated body and face, with distended abdomen; physical and mental debility; dry scurfs on the head; inflammation of the eyes and eyelids; herpes in the face; frequent sore throat; great disposition to take cold, &c.

Belladonna: Hard, swollen and ulcerated glands; muscular debility, with difficulty of learning to walk; photophobia; inflammation of the eyes and eyelids; cough with mucous rattling; otorrhœa; emaciation and atrophy; ulcers; inflammatory swelling of the nose; swelling of the lips; frequent bleeding of the nose; cancerous affections; *pale and bloated*; frequent sore throat with swelling; asthmatic affections; distended and hard abdomen; inability to retain the urine; disposition to wet one's bed; premature development of the mind; blue eyes and blond hair.

Calcarea: Large head with open fontanelles, curvature of the back and vertebræ, or *other rhachitic affections;* herpes, scald-head, crusts in the face; hard or suppurating glandular swellings; ulcers, exostoses or caries; hard and enlarged abdomen, with swelling of the mesenteric glands; emaciation and voracious appetite; thin and wrinkled face, with dim eyes; dry and flaccid skin; difficulty of learning to walk; difficult dentition; ophthalmia, photophobia and blepharophthalmitis; otorrhœa; *red swelling of the nose;* swelling of the upper lip; frequent bleeding of the nose; *pale* and *bloated;* constipation, or frequent diarrhœa, &c.

Cina: Worm-affections, pale face, emaciation, *voracious appetite,* inability to retain the urine.

Conium: Constipation and induration of the glands; herpes; ophthalmia; photophobia; frequent blennorrhœa from the lungs; dry cough; asthma; cancerous affections, &c.

Hepar: Pale and bloated, with induration and suppuration of the glands; atrophy; scaldhead; herpes; ophthalmia; otorrhœa; swelling of the nose or upper lip; cancerous ulcers; disposition to phlegmonous sore throat, catarrh or bronchitis; disposition of the skin to ulcerate, &c. (Suitable before or after: *Bell. sil. lach. merc.*)

Iodium: Emaciation; swelling and induration of the glands, the whole of the lymphatic system being involved; rhachitic affections; inflammation of the eyes and eyelids; otitis and otorrhœa; swelling of the mesenteric glands; frequent catarrh, bronchial catarrh, &c.

Lycopodium: Swelling and suppuration of the glands; disposition to catarrh, bronchitis, &c.; inflammation, curvature and other affections of bones; atrophy; herpes and ulcers; scabs on the hairy scalp; ophthalmia; otitis and otorrhœa; pale and bloated; frequent sore throat; obstinate constipation, &c. (Frequently suitable after *Calc.*)

Mercurius: Disturbed reproduction, with bodily and mental weakness; disposition to take cold, to sweat catarrh, bronchial catarrh, &c.; pale and bloated; swelling and suppuration of the glands; rhachitic affections; exostoses; curvature, caries and other affections of bones; eruptions and corrosive herpes with crusts; tinea capitis; crusts in the face; ophthalmia; blepharophthalmitis; otitis; otorrhœa; frequent sore throat; *slimy* diarrhœa, &c. (Is frequently suitable after or before: *Bell. dulc. jod. rhus-t.*

Rhus tox.: Swelling of the glands; scaldhead, herpes in the face, and other eruptions discharging pus or forming crusts; emaciation; hard and distended abdomen; frequent catarrh; ophthalmia; otorrhœa; frequent diarrhœa, &c. (Frequently suitable after *Merc.*)

Silicea: Swelling and suppuration of the glands; exostoses, curvature, caries, and other diseases of the bones; pale and bloated; cancerous affections; disposition of the skin to ulcerate; swelling of the nose or upper lip; scabs on the hairy scalp; otorrhœa, &c. (Is frequently suitable after: *Lyc. hep.* or *sulph.*)

Sulphur: In almost every case, at the commencement of the treatment, especially when the patient complains of: Eruptions, herpes, *swelling*, *suppuration* or *ulceration* of *glands;* disposition to take cold, or to *diarrhœa with colic*, or to *constipation*, also to catarrh and other *blennorrhœas:* disposition to sweat easily and profusely; morbid reproduction; spongy and flabby flesh; physical and mental debility; difficulty of learning to walk; inflammation of the eyes and eyelids; otorrhœa; pale and bloated, &c. (Suitable after *Bell. merc. jod. rhus-t.*, &c.)

§ 4. Other remedies:

Aurum muriaticum: For crusts and ulcers on the nose and lips.

Carbo animalis and veget.: *Swollen* and *hard glands.*

Cistus: Swollen and suppurating glands; ulcers; otorrhœa; caries of the jaw, &c.

Dulcamara: Swelling, induration and suppuration of glands.

Graphites: Herpes, ophthalmia, ulcers, swelling, induration and suppuration of glands., &c.

Kreosotum: Swelling of glands, ophthalmia, herpes, &c.

Lachesis: *Swelling of glands*, ophthalmia, sore throat with swelling, ulcers, &c.

Pinus: Weakness of the joints, with difficulty of learning to walk.

Staphysagria: Swelling, induration and suppuration of glands; frequent catarrh with ulcerated nostrils; disposition of the skin to ulcerate; scrofulous enlargement of the abdomen: emaciation, &c.

§ 5. Compare: Atrophy; Glandular affections; Bones, diseases of the; Rhachitis; Ophthalmia; Otorrhœa; Herpes; Ulcers, &c.

SCURVY. — Principal remedies for scorbutic affections: 1) *Amm. amm-m. merc. mur-ac. n-vom. staph. sulph.* 2) *Ars. canth. carb-an. caust. cist. hep. natr-m. nitr-ac. phosph. sep. sulph-ac.*

See: Gums, diseases of the, and: Ulcers.

SEA-SICKNESS.—Principal remedies: 1) *Sulph.* 2) *Ars. cocc. petr.;* or: 3) *Colch. ferr. n-mosch. sep. sil. tabac. therid.*

For ailments occasioned by *riding in a carriage,* give: 1) *Cocc. sep.* 2) *Borax. hep. ign. n-mosch. petr. selen. sil.*

For nausea and vomiting, caused by *swinging,* give: *Cocc. petr.*

SECRETIONS, SUPPRESSION OF; ERUPTIONS, BLENNORRHŒA.

§ 1. The principal remedies for the ailments arising from this cause, are: 1) *Acon. bell. bry. calc. chin. lyc. n-vom. puls. sulph.* 2) *Ars. carb-veg. caust. cham. dulc. graph. kal. lyc. phosph. phos-ac. rhus. sep. sil. stram.* 3) *Amb. amm. ant. arn. aur. baryt. cin. cocc. cupr. ferr. hep. hyos. ign. ipec. merc. mur-ac. natr. natr-m. nitr-ac. n-mosch. ran. seneg. spong. veratr. zinc.*

§ 2. Give more particularly:

a) After suppression of *eruptions* and *herpes:* 1) *Bell. bry. dulc. graph hep. ipec. phos-ac. puls. sulph.* 2) *Acon. amb. ars. carb-veg. caust. cham. lach. lyc. merc. natr. n-mosch. phosph. rhus. sassap. sep. sil. staph. thuj.*

b) Suppression of *hæmorrhage* or abandoning habitual depletions: 1) *Acon. bell. chin. ferr. n-vom. puls. sulph.* 2) *Arn. aur. bry. calc. carb-veg. graph. hyos. lyc. natr-m. nitr-ac. phosph. ran. rhus. seneg. sep. sil. spong. stram.*

c) Suppression of *ulcers* and purulent discharges: 1) *Bell. hep. lach. sil. sulph.* 2) *Ars. carb-veg. lyc. merc. natr-m. phos-ac. rhus. sep. staph.*

d) Suppression of *piles:* 1) *Acon. calc. carb-veg. n-vom. puls. sulph.* 2) *Amb. amm. ant. ars. bell. caps. caust. chin. coloc. graph. ign. kal. lach. mur-ac. nitr-ac. petr. rhus. sep. sil.*

e) Suppression of *lochia:* 1) *Coloc. hyos. n-vom. plat. rhus. sec. veratr. zinc.* 2) *Bell. bry. con. dulc. puls. sep. sulph.*

f) Suppression of *milk:* 1) *Bell. bry. dulc. puls.* 2) *Acon. calc. cham. coff. merc. rhus. sulph.*

g) Suppression of *menses:* 1) *Acon. bry. con. dulc. graph. kal. lyc. puls. sep. sil. sulph.* 2) *Amm. ars. baryt. bell. calc. caust. cham. chin. cocc. cupr. ferr. jod. merc. natr-m. n-mosch. op. plat. phosph. rhod. sabin. staph. stram. val. veratr. zinc.*

h) Suppression of *catarrh* or some other blennorrhœa: 1) *Acon. ars. bell. bry. calc. chin. cin. n-vom. puls. sulph.* 2) *Amb. amm. carb-veg. con. dulc. graph. ipec. kal. lyc. natr-m. nitr-ac. n-mosch. phosph. rhod. samb. sulph.*

i) Suppression of *sweat:* 1) *Bell. bry. cham. chin. dulc. lach. sil. sulph.* 2) *Acon. ars. calc. graph. lyc. merc. n-mosch. n-vom. op. phosph. puls. rhus. sep.*

k) Suppression of *foot-sweat:* 1) *Cupr. nitr-ac. puls. sep. sil.* 2) *Cham. merc. natr. rhus.*

§ 3. Compare: ERUPTIONS, PILES, NURSING, CONFINEMENT, AMENIA, CATARRH, COLD, &c.

SEXUAL INSTINCT, MORBID CONDITIONS OF THE.

§ 1. The remedies which affect the sexual functions principally, are: 1) *Canth. caust. chin. con. lyc. merc. natr. natr-m. nitr-ac. n-vom. phosph. plat. puls. selen. staph. thuj. veratr.* 2) *Arn. ars. bell. calc. cann. carb-veg. clem. coff. graph. hep. hyos. kal. lach. magn-arct. magn-c. mosch. mur-ac. n-mosch. op. phos-ac. plumb. rhus. ruta. sabin. sep. sil. stram. sulph. zinc.*

§ 2. For the *male* sex: 1) *Arn. cann. canth. merc. nitr-ac. natr. natr-m. n-vom. phosph. phos-ac. puls. sulph. thuj.* 2) *Agn. amb. ars. carb-veg. caust. chin. clem. graph. hep. ign. kal. lyc. petr. rhus. sep. staph.*

For the *female:* 1) *Amb. bell. con. croc. ferr. graph. hyos. ign. kreos. mosch. n-mosch. n-vom. plat. puls. sabin. sec. sep. sulph. thuj.* 2) *Acon. alum. asa. aur. calc. carb-veg. cham. chin. coccul. kal. lyc. magn-m. natr-m. nitr-ac. rhus. staph.*

§ 3. For *excessive* sexual excitement: 1) *Canth. chin. magn-arct. n-vom. phosph. plat. puls. veratr.* 2) *Ant. aur. calc. cann. graph. hyos. ign. lach. lyc. merc. mosch. natr. natr-m. op. sabin. sil. stram.*

Satyriasis: 1) *Canth. merc. natr-m. n-vom. sulph.* 2) *Hyos. phosph. stram. veratr.*

Nymphomania: 1) *Hyos. phosph. stram. veratr.* 2) *Bell. canth. merc. natr-m. n-vom. puls. sulph.*

Erections from physical excitement, even *priapism:* 1) *Canth. coloc. graph. natr. natr-m. nitr-ac. n-vom. phosph. plat. puls. rhus. sil.* 2) *Cann. ign. kal. magn-arct. op. phos-ac. plat. staph. thuj.*

§ 4. Disposition to *onanism:* 1) *Calc. n-vom. sulph.;* or, 2) *Chin. coccul. merc. natr-m. phosph.;* or, 3) *Ant. carb-veg. plat. puls.*

For the consequences of this vice, give: *Chin. n-vom. phos-ac.* or *staph.*, especially when they seem to be of an acute nature, and resulting from excessive rather than long-continued abuse.

Slow, chronic ailments, require: *Calc. n-vom. sulph.*, at long intervals. Some cases require: 1) *Cocc. merc. phosph.;* or, 2) *Ant. carb-veg. plat. puls.*

§ 5. For excessive *nocturnal emissions,* give: 1) *Chin. phos-ac.*

selen. sulph. 2) *Carb-veg. caust. con. kal. lyc. nitr-ac. n-vom. petr. phosph. puls. sep.* 3) *Bell. calc. graph. merc. stann.*—If caused by *onanism* or sexual abuse, give: 1) *Chin phos-ac. sulph.* 2) *N-vom. phosph. puls. sep.*

For discharge of *prostatic juice*, give: 1) *Calc. hep. phos-ac. sep. sil. sulph.* 2) *Agn. anac. natr. nitr-ac. puls. selen. staph. thuj.*

SEXUAL POWER, DEBILITY OF.

§ 1. Principal remedies: 1) *Agn. baryt. calad. calc. cann. con. graph. ign. lyc. mosch. mur-ac. natr-m. selen. sulph.* 2) *Ant. camph. caust. chin. kal. nitr-ac. n-mosch. phosph. sep.*

§ 2. *Impotency* of males: 1) *Baryt. calad. calc. can. con. lyc. mosch. mur-ac. natr-m. selen. sulph.* 2) *Agn. ant. camph. caust. chin. graph. hyos. lach. magn-aust. n-mosch. petr. sep.*

§ 3. *Sterility:* 1) *Borax. calc. cann. merc. phosph.* 2) *Amm. caust. con. graph. natr-m. sulph. sulph-ac.;* or: 3) *Agn. cic. croc. dulc. ferr. hyos. merc. natr. plat. ruta.*

Compare: MENSTRUAL DIFFICULTIES, and MISCARRIAGE.

§ 4. If an embrace causes *unpleasant feelings:* 1) *Agar. calc. kal. sep.* 2) *Alum. bov. carb-veg. chin. graph. merc. natr. n-vom. phos-ac. puls. selen. staph.*

§ 5. Compare: DEBILITY, LASSITUDE; and, under CAUSES: EXCESSES, ONANISM, &c.

SKIN, COLOUR OF, ULCERATIONS OF THE, see: CYANOSIS, CHLOROSIS, JAUNDICE, MACULÆ, ERYSIPELAS, &c.

SKIN, SORE, UNHEALTHY.—The principal remedies for a disposition of the skin to ulcerate when the least wound is inflicted upon it, are: 1) *Cham. hep. lach. petr. sil. sulph.* 2) *Alum. baryt. borax. calc. graph. lyc. mang. nitr-ac. staph.*

SKULL, DISEASES OF THE BONES OF THE.

§ 1. The principal remedies for *exostoses* are: *Aur. daph. merc. mez. phosph. phos-ac.*

Mercurial exostoses require: *Aur. daph. phosph. phos-ac.*—*Mez.*

Syphilitic: Aur. merc. mez.

§ 2. Large head of scrophulous children, with retarded closing of the fontanelles, require: *Calc. puls. sil.*

§ 3. See: BONES, DISEASES OF.

SLEEP, MORBID.

§ 1. Principal remedies for this state, though generally a mere symptom: 1) *Ars. bry. calc. cham. chin. coff. hep. kal. merc. phos. puls. rhus. sep. sil. sulph.* 2) *Acon. bell. borax. carb-v. caust. con. graph. hyos. ign. kreos. lach. lyc. magn-c. magn-m. natr. natr-m. nitr-ac. n-vom. op. thuj.* 3) *Amb. amm. amm-m. aur. baryt. camph. cann. carb-an. cocc. dulc. ipec. led. magn-arct. mosch. phos-ac. plat. rhod. sabin. samb. sassap. spong. staph. sulph-ac. veratr.*

§ 2. Use more particularly for:

a) *Anxious* sleep: 1) *Cocc. dulc. graph. lyc. magn-c. natr-m. phos. spong. veratr.* 2) *Acon. ars. bell. ferr. hep. kal. petr. rhus.*

b) *Stupefied* sleep: 1) *Bell. bry. camph. cham. con. croc. graph. hep. led. n-mosch. op. phos. puls. sec.* 2) *Calc. carb-v. cic. hyos. ign. lach. magn-arct. magn-c. nitr. n-vom. plat. spig. sulph. tart. veratr.*

c) *Deep*, heavy: 1) *Bell. ign. n-mosch. op. stram. tart.* 2) *Alum. ant. ars. con. croc. cupr. hyos. led. magn-arct. phos. phos-ac. puls. sec. sep. veratr.*

d) *Light*, like *slumber:* 1) *Ars. cham. graph. ign. n-vom. op. petr. sulph.* 2) *Calc. coff. kal. lach. lyc. nitr. puls. sil. veratr.*

e) *Comatose:* 1) *Bell. bry. camph. croc. hell. n-mosch. op. sec. stram. tart. veratr.* 2) *Arn. caps. carb-v. coloc. con. hyos. lach. led. magn-arct. mosch. phos. phos-ac. puls. rhus. samb.*

f) *Short*, with early waking: 1) *Ars. caust. dulc. kal. merc. natr. nitr-ac. n-vom. sep. sil.* 2) *Aur. borax. bry. calc. chin. coff. croc. graph. lyc. magn-arct. mur-ac. sulph-ac.*

g) *Too long*, waking late: 1) *Calc. caust. graph. magn-m. n-vom. phos. sep. sulph.* 2) *Alum. ant. con. hep. kal. lach. magn-arct. merc. natr. natr-m. phos-ac. puls. sec. sil. stann.*

h) *Raving*, with many fancies: 1) *Acon. calc. carb-v. graph. kal. lyc. natr. natr-m. n-vom. petr. puls. sil. sulph. zinc.* 2) *Carb-an. chin. con. hell. ign. nitr. nitr-ac. op. sep.*

i) With many *dreams:* 1) *Alum. bell. bry. calc. chin. con. kal. kreos. lyc. magn-c. nitr-ac. n-vom. phos. phos-ac. puls. sil. sulph.* 2) *Amm. amm-m. arn. bry. camph. carb-v. cham. coloc. ferr. graph hep. ign. magn-arct. magn-m. merc. mez. natr. natr-m. rhus. sep. spong. staph.*

k) Not *refreshing:* 1) *Alum. bry. chin. con. graph. hep. kreos. lyc. op. phosph. sep. sulph.* 2) *Amb. baryt. bell. calc. cann. caps. carb-an. carb-v. caust. cic. ign. lach. magn-m. natr-m. nitr-ac. petr. sabad. sil. squill. staph. thuj.*

l) *Restless, tossing about:* 1) *Amb. ars. baryt. calc. chin. kal. lyc. phos. rhus. sabad. sabin. sil. sulph.* 2) *Amm-m. aur. bell. bry. cham. coff. colch. coloc. dig. dulc. ferr. graph. hep. hyos. ign. ipec. led. magn-c. merc. mur-ac. natr. natr-m. nitr. nitr-ac. n-vom. petr. phos-ac. puls. samb. sassap. sec. seneg. spig. squill. staph. stram. tart. thuj.*

m) *Interrupted* by frequent waking: 1) *Bell. calc. graph. hep. kal. lach. lyc. merc. nitr-ac. n-vom. phos. puls. sep. sulph.* 2) *Amb. ars. carb-an. carb-v. caust. chin. ign. magn-arct. oleand. rhus. sil. staph.*

§ 3. When the patient *stretches his arms above his head* during sleep: *Chin. nitr-ac. n-vom. plat. puls. rhab. sulph. veratr.*—When laying them *under his head: Acon. cocc. magn-aust. phos. phos-ac. plat. tart.*—When on his *belly: Magn. plat. puls.*

b) When drawing up his *legs: Carb-v. plat. puls. stram.*—When *opening* them: *Cham. magn. puls.*—When *stretching* them: *Plat. stann.*—When *bending the knees: Amb. magn. viol-od.*

c) When *bending the head forwards: Acon. phos. puls.*—When *sideways: Cin. spong.*—When bending it *backwards: Bell. chin. hell. hep. n-vom. rhab.*

d) When lying on his *back* generally: 1) *Bry. n-vom. puls. rhus.* 2) *Acon. ant. aur. calc. chin. cic. coloc. dig. dros. ferr. ign. lyc. magn-arct. plat. sulph.*

e) When he is unable to lie on the *left* side: *Kal. lyc. natr. phos. sil.*—Not on the *right: Aur. merc. puls.*—Not on the *back: Acon. alum. baryt. caust. colch. merc. natr. magn-m. n-vom. phos. spig. sulph.*—When he is only able to sit in bed: *Acon. ars. chin. cin. hep. lyc. magn-aust. phos. puls. rhus. sabin. spig. sulph. tart.*

§ 4. a) For *frightful dreams*, causing anxiety: 1) *Acon. arn. bell. calc. caust. chin. graph. kal. lyc. magn-c. n-vom. phos. puls. rhus. sil. sulph.* 2) *Anac. ars. aur. bry. carb-v. hep. ign. kreos. magn-m. merc. natr-m. nitr-ac. rhus. sep. stram. sulph-ac. thuj. veratr. zinc.*

b) For *vexatious* dreams: *Bry. caust. cham. chin. magn-arct. magn-c. natr. natr-m. nitr-ac. n-vom. phos. rhab. sep.*

c) *Agreeable, merry* dreams: *Alum. ars. aur. caust. magn-c. magn-m. merc. natr. nitr-ac. n-vom. op. phos. phos-ac. plat. puls. sep. staph. sulph.*

d) *Disgusting* dreams about dirt, vermin, diseases, pus, &c.: 1) *Mur-ac. n-vom. phos.* 2) *Amm. anac. kreos. magn-m. natr-m. puls. sulph. zinc.*

e) Dreams with *fixed* ideas, dreaming about one and the same object: *Acon. ign. puls. stann.*

f) Dreams which *continue* after waking: 1) *Chin. graph.*

phos. sil. sulph. 2) *Amm. bry. calc. caust. ign. lach. led. natr-m. nitr-ac.*

g) *Lascivious*, amorous dreams: 1) *Graph. lach. natr. natr-m. n-vom. op. sil. staph.* 2) *Ant. canth. chin. coloc. con. ign. kal. lyc. merc. nitr-ac. oleand. phos. phos-ac. puls. sep. spig. stann. thuj.*

h) Dreams which *fatigue* the head, about scientific things, &c. 1) *Bry. graph. ign. lach. magn-arct. magn-aust. n-vom. phos. puls.* 2) *Acon. alum. anac. arn. aur. bell. calc. carb-an. carb-v. cham. chin. natr-m. op. phos-ac. sabin. stann. sulph. zinc.*

i) *Vivid* dreams: 1) *Anac. calc. cocc. lyc. natr. natr-m. petr. phos. puls. rhus. sil. stann. sulph.* 2) *Acon. agar. arn. bell. bry. carb-an. carb-v. cham. cic. coff. con. dros. graph. laur. lyc. magn-arct. merc. mur-ac. n-vom. phos-ac. spig. staph. stram.*

k) *Fanciful* dreams: 1) *Calc. graph. kal. lyc. natr. natr-m. n-vom. op. petr. sep. sil. sulph.* 2) *Acon. baryt. carb-an. carb-v. cham. chin. con. hell. ign. nitr. nitr-ac. puls. spong. zinc.*

l) Dreams about the common *affairs of the day*, and other indifferent things: 1) *Bry. graph. lach. puls. rhus. sil.* 2) *Anac. bell. cic. cin. croc. kal. lyc. magn-c. merc. natr-m. n-vom. phos-ac. sassap. staph. sulph.*

m) *Confused* dreams: 1) *Chin. cic. croc. lyc. natr. puls. stann. val.* 2) *Acon. alum. baryt. bry. cann. caust. hell. magn-aust. mang. phos. sil.*

n) Dreams in a waking state: *Acon. arn. bry. cham. hep. ign. magn-arct. merc. n-vom. op. petr. rhab. sep. sil. stram. sulph.*

§ 5. Dreams about thieves and robbers: 1) *Magn-c. merc. natr. sil.* 2) *Alum. aur. bell. magn-m. petr. phos. veratr. zinc.* —About *ghosts, demons*, &c.: *Alum. carb-v. ign. kal. lach. magn-c. natr. op. sassap. sep. spig. sil. sulph.*—About defunct persons, burials, &c.: 1) *Anac. ars. calc. kal. magn-c. phosph. phos-ac. thuj.* 2) *Amm. arn. aur. bry. caust. con. graph. magn-m. nitr-ac. n-vom. op. phos-ac. plat. sulph-ac.*

b) Dreams about misfortunes, adverse circumstances, chagrin, danger, &c.: *Anac. arn. ars. chin. graph. jod. kreos. lyc. n-vom. phos. puls.*—About diseases: *Amm. anac. borax. calc. con. kal. natr. n-vom. sil.*—About quarrels, disputes: *Alum. arn. baryt. bry. calc. caust. cham. hep. kal. magn-c. merc. n-vom. phos. phos-ac. puls. stann. staph.*—About war, bloodshed: *Amm-m. ferr. hep. merc. plat. spong. thuj. verb.*—About *murder*: *Amm-m. calc. carb-an. guaj. ign. kal. natr-m. phos. petr. sil. staph.*

c) About *animals*, dogs, cats, &c.: 1) *Arn. puls.* 2) *Amm. amm-m. bell. calc. hyos. lyc. merc. n-vom. sil. sulph. sulph-ac.*—About serpents: *Alum. kal. sil.*—About *vermin*, &c.: *Amm. ars. calc. hell. mur-ac. n-vom. phos.*

d) About water and danger of water: *Alum. amm-m. ars. dig. graph. ign. kal. magn-c. magn-m. merc. natr. sil.*—Fire and danger of fire: *Alum. anac. ars. calc. hep. kreos. magn-c. magn-m. natr. natr-m. phos. rhod. rhus. spig. spong. sulph.*

§ 6. When the patient moans a good deal during sleep: 1) *Caust. cham. chin. cin. ign. lach. lyc. nitr-ac. n-vom. rhab.* 2) *Arn. ars. aur. bry. hyos. ipec. magn-c. merc. mur-ac. natr-m. op. phos. phos-ac. rhab. sulph. veratr.*

b) When he starts a good deal: 1) *Ars. bell. cham. graph. hyos. kal. lach. lyc. merc. nitr-ac. n-vom. op. petr. puls. samb. sec. sil. sulph.* 2) *Arn. bry. calc. carb-an. caust. chin. cupr. dros. hep. ign. magn-arct. magn-c. natr. natr-m. phos. rhus. sep. veratr. zinc.*

c) For *screams* during sleep: 1) *Bell. bry. cham. hep. puls. rhab. rhus. sil. sulph. zinc.* 2) *Arn. aur. borax. calc. caps. carb-an. caust. cocc. croc. graph. hep. lyc. magn-c. magn-m. natr. sep. staph. tart.*

d) *Talking* during sleep: 1) *Ars. baryt. calc. cham. ign. n-vom. puls. sil. sulph. zinc.* 2) *Arn. calc. graph. kal. lyc. magn-c. merc. natr-m. phos. phos-ac. plumb. rhab. rhus. sabin. sep. spong. stann. tart. thuj.*

e) *Weeping* during sleep: 1) *Cham. ign. kal. natr-m. nitr-ac. n-vom. puls.* 2) *Calc. carb-an. caust. kal. lyc. magn-arct. magn-c. phos. puls. sil.*

§ 7. When the patient *snorts* a good deal during sleep: 1) *Bell. camph. carb-v. op. rhus. sil. stram.* 2) *Calc. caps. cham. chin. dros. dulc. hyos. ign. mur-ac. nitr-ac. puls. rhab. sulph.*

b) When the eyes are only half-closed or entirely open: *Bell. caps. chin. coloc. hell. ign. ipec. op. phos-ac. samb. stram. sulph.*

c) Sleeping with the mouth open: *Cham. dulc. ign. magn-arct. magn-aust. merc. op. rhus. samb.*—For *chewing* and *swallowing* during sleep: *Bry. calc. ign.*

d) For distorting one's features, quivering of the lips, distortion of the eyes, and other convulsive motions during sleep: *Bell. bry. cham. chin. cocc. hell. hyos. ign. ipec. op. phos-ac. puls. rhab. rhus. samb. veratr.*

§ 8. Compare: Sleeplessness and Sopor.

SLEEPLESSNESS, Insomnia.

§ 1. Generally a mere symptom, though in some cases the principal complaint of the patient, arising from an excess of irritation or stimulation. The principal remedies for sleeplessness generally are:

§ 2. 1) *Acon. ars. bell. bry. calc. carb-v. chin. coff. con. graph. hep. hyos. ign. kal. lach. lyc. merc. natr. natr-m. n-vom. phos. puls. sep. sil. sulph.* 2) *Alum. anac. camph. caust. cin. cocc. ipec. led. magn-arct. magn-c. magn-m. mosch. nitr-ac. op. phos-ac. plat. rhus. staph. sulph-ac. thuj. veratr.*

§ 3. If sleeplessness be the only or principal symptom, give: *Acon. bell. coff. hyos. ign. mosch. n-vom. op. puls.*

Particular indications:

Aconite: For sleeplessness caused by anxiety or alarming events, by fear, fright, &c.

Belladonna: The patient is sleepy, but is unable to sleep; with great anguish, restlessness, frightful visions, dread of things which are near him, &c., or when the patient is really sleepy in the morning or evening, but no sleep follows.

Coffea: Sleeplessness caused by *joy*, or an agreeable surprise; or suitable for the sleeplessness of children, or for sleeplessness caused by long watching; also suitable to persons that have indulged in excessive use of coffee.

Hyoscyamus: Sleeplessness from nervous excitement, especially after violent diseases, or suitable to irritable and easily excited individuals.

Ignatia: Sleeplessness caused by grief, care, sadness, anxious thoughts and depressing emotions.

Moschus: Sleeplessness from nervous excitement, without any other ailment; suitable to hysteric or hypochondriac individuals.

Nux vom.: Sleeplessness caused by excessive thinking, reading, &c., until late at night, or when caused by abuse of coffee, or when all sorts of ideas crowd upon the person's mind.

Opium: Sleeplessness after emotions, such as *fear, fright,* &c.; or when the patient is troubled with visions of ghosts, strange figures, &c., or suitable to old people.

Pulsatilla: Suitable to individuals that have eaten too much at supper; or when the sleeplessness is attended with orgasmus sanguinis, congestion of blood to the head; heat causing anxiety, &c.

§ 4. For the sleeplessness of children, with cries, colicky pains, restless tossing about, &c., the best remedies are: 1) *Acon. bell. cham. coff. jalap. rhab.*; or, 2) *Borax. cin. ipec. senn.*

Aconitum and Coffea: For great restlessness and feverish heat.

Belladonna: The child cries for days and hours, without any perceptible cause.

Chamomilla: Deserves a preference when the child complains of sleeplessness, with headache and otalgia.

Jalappa: Suitable for colic and diarrhœa.

RHUBARB: Suitable for frequent urging to stool, with tenesmus and colic.

§ 5. Use moreover:

a) For sleeplessness caused by pains which set in in the evening or at night: 1) *Ars. bry. calc. carb-an. carb-v. chin. hep. lyc. n-vom. phos. puls. rhus. sep. sulph.* 2) *Arn. bell. caust. cocc. graph. kal. merc. phos-ac. thuj.*

b) If caused by *nervousness*, mental excitement: 1) *Calc. chin. coff. hep. lach. lyc. mosch. n-vom. plat. puls. sep.* 2) *Borax. bry. caust. cocc. con. graph. hyos. kal. magn-arct. phos-ac. rhus. sil. spong. staph. sulph.*

c) If caused by nightly restlessness, agitation of the blood, heat, &c.: 1) *Acon. bell. bry. calc. carb-v. cin. graph. kal. lach. lyc. merc. n-vom. phos. puls. rhab. senn. sep. sil.* 2) *Alum. amb. ars. aur. carb-an. caust. chin. con. magn-c. magn-m. natr-m. nitr-ac. op. rus. sec. thuj.*

d) If caused by *pains:* 1) *Acon. alum. aur. bell. cham. chin. coff. hep. lach. lyc. magn-c. merc. nitr-ac. puls. sil. sulph.* 2) *Amm. ars. calc. carb-v. magn-m. mur-ac. natr-m. phos. rhus. sep.*

e) If by *cold feet: Amm-m. bry. carb-v. kal. nitr-ac. petr. phos. sulph. zinc.*

§ 6. a) If the sleeplessness occur principally *before midnight:* 1) *Alum. ars. bry. calc. carb-v. chin. con. graph. lach. lyc. merc. natr. natr-m. n-vom. phos. puls. rhus. sep. sil. sulph.* 2) *Anac. arn. bell. borax. carb-an. caust. hep. ign. kal. led. magn-c. magn-m. mur-ac. natr. natr-m. nitr-ac. op. phos-ac. plat. sassap. spig. staph. sulph-ac. thuj.*

b) If the patient wake soon after midnight, and be unable to go to sleep again: 1) *Ars. caps. coff. hep. nitr-ac. n-vom. sil.* 2) *Aur. bry. cann. caust. dulc. graph. lach. magn-c. natr. phos-ac. sep. sulph-ac.*

c) Remaining awake for hours at night, and not being able to go to sleep again: 1) *Natr-m. phos. sep. sil. sulph.* 2) *Ars. aur. bell. calc. caust. dulc. graph. magn-c. merc. mur-ac. natr. n-vom. puls. sassap. sulph-ac.*

d) Sleeplessness the *whole night:* 1) *Ars. chin. cin. coff. con. hyos. magn-c. mosch. n-vom. op. rhus. sil. sulph.* 2) *Amm. aur. bell. camph. carb-v. cham. clem. coloc. dulc. graph. hep. kreos. merc. natr-m. nitr-ac. op. phos. sec. sep. spig. squill. spong. staph. sulph-ac. thuj.*

e) Great *drowsiness,* but no *sleep:* 1) *Bell. cham. lach. op. phos. puls. sep.* 2) *Ars. bry. calc. carb-v. caust. chin. clem. cocc. con. hep. kal. magn-aust. merc. natr. natr-m. n-vom, phos-ac. samb. sulph, thuj.*

§ 7. For further particulars, see: "SYMPTOMEN-CODEX."

SMELL, BAD, OF THE MOUTH.

§ 1. Though only a symptom, yet it is of great importance in the selection of a remedy, and generally points to: 1) *Arn. ars. aur. carb-veg. merc. puls. sep. sulph.* 2) *Bell. bry. cham. chin. dulc. hyos. nitr-ac. n-vom. petr. rhus. sil. stann.* 3) *Acon. amb. anac. carb-an. coff. graph. ipec. spig.*

§ 2. If affecting *young girls* at the age of pubescence, *Aurum* is generally suitable; or: *Bell. hyos. puls. sep.*

If perceived only *in the morning*, try: *Arn. bell. n-vom. sil. sulph.*

If *after a meal: Cham. n-vom. sulph.*

If in the *evening* and at *night*: *Puls.* or *Sulph.*

If caused by *abuse* of *Mercury: Aur. carb-veg. lach. sulph.*; or: *Arn. bell. hep.*

SMELL, EXCESSIVE SENSITIVENESS and ILLUSIONS of.—Principal remedies: 1) *Aur. bell. calc. graph. lyc. magn-arct. n-vom. phosph. sep. sulph.* 2) *Acon. cham. chin. coff. hep. puls.*

For great *sensitiveness*, give: 1) *Aur. bell. con. graph. hep. lyc. phosph. phos-ac. plumb. sil. sulph.* 2) *Acon. baryt. cham. coff. con. kal. n-vom. sep.*

For *illusions of smell*, such as of *bad eggs, putrid substances, decayed cheese, manure*, or generally for *bad* and *fetid* smell, give: *Aur. bell. calc. magn-arct. men. merc. nitr-ac. n-vom. phosph. veratr.*—For smell as of *chalk* or *clay*: *Calc. magn-arct.*—As of *herrings: Agn. bell.*—As of *pitch* or *tar: Ars. con.*—As of *sour* things: *Alum.*—As of *old coryza: Graph. ars. sulph.*—As of *sweetish* things: *Aur.*—As of *Sulphur*, or *burning sponge*, or *gunpowder: Anac. ars. calc. graph. n-vom.*—As of *burnt* or *burning* substances: *Anac. aur. graph. n-vom. sulph.*

SOFTENING OF THE STOMACH, GASTROMALACIA.—We may try: 1) *Calc.* 2) *Ant. ars. baryt. carb-veg. n-vom. puls. sulph.*, &c.*

SOPOR, SOMNOLENCE, CATAPHORA, COMA, COMA VIGIL, LETHARGY, &c.

§ 1. These various states being all characterized by a disposition to sleep between the regular hours of sleep, we will comprehend them under the same head, and first indicate the general remedies for this condition. They are: 1) *Ant. bell. bry. calc.*

* Also *Kreasotum.—Hempel.*

carb-veg. con. croc. lach. n-vom. op. phosph. phos-ac. puls. rhus. sep. sulph. tart. 2) *Acon. anac. arn. ars. camph. carb-an. caust. chin. cin. coloc. graph. hell. hep. kal. laur. magn-arct. merc. mosch. natr. natr-m. sabad. samb. sec. sil. stram. veratr.* 3) *Amm. amm-m. cann. dig. ferr. magn-c. magn-m. merc. nitr-ac. petr.*

§ 2. Give: a) for common *drowsiness* in the day-time: 1) *Bell. calc. carb-veg. chin. con. graph. hep. kal. lach. merc. natr. natr-m. n-vom. phosph. sulph.* 2) *Amm. amm-m. anac. bry. cann. caust. cham. cin. dig. ferr. magn-c. magn-m. nitr-ac. puls. sabad. sep. sil. stram. zinc.*

b) For drowsiness *after rising* in the morning, or in the *forenoon:* 1) *Ant. calc. carb-veg. graph. hep. natr. natr-m. n-vom. phosph. phos-ac. sep. sulph.* 2) *Caust. con. magn-arct. magn-m. merc. puls. rhus. sil. spig. sulph-ac. tart. zinc.*

c) Drowsiness after *dinner*, or in the *afternoon:* 1) *Chin. graph. lach. n-vom. phosph. rhus. sulph.* 2) *Acon. agar. amm. anac. baryt. carb-veg. chin. croc. kal. natr. natr-m. n-mosch. phos-ac. puls. ruta. sil. staph.*

d) *Early in the evening:* 1) *Ars. bell. calc. con. croc. kal. lach. n-vom. phos-ac. puls. sil. sulph.* 2) *Amm-m. anac. arn. cin. cycl. natr. nitr-ac. phosph. rhus. ruta. sep. thuj.*

e) For *excessive sleepiness*, drunk with sleep: *Bell. bry. camph. carb-veg. coff. con. croc. magn-arct. n-mosch. op. phosph. phos-ac. puls. tart.*

§ 3. a) *Sopor*, or constant somnolence, generally requires: 1) *Bell. croc. lach. n-mosch. n-vom. op. puls. tart. veratr.* 2) *Ant. arn. ars. baryt. bry. camph. cham. cocc. con. croc. cupr. hell. hep. hyos. laur. led. magn-arct. merc. phosph. phos-ac. plumb. rhus. samb. sec. sep. stram.*

b) *Coma somnolentum, cataphora, carus:* 1) *Bell. led. n-mosch. op. n-mosch.* 2) *Ant. baryt. camph. carb-veg. cham. con. croc. hep. laur. magn-arct. n-vom. phosph. phos-ac. plumb. puls. sec. stram. tart. veratr.*

c) *Coma vigil, agrypnocoma, typhomania:* 1) *Ars. bell. cham cocc. hep. hyos. lach. n-vom. op.* 2) *Acon. anac. ant. bry. ign laur. magn-arct. phosph. spong. sulph. veratr.*

d) *Lethargy, lethargus, veternus*, with fever and delirium: 1) *Bell. lach. op. stram.* 2) *Ant. bry. cham. carb-veg. merc. plumb. puls. tart.*

§ 4. Particular indications:

Aconite: Stupid drowsiness, hot head, dilated pupils, cold hands and feet, feeble, quick pulse, or feeble and slow (*Hempel*).

Baryta: Stupid sleep, with restlessness, moaning and muttering, insensible pupils, feeble and quick pulse.

Belladonna: Deep or long sleep, with immobility, subsultus tendinum, pale and cold face, cold hands, small and quick pulse, moaning, convulsive motions and twitchings of the limbs, &c., hunger, furious look on waking; burning heat and dryness of the mouth after the paroxysm. (Suitable before or after *Lach.* or after *Op.*)

Chamomilla: Suitable to children, for great restlessness, tossing about; sudden starting from sleep; jactitation of the limbs; shortness of breath, feverish heat and redness, at times on one, at times on the other cheek; screams, colic, greenish diarrhœa, &c.

Lachesis: Long sleep, or alternation of sopor and sleeplessness; or: deep sleep, with grinding of teeth, tremulous and intermitting or completely suppressed pulse.

Nux vom.: Deep sleep, with sudden starting, sighing, loud snoring, bleareyed, dimness of sight, depression of the lower jaw, ptyalism, &c.

Opium: Deep sleep, with open and distorted eyes; red and bloated face, depression of the lower jaw, loss of consciousness; heavy, slow and intermitting breathing; slow or completely suppressed pulse; convulsive motions of all the extremities, facial muscles and corners of the mouth, &c.

Pulsatilla: Constant drowsiness, loss of consciousness, delirium, heat and restlessness, tossing about, involuntary motions of the mouth, hands and fingers, &c. (Suitable after *Cham.* or *Tart.*)

Compare: Sleep, Apoplexy, Typhus, Meningitis, &c.

SORE SKIN, Intertrigo.

Principal remedies: 1) *Cham. chin. graph. ign. lyc. puls. sep. sulph.* 2) *Acon. arn. bell. calc. carb-v. caust. hep. mang. merc. oleand. petr. phos. phos-ac. ruta. sulph-ac.*

Soreness of *full-grown* persons in the summer season, is frequently cured by: *Arn. carb-v. n-vom. lyc. sulph.*

Bedsores require: *Arn. carb-v. chin. plumb. sulph-ac.*

Soreness of the *nipples:* 1) *Arn. sulph.;* or, 2) *Calc. caust. cham. graph. lyc. n-vom. sep.*

Soreness of *children:* 1) *Acon. cham. lyc. sulph.;* or, 2) *Chin. graph. ign. merc. puls. ruta. sep.*—If *chammomile-tea* had previously been used in quantities, give *Ign.* or *Puls.*

SORE THROAT, Angina faucium.

§ 1. Principal remedies: 1) *Acon. bell. cham. lach. merc. n-vom. puls.* 2) *Baryt. bry. caps. chin. cic. coccul. coff. dulc. ign. rhus. sabad. sep. sulph. veratr.* 3) *Alum. amm. ars. calc. canth.*

carb-v. gran.? kreos.? lyc. mang. nitr-ac. n-mosch. seneg. staph. thuj.

§ 2. Common sore throat without fever, as occurs frequently after a cold, generally yields to: 1) *Bell. merc.* 2) *Cham. n-vom. puls. sulph.*

Acute angina requires: 1) *Aconite,* when there is fever; after which may be given: 2) *Bell. bry. cham. coff. ign. merc. n-vom. puls. rhus.*; or, 3) *Ars. baryt. canth. caps. chin. dulc. hep. lach. mang. staph.*

Chronic or habitual angina requires: 1) *Alum. baryt. calc. carb-v. hep. lach. lyc. sep. sulph.* 2) *Bell. chin. mang. natr-m. nitr-ac. n-vom. sabad. seneg. staph. thuj.*

§ 3. As regards varieties, give for *simple catarrhal* or *rheumatic* angina: 1) *Bell. cham. merc. n-vom. puls. sulph.* 2) *Acon. carb-v. caps. dulc. hep. rhus. seneg.*

Phlegmonous angina, with inflammation and swelling of the affected parts, requires: 1) *Acon. bell. hep. ign. merc. n-vom. sulph.*; or, 2) *Alum. baryt. calc. canth. coff. lach. sep. thuj.*

For *polypus* or *membranous* inflammation of the fauces, prescribe: *Alum. bell. chin. hep. merc. puls. spong.*; and *Acon.* when there is fever.

For *croup,* (see: CROUP.)

Gangrenous angina indicates: 1) *Amm. ars. lach.*; or, 2) *Con. euphorb. kreos. merc. sulph.*

§ 4. As regards *external causes,* give:

a) For angina after *acute* exanthemata, such as, *scarlatina, measles, variola,* &c.: *Ars. bar-c. bell. carb-v. ign. merc. puls.*

b) After *abuse of Mercury*: *Arg. bell. carb-v. hep. lach. lyc. staph. sulph.*

c) After a *cold*: *Bar-c. bell. bry. cham. coff. dulc. ign. lach. merc. n-vom. puls. sulph.*

d) In consequence of *syphilis*: 1) *Merc. nitr-ac. thuj.*; or, 2) *Carb-v. lach. phos.*

e) In consequence of *wounds* or *injuries* by foreign bodies, splinters, &c., which have got into the throat: 1) *Acon. bell. cham. cic. ign.* or *merc.*; or, 2) *Carb-v. con. nitr-ac. puls. sulph-ac.*

§ 5. Symptomatic indications:

BELLADONNA: For almost every kind of angina, especially when the following symptoms are present: *Sore pains, scraping,* sensation of thickness, burning or stinging in the throat, especially during deglutition; pains which extend into the ears; *contraction* and *spasmodic constriction of the fauces,* with constant desire to swallow, or else difficult, almost impossible deglutition; absence of thirst or else violent thirst, with aversion to drink, or with inability to drink, because the liquid returns by the nostrils; vivid, frequently yellowish redness of the affected parts, without swelling; or swelling and inflammatory redness of the velum palati, uvula or tonsils, even with suppuration; rapidly spreading ulcers; profuse accumulation of viscid, whitish mucus in the throat, mouth, and on the tongue; ptyalism; swelling of the muscles and cervical glands; violent fever, with hot, red and bloated face; violent aching pain in the forehead; whining mood and obstinacy. (Compare *Mercury*, which is sometimes indicated before and after *Bell.*)

CHAMOMILLA: Suitable to children, or when the disease is occasioned by suppression or interruption of the cutaneous action; or for: swelling of the parotid or submaxillary glands, or tonsils; stitching, burning pains, or sensation as if a foreign body were sticking in the throat; dark redness of the affected parts; inability to swallow solids, especially when lying; thirst, with dry mouth and throat; *tickling in the larynx*, with cough; roughness, hoarse voice; fever towards evening, with alternation of heat and chilliness; *red* cheeks, or only *one* cheek red; great restlessness, tossing about, crying, moaning.

LACHESIS: *Bell.* and *Merc.* being insufficient, for: sore pain, burning and dry throat, at one spot or all over as far as the ears, larynx, tongue, nose, gums, with suffocative breathing, ptyalism, &c.; swelling, redness and swelling of the tonsils and velum; constant desire to swallow, with spasms in the throat, or with sensation as if a lump were sticking in the throat; aversion to drink, the liquid frequently returning by the nose; aggravation in the afternoon, morning, or after sleeping, also by contact; relief by eating.

MERCURIUS: Frequently in alternation with *Bell.*, for: violent stitches in the throat and tonsils, especially when swallowing, the stitches extending to the parotid glands, ears and submaxillary glands; burning in the throat, with soreness; swelling, and intense inflammatory redness of the affected parts; elongation of the uvula; constant desire to swallow, with sensation as of a lump in the throat that ought to be swallowed down; *difficult deglutition*, especially as regards drinks, which frequently return by the nostrils; bad taste in the mouth; *ptyalism;* swelling of the gums and tongue; suppuration of the tonsils, or slowly spreading ulcers in the throat; aggravation *at night*, or in the evening, or in *the open air* and when talking; *chill towards evening*, or alternation of chilliness and heat; sweat, without relief; rheumatic, tearing or drawing pains in the head and nape of the neck.

Nux vom.: Frequently after *Cham.*, or suitable to thin, bilious and choleric individuals, or persons of a sanguine temperament, especially for: scraping and sore pain in the throat, particularly when swallowing or taking an inspiration; *pain during empty deglutition*, as if the pharynx were contracted, or as if a plug were sticking in the throat; stitches extending to the inner ears, especially when swallowing; swelling of the uvula, palate and tonsils; or *sensation of swelling*, with stitches and pressure; dry cough, with headache and pains in the hypochondria when coughing; small *fetid* ulcers in the mouth and throat.

Pulsatilla: Suitable to females and persons of a bland and phlegmatic temper, for: bluish redness of the throat, tonsils or uvula, with sensation of swelling in these parts, or sensation of a lump in the throat; scraping, soreness and dryness in the throat, without thirst; stitches in the throat, especially between the acts of deglutition, with pressure and tension during empty deglutition *chill towards evening*, with increase of soreness; varicose swelling of the cervical veins; accumulation of tenacious mucus on the affected parts.

§ 6. Give moreover:

Aconitum: For violent fever, with dry heat, red cheeks, restlessness, despair; dark redness of the affected parts, with troublesome and painful deglutition; burning, choking, *creeping* and contraction of the throat; painful sensitiveness of the throat when talking; burning thirst.

Bryonia: Painful sensitiveness of the throat to contact, and when turning the head; painful and troublesome swallowing, as if a hard body were sticking in the throat; *stitches, soreness and dry feeling in the throat*, rendering talking difficult; fever, with or without thirst, or chilliness and feeling of coldness; irritable mood.

Capsicum: Fever, with chill and thirst, and subsequent heat; aching pains with spasmodic constriction of the throat; soreness and ulceration of the mouth and throat; painful cough; constant desire to lie down and sleep, with dread of the open air and cold.

Coffea: Coryza, irritation in the throat, inducing cough; sleeplessness, heat, whining and moaning; swelling of the velum and elongation of the uvula; the affected parts are very sensitive; short, dry cough, &c.

Hepar: After *Bell.* or *Merc.*, for: dryness, sensation of a lump, or stitches in the throat, as from splinters, especially when swallowing, coughing, breathing or turning the head; painful scraping, difficult deglutition, pressure in the throat with danger f suffocation; swelling of the tonsils.

IGNATIA: Red and inflammatory swelling of the palate or tonsils; sensation as of a lump in the throat, or stitches extending to the inner ears, especially between the acts of deglutition, with burning or sore pain when swallowing; it is more difficult to swallow liquids than solids; the tonsils are hard or covered with little ulcers. (Compare: *Cham. nux-v. puls.;* or, *Bell. merc. sulph. hep.*)

RHUS TOX.: *Bryonia* being insufficient; rather whining disposition; pressure and stitches *during deglutition;* beating pain at the base of the pharynx; sensation of contraction in the throat during deglutition; sensation of swelling in the throat, with contusive pain even when talking.

SULPHUR: Swelling of the throat, tonsils or uvula; scraping and *dryness, sore pain;* burning and stitching in the throat, during and between the acts of deglutition; pressure in the throat as from a lump, or painful sensation of contraction, with difficult deglutition; swelling of the cervical glands.

§ 7. Try moreover:

BARYTA CARB.: The sore throat sets in every time after taking cold, with swelling and hardness of the tonsils and disposition to suppurate.

CHINA: Swelling of the palate and uvula, with stitches in the throat, especially when swallowing, or with restless sleep at night; the pain increases by the least exposure.

CICUTA: Excessive swelling of the throat in consequence of a foreign body having penetrated into it, *Bell.* being insufficient.

COCCULUS: Pains in the œsophagus, with dryness extending down to the chest; gurgling noise when drinking.

DULCAMARA: Catarrhal sore throat, with excessive secretion of mucus; *Merc.* being insufficient.

SABADILLA: Obstinate sore throat, with pressure, burning, sensation of a lump in the throat or of constriction, between and during the acts of swallowing; dryness, scraping and roughness in the throat, with constant desire to swallow.

SEPIA: Soreness, stitches when swallowing, with frequent rattling and secretion of mucus.

VERATRUM: Dry throat, with burning, roughness, scraping, or constrictive pain; choking, pressure and spasm when swallowing.

§ 8. As regards symptoms, give:

a) When the *velum* is principally affected: 1) *Acon. bell. coff. lach. merc. natr-m. phos. phos-ac.* 2) *Arg. carb-v. stram. sulph.*

b) When the *uvula:* 1) *Bell. calc. carb-v. coff. merc. n-vom. puls.* 2) *Caust. jod. lyc. natr-m. sil. sulph.*

c) When the *tonsils :* 1) *Bell. lach. merc.* 2) *Amm. cham. ign. n-vom. puls. staph.* 3) *Alum. baryt. calc. hep. lyc. nitr-ac. phos. sep. sulph. thuj.*

d) When the *larynx* is involved: *Acon. ars. bell. bry. carb-veg. dros. hep. jod. n-vom. phosph. spong.*

e) When the *œsophagus: Amm. ars. asa. canth. carb-veg. coccul. lach. natr.*

f) When the *fauces: Alum. bell. carb-veg. ign. lach. merc. n-vom. phosph. puls. sulph.*

§ 9. a) For *burning* pains: *Alum. ars. bell. carb-veg. lach. merc. nitr-ac. n-vom. puls. rhus. seneg.*

b) *Aching: Alum. caust. hep. merc. nitr-ac. phosph. puls. sep. sulph.*

c) Sensation of *swelling*, without any swelling being present: *Chin. lach. nitr-ac. puls. sulph.*

d) For *tickling* and titillation: *Carb-veg. lach. sep.*

e) For *scraping* and *roughness:* 1) *Acon. amm. carb-veg. n-vom. phosph. puls. sulph.* 2) *Alum. ars. caust. con. graph. sabad. sep.*

f) Sensation as of a *plug, lump,* &c., in the throat: 1) *Bell. cham. ign. lach. merc. natr-m. n-vom. puls. sulph.* 2) *Amm. caust. nitr-ac. sep.*

g) *Tearing* pains: *Amm. ars. jod. lyc.*

h) Pains as if *raw* and *sore:* 1) *Alum. calc. carb-veg. caust. ign. lach. merc. mur-ac. nitr-ac. phosph. puls. sep.* 2) *Amm. caps. carb-an. graph. kal. lyc. n-vom. phos-ac. sep. staph.*

i) *Cutting* pains: *Puls. sep. stann.*

k) *Stitching* pains: 1) *Acon. bell. ign. merc. puls.* 2) *Calc. cham. hep. lach. lyc. natr-m. nitr-ac. sulph. thuj.*

l) Sensation of *contraction*. 1) *Bell. dros. puls. rhus. sulph.* 2) *Alum. calc. carb-veg. caust. chin. natr-m. veratr.*

m) *Constrictive* sensation and spasm in the fauces: 1) *Bell. ign. n-vom. stram. sulph.* 2) *Alum. ars. caps. carb-veg. coccul. con. natr-m. sabad. seneg. veratr.*

§ 10. a) For *swelling* of the affected parts: 1) *Amm. bell. calc. lach. merc. n-vom. staph.* 2) *Alum. baryt. cham. chin. coff. graph. hep. lyc. nitr-ac. phosph. sabad. sil. sulph. thuj.*

b) *Suppuration: Bell. lach. hep. merc.*

c) *Ulcers* in the throat: 1) *Alum. bell. ign. lach. merc. natr-m. nitr-ac. n-vom. thuj.* 2) *Borax. calc. staph.*

d) *Redness:* 1) *Acon. alum. amm. bell. cham. ign. merc. n-vom. puls. sulph.* 2) *Baryt. coff. hep. lach. lyc. staph.*

e) Profuse *secretion of mucus: Alum. bell. calc. caps. caust. cham. chin. con. ign. kal. lach. lyc. n-vom. phosph. puls. seneg. staph. sulph.*

f) *Mucous lining* on the affected parts: *Bell. canth. chin. merc. plumb. puls.*

g) *Ptyalism:* 1) *Acon. bell. chin. merc. n-vom. phosph. puls. rhus. sulph.* 2) *Alum. amb. ant. arg. bry. calc. cham. ign. lach. lyc. natr-m. nitr-ac. sep. sil.*

h) *Dryness* of the mouth and throat: *Acon. bell. bry. calc. cham. ign. merc. nitr-ac. n-vom. phosph. puls. rhus. seneg. sep. sil. sulph.*

i) *Varicose* condition of the throat: *Carb-veg. puls.*

k) *Soreness: Alum. amb. carb-veg. graph. kal. lach. merc. mez. mur-ac. nitr-ac. phosph. phos-ac. sabad. sil.*

§ 11. a) For *constant desire* to swallow: 1) *Bell. cham. ign. lach. lyc. n-vom. phosph. puls.* 2) *Alum. calc. caps. caust. chin con. kal. seneg. staph. sulph.*

b) *Painful* deglutition: *Bell. bry. hep. merc. n-vom. phosph. puls. rhus. sep. staph. thuj.*

c) Pain during *empty* deglutition: *Bry. coccul. lach. hep. merc. n-vom. puls. rhus. sulph.*

d) Pain when swallowing *food: Alum. baryt. bry. cham. hep. nitr-ac. n-vom. phosph. rhus. sep. sulph.*

e) Difficulty in *swallowing liquids: Bell. canth. cupr. ign. jod. lach. merc. natr-m. phos. sil.*

f) Deglutition being altogether *prevented* or rendered very *difficult:* 1) *Acon. bell. canth. hyos. lach. lyc. merc. stram.* 2) *Alum. amm. ars. bry. calc. canth. carb-veg. caust. cham. cic. cin. con. cupr. dros. hep. ign. n-vom. phosph. phos-ac. puls. sep. sil.*

g) Pain *not increased* by swallowing: 1) *Ign.* 2) *Alum. amb. caps. graph. lach. merc. mez. n-vom. puls. spong. stann. staph.*

§ 12. Comp.: STOMACACE, PTYALISM, BRONCHITIS, CATARRH, COUGH, &c.

SPASMS, CONVULSIONS.

§ 1. We have arranged under one head the various spasmodic affections, such as: catalepsy, epilepsy, chorea, hysteric convulsions, eclampsia, tetanus, &c., because they frequently indicate the same remedy, provided the secondary symptoms correspond to it. The reader is thus enabled to discover more easily the characteristic indications for the respective remedies.

§ 2. Principal remedies for spasmodic affections: 1) *Bell. calc. caust. cham. cupr. hyos. ign. ipec. lach. n-vom. op. sil. stram.* and *sulph.* 2) *Acon. ang. arn. ars. camph. cic. citr. cocc. croc.*

merc. mosch. plat. rhus. sil. stann. sulph. veratr. zinc. 3) *Agar. Arg. coccul. hell. hyos. laur.*

§ 3. *Recent* spasms require: *Acon. ang. arn. bell. camph. cham. cic. citr. cocc. croc. hyos. ign. ipec. merc. mosch. n-vom. op. rhus. stram. veratr.*

For *chronic* spasmodic affections, use: *Ars. calc. caust. cupr. lach. plat. sil. stann. sulph. zinc-sulph.*; unless: *Bell. cocc. croc. hyos. merc. n-vom. rhus. stran.* or *veratr.* should be indicated.

§ 4. For *catalepsy*, use: 1) *Cham. ipec. plat. stram.* 2) *Acon. agar. bell. cic. hyos. mosch. veratr.* 3) *Asa. camph. coloc. dros. ign. merc. op. petr.*

For *chorea* St. Viti: 1) *Bell. caust. cocc. croc. cupr. hyos. ign. n-vom. stram. zinc.;* or, perhaps, 2) *Asa. ars. chin. cic. coff. dulc. jod. puls. sabin. sep. sil.;* or, 3) *Agar. laur. electr.*

For *eclampsia:* 1) *Bell. caust. cham. ign. n-vom. plat.;* or, 2) *Cic. cin. magn-c. n-mosch. phosph. stram.;* or, 3) *Arg. canth. hell. kal. nitr-ac. sulph.*

Recent attacks of epilepsy frequently yield to *Bell. ign. n-vom. op.*, &c.; *chronic* cases require: *Sulph.*, to be followed by: *Calc. caust. cupr.* or *sil.;* or *Bell.*, to be followed by: *Lach. hep.* or *sil.*, &c.—With more or less success have been employed: *Agar. ars. camph. cic. cin. hyos. natr-m. nitr-ac. plumb. sep. stann. stram.* (These remedies should be given at long intervals, and the effect of each remedy should be carefully observed.)

Tetanus generally sets in in consequence of wounds, poisoning, &c., and points to the following remedies: 1) *Ang. bell. bry. camph. cham. ipec. mosch. op. plat. sec. stram.;* or, 2) *Acon. arn. cann. canth. cic. cocc. cin. grat. hyos. ign. lach. laur. n-vom. rhus. stann.*

§ 5. *Convulsions of children* require: *Acon. caust. cham. cin. coff. cupr. ign. ipec. lach. merc. n-vom. op. stann. sulph.*—If caused by *dentition: Bell. calc. cham. cin. ign. stann. sulph.*—If by *worms: Cic. cin. hyos. merc. sulph.*

Hysteric females principally require: 1) *Aur. bell. cocc. ign. ipec. mosch. stram. veratr.;* or, 2) *Bry. calc. caust. cham. cocc. con. magn-c. magn-m. plat. sec. sep. stann. sulph.*—If the spasms depend upon the menses, give: *Coff. cocc. cupr. ign. puls.;*—and spasms of lying-in females require: *Bell. cham. cic. hyos. ign.*

§ 6. If the spasms depend upon wounds or other external injuries, give: *Arn.* or *Ang.;* or: *Puls. rhus-t.* and *sulph.*

Spasms caused by fright or some other emotion, require: *Cham. cupr. hyos. n-vom. op. plat.*—In one case of epilepsy after fright, *Artem.* has been given with success.

Spasms caused by *onanism*, or other debilitating concussions of the nerves, require: 1) *Sulph. calc. lach. sil. n-vom.;* or, 2) *Arn. chin. phos-ac.*, &c.

If caused by abuse of *narcotics*, wine, opium, beer, (adulterated with belladonna, cocculus, &c.) tobacco, &c., give: *Bell. cupr. cham. citr. coff. cupr. hyos. ign. n-vom. op.*, &c.

If caused by *retrocession* of some eruption, give: *Calc. caust. ipec. lach. n-vom. stram. sulph.*

If by a *cold*, or by suppression of the cutaneous secretions, give: *Acon. bell. cham. chin. cic. lach. n-vom. sil.*, &c.

If by mercurial vapours, give: *Bell. stram.;* and if by the vapours of copper or arsenic, give *Camph. merc.;* give *Ars.* for copper, and *Cupr.* for arsenic.

§ 7. Symptomatic indications:

Belladonna: For tetanus, trismus, hysteric spasms, convulsions of little children, eclampsia, chorea, epilepsy, &c.; when the convulsions commence in the upper extremities, with creeping and feeling of rigidity in the same, twitching of one or more of the extremities, especially of the arms; convulsive motion of the mouth, facial muscles and eyes; congestion of blood to the head, with vertigo, dark-red, hot and bloated face, or with pale and cold face and shuddering; photophobia; distorted or staring eyes, dilated pupils; spasms in the larynx and fauces, with inability to swallow and with danger of suffocation; foam at the mouth; involuntary passage of fæces, or diarrhœic stools with undigested food; oppression of the chest and anxious breathing; the spasms are excited again by the least touch or the least contradiction; stupefaction or complete loss of consciousness; sleeplessness between the paroxysms, with restless tossing about; deep or comatose sleep, with smiling and distortion of features; sudden starting from sleep, with a cry; obstinate, weeping; malicious desire to bite and tear every thing; or great anxiety, fear, frightful visions. (Comp. *Cham. Hyoscyam. Ign. Op. Stram.*)

Causticum: Epileptic convulsions, chorea St. Viti, with screams, violent movements of the extremities, grinding of the teeth, laughing or weeping, involuntary or frequent emission of urine; cold water brings the paroxysms on again.

Chamomilla: For spasms of children and lying-in females, when characterized by: Stretching of the limbs, convulsions of the extremities, eyes, eyelids and tongue; convulsive starting during sleep; red, bloated face, or one cheek is red and the other pale; dry and burning heat of the skin, with burning thirst; hot sweat on the forehead and hairy scalp; anguish, moaning and lamenting; anxious, hurried, rattling breathing; dry and rattling, short cough; colicky pains, distended abdomen, diarrhœic, green stools. (Comp.: *Bell. ign.*)

CUPRUM: For convulsions of children, tonic spasms, epilepsy, St. Vitus' dance; and for: convulsions commencing at the fingers or toes, or in the arms; clenching the thumbs; loss of consciousness and speech; ptyalism, sometimes like froth; suffocative paroxysms (especially with previous weeping); fequent emission of urine; turbid urine; *red face and eyes*, weeping and anguish, or strange demeanour, disposition to hide himself; the paroxysms return every month, especially after the menses.

HYOSCYAMUS: Clonic spasms, chorea, epilepsy, &c., especially for: Bluish colour and bloatedness of the face, foam at the mouth, protruded eyes, convulsive movements of some parts or of the whole body; violent tossing about; clenching of the thumbs; the spasms come on again every time he attempts to swallow liquids; great anxiety with cries and grinding of the teeth; loss of consciousness; oppression of the chest, involuntary emission of urine, congestion of blood to the brain; deep and comatose sleep, with stertorous breathing; feeling of hunger and gnawing in the stomach; dry cough at night; desire to laugh at every thing; running about from place to place between the spasms; delirium. (Comp. *Bell. op.*)

IGNATIA: Clonic and tonic spasms, hysteric spasms, convulsions of little children, epilepsy, chorea St. Viti, &c.; and for: Convulsive movements of the extremities, eyes, eyelids, facial muscles and lips; opisthotonos; clenching the thumbs; bluish, or very red face, or one cheek red, the other pale, or alternate redness and paleness; foamy saliva; spasms of the pharynx and larynx, with suffocative fits, difficult deglutition; loss of consciousness with involuntary screams and laughter; frequent yawning or sopor; anxiety and deep sighs; the spasms recur every day; bland, sensitive disposition; fitful mood; quiet temper.

IPECACUANHA: Clonic and tonic spasms, especially of children, and hysteric females; especially for: opisthotonos, loss of consciousness, screams; pale, bloated face, distortion of the facial muscles, and of the half-closed eyes, or convulsive movements of the facial muscles, lips, eyelids and extremities; asthmatic ailments, with mucous rattling, nausea, loathing, paroxysms of vomiturition, vomiting or diarrhœa.

LACHESIS: Epileptic convulsions and other clonic or tonic spasms, when characterized by: Cries, falling down without consciousness, foam at the mouth, cold feet, eructations, pale face, vertigo, heavy and painful head, palpitation of the heart, distended abdomen, comatose condition, nausea, &c, suitable to children and young people, also to men in full manhood.

NUX-VOMICA: Clonic and tonic spasms, epilepsy, chorea, &c., especially when characterized by: cries, opisthotonos, trembling or convulsive twitching of the limbs or muscles; the spasms are excited by chagrin or mortification; involuntary discharge of fæces and urine; feeling of rigidity in the limbs, and as if they would go to sleep; vomiting; copious sweat; oppression of the chest; constipation, ill humour and irritable disposition.

Opium: Tonic and clonic spasms, epilepsy, &c., with: setting in of the paroxysms at night and in the evening; opisthotonos, or violent motions of the extremities, especially the arms; loss of consciousness; insensibility; cries; clenching of the fists; suffocative paroxysm, *deep and comatose sleep.* (Comp.: *Bell. hyos. ign.*)

Stramonium: Clonic and tonic spasms, catalepsy, eclampsia, chorea, hysteric spasms, &c., especially for: opisthotonos, convulsive motions of the extremities, especially the upper; *risus sardonius;* stuttering or loss of speech; pale, worn out appearance, with a stupid-friendly look; or red and pale face; loss of consciousness and sensation, sometimes with cry, furious or religious motions, frightful visions, laughter, lamentations, singing, desire to escape, &c.; the spasms are excited again by contact, or by the sight of bright or shining objects. (Comp. *Bell.*)

§ 8. Use likewise:

Aconitum: For tetanus, trismus, and other tonic spasms, with alternately pale and red face, cries, grinding of the teeth, and convulsive hiccough; also for spasms of young plethoric people (especially young girls) who lead a sedentary life.

Angustura: Tonic spasms, with opisthotonos, trismus, &c.

Arnica: Tonic spasms, especially in consequence of wounds, with palpitation of the heart, trismus, opisthotonos, &c.

Arsenicum: Epilepsy, with burning in the stomach, spine and abdomen.

Calcarea: Epilepsy, chorea, &c., especially for nocturnal paroxysms. (After *Sulphur.*)

Camphora. For some kinds of epilepsy, with stertorous breathing, red and bloated face, coma.

Cicuta: Clonic and tonic spasms, epilepsy, catalepsy, eclampsia, &c., with pale or yellowish complexion, trismus, distortion of the extremities, cries, frothy saliva, colic as if from worms, &c.

Citric acid.: Convulsions caused by eating Stramonium.

Cocculus: Epilepsy, chorea and other spasms, especially during the menses, or in consequence of some external injury.

Crocus: Chorea and other convulsions, with laughing and springing, especially when the convulsions alternate with paroxysms of whooping-cough.

Mercurius: Epilepsy and other convulsions, with cry, rigidity of the body, bloated abdomen, itching of the nose, thirst and nocturnal paroxysms.

MOSCHUS: Hysteric spasms, especially when pulmonary spasms are present at the same time.

PLATINA: Catalepsy and eclampsia, without loss of consciousness, with trismus, loss of speech, convulsive motions of the eyes, corners of the mouth and eyelids, the paroxysms set in at dawn of day.

RHUS-T.: *Tonic* spasms, chorea, &c.

SILICEA: Chronic epilepsy. (After *Calc.*)

STANNUM: Epilepsy, with tossing of the extremities, clenching of the thumbs, pale face, *opisthotonos*, loss of consciousness; the paroxysms occur in the evening.

SULPHUR: Chronic epilepsy, with creeping sensation in the muscles, with cries, stiffness of the body; the spasms are caused by fright or excessive running.

VERATRUM: Clonic and tonic spasms, with loss of sense and motion; convulsive motions of the eyes and eyelids; *anguish*, loss of spirits and despondency.

SPEECH, DIFFICULT, STUTTERING, DUMBNESS, &c.

§ 1. Principal remedies: 1) *Bell. caust. con. dulc. euphr. hyos. lach. laur. merc. n-vom. op. stram. sulph.* 2) *Acon. amm. anac. bov. bry. calc. cann. carb-an. carb-veg. chin. cic. cupr. hep. lyc. mez. natr-m. oleand. plumb. ruta. sec. sil. stann. thuj. veratr.*

§ 2. a) For difficult speech, *stammering*, &c.: 1) *Bell. caust. dulc. euphr. graph. lach. merc. natr. n-vom. stram. sulph.* 2) *Acon. ars. cic. con. natr-m. op. ruta. sec. stann.* 3) *Anac. arg. calc. cann. carb-an. carb-veg. hep. lyc. oleand. plumb. thuj. veratr.*

b) For *nasal* twang: *Alum. bell. bry. lach. lyc. phos-ac. sil. staph.*

c) *Loss of speech, dumb:* 1) *Dulc. euphr. hyos. lach. laur. merc. op. plumb. stram.* 2) *Bell. caust. chin. cic. con. cupr. euphr. oleand. ruta. sec. veratr.*

§ 3. If this condition be accompanied with inflammatory affections of the organs of speech, give: 1) *Acon. bell. cann. dulc. lach. merc. n-vom. sulph.* 2) *Alum. ars. bry. calc. canth. hep. lyc. natr-m. sil. staph.*

If depending upon *spasms:* 1) *Bell. canth. hyos. op. stram. veratr.* 2) *Cic. con. cupr. lach. laur. ruta. sec.*

If upon *paralysis:* 1) *Bell. caust. dulc. euphr. graph. hyos. lach. laur. n-vom. natr-m. stram.* 2) *Canth. carb-veg. chin. stann. staph. zinc.*

§ 4. Comp.: SORE THROAT, SPASMS, PARALYSIS, &c.

STOMACACE, INFLAMMATION OF ULCERATION OF THE MOUTH.

§ 1. Principal remedies: 1) *Merc. n-vom.;* or, 2) *Ars. borax. caps. carb-veg. dulc. natr-m. nitr-ac. staph. sulph. sulph-ac.;* or, 3) *Chin. gran. hep. jod. n-mosch. sep. sil.*

If caused by *Mercury:* 1) *Carb-veg. dulc. hep. nitr-ac. staph. sulph.;* or, 2) *Chin. jod. natr-m.*

If by abuse of *kitchen-salt: Carb-veg. nitr-sp.*

For simple *aphthæ:* 1) *Borax. sulph-ac.* 2) *Merc. n-vom. sulph.*

§ 2. Particular indications:

Arsenicum: The edges of the tongue are ulcerated, aphthæ, violent burning pains; swollen and readily-bleeding gums, looseness of the teeth; *debility* and *sinking.*

Borax: Ulcerated gums; *aphthæ in the mouth or on the tongue,* which bleed readily; tenacious mucus in the throat; acrid *fetid urine.* (Suitable to little children.)

Capsicum: Suitable to large, phlegmatic, plethoric persons, who lead a sedentary life; especially for: burning vesicles in the mouth and on the tongue, swelling of the gums, &c.

Carbo-veg.: The gums stand off, are *sore and ulcerated,* bleed profusely, with loose teeth, heat in the mouth, bad smell of the ulcers, sore and stiff tongue.

Dulcamara: The least cold brings the disease on, with swelling of the cervical glands.

Mercurius: Red, spongy, receding, ulcerated gums, with *burning pains at night,* and soreness, especially when touched; *loose teeth, inflamed, sore, ulcerated, tongue and mouth,* sometimes covered with aphthæ; fetid, cadaverous smell of the mouth and ulcers; profuse discharge of *fetid,* and even *bloody* saliva; with ulceration of the orifice of the Stenonian duct; the tongue is swollen, stiff, hard, or moist and covered with white mucus; pale face and chills; burning diarrhœic stools.

Natrum-mur.: Swollen, readily bleeding gums, with great sensitiveness to cold or warm substances; ulcers and blisters in the mouth, on the tongue and gums, with burning pains and impeded speech; ptyalism, rigidity of the tongue; especially on one side.

Nitric-acid.: Bleeding, white and swollen gums, loose teeth; sore mouth, with stinging pains; *fetid smell* of the mouth; ptyalism.

Nux-vom.: Suitable to thin persons of lively temper and sedentary habits; especially for: foul and painful swelling of the gums, with burning or beating pains; fetid ulcers, pimples and painful blisters in the mouth, on the gums, palate or tongue; ptyalism at night; bloody saliva; tongue white and thickly coated with mucus; *fetid odour from the mouth;* pale face with sunken cheeks and dim eyes; emaciation, constipation, angry, irritable mood.

STAPHYSAGRIA: Pale, white, ulcerated, or painful and swollen gums; *readily bleeding spongy excrescences* on the gums and in the mouth; mouth and tongue are ulcerated and covered with blisters; discharge of saliva which is at times bloody; stinging pains on the tongue; sickly complexion, with sunken cheeks hollow eyes, surrounded with blue rings; swelling of the cervical glands, and blisters under the tongue.

SULPHUR: Readily bleeding, receding and swollen gums, with beating pains; blisters and *aphthæ* in the mouth and on the tongue, with burning and soreness, especially when eating; *fetid and sour smell* of the mouth; ptyalism, or bloody saliva; tongue thickly coated, whitish or brownish; slimy, greenish stools, with tenesmus; rash; restlessness at night, &c.

SULPHURIS-ACIDUM: Aphthæ in the mouth; swollen, ulcerated and readily bleeding gums; profuse *ptyalism,* &c.

§ 3. Compare: PTYALISM, GUMS, DISEASES OF THE, SCURVY, MERCURY, &c.

STOMACH, WEAKNESS OF THE, DYSPEPSIA.

§ 1. This affection is characterized by weak digestion, deficient or irregular appetite, distress in the region of the stomach, eructations, flatulence, ill humour, drowsiness, and other unpleasant feelings after a meal; disposition to gastric derangement; acidity and accumulation of mucus in the intestines.

Dyspepsia is of very frequent occurrence, and therefore deserves particular attention in a work of this kind.

§ 2. *Hep.* and *Sulph.* are excellent remedies for dyspepsia, and frequently effect a cure, provided the remedies are given at long intervals.

The following remedies are likewise indicated in many cases: 1) *Arn. bry. calc. chin. lach. merc. n-vom. puls. rhus.;* or, 2) *Carb-veg. natr. natr-m. ruta. sep. sil.;* or, 3) *Amm. anac. ars. aur. baryt. bell. con. dros. ferr. graph. hyos. ign. kal. kreos. lyc. n-mosch. petr. phosph. staph. veratr.*

§ 3. *Dyspepsia* of children requires: *Baryt. calc. ipec. lyc. merc. n-vom. puls. sulph;* or, *Hyos. jod.*

Of *old people:* 1) *Baryt. cic.;* or, 2) *Ant. carb-veg. chin. n-mosch. n-vom.*

Of *hypochondriacal people:* 1) *N-vom. sulph.;* or, 2) *Bry. calc. chin. con. lach. natr. staph. veratr.,* &c.

Of *hysteric individuals :* 1) ***Puls. sep.;*** or, 2) ***Bell. bry. calc. con. hyos. ign. lach. n-mosch. phosph. sep. sulph. veratr.,*** &c.

Of *pregnant females : Acon. ars. con. ferr. ipec. kreos. lach. magn-m. natr-m. n-mosch. n-vom. petr. phosph. puls. sep.*

§ 4. Dyspepsia in consequence of *sedentary habits :* ***Bry. calc. n-vom. sep. sulph.;***—in consequence of *watching:* ***Arn. carb-veg. cocc. n-vom. puls. veratr.;***—of long *studying :* ***Arn. calc. lach. n-vom. puls. sulph.;*** or, *Cocc. veratr.*

Dyspepsia caused by *loss* of *animal fluids,* abuse of cathartics, vomiting, bloodletting, &c., requires: *Chin. carb-veg. ruta.;* or, *Calc. lach. n-vom. sulph.*—By *sexual abuse : Calc. merc. n-vom. phos-ac. staph.*

By *overloading* or deranging the stomach : ***Ant. ars. ipec. n-vom. puls.***—By abuse of *wine* or *spirits : Carb-veg. lach. n-vom. sulph. ;* or, *Ars. bell. chin. merc. natr. puls.*—By *abuse* of *coffee : Cocc. ign. n-vom. ;* or, *Carb-veg. cham: merc. puls. rhus. sulph.*—By abuse of *tea : Ferr.* or *Thuja.*—By abuse of *tobacco : Cocc. merc. ipec. n-vom. puls. staph.*

Dyspepsia in consequence of external injuries, : a blow on the stomach, heavy lifting, strain, &c., requires: *Arn. bry. rhus-t.* or, *Amm. calc. con. ? puls. ruta.*

In consequence of *depressing emotions,* such as: chagrin, *anger,* &c.: *Bry. cham. chin. coloc. n-vom. phos-ac. staph.* &c.

§ 5. Symptomatic indications :

Arnica: After *Chin.,* if thif should not suffice, and for: Nervousness ; dry or yellow-coated tongue ; sour, foul or bitter taste; bad smell of the mouth : frequent eructations, sometimes tasting of putrid eggs ; desire for acid things ; fullness in the epigastrium, flatulence and distention of the abdomen after a meal ; feeling of indolence in the extremities ; vertigo ; dulness of the head, especially in the forehead, over the eyes ; stupefaction and heat in the head ; disturbed sleep, with sudden starting, frequent waking, anxious and heavy dreams ; *yellowish, livid* complexion ; frequent nausea, with desire to vomit, especially in the morning or after eating ; *hypochondriac mood.* (After *Arn. n-vom.* is sometimes suitable ; comp. *Bry.* and *Rhus.*)

Bryonia: For dispepsia which principally occurs in the summer or in damp and hot weather ; or for: loss of appetite, alternating with canine hunger even at night, or loss of appetite after swallowing or mouthful ; desire for wine, coffee and acids ; loathing of food, sometimes so violent that even the smell of food is intolerable ; *frequent eructations, especially after a meal,* generally a mere rising of air, or with sour or bitter taste; oppression and distention of the pit of the stomach; colicky pains, regurgitation or vomiting *of the ingesta;* bread and milk spoil the stomach easily; discharge of water from the mouth, like waterbrash; painful sensitiveness of the region of the stomach to contact; inability to bear the pressure of the clothes; constipation or hard stools; restless irritable, vehement disposition. (Comp.: *Arn. Chin. Rhus-t.*

Calcarea: Sticky or dry mouth, with sour or bitter taste; continual thirst, with feeble appetite; food has no taste; hunger after a meal; paroxysms of canine hunger, especially early in the morning; *aversion to meat* and warm food, with desire for wine and dainties; nausea or sour regurgitation after eating milk; heat, distention, headache, pain in the stomach and abdomen, or drowsiness after eating; *heartburn* and *acidity, accumulation of mucus in the stomach,* fullness and swelling in the region of the stomach, with great sensitiveness to contact; tension in the hypochondria, and inability to wear tight clothes; stool every two, three or four days; or two or three stools a day; general debility; stitching or aching pain in the head, with *feeling of coldness* in the head; plethoric, fat constitution. (Frequently suitable after *Sulph.*)

China: Dyspepsia from loss of animal fluids, noxious miasms in the air, in the spring and fall, in the neighbourhood of canals, marshes, &c., for: aversion to food or drink, as if one had eaten enough; desire for wine, pungent, spiced, sour and refreshing things; frequent derangement of the stomach, caused by the least irregularity and especially by a late supper; *malaise, drowsiness, hypochondriac mood, fullness, distention,* eructations, or even vomiting of the ingesta; debility, with constant desire to lie down, *after every,* even the *least meal;* chilliness and great sensitiveness to the least draught of air; remaining awake in bed late in the night; *easily disturbed night-sleep;* ill humour and indisposition to do any thing. (Compare: *Arn. Bry. Rhus.*)

Hepar: Chronic dyspepsia, especially when the patient had taken much mercury, or when he complains of: liability to derange his stomach, in spite of the most careful diet, with desire for wine, or sour, pungent, refreshing things; frequent nausea, especially in the morning, with desire to vomit and eructations, or *vomiting of acid, bilious or slimy substances; accumulation of mucus in the throat;* colic; *hard, difficult, dry stools;* pressure, distention and heaviness in the epigastrium; bitter taste in the mouth and of the food while eating; aversion to fat; great thirst; the clothes press on the hypochondria and feel tight. (After *Hep., Lach.* and *Merc.* are sometimes suitable.)

Lachesis: Chronic dyspepsia, especially after *Hepar,* for: irregular appetite; aversion to bread, desire for milk and wine, though these substances do not agree; nausea, eructations, vomiting of the ingesta; malaise, indolence, repletion, pains in the stomach after eating, &c.; flatulence, constipation or hard stools; livid complexion, fullness in the hypochondria and epigastrium; with sensitiveness to contact. (After *Lach.*, *Merc.* is sometimes suitable.)

Mercurius: Foul, sweetish or bitter taste, especially early in the morning; loss of appetite, or voracious appetite, with speedy repletion after eating; *aversion to solid food, meat, warm food,* with *desire for refreshing things,* milk, cold drinks, or wine and brandy; *pressure in the epigastrium,* eructations, heartburn, and other unpleasant feelings after a meal; *eructations,* nausea, desire to vomit; painful sensitiveness, fullness, pressure and tension in the region of the stomach; flatulence; constipation, frequently with ineffectual urging to stool, and tenesmus; sadness, hypochondria, suspicious and vehement mood.

Nux vom.: Suitable to persons that are disposed to piles, and for: *sour* or bitter taste in the mouth and of the food, especially bread, or the food has no taste; aversion to food with desire for beer, milk, wine, brandy; or insatiable hunger, though satiated very soon; nausea, eructations, *regurgitation* or *vomiting of food,* flatulence, dullness of the head, vertigo, malaise, hypochondriac mood; languor, indolence, drowsiness after eating; distention, fullness and tension in the epigastrium, with great sensitiveness to contact and unpleasant pressure of the clothes on the hypochondria; liquids, rye-bread, and acids, do not agree; sour eructations and regurgitation of food; frequent nausea and desire to vomit; accumulation of mucus in the stomach; heartburn; heaviness of the head, with inability to perform mental labour; frequent *heat* and *redness of the face;* restless, quarrelsome, vehement mood; lively and choleric temperament; *yellowish, sallow complexion; constipation, hard stools.* (After *Nux-v.*, *Sulphur* is frequently suitable.

Pulsatilla: Suitable to females or persons of a phlegmatic temperament and bland disposition, with disposition to excessive secretion of mucus in the primæ viæ; acidity, with sour, bitter or foul taste in the mouth and of the food; aversion to warm or boiled food, with desire to sour, pungent or stimulating substances, wine, brandy, &c. *No thirst; nausea, desire to vomit, eructations* or vomiting; difficulty of breathing, sadness and melancholy after a meal; bread disagrees; bitter or sour eructations, or eructations tasting of the ingesta; *water-brash;* frequent hiccough; frequent diarrhœic stools, or slow stools; colicky pains with rumbling in the abdomen. (After *Puls.*, *Sulphur* is frequently suitable.)

Rhus-tox.: *Bry.* being insufficient, and for the following

symptoms: Flat, viscid taste in the mouth; foul, or sweetish, or bitter taste of the food; no appetite, as if one had eaten enough, with aversion to bread and meat, or desire for dainties; liquids, bread and beer disagree; *sleep, fullness, eructations*, nausea, languor, vertigo after eating; frequent, *empty, violent* and *painful eructations;* waterbrash; pressure and distention in the region of the stomach; frequent emissions of fetid flatulence; gastric ailments at night; hypochondriac mood, melancholy, despondency, dread of the future, uneasiness about one's affairs, &c. (Compare: *Arn.* and *China.*)

SULPHUR: Chronic dyspepsia, after *Nux-v.* and *Puls.*, for: Sour, foul, or sweetish taste in the mouth, especially early in the morning; food has no taste, or tastes too salt; aversion to food, especially *meat*, bread, fat, and milk; with desire for sour things and wine; meat, fat, *milk, acids, sweets* and flour, disagree; after a meal: *heavy breathing, nausea, pain in the stomach*, regurgitation or vomiting of the ingesta, languor, chilliness, &c., and frequent eructations; acidity, heartburn and waterbrash; disposition to mucous derangements in the primæ viæ; flatulence, slow action of the bowels; great thirst; sad hypochondriac, or peevish and vehement disposition. (After *Sulph.* are frequently suitable: *Calc.* and *merc.*

§ 6. Of other remedies, use:

CARBO VEG.: For bitter taste in the mouth, aversion to meat, milk or fat, sour stomach in consequence of eating these things; frequent, sour, bitter or empty eructations; accumulation of mucus in the stomach; *frequent flatulence*, with heavy breathing, &c.

NATRUM: *Bry. chin. nux-v.* being insufficient, with pressure in the stomach, *intractable disposition* after a meal; milk and liquids disagree, with constant nausea.

NATRUM MURIATICUM: Fat, milk, acids and bread disagree, with irregular appetite, which is at times wanting, at others excessive; frequent waterbrash or vomiting of the ingesta, &c.

RUTA: Food has no taste; foul eructations after eating meat; frequent attacks of sudden nausea while eating, with vomiting of the ingesta; bread disagrees, &c.

SEPIA: No appetite, aversion to meat or milk, or else excessive appetite, voracious; fat, milk and acids disagree; acid stomach, especially after eating; waterbrash, especially after drinking, &c.

SILICEA: Bitter taste in the morning; *nausea*, especially *in the morning* or *after a meal;* aversion to cooked food, especially meat; vomiting after drinking; *pains in the stomach, with waterbrash, great thirst, &c.*

§ 7. Use more particularly:

a) For the ill effects from *beer:* 1) *Ars. bell. coloc. ferr. n-vom. puls. rhus. sep. sulph.* 2) *Alum. asa. ign. mez. mur-ac. stann. veratr.*—From *lemonade: Selen.*—*Brandy:* 1) *N-vom. op.* 2) *Ars. calc. cocc. hep. ign. lach. led. stram. sulph. veratr.* —*Wine:* 1) *Ars. calc. coff. lach. lyc. n-vom. op. sil. zinc.* 2) *Ant. arn natr. natr-m. puls. selen. sulph.*—*Spirits* generally: 1) *Ars. calc. carb-veg. hell. hyos. lach. n-vom. op. puls. sulph.* 2) *Ant. bell. chel. chin. coff. ign. led. lyc. merc. natr. natr-m. n-mosch. rhus. selen. sil. stram. veratr.*

b) From *coffee:* 1) *Cham. coccul. ign. merc. n-vom.* 2) *Canth. carb-veg. caust. chin. coccul. hep. ipec. lyc. puls. rhus. sulph.* —*Tea:* 1) *Chin. ferr. selen.* 2) *Ars. coff hep. lach. veratr.*—*Chocolate: Bry. caust. lyc. puls.*—*Milk:* 1) *Bry. calc. n-vom. sulph.* 2) *Amb. ars. carb-veg. chin. con. cupr. ign. kal. lach. lyc. magn-c. natr. natr-m. nitr. nitr-ac. phosph. puls. rhus. sulph-ac.*—*Water:* 1) *Chin. merc. puls. rhus. sulph-ac.* 2) *Ars. caps. cham. ferr. natr. n-vom. veratr.*

c) When *bread* disagrees: 1) *Baryt. bry. caust. chin. merc. natr-m. phos-ac. puls. rhus. sep. staph.* 2) *Cin. coff. kal. merc. nitr-ac. n-vom. phosph. sulph. zinc.*—*Butter: Ars. carb-veg. chin. hep. nitr-ac. puls. sep.*—*Fat:* 1) *Ars. carb-veg. chin. natr-m. puls. sep. sulph. tarax. thuj.* 2) *Colch. cycl. ferr. hell. magn-m. nitr-ac.*—*Meat: Calc. ferr. merc. puls. ruta. sep. sil. sulph.*—*Veal: Calc. caust. ipec. nitr. sep.*—*Pork: Carb-veg. colch. dros. natr-m. puls. sep.*—*Spoiled sausage: Ars. bell. bry. phos-ac. rhus.*—*Fish: Carb-an. kal. plumb.*—*Oysters: Puls.*, drinking at the same time quantities of milk, when dangerous symptoms set in, in consequence of the stomach being overloaded with oysters.—*Foul fish:* 1) *Carb-veg. puls.* 2) *Chin. rhus.*—*Poisonous muscles: Bell. carb-veg. cop. euphorb. lyc. rhus.*

d) *Flatulent* food: 1) *Carb-veg. chin.* 2) *Bry. chin. cupr. lyc. petr. puls. sep. veratr.*—*Potatoes: Alum. amm. sep. veratr.* —*Fruit,* &c.: 1) *Ars. bry. puls. veratr.* 2) *Chin. magn-m. merc. natr. selen. sep.*—*Pastry,* &c.: 1) *Bry. puls. sulph.* 2) *Ars. carb-veg. kal. veratr.*—*Eggs: Colch. ferr. puls.*—*Acid things:* 1) *Acon. ars. carb-veg. hep. sep.* 2) *Ant. ferr. lach. natr-m. n-vom. phosph. phos-ac. sulph. sulph-ac.*—*Salt: Ars. calc. carb-veg. dros. lyc. nitr-sp.*—*Sweets: Acon. cham. ign. merc. selen. zinc.*

e) *Ice: Ars. carb-veg. puls.*—*Pepper: Ars. chin. cin. n-vom.* —*Onions: Thuj.*

f) *Tobacco:* 1) *N-vom. puls.* 2) *Ign. spong. staph.* 3) *Acon. ant. arn. bry. cham. chin. clem. coccul. coloc. cupr. euphr. ipec. lach. merc. natr. natr-m. phosph. veratr*

g) Every kind of food disagrees shortly after taking it : 1) *Calc. carb-veg. caust. chin. natr-m. n-vom. sulph.* 2) *Amm. ars. bry. con. cycl. graph. kal. lach. lyc. natr. nitr-ac. petr. phosph. phos-ac. puls. rhus. sep. sil.*

§ 8. Compare: Loss of appetite; Hunger; Vomiting; Heartburn; Gastric Derangement; Stomach, Derangement of; Colic; Diarrhœa, &c.

STRABISMUS.—Principal remedies: *Bell. hyos.*, or *alum.*

STRAMONIUM, ill effects of.—Poisoning with large doses: 1) *Black coffee;* 2) *Vinegar* and *lemon-juice;* and if no vomiting should set in: 3) *Injections of tobacco.*

For the remaining symptoms: 1) *N-vom.* 2) *Bell. hyos.*

STRICTURE OF THE URETHRA.—Principal remedies: 1) *Carb-veg. clem. dig. dulc. n-vom. petr. puls. rhus. sulph.;* or, 2) *Bell. camph. canth. chin. cic. coccul. merc.? phosph.? spong.?;* or, 3) *Arn.? calc.? con.? graph.? lyc.? magn-m.? sil.?*

Spasmodic stricture: 1) *Canth. n-vom. puls.* 2) *Bell. camph. cic. coccul.*

Callous stricture, as after gonorrhœa: 1) *Clem. dig. dulc. petr. puls. rhus.;* or, 2) *Camph. carb-veg. canth. cic. merc. phosph. spong.?;* or, 3) *Arn.? calc.? con.? graph.? lyc.? magn-m.? sil.?*

STYE,—Principal remedies: 1) *Puls.*, or *staphys.;* or, 2) *Amm-c. bry. calc. con. ferr. graph. lyc. phosph. phos-ac. rhus. sep. stann.*

Compare: Blepharophthalmia.

SUBSTANCES, ALKALINE, poisoning by.

Hering recommends: *Vinegar*, two tablespoonfuls mixed with eight to ten ounces of water, drinking a tumblerful every quarter of an hour. 2) *Lemon-juice* or other vegetable acids, sufficiently diluted; 3) *Sour-milk;* 4) *Mucilaginous* drinks and injections.

In a case of poisoning with *barytes*, pure vinegar is hurtful; but *Glauber salt*, dissolved in vinegar and diluted with water, will be frequently found excellent.

The effects of poisoning with *potash*, are best antidoted by *Coffea* or *Carb-v.;* and with *Sal ammoniacum*, by *Hep.*

SULPHUR, ill effects of.

Principal remedies: 1) *Merc. puls. sil.* 2) *Chin. n-vom. sep.*

For the consequences of the *vapours of sulphur*, give: ***Puls.***; for *sulphurated* wine: *Merc. puls.*—*Ars. chin. sep.*

SUMACH, ILL EFFECTS OF.

The eruptions require: *Bell. bry.*; or, *Ars. merc. puls. sulph.*

SUPPURATION.

§ 1. The principal remedies for suppurating wounds and ulcers are: 1) *Asa. hep. lach. merc. puls. sil. sulph.* 2) *Ars. bell. calc. canth. carb-v. caust. cist. dulc. kreos. lyc. mang. nitr-ac. phos. rhus. staph. sulph-ac.*

§ 2. Give more particularly for *bloody* pus: 1) *Asa. hep. merc.* 2) *Ars. carb-v. caust. nitr-ac. puls. sil.*
For *jelly-like*: *Cham. merc. sil.*
Ichorous: 1) *Ars. asa. carb-v. chin. merc. nitr-ac. rhus. sil.* 2) *Calc. caust. kreos. phos. sulph.*
Watery, thin: 1) *Asa. caust. merc. sil. sulph.* 2) *Ars. carb-v. lyc. nitr-ac. ran. rhus. staph.*
Fetid, cadaverous: 1) *Asa. carb-v. chin. hep. sil. sulph.* 2) *Ars. calc. graph. kreos. lyc. n-vom. phos-ac. sep.*
Viscid: *Asa. con. merc. phos. sep.*

§ 3. *Brown, brownish*: *Ars. bry. carb-v. rhus. sil.*
Yellow: 1) *Hep. merc. puls. sil. sulph.* 2) *Ars. calc. carb-v. caust. phos. rhus. sep. staph.*
Greenish: *Asa. aur. caust. merc. puls. rhus. sep. sil.*
Gray: *Ars. caust. merc. sil.*
Leaving a black *stain*: *Chin.*

§ 4. *Sour-smelling*, or *causing an acid taste*: *Calc. hep. merc kal. sulph.*
Salt: 1) *Amb. ars. calc. graph. lyc. puls. sep. staph. sulph.*
Acrid, corrosive: 1) *Ars. caust. merc. nitr-ac. ran. rhus. sep. sil.* 2) *Carb-v. cham. clem. lyc. natr. petr. staph. sulph. sulph-ac.*

§ 5. *Laudable pus*: *Hep. lach. merc. puls. sil. sulph.* 2) *Bell. calc. mang. phos. rhus. staph.*
Malignant pus: 1) *Asa. chin. hep. merc. phos. sil.* 2) *Ars. calc. carb-v. caust. kreos. nitr-ac. rhus. sulph. sulph-ac.*
Too *profuse*: 1) *Asa. hep. merc. phos. puls. sep. sulph.* 2) *Ars. calc. chin. lyc. rhus. sil.*
Suppressed or prematurely stopping: *Calc. hep. lach. merc. sil.*
Suppuration of *membraneous* tissues: *Sil.*

§ 6. See : Abscess, Gangrene, Tumours, Ulcers, Wounds, &c.

SWEAT, BLOODY.

This symptom points to : 1) *Arn. calc. n-vom.* 2) *Cham. clem. coccul. crotal. lach. n-mosch.*

SWEAT, MORBID, Nightsweats, liability to Sweat, &c.

§ 1. Mere symptoms, but of great importance, and pointing to : 1) *Bell. bry. calc. carb-an. carb-v. caust. cham. chin. graph. hep. kal. merc. natr-m n-vom. op. puls. rhus. samb. selen. sep. sulph. veratr.* 2) *Acon. ars. borax. cocc. coff. guaj. ign. lyc. natr. nitr-ac. phos. phos-ac. sabad. sil. stann. staph. thuj.* 3) *Amb. amm. amm-m. baryt. caps. coloc. con. dros. dulc. ferr. hell. hyos. lach. magn-arct. magn-aust. nitr. rhab. rhod. spig. spong. sulph-ac. tart.*

§ 2. a) For *profuse nightsweats:* 1) *Amm-m. ars. baryt. bry. calc. carb-an. caust. chin. graph. ipec. kal. lyc. nitr-ac. petr. phos. puls. rhus. sep. sil. stann. staph. sulph.* 2) *Alum. amb. amm. anac. arn. bell. canth. carb-v. dig. dros. dulc. ferr. hep. jod. lach. magn-arct. merc. natr. natr-m. nitr. n-vom. sabin. samb. sep. veratr.*

b) Sweat setting in as soon as one gets *into bed : Ars. calc. carb-an. carb-v. cham. con. hep. magn-c. merc. mur-ac. op. phos. rhus. veratr.*

c) *Morning sweats :* 1) *Bry. calc. caust. chin. con. ferr. lyc. natr-m. n-vom. phos. puls. rhus. sep. sil. stann. sulph.* 2) *Amm. amm-m. ars. canth. carb-an. carb-v. guaj. hell. hep. jod. kal. magn-c. natr. nitr. nitr-ac. n-vom. op. phos-ac. veratr.*

d) Sweat in day-time from *the least exertion* or exercise: 1) *Calc. carb-an. carb-v. caust. chin. hep. kal. natr. natr-m. puls. selen. sep. sulph. veratr.* 2) *Amm-m. asar. bell. bry. ferr. graph. lach. lyc. merc. nitr-ac. n-vom. petr. phos. phos-ac. rhod. rhus. spig. staph. sulph-ac. zinc.*

e) Sweat in the day-time, even *during rest :* 1) *Anac. rhus. sep. sulph.* 2) *Asar. calc. con. ferr. phos-ac. spong. staph. sulph-ac.*

f) Sweat during *mental exertions*, conversations, &c.: *Borax. graph. hep. sep. sulph.*

§ 3. *Partial* sweats, a) On *one side : Amb. baryt. bry. cham. ign. n-vom. puls. rhab. rhus. spig. sulph.*

b) About *the head only :* 1) *Bell. bry. calc. cham. chin. merc. puls. sil. veratr.* 2) *Graph. kal. n-vom. op. phos. rhab. rhus. sassap. staph. val.* 3) *Camph. dulc. guaj. hep. magn-m. sabad. sep. spig.*

c) In the *face* only: 1) *Carb-v. ign. puls. rhus. samb. spong. veratr.* 2) *Alum. bell. borax. carb-an. chin. cocc. coff. dros. dulc. magn-arct. merc. phos. rhab. ruta. sep. sil. stram. sulph.—Under* or *around* the nose: *Bell. n-vom. rhab.*

d) Sweat on the *neck* and nape of the neck: 1) *Bell. nitr-ac. sulph.* 2) *Ars. kal. mang. n-vom. phos-ac. rhus. stann.*

e) On the *back:* 1) *Chin. petr. phos-ac.* 2) *Ars. calc. dulc. guaj. hep. lach. natr. sep. sil. veratr.*

f) On the *chest: Agar. arn. canth. chin. cocc. graph. hep. lyc. nitr. nitr-ac. phos. phos-ac. selen. sep. sil.*

g) On the *abdomen: Amb. anac. arg. canth. dros. phos. plumb. staph.*

h) About the *sexual* parts: 1) *Aur. hep. sep. sil. sulph. thuj.* 2) *Amm. baryt. bell. canth. con. ign. magn-m. merc. n-vom. phos-ac. rhod. selen. staph.*

i) In the *axillæ:* 1) *Hep. kal. lach. nitr-ac. petr. sep. sulph.* 2) *Bry. caps. carb-an. dulc. rhod. selen. squill. thuj. zinc.*

k) On the *hands:* 1) *Calc. con. hep. sep. sil. sulph.* 2) *Baryt. carb-v. dulc. ign. jod. led. nitr-ac. n-vom. petr. puls. rhab. thuj. zinc.*

l) On the *feet:* 1) *Calc. carb-v. kal. lyc. nitr-ac. sep. sil. sulph.* 2) *Amm. baryt. cupr. dros. graph. lach. magn-m. natr-m. petr. phos-ac. puls. sabad. sabin. thuj. zinc.*—And if this sweat should smell badly: *Baryt. graph. kal. nitr-ac. sep. sil. zinc.*

§ 4. a) *Exhausting* sweats: 1) *Ars. carb-an. chin. ferr. natr-m. nitr. phos. sep. sil. stann. sulph.* 2) *Calc. cocc. jod. lyc. merc. n-vom. samb. veratr.*

b) Profuse sweats, not affording any relief, especially with pains in the limbs, catarrhal or rheumatic fevers, &c.: *Chin. dulc. lach. lyc. merc. nitr. sep.*

c) *Oily, fatty* sweats: *Bry. chin. magn-c. merc. stram.*

d) Warm or *hot* sweats: *Bell. bry. camph. cham. lach. op. phos. sabad. stann.*

e) *Cold* sweats: 1) *Ars. camph. carb-v. chin. cin. hyos. ipec. sec. veratr.* 2) *Aur. cupr. ferr. hep. ign. lach. magn-arct. n-vom. petr. puls. sabad. sep. staph. stram. tart.*

f) *Sticky* sweats: *Acon. anac. ars. bry. calc. camph. carb-an. cham. chin. ferr. hep. lyc. merc. n-vom. phos. phos-ac. plumb. sec. spig. veratr.*

g) Sweat leaving a *stain on the linen: Ars. bell. carb-an. graph. lach. merc. rhab. selen.*

§ 5. a) *Fetid* sweats: 1) *Amm-m. baryt. dulc. graph. hep. led. lyc. nitr-ac. n-vom. phos. rhus. selen. sep. sil. staph. sulph.* 2)

Bell. canth. carb-an. ferr. kal. magn-c. merc. puls. rhod. spig. veratr.

b) *Sour-smelling ;* 1) *Ars. asar. bry. lyc. nitr-ac. sep. sil. sulph. veratr.* 2) *Arn. bell. carb-v. cham. ferr. hep. ipec. kal. led. magn-c. merc. n-vom. rhus.*

c) Bitter-smelling: *Veratr.*—With smell as of *blood : Lyc.*—*Empyreumatic* smell: *Bell. magn-arct. sulph.*—*Fetid* smell: *Carb-v. n-vom. staph. stram.*—*Acrid* smell: *Rhus-t.*

SWELLING OF THE CHEEK.

For swelling in consequence of tooth-ache: 1) *Arn. cham. merc. magn-arct. n-vom. puls. sep. staph.;* or, 2) *Ars. aur. bell. bry. carb-v. caust. sulph.*, &c.

For *red* and *hot swelling : Arn. bell. bry. cham. merc.*

Hard swelling: *Arn. bell. cham.*

Pale swelling: *Bry. n-vom. sep. sulph.*

Erysipelatous : 1) *Cham. sep.* 2) *Bell. graph. hep. lach. rhus. sulph.*—and other remedies indicated for erysipelas.

If remedies had been administered for the toothache before the swelling set in, give after *Merc.* and *Cham. : Puls. ;* or after *Puls.* or *Bell., Merc.; Bell.* after *Merc. ;* or *Sulph.* after *Bell. bry.*, &c.

Compare: TOOTHAQHE.

SWELLING OF THE LABIA, (VULVA.)

The lymphatic swelling of the *labia* requires: *Merc. sep. sulph.*

Swelling of the prepuce, if not caused either by gonorrhœa or syphilis, requires: *Acon. arn. merc. rhus. sep. sulph.*

See: SYPHILIS, GONORRHŒA, PHIMOSIS, HERPES PRÆPUTIALIS, &c.

SWELLING OF THE LIPS.

Scrofulous swelling of the lips requires: *Aur. bell. bry. hep. lach. merc. sil. staph. sulph.*, &c.

Swelling and *eversion* of the lip: *Bell. merc.*

Crusts and *ulceration* of the lips: 1) *Bell. hep. merc. sep. sil. staph. sulph. ;* or, 2) *Ars. aur. cic. clem. graph. natr-m. nitr-ac.*, &c.

Scirrhous indurations and *cancerous* ulcers: 1) *Bell. sil. sulph.* 2) *Ars. clem. con.*

Compare: *Eruptions* in the face and *swelling* of the face.

SYCOMA, SYCOSIS MENTI ET CAPILLICII.

Principal remedies: 1) *Ars. carb-v. cic. graph. hep. sil.* 2) *Con.? staph.? sulph.? thuj.?*

SYCOSIS HAHNEMANNI, Venereal figwarts.

Principal remedies: *Nitr-ac.* and *Thuja;* moreover: *Cinn. euphr. lyc. phos-ac. sabin. staph.;* or, *N-vom. sassap.*

The *suppurating, horny* and *crest-shaped* warts seem to require *Thuja;* the *pediculated, Lyc.;* and the *flat* ones: *Sassap. sulph.*

(See: Syphilis.)

SYNCOPE, Lypothymia, Fainting.

§ 1. Principal remedies for fainting, sudden loss of consciousness, hysteric weakness, &c., require: *Acon. camph. carb-v. cham. hep. ign. lach. mosch. n-vom. phos-ac. veratr.*

§ 2. If caused by *fright* or some other emotion, give: *Acon. amm. camph. cham. coff. ign. lach. op. veratr.*

If by *violent* pain: *Acon.* or *Cham.*

If by the *least* pain: *Hep. n-mosch.*

To *hysteric persons* give: *Cham. cocc. ign. mosch. n-mosch. n-vom.;* or, 2) *Ars. natr-m.*

If caused by *debilitating* losses, or *acute* diseases, give: *Carb-v. chin. n-mosch. n-vom. veratr.*

If by *abuse of Mercury: Carb-v.;* or, *Hep. lach. op.*

§ 3. Give more particularly:

Aconitum: For: violent palpitation of the heart, congestion of blood to the head, buzzing in the ears; and if the fainting takes place as soon as the patient raises himself from a recumbent posture, with chills and deadly paleness of the face, which was red previously.

Carbo veg.: The paroxysms set in after sleeping, after *rising* in the morning, or while yet in bed.

Chamomilla: The paroxysm is accompanied with vertigo, darkness of sight, hard hearing, sensation of qualmishness and flatness in the pit of the stomach, &c.

Coffea: Suitable to sensitive persons, and if the symptoms caused by fright do not yield to *Acon.*

Hepar: The paroxysms set in in the evening, preceded by vertigo.

Lachesis: Asthmatic affections, vertigo, pale face, *nausea,* vomiting, *pains and stitches* in the region of *the heart, cold sweat,* spasms, trismus, stiffness and swelling of the body, &c.

Moschus: The paroxysms set in at night, or in the open air, with *pulmonary spasms,* or *succeeded by headache.*

Nux vom.: The paroxysms set in principally in the morning, or *after a meal;* also suitable to pregnant females or persons worn out by mental labour or addicted to the use of spirits; and generally, when nausea, pale face, scintillations before the eyes, or obscuration of sight, pains in the stomach, anguish, trembling and congestion of blood to the head or chest are present.

Phosphori acid.: The paroxysms set in after a meal, *Nux-v.* being insufficient.

Veratrum: The paroxysms set in after the least motion, or are preceded by great *anguish* or despondency; or attended by spasms, lock-jaw, convulsive motion of the eyes and eyelids, &c.

SYPHILIS AND SYCOSIS.

The principal remedy is *Mercurius* 3, a dose every day or every other day. After eight or ten days, (or even after two or three days,) red tips, being healthy granulations, can be perceived at the bottom of the ulcer, which continue to increase. During this time the ulcer sometimes bleeds and the edges become depressed.

After the syphilitic character of the ulcer, that is, its lardaceous appearance, has disappeared, and the cicatrix should not form properly, or proud flesh should start up from the ulcer, *Nitr-ac.* can be given with excellent effect.

Nitric-ac. is likewise excellent for chancres that had been ineffectually treated with large doses of Mercury. It should not be given when the chancres heal of *themselves*, without Mercury.

§ 3. Every chancre which is not treated, or improperly treated with *Mercury*, becomes chronic after the lapse of from six to eight weeks, losing its lardaceous appearance and raised edges, and exhibiting a red surface with a hard bottom, and secreting a thin, bad pus. *Nitr-ac.* should not be given for such chancres, for it favours the breaking out of general syphilis, the symptoms of which are roseola on the abdomen, and pimples on the forehead and region of the stomach. The principal remedy is *Mercurius*, which should be continued, giving one dose every forty-eight hours until the chancre and the spots and pimples have disappeared. Should doubtful symptoms develop themselves after the disappearance of the chancre, and should their true nature, whether mercurial or syphilitic, not be apparent, give: *Aur. carb-v. lach. nitr-ac. phos-ac. thuj.*

§ 4. *Secondary chancres* in the throat require the same treatment as the primitive chancre; sometimes a few doses of *Thuja* may be given, if the patient should have taken much Mercury.

Buboes require *Mercurius*, the same as the chancre; but if the patient should have been drugged with large doses of Calomel, give *Nitr-ac.*, or sometimes *Aurum* or *Carb-veg.*

§ 5. Constitutional syphilis requires *Mercury*; or, if the patient should have been drugged with it: *Alum. bell. carb-veg. clem. dulc. guaj. hep. jod. lyc. phos-ac. sassap. staph.*

Syphilitic *bone-pains* require: *Aur. merc. lach.*;—*spots* and *herpes*: *Merc. lach. nitr-ac. thuj.*;—syphilitic *ophthalmia*: *Merc* or *Nitr-ac.* *

TASTE, ALTERATIONS OF.

§ 1. Changes of taste are mere symptoms, which, however, point to the following remedies: 1) *Acon. ant. arn. ars. bell. bry. cham. chin. coccul. ipec. merc. n-vom. puls. rhus.* 2) *Bry. caps. carb-veg. hep. kal. natr. nat-m. n-vom. petr. phosph. rhab. sabin. sep. squill. staph. sulph. tart. veratr.* 3) *Asa. asar. calc. cupr. ign. lach. lyc. magn-m. sil. stann. sulph-ac. tarax.*

§ 2. Use more particularly:

a) For *bitter* taste: 1) *Acon. arn. ars. bry. calc. cham. chin. merc. natr. natr-m. n-vom. puls. sabad. sep. sulph. veratr.* 2) *Amm. carb-an. carb-veg. coloc. con. dros. ferr. ipec. kal. lach. lyc. magn-m. sil. spong. staph. tart.*

b) Taste as of *blood*: 1) *Ipec. sil. zinc.* 2) *Alum. amm. ferr. kal. natr. sabin.*

c) *Empyreumatic*: *Cycl. puls. ran. squill. sulph.*

d) As of *pus*: *Merc. natr. puls.*

e) *Clayey*: *Cann. chin. ferr. hep. ign. phosph. puls. stann.*

f) *Flat*: *watery*, insipid: 1) *Bry. chin. ign. natr-m. puls. staph.* 2) *Acon. ant. arn. ars. bell. caps. ipec. kal. lyc. magn-m. natr. petr. phosph. phos-ac. rhab. rhus. ruta. stann. sulph.*

g) *Foul*, as of bad eggs, cheese, &c.: 1) *Acon. arn. merc. puls. rhus. sulph.* 2) *Bell. bry. carb-veg. cham. con. natr-m. n-vom. petr. phosph. sep. veratr.*

* The specific remedy for syphilitic diseases is undoubtedly *Mercury*, the lower triturations of which are generally used. The *red precipitate* acts more intensely than the *Merc. sol. Hahnem.*, and Mueller reports a case where both these preparations failed, and *Cinnabaris* effected a cure. Cinnabaris is likewise effectual in gonorrhœa, even in cases where the other mercurial preparations fail. Goullon of Weimar recommends *Merc. corr.* for chancres, one half of a grain, 1st trit., with eight ounces of pure water and half an ounce of spirits of wine, a tablespoonful morning and evening (diminishing the quantity when vomiting followed the first dose or two.) He recommends baths of *Merc. corrosiv.* for syphilitic eruptions, scrofula, &c. except when much Mercury had been used previously, in which case *Acid. nitr.* is recommended. In sore throat *Lyc.*, in ostitis and exostitis *Sil.*, and in tetters and herpetic sores *Sassapar.* (ptisan) proved the most serviceable. Attomyr recommends the following remedies for chancre: *Merc. sol.*, *merc. dulc. merc-corr. acid. nitr. thuj. hep. corollia rubra, acid-phosph. sulph. caust. staph.* He cured a case of syphilitic orchitis with *Clematis* and a case of mismanaged condylomata on the anus with *Staphysagria*. *Mezereum* should not be forgotten in the treatment of nodes. A great many homœopathic physicians in this city, use strong injections of *nitrate of silver* for the cure of gonorrhœa. *Hempel.*

h) *Greasy*, oily: *Alum. asa. caust. lyc. mang. puls. rhus. sabin. sil. val.*

i) *Herby: N-vom. phos-ac. puls. sassap. veratr.*

k) *Metallic*, brassy, &c.: 1) *Agn. amm. calc. coccul. cupr. lach. natr. natr-m. n-vom. rhus.* 2) *Alum. coloc. magn-aust. ran. sassap. seneg. sulph. zinc.*

l) *Pappy*, viscid, slimy: *Cham. chin. dig. lyc. magn-c. magn-m. merc. n-vom. petr. phosph. puls. rhab. rhus.*

m) *Rancid: Alum. amb. asa. bry. cham. ipec. mur-ac. petr.*

n) *Salt:* 1) *Ars. carb-veg. merc. phosph. puls. sep. zinc.* 2) *Chin. lach. lyc. natr. rhus. sulph. veratr.*

o) *Sour:* 1) *Amm. bell. calc. chin. kal. merc. natr-m. n-vom. phosph. puls. sulph.* 2) *Alum carb-an. cham. chin. coccul. con. graph. ign. lach. lyc. magn-c. magn-m. natr. nitr. nitr-ac. petr. phos-ac. rhus. sep. stann. tarax.*

p) *Bad* taste *generally*, as from a spoiled stomach: 1) *Bry. calc. kal. merc. n-vom. puls. sep.* 2) *Ars. asa. caust. chin. ign. natr-m. petr. stann. sulph-ac. val. zinc.*

q) *Sweetish:* 1) *Bell. bry. chin. dig. nitr-ac. phosph. plumb. puls. sabad. squill. stann. sulph.* 2) *Acon. alum. amm. chin. cupr. ferr. ipec. kal. lyc. merc. n-vom. rhus. sassap. sulph-ac.*

§ 3. Comp.: Gastric derangement, Weak stomach, &c.

TEA, ill effects of.—Principal remedies: 1) *Ferr. selen. thuj.* 2) *Chin. coff. lach. veratr.*

THICKENING OF THE BLADDER.—Principal remedies: *Dulc. merc. puls. sulph.*—See Catarrh of the Bladder, and Cystitis.

TIN, ILL EFFECTS OF.—Poisoning with large doses requires: 1) *White of an egg:* 2) *Sugar;* 3) *Milk.* —The chronic ailments require: *Puls.;* or: *Carb-veg. hep. ign.*

TINEA CAPITIS.—Principal remedies: 1) *Ars. calc. hep. lyc. rhus. sulph.;* or, 2) *Bar-c. cic. graph. oleand. phosph. sep. staph. vinc.*

For *dry scaldhead* (*tinea furfuracea, amiantacea, favosa? granulata*) give: 1) *Sulph.* or, *Calc.;* or, 2) *Ars. hep. phosp. rhus-t.*

For *humid scaldhead* (*achor tinea capitis et faciei musciflua*): *Lyc. sulph.;* or, 2) *Hep. rhus. sep.;* or, 3) *Bar-c. calc. cic. graph. oleand. staph. vinc.*

If other *scrofulous ailments* should be present at the same time, such as: swelling of the cervical glands, &c., give: 1) *Amm. ars. baryt. calc. staph.;* or, 2) *Bry. dulc.*

The best mode of classifying tinea, is as follows:

1) *Tinea granulata*, the real *dry* scaldhead, resembling *favus*, except that the tips are arched, not depressed in the shape of a goblet.

2) *Tinea muciflua*, humid scaldhead, groups of pustules, with copious secretion of moisture, which, on drying, causes the hairs to stick together and covers the head like a layer.

3) *Tinea favosa*, s. favus, a sort of fungous growth, in the shape of small pustules depressed at their tips.

4) *Tinea annulata*, circular groups of yellowish pustules, through whose centre a hair passes; with destruction of the follicles.

5) *Tinea amiantacea*, or eczema of the hairy scalp, generally affecting old people.

It might perhaps be desirable that we should finally succeed in prescribing certain remedies for certain forms of tinea, though I (Jahr) think that the constitutional symptoms of the patient are better indications for the selection of a remedy than the form of the eruption.

TOBACCO, ILL EFFECTS OF.

§ 1. Principal remedies: *Acon. bry. cham. chin. cocc. coloc. cupr. merc. n-vom. puls. staph. veratr.*

§ 2. For the immediate consequences, give: *Acon. cham. cocc. cupr. n-vom. puls. staph. veratr.*

The *chronic* ailments require: *Cocc. merc. n-vom. staph.*

For the effects of *chewing*, give: *Cham. cocc. cupr. n-vom. puls.*

For working in *tobacco-manufactories: Ars. coloc. cupr.*

§ 3. Use more particularly:

Aconitum: Violent headache with nausea.

Chamomilla: Vertigo, stupefaction, fainting, bilious vomiting, diarrhœa, &c.

Cocculus: Bad digestion, great sensitiveness of the nerves.

Nux vom.: Bad digestion, nausea, nervousness and obstinate constipation.

Pulsatilla: Nausea, loss of appetite, thick saliva in the mouth, diarrhœa and colic.

Staphysagria: Anxiety and restlessness, nausea, obstinate constipation, &c.

Veratrum: Weakness, fainting turn, diarrhœa, icy coldness of the extremities and body, &c.

§ 4. For the *toothache*, give: *Bry.* or, *Chin.;* for the *nausea: Ign.;* and for the *constipation: Mercury.*

TONGUE, DISEASES OF THE.

§ 1. Most of them, from a simple coating up to inflammation, suppuration and gangrenous disorganization, are mere symptoms, induced by digestive derangements, fevers, poisonous substances, dyscrasias, &c.; nevertheless, in selecting a remedy, these symptoms deserve particular attention, inasmuch as they generally indicate specific remedies.

§ 2. *Coating* of the tongue: 1) *Ant. arn. bell. bry. cham. chin. dig. ign. ipec. merc. phosph. plumb. puls. rhus. sabad. sep. sil. sulph.* 2) *Acon. amb. ars. carb-veg. cin. dig. dulc. hep. hyos. jod. lach. natr. natr-m. nitr. nitr-ac. n-vom. petr. sabin. sec. seneg. staph. tart. thuj. veratr. verb.*

Brown coating: *Bell. carb-veg. hyos. n-vom. sabin. sil. sulph. verb.*—*Thick* coating: *Baryt. bell. bry. cham. chin. lach. merc. phosph. sec. sabad. sabin. selen.*—*Yellowish* coating: *Bell. bry. carb-veg. cham. chin. coloc. ipec. lach. mez. n-vom. plumb. puls. sabad. sabin. seneg. veratr. zinc.*—*Gray: Amb. puls. tart.*—*Greenish: Magn-c. magn-m. plumb. rhod.*—*Slimy: Bell. chin. cupr. dig. dulc. lach. magn-arct. natr. n-mosch. n-vom. phosph. puls. seneg. sep. sil. stann. stront. sulph.*—*White: Arn. ars. bell. calc. carb-veg. cham. chin. croc. dig. ign. ipec. merc. n-mosch. n-vom. oleand. petr. phosph. puls. staph. thuj.*

Bluish colour of the tongue requires: *Ars. dig. mur-ac*—*Brown: Ars. lach. n-vom plumb. rhus. sec. sulph.*—*Paleness: Agar. lach. merc. natr.*—*Red: Ars. bell. cham. hyos. rhus. stann. sulph. veratr.*—*Black: Ars. chin. lach. n-vom. op. sec. rhus. veratr.*—*White: Ars. bell. bry. coloc. graph. hell. lach. nitr-ac. n-vom. op. petr puls. sep. sulph.*

Dryness of the tongue and mouth: 1) *Acon. ars. bell. bry. carb-veg. cham. cist. dulc. hyos. phosph. rhus.* 2) *Arn. calc. caps. hell kal. merc. natr. natr-m. nitr-ac. plumb. puls. staph. stram. sulph. sulph-ac. veratr*—*Feeling of dryness* when the tongue is moist: *Acon. ars. bell. Camph. caps. chin. coff. n-mosch. phosph. rhab. rhus. stront. sulph-ac.*

§ 3. *Inflammation* of the tongue: *Canth. plumb. ran-sc.*—*Blisters* or pimples on the tongue: *Amm. ant. calc. canth. carb-an. caust. cham. graph. hell. merc. mez. mur-ac. natr. natr-m. nitr-ac. n-vom. sabad. sep. spig. squill. thuj. zinc.*—*Ulcers: Bov. cic. dig. graph. lyc. merc. mur-ac. natr-m. op.*—*Apthæ: Agar. borax. cham. hell. merc. mur-ac. n-vom. sassap. sulph. sulph-ac. thuj.*—*Soreness: Agar. carb-veg. dig. kal. lach. lyc. merc. mez. mur-ac. natr-m. nitr-ac. phosph. phos-ac. sabad. sil.*

Swelling of the tongue: *Calc. con. dig. dros. dulc. hell. kal.*

lach. lyc. merc. natr-m. phos-ac. sec. sil. stram. thuj.—*Suppuration: Canth. merc.*

§ 4. *Paralysis: Acon. ars. bell. caust. dulc. graph. hyos. lach. n-mosch. op. stram.*

Stiffness: Borax. colch. euphr. lach. natr-m.

Difficulty of moving the tongue: *Anac. bell. calc. con. lyc.*

Heaviness of the tongue: *Anac. bell. carb-veg. colch. lyc. mur-ac. natr-m. plumb.*

§ 5. See: STOMACACE, SPEECH, DIFFICULTIES OF, ANGINA FAUCIUM, &c.

TONSILLITIS.—Principal remedies: 1) *Baryt. bell. hep. ign. lach. merc. nitr-ac. n-vom. sulph.;* or, 2) *Calc. canth. cham. gran.? lyc. sep. thuj.*

Suppuration and *ulceration* of the tonsils: *Bar-c. bell. ign. lach. lyc. merc. nitr-ac. sep.*

Induration: Baryt. calc. ign. sulph.

Inflammatory swelling which threatens to terminate in suppuration: 1) *Acon. bell.;* then, 2) *Hep. lach. merc.;* 3) *Ign. n-vom. sulph.* See: SUPPURATION.

TOOTHACHE.

§ 1. Principal remedies: 1) ***Bell. cham. merc. n-vom. puls. sulph.*** 2) *Bry. calc. chin. hyos. ign. mez. rhus. spig. staph. magn-arct.* 3) *Acon. ant. arn. ars. carb-veg. coff. hep. sep. sil. veratr.* 4) *Baryt. caust. cycl. dulc. euphorb. magn-c. nitr-ac. phos-ac. plat. sabin.*

§ 2. For pains in *hollow* teeth: 1) ***Ant.*** 2) ***Magn-arct. mez.*** *sep. staph.* 3) *Acon. bell. borax. chin. merc. natr. n-vom. puls.* 4) *Baryt. bry. calc. cham. coff. hyos. kreos. lach. lyc. magn-c. phosph. phos-ac. plat. plumb. rhus. sabin. sil. sulph.*—It is very difficult to discover the suitable remedy; if no proper remedy can be found, introduce a little cotton moistened with one drop of the *tincture of Aconite* into the hollow tooth, or in some cases, *Bell.* instead of the *Acon.* This frequently affords instantaneous relief.

§ 3. If *several teeth* at once, or a whole jaw should be affected, give: *Cham. merc. rhus. staph.;* or for pains on *one* side: 1) *Cham. merc. puls. rhus.* 2) *Calc. chin. ign. mez. phos-ac. plat. spig. sulph.*

Toothache with pain in the *facial bones,* requires: *Clem. hyos. magn-c. merc. n-vom. rhus. spig. sulph.*—If the pain extends to the *eyes: Cham. calc. clem. puls. spig.*—To the *ears: Ars. bell.*

cham. clem. kreos. merc. puls. sep. sulph.—To the *head: Ant. ars. bell. cham. hyos. merc. n-vom. puls. rhus. sulph.*

Toothache with *swelling* of the *cheeks*, requires: 1) *Arn. cham. lyc. magn-arct. magn-c. merc. n-vom. puls. sep. staph.* 2) *Ars. aur. bell. bry. carb-veg. caust. sulph.*—Swelling of the *gums: Acon. bell. cham. chin. hep. hyos. merc. n-vom. phos-ac. rhus. sep. staph. sulph.*—Swelling of the *submaxillary glands: Carb-veg. cham. merc. n-vom. sep. staph.*

§ 4. Toothache from *congestion of blood:* 1) *Acon. bell. calc. cham. chin. hyos. mez. puls. sep.*; or, 2) *Aur. phosph. plat. sulph.*

Rheumatic or *arthritic* toothache: 1) *Acon. bell. caust. cham. chin. merc. n-vom. puls. staph. sulph.*; or, 2) *Arn. bry. cycl. hep. lyc. magn-c. phosph. rhus. sabin. veratr. magn-arct.*

Nervous toothache requires: 1) *Acon. bell. cham. coff. hyos. ign. n-vom. plat. spig. magn-arct.*; or, 2) *Ars. magn-c. mez. sulph. veratr.*, &c.

§ 5. Toothache from *abuse of coffee:* 1) *Cham. ign. n-vom.*; or, 2) *Bell. carb-veg. merc.*; or, 3) *Cocc. puls. rhus.*

From *smoking:* 1) *Bry. chin. spig.*; or, 2) *Cham. merc. sassap.*

From *abuse* of *mercury:* 1) *Carb-veg. nitr-ac.*; or, 2) *Bell. chin. hep. puls. staph. sulph.*

From a *cold:* 1) *Acon. bell. cham. coff. dulc. ign. merc. n-vom. puls.*; or, 2) *Baryt. calc. chin. hyos. magn-arct. n-mosch. phosph. rhus. sulph.*—From exposure to *cold* and *damp* air: 1) *N-mosch. puls.*; or, 2) *Bell. calc. hyos. merc. sil. staph. sulph.*—From the *water* which one drinks: 1) *Bry. carb-veg. merc. staph. sulph.* 2) *Calc. cham. mosch. n-vom. puls. sil. sulph.*

§ 6. Toothache of *nervous* and *sensitive* persons requires: *Acon. bell. coff. hyos. ign. n-vom. plat. spig.*

Toothache of *females: Acon. bell. calc. cham. chin. coff. hyos. ign. plat. puls. sabin. sep. spig.*—Of *plethoric* young *girls: Acon. bell. calc.*—At the time of the *menses:* 1) *Amm. baryt. calc. carb-veg. cham. graph. lach. magn-c. natr-m. nitr-ac. phosph. sep.*—During *pregnancy:* 1) *Bell. calc. magn. n-mosch. n-vom. puls. sep. staph.* 2) *Alum. hyos. rhus.*—During *nursing: Chin.*—Of *hysteric females: Ign. sep.*

Toothache of *children: Acon. bell. calc. cham. coff. ign. merc. sulph.*

§ 7. Symptomatic indications:

Belladonna: Anxiety driving one to and fro; or for: sadness, whining mood; pains in the gums and teeth as if ulcerated; tearing, cutting, stitching or drawing pains in the teeth, face and ears, worse in the evening, after lying down, and especially at night; boring in the carious teeth, as from congestion of blood, with bleeding on sucking at the teeth; painful swelling of the gums, with heat, itching, vesicles, and burning; swelling of the cheeks; *ptyalism*, or dryness of the throat and mouth, with great thirst; the pains are renewed by mental labour, or after a meal; *aggravation in the open air* and by the *contact of food* (while chewing, &c.); *hot* and *red face*; *beating in the head* or cheeks; burning and redness of the eyes. (After ***Bell.*** are sometimes suitable: ***Merc. hep.***, or *cham. puls.*)

Chamomilla: Irritable and whining mood during the pain; violent drawing, jerking, or *beating* and *stitching* pains; *pains that seem intolerable*, especially at night, in bed, driving one to despair, with *hot swelling of the cheeks*, and redness, shining swelling of the gums, and swelling of the submaxillary glands; pains in one whole side of the jaw without the patient being able to point out the tooth which is affected; digging and gnawing in a carious tooth, with looseness; stitching or beating semilateral pains in the whole side of the head which is affected, in the ear and face; aggravation or renewal of the pains from eating or drinking any thing cold or *warm*, especially *coffee;* pains with heat and redness, especially of *one cheek;* warm sweat, even in the hairs; anxiety, restlessness, or weakness unto fainting, &c.

Mercurius: Tearing, stitching pains in the carious teeth, or in the roots of the teeth, affecting the whole side of the head and face, even to the ears; painful swelling of the cheek or submaxillary glands; *ptyalism;* aggravation in the evening or at night, *in bed;* the pains are excited by cool and damp air, or by eating or drinking any thing hot or cold; dullness, looseness and sensation of elongation of the teeth; swollen, whitish, ulcerated, and colourless gums, readily bleeding, with itching, burning and soreness to the touch; *night-sweats*, vertigo, rheumatic pains in the limbs: peevish or whining mood; chilliness, red cheeks, &c. (Is frequently suitable before or after ***Bell.*** or *dulc.*, or before ***Hep.*** or *carb-veg.*)

Nux vom.: Suitable to persons of a lively, choleric temperament, with bright complexion; also to individuals who indulge in coffee, wine, brandy, or who lead a sedentary and confined life; sore pains or jerking drawing, with stitches in the teeth and jaw, or only in the carious teeth; pains extending to the head, ears and malar bones, with painful swelling of the submaxillary glands: *swelling* and sensitiveness of the gums, with beating as if in an ulcer; red and hot spots on the cheeks and neck; aggravation or renewal of the pains at night, or *early after waking*, or after dinner, during a walk in the open air, when reading, thinking, or performing any other mental labour, or in a warm room; relief in the open air; lamenting and despairing, or irritable, quarrelsome, peevish humour.

Pulsatilla: Suitable to individuals of a bland, quiet and timid disposition, and who cry easily; *toothache with otalgia* and *hemicrania;* tearing, drawing, stitching or jerking pains, as if the nerves were put upon the stretch, and then suddenly let go again; or beating, digging and gnawing pains, with creeping in the gums; pains which extend to the face, head, eye and ear of the affected side, with *pale* face, heat in the head, chilliness of the body, and asthma; aggravation or renewal of the pains in the evening or at night, *after midnight*, in bed and in a warm room, or from eating or drinking any thing warm, when sitting or picking the teeth; *relief by cold water* (which sometimes aggravates the pain), and by *cool, fresh air.*

§ 8. Bryonia: Suitable to persons of a lively and choleric disposition, or to vehement and obstinate people; pains in carious and still more in the sound teeth; jerking and drawing pains, with *looseness of the teeth* and *sensation of elongation*, especially during and after a meal; stitches in the ear; pains, with desire to lie down; worse at night or by introducing any thing warm into the mouth, or by lying on the sound cheek, relief being obtained by turning to the affected side; soreness of the gums.

Calcarea: Toothache, with *congestion of blood to the head*, especially at night; with *beating*, stitching, boring pains, or soreness; gnawing and digging, both in the carious and sound teeth; swelling, painful sensitiveness of the gums, with liability to bleed; aggravation or renewal of the pains by a draught of air, or *cold air*, or by drinking any thing *warm* or cold, or by the least noise, cold, and when the menses make their appearance.

China: After debilitating losses of animal fluids, while nursing, &c.; or if the pains should cause ill, quarrelsome humour; or for dull, distressing pains in the carious teeth; or beating, drawing and jerking pains; the pains come on or get worse after a meal, or *at night*, or after the least contact; they return in the open air, or in a draught, and abate by pressing the teeth firmly together; swelling of the gums; dry mouth with thirst; congestion of blood to the head, with swelling of the veins on the forehead and hands; restless sleep at night.

Hyoscyamus: Violent tearing and beating pains, extending rom the cheek to the forehead; swelling of the gums, with tearing pains and buzzing in the tooth, which appears to be loose; the pains come on in cold air, or early in the morning; congesion of blood to the head, with heat and redness of the face;

spasms in the throat, or convulsive twitching of the fingers, hands or arms; nervousness; red and shining eyes.

IGNATIA: In many cases where *N-vom.* and *puls* seem to be indicated, or suitable to persons of a bland disposition, or who are now disposed to weep, then to be merry and cheerful, but especially to persons who are apt to give themselves up to grief; the teeth feel bruised, loose; the pains are particularly felt towards the end of the meal, or are even worse; or they are aggravated by coffee, smoking, after lying down in bed in the evening, or on waking in the morning.

MAGNETIS POL. ARCTICUS: Pains in the carious teeth, *as if they would be pulled out*, or painful jerks and shocks through the periosteum of the jaw, with drawing, aching, tearing, digging, burning or stitching pains; swelling and painfulness of the gums to contact, or the gums feel numb when the pains abate; aggravation of the pains after eating, and in warmth; relief in the open air and when walking; red and hot swelling of the cheek; chilliness of the body; nervousness, tremour of the limbs

MEZEREUM: The carious teeth are principally affected, with burning, boring or drawing stitches, extending to the facial bones and temples; sensation as if the teeth were too dull, and elongated; aggravation of the pains by contact, motion, or in the evening, with chilliness, rushes of blood, congestion of blood to the head; feeling of rigidity and drawing pains in the affected side of the head; constipation, loss of appetite, ill-humour.

RHUS TOX.: Suitable to persons of a quiet, melancholy or anxious disposition; for *tearing, jerking* or *stitching* pains, or for digging and *creeping*, and sore pains in the teeth; the pains get worse, or come on in the open air, or *at night*, when they are intolerable; relief by applying something warm; the gums are painful, and burn; the teeth are loose, and the carious teeth smell badly. (Comp. *Bell.* and *Bry.*)

SPIGELIA: Aching, distensive pains, or jerking, *beating, tearing*, especially in the carious teeth; the pains set in immediately after eating, or at night, obliging the patient to get up; worse by applying cold water or going into the open air; particularly useful for: burning, jerking and tearing pains in the malar bones; bloatedness of the face, with yellowish colour around the eyes; pains in the eyes; frequent desire to urinate, palpitation of the heart, chilliness, restlessness.

STAPHYSAGRIA: The teeth are becoming black, carious, and commence crumbling, with *pale, white, ulcerated, swollen* and *painful gums*, readily bleeding, with tubercles and excrescences; swelling of the cheek and submaxillary glands; aching, tearing and drawing pains in the gums, in the carious teeth and in the roots of the sound teeth; the pains are worse or set in when chewing, or immediately *after drinking any thing cold,* or *after eating*, or by exposure to *cold air*, or *early in the morning*, or at night.

Sulphur: For *tearing, jerking* and *beating* pains, in sound or *carious* teeth; pains which extend to the ears and head, with swelling of the cheeks, congestion of blood to the head, headache, inflammatory redness of the eyes and nose; *stitches in the ears;* constipation, with frequent but ineffectual urging to stool; pains in the small of the back; restlessness in the extremities; drowsiness in the daytime, chilliness; aggravation or renewal of the pains in the evening, or at night in bed, or in the open air, in a current of air; also by applying *cold water*, when eating or chewing; looseness, elongation or dullness of the teeth; the gums bleed readily, recede from the teeth, are swollen, with beating pains. (Suitable after *Coff.* or *Acon.*)

§ 9. Consider likewise:

Aconitum: When it is difficult to describe the pains, the patient is beside himself, *Coff.* being insufficient; stitching jerks or shocks, or throbbing pains, with congestion of blood to the head, heat in the face, red cheeks and great restlessness.

Antimonium: Pains in *carious* teeth, followed by jerking and gnawing, extending up to the head, especially *in the evening, in bed;* the pains are worse after eating, or by applying cold water; relief in the open air; the gums bleed readily and recede from the teeth.

Arnica: Toothache after an operation; or for *pain as if sprained* in the teeth; or for drawing and pulling in the teeth, while eating; or when the cheek is *swollen, red* and *hard*, with beating and tingling in the gums.

Arsenicum: Elongation and painful looseness of the teeth; drawing, jerking pains in the teeth and gums, extending to the ears, cheek and temples; the pains are so great, that they drive the patient to despair; the pains come on at night, are aggravated by *lying on the affected side;* relief near the warm stove.

Carbo veg.: *Ars.* or *merc.* being insufficient, for receding and bleeding gums, with ulcers; the teeth are loose and sensitive to contact, especially after eating; drawing, tearing or beating pains, especially when the teeth are touched by hot, cold or salt things.

Coffea: Excessive pains, with weeping, trembling, anguish and tossing about; indescribable pains, or tearing and jerking, especially at night or after a meal. (If *Coff.* should not be sufficient, give *Acon.* or *hyoscyam. sulph. veratr.*)

Hepar: Frequently after *Merc.* or *bell.*, especially for painful or erysipelatous swelling of the cheeks; jerking and drawing pains in the teeth, worse when pressing the teeth together, when eating, in a warm room, or *at night.*

Sepia: Beating and stitching pains, especially when the patients have a yellowish complexion; pains which extend to the ears, and along the arm, to the fingers, where they terminate in a creeping sensation; particularly when the pains are attended with *swelling of the cheeks,* cough, and swelling of the submaxillary glands.

Silicea: Stitching pains, with swelling of the jaw-bone or only the *periosteum;* pains affecting the jaw rather than the teeth; or nightly pains, with sleeplessness; unhealthy skin; aggravation of the pains at night, or by the contact of any thing hot or cold.

Veratrum: Pains with swelling of the face, cold sweat on the forehead, nausea or even vomiting of bile; rigidity of the extremities; fainting, coldness of the whole body, with internal heat and excessive desire for cold water; beating pains, or pressure and feeling of heaviness in the teeth.

§ 10. Or try, lastly:

Baryta carb.: The gums and cheeks are pale and swollen, with beating in the ears, especially at night; or burning stitches in the teeth, when touched by any thing warm.

Causticum: Beating or stitching pains, with painful or readily bleeding gums, and rheumatic pains in the facial muscles, eyes and ears.

Cyclamen: Stitching and boring pains, or dull jerking, especially at night, in arthritic patients.

Dulcamara: Toothache from cold, with diarrhœa, *Cham.* being insufficient; or dullness of the head, with ptyalism, and receding, spongy gums, *Bell.* and *merc.* being insufficient.

Euphorbium: Aching, stitching or boring pains, with erysipelatous swelling of the cheek, or with crumbling of the teeth.

Magnesia carbon.: *Boring pains* at night, or tearing and jerking pains, or ulcerative pains; intolerable pains during rest, obliging the patient to get up and walk the room, with swelling of the cheek.

Nitri acidum: Beating, or jerking, stitching and drawing pains, especially in the evening, *in bed.*

Phosphori acidum: Swollen, receding and bleeding gums, with tearing pains, worse in bed and by the contact of hot or cold things; violent pains in the incisores at night.

Platina: Beating and digging pains in the teeth, worse in the evening and during rest; *crampy sensation* and *numb pain* in the affected side of the face; proud, overbearing disposition.

Sabina: Beating or aching pains, setting in in the evening or at night, *in bed,* and after eating, *with sensation as if the tooth would fly to pieces*, or *would be torn out*; beating in the whole body; frequent eructations and loss of blood from the uterus.

§ 11. Use more particularly for: a) Feeling of fullness, swelling, *distensive sensation* in the teeth: *Amb. amm. graph. mur-ac. n-vom. phos-ac. puls. ran. rhod. sabin. spig. spong.*—Sensation as if the teeth would *start* or be *torn* out of their sockets: *Bry. cocc. magn-arct. mez. mur-ac. natr. natr-m. sulph.*—*Boring* and digging in the teeth: *Bell. calc. cham. cycl. laur. magn-arct. magn-c. mez. natr. natr-m. n-vom. plat. puls. sil. sulph.*—*Burning* pains: *Baryt. cham. kal. magn-arct. merc. mez.*—*Buzzing* and roaring, whizzing in the teeth: *Hyos. magn-arct. n-vom. sep. sulph.*—*Aching* pains: 1) *Ars. carb-veg. caust. magn-arct. n-mosch. sep.* 2) *Anac. asa. chin. graph. kal. natr-m. phosph. staph. sulph.*—Sensation of *gnawing*: *Carb-veg. cham. kal. puls. staph. thuj.*—*Ulcerative* pain: *Alum. amm. bell. carb-veg. caust. graph. magn-c. mang. natr. phosph. sil.*—*Bubbling* in the teeth: *Lyc. nitr-ac. spig.* — *Digging*, griping in the teeth: *Amm. ant. borax. carb-an. ign. kal. magn-m. rhus. sulph-ac.*—*Shifting* pains: *Amb. bell. graph. hep jod. magn-c. nitr-ac. puls. tab.*—*Feeling of coldness* of the teeth: *Nitr-ac. phos-ac. sep.*—Sensation as if the tooth were *jammed*: *Amb. anac. carb-veg. cham. magn-arct. plat. spig.*—*Beating* pains: 1) *Caust. chin. kal. magn-arct. natr-m. nitr-ac. sep.* 2) *Acon. amm. bell. cham. coloc. hyos. magn-c. plat. puls. spig. sulph.*—*Tingling* in the teeth: *Acon. arn. baryt. rhus.*—*Feeling of looseness*: 1) *Acon. arn. aur. hyos. ign. merc. nitr-ac. n-mosch. rhus. sulph.* 2) *Alum. amm. baryt. carb-an. carb-veg. caust. hep. hyos. ign. natr-m. n-vom. puls. rhus. sil. staph. sulph.* —*Tearing* in the teeth: 1) *Bell. cupr. hyos. lach. magn-arct. merc. n-mosch. n-vom. puls. rhus. sil.* 2) *Amm. amm-m. borax. carb-veg. caust. chin. mur-ac. sep. staph. sulph-ac.*—*Jerks* in the teeth: *Baryt. bell. calc. magn-arct. merc. sep. spig. sulph.*—Feeling of *weakness* in the teeth: *Amm. merc.*—Feeling of *heaviness*: *Sep. veratr.*—*Stitching* pains: 1) *Baryt. bell. calc. caust. cham. con. cycl. graph. kal. lach. magn-aust. merc. mez. n-mosch. n-vom. phosph. puls. sep. sulph.* 2) *Amm. clem. laur. natr-m. nitr-ac.*—Feeling as if *set on edge*: 1) *Amm. merc. mez. sulph. sulph-ac.* 2) *Aur. dulc. caps. kal. lyc. natr-m. nitr-ac. n-mosch. phosph. phos-ac. sep. sil. staph.*—*Numb* feeling: *Arn. chin. ign. magn-arct. natr-m. plat.*—Sensation as if *elongated*: 1) *Bell. caust. cham. hyos. kreos. mez. stann. sulph.* 2) *Alum. carb-an. carb-veg. lach. magn-arct. magn-c. magn-m. nitr-ac. petr. sep.*—Sensation as if *sprained*: *Arn. merc. n-vom.*—*Digging* pains, see: *Boring.*—Sensation as if they were *soft*: *Alum. caust. ign. lyc.* —*Soreness*: 1) *Bell. n-vom. rhus. thuj. zinc.* 2) *Carb-veg. graph. ign. lach. sep. sil. staph.*—Pain as if *bruised*: *Alum.*

caust. ign. lyc.—*Drawing* pains, see : *Tearing.*—*Jerking* pains : 1) *Cham. clem. coff. magn-arct. nitr-ac. n-vom. puls. sil. spig.* 2) *Bry. chin. rhus.*

§ 12. *Crumbling* of the teeth: *Bell. borax. euphorb. lach. plumb. sabad. staph.*—When they *bleed* readily: *Amb. amm. ant. baryt. bell. carb-v. lach. phos. phos-ac. sep. sulph.*—*Smooth* teeth : *Phos. selen.*—*Yellow : Lyc. nitr-ac. phos-ac.*—*Elongated :* 1) *Bell. caust. cham. hyos. kreos. mez. stann. sulph.* 2) *Alum. carb-an. carb-v. lach. magn-arct. magn-c. magn-m. nitr-ac. petr. sep.*—*Loose :* 1) *Alum. amm. carb-v. caust puls. sulph.* 2) *Baryt. carb-an. hep. merc. natr-m. nitr-ac. n-vom. rhus. sil. sulph.*—Covered with *sordes : Alum. arn. cham. hyos. jod. mez. petr. plumb. sulph.*—*Black : Merc. plumb. sep. squill. staph.*

§ 13. When the *molar* teeth are principally affected: 1) *Amm. bry. carb-v. chin. con. ign. jod. kreos. magn-arct. magn-c. magn-m. meph. natr. nitr-ac. n-vom. phos. rhus. sil. staph. sulph. zinc.*—The *upper* teeth : *Acon. aur. bell. carb-v. chin. kreos. magn-c. magn-m. natr-m. nitr-ac. petr. phos. sep. zinc.*—The *incisores : Agar. alum. carb-v. chin. ign. kal. magn-arct. merc. natr-m. n-mosch. phos. rhus. sep. sulph.*—*Cuspidati : Calc. mur-ac. n-vom. petr. rhus. sep. squill. sulph-ac.*—*Lower* teeth : *Amb. amm. anac. arn. aur. bell. carb-an. carb v. caust. cham. chin. magn-arct. natr. nitr-ac. petr. phos. rhus. ruta. sabad. sabin. spig. sulph-ac. thuj. zinc.*

§ 14. Aggravation in the *evening : Alum. hep. kal. lyc. magn-c. magn-m. merc. mez. natr. nitr-ac. petr. phos. puls. rhus. sabin. sassap. sulph.*—In the evening *in bed : Amm. bell. calc. cham. chin. coff. graph. kal. magn-c. merc. n-mosch. n-vom. phos. puls. rhus. sabin. sil. staph. sulph.*—Relief by *pressing* the teeth together : *Chin. coff. euphorb. magn-m.*—Aggravation *when eating : Aur. bell. bry. carb-v. caust. cham. graph. kal. lach. magn-arct. magn-c. magn-m. merc. n-vom. phos. puls. sep. sil*—*Relief by eating : Amb. amm. cham. magn-arct. nitr-ac. phos-ac. rhod. sil.*—Aggravation by *riding* in a *carriage : Calc. magn-c.*—The pains are *worst in the open air : Alum. amb. amm. caust. con. graph. magn-c. natr. n-vom. petr. phos. staph.*—*Relief* in the *open air : Bry. hep. magn-arct. magn-m. n-vom. sabad. stann.*—The pains set in *early in the morning : Ars. baryt. bry. caust. dros. hyos. ign. kreos. magn-c. magn-m. merc. mez. nitr. n-vom. petr. phos. phos-ac. sabin. sep. sil. staph. sulph. tart. thuj.*—Aggravation by *mental labour*, reading, thinking, &c. : *Bell. ign. n-vom.*—Aggravation by *coffee : Bell. cham. ign. merc. n-vom.*—Aggravation by *cold*, relief by warmth : *Calc. lyc. magn-c. nitr-ac.*—Relief by *cold*, see : aggravation by *warmth :*—Aggravation by eating or drinking anything *cold : Baryt. calc. carb-*

v. cham. con. magn-m. merc. mur-ac. nitr. nitr-ac. n-vom. phos-ac. puls. thuja.—*Relief* by eating or drinking anything *cold : Amb. magn-c. magn-m.*—Aggravation by cold drinks, &c. : *Bry. calc. cham. graph. n-mosch. n-vom. puls. rhus. sep. sil. spig. sulph.*—Relief by cold drinks : *Bry. clem. puls.*—Aggravation by *cold air : Bell. calc. chin. hyos. magn-arct. merc. nitr. n-mosch. n-vom. petr. sassap. sep. sil. staph. sulph.*—Relief by *cold air : N-vom. puls. sep.*—Aggravation by *exposure to air : Amm. ant. aur. bell. bry. calc. caust. chin. hyos. magn-arct. merc. natr-m. n-mosch. n-vom. petr. phos. sep. sil. spig. staph. sulph.* —The pains set in at *night : Amm. bell. calc. cham. chin. clem. coff. graph. kal. lyc. magn-c. merc. natr. natr-m. nitr-ac. n-mosch. n-vom. oleand. phos. puls. rhus. sabin. sil. staph. sulph.*—Aggravation by exposure to *wet*, by wet and damp weather: *Amm. borax. natr. n-mosch. rhod. rhus.*—When the pains appear principally at the time of the *menses : Amm. baryt. calc. carb-v. cham. graph. lach. magn-c. natr-m. nitr-ac. phos. sep.*—The pains set in while *cleaning* the teeth : *Carb-v. graph. lach. lyc. phos-ac. ruta. staph.*—Aggravation by salt things : *Carb-v.* —Relief by salt things: *Magn-c.*—Aggravation by sucking at the teeth : *Amm. bell. carb-v. kal. nitr-ac. n-mosch. n-vom. zinc.* —Relief by sucking : *Clem.*—Aggravation or renewal of the pain by *picking* the teeth : *Puls.*—*Relief* by picking : *Amm. sassap.* —The pain is excited by sweet things : *Natr.*—Aggravation by *smoking : Bry. chin. clem. sabin. sassap. spig.*—Relief by smoking: *Borax. merc. natr. spig.*—Aggravation by drinking, warm or cold : *Amm. caust. cham. dros. lach. rhus. sabin. sil. spig.*—Aggravation by eating or drinking anything warm : *Agn. amb. anac. baryt. bry. calc. carb-v. magn-arct. kal. lach. merc. puls. sep. sil. sulph.*—*Relief* by warm food or drink : *Magn-m. nitr-ac. phos. sil.*—Aggravation by *warm drink : Amm. cham. dros. lach. magn-aust. n-mosch. n-vom. puls. sil.*—Relief by warm drink : *Lyc. n-mosch. sulph.*—Aggravation by *warmth* generally : *Cham. hep. magn-arct. magn-c. n-vom. puls. rhod.*—Relief by *warmth : Ars. kal. natr. n-mosch. n-vom. rhus. sulph-ac.*—Aggravation in a *warm room : Cham. hep. magn-arct. magn-c. n-vom. puls.*—Aggravation in *bed : Cham. graph. magn-c. merc. phos. phos-ac. puls. sabin. spig. sulph-ac.*—*Relief* in bed : *Amm. bry. lyc. n-vom.*—Aggravation in the wind : *Acon. graph. puls. sil.*—Aggravation by a *draught of air : Bell. calc. chin. sassap. sep. sulph.*—Aggravation by *pressing* the teeth against each other, or by *chewing : Alum. amm. bry. graph. guaj. hep. hyos. lyc. natr-m. nitr-ac. phos. phos-ac. puls. rhus. sil. spong. staph. sulph.*—Relief by *chewing : Bry. chin. coff. seneg.*

Compare : PROSOPALGIA, HEADACHE, PAINS, PAROXYSMS OF, CONDITIONS, CAUSES.

TRACHEAL PHTHISIS.

Principal remedies: 1) *Ars. calc. carb-v. caust. cist. phos.* 2) *Dros. hep. kreos. led. mang. nitr-ac.*

See : HOARSENESS, COUGH, BRONCHITIS, LARYNGITIS, &c.

TREMBLING, TREMOUR.

Generally a mere symptom, but sometimes indicating a more or less general paralysis of the muscles. Principal remedies: 1) *Alum. anac. arn. ars. bell. bry. calc. caust. jod. lach. merc. op. phos. plat. puls. sil. sulph.* 2) *Carb-v. cic. cocc. con. hep. kal. magn-arct. natr. natr-m. nitr-ac. n-vom. petr. rhus. sabad. sec. stram. zinc.*

The *trembling of the hands* of drunkards requires: ***Ars. lach.*** *n-vom. sulph.*

TUBERCLES, ABDOMINAL.

Principal remedies: 1) *Calc. hep. lach. sil. sulph.* 2) ***Amm.*** *caust. jod. kal. merc. nitr-ac. ol-jec. phos.*

TUBERCULOSIS.

§ 1. Principal remedies: 1) *Ars. calc. jod. kal. lyc. phos. puls. stann. sulph.* 2) *Acon. amb. bell. bry. carb-an. carb-v. chin. con. dros. ferr. hep. natr-m. nitr-ac. phos-ac. seneg. sep. sil. thuj.*

§ 2. For the stage of *irritation* and *inflammation* : ***Acon.*** *amm. bell. bry. calc. dros. lyc. phos.*

For the stage of *suppuration*, the real *consumptive* stage: 1) *Ars. calc. ferr. jod. hep. kal. lyc. nitr-ac. phos. puls. stann. sulph.* 2) *Carb-v. chin. con. nitr. phos-ac. sep. staph.*

§ 3. It is doubtful whether tubercles of the brain, lungs, intestines, require different remedies. Probably any tubercles should be treated with the same remedies, provided the totality of the symptoms corresponds.

TUMOURS.

§ 1. Principal remedies: 1) *Ars. bell. bry. cham. hep. merc phos. puls. rhus. sulph.* 2) *Ant. arn. carb-v. caust. chin. dulc kal. lach. led. lyc. nitr-ac. n-vom. rhod. rhus. sabin. samb. sep sil.*

§ 2. *Phlegmonous* tumours require: *Ars. bell. bry cham. hep. phos. puls. sulph.*—If given in time, these remedies will generally suffice to disperse the swelling before suppuration sets in ; ***Ars.*** is indicated by *burning :* ***Bry.*** by hot and tight, or *pale* or red tumours ; ***Bell.***, when the redness spreads over the adjacent parts ;

Hep. and *Rhus.* when the swelling is painful to the touch ; *Puls.* when it is surrounded by a red areola, &c.

For *hard* swellings give : *Baryt carb-an. carb-v. con. jod kal. ;* or, *Bry. cham. sulph.* If suppuration should have set in, give *Hep.* or *Lach.*, which will soon bring the swelling *to a head.*

If the suppuration should last *too long*, give : *Calc. hep. merc. phos. sil.*—*Phos* and *Sil.* more particularly if hectic fever supervene.

See : SUPPURATION and ULCERS.

§ 3. *Lymphatic* swellings and abscesses require : *Asa. bell. calc. carb-v. cocc. dulc. hep. lach. merc. phos. sep. sil. sulph.*—If *inflammatory*, give : 1) *Merc.* 2) *Bell. carb-v. hep. lach. sep. sil. phos.*—If *cold*, without inflammation, give : *Asa. bell. calc. coccul. dulc. merc. sulph.*

§ 4. *Lipomata* (lupiæ) require : 1) *Calc.* 2) *Graph. hep. sil.;* or, 3) *Baryt. caust. nitr-ac. sulph.*

Steatomata : *Bar-c.*

Ganglia : Arn. rhus.; or, *Amm. phos. phos-ac. plumb. ? sil. zinc.*

§ 5. *Phlegmasia alba dolens :* 1) *Bry. lyc.* 2) *Ant. ars. puls. rhus. sabin. sulph.;* or, 3) *Bell. calc. chin. jod. merc. rhus. sep. sil.*

Œdematous and *dropsical* swellings : 1) *Ant. ars. bry. chin. hell. lyc. merc. puls. squill. sulph.* 2) *Aur. baryt. bell. dig. dulc. ferr. kal. led. phos. rhod. rhus. sabin. samb. stram.*

Arthritic swellings : 1) *Acon. ant. arn. bry. chin. colch. merc. sulph.* 2) *Coccul. hep. kreos. n-vom. rhus.*

Rheumatic swellings : 1) *Acon. arn. bell. bry. cham. chin. colch. merc. n-vom. puls. sulph.* 2) *Coccul. hep. kreos. lach. rhus.*

Arthritic nodosities : 1) *Agn. ant. calc. carb-an. caust. graph. lyc. merc. puls. rhus. sabin. staph. sulph.* 2) *Acon. arn. aur. clem. cic. dig. hep. led. nitr-ac.*

§ 6. *Pale* swellings require : 1) *Baryt. bry. lyc. rhus.* 2) *Arn. calc. jod. merc. puls. sep.*

Blue-red : 1) *Arn. bell. cham. lach.* 2) *Ars. canth. con. kal. sil.*

Red-spotted : Chin. lyc. sep.

Erysipelatous : 1) *Bell. puls. rhus.* 2) *Acon. amm. arn. ars. hep. phos. sep.*

Black-blue : 1) *Ars. lach. puls.* 2) *Acon. arn. bell. dig. merc. op. veratr.*

§ 7. ***Hot***, red swellings: 1) *Arn. ars. bell. borax. bry. chin. coccul. hep. lach. lyc. merc. n-vom. phos. puls. rhus. sep. sil. sulph.* 2) *Acon. ant. asa. aur. cann. colch. led. mang. natr-m. nitr-ac.*

Suppurating: 1) *Calc. hep. merc. phos. sil.* 2) *Baryt. lach. lyc. mang. sulph.*

Hard, tight: *Arn. ars. bell. bry. calc. carb-an. cham. graph. lyc. phos. puls. rhus. sil. sulph.*

Shining: Arn. ars. bry. merc. sulph.

Cold: 1) *Ars. calc. bell. coccul. dulc. merc. sulph.* 2) *Asa. con. lach. puls. rhod. spig.*

§ 8. *Burning* and painful: 1) *Ars. bry. lyc. phos. sulph.* 2) *Acon. arn. bell. caust. lach. merc. puls. rhus. sep. sil.*

Creeping: Arn. colch. merc. puls. rhus. sep. sulph.

Stinging and painful: *Acon. bry. caust. nitr-ac. puls. sep sulph.*

§ 9. Compare: *Abscess, Glands*, diseases of, *Suppuration, Ulcers, Arthritic* ailments, *Erysipelas, Rheumatism, Lupia*, &c. Also all local swellings, such as: *Swelling* of the *cheeks, knee*, &c.

TYMPANITIS.

Principal remedy: *Chin.;* moreover: *Carb-v. coloc. lyc. n-vom. sulph.*

Compare: *Distention of the abdomen*, and *Colic.*

TYPHUS.

§ 1. Under this head we arrange all fevers with *typhoid* symptoms, such as: typhus gastricus, stupidus, versatitis, putridus, &c.; and even pneumo-typhus, for this is, after all, typhus affecting most particularly the lungs. Pneumonia may assume a typhoid character in consequence of excessive bleeding, but this would not be true pneumo-typhus, and the characteristic disorganization of the blood, as well as the regularity of the stages which we observe in true typhus, are wanting in such apparently typhoid diseases.

In *true typhus*, whether *putridus, petechialis*, &c., *Bry.* and *Rhus-t.* are the principal remedies; if, however, neither of these remedies should be indicated by the symptoms, we may resort to:—

§ 2 The following remedies: 1) *Bell. bry. hyos. lach. merc. n-vom. phos-ac. rhus. stram. sulph.* 2) *Acon. arn. ars. camph.*

carb-v. cham. chin. cocc. lyc. mur-ac. natr-m. nitr-sp. n-mosch. op. puls. sulph. 3) *Daph. gran. phos. sulph-ac.*

§ 3. *Pseudo-typhus*, that is, fevers with apparently typhoid symptoms, require: *Acon. arn. ars. bell. bry. chin. cocc. hyos. lach. lyc. merc. mur-ac. natr-m. phos-ac. rhus. stram. sulph.*

True typhus requires, as was said above: 1) *Bry.* or *Rhus-t.*; or, if these should be insufficient: *Ars. lach. merc. mur-ac. phos-ac. sulph-ac.*; or one of the remedies mentioned in § 2.

We may furthermore select:

a) For *typhus versatilis: Acon. bell. bry. cham. hyos. lyc. mur-ac. natr-m. n-vom. rhus. stram.*

b) *Typhus stupidus: Arn. ars. bell. bry. chin. cocc. hyos. lach. nitr-sp. n-vom. op. rhus. stram. veratr.*

c) *Typhus cerebralis:* 1) *Bry.* 2) *Acon. bell. hyos. lach. lyc. n-vom. op. phos-ac. rhus. stram.*

d) *Typhus pulmonaris:* 1) *Bry. rhus.*; or, 2) *Ars. bell. chin. hyos. sulph.*

e) *Typhus abdominalis, putridus:* 1) *Rhus-t.*; or, *Bry.*; or, 2) *Ars. chin. merc.*; or, 3) *Arn. carb-veg. n-mosch. puls. sulph.* 4) *Canth. mosch.*

§ 5. In the *precursory stage, Bry.* or *Rhus-t.* will sometimes cut the disease short.

The *inflammatory stage* requires: 1) *Bry.*; or, 2) *Acon. bell. cham. hyos. lyc. n-vom. stram.*

The *stage* of *debility* requires: 1) *Rhus.*; or, 2) *Ars. carb-veg. chin. merc. mur-ac.*; or, 3) *Arn. lach. n-mosch. phos-ac. sulph.*—*Carbo-veg.* particularly will sometimes bring about a favourable change, even if life seems almost extinct.

During the *stage of convalescence*, if the patient should be very weak, give: 1) *Cocc. chin. veratr.*; or, 2) *N-vom. sulph.*

§ 6. Symptomatic indications:

Belladonna: Alternate chill and heat, or internal and external heat, with redness and burning heat of the chceks or whole face; red, sparkling eyes; *dilated pupils; photophobia;* buzzing in the ears and hard hearing; *unsteady* or *furious look;* bloated face; *burning* thirst with aversion to drink, or with desire for drink and inability to swallow; restless sleep, sleeplessness; *starting during sleep*, or *on waking;* loss of consciousness, with muttering, *grasping at flocks*, or furious delirium *with frightful visions, fear, desire to escape;* violent *headache*, especially in the forehead; vertigo on raising the head; dry lips; ulcerated corners of the mouth; dry and red tongue, or covered with a dirty coating; bitter taste in the mouth; loss of appetite, *loathing of food* and nausea; anxiety and oppression in the pit of the stomach; no stool; bright-yellow or scanty, *red urine;* hurried breathing; frequent pulse; hurried, or feeble, indistinct speech; cold sweat in the face, especially on the forehead, under the eyes and around the nose; great languor; painfulness of all the limbs; cough with pains in the chest, &c. (Comp. *Hyosc.*)

BRYONIA: Chill, succeeded by constant heat all over the body, especially about the head, with *red face* and profuse sweat, or dry and chapped, or moist and clammy skin; *dry, brownish* and *cracked lips and tongue;* violent thirst; *aversion to food;* also with nausea and desire to vomit, or slimy and bilious vomiting; violent pain in the pit of the stomach when touched; constipation, or diarrhœa, yellow stools; *red-brown,* or bright-yellow urine, with yellowish sediment; *oppressive, stupefying headache,* or pain as if the brain were torn or bruised; gauze before the eyes; *stoppage of the ears* and hard hearing; copious accumulation of thick and tenacious mucus in the posterior nares and fauces; *prostration,* with trembling and *vertigo on raising* one's-self; *delirium,* day and night, with strange fancies and desire to escape from bed; sleeplessness, with *flushes of heat* and restless *tossing about;* or constant desire to sleep, and even coma, with sudden *starting* and *strange dreams; grasping at flocks;* hurried and frequent pulse, or irregular, small and intermitting pulse; short oppressed respiration; painfulness and lameness of all the limbs; *stitches in the chest or side;* irritable, vehement disposition, despair of one's recovery, dread of death, petechiæ. (Comp *Rhus-t.*)

HYOSCYAMUS: Furious delirium, with all sorts of visions; nervousness, with sleeplessness and restlessness, or comatose state, interrupted by delirium which is at times of a bland, at others of a furious character; listlessness, dullness, great debility, especially of the hands on moving them; jactitation of the muscles; grasping at flocks; desire to escape; pale, or *red and hot face,* with bluish cheeks; dim, *staring eyes,* with blue margins around the same; or *red* and *sparkling* eyes, with alternately dilated and contracted pupils; hardness of hearing, with buzzing and ringing in the ears; dry, parched tongue, covered with a brownish coating. (Comp. *Bell.*)

LACHESIS: Vertigo as often as the patient raises himself; lame eyelids, bitter mouth; pain in the chest, with dry cough; *coma;* depression of the lower jaw; *muttering delirium,* stupid looks; smooth and dry, or whitish, or parched or *yellowish-red* tongue; or *heavy tongue;* thirst with aversion to liquids; red-brown and copious urine.

LYCOPODIUM: Prostration; depression of the lower jaw; dim and half-closed eyes; slow breathing with open mouth; or alternate chills and heat; animation without heat or congestion of blood to the head or face; *circumscribed* redness of *the cheeks;* debilitating sweats; red tongue; *constipation;* quiet disposition, or *screams;* ill will, especially on waking.

Mercurius: Vertigo, stupefaction, fullness and confusion of the head; dullness, inability to think; *headache,* especially in the forehead and on the vertex; buzzing in the ears; the tongue is thickly coated, or dirty-yellow, or clean tongue with a bitter, *foul* taste; bleeding gums; nausea, desire to vomit, or vomiting of slimy and bitter substances; *great sensitiveness* and *painfulness* of the *pit of the stomach, region of the liver,* and abdomen around the umbilicus, with pains, especially at night; restlessness, anxiety, and tossing about; constipation, or *green, yellow, diarrhœic stools; dark, brownish urine;* burning and dry skin, or *copious, debilitating* and clammy sweats; debility; *sleeplessness;* no delirium, or scarcely perceptible.

Nux vomica: Excessive sensitiveness of all the organs, with prevailing gastric and bilious symptoms; *drowsiness,* as if intoxicated, with loss of consciousness; prostration; red and burning cheeks, and palms of the hands; white, or black dry tongue, with red and cracked edges, dry lips; thirst with aversion to liquids; foul or bitter taste, especially of liquids; aversion to food; tearing or aching pain in the head, with *vertigo;* colicky pains, palpitation of the heart, and anguish; painful pressure and tension in the region of the stomach and hypochondria; sensation in the limbs as if bruised and paralyzed; vehement, peevish disposition.

Phosphori acidum: Complete listlessness, stupefaction and *dullness;* prostration; *taciturn;* staring, dull looks, with glassy or hollow eyes; sleeplessness at night, with anguish and tossing about; or irresistible drowsiness and sleep, full of fancies, or muttering delirium and grasping at flocks; confusion and painful cloudiness of the head, especially on waking; violent buzzing in the ears, with hardness of hearing; dry tongue; dryness, burning and roughness of the skin; heat, especially towards evening; *diarrhœic stools,* or constipation, with heaviness and pressure in the abdomen; brown-red urine with reddish sediment; cold sweat in the face, pit of the stomach and on the hands, with anguish, &c. (Is sometimes suitable before or after *Opium.*)

Rhus-t: Prostration, the patient being scarcely able to turn about; sleeplessness, with anguish and frequent starting, or coma with muttering, stertorous breathing, and grasping at flocks; dry heat with anguish; silliness or confusion of ideas, or complete loss of consciousness; loquacious delirium with desire to escape, alternating with lucid intervals; stupefying headache; vertigo on raising one's head or turning about; burning and redness of the face or cheeks; red and burning, or staring and dim eyes; stopped ears and hardness of hearing; dry mouth and fauces; dry, chapped, brownish or blackish lips and tongue; or trembling and *red* tongue; great thirst; loss of appetite and aversion to food; hard and distended abdomen, with violent pains in the region of the stomach, especially when touching the part; constipation with ineffectual urging; or blood-coloured, diarrhœic stools; the urine is at first clear and becoming turbid after standing awhile, or it is hot and dark-coloured; dry heat, with anguish, or clammy sweat; petechiæ. (Comp. *Bry.*)

STRAMONIUM: Beating headache, especially on the vertex, with fainting turn, obscuration of sight and hardness of hearing; delirium with violent tossing about, frightful visions and illusions of sight and hearing, or with singing, whistling, talking in a foreign tongue, desire to escape from bed, &c.; loss of consciousness, the patient not knowing even his own family; dilated, insensible pupils; no stool or urine; coma with stertorous breathing, &c.

§ 7. ARNICA: Coma with delirium and grasping at flocks, stertorous breathing, involuntary discharges of fæces or urine, &c.

ARSENICUM: Patechiæ, coma, delirium, grasping at flocks, loss of consciousness, frequent, sudden starting and sighing; great prostration; depression of the lower jaw; open mouth; dim and glassy eyes, &c.

CAMPHORA: Violent delirium, dullness and heat of the head, with clammy, *cold skin;* debility; debilitating and clammy sweats; disposition to diarrhœa. (Sometimes suitable after ***Rhus.***)

CARBO-VEG.: Coma with rattling, hippocratic countenance, insensible pupils; small, almost extinct pulse; cold sweat in the hands, feet and in the face; involuntary stool with cadaverous smell; *dark-red* urine with a little flock in the centre, &c.

CHAMOMILLA: Spasmodic pains, cardialgia or spasmodic colic and diarrhœa, together with the other typhoid symptoms.

CHINA: Loss of appetite and earthy taste of food; dry, parched lips and tongue; diarrhœa day and night, with watery, yellow stools, or discharge of undigested food; constant sopor, or unrefreshing sleep, &c.

COCCULUS: Debility, headache, vertigo, fainting turns, cardialgia, lameness of the extremities, &c. (Is frequently suitable after ***Rhus-t.*** or *Camph.*)

MURIATIS ACIDUM: Prostration, headache as if the brain were bruised, putrid symptoms, distress in the side.*

* The principal indications for Muriatic acid have been omitted by Jahr; they are: *settling down in the bed,* while *digging with* the head into the pillow, turning up the whites, depression of the lower jaw, *slavering,* &c.—*Hempel.*

NATRUM MURIATICUM: Loss of consciousness, unquenchable thirst, dry tongue, debility.

NITRI SPIRITUS: Prostration, *listlessness*, stupidity, with starting, wild looks, deafness, dry, brownish lips, sleep, with delirium and muttering, &c.

NUX MOSCHATA: Putrid or colliquative diarrhœa, coma, delirium, stupidit y, &c.

OPIUM: *Coma with stertorous breathing*, open mouth, delirium, muttering. (After *Opium*, *Phos-ac.* is sometimes suitable.)

PULSATILLA: Loss of consciousness, with violent delirium, *whining* and *lamenting* with desponding looks.

SULPHUR: Constant heat, especially in the evening, with full, hurried pulse, great thirst, dry and brownish tongue; scanty, dark-red urine which soon deposits a sediment; sleeplessness; delirium, with open eyes; grasping at flocks; constipation.

§ 8. Comp.: INFLAMMATORY FEVER, GASTRIC FEVER, &c.

TYPICAL DISEASES: 1) *Ars. caps. chin. ign ipec. natr-m. n-vom. puls. sep. spig.* 2) *Alum. anac. ant. arn. baryt. bry. canth. carb-veg. coc lach. plumb. rhod. rhus-t. sabad. sep. staph. sulph. veratr.* See INTERMITTENT FEVER.

ULCERS.

§ 1. Ulcers, without an exception, depend upon a particular dyscrasia of the organism, and cannot be radically healed except by means of remedies which are capable of eradicating the dyscrasia, of which the ulcer is a mere symptom. Nevertheless, the character, configuration or other peculiarities of ulcers, should not be left out of consideration in selecting a remedy. These external characteristics of ulcers generally point to the following remedies: 1) *Ars. asa. hep. lach. lyc. merc. puls. sil. sulph.* 2) *Aur. bell. bry. calc. canth. carb-veg. cham. chel. clem. con. cupr. graph. nitr-ac. phosph. phos-ac. rhus. sep. staph. thuj.*

§ 2. We should use more particularly:

a) For *atonic* ulcers, as we find them among *old*, feeble and *cachectic* individuals, on the leg, &c.: 1) *Ars. lach. sil. sulph* 2) *Calc. carb-veg. graph. ipec. lyc. mur-ac. natr. phos-ac. puls. ruta.* 3) *Amm. amm-m.*

b) For *arthritic* ulcers: 1) *Bry. chin. lyc. sulph.* 2) *Calc. graph. rhus. staph.* (See: GOUT.)

c) For *impetiginous* ulcers: 1) *Calc. clem. graph. lyc. merc. rhus. sep. sil. sulph. zinc.* (See: HERPES.)

d) For *scorbutic* ulcers: 1) ***Ars. carb-an. carb-veg. lach. merc.***

mur-ac staph. sulph. 2) *Amm. amm-m. asa. clem. con. hep. phosph. sep. sil. thuj.*

e) For *scrofulous* ulcers: 1) *Ars. bell. calc. carb-veg. lyc. mur-ac. sil. sulph.* 2) *Aur. cist. graph. hep. lach. phosph.*

f) For *syphilitic* ulcers: 1) *Merc.* 2) *Aur. carb-veg. lach. nitr-ac. thuj.* 3) *Jod.? nux-jugl.? mez.?*

g) For *mercurial* ulcers: 1) *Asa. aur. bell. carb-veg. hep. lach. lyc. nitr-ac. phos-ac. sassap. sep. sil. sulph.*

§ 3. As regards the *structure* and *shape* of ulcers, give :

a) For *fistulous* ulcers : 1) *Ant. calc. lyc. phosph. sil. sulph.* 2) *Asa. bell. carb-veg. caust. con. nitr-ac. puls. ruta.*

b) For *flat*, superficial ulcers: 1) *Lach. merc. nitr-ac. thuj.* 2) *Ars. asa. bell. lyc. phos-ac. puls. sep. sil.*

c) For *hard, callous* ulcers, with callous edges: *Ars. asa. calc. carb-veg. hep. lach. lyc. merc. petr. sep. sil. sulph.*

d) For *carious* ulcers: 1) *Asa. lyc. merc. sil.* 2) *Aur. calc. hep. phos-ac. ruta. sabin. sulph.*

e) *Cancerous* ulcers, that is: ulcers which look like cancer, but are of a different nature: 1) *Ars. con. lach. merc. sil. sulph.* 2) *Aur. bell. calc. clem. hep. nitr-ac. sep. sil. squill. staph.*

f) *Fungous* ulcers: 1) *Ars. carb-an. lach. merc. petr. sep. sil. sulph.* 2) *Carb-veg. cham. clem. phosph. staph. thuj.*

g) *Lardaceous* ulcers: 1) *Ars. hep. merc. sabin.* 2) *Cupr. kreos. nitr-ac. sulph. thuj.*

h) *Deep* ulcers: 1) *Lach. merc. nitr-ac.* 2) *Bell. calc. con. lyc. sep. sil. sulph.*

i) *Varicose* ulcers: 1) *Carb-veg. puls. sulph.* 2) *Ars. caust. graph. lach. lyc.*

k) *Verminous* ulcers (with maw-worms): 1) *Merc. sil.* 2) *Ars. calc. sabad.*

l) *Indented* ulcers: 1) *Merc. phos-ac.* 2) *Hep. lach. sil. staph. sulph.*

m) *Shaggy* ulcers: 1) *Ars.* 2) *Petr. sil.*

§ 4. As regards *appearance* and *colour*, use :

a) For *bluish* ulcers: 1) *Asa. aur. con. hep. lach.* 2) *Ars. sil.*

b) *Spotted* ulcers: *Arn. con. lach. sulph-ac.*

c) *Yellow: Calc. carb-veg. puls. sil.*

d) *Gray: Ars. caust. merc. sil.*

e) *Greenish: Asa. aur. caust. merc. puls. rhus. sil.*

f) *Discoloured,* unclean, dirty ulcers: *Lach. merc. nitr-ac. sabin. thuj.*

g) Ulcers with red *areolæ: Ars. asa. calc. cham. hep. lach. lyc. merc. puls. rhus. sil. staph. sulph.*

h) Ulcers which turn *black:* ***Ars. asa. carb-veg. ipec. lach. sec.*** *sil. sulph.*

i) *Whitish*, white-spotted: ***Ars.*** *lach. merc. sil.*

§ 5. As regards the *pathological nature* of ulcers, select:

a) For *readily bleeding* ulcers: 1) *Ars. carb-veg. hep. kal. lach. lyc. nitr-ac. phosph. phos-ac. puls.* 2) *Con. sil. sulph.*

b) For *gangrenous* ulcers: 1) *Ars. bell. chin. lach. sil.* 2) ***Con. rhus.*** *sec. squill.*

c) *Suppurating* ulcers: 1) *Ars. hep. merc. puls. sil. sulph.* 2) *Asa. chin. con. lach. phosph. phos-ac.*

d) *Inflamed* ulcers: 1) *Ars. cham. hep. lyc. merc. phosph.* ***staph.*** 2) *Acon. bell. bry. nitr-ac. puls. rhus. ruta. sulph.*

e) ***Putrid*** ulcers: 1) *Ars. carb-veg. hep. merc. mur-ac.* ***puls. sil.*** *sulph.* 2) *Amm amm-m. asa. bell. calc. chin. phos-ac.* ***rhus.***

f) *Phagedenic* ulcers: 1) *Ars. hep. merc. mez. sil.* ***sulph.*** 2) *Carb-veg. caust. cham. clem. con. graph. nitr-ac. petr. ran.* ***rhus.*** *sep.*

g) *Torpid* ulcers: 1) *Carb-veg. con. lyc. phos-ac. sep. sulph.* 2) *Carb-an. cupr. op. sil.*

§ 6. As regards *pains*, give:

a) For very *painful* ulcers: 1) *Ars. carb-veg. graph. hep.* ***sil.*** 2) *Arn. asa. bell. lyc. merc. nitr-ac. phos-ac. puls.*

b) *Painless: Carb-veg. lach. phos-ac. sep. sulph.*

c) *Itching* or *smarting:* 1) *Ars. hep. lyc. puls. rhus.* ***sil. sulph.*** 2) *Ant. caust. chin. graph. nitr-ac. phos-ac.*

d) *Boring* pains: *Aur. bell. natr-m. sil. sulph.*

e) *Burning* pains: *Ars. carb-veg. merc. mez. puls. rhus.* ***sil. sulph.***

f) *Pressure* and *tension: Caust. con. graph. merc. phosph.* ***puls.*** *rhus. sil. spong. sulph.*

g) *Beating* and *throbbing: Asa. calc. clem. kal. lyc. merc.* ***sil. sulph.***

h) *Creeping* and *gnawing: Arn. cham. clem. con. dros. lach. lyc. merc. phosph. rhus. sep. staph. sulph.*

i) *Tearing* or *drawing: Ars. calc. lyc. sep. sil. sulph.*

k) *Stitching* or *cutting: Bell. calc. graph. lyc. merc. natr-m. nitr-ac. puls. sep. sil. staph. sulph.*

l) *Sore* pains: *Graph. hep. puls. sep. sulph.*

m) *Darting* (jerking) pains: *Asa. calc. caust. puls. rhus. sil.*

§ 7. Compare: SUPPURATIONS, ERUPTIONS, and HERPES; also: GOUT; SCURVY; SCROPHULA; SYPHILIS; MERCURIAL CACHEXIA; BONES, DISEASES OF; CANCER; VARICES; GLANDS, DISEASES OF; and the parts where ulcers are apt to break out.

URETHRITIS. — Principal remedies: *Acon. cann. canth. merc. sulph.*
See: CYSTITIS, URINARY DIFFICULTIES, GONORRHŒA.

URETHRORRHAGIA, HÆMATURIA.

§ 1. Principal remedies: *Arn. ars. cann. canth. chin. ipec. lyc. merc. mez. puls.;* or, 2) *Calc. caps. con. n-vom. phosph. sec. sep. zinc.*

§ 2. If caused by a badly managed gonorrhœa, give: *Cann. canth. puls.*
If by *suppression* of *herpes*, or itch: *Ars. calc. con. sulph.*
If by *external injuries: Arn. con. puls. rhus.*
If attended with *affections* of the *kidneys: Canth. lyc. puls. sulph.*
§ 3. See: URINARY DIFFICULTIES, GONORRHŒA, HÆMORRHAGES, NEPHRITIS, CYSTITIS, &c.

URINARY DIFFICULTIES, ISCHURIA, LYSURIA, ANURIA, &c.

§ 1. These various affections have been arranged under one head in order to avoid unnecessary repetitions. The principal remedies for these affections are: 1) *Acon. bell. camph. cann. canth. coloc. dulc. hep. merc. n-vom. puls. sulph.* 2) *Arn. ars. aur. baryt. caps. caust. colch. coloc. dig. graph. hell. hyos. kal. lyc. mur-ac. n-mosch. phosph. phos-ac. rhus. ruta. sabin. sassap. staph. sulph.*

§ 2 As regards the *varieties*, give:

a) For *dysuria*, with ineffectual urging: 1) *Acon. cann. canth. dulc. magn-aust. merc. n-vom. puls. sulph.* 2) *Arn. ars. aur. bell. calc. colch. con. dig. hyos. kal. n-mosch. phosph. sassap. staph.*
b) For *ischuria*, anuria: 1) *Arn. canth. lyc. n-vom. op. puls. stram.* 2) *Acon. aur. camph. con. dig. hep. hyos. lach. laur. plumb. rhus. ruta. sulph. veratr.*
c) For *enuresis:* 1) *Arn. bell. carb-veg. caust. cin. hep. hyos. magn-aust. natr-m. puls. rhus. ruta. sep. sulph. zinc.* 2) *Acon. cic. dulc. kreos. lach. laur. lyc. magn-c. merc. petr. sil. spig.*
d) For *enuresis nocturna:* 1) *Bell. caust. cin. puls. rhus. sep. sil. sulph.* 2) *Acon. amm. arn. ars. bry. calc. carb-veg. cham. chin. con. graph. hep. magn-aust. merc. natr-m. op. ruta. stram.*

§ 3. As regards the *pathological* state to which the urinary difficulty belongs, give:

a) For an *inflammatory* state : 1) *Acon. cann. canth. merc. n-vom. puls.* 2) *Bell. cop. dig. dulc. sassap. sabin. sulph.*

b) For a *spasmodic* state: 1) *N-vom. op. puls.* 2) *Bell. canth. caps. caust. cin. coloc. hyos. ign. lach. lyc. rhus. veratr.*

c) For *paralysis:* 1) *Ars. cin. dulc. hyos.* 2) *Acon. bell. caust. cic laur. magn-aust.*

d) *Strictures*, or *indurations* in the urinary passages: *Clem. dulc. merc. petr. puls. rhus. sulph.*

e) For *hæmorrhoids :* 1) *N-vom. puls. sulph.* 2) *Acon. ars. calc. carb-veg. lach. merc.*

f) During *pregnancy*, or when the menses are suppressed: 1) *Coccul phos-ac. puls.* 2) *Con. n-vom. sulph.*

g) *Lythiasis* or *gravel :* 1) *Lyc. sassap.* 2) *Calc. cann. n-vom. petr. phosph. sep. sil.*, &c. (See : LYTHIASIS.)

§ 4. As regards *external causes*, give :

a) When caused by a *cold: Acon. bell. dulc. merc. n-vom. puls.*

b) When by exposure to *wet* and *cold:* 1) *Puls. sassap.* 2) *Alum. calc. sulph.*

c) When by *abuse* of *spirits:* 1) *N-vom. puls. sulph.* 2) *Ars. bell. calc. hep. lach. merc.*

d) By *abuse* of *Cantharides:* 1) *Camph* 2) *Acon. puls.*

e) By *fright* or fear: *Acon. bell. hyos. op. veratr.*

f) By a *concussion* in consequence of a *fall, shock*, &c.: *Arn. cic. con. rhus. puls.*

§ 5. We may moreover prescribe, if the accompanying symptoms permit :

a) For frequent *urging* to urinate: 1) *Bell. bry. canth. carb-veg. caust. colch. graph. kal. lyc. n-vom. phos-ac. puls. rhus. ruta. sabin. sassap. squill. staph. sulph.* 2) *Acon. arn. baryt. caps. coccul. coloc. dig. dulc. guaj. hell. ign. merc. mur-ac. phosph. sabad. sep. spong.*

b) *Ineffectual* urging: 1) *Canth. caust. dig. n-vom. petr. puls. sassap. sep. sulph.* 2) *Acon. arn. camph. cham. chin. coloc. hyos. kal. lyc. merc. phosph. phos-ac. plumb. sil.*

c) *Urging* at night: 1) *Arn. ars. bell. calc. caust. graph. magn-aust. natr-m. puls. rhus. sep. sil. squill.* 2) *Alum. amm. baryt. bry. cin. cupr. dros. hep. magn-aust. merc. n-vom. op. ruta. stram.*

d) *Emitting* the urine in *drops* only: 1) *Bell. canth. dulc. magn-aust. n-vom. sulph.* 2) *Arn. camph. cann. caps. caust. clem. colch. con. merc. n-mosch. petr. puls. rhus. spig. staph. stram.*

e) *Inability to emit all the urine*, drops of which continue to full out: 1) *Calc. kal. selen.* 2) *Bry. lach. natr. petr. rhod. sil. staph. thuj.*

f) *Interrupted* or thin stream: 1) *Caust. clem. con. dulc magn-aust. sulph. zinc.* 2) *Carb-an. kal. phos-ac. thui.*

§ 6. Or for: a) ***Painful*** emission of urine: 1) ***Cann. canth. coloc. hep. lyc. merc. natr-m. phos-ac. puls. thuj.*** 2) ***Bell. clem.*** *colch. con. dulc. nitr-ac. n-vom. phosph. sassap. sep. sulph. veratr.*

b) *Burning* pains: 1) ***Ars.*** *calc. cann. lach. merc. natr. n-vom. phosph. phos-ac. seneg. sulph.* 2) *Canth. caps. carb-an. carb-veg. caust. con. hep. ign. lyc. nitr. nitr-ac. thuj. veratr.*

c) *Cutting* pains: 1) *Ant. cann. canth. con. dig. phos-ac.* 2) *Arn. calc. guaj. hep. merc. mur-ac. nitr-ac. petr. staph. thuj.*

d) *Stitching* pains: *Arn. cann. clem. lyc. nitr. n-vom. phosph. seneg.*

e) *Soreness* and *smarting:* 1) *Carb-veg. ign. phosph. sep.* 2) *Calc. hep. lyc. magn-c. mez. natr. nitr-ac. n-vom.*

§ 7. Compare: Secretion of Urine, Cystitis, Catarrh of the Bladder, Paralysis of the Bladder, Gonorrhœa, Lithiasis, &c.

URINE, Morbid secretion of.

§ 1. Under this head we have arranged a number of affections of the urinary organs, which, though differing from each other pathologically, yet, so far as their symptoms are concerned, all point to the remedies mentioned below.

§ 2. As regards the *secretion of urine* itself, give:

a) For *copious* micturition: 1) *Arg. carb-v. led. merc. mur-ac. natr-m phos-ac. puls. rhus. spig. squill. sulph. verb.* 2) ***Alum.*** *amb. ars. canth. carb-an. daph. guaj. ign. lach. natr. nitr. oleand. phos. seneg.*

b) *Frequent* urination: 1) *Arg. baryt. caust. kreos. lach. merc. nitr. oleand. phos-ac. rhus. ruta. sil. squill. staph.* 2) *Aur. bry. calc. coff. daph. kal. mur-ac. spig. veratr.*

c) *Scanty* secretion: 1) *Acon. arn. aur. bell. bry. canth. hyos. laur. n-vom. op. plumb. stram.* 2) *Ars. camph. chin. colch. hep. merc. puls. ruta. sec. sulph.*

d) *Diminished* secretion: 1) *Bell. canth. colch. dig. graph. hell. hyos. jod. laur. n-vom. op. plumb. ruta. sec. staph. stram. veratr.* 2) *Acon. alum. arn. bry. cann. carb-v. caust. dulc. hep. kal. merc. nitr-ac. phos. puls. rhus. sassap. sulph.*

e) *Suppression* of urine: 1) *Acon. bell. canth. hyos. jod. laur. op. plumb. sec. stram.* 2) *Alum. colch. dig. graph. hell. n-vom. ruta. sassap. veratr.*

§ 3. As regards the *nature* of the urine, give:

a) For urine with *ammoniacal smell : Asa. carb-v. jod. mosch. nitr-ac. petr. phos. stront.*

b) *Pale*, watery, colourless urine: 1) *Aur. coloc. con. mur-ac. nitr. phosph. phos-ac. puls. staph.* 2) *Alum. arn. bell. colch. dig. hep. ign. magn-c. mur-ac. natr-m. plat. rhus. sassap. sec. sep. stram. stront. sulph-ac.*

c) *Dark-coloured*, red, fiery, saturated urine: 1) *Acon. arn. bell. bry. carb-v. colch. merc. sep. sulph. tart. veratr.* 2) *Ant. calc. canth. caps. chin. dig. dros. hell. hep. ipec. kal. lach. n-vom. phos. puls. selen. staph.*

d) *Dark-brown*, red-brown, brown-red urine: 1) *Arn. bell. bry. dros. lach. phos. sulph.* 2) *Acon. amb. ars. calc. caust. colch. kreos. merc. nitr-ac. petr. puls.*

e) Dark *blood-coloured :* 1) *Calc. sep.* 2) *Coff. hep. petr. sulph-ac.*

f) *Yellow-coloured :* 1) *Amb. arn. bell. cham. chin. ipec. lach. rhab. sassap. zinc.* 2) *Agar. amm. ant. canth. carb-v. colch. hyos. ign. led. magn-m. nitr. samb. spong. veratr.*

g) *Greenish :* 1) *Ars. camph. rhab. ruta. veratr.* 2) *Aur. chin. jod. kal. magn-c. rhod. sulph.*

h) *Hot : Acon. ars. bry. canth. cham. colch. dig. hep. merc. nitr-ac. n-vom. phos-ac. sec. squill.*

i) *Cold* while being emitted : *Agar. nitr-ac.*

k) *Viscid : Arg. canth. coloc. cupr. kreos. phos-ac.*

l) *Milky, whitish*, as if stirred with milk, flour, or chalk: 1) *Phos-ac.* 2) *Aur. carb-v. cin. con. merc. mur-ac. nitr-ac. phos. sulph.* 3) *Alum. amm. arn. bell. cann. canth. caust. chin. dulc. hep. jod. natr-m. rhus.*

m) *Sour-smelling :* 1) *Amb. merc.* 2) *Calc. graph. natr. nitr-ac. petr.*

n) *Acrid* urine: 1) *Borax. cann. caust. hep. merc.* 2) *Arn. calc. clem. graph. jod. kal. natr-m. phos. rhus. seneg. thuj. veratr.*

o) *Foaming : Chinin. laur. lyc. seneg. spong.*

p) *Fetid :* 1) *Ars. carb-an. carb-v. guaj. merc. nitr-ac. puls. sulph.* 2) *Cupr. dulc. natr. petr. phos. phos-ac. sep. stann. viol-tr.*

q) *Turbid :* 1) *Chin. cin. con. dulc. merc. sabad. sep.* 2) *Amb. bell. cann. carb-an. carb-v. cham. ign. phos. puls. rhus.*

r) Becoming *turbid : Bry. caust. cham. cin. graph. hep. merc. mez. phos-ac. rhus. seneg. sulph.*

s) *Cloudy :* 1) *Amb. bry. caust. merc. nitr. petr. phos-ac. seneg. thuj.* 2) *Ant. chin. kal. lach. rhod. sassap.*

§ 4. As regards the *sediment* deposited by the urine, give:

a) For *bloody* urine: 1) *Canth. can. puls.* 2) *Arn. ars. chin.*

ipec. lyc. merc. mez. 3) *Calc. caps. con. n-vom. phos. sec. sep. sulph. zinc.*

b) *Bloody* sediment: 1) *Sep. sulph-ac.* 2) *Canth. dulc. lyc. phos-ac. puls.*

c) *Purulent: Cann. canth. clem. lyc. n-vom. puls. sep.*

d) *Fibrinous*, flocculent: *Cann. canth. merc. mez. nitr-ac. seneg. tart.*

e) *Opalescent* urine: *Calc. chin. hep. jod. par. petr. phos. puls. sulph.*

f) *Jelly-like* sediment: *Coloc. puls.*

g) *Yellow*-coloured: 1) *Baryt. cham. chin. cupr. lyc. phos. sil. spong. sulph-ac. zinc.* 2) *Amm. canth. lach.*

h) *Gray: Con. hyos. spong.*

i) Gravel, sand, or stone sediments: 1) *Lyc. sassap.* 2) *Calc. cann. n-vom. petr. phos. sep. sil.* 3) *Alum. amm. amb. ant. calc. canth. chin. lach. natr-m. nitr-ac. n-mosch. puls. thuj. zinc.*

k) *Loamy* sediment: *Amm-m. sassap. sep. sulph. sulph-ac. zinc.*

l) Sediment resembling *flour*, chalk or lime: *Calc. chin. graph. merc. natr-m. phos-ac. sulph tart.*

m) *Reddish*, brick-coloured sediment: 1) *Canth. chin. lyc. natr-m. phos. puls. sep. squill. val.* 2) *Acon. amb. ant. arn. dulc. lach. nitr-ac. sil.*

n) *Slimy* urine or sediment: 1) *Ars. dulc. merc. natr-m. puls. seneg.* 2) *Ant. canth. carb-v. coloc. con. hep. nitr-ac. n-vom. sassap. sulph.*

o) Mucous threads in the urine: *Cann. canth. merc. mez. nitr-ac. seneg. tart.*

p) *Whitish* sediment: *Colch. dulc. hep. nitr-ac. petr. phos. phos-ac. rhus. spig. sulph.*

§ 5. Compare: *Urinary* difficulties, *Gonorrhœa*, *Enuresis*, *Cystitis*, &c.

UTERUS, DISEASES OF THE.

§ 1. Principal remedies: 1) *Bell. cham. cocc. con. hyos. ign. magn. magn-m. n-vom. plat. puls. sep. sulph.*; or, 2) *Bry. caust. mosch. natr-m. n-mosch. stann. stram. veratr.*, &c. Comp.: Hysteria.

§ 2. *Metralgia* or *Hysteralgia:* 1) *Cocc. con. ign. magn. magn-m.*; or, 2) *Bell. bry. cham. caust. hyos. natr-m. n-vom. plat.? sep. stann.*, &c. (Comp.: *Menstrual colic* and *Hysterical spasms.*)

§ 3. *Prolapsus* of the uterus: 1) *Aur. bell. calc. n-vom. sep. stann.*; or, 2) *Gran.? kreos.? merc.? n-mosch.?*

§ 4. *Metritis.* (See this article.)

§ 5. *Swelling* of the uterus in old females, or women who have borne many children, require: 1) *Sep.*; or, 2) *Bell.? calc.? chin.? n-vom.? plat.?*
Meteorism of the uterus: *Phosph* or *Lyc.*

§ 6. *Hydatids* and *moles*: No remedies positively known; *moles* may require: *Bell.* or *Canth.*

§ 7. For *Polypi* of the uterus, *Staphys.* has been recommended; I prefer *Calc.*

§ 8. For scirrhous and cancerous affections of the uterus, see: *Cancer.*

§ 9. *Putrescence* of the uterus, as sometimes occurs in cachectic females after confinement, requires: *Sec.*
Vagina or *prepuce*, swelling of.—For lymphatic swelling of the labia: *Merc. sep. sulph.*— Swelling of the prepuce, not syphilitic: *Acon. arn. merc. rhus-t. sep. sulph.*—See: SYPHILIS, GONORRHŒA, PHIMOSIS, &c.

VALERIANA, ILL EFFECTS OF.—The best remedy is *Cham.*, after which *Coff.*; in some cases *N-vom.* or *Sulph.*

VAPOURS, NOXIOUS, ill effects of. Hering proposes:

§ 1. to counteract *sulphuretted hydrogen*: 1) Sprinkling with water and vinegar, which should at the same time be held under the patient's nose to inhale the vapour. 2) *Chlore-water*, when the patient shows signs of life after having been apparently dead; a few drops may be given internally. 3) *Black coffee*, when the dilute vinegar does not agree, and the patient complains of chilliness; 4) a few drops of good wine, when great heat and debility set in.

§ 2. The *vapours of coal* are antidoted by: 1) *Water and vinegar*; and, after return of consciousness: 2) By a few doses of *Opium*; or, 3) *Bell.* if *Op.* should be insufficient.
The ill effects of emanations from wood and loam-work in recently built houses, are best treated with *Sulph. ac.*

§ 3. The *vapours* of *chlore* require: 1) *tobacco-smoke*; 2) *brandy* or *wine*; 3) *loaf sugar.*

§ 4. See: SULPHUR, PRUSSIC ACID, MERCURY, &c.

VARICELLÆ.—Principal remedies: 1) *Acon. ant. bell. puls. rhus. tart.* 2) *Ars. canth. carb-veg con. ipec. merc. sep. sil. thuj.* 3) *Asa. caust. cycl. led. natr. natr-m. sec. sol-m. sulph.*

§ 2. As regards varieties, give for:

a) *Varicellæ emphysematicæ:* 1) *Acon. ant. bell. puls. tart.* 2) *Canth. con. merc. sec. sil. sol-m. thuj.*

b) For the so-called *swine-* or *water*-pox: *Acon. bell. led. puls. rhus.*

c) For the *acuminated* varicellæ: 1) *Acon. ant. bell. puls. rhus. tart.* 2) *Ars. carb-veg. ipec. sep. thuj.*

§ 3. In the inflammatory period give *Acon.*, no matter what form the eruption may have, or *Bell.* if the brain should be irritated.

The *tenesmus* or *ischuria* requires: *Canth. con. merc.*

Swelling of the *cervical glands: Bell. carb-veg. merc.*

Large *pustules* with profuse suppuration: *Ars. merc. puls. rhus. thuj.*

For slow development of the eruption, with *gastric* and *bilious* symptoms: 1) *Ant. puls. tart.* 2) *Ipec. rhus. sulph.*

§ 4. See: VARIOLA, EXANTHEMS, VARIOLOID.

VARICES.—Principal remedies: 1) *Arn. ars. calc. carb-veg. caust. lyc. n-vom. puls. sulph.* 2) *Ambr. ant. coloc. ferr. graph. kreos. laches. lycop. magn-aus. natr-m. silic. spigel. sulph-ac. zinc.*

VARIOLA.

§ 1. Principal remedies: 1) *Ars. merc. rhus.* 2) *Acon. bell. bry. camph. chin. sulph. tart.*

§ 2. *Precursory* stage: *Acon.*; or, *Coff. bry.* and *Rhus t.*

For *metastasis* to the brain: *Bell.*; and for *gastric ailments: Ars.* and *Ipec.*

If the eruption be accomplished, give *Sulph.* and *Merc.*, to promote the desiccation; if the eruption should be very violent, a dose of *Bell.* may be required; and if the suppurative fever should be very violent, give *Acon.* or *Bell.*; or *Cham.*, if there should be cough. If the pus should be ichorous, and gangrene threaten to set in, give *Ars.* and *Carb. v.*

Ptyalism requires *Merc.*; *catarrh* with cough and hoarseness: *Ars.* or *Merc.*; and *diarrhœa: Chin.*

§ 3. Generally speaking, use:

a) During the *fever-period*: 1) *Acon. bell.* 2) *Op. ars.*

b) During the *eruptive period:* 1) *Merc.* 2) *Ant-cr. stram. bell.*

c) *Maturity: Merc.*

d) Period of *desiccation:* 1) *Acon. bell. cham. puls.* 2) *Bry. nux.*

e) Black, *gangrenous* pocks: 1) ***Ars. carb-v.*** 2) ***Bell. hyos. lach. rhus sec. sil.***

§ 4. Symptomatic indications:

Arsenicum: Angina faucium, metastasis to the mouth and throat, in the last part of the eruptive period; also for *black pocks.*

Belladonna: After *Acon.*, for violent fever, congestion of blood to the head, furious delirium; ophthalmia; photophobia, meningitis.

Bryonia: Precursory stage, nausea, vomiting, &c.; or after the eruption is out, when ascites sets in.

China: *Black* pustules, diarrhœa, oppression, &c. during the eruption.

Coffea: ***Restlessness*** and bilious vomiting at the commencement of the disease.

Mercurius: Ptyalism, tendency of blood to the head, irritation of the mucous membranes in the eyes, nose and mouth, during maturity; diarrhœa in the last half of the period of desiccation.

VARIOLOID.—Principal remedies: *Bell.* and *Merc.;* or, ***Ars.*** and *rhus.*

Precursory stage, for violent *fever* and *headache*, ***Acon.*** and *Bell.*, and for pain in the *small of the back.*

To promote *desiccation*, give *Sulphur. bry.*

For subsequent *catarrh*, give *Merc.* or *Bell.;* or, when asthmatic affections are present, with mucous rattling: *Tart. emet.* and *senega.*

The *affections* of the *bones* require: *Sil.* or ***Phosph-ac.;*** and those of the *joints: Bell. bry. merc.*

VEINS, SWELLING OF THE.—Principal remedies: 1) ***Bellad.*** *china. crocus. ferr. hyosc. phosph. pulsat. sulph. thuj.* 2) *Amm. arn. baryt. calc. chelid. cicut. coloc. coni. cyclam. laches. lycop. magn-arc. meny. natr-m. n-vom. phos-ac. sassap. sepia. spigel. spong.*

VERTIGO.

§ 1. The principal remedies for vertigo and the affections of which it is sometimes the most prominent symptom, are: 1) ***Acon.*** *arn. bell. calc. chin. con. hep. lach. lyc. merc. n-vom. op. phosph. puls. rhus. sil. sulph.* 2) *Ant. baryt. bry. carb-an. cham. cic. cin. cocc. ign. kal. natr-m. nitr-ac. petr. sec. sep. stram. veratr. zinc.*

§ 2. For vertigo proceeding from the stomach, the best remedies are: *Acon. ant. arn. bell. cham. merc. n-vom. puls.* ***rhus.***

Vertigo from *cerebral irritation* or debility, requires: *Arn. bell. cham. chin. cin. hep. mosch. n-vom. puls.* and *rhus.*

From *congestion* of *blood* to the brain: *Acon. arn. bell. chin. con. lach. merc. n-vom. op. puls. rhus. sil. sulph.*

From *suppression* of *ulcers* or cutaneous eruptions: 1) *Calc. sulph.* 2) *Bell. bry. carb-veg. cham. hep. ipec. lach phosph. puls.*

From *riding in a carriage:* 1) *Hep. sil.;* or, 2) *Cocc. petrol.*

§ 3. Symptomatic indications:

Aconitum: Vertigo on raising one's head when lying or stooping, and when attended with: nausea, eructations, vomiting, obscuration of sight, loss of consciousness, dizziness.

Antimonium: Derangement of the stomach, nausea and vomiting, aversion to food, &c.

Arnica: Vertigo in consequence of too copious meal, or during a meal, with nausea, obscuration of sight, dizziness, red face, &c.

Belladonna: Vertigo with anguish, stupefaction or absence of mind, darkness; or vacillation, nausea, trembling of the hands, and scintillations; or when the vertigo is caused by *stooping* or *raising one's-self.*

Chamomilla: Vertigo on rising in the morning, or after eating, and especially after drinking coffee; with obscuration of sight, or *fainting turns.*

China: Vertigo on raising one's head (or during motion), with sensation of weakness of the head, which the patient is not well able to hold erect.

Conium: *Vertigo* causing the patient to fall to one side, especially when *looking about;* sensation of heaviness and fullness of the head; weak memory.

Hepar: Vertigo from riding in a carriage, or moving the head; or vertigo with nausea, stupefaction, fainting turn and obscuration of sight.

Lachesis: Vertigo with pale face, fainting, vomiting, bleeding at the nose, &c., especially when the vertigo is felt early *on waking,* or when it is attended with absence of mind, stupidity, intoxication, &c.

Mercurius: Vertigo on rising, or raising one's head; or in the evening, with *nausea,* obscuration of sight, heat, anguish, desire to lie down.

Nux vom.: Vertigo *during* or *after* a meal, or when walking in the open air, stooping or thinking; or in the morning, or evening in bed, when lying on the back, with sensation as if the head were turning and with danger of falling; or with buzzing in the ears, obscuration of sight; or fainting turn and loss of consciousness.

Opium: Vertigo from fright, especially when attended with:

Trembling, debility, *stupefaction*, *buzzing*, obscuration of sight; the vertigo comes on by raising one's-self in bed, and obliges one to lie down again.

PULSATILLA: Vertigo causing the patient to fall, especially on *lifting one's eyes*, or when sitting or stooping, especially in the evening in bed or after a meal; with heaviness of the head, buzzing in the ears, heat or paleness of the face, obscuration of sight; nausea and desire to vomit.

RHUS T.: Vertigo on lying down in the evening, with fear that he will fall or die.

SILICEA: Vertigo in the morning, or on lifting up one's eyes, when riding in a carriage, or stooping, and *after an emotion*, with fear of falling, nausea; or when the vertigo seems to rise from the back to the nape of the neck and thence to the head.

SULPHUR: Vertigo especially when sitting, ascending an eminence, or after a meal, *in the morning*, evening, or *at night;* with nausea, fainting, or bleeding of the nose.

§ 4. Comp.: CONGESTIONS of the Head, APOPLEXY, SPASMS, &c.

VINEGAR, ILL EFFECTS OF.—Principal remedies: *Acon. ars. asar. ign. n-vom. puls. sep.*

VOMIT, BLACK, MELÆNA.—This disease, which is characterized by discharge of *black blood* by the mouth or rectum, requires: 1) *Ars. chin. veratr;* or, 2) *Ipec. n-vom. petr. phosph. plumb. sulph-ac. ?*

Comp.: BLACK and BLOODY evacuations under DIARRHŒA and VOMITING.

VOMITING and NAUSEA.

§ 1 The remedies which are generally indicated by these symptoms are: 1) *Ipec. n-vom. puls.* 2) *Ars. bry. cham. cupr. ferr. sil. sulph. veratr.* 3) *Ant. arn. bell. calc. chin. cin. con. dig. dros. dulc. hyos. ign. lach. merc. phosph. plumb. sec. sep. tart.* 4) *Amb. carb-veg. caust. cic. cin. coloc. guaj. lyc. merc. natr-m. op. petr. rhus. sabad. stann.*

§ 2. Vomiting of the *ingesta:* 1) *Ars. ferr. hyos. n-vom. puls. sil. sulph.* 2) *Bell. bry. calc. cocc. cin. cupr. dros. graph. kal. lach. natr-m. phosph. rhus. sep. stann. veratr.*

Hæmatemesis: 1) *Acon. arn. ferr. hyos. ipec. n-vom.;* or, 2) *Amm-c. bell. bry. canth. carb-veg. caust. chin. lach. lyc. mez. mill. plumb. puls. sulph. veratr.*

Melæna: *Ars. calc. chin. veratr.;* or, *Ipec. n-vom. raph. sulph.*, &c.

Vomiting of *fæcal matter* (*iliac passion, chordapsus, miserere, ileus,* &c.): 1) *Bell. n-vom. op.* 2) *Acon.? *bry. plumb. raph. sulph.? thuj.?*

Comp. Ileus.

§ 3. The vomiting of *pregnant females* requires: 1) *Ipec. n-vom.*; or, 2) *Acon. ars. con. ferr. kreos. lach. magn-m. natr-m. n-mosch. petr. phosph. puls. sep. veratr.*

Vomiting of *drunkards*: 1) *Ars. lach. n-vom. op.*; or, 2) *Calc. sulph.*

Vomiting in consequence of *passive motion,* such as: *riding in a carriage, sailing,* &c., requires: 1) *Ars. coccul. colch. ferr. petr.* 2) *Bell. croc. n-mosch. sec.*

If caused by *worms,* give: 1) *Acon. cin. ipec. merc. n-vom. puls. sulph.*; or, 2) *bell. carb-veg. chin. lach.*

If by *overloading the stomach,* or by eating indigestible food: 1) *Ipec. puls.* 2) *Ant. bry. n-vom. sulph.* 3) *Ars. bell. ferr. rhus.*

§ 4. Use more particularly:

For vomiting of *bile,* with bitter taste and *greenish* look: 1) *Ars. bell. bry. cham. ipec. merc. n-vom. phosph. puls. sep. veratr.* 2) *Ant. arn. cann. chin. cin. coloc. con. cupr. dros. dulc. ign. lach. lyc. petr. raph. sec. sulph.*

For *sour*-smelling and tasting vomiting: 1) *Calc. cham. chin. n-vom. phosph. phos-ac. puls. sulph.* 2) *Ars. bell. ferr. ipec. lyc. sulph-ac. tart.*

Vomiting of *mucus*: 1) *Ars. bell. dros. n-vom. puls. sulph.* 2) *Acon. ant. calc. cham. chin. cin. con. guaj. hep. hyos. ign. merc. sec. veratr.*

Watery vomiting: 1) *Bell. bry. caust. ipec.* 2) *Arn. ars. chin. cupr. n-vom. puls. sulph.*

§ 5. Vomiting by *motion*: *Ars. bry. n-vom. veratr.*

Vomiting with *diarrhœa*: *Ars. bell. coloc. cupr. dulc. ipec. phosph. puls. veratr.*

Worse after eating: 1) *Ars. ferr. n-vom. puls. sulph.* 2) *Acon. arn. hyos. ipec. natr-m.*

Vomiting every *morning*: 1) *Ars. dros. n-vom.* 2) *Hep. lyc. natr-m. sil. veratr.*

At night: *Ars. ferr. chin. n-vom. sil. sulph.*

After *drinking*: 1) *Ars. ferr. chin.* 2) *Acon. arn. bry. cham. n-vom. sil.*

§ 6. Comp.: Gastric Derangement, Stomach, Derangement of, Weak Stomach, Gastritis, Diarrhœa, Cholera, Colic, Worm-affections, &c.

WARMTH, DEFICIENT, TENDENCY TO FEEL CHILLY, &c. —§ 1. Principal remedies for this symptom: 1) *Ars. bry. camph. carb-veg. con. dulc. ipec. lyc. natr. natr-m. puls. ran. rhus. veratr.* 2) *Acon. alum. ang. arn. calc. caps. caust. chel. chin. euphorb. ferr. led. merc. natr. natr-m. nitr. nitr-ac. n-vom. oleand. op. phosph. sabad. sassap. sep. staph. stram. sulph. thuj.* 3) *Aur. baryt. bell. carb-an. cic. graph. hell. hyos. kal. magn-arct. sec. squill. staph. tart.*

§ 2. When there is an excessive *want* of *animal heat:* 1) *Ars. chel. con. phosph. puls. ran. rhus. sep. veratr.* 2) *Acon. alum. ang. calc. camph. caps. caust. chel. chin. euphorb. ferr. ipec. led. lyc. natr. natr-m. nitr. nitr-ac. n-vom. oleand. op. sabad. sassap. staph. stram. sulph. tart. thuj.*

b) For great *sensitiveness* to the *open air:* 1) *Amm. calc. caps. carb-an. caust. cham. cocc. coff. mez. natr. n-vom. puls. rhus.* 2) *Agar. alum. anac. aur. bell. cycl. dulc. lach. lyc. natr-m. nitr-ac. n-mosch. rhod.*

c) *chilliness,* disposition to feel chilly, even in a room, &c.: 1) *Ars. bry. carb-veg. caust. chin. magn-arct. merc. natr-m. n-vom. phosph. puls. sil. sulph.* 2) *Agn. alum. anac. asar. calc. cham. cocc. hep. ipec. kreos. mez. natr. nitr-ac. n-mosch. petr. ran. rhus. sabad. sep. spig. veratr.*

d) frequent *shuddering:* 1) *Acon. ars. bell. chin. cocc. ign. merc. n-vom. puls. rhus. sep. staph.* 2) *Aur. bry. calc. caust. clem. coff. hep. kal. magn-arct. magn-aust. magn-m. natr. natr-m. phosph. plat. rhab. sabad. sabin. spig. sulph. thuj. veratr.*

§ 3. a) *External* coldness: 1) *Arn. ign. merc. mosch. n-vom. phosph. plat. rhus. sec. veratr.* 2) *Calc. caust. chin. lyc. mez. mur-ac. puls. rhod. sabad. sec. staph. sulph.*

b) *Internal* coldness: 1) *Ars. calc. chin. laur. lyc. n-vom. puls. sep.* 2) *Agn. alum. amb. bell. bry. chin. colch. ign. men. merc. mez. phosph. spig. sulph. veratr.*

c) *Coldness* or chilliness on one side: 1) *Caust. n-vom. puls. rhus.* 2) *Baryt. bell. bry. verb.*

d) *Constant coldness* or chilliness about the *head:* 1) *Bell. calc. phosph. sep. sulph. veratr.* 2) *Acon. arn. dulc. mosch.*

e) Constant coldness or chilliness in the *back:* 1) *Bell. calc. caps. chin. lach. natr-m. n-vom. sep. sil. stann. sulph.* 2) *Amm-m. camph. croc. dig. dulc. hep. lyc. phosph. rhus. sec. staph. thuj.*

f) Constant coldness of the *hands:* 1) *Jod. lach. natr. natr-m. sulph.* 2) *Amb. aur. calc. carb-an. carb-veg. caust. chin. coloc. con. dros. graph. merc. natr. natr-m. n-vom. ran. sassap. spig. thuj.*

g) Coldness of the *feet:* 1) *Amm. amm-m. calc. caust. con. graph. kal. lach. lyc. mur-ac. natr. natr-m. petr. phosph. plat.*

sil. sulph. veratr. 2) *Amb. ars. carb-an. carb-veg. ferr. hep hyos. ign. kreos. merc. nitr-ac. oleand. sep. stront. zinc.*

WARTS, VERRUCÆ.

§ 1. Principal remedies: 1) *Calc. caust. dulc. natr. nitr-ac. rhus. sep. sulph. thuj.* 2) *Ars. baryt. bell. hep. lyc. natr-m. phos-ac. sil. staph.*

Warts on the hands of onanists require: *Nitr-ac. sep. sulph. thuj.*

§ 2. Use moreover:

For *old* warts: *Calc. caust. nitr-ac. rhus. sulph.*

Bleeding warts: *Magn-aust. natr. nitr-ac. thuj.*

Inflamed warts: 1) *Caust. natr. nitr-ac. sil. sulph.* 2) *Amm. calc. rhus. sep. staph.*

Ulcerated warts: 1) *Calc. caust. hep. natr. thuj.* 2) *Ars. phosph sil.*

Itching warts: *Euphr. kal. nitr-ac. phosph. thuj.*

Painful warts: 1) *Calc. caust. petr. phosph. rhus.* 2) *Lyc. nitr-ac. sep. sil. sulph.*

§ 3. *Flat* warts require: *Dulc. lach.*

Large warts: *Caust. dulc. kal. natr. nitr-ac. sep.*

Small warts: 1) *Calc. nitr-ac. rhus. sassap. sep. sulph. thuj.* 2) *Dulc. ferr. hep. lach.*

Hard, horny warts: *Ant. borax. dulc. graph. ran. sulph. thuj.*

Pediculated: Dulc. lyc. thuj.

§ 4. Warts in the *face: Caust. dulc. kal. nitr-ac. sep. sulph.* —In the *eyebrows: Caust.*—On the *eyelids: Nitr-ac.*—Under the *eyes: Sulph.*—On the nose: *Caust.*

Warts on the *arms: Calc. caust. nitr-ac. sep. sulph.*

Warts on the *hands: Calc. dulc. lach. lyc. nitr-ac. rhus. sep. sulph. thuj.*

Warts on the *fingers: Lach. nitr-ac. rhus-t. sep. sulph. thuj.*

WHOOPING-COUGH.

§ 1. Principal remedies: 1) *Acon. arn. bell. carb-veg. cin. cupr. dulc. hep. ipec. merc. n-vom. puls. veratr.* 2) *Bry. cham. con. jod. lact. led. sep. sulph. tart.;* or, perhaps: 3) *Anac. ars. ferr. lach. nitr-ac. samb.*

§ 2. In the *first* period, period of incubation, give: *Acon. carb-veg. dulc. ipec. n-vom. puls.*

ACONITUM: Dry and wheezing cough, with fever, or burning pains in the larynx or trachea.

CARBO VEG.: *Convulsive* cough, especially in the evening or before midnight, with red neck, pain in the throat when swallowing, lachrymation; or stitches in the head, pains in the chest and throat, or when an eruption breaks out on the head or abdomen.

DULCAMARA: Moist cough from the commencement, with easy expectoration and hoarseness, and when the cough was brought on by taking cold.

IPECACUANHA: The cough is accompanied by great anguish, suffocative symptoms and bluish face; *Nux v.* being insufficient.

NUX VOM.: *Dry* cough from midnight till morning, with vomiting, anguish, suffocation, bluish face, bleeding from the mouth and nose.

PULSATILLA: *Moist cough* from the first, with vomiting of mucus or of the ingesta, or mucous diarrhœa.

§ 3. In the *spasmodic* period, with vomiting and *bleeding from nose and mouth*, the best remedies are: 1) *Cin. cupr. dros. veratr.;* or: 2. *Bell. merc.*

CINA: During the paroxysm the children suddenly become rigid, and the paroxysm is followed by a gurgling noise from the throat to the abdomen. This remedy is a specific, when the children are affected with the usual worm-symptoms, such as: Cutting in the bowels, itching of the anus, desire to rub one's nose or to bore with the finger in it.—*Merc.* is likewise suitable for these symptoms.

CUPRUM: The body becomes rigid during the paroxysm, with arrest of breathing and loss of consciousness; vomiting after the paroxysms, and rattling of mucus in the chest between the paroxysms. (After *Cupr.*, *Veratr.* is frequently suitable.)

DROSERA: Excessive violence of the paroxysms, wheezing cough; no fever, or else: high fever with chills and heat, thirst only after the chills, the sweat is rather hot than cool, and sometimes sets in only at night; aggravation during rest, relief from motion. *Drosera* is generally the best remedy for fully developed whooping-cough, with vomiting of food or mucus, and bleeding from the mouth and nose. (After *Dros.*, *Veratr.* is sometimes suitable.)

VERATRUM: *Dros.* and *Cupr.* being insufficient, or sometimes before these medicines have been given, especially when the children are very feeble, with a sort of hectic fever, cold sweat, especially on the forehead; small, hurried and feeble pulse; great thirst; or the coughing causes an involuntary emission of urine, and pain in the chest and loins; between the paroxysms the patients are in a comatose state, and care not either to move or converse; excessive weakness of the neck, so that the children are scarcely able to keep their head erect; attended with rash over the whole body, or only in the face and on the hands.

§ 4. The convulsive form of whooping-cough is not always fully developed, and it frequently happens that, at a period when the whooping-cough is epidemic, children are seized with a spasmodic cough which is without a great many of the characteristic symptoms of whooping-cough. The best remedies for such a cough are: *Bell. bry. jod. merc. sulph. tart.*

Belladonna: Cerebral irritation, or the cough is preceded by a painful sensation in the region of the stomach, with bleeding of the nose and mouth, or ecchymoses in the eye; or when other spasmodic symptoms, such as: tetanus, convulsive asthma, &c. are present; or when the paroxysms terminate in sneezing.

Bryonia: The paroxysms set in principally in the evening or at night, or after eating or drinking, with loss of breath, want of air, and vomiting of the ingesta.

Jodium: The cough is excited by tickling in the bronchi, with undulating inspirations during the paroxysms, which are preceded by great anguish, attended with great exhaustion, emaciation.

Lactuca: Violent cough, with vomiting after every paroxysm, but without any other characteristic symptoms.

Mercurius: Cough only at night or only in the day-time, two paroxysms succeeding each other closely, and separated from the next two paroxysms by a longer interval of repose; or suitable for the *real whooping-cough*, when the children, during the vomiting, bleed profusely from nose and mouth, with profuse sweat at night and great nervousness; especially when the children are affected with worms and are liable to convulsions. (The last mentioned symptoms sometimes require *Carb. veg.* after *Merc.*)

Sulphur: The paroxysms are accompanied with vomiting, and do not yield to any of the above-mentioned remedies.

Tartarus: The vomiting is accompanied by diarrhœa, with great prostration, or the children vomit up their supper in the first hours after midnight.

§ 5. If the convulsive period have run its course, and *catarrhal* symptoms remain, use: *Arn. carb-veg. dulc. hep. puls.*

Arnica: The children weep much after coughing, or the paroxysms are preceded by screams and crying, or they are caused by these screams.

CARBO VEG.: The catarrhal cough frequently becomes spasmodic, or the vomiting keeps up though the other symptoms of whooping-cough have disappeared.

DULCAMARA: The catarrhal cough is accompanied by profuse expectoration of mucus.

HEPAR: The cough abates, but is hacking, dry and rough, with desire to vomit after the paroxysms, and frequent weeping.

PULSATILLA: Moist cough, with easy expectoration of serous mucus.

§ 6. Although we have distinguished whooping-cough into stages, yet it must not be supposed that the remedies which have been respectively indicated for the different stages, cannot be used for any other; on the contrary, many of the remedies which we have mentioned for the spasmodic stage, may, in many cases, be required in the precursory stage, and vice versa. Let it be remembered, that the selection of a remedy does not depend upon the *name* of the disease, but upon the symptoms, the pathological character of the disease, and the state of the patient.

Compare: BRONCHITIS, CROUP, LARYNGITIS, COUGH, &c.

WORM-AFFECTIONS, HELMINTHIASIS.

§ 1. Principal remedies: 1) *Acon. cin. merc. sulph.* 2) *Calc. carb-veg. chin. cic. ferr. fil. graph. ign. n-mosch. n-vom. sabad. sil. spig.* 3) *Ars. kal. natr-m. petr. phosph. puls. ruta. sabin. val.*

§ 2. For *tænia*, give a dose of *Sulphur*, when the moon is on the decline; at the next full moon give a dose of *Mercury;* then again, in eight days, a dose of *Sulphur;* and so on for some time.

If this treatment should prove unsuccessful, give: 1) *Calc. carb-veg. graph. magn-m. n-vom. puls. sabad. sil.* 2) *Ign. merc. petr. phosph.* 3) *Fil. fragar-vesc. gran.*

§ 3. The best remedies for *maw-worms* are: 1) *Acon. cin. merc. sabad.* 2) *Sulph.;* or: 3) *Bell. calc. cham. chin. cic. graph. hyos. lyc. natr-m. n-vom. rhus. ruta. sil. spig.*

Fever with colic, disposition to vomit, hard and distended abdomen, tenesmus or small slimy stools, require *Acon.;* after which, in a few hours, *Cin.* may be given; and, if necessary, in 24 hours, *Merc.*

If the fever and colic should be attended with great thirst, nervousness, sudden starting from sleep, and tendency to start, give *Bell.*, or *Lach.* if *Bell.* should not suffice.

For the *fever*, some have successfully given: *Chin. cic. sil. spig.*—For the *colic* and *convulsions: Cic.*—For *worm-colic* with canine hunger, diarrhœa and chilliness: *Spig.*—For the *fever-paroxysms* of scrofulous patients: *Sil.*

After these paroxysms have been subdued, a dose of *Sulphur* may be given, allowing it to act 4, 5, 6 weeks; and if, after the lapse of this period, worm-symptoms should still manifest themselves, such as: *Loss of flesh*, voracious appetite, pale face, &c. give: *Baryt. calc. graph. lyc.*, or *natr-m.*

§ 4. The best remedies for the ailments caused by ascarides, are: 1) *Acon. calc. chin. ferr. ign. merc. sulph.;* or 2) *Graph. n-vom. phosph. teucr.*

For feverish restlessness at night, tossing about, give: *Acon.;* and, if this should not suffice, *Ign.*

If *Acon.* and *Ign.* should not help, and if the distress should return at new or full moon, *Sulph.* should be given, either during the decline or increase of the moon; or else: *Calc. ferr. chin.*

WORN OUT. See Lassitude and Debility.

WOUNDS, Injuries, Sprains, &c.

§ 1. Principal remedies: 1) *Arn. cic. con. hep. lach. puls. rhus. sulph-ac.* 2) *Acon. amm. bry. calc. caust. cham. euphr. nitr-ac. n-vom. phosph. ruta. sil. staph. sulph. zinc.* 3) *Alum. bell. borax. carb-veg. dulc. jod. petr. sil.*

§ 2. For *sprains, luxations*, &c., give: *Arnica*, 10 drops of the tincture in a tumblerful of water, before and after the necessary manual operations, such as: reduction of the dislocation, &c. If the contusion or luxation should be very bad, *Arnica* 30 may likewise be given internally; and if no result should have been obtained in 24 hours, *rhus-t.*, one dose, allowing it to act until an improvement takes place. A second dose of *Rhus.* may be given after the first ceases to act; or, if a pain should occasionally be experienced in the sprained joint, *Amm. ruta.* should be resorted to; or: *Agn. bell. bry. puls.*; or, *Calc. carb-an. carb-veg. ign. lyc. magn-aust. natr. natr-m. nitr-ac. n-vom. petr. phosph. sep. sulph.*

If the patient should have injured himself by *lifting heavy weight*, the principal remedy is *Rhus t.*, especially when the dorsal and cervical muscles and the vertebral column are affected, and headache, pains in the back or gastric ailments are experienced. If *Rhus* should not suffice, give: *Calc. cocc. natr.*

n-vom. sulph.; or: *Arn. bry. carb-an. carb-veg. graph. kal. lyc. sep. sil.*—If *hernia inguinalis* should have been caused by lifting heavy weight, or by straining the body, give: 1) *N-vom. sulph-ac.* 2) *Cocc. sulph.*—If a prolapsus of the womb should have been occasioned by these causes, *N-vom.* is almost a specific remedy, and should be resorted to before *Bell.* or *Sep.* are given.

The ill effects of missing a step or pressing the foot to the floor with too much violence, require: 1) *Bry.* 2) *Cic. con. puls. rhus.* 3) *Arn. spig.*

§ 3. Parts which have been injured by a contusion, fall or blow, should be bathed with a solution of *Arnica; Arnica* being likewise taken internally if the contusion be very bad, or if the head, chest, abdomen, &c., should have been violently concussed. If *Arnica* should be insufficient, give:

For simple *contusion* without concussion: 1) *Euphr. jod. puls. ruta. sulph-ac.* 2) *Croc. hep. mez. petr. phosph. sulph.*

For *concussion* from blow, shock, fall, or other causes; 1) *Cic. con. puls. rhus.* 2) *Euphr. jod. lach. sulph. sulph-ac.*

Concussion *of the whole body* by a fall: *Bry. cic. con. puls. rhus. sulph-ac.*

Ecchymosis which does not yield to *Arnica:* 1) *Bry. rhus. sulph-ac.* 2) *Con. dulc. lach. n-vom. puls. sulph.*

Swelling of the injured parts: 1) *Bry. puls. rhus. sulph.* 2) *Bell. n-vom. sulph-ac.*

§ 4. If there should be a solution of continuity (as in wounds, &c.) apply first *Arnica* as a wash; and if this should be insufficient, apply:

For *bites*, not of poisonous animals: *Arn. sulph-ac.*—And of poisonous animals: 1) *Amm. ars. bell.* 2) *Caust. lach. natr-m. puls. seneg.*

Contused wounds, see: Contusion in the preceding paragraph.

Excoriations, bedsores: 1) *Arn. sulph-ac.* 2) *Carb-veg. chin. puls.*

Cut-wounds: 1) *Staph. sulph.* 2) *Natr. plumb. sil. sulph-ac.*

Gun-shot-wounds: 1) *Euphr. nitr-ac. plumb. sulph-ac.* 2) *puls. ruta. sulph.*

Splinters: 1) *Acon. carb-veg. sic. hep. nitr-ac. sil.* 2) *Lach. sulph.*

Stab-wounds: 1) *Carb-veg. cic. lach. nitr-ac. sil.* 2) *Con. hep. plumb. sulph.*

Burns: Acon. ars. carb-veg. caust. lach. stram. urtic.—Relief is sometimes obtained by washing the burn with *soap-spirits.*—Burns of the *tongue* sometimes are cured by a small dose of *Ars.* or *Caust.*

§ 5. Employ more particularly

For readily *bleeding* wounds: 1) *Acon. arn.* ***chin. phosph.*** 2) ***Carb-veg. diadem. lach. sulph. sulph-ac.***

For *profuse suppuration :* 1) *Bell. chin. merc.* ***puls. sulph.*** 2) *Bell. hep. lach. plumb.*

For *inflamed, angry, ulcerated* wounds, give: 1) ***Cham. sil.*** 2) *Borax. graph. hep. lach. merc. nitr-ac.* ***puls. rhus. sulph. sulph-ac.***

Gangrenous wounds: 1) ***Ars. chin. lach. sil.*** 2) ***Acon.*** *amm. bell. carb-veg. euphorb.*

§ 6. If the *muscles* and *soft* parts alone were injured, give: 1) *Arn. euphr. hep. puls. sulph-ac.* 2) *Con. dulc. lach.* ***n-vom. sulph.***

If the tendons, *ligaments* or *synovial* membranes: 1) ***Amm.*** *arn. bry. rhus. ruta.* 2) *Calc.* ***natr.*** *natr-m. phosph.* 3) ***Agn.*** *carb-an. carb-veg. lyc. magn-aust. n-vom. petr. sep.*

Wounds of *glandular* organs require: 1) *Con.* ***jod. kal. phosph.*** 2) *Cic. hep. merc. puls. sil. sulph.*

Wounds of *bones* or the *periosteum :* 1) *Calend.* ***phos-ac. puls. ruta.*** 2) *Calc. phosph. sil. staph.*

Fractures : Calc. calend. ruta. sil. symphitum ***officinale.***

§ 7. *Traumatic* convulsions (tetanus) require: ***Ang. bell. cic. cocc.***

Traumatic (wound) *fever : Acon. bry. rhus-t.*, provided ***Arn.*** is insufficient.

Nervous symptoms, after violent concussion of the brain or spinal marrow, require: 1) *Cic. con.* 2) *Bell.* ***calc. cin. hep.***, provided *Arn.* is insufficient.

§ 8. See: Poisoning, Bites of poisonous animals, &c.

YAWNING, SPASMODIC.

The principal remedies for this symptom are: 1) ***Ign. magn-arct. natr-m. plat.*** *rhus. sulph.* 2) *Amm. caust.* ***cham. cocc. croc. euphr. lach. magn-c. nitr-ac. tart. veratr.***

ZONA, ZOSTER, ignis sacer.

This disease only occurs on the trunk, and should not be confounded with common vesicular erysipelas. The principal remedies for this disease are: 1) *Rhus-t.* 2) *Graph.*—These two remedies generally suffice in recent cases. In old cases, which had been mismanaged with other medicines, we may try: ***Ars.;*** or: ***merc. puls.*** or: *Bry.* ***cham. natr. selen. sil. sulph.***

CHARACTERISTIC SYMPTOMS

OF THE MOST IMPORTANT

HOMŒOPATHIC REMEDIES.

(For a full description of the Symptoms, the reader is referred to *Hempel's Jahr.*)

A.

ACON.—ACONITUM NAPELLUS.—Stitching pains or pains confined to a small spot; painful sensitiveness of the body, or especially of the affected part, to contact; *great nervous and vascular excitement*, or great debility and fainting fits; dry, burning heat of the skin and swollen parts; burning, red, inflamed eruptions; *dry heat all over*, with thirst, short breathing, full, hard, *hurried pulse*, redness of the face or cheeks, disposition to uncover one's-self, chills when uncovering one's-self ever so little; anguish and forebodings, lamentations; apprehensions of death, designation of the day when one is to die; tendency to start; zoomagnetic state of the mind; delirium; frequent paroxysms of vertigo, or fainting, with vanishing of sight; *rush of blood* to the head, with heat in the head, and red face; beating headache or stupefying tightness in the forehead; sensation on the vertex as if the hairs were pulled; inflamed and painful eyes; hard, red swelling of the lids; photophobia; dilated pupils; sensitiveness to noise and odours; bleeding of the nose; bloated and red face, or pale face on raising the head; dry and parched lips; dry mouth; inflamed fauces, with stinging, burning and dark redness; loathing of food, or *burning thirst;* bitter taste in the mouth and of food and drink, except water; vomiting of mucus, blood or ascarides; *pressure as from a stone* in the pit of the stomach; *distended abdomen*, or the abdomen is painful to contact; *small soft stools* with tenesmus; white stools with red urine; *red, hot, fiery* and *scanty* urine; suppression of urine; *profuse menses;* short, hurried breathing; suffocative fits, as if from anguish, or compression of the chest; *short* and dry cough, with expectoration of blood or bloody mucus; *stitches in the chest*, especially in *the side*, when breathing, coughing or moving; *palpitation of the heart*, with great anguish iu the chest.

AGAR.—Agaricus Muscarius.—Convulsions, epilepsy, miliary eruptions, chilblains, prosopalgia, toothache, &c.

AGN.—Agnus Castus.—Impotence; gleet; sterility; suppressed menses; swelling and *induration* of the spleen; ascites: soreness of the anus; swelling and induration of the testicles; leucorrhœa, &c.

ALUM.—Alumina.—Constrictive sensation in various organs: soreness of the *mucous membranes;* itching of the skin in the evening; *humid herpes* and *scurfs;* rhagades; sad mood, whining and moaning; profuse secretion of mucus in the eyes; purulent otorrhœa; blennorrhœa of the nose, with *ulcerated nostrils;* heaviness of the face, and tightness of the skin of the face as if covered with the white of an egg; toothache, specially when chewing, with sensation as if the teeth were loose and elongated: *difficult deglutition,* as if the fauces were constricted; irregular appetite; heartburn; pressing and pulsations in the abdominal ring; slow stool as from inaction of the bowels; itching of the anus, increased sexual desire, with erections and nocturnal emissions; scanty and pale menses; slimy and corrosive leucorrhœa; hoarseness; orthopnœa, as if from constriction of the chest; irregular beating and shocks of the heart.

AMB.—Ambra Grisea.—Crampy pains in the muscles and tearing in the joints: pains as if strained; numbness of the skin; itching and burning as if one had the itch; dreams; chills in some parts; nervousness; despondency; mental debility; vertigo; *rush of blood to the head,* especially when listening to music; falling off and soreness of the hair; buzzing and ringing in the ears; obstruction of the nose; *jaundiced complexion,* and red spots on the face; twitching of the lips and wings of the nose: bad smell from the mouth; sore blotches under the tongue; feeling of coldness in the abdomen; irregular stools; turbid urine: sour smell of the urine; pleasurable sensation in the interior sexual organs; erections; soreness, swelling and itching of the labia; leucorrhœa, with discharge of pieces of bluish-white mucus; hoarseness, with tenacious mucus in the throat; palpitation of the heart, with pale face, arrest of breathing.

AMM.—Ammonium Carbonicum. *Ulcerative pains,* or stinging and tearing, less in bed; drawing in the joints as from shortening of the tendons; sensitiveness to cold and open air; burning pimples; rash, scarlet-redness of the skin; freckles; frightful dreams about dying, death and dead bodies; chills in the evening; sad, anxious mood; absence of mind, vertigo in the morning; headache as *if the forehead would split;* feeling of coldness or burning in the eyes; lachrymation; itching and suppuration of the ear; pale face, itching eruptions in the face; *ulcerative pain* of the roots of teeth; blisters and ulcers in the mouth; ptyalism;

heartburn; feeling of coldness or burning in the stomach; costiveness; wetting the bed; urine with sandy sediment; swelling, itching and burning of the pudendum; hoarseness and aphonia; *dry night-cough* as if from feather-dust in the throat; bloody expectoration; heaviness on the chest as if from too much blood; asthma with palpitation of the heart.

Ammonium has been advantageously used for: hemicrania; styes; parotitis; scurvy; dyspepsia; cardialgia; hæmorrhoids; *asthma;* hydrothorax; goïtre; gout; angina faucium; scrophula; rickets; rash; *scarlet-fever;* typhus; herpes furfuraceous, &c.

AMM. M.—Ammonium Muriaticum.—*Jerking tearing* in the limbs, especially the fingers and toes, with throbbing as if suppurating; rash, or blotches which burn after being scratched; burning of the eyes at twilight, going off when the lamps (candles) are lighted; muscæ volitantes; sore nose with thick mucus; pale face; rhagades of the lips; *distention of the inguinal region,* with ulcerative pain when touched; sore pain in the rectum, and discharge of blood from the anus; premature menses; leucorrhœa, like brown mucus or the white of an egg; violent dry cough; asthma, especially when moving the arms much, &c.

ANAC.—Anacardium Orientale.—*Pressure as from a plug,* or crampy jerking; prostration; lameness; sensitiveness to cold and draughts of air; anxious dreams about fire, loathsome diseases, &c.; *hypochondria,* foreboding of danger; want of feeling; laughing at serious things, and vice versa; weakness of mind and memory, with bruised pain in the head when reflecting; hardness of hearing and want of smell: pale face, with hollow eyes; dyspepsia, with heat in the face, hypochondria, &c., after eating; sexual excitement with discharge of prostatic juice; racking cough like whooping-cough, especially at night, with rush of blood to the head.

ANG.—Angustura.—Spasmodic pains, traumatic tetanus; tetanic spasms with blue cheeks and lips; caries and painful ulcers attacking the bones.

ANT.—Antimonium Crudum.—Adiposis, or emaciation; dropsical swellings; *pustules like chickenpox;* tumours and blisters as when bitten by insects; brown spots and freckles; horny excrescences; red, hot swellings; night- and morning-sweats, especially every other day; inflammatory redness of the eyes and lids; sore nostrils and corners of the mouth; pustulous eruption on the cheeks and chin, with yellow scurfs; ptyalism; *loss of appetite; eructations tasting of the ingesta, nausea, vomiting* of bile and mucus; *oppression of the stomach* from overloading it; cardialgia; agonizing burning in the pit of the stomach; hard stool with pressing; discharge of yellow mucus from the anus; frequent micturition with discharge of mucus; red sediment in the urine;

sexual excitement, with erections and emissions; hoarseness and aphonia, especially during warmth; paroxysms of suffocative asthma; burning in the chest, when coughing.

ARG.—Argentum.

ARN.—Arnica.—Stinging creeping, or laming and bruised pains in the affected parts; pains as if *sprained, contused, hurt; red, shining, hot swellings;* a number of small boils; the lower parts of the body feel cold, the upper hot; *tensive pressure* in the forepart of the head, as if the brain were squeezed up in a lump; itching tearing or stitching in the head; immobility of the scalp; one cheek is hard and swollen; creeping in the face, nose, scalp, lips and gums; toothache as if the teeth were sprained and loose; white-coated tongue; foul smell from the mouth; foul eructations; vomiting of coagulated blood; spasmodic pressure in the stomach; splenetic stitches when walking; fetid flatulence; frequent small mucous stools; nocturnal enuresis; brown urine with brick-dust sediment; inflammatory swelling of the scrotum and spermatic cord; hæmoptoë with discharge of bright-red blood or black lumps; stitches in the chest, especially when coughing or moving about; fetid breath; stitches in the region of the heart, with paroxysms of fainting.

ARS.—Arsenicum album.—Relief by *moving the affected part; burning pains; sudden prostration;* cold, parchment-like, dry skin; also with blueness; *burning eruptions* aud *ulcers*, flat and ichorous; frightful dreams; *coldness all over*, also with cold, clammy sweat; religious melancholy; excessive anguish and agony, particularly at *night;* swelling of the head; beating headache, especially over the root of the nose; suppurating crusts on the hairy scalp; dim, œdematous eyes; yellowness of the whites; burning coryza; *sunken, pale, livid, cadaverous countenance*, with hollow eyes surrounded by blue margins, and with pointed nose; swelling of the face, especially under the eyes; jaundiced appearance; blackish, cracked, swollen or ulcerated lips; spasmodic grinding of the teeth; bluish, brown, or blackish, trembling tougue; *thirst, but can drink only* a *few drops at a time;* excessive nausea; vomiting of blood or black substances; vomiting of the ingesta; burning in the stomach, anguish, painfulness of the pit; cardialgia; colic, spasmodic or cutting, driving one to despair; *burning* or watery diarrhœa, with *tenesmus* and colic; burning varices of the anus; profuse and premature menses; corrosive leucorrhœa; cough after drinking; orthopnœa; nightly suffocative paroxysms.

ASA.—Asa Fœtida.—Intermittent, pulsative pains from within outwards; stitching, tearing, and changed by contact; ulcers penetrating to the bones, discharging a thin, fetid ichor.

ASAR.—ASARUM EUROPÆUM.—Hemicrania, bilious and gastric affections, lienteria.

AUR.—AURUM FOLIATUM.—Bruised pains, especially in the joints; laming pains; formication; laming tearing in the bones; restless sleep with frightful dreams; *religious melancholy*, longing for death, *suicidal mania;* congestion of blood to the head, with *roaring;* vertical half-sightedness; muscæ volitantes; dark, brown-red spots on the nose, and ulcerated, scurfy nostrils, with swelling of the nose; swelling of the cheek and lip, with drawing tearing in the bones; gumboil with swelling of the cheek; fetid odour from the mouth; disposition of exciting hernia to protrude; sexual excitement; swelling and contusive pain in the testes; nocturnal asthma and constrictive oppression of the chest; palpitation of the heart, with congestion of blood to the chest; shaking of the heart when walking as if it were loose.

AUR. M.—AURUM MURIATICUM.

B

BARYT.—BARYTA CARBONICA.—General debility of the body, nerves, senses and mind; unhealthy skin; glandular swellings and indurations; irresoluteness, despondency; headache over the eyes or in the occiput; eruption behind the ears; sensation as if the face were covered with cobweb; swelling of the *upper lip* and *submaxillary glands;* pale-red swelling of the gums; inflammation of the throat and tonsils with suppuration; burning blisters on the tongue; suppression of the sexual desire; feeble and short menses; hoarseness and aphonia.

BELL.—BELLADONNA.—Stinging or burning pains, with bruised pain and swelling in the affected parts; spasmodic paroxysms with screams, creeping in the muscles; rush of blood to the affected part, with sensation of fullness and pressure from within outwards; lethargy, or sleeplessness with unsuccessful attempts at sleeping; alternate heat and chilliness; anguish and restlessness, or excessive irritation of the senses, with whining and lamenting; *furibond delirium;* violent pain in the forehead as if it would split; or burning stinging over the eyes; headache, with throbbing of the carotids, vertigo and buzzing in the ears; red shining and protruded, or faint and distorted eyes; *dilated* or extremely contracted pupils; inflammation of the eyes, with photophobia and smarting lachrymation; *bloated, red and hot* face; constriction of the throat; violent thirst, frequently with aversion to drinks; colic, as if a spot were seized with nails and spasmodically drawn to one lump; pressing towards the female sexual organs as if every thing would protrude; painfulness of the abdomen to contact, as if sore and ulcerated; painfulness of the larynx with danger of suffocation when touching it; short spasmodic cough with stitches in the abdomen and chest; painful stiffness of the neck and nape of the neck.

BORAX.—Borax Veneta.—Phagedenic blisters; anxious sleep with starting; plica polonica; blepharophthalmitis, with lachrymation in the daytime and nightly suppuration; inflammation and swelling of the ears, and discharge of pus; ulcerated nostrils, with soreness and swelling of the tip of the nose; discharge of green, thick mucus from the nose; scurfy upper lip and herpetic spots around the mouth; *aphthæ;* dyspepsia; vomiting of mucus; discharge of mucus from the anus, during and between the stools, with pains in the small of the back; yellow mucous diarrhœa; *fetid urine,* with *acrid smell;* easy conception; pains in the small of the back.

BRY.—Bryonia Alba.—Tension, drawing and tearing in the affected part, which does not bear motion; sweats during rest and trembles when the pains abate; *bruised pain* as if ecchymosed, or as if the flesh had been detached from the bones by blows; great nervousness, obliging one to lie down; *aggravation of the pains* by *contact or motion;* tight, red, hot swellings; erysipelatous inflammation in the joints; nightly rushes of blood, with heat, dreams and delirium; *chilliness,* frequently with red face; *sweat,* day and night, sometimes greasy, or dry heat and thirst; *disposition to be angry;* rush of blood to the head, with heat in the head; headache with nausea, vomiting, worse even by moving the eyes; the hair of the head is very greasy; face red and bloated or yellow and livid, or circumscribed redness of the cheeks; *aversion to food;* desire for wine, acids or coffee; *vomiting of food* or of bitter substances; painful pressure in the region of the stomach; painful sensitiveness of the liver; *obstinate constipation,* or yellow, nightly or morning-diarrhœa; foul diarrhœic stools; scanty, brown, hot urine; dry coryza; *dry cough,* racking, or with vomiting of food; coughs up coagulated or brownish blood; *stitches in the* chest and *sides of the chest,* painful when coughing, breathing or moving; deep, panting, or anxious and hurried breathing.

C.

CALC.—Calcarea Carbonica.—Debility and atrophy; *contraction of the fingers and toes;* numbness and deadness of various parts; nervousness; sensitiveness to cold and damp air; rough and dry skin; rash; warts; scurfy eruptions and herpes; rhagades; fetid ulcers; melancholy mood; anxiety and fear, especially at twilight; scurfs on the hairy scalp; sore nose; pale and thin, wrinkled face; swelling of the submaxillary and cervical glands; large abdomen with swelling of the mesenteric glands; aversion to meat; desire to wine and dainties; costiveness; profuse and premature menses; cough with fetid purulent expectoration; chronic hoarseness.

CAMPH.—CAMPHORA.—Asiatic cholera, influenza; epilepsy; typhus; dropsical affections; insolation, &c.; also for: excessive prostration, convulsions and tetanic spasms with loss of consciousness, and vomiting; coma; coldness all over, with pale face, blue skin and cold sweats; burning in the mouth, fauces and stomach; internal heat and external chilliness; want of sexual power and weakness of the sexual organs; accumulation of mucus in the air-passages, even unto arrest of breathing.

CANN.—CANNABIS.—*Cataract;* obscuration and specks of the cornea; succulated ascites; chronic constipation; cystitis and nephritis; urinary difficulties; *hæmaturia; acute gonorrhœa;* leucorrhœa; sterility; affections of the heart, &c.

CANTH.—CANTHARIDES.—Burning sore pains, especially in the mucous membranes; convulsive tossing of the limbs, with shrieking and roaring; paroxysms of rage, with convulsions, renewed by the sight of water; miserable looks; hippocratic countenance; frothy ptyalism; difficult deglutition; burning thirst, with aversion to drinks; hæmatemesis; *violent pains in the neck of the bladder;* suppression of urine; constant urging to urinate with drop-discharges; priapism; inflammation and gangrene of the sexual parts; feeling of weakness in the chest, with faint speech.

CAPS.—CAPSICUM ANNUUM.—Laziness and dread of motion; chilliness and coldness of the body; mental weakness as if the head were empty; slimy stools with tenesmus.

CARB. AN.—CARBO ANIMALIS.—Being unable to point out the difference between Carbo animalis and vegetabilis, I refer the reader to:

CARBO VEG.—CARBO VEGETABILIS.—*Burning pains,* especially in the joints and bones; *fine rash;* readily bleeding, fetid, burning, ichorous ulcers; *drowsiness in the day-time;* chilliness, *with paroxysms of flushes of heat;* disposition to sweat; despondency; fear (of ghosts); tendency to start; confusion of the brain; *painfulness of the scalp,* even when merely touching the hair; *shortsightedness;* pale, gray-yellow complexion; loose teeth, and receding, readily bleeding gums; dyspepsia; cardialgia; *flatulence;* discharge of mucus from the rectum, during and between stools; lascivious fancies; cough when taking the least cold; cough with expectoration of mucus, also greenish, purulent mucus; soreness in the chest.

CAUST.—CAUSTICUM.—Contraction of single parts, or numbness and deadness; rushes of blood; tremulous weakness; lameness, especially of the organs of speech and deglutition; *itchlike eruptions; warts* and varices; *profuse sweats* and chilliness; stoppage of the nose and constant coryza; yellow, discoloured complexion; chronic costiveness; involuntary emission of urine;

uterine spasms; chronic hoarseness and aphonia; soreness in the chest and larynx, especially when coughing; glandular swelling on the neck, resembling goïtre.

CHAM.—CHAMOMILLA.—Lameness and numbness of the affected parts, with constant disposition to move them; nervous irritation with intolerance of pain; excessive prostration as soon as the pains commence; convulsive twitchings of the lips, facial muscles, eyes and lids; unhealthy skin; painful ulcers, with nightly burning and creeping; yellow skin; restless sleep; coma vigil; *shuddering*, with internal heat; *feverish heat*, with red cheeks and hot sweat on the forehead and head, even in the hairs; anguish and tossing about as if in despair; hypochondriac, vexed mood; *redness and heat of one cheek;* frequent change of colour in the face; fetid smell from the mouth, especially after a meal; red and cracked tongue; foul taste in the mouth; vomiting of bile or acids; *violent pressure in the pit of the stomach;* greenish diarrhœa, like stirred eggs.

CHEL.—CHELIDONIUM.—Has been used for obscuration of the cornea, herpes facialis, &c.

CHIN.—CHINA, CINCHONA OFFICINALIS.—*Jerking tearing, increased by contact*, and with lameness of the affected parts; *bruised pain of the bones in the joints, especially when lying*, less when moving about; aggravation of the pains, especially by contact, also *at night* or after a meal; nervousness, with feeling of debility; painful weariness in the joints, with pressure as if from a weight; lameness and tremulous weakness; emaciation; dropsical swellings, or hard, red inflammatory swellings; drowsiness in the day-time, but no sleep at night in consequence of fancies; disturbed sleep with heavy anxious dreams; thirst during and after the cold stage, and during the sweaty stage; nightly pressure in the head, or sore and bruised pain of the brain, during mental labour; painful sensitiveness of the hairy scalp when touched; ringing in the ears; dimness and weakness of sight; yellow, livid complexion; pale, sunken face, with hollow eyes and pointed nose; foul smell from the mouth, especially early in the morning; bitter taste of food; dyspepsia; desire for dainties and wine; swelling and hardness of the region of the liver; copious and fetid flatulence; sexual excitement; suffocative fits at night; pressure between the scapulæ as if from a stone.

CIC.—CICUTA VIROSA.—Sore pains as if bruised; catalepsy; convulsions; confluent pustules with yellow scurfs; nervousness; foolish exhibitions of craziness; vertigo and loss of sense, with vanishing of sight; frequent staring as if from absence of mind; diplopia and blackness of sight; suppurating herpes facialis; trismus and grating of the teeth; foam at the mouth; desire for charcoal; hæmatemesis; involuntary emission of urine, as if from paralysis of the bladder; arrest of breathing as if the chest would be pressed asunder.

CIN.—Cina.—Atrophy; scrofula; convulsions; intermittent fevers; acute hydrocephalus; amaurosis, specks on the cornea; gastric symptoms; worm-affections; wetting the bed.

CINN.—Cinnab.—Cinnabaris.

CIST.—Cistus—Glandular swellings; scrophula; *scurvy;* caries of the lower jaw; laryngeal phthisis.

CLEM.—Clematis Erecta.—Ailments from abuse of Mercury; acute articular rheumatism after gonorrhœa; strictures of the urethra, after gonorrhœa; swelling and induration of the testicles; glandular swellings, also glandular indurations.

COCC.—Cocculus.—Painful stiffness of the joints, with cracking semilateral pains and distresses; aggravation of the pains from drinking, smoking, contact and riding in a carriage; excessive prostration; spots on the skin as if from red wine; cold glandular swellings with stinging pains; chlorotic colour of the skin; coma vigil; melancholy, and foreboding anguish; headache as if the head were constricted or as if the eyes would be pulled out; the head feels empty and hollow; redness and heat of the cheeks, with burning; pain and burning in the œsophagus; *nausea* unto fainting, *especially when riding in a carriage;* cardialgia after eating; distressing flatulence; disposition to inguinal hernia; suppression of the menses, with a good deal of distress.

COFF.—Coffea Cruda.—Excessive nervousness, with sensitiveness to pain; extreme mobility of the muscles; aversion to open air; sleeplessness from excessive mental and bodily wakefulness; anguish with trembling; excessive pain, driving one to despair; sensation as if the brain were torn, or as if a nail were driven into the head; sexual excitement.

COLCH.—Colchicum Autumnale.—Sudden *tearings* or *stitching pains even through the periosteum,* with lameness of the affected part; aggravation of the pains by mental exertions, especially in the night or evening, frequently driving one to despair; tearing in the limbs in warm weather, and stitching in cold weather; sensitiveness of the body to contact; lameness of the knee-joints, causing them to give way; *creeping* as if frozen, especially when the weather changes; œdematous and dropsical swellings; otorrhœa with tearing; yellow spots in the face; bloated face; nausea, even from the mere smell of broth and eggs; burning, or sensation of icy-coldness in the stomach; dysenteric stools of white mucus or membranous substances, with tenesmus; constipation with unsuccessful urging; brown, dark urine.

COLOC.—Colocynthis.—*Crampy* pains, internally and externally; muscular contractions; desquamation of the epidermis; urinous smell of the night-sweat; hemicrania with vomiting;

spasmodic, constrictive colic, as if the bowels were pressed between stones, with diarrhœa; tympanitic distention of the abdomen; yellow diarrhœic stools, after taking the least food or drink; dysenteric stools with mucus and blood; fetid urine, which becomes turbid and jelly-like soon after standing; spasmodic constriction of the chest.

CON.—Conium Maculatum.—Cramp and spasmodic pains in various parts; debility in the open air; pains as from a blow; blue, yellow-green spots as if ecchymosed; swelling and indurations of glands; anthropophobia with aversion to solitude; pale or bluish, bloated face; photophobia; ulcers of the lips; herpes facialis; spasms of the œsophagus; sexual weakness; uterine spasms; acrid mucous leucorrhœa; spasmodic-cough; suffocative fits as if the throat were obstructed.

COP.—Copaivæ Balsamum.—Used for gonorrhœa, nettle-rash, ill effects of poisonous muscles.

CROC.—Crocus Sativus.—Bounding sensation in the affected parts as of something alive; hæmorrhage of tenacious, black blood; scarlet-red spots upon the skin; remarkable alternation of weeping and laughing, quarrelling and singing; *disposition to mirth and jest;* livid complexion and burning-red spots in the face.

CUPR.—Cuprum Metallicum.—Spasms and convulsions with piercing shrieks, or commencing at the fingers and toes; epilepsy; pains in the bones as if broken; coma with convulsions; itch-like and leprous eruptions; paroxysms of rage, with pride, rage or fear, red and inflamed eyes; blue face and lips; cold tip of the tongue; violent retching and vomiting, with abdominal spasms and convulsions; hoarseness; asthma and spasmodic suffocative fits.

D.

DAPH.—Daphne Indica.—Rheumatic and arthritic pains, with stitching; bone-pains and exostoses; weak sight, as if a pellicle were drawn over the eyes; diplopia; cough with vomiting, and yellow, frothy, blood-streaked expectoration.

DIG.—Digitalis Purpurea.—*Jaundice; chlorosis; dropsical affections;* gastric, bilious and mucous fevers; organic diseases of the heart; *ascites;* hydrocele; hæmoptysis.

DROS.—Drosera Rotundifolia.—*Fever* with nausea and gastric symptoms; gauze before the eyes, print looks pale when reading; frequent bleeding of the nose; bleeding from the mouth; creeping in the larynx as from a soft body; hoarseness and deep bass-voice, with rough and scraping feeling of dryness in the throat; pain in the larynx when talking; dry, *spasmodic cough,* evening and night, with retching, bleeding from the mouth and nose, blue face and suffocative fits; cough with discharge of bright-red or black blood; purulent expectoration.

DULC.—DULCAMARA.—Ailments from abuse of Mercury; ill effects of exposure to wet and cold weather; scrofulous affections with swelling and induration of single glands; lameness; *herpes;* vesicular eruptions; scarlet and purple-rash; crusta lactea; scrofulous ophthalmia; diarrhœa from cold; *catarrh of the bladder;* scrofulous buboes; herpes præputialis; mucous asthma; hydrothorax, &c.

E.

EUPHORB.—EUPHORBIUM.—Ptyalism; mercurial affections; old, torpid ulcers; vesicular erysipelas; œsophagitis; adhesion of the pleura, &c.

EUPHR.—EUPHRASIA OFFICINALIS.—*Ophthalmia,* also traumatic, chronic blennorrhœ; diseases of the cornea; incipient amaurosis; moist cough after influenza; figwarts.

F.

FERR.—FERRUM METALLICUM.—Rushes of blood, congestions, hæmorrhage, with vascular irritation; tearing and stitching, especially at night, with disposition to move the affected parts; debility with trembling, heaviness of the limbs, constant disposition to be lying down; emaciation; livid complexion; dropsy; burning and soreness of a great many spots on the skin; night-sweat with strong smell; vertigo on looking at flowing water; congestion of blood to the head, with throbbing and hammering; *pale, sunken countenance with pale lips* and hollow eyes; livid complexion, with blue spots in the face, or fiery redness with swollen veins; bloated face, especially around the eyes; load in the stomach after eating; watery diarrhœa and lienteria; *discharge of ascarides;* disposition to miscarriage; uterine hæmorrhage with labour-pains in the abdomen and small of the back; spasmodic cough with vomiting of mucus or food; hæmoptysis and purulent expectoration; asthma as if from constriction of the chest.

G.

GRAPH.—GRAPHITES.—Crampy pains, with red swelling, hardness and painfulness of the swollen part; *tension as if the muscles were contracted;* sudden darting pains; *liability to take cold;* pulsations in the whole body after slight exercise; nervousness with tremulousness, or moaning; dryness of the skin and deficient exhalation; erysipelas, steatoma, glandular swellings; moist herpes, phagedenic blisters, sore places, disfigured nails, fetid ulcers and other diseases of the skin; disposition to grief and despondency; humid eruptions on the hairy scalp; photophobia; soreness behind the ears; *scurfy eruptions around the mouth and chin;* foul, urinous smell from the mouth; *dyspepsia;* excessive flatulence; chronic costiveness or diarrhœa; sexual excitement; suppressed, or scanty and pale menses; soreness of the pudendum; painful, inflammatory swelling of the ovaries; soreness of the nipples with humid blisters; fetid sweat of the feet.

GUAJ.—Guajacum.—Stitching and tearing with contraction of the affected parts and renewal of the pains by the least motion; creeping pains in the bones, also with swelling and interstitial distention; stitches in the brain, or stitching and tearing in one side of the head; constant urging to urinate with copious discharge of fetid urine; shuddering of the mammæ; bad cough with fetid purulent expectoration and stitches in the chest.

H.

HELL.—Helleborus.—Lancinations in the joints or across parts; stitching *boring* in the periosteum and other parts, increased by eating and drinking, cool air and bodily exertions; paroxysms of sudden muscular relaxation, with sudden prostration, especially when not thinking of the action of the muscles; convulsions and spasmodic rigidity of the limbs, with shaking of the head; dropsy; falling off of the hair and nails; silent melancholy and moaning; frequent staring; burning heat in the head, and pale face; œdema of the face; blisters and aphthæ in the mouth and on the tongue; ulcerative pain in the stomach after eating, and soreness of the pit of the stomach when coughing or stepping; sensation of coldness and heaviness in the abdomen; diarrhœa, of white, jelly-like mucus; complete loss of sexual desire.

HEP.—Hepar Sulphuris Calcareum.—Drawing, tearing and stitching in the limbs and joints, especially on waking early in the morning; chronic suppurations; glandular swellings and suppurations; erysipelas, rhagades, unhealthy skin, fetid ulcers and cutaneous affections generally; hot and red swellings with strained feeling; *sore* and bruised pain when touching the parts; sleeplessness, or the sleep is disturbed by thoughts passing through the head like clouds; pimples on the hairy scalp, sore to the touch; erysipelatous ophthalmia; fetid otorrhœa; *yellow complexion* with blue margins around the eyes; painful sensation as of a plug in the throat, or stitching as from a splinter; dyspepsia; slow stool as if from inaction of the bowels; soreness of the pudendum; weakness of the larynx with hectic fever; *dry cough* with spasmodic retching and vomiting, or *moist cough* with mucous rattling in the chest; anxious, wheezing breathing, with danger of suffocation when lying down.

HYOS.—Hyoscyamus Niger.—Spasms and convulsions with diarrhœa, enuresis and coldness of the body, shriek, anguish, oppression of the chest and renewal of the paroxysm on attempting to swallow liquids; sudden falling down with a shriek and convulsions; hemiplegia; pustules like smallpox; boils, brown spots and gangrenous blisters; coma with convulsions, or sleeplessness from anguish and nervousness; fearfulness and anxiety, with dread of men; *frenzy and rage*, with beating, murderous disposition and great physical strength; quarrelsome and reproachful; *complete loss of consciousness;* absurd laughing and prating; demeanour, as if possessed of the devil; *red, sparkling eyes and staring look;* objects look red and larger than usual; dilated pupils; pale-bluish, cold face, or blood-red and brown-red face; froth at the mouth; red, dry and parched tongue; paralysis of the tongue; *inability to swallow* on account of a spasmodic constriction and swelling of the throat; *aversion to liquids;* vomiting of mucus, blood or food; constipation or involuntary stools; whitish, slimy diarrhœa; suppressed or involuntary emission of urine; nightly, dry, spasmodic cough, especially when lying; spasms of the chest.

I.

IGN.—Ignatia Amara.—Distensive or constrictive sensation in the cavities of the body; *contusive* and *bruised* pain, especially in the periosteum or long bones, particularly when lying on one side, and going off in a recumbent posture; *aggravation* by smoking, coffee, brandy; *improvement* by a change of position, lying on the back or the affected part; *opisthotonic spasms*, with blue-red face, spasms of the fauces, suffocative fits, loss of consciousness, foam at the mouth; sore places on the skin; a good deal of yawning, as if the lower jaw would be dislocated; itching nettle-rash; *restless night-sleep*, with moaning, talking, twitching of the limbs; heat and redness, externally, with intolerance of warmth; whining melancholy and internal grief, with moaning; obstinate and irritable, cannot bear being contradicted; *alternate redness and paleness of the face*, or livid sunken countenance with hollow eyes; *redness* and *burning heat of one cheek; bites his tongue easily when chewing or talking;* stitches or sensation as of a lump in the throat, almost only between the acts of deglutition; constipation, with much urging and *disposition of the rectum to protrude;* ascarides; sexual debility, but much desire; uterine spasms with lancinating and labour-like constriction; constriction of the chest and throat, with dry cough.

IOD.—Iodium.—Ailments from abuse of Mercury; scrophula; rickets; blepharophthalmitis; ptyalism and ulcers in the mouth after abuse of Mercury; abdominal phthisis; laryngeal phthisis;

inflammatory swelling of the knee; goïtre; hydrarthrus; white swelling of the limbsand joints.

IPEC.—Ipecacuanha.—Cracking in the joints; debility with pale face and blue margins around the eyes; *paroxysms of sudden debility with nausea and loathing;* opisthotonic spasms with distortion of the features, redness and bloating of the face, twitching of the facial muscles, lips and eyelids; *hæmorrhage* of bright-red blood; *rash;* chilliness and coldness; sudden attacks of heat with sweat; bruised pain of the brain and skull, with nausea; yellow, livid complexion, or *pale*, bloated face, with blue margins around the eyes; red skin around the mouth; sweet taste in the mouth as of blood; *aversion to food;* vomiting of mucus, bile and food; hæmatemesis; excessive pain in the stomach and pit of the stomach; yellow, slimy, or green diarrhœa, as if fermented; pitch-like stools; spasmodic suffocative cough, with blueness of the face and rigidity of the body; asthma and spasmodic suffocative fits; panting breathing; mucous rattling in the chest.

K.

KAL.—Kali Carbonicum.—Drawing pain in the limbs, with great paleness and chilliness after the attack; *stitches in the joints, tendons and muscles;* want of exhalation and inability to sweat; *rushes of blood*, and pulsations through the whole body; glandular swellings and indurations; *dropsical* and *œdematous swellings;* bluish chilblains; ulcers bleed readily, especially at night; old warts; drowsiness in the day-time and sopor; light and restless night-sleep with anxious dreams; a good deal of vertigo, as if proceeding from the stomach; sacculated swelling between the eyebrows and eyelids; lachrymation and nightly agglutination; feeling of coldness in the lids; *cold ears;* inflammation and swelling of the parotids; sore nostrils with discharge of fetid matter; yellow or pale face, with hollow eyes and pale lips; fetor from the mouth like old cheese; flatulence; costiveness, on account of want of action in the bowels; urging to urinate with increased secretion; itching, gnawing and soreness of the pudendum; cough with *expectoration of mucus and pus;* spasmodic asthma.

KREAS.—Kreasotum.—Pains as if sore, contused, and bruised; stitching in the joints; great agitation in the body as if the parts were all in motion; pustules resembling smallpox or itch; dry and humid herpes; despair of one's recovery; swelling of the margins of the eyelids, suppuration of the eyes and profuse discharge of acrid, smarting tears; inflammation of the outer ear with bright redness, swelling and burning pain; humid herpes of the ears; livid complexion; acne rosacea and scaly herpes on the eyelids, cheeks and around the mouth; drawing from the teeth to the temples; painful, hard spot in the region of the pylorus; spasmodic labour-pains, ulcerative pain and painful feeling of coldness in the abdomen; fetid, brown or reddish urine with red sediment; liability of the uterus to descend; premature menses with profuse discharge of dark blood; discharge of acrid-smelling, bloody, corrosive ichor after the menses; white and painless, or corrosive, yellow, foul-smelling leucorrhœa; dry, whizzing cough, also with retching; stitches about the heart.

L.

LACH.—Lachesis.—Emaciation; tearing in, and contraction of the affected joints; *dread of exercise;* tubercles, nettle-rash, rash, pimples and warts; yellowish complexion; deeply-penetrating suppurations; anxiety and despair of one's recovery; quarrelsome; jealous; *fancies; frequent bleeding* of the *nose;* sensation of a lump in the throat, from which all the pains seem to emanate; *obstinate constipation;* violent sexual desire and lascivious ideas, with feeble erections; scanty and suppressed menses; *sensitiveness of the larynx* to contact; *palpitation* of the heart accompanying other ailments.

LAUR.—Laurocerasus.—Cyanosis, florid phthisis and cholera.

LED.—Ledum Palustre.—Rheumatic and arthritic complaints; dropsical affections; hardness of hearing from taking cold in the head.

Lyc.—Lycopodium.—Painful sensitiveness of the limbs; drawing and tearing in the affected parts, especially every other day, or in windy, wet weather; frequent attacks of distressing feeling of coldness, as if the blood became cold, or the circulation were arrested; spasmodic extension and contraction of single limbs and muscles; tremulous languor; emaciation; hepatic spots; large boils, periodically; *arthritic nodosities;* glandular swellings; softening, contraction and curvature of bones; nightly bone-pains; melancholy sadness, grief, and whining mood; anxiety in the evening, with dread of men, and fear of solitude; frenzy, with pride and desire to command; absence of mind, using one word for another in talking, and one letter for another in reading; suppurating eruptions on the scalp; *falling off* of the hair; vertical half-sightedness; excessive sensitiveness of hearing and sight; pale, livid complexion; pimples, freckles and itching herpes in the face; the teeth become yellow; tightness of the hypochondria as from a band; pains in the liver; *chronic costiveness and constipation,* also with ineffectual urging; gravel; chronic dryness of the vagina; gray, salt-tasting mucous or purulent expectoration; hepatic spots on the chest; yellow skin in the nape of the neck.

M.

MAGN. ART.—Magnes Artificialis.

MAGN. ARCT.—Magnetis Polus Arcticus.

MAGN. AUST.—Magnetis Polus Australis.

MAGN. C.—Magnesia Carbonica.—Pains as if bruised or luxated, or great weakness, especially in the lower limbs; lameness and paroxysms of fainting, with falling down without loss of consciousness; itching creeping in the skin; phagedenic blisters; small, red, scaly herpes; small boils; sour, or fetid and greasy sweat; vexed and peevish mood; tearing, stitching and boring in the head; burning of the eyes, with photophobia; obscuration of the cornea; swelling of the eyeball as if dropsical; pale livid complexion; bloatedness and tubercles of the face; digging tearing toothache at night, increased by cold; longing for greens and aversion to meat; sour smell from the mouth, and sour eructations; frothy, sour and green diarrhœa, with colic; ascarides; increased, pale or greenish urine; delaying or *suppressed* menses, or else profuse and premature; white-slimy, smarting leucorrhœa, with abdominal spasms; nightly spasmodic cough.

MAGN. M.—Magnesia Muriatica.—Hysteric ailments and spasmodic paroxysms; throbbing in the ears; troublesome dryness of the nose, or else discharge of corrosive water; frequent nausea with livid complexion, nervousness and weeping; *chronic hepatitis*, with hardness and aching pains; abdominal spasms, especially during the menses and leucorrhœal discharge; painful hardness in the abdomen, and constant distention of the same; chronic costiveness with difficult stool like sheep's-dung; chronic looseness; *uterine spasms* with leucorrhœa; scirrhous indurations of the neck of the uterus; sweaty feet; aching pain in the knees.

MANG.—Manganum.—Intolerable pains of the periosteum and joints; arthritis of the joints, with *digging*, tension and drawing, jerking or drawing, generally on one side or crosswise, on the right and left side; *soreness in the folds of the joints;* inflammatory swellings with suppuration; dryness, heat and nightly agglutination of the eyes; hardness of hearing as if from stoppage of the ears, the ears opening by blowing the nose; whizzing in the ears, or reports when blowing the nose; chronic angina faucium, with cutting soreness; diseases of the larynx and trachea, with roughness and dryness of the throat, and rough speech.

MEN.—Menyanthes Trifoliata.—Arthritic complaints; fever and ague with coldness in the abdomen; otorrhœa after exanthemata.

MEPH.—Mephitis Putorius.

MERC.—Mercurius.—Congestions of blood, hæmorrhage; bruised pain in all the limbs, especially the thighs, and pain in all the bones; drawing and jerking tearing in the limbs, especially at night, or with profuse sweat which affords no relief; restlessness and twitching in the limbs, *with constant disposition to move them;* great exhaustion and debility, with inexpressible malaise of body and soul; emaciation; aggravation of the pains in the evening or at night, in bed; nocturnal, inflammatory bone-pains; stitching pains in the limbs and joints, with feeling of coldness in the affected parts; *hot, inflammatory swellings;* inflamed, swollen, suppurating glands; inflammatory swellings with slow suppuration; much chilliness and shuddering, especially at night; disposition to sweat and constant sweating during the pains; obstinate, quarrelsome, hypochondriac forebodings; semilateral tearing and stitching in the head; *ulcerated margins of the eyelids;* with scurfs around the eyes; photophobia and scintillations; stitching and tearing pain in the ears; purulent otorrhœa; ulceration of the concha; parotitis; shining swelling of the nose; *livid complexion;* cracked, *ulcerated lips; swollen, ulcerated, white, indented,* receding gums, with nightly burning, and soreness; looseness and falling out of the teeth; fetid smell from the mouth; aphthæ; fetid ptyalism; husky voice; unquenchable thirst for cold liquids; weak digestion with constant hunger; inflammatory swelling and suppuration of the inguinal glands; much urging to stool with tenesmus; dysenteric stools, or acrid, corrosive stools of bloody mucus; excessive emission of urine; dark-red, fetid urine; painful erections at night; profuse menses with anguish and colic; purulent, corrosive leucorrhœa; dry, racking cough, as if head and chest would split.

MEZ.—Mezereum.—Diseases of the bones and mucous membranes; rheumatic tearing; drawing and tightness in the limbs; tertian fever, with hard swelling of the spleen, and great sensitiveness to cold air; bone-pain of the skull, with drawing and feeling of numbness; crampy, or stupefying-aching prosopalgia; drawing burning or boring stitching in hollow teeth; *slimy, corrosive gonorrhœa.*

MOSCH.—Moschus.—Nervous, hypochondriac, and hysteric ailments; nervous paroxysms; impotence; asthma Millari.

MUR. AC.—Muriatis Acidum.—Scrofulous affections; putrid, torpid typhus; scorbutic gums; angina faucium, with raw feeling in the fauces; abdominal spasms; flatulence; varices of the anus, with burning soreness, &c.

N.

NATR.—Natrum Carbonicum.—Rheumatic ailments with muscular contractions; paroxysms of pain with trembling, anguish and sweat; *dryness of the skin,* with profuse sweat from the least exertion; bleeding, large warts; ulcerated phagedenic blisters; night-sweat, alternating with dry skin; fistula lachrymalis; yellow spots on the forehead and upper lip; dyspepsia, with hypochondriac mood after eating; pressing on the pudendum; fetid leucorrhœa; discharge of mucus from the vagina after an embrace; cramp in the calves. *

NATR. M.—NATRUM MURIATICUM.—Stiffness and cracking in the joints; spasmodic sensation in the limbs as if gone to sleep; hysteric ailments; muscular twitchings; *dread of exercise;* emaciation; painful sensitiveness of the skin; great drowsiness in the day-time and sleeplessness at night; irregular, and frequently intermittent pulse; *constant chilliness;* hypochondriac anxiety; *sensation as if the head would split;* falling off of the hair, even of the whiskers; ulcerated eyelids; smarting lachrymation; painful swelling of one half of the nose; cracked lips; fistula dentalis; burning blisters in the mouth and on the tongue; *constant thirst,* with distress after drinking; weak digestion, with sour eructations; red spots on the pit of the stomach; flatulence; constipation and difficult evacuations with stitches in the rectum; constant urging to urinate, with profuse emission; erections and excessive sexual excitement; delaying or suppressed menses; acrid leucorrhœa with yellow complexion; hang nails.

NITR.—NITRUM.—Loss of appetite with thirst; painless diarrhœa; neglected pneumonia; stitches in the chest during a deep inspiration.

NITR. 'AC.—NITRI ACIDUM.—Inflammatory pains in the periosteum; pains in the joints as if sprained, with cracking; stitching pains as if froms plinters; *pains when the weather changes;* tremulous weakness; *glandular swellings;* black pores; brown-reddish spots on the skin and frequent boils; *pains which are felt during sleep;* anxious, lascivious dreams; sadness; headstrong; weak memory; bone-pains of the skull; ulcerated eruptions on the scalp; ulcerated eyes, with stitching; *specks on* the *cornea;* hardness of hearing; buzzing and roaring in the ears; soreness of the nostrils, and fetor from the nose; pale face; yellowness around the eyes; bloat around the eyes; pimpless, herpes and pustules in the face; burning and ulcers in the throat; desire for clay, chalk and lime; stitches and throbbing in the pit of the stomach; suppuration of the inguinal glands; chronic looseness; *fetid urine;* enuresis; red, scurfy spots and ulcers on the glans;

* Jahr contends in a note for the identity of the symptoms of Natrum carb. and Natr. mur., Magn. c. and mur., Amm. c. and mur., Kali and Kali nitr., acetates and carbonates of the same substance; according to Jahr, the symptoms produced by those preparations belong to the *base.* This seems even to be true in regard to the mercurial preparations, though this observation does not apply to basic preparations, such as *Cinnabaris, hepar sulph.,* for these manifest different properties from those of their constituent elements. Jahr's remarks should be taken *cum grano salis.*—*empel.*

excessive sexual desire, with discharge of prostatic fluid; cherry-brown, fetid leucorrhœa; *purulent expectoration;* pains in the back and small of the back.

NITR. SP.—NITRI SPIRITUS DULCIS.

N. MOSCH.—NUX MOSCHATA.—Rheumatic pains caused by cold; pains with drowsiness and disposition to faint; fever and ague, with simple and double type; nervous affections of the brains; toothache from exposure to damp evening-air, or stitching and tearing, in pregnant females; oppression of the chest proceeding from the pit of the stomach; palpitation of the heart with fainting fits.

N. VOM.—NUX VOMICA.—Rheumatic pains, especially of the muscles of the back, loins, chest and small of the back; dartings through the whole body; stitching and tearing in the joints, worse when the weather changes; drawing and tearing, especially at night, or with *numbness of the affected parts;* pains of the joints and limbs as if bruised, especially during motion, or early in bed; sensation of spasmodic drawing to and fro in the muscles, as if something were moving about in them; trembling of the limbs, with fluttering of the heart and tremour; convulsions and spasms; *languor, dread of exercise;* nervous debility; aggravation by coffee, wine, tobacco, watching and mental exertions; blue spots on the body, like ecchymosis; boils; chilblains; cold and blue skin, with blue nails; excessive anguish, as if one must kill one's-self; sensitiveness to noise, talk, odours, and light; *vehement, malicious;* the head is easily fatigued by mental exertions; *congestion of blood to the brain with heat and redness of the face;* livid, yellowish complexion and yellowish colour around the mouth and nose; tongue coated with white slime; *sour taste,* after eating or drinking; herby or foul taste; the clothes feel tight round the hypochondria; sanguineous congestion and heaviness in the abdomen; the abdominal muscles feel as if bruised; *constipation* as from constriction of the rectum, with ineffectual urging; large, hard fæces, or frequent stools consisting of mucus and attended with tenesmus; prolapsus of the rectum; painful urging to urinate, with drop-discharge of the urine; *sexual excitement; the menses are profuse and too long,* with much distress; *dry cough,* with vomiting of mucus; asthmatic constriction across the chest; slight paroxysms of palpitation of the heart, with rushes of blood.

O.

OLEAND—OLEANDER.—Buzzing sensation in all the limbs; *laming rigidity of all the limbs;* painless paralysis; *scurfy* pimples; dullness and absence of mind; scurfy, scaly or humid eruptions on the hairy scalp; *humid, fetid sores behind the ears*, with red, rough, herpetic spots in front of the ears; brownish, burning urine with white sediment; cold feet; lameness of the feet and legs.

OP.—OPIUM.—Ill effects of wine; ill effects of fright or mortification; apparent death; general torpor of the nervous system and insensibility to medicinal action; absence of pain during the complaint; epileptic convulsions; tetanic spasms; drowsiness, *coma*, with stertorous breathing; profuse sweat, with itching and eruption on the skin; fearful, with tendency to start; stupor, complete loss of consciousness and sensibility; visions of mice, scorpions, &c.; intoxication, paroxysms of vertigo; pulsation of the carotids; eyes red, as if inflamed, staring and shining; pupils dilated and immoveable; bluish face; *stupid appearance*, with relaxed appearance of the facial muscles; red and bloated face; spasmodic motion of the facial muscles; vomiting of fæces and urine; tympanitis; *constipation* and *costiveness;* hard stool, in small lumps; suppression of the urinary secretions; suppression of labour-pains; stertorous breathing.

P.

PAR.—PARIS.

PETR.—PETROLEUM.—Ailments from riding in a carriage; debility after making an exertion, with vanishing of sight, trembling of the body, buzzing in the ears, and nausea; *brown* and *yellow spots on the skin;* itching, burning pustules; sore, humid spots on the skin; *rhagades;* corns; chilblains; *irresolute;* hardness of hearing, from paralysis of the auditory nerves; canine hunger, though one is soon satiated; *nausea from riding in a carriage;* hard, lumpy stool; tænia; enuresis nocturna, with itching and dampness of the scrotum; discharge of prostatic juice, and a number of erections; leucorrhœa, with many dreams; cracked skin on the hands, with rhagades; chilblains on the fingers; cold feet.

PETROS.—PETROSELINUM.

PHOSPH.—PHOSPHORUS.—Burning pains; rheumatic tearing and stitching after taking cold; *pains when the weather changes;* frequent rushes of blood; indolence and heaviness of the body; nervous debility with languor of the lower limbs; *sudden prostration;* trembling; *emaciation*, especially of the hands; formication in the paralyzed parts; brown, yellow or brown spots; petechiæ; small wounds bleed profusely; lymphatic abscesses full of fistulous passages; night- and morning-sweats; sensitiveness of the senses and tendency to start; vertigo of various kinds; congestion of blood to the head, with buzzing, and heat in the head; lachrymation in the open air; photophobia; *pale, dirty complexion, with deep, hollow eyes;* weak stomach; frequent eructations with sensation as if the hypochondriac regions were filled with air; *painfulness of the stomach* when touching it or walking; large, yellow spots and boils on the abdomen; *frequent stools, soft;* watery, colourless urine in large quantity; *excessive sexual desire,* with erections and nocturnal emissions; profuse, and premature menses with a good deal of distress; cough as from tubercles, with expectoration of salt mucus; oppression, anguish and heaviness on the chest; yellow spots on the chest; numbness of the fingers; pains of the soles as if ulcerated.

PHOS. AC.—Phosphori Acidum.—Disease of the bones, especially interstitial distention, inflammation and caries; debility, with pale complexion; ulcers, itching or flat, with dirty pus and indented bottom; *taciturn;* inability to perform any mental labour; yellow spot on the sclerotica; burning in the skin of the cheeks; pimples on the forehead and chin; the teeth become dull and yellow; painful tubercles on the gums; tenacious, viscid mucus in the mouth; sensation in the stomach as if something were heaving up and down; flatulence, especially after acids; distention of the uterus as if from air; greenish-white diarrhœa; milky urine, with jelly-like lumps; cough with purulent, fetid expectoration; old, itching ulcers on the legs.

PLAT.—Platina.—Neuralgia with pulsative throbbing, and crampy, creeping numbness of the affected parts; spasmodic pains of the female sex and especially of hysteric women; *sadness,* especially in the evening, with disposition to weep; agony, with fear of death which she believes to be near; over-estimation of herself, she thinks herself much above those near her; delirium, compressive sensation in the temples, with heat and redness of the face; pale, sickly complexion; excessive sexual desire and voluptuous titillation in the sexual parts; pressing towards the pudendum; profuse and premature menses, with thick, dark blood; aphonia; short, difficult breathing.

PLUMB.—Plumbum.

PRUN.—Prunus Spinosa.

PULS.—Pulsatilla.—Pains in the limbs, tearing, drawing, or jerking in the muscles, with numbness, lameness and swelling of the affected parts, stitching and feeling of coldness in the affected parts when the weather changes; *erratic pains,* shifting rapidly from one part to another, with swelling and redness in the joints; *paroxysms of pains,* with chilliness; asthma, paleness of the face; aggravation of the pains when sitting, rising from the seat, or during rest, or when lying on one side; the pains are worse before midnight, or every other evening; *chickenpox;* erysipelas with swelling; disposition to blennorrhœa; coldness, shuddering, chilliness and continual internal chilliness; melancholy with weeping, and dread of death; timid disposition; despair of one's salvation; confusion of the head, with pain as after intoxication or watching; redness and swelling of the eyelids, with stye; dimness of sight, as if something were hanging over the cornea which might be wiped off; purulent otorrhœa; catarrh with profuse discharge of mucus; *pale* face, and alternate redness and paleness; toothache with otalgia; slimy, foul taste in the mouth; *bitter taste when chewing; pulsations* in the pit of the stomach; tenesmus of the bladder; watery urine; excessive sexual excitement, almost like priapism; suppression of the menses; distress during the menses, especially chilliness and paleness of face, with thick and black blood; cough with expectoration of thick mucus, asthma in a horizontal position as if the throat would be constricted; paroxyms of palpitation of the heart, with anguish.

R.

RAN.—Ranunculus Bulbosus.

RAN. SC.—Ranunculus Sceleratus.

RHAB.—Rhabarbarum.—Diseases of children, especially during dentition; the child tosses about, screams, is quarrelsome, has convulsive drawing in the fingers, facial muscles and eyelids, cries and asks for a variety of things with impetuosity; agony; twitching of the facial muscles, corners of the mouth and eyelids; tenesmus; diarrhœa of lying-in women, or papescent, sour diarrhœa preceded by urging.

RHOD.—Rhododendron.—Arthritic and rheumatic pains in the limbs, caused by rough and stormy weather, worse during rest and in bed; violent tearing in the limbs, after abuse of Mercury, with swelling and redness, and aggravation of the pains at night and in the morning; pains in the bones or periosteum, generally at small spots, when the weather changes; swelling and redness of the joints affected with gout; swelling of the testes, with drawing pressing, also after suppression of gonorrhœa and cold; hydrocele.

RHUS. –Rhus Toxicodendron.—Affections of the ligaments, tendons and synovial membranes; tension, drawing and tearing in the limbs, worse during rest, and in the cold season, or at night, in bed, frequently attended with numbness of the affected part after moving it; *creeping pains;* sensation in inner organs as if something would be torn loose; lameness and paralysis, also hemiplegia; vesicular erysipelas; rhagades; pustules which break and discharge a fluid; *hang-nails;* red, shining swelling; violent and *spasmodic yawning;* evening fever, with diarrhœa; sweat during the pains, frequently with violent trembling; illusions of the fancy, and delirium; pain as if the brain would be torn; painful creeping in the head; swelling of the head; phagedenic scald-head; small, soft tumours on the hairy scalp; swelling and inflammation of the parotid glands; acne rosacea around the mouth and chin; nightly discharge of yellowish, or bloody saliva; ulcerative pain in the pit of the stomach as if something would be torn off, especially when stooping or making a false step; the small of the back feels as if bruised, especially when lying still on it.

RUT.—Ruta Graveolens.—Burning and gnawing pains in the periosteum; pains as if bruised or contused in the limbs, joints and bones; inflamed ulcers; liability to become sore, when riding on horseback, &c.; contusions and injuries of the bones and periosteum; *debility of the eyes* from reading too much; incipient amaurosis, with mistiness and complete darkness at a distance; eructations of hysteric females; prolapsus of the rectum, at every alvine evacuation; frequent urging to urinate, with scanty emission, also of green urine, or with renewed ineffectual urging after micturition; gravel; miscarriage, sterility; corrosive leucorrhœa after suppression of the menses.

S.

SABAD.—Sabadilla.—Laming drawing through all the limbs; fever and ague, with thirst between the chilly and hot stage; fluent coryza, with disfigured countenance and dullness of the head; scalding sensation in the mouth; red spots upon the abdomen, chest and hands; the cough is attended with vomiting, stitches in the vertex, pains in the stomach, &c.

SABIN.—Sabina.—Acute and chronic arthritis; pressing in the tooth as if it would fly to pieces; profuse menses with lumps of coagulated blood; metrorrhagia after confinement and miscarriage; leucorrhœa after suppression of menses, or starchlike, yellow, ichorous, fetid leucorrhœa, with painful discharges of blood, like serum, with a fetid smell.

SAMB.—Sambucus.—Dropsical swelling of the whole body; fever and ague, with excessive sweat; tracheitis; cough with profuse expectoration of salt or also sweetish mucus; wheezing and hurried breathing; asthma Millari; angina pectoris.

SASSAP.—Sassaparilla.—Arthritic and rheumatic pains with diminished secretion of urine, or after suppression of gonorrhœa, or exposure in the water; obstinate constipation with urging to urinate; lithiasis.

SEC.—Secale Cornutum.—Spasms of the upper and lower limbs, with convulsions; sweats, from the head to the pit of the stomach, also clammy; *sunken eyes;* hippocratic countenance; ugly spots in the face; tongue coated with thick mucus, discoloured, brown, and lastly black; colic with pain in the back and thighs, eructations, vomiting, and cutting and tearing in the abdomen; seated burning in the region of the spleen and loins; diarrhœa, with great prostration; suppression of urine; hot, scanty urine; *metrorrhagia,* when moles are present in the uterus, after miscarriage, confinement, with black, fluid blood; chronic uteritis, after suppression of the lochia; gangrene of the uterus; threatening miscarriage; irregular, feeble, or suppressed, or even spasmodic labour-pains; adhesion of the placenta; cramps in the calves and soles of the feet.

SELEN.—Selenium.

SENEG.—Senega.

SENN.—Senna.

SEP.—Sepia.—Affections of the *capillary vessels;* stitching or burning pains; drawing tearing from below upwards; inflexibility of the joints; *rushes of blood,* with perceptible throbbing in the body; the pains abate during motion; hysteric debility; fainting fits; itching pimples in the joints; pemphigus; brown, reddish, herpetic spots upon the skin; herpes circinnatus; chilliness; sadness and weeping, *melancholy;* hemicrania with vomiting; *involuntary shaking of the head;* pustules on the cornea; paralysis of the lids; incipient amaurosis with contracted pupils; plugs in the nose, and painful eruption on the tip; *pale face;* sickly complexion, with dim, red eyes; yellow spots in the face, and yellow saddle across the cheeks and nose; *excessive appetite* and painful feeling of hunger in the stomach; weak digestion; ineffectual urging, and hard, insufficient stool; oozing from the rectum; *frequent* micturition; excessive sexual desire, with erections; dampness and soreness of the pudendum; leucorrhœa, soreness and itching in the vagina; congestion of blood to the chest, with palpitation of the heart and intermission of the beats of the heart; claret-red spots on the neck and under the chin; painful ulcers at the tips of the fingers; corrosive, fetid sweat of the feet.

SIL.—Silicea.—Nightly stinging in the joints; twitching of the limbs day and night; nervous debility and fainting; lymphatic tumours and abscesses; glandular swellings with suppuration or induration; scirrhous indurations; benign and malignant suppurations, especially in membranous parts; unhealthy skin; ganglia; panaritia; diseases of bones; *night-sweats;* vertigo, tension, and pressing in the head, as if the head would split; ulcers of the cornea; obscuration of sight, as if seeing through a gray cover, and sudden paroxysms of blindness; stoppage of the ears, sometimes going off with a report; vomiting after drinking; distention and heat of the abdomen; *constipation with ineffectual urging;* cough with purulent expectoration; panaritia; fetid sweat of the feet.

SOL. NIGR.—Solanum Nigrum.

SPIG.—Spigelia.—Tearing in the limbs, also arthritic, stitching tearing; worm-fevers; *nervous pains in and above the eyes,* especially deep in the orbits, with pain of the eyeballs on moving them, as if too large; stitching in the eyes, with boring in the head, and pain driving one to despair; luminous flashes before the eyes; amaurosis; cataract; *pale face,* with yellow margins around the eyes; prosopalgia, with shining swelling of the affected part; canine hunger, with nausea and thirst; nausea, with sensation as if something were rising from the stomach into the throat; ascarides; asthma when stirring in bed, can only lie on the right side and with the trunk raised; suffocative danger, on making the least motion, especially when raising the arms; spasmodic sensation in the chest, as if from the pit of the stomach, with arrest of breathing; undulating motion of the heart; stitches in the region of the heart; purring sensation in the region of the heart; aneurysms of the heart.

SPONG.—Spong. Tosta.—Diseases of the lymphatic vessels and glands; heat, with dry, hot skin, thirst, headache and delirium; redness of the eyes, with burning and lachrymation; frequent eructations, with cutting and tearing in the stomach; relaxed feeling in the stomach, as if the stomach were open; orchitis; induration of the testes; pain in the larynx on touching it and turning the head; burning in the larynx and trachea; dryness, husky and hoarse voice; inflammation of the larynx, trachea and bronchi; croup; laryngeal and tracheal phthisis; cough, deep from the chest, with soreness and burning, or chronic cough with yellowish expectoration and hoarseness; wheezing inspirations; asthma with amenorrhœa; goitre; hard goitre.

SQUILL.—Squilla Maritima.—Dropsy; heat, with chilliness when uncovered ever so little; pale face after the heat; dark redness of the face.

STANN.—Stannum.—Excessive mental and physical debility; spasms, also hysteric or epileptic spasms of children during dentition; excessive emaciation; hot sweats over the whole body, with complete prostration, even after the least exertion; heaviness in the head, and stupefying pressure in the brain; *pale and sunken face,* with hollow eyes; leucorrhœa with great debility; roughness of the throat, with hoarseness; racking cough, with bruised pain in the pit of the stomach, or retching and vomiting of the ingesta; *cough* with *much mucus;* yellow, salt or foul-tasting expectoration; oppressive weight on the chest, obliging one to take deep breath, with feeling of emptiness in the pit of the stomach; hydrothorax.

STAPH.—Staphysagria.—Scorbutic affections; *ill effects of chagrin,* with indignation, or of *grief and care;* bone-pains, also inflammatory; drawing tearing in the muscles; bruised pain of the body, as after a long journey on foot; rash, with nightly convulsions; itch-like and herpetic eruptions; unhealthy skin; frequent boils; swelling of bones; disposition to sweat, or else inability to sweat, even during the greatest exertions, with pale face and headache; *melancholy* and *sad* mood; *pushes away every thing near him, from sheer indignation;* pimples around the inflamed eye; tubercles in the margins of the eyelids; hardness of hearing, from enlargement of the tonsils; worn-out, pointed countenance, with hollow eyes, as after a night's revel, or in consequence of some violent emotion; inflammatory pains of the facial bones; ulcer of the lip, with gnawing-drawing pain; swelling and tubercles of the gums; canine hunger, even with full stomach, with waterbrash; feeling of weakness in the abdomen, as if it would fall off; swelling of the inguinal glands; constipation and delaying stool, owing to a deficiency of peristaltic motion; excessive sexual desire, with noctural emissions and dreams; cough, with yellow purulent mucus.

STRAM.—Stramonium.—Painful sensation as if the joints were loose: spasmodic movements and convulsions, on looking at bright objects; epileptiform convulsions with consciousness; spasms after fright; St. Vitus' dance; cataleptic immobility, with loss of consciousness; debility, with vacillating gait; *wakes with a solemn air, an air of importance;* coma, with stertorous breathing, bloody froth at the mouth and dark-brown face: great coldness of the extremities and trunk; *melancholy, desire for company, light, sunshine, the symptoms being aggravated by darkness and solitude;* believes all the time that he is alone, and is afraid; paroxysms of rage; *frightful fancies,* such as shapes of dreadful animals, &c.; loquacious delirium; alternation of ludicrous demeanour and sadness; violent headache, with obscuration of sight and hard hearing; optical illusions; *distorted features.* as if by pain or fear and anxiety, with deep furrows and wrinkles on the forehead; red face, with staring eyes; swelling of the face, as if turgid with blood, with friendly look; blue and swollen lips; speech as if paralyzed, utters inarticulate sounds; spasmodic constriction of the fauces; violent singultus; *aversion* to *liquids;* cadaverous stools; suppression of urine; lascivious disposition; spasms of the chest.

STRONT.—Strontiana Carbonica.

SULPH.—Sulphur.—Pains in the limbs, with weakness and numbness, and stitching in the joints and rigidity; drawing and tearing, becoming intolerable under a feather-bed; *talking fatigues him and causes pain; sensitiveness to wind and open air;* orgasmus sanguinis, with swelling of the veins of the hands; epilepsy, after a fright or after running about; emaciation; *itch-like eruptions;* hepatic spots; moles; rhagades; unhealthy skin; readily bleeding ulcers; glandular affections; diseases of bones; chlorosis; dropsy; red, hot swellings; *drowsiness in the day-time; nightmare; chilliness;* sweats readily; melancholy, despair of one's salvation; disposition to philosophic and religious meditations; pain of the roots of the hairs, especially on touching them; ulcerated margins of the eyelids; pale and bloated face; livid complexion; blue margins around the eyes; hot face with red spots (between the eye and ear); rough skin in the face; *black pores* of the nose, lip and chin; teeth loose and elongated; *aphthæ;* excessive hunger; acid stomach; regurgitation of food; *hæmorrhoidal colic; constipation;* insufficient stool, with sensation as if something had remained behind; lienteria; painful micturition; *enuresis nocturna;* impotence; emissions; suppression of the menses; burning, corrosive leucorrhœa; much mucus in the chest and throat; feeling of heaviness on the chest, as from a lump; hang-nails; cold feet.

SULPH. AC.—Sulphuris Acidum.—Red and bluish spots on the skin; sore places on the skin, with gangrenous ulceration; ill effects of mechanical injuries; chronic ophthalmia; aphthæ; acidity in the throat, and heartburn; premature and profuse menses; chronic hæmoptysis.

T.

TARAX.—Taraxacum.

TART.—Tartarus Emeticus.—Pustulous eruption, like variola; varioloids; variola; fever and ague, with absence of thirst and great drowsiness; pale and sickly complexion; nausea, vomiting, diarrhœa and great debility; sour vomiting of food; yellow-brown, or slimy diarrhœa; the larynx is painful to contact; croup; catarrh, with mucous rattling in the air-passages; paralysis of the lungs; suffocative catarrh.

THER.—Theridion.

THUJ.—Thuja Occidentalis.—Tearing and beating in the affected parts, as if ulcerated; sensation as if the whole body were very thin and delicate, and might easily fall to pieces; the pains are worst during rest and in bed; eruption like chicken-pox, with red areola; *brown spots on the skin; figwarts;* slow comprehension; headache, as if a nail were driven into the crown; tensive drawing in the nasal bones; ulceration and painful scurfs high up in the nose; ranula; swelling of the parotid glands; pain as from intussusception of the bowels; motions in the abdomen as of something alive; constipation as if from intussusception of the bowels; sensation in the urethra, as if drops of urine were running along; round, flat, unclean ulcers on the glans; *figwarts,* especially horny or humid, suppurating and itching; constant erections and emissions, with sensation of stricture in the urethra; wart-shaped excrescences on the os tincæ; the region of the heart is painful; warts on the hands.

V.

VAL.—Valeriana.—Jerking drawing in the limbs and bones; pains which appear suddenly, concussive, or shifting from one part to another; the pains are mitigated by friction and rubbing; morbid nervousness; hypochondriac despair; taste as of fetid tallow; ulcerative pain in the abdomen, and distensive sensation.

VERAT.—VERATRUM ALBUM.—Paroxysms of pain, causing delirium and rage for a short time; *pains in the limbs*, which become worse in bed, decrease on rising, cease entirely by walking about, and generally appear early in the morning; aggravation of the pains by the talking of others; trembling with anguish, and disposition to faint; concussions like electric shocks, with profuse sweat; spasms and convulsions, with contraction of the palms of the hands and soles of the feet; catalepsy, with lock-jaw; laming prostration and disposition to faint, from the least exercise; *flaccid* skin; coma vigil; coldness of the whole body, with cold, clammy sweats; hot face, with redness and shuddering; slow and almost extinct pulse; *anguish* as from an evil conscience; fearfulness, running about from anxiety; mania, religious or amorous, with foolish demeanour; *sensation as if a piece of ice were lying on the crown of the head;* hemeralopia; red spots on the nose; *cold, cadaverous countenance, with pointed nose and sunken cheeks;* bluish or yellowish face; acne rosacea in the face, around the mouth and on the chin; lips dry, blackish and cracked; lock-jaw; discharge of mucus from the mouth, and froth at the mouth; tongue red and swollen, or dry, blackish and cracked; *canine hunger;* black vomit; vomiting with diarrhœa, and pressure in the pit of the stomach; *painful sensitiveness of the pit and region of the stomach* and *great anguish in the pit of the stomach;* cutting in the abdomen, or burning as if from hot coal; *chronic constipation as if from want of action of the bowels;* green, watery stools, mixed with flocks, or brownish and blackish stools; violent palpitation of the heart, and great anguish about the heart; creeping in the hands and fingers; icy-cold feet.

VERB.—VERBASCUM.

VIOL. OD.—VIOLA ODORATA.

VIOL. TR.—VIOLA TRICOLOR.

Z.

ZINC.—ZINCUM.—Feeling of coldness in the bones; chronic eruptions; herpetic ulcers; loud shrieks during sleep; night-sweats; soreness in the head; buzzing in the head; pain of the hairy scalp as if from subcutaneous ulceration; paralysis of the upper lids; bleeding gums; bluish herpes in the throat, after neglected gonorrhœa; constipation; gravel; leucorrhœa, preceded by cutting colic; spasmodic asthma; tension in the sternum; palpitation and shocks of the heart, with intermission of the beats of the heart and arrest of breathing; pain in the small of the back.

ALPHABETICAL INDEX

OF THE

LATIN AND GERMAN NAMES

OF THE DISEASES

MENTIONED IN THIS REPERTORY.

(The numbers refer to the page in the Repertory, where the article commences.)

A.

B.

C.

D.

E.

F.

G.

I & J.

L.

N.

T.

U.

V.

W.

Y.

Z.

WILLIAM RADDE,

322 BROADWAY, NEW-YORK,

Respectfully informs the Homœopathic Physicians, and the friends of the System, that he is the sole agent for the Leipzig Central Homœopathic Pharmacy, and that he has always on hand a good assortment of the best Homœopathic Medicines, in complete sets, or by single vials, in *Tinctures*, *Dilutions*, and *Triturations; also Pocket Cases of Medicines; Physicians'* and *Family Medicine Chests* to *Laurie's Domestic* (60 Remedies —EPPS' (58 Remedies)—HERING'S (82 Remedies).— *Small Pocket Cases* at $3 with Family Guide and 27 Remedies.—*Cases* containing 415 Vials with Tinctures and Triturations, for Physicians.—*Cases* with 268 Vials of Tinctures and Triturations to Jahr's New Manual, or Symptomen-Codex.—POCKET CASES with 60 Vials of Tinctures and Triturations.—*Cases* from 100 to 400 Vials with low and high dilutions of Medicated Pellets.—*Cases* from 50 to 80 Vials of low and high dilutions, &c. &c. Homœopathic Chocolate, Refined Sugar of Milk, pure Globules, &c. *Arnica Tincture*, the best specific remedy for bruises, sprains, wounds, &c. *Arnica Plaster*, for *Corns, &c* *Urtica Urens*, for *Burns; Homœopathic Tooth-Powder;* as well as Books, Pamphlets, and Standard works on the System, in the English, French, and German languages.

HOMŒOPATHIC BOOKS.

JAHR'S NEW MANUAL OF HOMŒOPATHIC PRACTICE, Edited, with annotations, by A. Gerald Hull, M. D., from the last Paris edition. This is the fourth American edition of a very celebrated work, written in French, by the eminent Homœopathic Professor Jahr, and it is considered the best practical compendium of this extraordinary science that has yet been composed. After a very judicious and instructive introduction, the work presents a table of the Homœopathic Medicines, with their names in Latin, English, and German; the order in which they are to be studied, with their most important distinctions, and clinical illustrations of their symptoms and effects upon the various organs and functions of the human system.—The second volume embraces an elaborate analysis of the indications in disease, of the medicines adapted to cure, and a glossary of the technics used in the work, arranged so luminously as to form an admirable guide to every medical student. The whole system is here displayed with a modesty of pretension, and a scrupulosity in statement, well calculated to bespeak candid investigation. This laborious work is indispensable to the students and practitioners of Homœopathy, and highly interesting to medical and scientific men of all classes. Repertory, 1 vol, bound. 1849. Price $3.

JAHR'S NEW MANUAL; originally published under the name of Symptomen-Codex. (Digest of Symptoms.) This work is intended to facilitate a comparison of the parallel symptoms of the various homœopathic agents, thereby enabling the practitioner to discover the characteristic symptoms of each drug, and to determine with ease and correctness what remedy is most homœopathic to the existing group of symptoms Translated, with important and extensive additions from various sources, by Charles Julius Hempel, M D, assisted by James M. Quin, M. D.; with revisions and clinical notes by John F. Gray, M. D.; contributions by Drs. A. Gerald Hull, and George W. Cook, M. D., of New-York; and Drs. C. Hering, J. Jeanes, C. Neidhard, W Williamson, and J. Kitchen, of Philadelphia. With a Preface by Constantine Hering, M. D. 2 vols. $11.

HAHNEMANN'S ORGANON, by Chs. Hempel, M. D. $1.

RAU'S ORGANON. Translated by C. J. Hempel, M. D. $1 25.

BECKER, M. D. On Consumption Translated from the German. 1848. 38cts.

—— —— On Diseases of the Eye. 1848. 38cts.

—— —— On Constipation. 1848. 38cts.

—— —— On Dentition. 1848 38cts.

HEMPEL'S BŒNNINGHAUSEN for Homœopathic Physicians; to be used at the bedside of the patient, and in studying the Materia Medica Pura. Most complete edition, including the Concordances of Homœopathic Remedies. Translated and adapted to the use of the American Profession. by C. J. Hempel, M.D. 1847. $1 50.

HARTMANN'S ACUTE AND CHRONIC DISEASES, by Chs. J. Hempel, M.D. 4 vols. $6

JAHR, G. H. G., M D. Short Elementary Treatise upon Homœopathia and the manner of its Practice; with some of the most important effects of ten of the principal Homœopathic Remedies, for the use of all honest men who desire to convince themselves, by experiment, of the truth of the doctrine Second French edition, corrected and enlarged. Translated by Edward Bayard, M. D. Bound, 38 cts.

HAHNEMANN, Dr S. Materia Medica Pura. Translated and edited by Charles Julius Hempel, M D. 4 vols. 1846. $6.

HAHNEMANN, Dr S. The *Chronic Diseases*, their specific nature and *Homœopathic Treatment*. Translated and edited by Chs. J. Hempel M. D., with a Preface, by Constantine Hering, M. D., Philadelphia. 8vo. 5 vols. Bound. 1845. $7.

BŒNNINGHAUSEN'S Essay on the Homœopathic Treatment of Intermittent Fevers. Translated and edited by Charles Julius Hempel, M D. 1845. 38 cts.

A TREATISE *on the use of Arnica* in cases of Contusions, Wounds, Strains, Sprains, Lacerations of the Solids, Concussions, Paralysis, Rheumatism, Soreness of the Nipples, &c. By Charles Julius Hempel, M D. 1845. 19 cts.

HOMŒOPATHIC COOKERY, second edition. Designed chiefly for the use of such persons as are under homœopathic treatment. 50 cts.

RUECKERT'S THERAPEUTICS; or Successful Homœopathic Cures, collected from the best Homœopathic periodicals. By C. J. Hempel M. D One large 8vo vol. $3.

THE HOMŒOPATHIC EXAMINER By Drs. Gray and Hempel. 2 vols. New Series. 1846 and 1847. Bound in two volumes, $6.

TRANSACTIONS of the American Institute of Homœopathy. 1846. Bound, $1 50.

HOMŒOPATHIC BOOKS.

LAURIE, DR. J., HOMŒOPATHIC DOMESTIC MEDICINE. with the Treatment and Diseases of Females, Infants, Children, and Adults. 5th American edition, much enlarged with additions by A. Gerald Hull, M. D. 1849. Bound, $1 50.

CHEPMELL'S HOMŒOPATHIC DOMESTIC, with additions and improvements, by S. B. Barlow, M. D. 1849. 50 cts.

E. STAPF'S ADDITIONS to the Materia Medica Pura. Translated by C. J. Hempel, M. D. $1 50.

C. HERING'S DOMESTIC PHYSICIAN. Fourth American edition, revised, with additions from the Author's manuscript of the sixth German edition. The part relating to the Diseases of Females and Children, by Walter Williamson. M D. 1848. $2 00.

RUOFF'S REPERTORY OF HOMŒOPATHIC MEDICINE, nosologically arranged. Translated from the German, by A. H. Okie, M. D, translator of Hartmann's Remedies. Second American edition, with additions and improvements, by G Humphrey, M. D., etc. 1844. Bound. $1 50.

EPPS, Dr. J. DOMESTIC HOMŒOPATHY: or, Rules for the Domestic Treatment of the Maladies of Infants, Children, and Adults, etc. Third American from the fourth London edition. Edited and enlarged by George W. Cook, M. D. 1848. Bound, 75 cents.

W. WILLIAMSON, M. D. Diseases of Females and Children, 38 cents.

WM. HENDERSON, M. D. Homœopathic Practice. 1846. 50 cents.

FORBES, M. D. Homœopathy, Allopathy, and Young Physic. 1846. 19 cents.

WM. HENDERSON, M. D. Letter to John Forbes. 1846. 19 cents.

☞ The above three books, bound in one volume, $1 00.

THE FAMILY GUIDE to the Administration of Homœopathic Remedies. Third edition, after the second London edition, with additions. Retail price 25 cents.

ON ECLECTICISM IN MEDICINE: or a Critical Review of the Leading Medical Doctrines. An inaugural thesis, presented at the New-York University, on the first of March, 1845. By Charles J. Hempel, M. D. 25 cts.

REASONS why Homœopathy should receive an Impartial Investigation from the Medical Profession and the Public. By B. F. Bowers, M. D. 18 cents.

DEFENCE OF HAHNEMANN AND HIS DOCTRINES, including an Exposure of Dr. Alexander Wood's "Homœopathy Unmasked." London, 1844. 50 cents.

SHERRILL'S MANUAL OF HOMŒOPATHY. 37½ cts.

F. A. GUENTHER'S New Manual of Homœopathic Veterinary Medicine; or, the Homœopathic Treatment of the Horse, the Ox, the Sheep, the Dog, and other Domestic Animals. $1,25.

www.ingramcontent.com/pod-product-compliance
Lightning Source LLC
LaVergne TN
LVHW021145110826
845150LV00005B/1131

* 9 7 8 1 4 2 5 5 4 7 1 8 9 *